1971	1972	1973	1974	1975	1976	1977	1978	1979	1980	1981	1982	1983
1,127.1	1,238.3	1,382.7	1,500	1,638.3	1,825.3	2,030.9	2,294.7	2,563.3	2,789.5	3,128.4	3,255	3,536.7
3,898.6	4,105	4,341.5	4,319.6	4,311.2	4,540.9	7,450.5	5,015	5,173.4	5,161.7	5,291.7	5,189.3	5,423.8
3.4	5.3	5.8	−0.5	−0.2	5.3	4.6	5.6	3.2	−0.2	2.5	−1.9	4.5
701.9	770.6	852.4	933.4	1,034.4	1,151.9	1,278.6	1,428.5	1,592.2	1,757.1	1,941.1	2,077.3	2,290.6
178.2	207.6	244.5	249.4	230.2	292	361.3	438	492.9	479.3	572.4	517.2	564.3
246.5	263.5	281.7	317.9	357.7	383	414.1	453.6	500.8	566.2	627.5	680.5	733.5
4.4	3.2	6.2	11	9.1	5.8	6.5	7.6	11.3	13.5	10.3	6.2	3.2
228.3	249.1	262.9	274.2	287.1	306.2	330.9	357.3	381.8	408.5	436.7	474.8	521.4
4.67	4.44	8.74	10.51	5.82	5.05	5.54	7.91	11.2	13.35	16.39	12.24	9.09
5.73	5.25	8.03	10.81	7.86	6.84	6.83	9.06	12.67	15.26	18.87	14.85	10.79
207.7	209.9	211.9	213.8	216	218	220.2	222.6	225.1	227.8	230	232.2	234.3
370.5	384.7	400.1	394.9	386.2	398.6	462.3	601.4	460.3	530.6	596.6	594.1	559.8
84.4	87	89.4	91.9	93.8	96.2	99	102.3	105	106.9	108.7	110.2	111.6
79.4	82.2	85.1	86.8	85.8	88.8	92	96	98.8	99.3	100.4	99.5	100.8
5.9	5.6	4.9	5.6	8.5	7.7	7.1	6.1	5.8	7.1	7.6	9.7	9.6
−23	−23.4	−14.9	−6.1	−53.7	−73.7	−53.7	−59.2	−40.7	−73.8	−79	−128	−207.8
406.2	435.9	466.3	483.9	541.9	629	706.4	776.6	829.5	909	994.8	1,137.3	1,371.7
2.03	2.29	3.05	10.73	10.73	11.51	12.39	12.7	17.25	28.64	32.51	32.38	29.04
3.9	4.14	4.43	4.73	4.73	5.06	5.44	5.87	6.33	6.84	7.43	7.86	8.19
36.8	36.9	36.9	36.4	36	36.1	35.9	35.8	36.6	35.2	35.2	34.7	34.9
4.1	4.3	4.7	5.5	4.6	5.4	5.3	5.4	5.7	4.8	4.7	3.5	4.1
17.8	19	20.7	22.2	23.5	26.1	28.9	32.2	37.1	43.2	43.2	57.2	63.7
15	19.5	34.4	27.3	25.5	20.2	19.9	25.2	27.4	16.1	26.9	23.8	14.3
1.6	1.6	1.6	2	2.1	2.3	2.3	2.65	2.9	3.1	3.35	3.35	3.35
12.5	11.9	11.1	11.2	12.3	11.8	11.6	11.4	11.7	13	14	15	15.2
0.396	0.401	0.397	0.395	0.397	0.398	0.402	0.402	0.404	0.403	0.406	0.412	0.414
4.1	3.2	3.0	−1.6	3.5	3.1	1.7	1.1	0	−0.2	2.1	−0.8	3.6
−1.3	−5.4	1.9	−4.3	12.4	14.8	−27.2	−29.8	−24.6	−19.4	−16.2	−24.2	−57.8

Essentials of Economics

Stanley L. Brue
Pacific Lutheran University

Campbell R. McConnell
University of Nebraska at Lincoln

Boston Burr Ridge, IL Dubuque, IA Madison, WI New York San Francisco St. Louis
Bangkok Bogotá Caracas Kuala Lumpur Lisbon London Madrid Mexico City
Milan Montreal New Delhi Santiago Seoul Singapore Sydney Taipei Toronto

ESSENTIALS OF ECONOMICS
Published by McGraw-Hill/Irwin, a business unit of The McGraw-Hill Companies, Inc., 1221 Avenue of the Americas, New York, NY, 10020.

This book is printed on acid-free paper.

2 3 4 5 6 7 8 9 0 VNH/VNH 0 9 8 7 6

ISBN-13: 978-0-07-301967-3
ISBN-10: 0-07-301967-4

Publisher: *Gary Burke*
Executive sponsoring editor: *Lucille Sutton*
Editorial coordinator: *Jackie Grabel*
Senior marketing manager: *Martin D. Quinn*
Lead producer, Media technology: *Kai Chiang*
Senior project manager: *Lori Koetters*
Production supervisor: *Gina Hangos*
Director of design BR: *Keith J. McPherson*
Photo research coordinator: *Lori Kramer*
Photo researcher: *Keri Johnson*
Lead media project manager: *Becky Szura*
Senior supplement producer: *Carol Loreth*
Cover and interior design: *Kiera Pohl*
Cover illustration: *Kiera Pohl/Gettyimages*
Typeface: *10/12 Jansen*
Compositor: *TechBooks/GTS, York, PA*
Printer: *Von Hoffmann Corporation*

Library of Congress Cataloging-in-Publication Data

Brue, Stanley L., 1945-
Essentials of economics / Stanley Brue, Campbell McConnell.—1st ed.
p. cm.
Includes index.
ISBN-13: 978-0-07-301967-3 (alk. paper)
ISBN-10: 0-07-301967-4 (alk. paper)
1. Economics. I. McConnell, Campbell R. II. Title.

HB171.B778 2007
330–dc22 2005049644

www.mhhe.com

About the Authors

Stanley L. Brue

Stanley L. Brue did his undergraduate work at Augustana College (S.D.) and received its Distinquished Achievement Award in 1991. He received his Ph.D. from the University of Nebraska–Lincoln. He is a professor at Pacific Lutheran University, where he has been honored as a recipient of the Burlington Northern Faculty Achievement Award. Professor Brue has also received the national Leavey Award for excellence in economic education. He has served as national president and chair of the Board of Trustees of Omicron Delta Epsilon International Economics Honorary. He is coauthor of *Economics*, sixteenth edition (McGraw-Hill/Irwin), *Economic Scenes*, fifth edition (Prentice-Hall), *Contemporary Labor Economics*, seventh edition (McGraw-Hill/Irwin), and *The Evolution of Economic Thought*, seventh edition (South-Western). For relaxation, he enjoys international travel, attending sporting events, and skiing with family and friends.

Campbell R. McConnell

Campbell R. McConnell earned his Ph.D. from the University of Iowa after receiving degrees from Cornell College and the University of Illinois. He taught at the University of Nebraska–Lincoln from 1953 until his retirement in 1990. He is coauthor of *Economics*, sixteenth edition (McGraw-Hill/Irwin), *Contemporary Labor Economics*, seventh edition (McGraw-Hill/Irwin), and has edited readers for the principles and labor economics courses. He is a recipient of both the University of Nebraska Distinguished Teaching Award and the James A. Lake Academic Freedom Award and is past president of the Midwest Economics Association. Professor McConnell was awarded an honorary Doctor of Laws degree from Cornell College in 1973 and received its Distinguished Achievement Award in 1994. His primary areas of interest are labor economics and economic education. He has an extensive collection of jazz recordings and enjoys reading jazz history.

Brief Contents

PART ONE
Introduction

1 Limits, Alternatives, and Choices 3

2 The Market System and the Circular Flow 26

PART TWO
Price, Quantity, and Efficiency

3 Demand, Supply, and Market Equilibrium 48

4 Elasticity of Demand and Supply 70

5 Market Failure: A Role for Government 90

PART THREE
Product Markets

6 Businesses and Their Costs 114

7 Pure Competition 140

8 Pure Monopoly 166

9 Monopolistic Competition and Oligopoly 190

PART FOUR
Resource Markets

10 Wage Determination 216

11 Income Inequality and Poverty 242

PART FIVE
Macroeconomic Measurement, Models, and Fiscal Policy

12 Introduction to GDP, Growth, and Instability 264

13 Aggregate Demand and Aggregate Supply 290

14 Fiscal Policy, Deficits, and Debt 312

PART SIX
Money, Banking, and Monetary Policy

15 Money and Banking 338

16 Monetary Policy 366

PART SEVEN
Economic Growth and International Economics

17 Economic Growth 388

18 International Trade 410

Contents

Preface xiii
Reviewers xviii

PART ONE
Introduction

1 Limits, Alternatives, and Choices 3

The Economic Perspective 4
Scarcity and Choice
Illustrating the Idea Did Gates, Winfrey, and Rodriquez Make Bad Choices? 4
Purposeful Behavior / Marginalism: Benefits and Costs
Applying the Analysis Fast-Food Lines 6
Theories, Principles, and Models 6
Microeconomics and Macroeconomics 8
Microeconomics / Macroeconomics
Individual's Economic Problem 9
Limited Income / Unlimited Wants / A Budget Line
Society's Economic Problem 12
Scarce Resources / Resource Categories
Production Possibilities Model 14
Production Possibilities Table / Production Possibilities Curve / Law of Increasing Opportunity Cost / Optimal Allocation
Applying the Analysis The War on Terrorism 18
Unemployment, Growth, and the Future 19
A Growing Economy
Applying the Analysis Information Technology and Biotechnology 21
Present Choices and Future Possibilities
Summary
Terms and Concepts
Study Questions
Website Questions

2 The Market System and the Circular Flow 26

Economic Systems 27
The Command System / The Market System
Characteristics of the Market System 28
Private Property / Freedom of Enterprise and Choice / Self-Interest / Competition / Markets and Prices / Technology and Capital Goods / Specialization / Use of Money / Active, but Limited, Government
Four Fundamental Questions 34
What Will Be Produced?
Applying the Analysis McHits and McMisses 35
How Will the Goods and Services Be Produced? / Who Will Get the Output? / How Will the System Promote Progress?
Applying the Analysis The "Invisible Hand" 36
Applying the Analysis The Demise of the Command Systems 37
The Circular Flow Model 39
Resource Market / Product Market
Applying the Analysis Some Facts about U.S. Businesses 40
Applying the Analysis Some Facts about U.S. Households 42
Summary
Terms and Concepts
Study Questions
Website Questions

PART TWO

Price, Quantity, and Efficiency

3 Demand, Supply, and Market Equilibrium 48

Demand 49

Law of Demand / The Demand Curve / Market Demand / Changes in Demand / Changes in Quantity Demanded

Supply 54

Law of Supply / Market Supply / Determinants of Supply / Changes in Supply / Changes in Quantity Supplied

Market Equilibrium 58

Equilibrium Price and Quantity / Rationing Function of Prices

Applying the Analysis Ticket Scalping 60

Changes in Demand, Supply, and Equilibrium 60

Changes in Demand / Changes in Supply / Complex Cases

Government-Set Prices 63

Applying the Analysis Price Ceilings on Gasoline 63

Applying the Analysis Rent Controls 64

Applying the Analysis Price Floors on Wheat 65

Summary

Terms and Concepts

Study Questions

Website Questions

4 Elasticity of Demand and Supply 70

Price Elasticity of Demand 71

The Price-Elasticity Coefficient and Formula / Interpretations of E_d / The Total-Revenue Test

Illustrating the Idea A Bit of a Stretch 74

Price Elasticity along a Linear Demand Curve / Determinants of Price Elasticity of Demand

Applying the Analysis Fluctuating Farm Income 79

Applying the Analysis Excise Taxes and Tax Revenue 80

Applying the Analysis Decriminalization of Illegal Drugs 81

Applying the Analysis Price Elasticity of Demand and College Tuition 81

Price Elasticity of Supply 82

Price Elasticity of Supply: The Market Period / Price Elasticity of Supply: The Short Run / Price Elasticity of Supply: The Long Run

Applying the Analysis Antiques and Reproductions 85

Applying the Analysis Volatile Gold Prices 86

Income Elasticity of Demand 86

Normal Goods / Inferior Goods

Applying the Analysis Income Elasticity and Insights about the Economy 87

Summary

Terms and Concepts

Study Questions

Website Questions

5 Market Failure: A Role for Government 90

Private Goods 91

Profitable Provision / Efficient Allocation

Public Goods 92

Illustrating the Idea Art for Art's Sake 93

Optimal Quantity of a Public Good / Measuring Demand / Comparing Marginal Benefit and Marginal Cost

Applying the Analysis Cost-Benefit Analysis 95

Externalities 96

Negative Externalities / Positive Externalities / Individual Bargaining: Coase Theorem

Illustrating the Idea A Forest Tale 98

Liability Rules and Lawsuits / Government Intervention

Applying the Analysis Lojack: A Case of Positive Externalities 102

A Market-Based Approach

Applying the Analysis Tradable Emission Allowances 105

Financing the Public Sector: Taxation 106

Apportioning the Tax Burden / Benefits Received versus Ability to Pay / Progressive, Proportional, and Regressive Taxes / Tax Progressivity in the United States

Government's Role: A Qualification 109

Summary

Terms and Concepts

Study Questions

Website Questions

PART THREE

Product Markets

6 Businesses and Their Costs 114

The Business Population 115

Advantages of Corporations / The Principal-Agent Problem

Applying the Analysis Unprincipled Agents 117

Economic Costs 117

Explicit and Implicit Costs / Normal Profit as a Cost / Economic Profit (or Pure Profit) / Short Run and Long Run

Short-Run Production Relationships 121

Law of Diminishing Returns / Relevancy for Firms

Illustrating the Idea Diminishing Returns from Study 122

Tabular and Graphical Representations

Illustrating the Idea Exam Scores 125

Short-Run Production Costs 125

Fixed, Variable, and Total Costs

Applying the Analysis Sunk Costs 127

Per-Unit, or Average, Costs / Marginal Cost

Applying the Analysis Rising Cost of Insurance and Security 130

Long-Run Production Costs 130

Firm Size and Costs / The Long-Run Cost Curve / Economies and Diseconomies of Scale

Applying the Analysis The Verson Stamping Machine 134

Minimum Efficient Scale and Industry Structure

Applying the Analysis Aircraft Assembly Plants versus Concrete Plants 136

Summary

Terms and Concepts

Study Questions

Website Questions

7 Pure Competition 140

Four Market Models 141

Pure Competition: Characteristics and Occurrence 142

Demand as Seen by a Purely Competitive Seller 143

Perfectly Elastic Demand / Average, Total, and Marginal Revenue

Profit Maximization in the Short Run 145

Profit Maximization / Loss Minimization and Shutdown

Applying the Analysis The Still There Motel 150

Marginal Cost and Short-Run Supply 151

Generalized Depiction / Firm and Industry: Equilibrium Price

Profit Maximization in the Long Run 154

Assumptions / Goal of Our Analysis / Long-Run Equilibrium

Applying the Analysis The Exit of Farmers from U.S. Agriculture 157

Long-Run Supply for a Constant-Cost Industry / Long-Run Supply for an Increasing-Cost Industry / Long-Run Supply for a Decreasing-Cost Industry

Pure Competition and Efficiency 160

Productive Efficiency: P = Minimum ATC / Allocative Efficiency: P = MC

Summary

Terms and Concepts

Study Questions

Website Questions

8 Pure Monopoly 166

An Introduction to Pure Monopoly 167

Barriers to Entry 168

Economies of Scale / Legal Barriers to Entry: Patents and Licenses / Ownership or Control of Essential Resources / Pricing and Other Strategic Barriers to Entry

Monopoly Demand 170

Marginal Revenue Is Less than Price / The Monopolist Is a Price Maker

Output and Price Determination 172

Cost Data / MR = MC Rule / Misconceptions Concerning Monopoly Pricing

Economic Effects of Monopoly 175

Price, Output, and Efficiency / Income Transfer / Cost Complications

Applying the Analysis Is De Beers' Diamond Monopoly Forever? 179

Price Discrimination 180

Conditions / Examples / Graphical Analysis

Applying the Analysis Price Discrimination at the Ballpark 182

Monopoly and Antitrust Policy 183

Not Widespread / Antitrust Policy

Applying the Analysis *United States v. Microsoft* 185

Summary

Terms and Concepts

Study Questions

Website Questions

9 Monopolistic Competition and Oligopoly 190

Monopolistic Competition 191

Relatively Large Number of Sellers / Differentiated Products / Easy Entry and Exit / Advertising / Monopolistically Competitive Industries

Price and Output in Monopolistic Competition 193

The Firm's Demand Curve / The Short Run: Profit or Loss / The Long Run: Only a Normal Profit

Monopolistic Competition and Efficiency 196

Neither Productive nor Allocative Efficiency / Excess Capacity / Product Variety and Improvement

Oligopoly 197

A Few Large Producers / Either Homogeneous or Differentiated Products / Control over Price, but Mutual Interdependence

Illustrating the Idea Creative Strategic Behavior 198

Entry Barriers / Mergers

Oligopoly Behavior: A Game-Theory Overview 200

Mutual Interdependence Revisited / Collusive Tendencies / Incentive to Cheat

Kinked-Demand Model 201

Kinked-Demand Curve / Price Inflexibility / Price Leadership

Applying the Analysis Challenges to Price Leadership 204

Collusion 205

Joint-Profit Maximization

Applying the Analysis Cartels and Collusion 206

Obstacles to Collusion

Oligopoly and Advertising 208

Positive Effects of Advertising / Potential Negative Effects of Advertising

Oligopoly and Efficiency 210

Inefficiency / Qualifications

Applying the Analysis Oligopoly in the Beer Industry 211

Summary

Terms and Concepts

Study Questions

Website Questions

PART FOUR Resource Markets

10 Wage Determination 216

A Focus on Labor 217

Labor Demand 217

Marginal Revenue Product / Rule for Employing Labor: MRP = MRC / MRP as Labor Demand Schedule

Market Demand for Labor 220

Changes in Labor Demand 220
Changes in Product Demand / Changes in Productivity / Changes in the Prices of Other Resources

Applying the Analysis Occupational Employment Trends 222

Elasticity of Labor Demand 224
Ease of Resource Substitutability / Elasticity of Product Demand / Ratio of Labor Cost to Total Cost

Market Supply of Labor 225

Wage and Employment Determination 226

Monopsony 227
Upward-Sloping Labor Supply to Firm / MRC Higher than the Wage Rate / Equilibrium Wage and Employment

Applying the Analysis Monopsony Power 229

Union Models 230
Exclusive or Craft Union Model / Inclusive or Industrial Union Model / Wage Increases and Unemployment

Wage Differentials 233
Marginal Revenue Productivity / Noncompeting Groups

Illustrating the Idea My Entire Life 236

Compensating Differences

Applying the Analysis The Minimum Wage 237

Summary
Terms and Concepts
Study Questions
Website Questions

11 Income Inequality and Poverty 242

Facts about Income Inequality 243
Distribution by Income Category / Distribution by Quintiles (Fifths) / The Lorenz Curve and Gini Ratio / Income Mobility: The Time Dimension / Effect of Government Redistribution

Causes of Income Inequality 247
Ability / Education and Training / Discrimination / Preferences and Risks / Unequal Distribution of Wealth / Market Power / Luck, Connections, and Misfortune

Income Inequality over Time 249
Rising Income Inequality since 1970 / Causes of Growing Inequality

Equality versus Efficiency 252
The Case for Equality: Maximizing Total Utility / The Case for Inequality: Incentives and Efficiency / The Equality-Efficiency Tradeoff

Illustrating the Idea Slicing the Pizza 254

The Economics of Poverty 254
Definition of Poverty / Incidence of Poverty / Poverty Trends / Measurement Issues

The U.S. Income-Maintenance System 257
Social Insurance Programs / Public Assistance Programs

Applying the Analysis Welfare Reform 260

Summary
Terms and Concepts
Study Questions
Website Questions

PART FIVE
Macroeconomic Measurement, Models, and Fiscal Policy

12 Introduction to GDP, Growth, and Instability 264

Gross Domestic Product 265
A Monetary Measure / Avoiding Multiple Counting / Excluding Secondhand Sales

Measuring GDP 267
Personal Consumption Expenditures (C) / Gross Private Domestic Investment (I_g) / Government Purchases (G) / Net Exports (X_n) / Adding It Up: GDP $= C + I_g + G + X_n$

Nominal GDP versus Real GDP 269

Applying the Analysis The Underground Economy 270

Growth and the Business Cycle 272
Growth as a Goal / Arithmetic of Growth

Illustrating the Idea Growth Rates Matter! 273

Main Sources of Economic Growth / Growth in the United States

Business Cycles 275

Unemployment 276

Measurement of Unemployment / Types of Unemployment / Definition of Full Employment / Economic Cost of Unemployment / International Comparisons

Inflation 279

Meaning of Inflation / Measurement of Inflation / Facts of Inflation / Types of Inflation

Illustrating the Idea Clipping Coins 282

Redistribution Effects of Inflation 283

Who Is Hurt by Inflation? / Who Is Unaffected or Helped by Inflation? / Anticipated Inflation

Does Inflation Affect Output? 285

Cost-Push Inflation and Real Output / Demand-Pull Inflation and Real Output

Applying the Analysis Hyperinflation 286

Summary

Terms and Concepts

Study Questions

Website Questions

13 Aggregate Demand and Aggregate Supply 290

Aggregate Demand 291

Changes in Aggregate Demand 291

Consumer Spending

Applying the Analysis What Wealth Effect? 293

Investment Spending / Government Spending / Net Export Spending

Aggregate Supply 297

Aggregate Supply in the Long Run / Aggregate Supply in the Short Run

Changes in Aggregate Supply 299

Input Prices / Productivity / Legal-Institutional Environment

Equilibrium Price Level and Real GDP 302

Changes in the Price Level and Real GDP

Applying the Analysis Demand-Pull Inflation 304

Applying the Analysis Cost-Push Inflation 305

Downward Price-Level Inflexibility

Illustrating the Idea The Ratchet Effect 307

Applying the Analysis Recession and Cyclical Unemployment 308

An Important Caution

Summary

Terms and Concepts

Study Questions

Website Questions

14 Fiscal Policy, Deficits, and Debt 312

Fiscal Policy and the AD-AS Model 313

Expansionary Fiscal Policy / Contractionary Fiscal Policy

Built-In Stability 316

Automatic or Built-In Stabilizers / Economic Importance

Evaluating Fiscal Policy 317

Applying the Analysis Recent U.S. Fiscal Policy 320

Problems, Criticisms, and Complications 322

Problems of Timing / Political Considerations / Future Policy Reversals / Offsetting State and Local Finance / Crowding-Out Effect / Current Thinking on Fiscal Policy

The Public Debt 325

Ownership / Debt and GDP / International Comparisons / Interest Charges

False Concerns 327

Bankruptcy / Burdening Future Generations

Substantive Issues 328

Income Distribution / Incentives / Foreign-Owned Public Debt / Crowding Out Revisited

The Long-Run Fiscal Imbalance: Social Security 331

The Future Funding Shortfall / Policy Options

Summary

Terms and Concepts

Study Questions

Website Questions

PART SIX
Money, Banking, and Monetary Policy

15 Money and Banking 338

The Functions of Money 339

The Components of the Money Supply 339

Money Definition: *M*1 / Money Definition: *M*2

What "Backs" the Money Supply? 343

Value of Money

Illustrating the Idea Are Credit Cards Money? 344

Money and Prices

The Federal Reserve and the Banking System 346

Board of Governors / The 12 Federal Reserve Banks / FOMC / Commercial Banks and Thrifts / Fed Functions and Responsibilities / Federal Reserve Independence

The Fractional Reserve System 350

Illustrating the Idea The Goldsmiths 350

A Single Commercial Bank 351

Transaction 1: Creating a Bank / Transaction 2: Acquiring Property and Equipment / Transaction 3: Accepting Deposits / Transaction 4: Depositing Reserves in a Federal Reserve Bank / Transaction 5: Clearing a Check Drawn against the Bank / Transaction 6: Granting a Loan (Creating Money)

The Banking System: Multiple-Deposit Expansion 358

The Banking System's Lending Potential / The Monetary Multiplier / Reversibility: The Multiple Destruction of Money

Applying the Analysis The Bank Panics of 1930 to 1933 362

Summary

Terms and Concepts

Study Questions

Website Questions

16 Monetary Policy 366

Interest Rates 367

The Demand for Money / The Equilibrium Interest Rate

Illustrating the Idea That Is Interest 370

Tools of Monetary Policy 371

Open-Market Operations / The Reserve Ratio / The Discount Rate / Easy Money and Tight Money / Relative Importance

Monetary Policy, Real GDP, and the Price Level 375

Cause-Effect Chain / Effects of an Easy Money Policy / Effects of a Tight Money Policy

Monetary Policy in Action 380

The Focus on the Federal Funds Rate

Applying the Analysis Recent U.S. Monetary Policy 381

Problems and Complications

Illustrating the Idea Pushing on a String 383

"Artful Management" or "Inflation Targeting"?

Summary

Terms and Concepts

Study Questions

Website Questions

PART SEVEN
Economic Growth and International Economics

17 Economic Growth 388

Ingredients of Growth 389

Supply Factors / Demand Factor / Efficiency Factor

Production Possibilities Analysis 390

Growth and Production Possibilities / Production Possibilities and Aggregate Supply / Inputs and Productivity

Applying the Analysis U.S. Economic Growth Rates 393

Accounting for Growth 394

Labor Inputs versus Labor Productivity / Technological Advance / Quantity of Capital / Education and Training / Economies of Scale and Resource Allocation / Other Factors

The Productivity Acceleration: A New Economy? 398

Reasons for the Productivity Acceleration / Implication: More-Rapid Economic Growth /

Skepticism about Permanence / What Can We Conclude?

Is Growth Desirable and Sustainable? 403

The Antigrowth View / In Defense of Economic Growth

Applying the Analysis Growth in the Low-Income Nations 405

Summary

Terms and Concepts

Study Questions

Website Questions

18 International Trade 410

Trade Facts 411

Comparative Advantage and Specialization 412

Illustrating the Idea A CPA and a House Painter 413

Comparative Advantage: Production Possibilities Analysis / Trade with Increasing Costs

The Foreign Exchange Market 418

Exchange Rates / Depreciation and Appreciation / Determinants of Exchange Rates

Government and Trade 422

Trade Protections and Subsidies / Economic Impact of Tariffs / Net Costs of Tariffs / So Why Government Trade Protections?

Illustrating the Idea Buy American? 425

Three Arguments for Protection 425

Increased Domestic Employment Argument / Cheap Foreign Labor Argument / Protection-against-Dumping Argument

Trade Adjustment Assistance 427

Applying the Analysis Is Offshoring Bad? 428

Multilateral Trade Agreements and Free-Trade Zones 429

General Agreement on Tariffs and Trade / World Trade Organization

Applying the Analysis The WTO Protests 429

European Union / North American Free Trade Agreement

U.S. Trade Deficits 432

Causes of the Trade Deficits / Implications of U.S. Trade Deficits

Summary

Terms and Concepts

Study Questions

Website Questions

Appendix: Graphs and Their Meaning 438

Construction of a Graph / Direct and Inverse Relationships / Dependent and Independent Variables / Other Things Equal / Slope of a Line

Glossary 445

Index 464

Preface

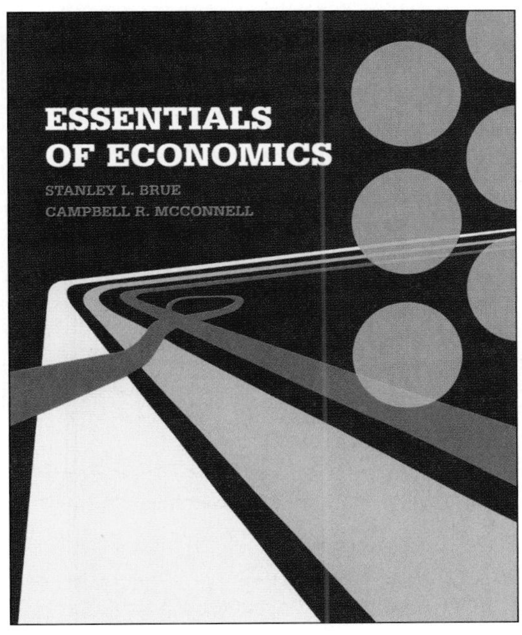

Welcome to *Essentials of Economics*, a one-semester principles of economics text derived from McConnell-Brue *Economics*, the best-selling two-semester economics textbook. Over the years numerous instructors have requested a short, one-semester version of *Economics* that would cover both microeconomics and macroeconomics. While some other two-semester books simply eliminate chapters, renumber those that remain, and offer the "cut and splice" version as a customized book, this methodology does not fit with our vision of a tightly focused, highly integrated book. We built this new text from scratch, incorporating the core content from *Economics* in a format designed specifically for the one-semester course. This book has the clear and careful language and the balanced approach that has made its two-semester counterpart a best-seller, but the pedagogy and topic discussion are much better suited to the needs of the one-semester course.

We think *Essentials of Economics* will fit nicely in various one-term courses. It is sufficiently lively and focused for use in principles courses populated primarily by nonbusiness majors. Also, it is suitably analytical and comprehensive for use in combined micro and macro principles courses for business and potential economics majors. Finally, we think this book—if supplemented with appropriate lecture and reading assignments—will work well in refresher courses for adult students returning to MBA programs.

However the book is used, our goals remain the same:

- Help the student master the principles essential for understanding the economic problem, specific economic issues, and policy alternatives.
- Help the student understand and apply the economic perspective and reason accurately and objectively about economic matters.
- Promote a lasting student interest in economics and the economy.

Distinguishing Features

Essentials of Economics includes several features that we think add up to a unique whole.

State-of-the-Art Design and Pedagogy

Essentials incorporates a single-column design with a host of pedagogical aids, including a strategically placed "To the Student" statement, chapter opening objectives, definitions in the margins, combined tables and graphs, complete chapter summaries, lists of key terms, carefully constructed study questions, connections to our Website, an appendix on graphs, an extensive glossary, and historical statistics on the inside covers.

Focus on Core Models

Essentials of Economics shortens and simplifies explanations where appropriate but stresses the importance of the economic perspective, including explaining and applying core economic models. Our strategy is to develop a limited set of essential models, illustrate them with analogies or anecdotes, explain them thoroughly, and apply them to real-world situations. Eliminating unnecessary graphs and elaborations makes perfect sense in the one-semester course, but cutting explanations of the truly *essential* graphs does not. In dealing with the basics, brevity at the expense of clarity is false economy.

We created a student-oriented one-semester textbook that draws on the methodological strengths of the discipline and helps students improve their analytical reasoning skills. Regardless of students' eventual majors, they will discover that such skills are highly valuable in their workplaces.

To the Student

This book and its ancillaries contain several features designed to help you learn economics:

- ***Icons in the margins*** A glance through the book reveals many pages with symbols in the margins. These icons are designed to alert you to helpful learning aids available with the book. The graph icon denotes "Interactive Graphs" found at the text's Website, www.brueonline.com. Brief exercises have you interact with the graphs, for example, by clicking on a specific curve and dragging it to a new location. These exercises will enhance your understanding of the underlying concepts. The light-bulb icon, in contrast, stands for "Origin of the Idea." Each of these pieces traces a particular idea to the person or persons who first developed it.

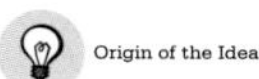

- ***Other Internet aids*** Our Internet site contains many other aids. In the student section at the Online Learning Center, you will find self-testing multiple-choice quizzes, links to relevant news articles, and much more.
- ***Appendix on graphs*** To understand the content in this book, you will need to be comfortable with basic graphical analysis and a few quantitative concepts. The ap-

FIGURE 13.5
Changes in aggregate supply. A change in one or more of the listed determinants of aggregate supply will shift the aggregate supply curve. The rightward shift of the aggregate supply curve from AS_1 to AS_2 represents an increase in aggregate supply; the leftward shift of the curve from AS_1 to AS_3 shows a decrease in aggregate supply.

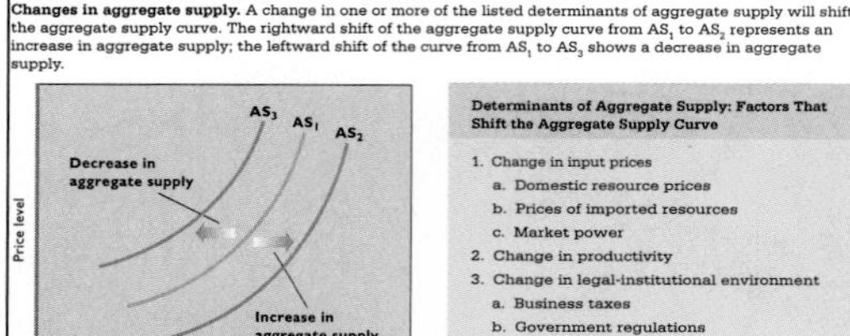

Illustrating the Idea

We included numerous analogies, examples, and anecdotes to help drive home central economic ideas in a lively, colorful, and easy-to-remember way. For instance, elastic versus inelastic demand is illustrated by comparing the stretch of an Ace bandage and that of a tight rubber tie-down. McDonald's sandwich "McHits" and "McMisses" over the years explain the concept of consumer sovereignty. Public goods and the free-rider problem are illustrated by public art, while a pizza analogy walks students through the equity-efficiency tradeoff. Inflation as a hidden tax is illustrated by a story of the prince of the realm clipping coins. These brief vignettes flow directly from the preceding content and segue to the content that follows, rather than being "boxed off" away from the flow and therefore easily overlooked.

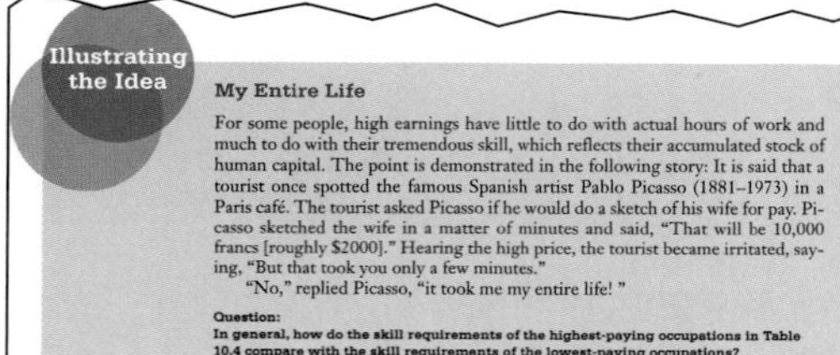

Illustrating the Idea

My Entire Life

For some people, high earnings have little to do with actual hours of work and much to do with their tremendous skill, which reflects their accumulated stock of human capital. The point is demonstrated in the following story: It is said that a tourist once spotted the famous Spanish artist Pablo Picasso (1881–1973) in a Paris café. The tourist asked Picasso if he would do a sketch of his wife for pay. Picasso sketched the wife in a matter of minutes and said, "That will be 10,000 francs [roughly $2000]." Hearing the high price, the tourist became irritated, saying, "But that took you only a few minutes."

"No," replied Picasso, "it took me my entire life! "

Question:
In general, how do the skill requirements of the highest-paying occupations in Table 10.4 compare with the skill requirements of the lowest-paying occupations?

Applying the Analysis

A glance though this book's pages will demonstrate that this is an application-oriented textbook. *Applying the Analysis* pieces immediately follow the development of economic analysis and are part of the flow of the chapters, rather than segregated from the main-body discussion in a traditional boxed format. For example, the basics of the economic perspective are applied to why customers tend to try to wait in the shortest checkout lines. The book illustrates inelasticity of demand (with changing supply) with an explanation of fluctuating farm income. Differences in elasticity of supply are contrasted by the changing prices of antiques versus reproductions. Hidden car-retrieval systems (such as Lojack) explain the concept of positive externalities. The book describes the principal-agent problem via the

Applying the Analysis

Price Ceilings on Gasoline

A **price ceiling** sets the maximum legal price a seller may charge for a product or service. A price at or below the ceiling is legal; a price above it is not. The rationale for establishing price ceilings (or ceiling prices) on specific products is that they purportedly enable consumers to obtain some "essential" good or service that they could not afford at the equilibrium price.

Figure 3.8 shows the effects of price ceilings graphically. Suppose that rapidly rising world income boosts the purchase of automobiles and increases the demand for gasoline so that the equilibrium or market price reaches $2.50 per gallon. The rapidly rising price of gasoline greatly burdens low- and moderate-income households, which pressure government to "do something." To keep gasoline affordable for these households, the government imposes a ceiling price of $2 per gallon. To impact the market, a price ceiling must be below the equilibrium price. A ceiling price of $3, for example, would have had no immediate effect on the gasoline market.

price ceiling
A legally established maximum (below-equilibrium) price for a product.

problems of corporate accounting and financial fraud. The idea of minimum efficient scale is applied to ready-mix concrete plants and assembly plants for large commercial airplanes. The difference in adult and child pricing for tickets to a ballgame compared to the pricing at the concession stands illustrates the concept of price discrimination. The aggregate demand model is applied to specific periods of inflation and recession, while the trade theory discussion touches on the issue of the offshoring of U.S. jobs. These and the many other applications clearly demonstrate to beginning students the relevance and usefulness of mastering the basic economic principles and models.

Photo Ops

Photo sets called *Photo Op* are included throughout the book to add visual interest, break up the density, and highlight important distinctions. Just a few of the many examples are sets of photos on complements versus substitutes in consumption, homogeneous versus differentiated products, economic stocks versus economic flows, substitute resources versus complementary resources, consumer durables versus nondurables versus services, and intermediate versus final goods.

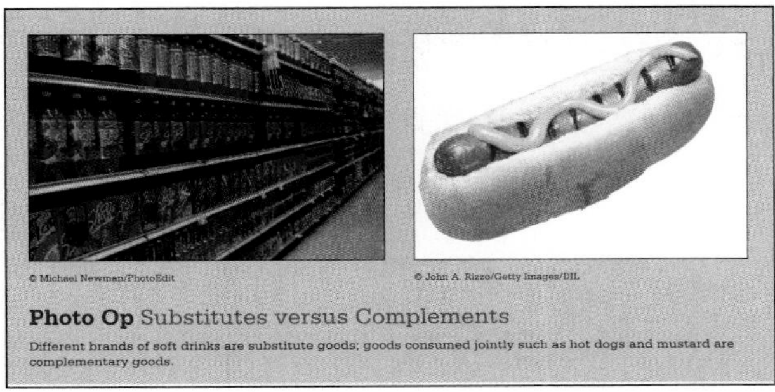

© Michael Newman/PhotoEdit © John A. Rizzo/Getty Images/DIL

Photo Op Substitutes versus Complements

Different brands of soft drinks are substitute goods; goods consumed jointly such as hot dogs and mustard are complementary goods.

Web Buttons

We link the book directly to our Website, www.brueonline.com, via icons that appear throughout the book to indicate that additional content on a subject can be found online. There are two Button types:

- The symbol to the right directs students to **Interactive Graphs.** Developed under the supervision of Norris Peterson of Pacific Lutheran University, this interactive feature depicts major graphs and instructs students to shift the curves, observe the outcomes, and derive relevant generalizations. There are 20 Interactive Graph icons scattered throughout the book.

- The light-bulb symbol directs students to **Origins of the Idea.** These brief histories were written by Randy Grant of Linfield College and examine the origins of scores of major ideas identified in the book. Students will find it interesting to learn about the economists who first developed such ideas as opportunity costs, equilibrium price, creative destruction, comparative advantage, and elasticity.

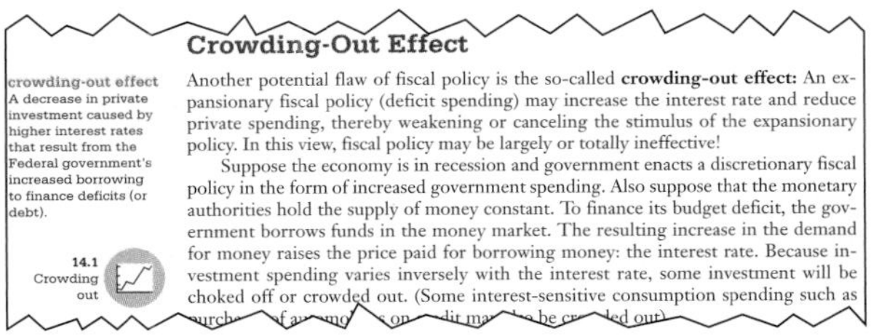

Crowding-Out Effect

crowding-out effect A decrease in private investment caused by higher interest rates that result from the Federal government's increased borrowing to finance deficits (or debt).

Another potential flaw of fiscal policy is the so-called **crowding-out effect:** An expansionary fiscal policy (deficit spending) may increase the interest rate and reduce private spending, thereby weakening or canceling the stimulus of the expansionary policy. In this view, fiscal policy may be largely or totally ineffective!

Suppose the economy is in recession and government enacts a discretionary fiscal policy in the form of increased government spending. Also suppose that the monetary authorities hold the supply of money constant. To finance its budget deficit, the government borrows funds in the money market. The resulting increase in the demand for money raises the price paid for borrowing money: the interest rate. Because investment spending varies inversely with the interest rate, some investment will be choked off or crowded out. (Some interest-sensitive consumption spending such as

14.1 Crowding out

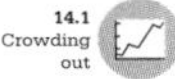

The outcome, as shown in Figure 5.1b, is that the equilibrium output Q_e is less than the optimal output Q_o. The market fails to produce enough vaccinations, and resources are *underallocated* to this product.

5.1 Externalities

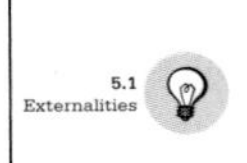

Economists have explored several approaches to the problems of negative and positive externalities. Let's first look at situations where government intervention is not needed and then at some possible government solutions.

Individual Bargaining: Coase Theorem

Coase theorem The idea that externality problems can be resolved through private negotiations by the affected parties when

In the **Coase theorem,** conceived decades ago by economist Ronald Coase at the University of Chicago, government is not needed to remedy negative or positive externalities where (1) property ownership is clearly defined, (2) the number of people involved is small, and (3) bargaining costs are negligible.

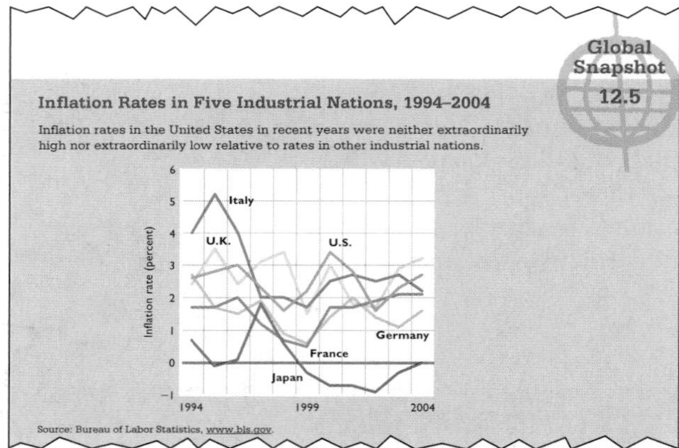

Global Snapshot 12.5
Inflation Rates in Five Industrial Nations, 1994–2004
Inflation rates in the United States in recent years were neither extraordinarily high nor extraordinarily low relative to rates in other industrial nations.
Inflation rate (percent)
Italy
U.K.
U.S.
Germany
France
Japan
1994
1999
2004
Source: Bureau of Labor Statistics, www.bls.gov.

Global Snapshots

Global Snapshot pieces show bar charts and line graphs that compare data for a particular year or other time period among selected nations. Examples of lists and comparisons include income per capita, the world's 10 largest corporations, the world's top brand names, standardized budget deficits or surpluses, the index of economic freedom, sizes of underground economies, rates of economic growth, exports as percentages of GDP, and so forth. These Global Snapshots join other significant international content to help convey that the United States operates in a global economy.

Supplements for Students

Essentials of Economics is accompanied by two high-quality supplements that help students master the subject.

- ***Study Guide*** One of the world's leading experts on economic education—William Walstad of the University of Nebraska at Lincoln—has prepared the *Study Guide.* Each chapter contains an introductory statement, a checklist of behavioral objectives, an outline, a list of important terms, fill-in questions, problems and projects, objective questions, and discussion questions. The text's glossary is repeated in the *Study Guide* so that the student does not have to go back and forth between books. Many students will find this "portable tutor" indispensable.
- ***Brue-McConnell Website*** (www.brueonline.com) Along with the Interactive Graphs and Origin of the Idea pieces, the student portion of the Website includes many learning aids for students. For example, there are Web-based study questions, self-grading quizzes, weekly news updates, and an interactive glossary—all specific to *Essentials of Economics*. For math-minded students, there is a "Want to See the Math?" section, written by Professor Norris Peterson, where they can explore the mathematical details of the concepts in the text.

Supplements for Instructors

Several supplements help instructors implement and customize their courses.

- ***Instructor's Manual*** Randy Grant of Linfield College has prepared the *Instructor's Resource Manual*. It includes chapter learning objectives, outlines, and summaries; numerous teaching suggestions; discussions of "student stumbling blocks"; listings of data and visual aid sources with suggestions for classroom use; and answers to the end-of-chapter study questions.

  Also available is an MS-WORD version of the *Manual*. Instructors can print out portions of the *Manual*'s contents, complete with their own additions and alterations, for use as student handouts or in whatever ways they wish. This capability includes printing out answers to the end-of-chapter questions.

- ***PowerPoints*** Darlene DeVera of Miami University created these in-depth slides to accompany lectures. The slides hit upon all the main points of the text and include the key figures and tables from the text.
- ***Instructor's Resource CD-ROM*** This CD contains everything the instructor needs, including PowerPoint slides, transparencies of the text graphs and charts, the Test Bank, and the *Instructor's Resource Manual.*
- ***Test Bank*** The Brue-McConnell Test Bank, compiled by Professor Grant, contains over 3,700 multiple-choice and true-false questions. For all test items, the kind of question is identified (for example, G = graphical, C = complex, etc.), as are the numbers of the text's pages that are the basis for each. Also, each chapter of the Test Bank has an outline or table of contents that groups questions by topics. Finally, the test items are coded for estimated degree of difficulty.

  The Test Bank is available in computerized EZ Test versions, as well as in MS Word. EZ Test systems can produce high-quality graphs from the Test Bank and feature the ability to generate multiple tests, with versions "scrambled" to be distinctive. This software will meet the various needs of the widest spectrum of computer users.
- ***Instructor Center at the Website*** The password-protected Instructor's Edition of the OnLine Learning Center at the Brue-McConnell Website, www.brueonline.com, contains a wealth of other supporting resources for instructors, including the *Instructor's Resource Manual*, PowerPoint slides, current news articles, information on the "clicker" system (CPS by eInstruction), and overhead transparencies.

Acknowledgments

We give special thanks to Norris Peterson of Pacific Lutheran University and Randy Grant of Linfield College, who teamed up to create the "button" content on our Website. We also thank Robert Jensen of Pacific Lutheran University for his meticulous help in proofreading the entire manuscript. Finally, we wish to acknowledge William Walstad and Tom Barbiero (the coauthor of the Canadian edition of *Economics*) for their ongoing ideas and insights.

We are greatly indebted to an all-star group of professionals at McGraw-Hill—in particular Gary Burke, Lucille Sutton, Erin Strathmann, Jackie Grabel, Keith McPherson, Martin Quinn, and Lori Koetters for their publishing and marketing expertise.

We thank Keri Johnson for her selection of Photo Op images. Kiera Pohl provided the vibrant interior design and cover.

Essentials of Economics has benefited from a number of unusually perceptive reviews. The contributors, listed at the end of the Preface, were a rich source of suggestions for this book. To each of you, thanks for your help and encouragement in completing this project. If *Essentials of Economics* helps a wider range of students to understand and apply economics, that educational outreach will be our most valued reward.

Stanley L. Brue
Campbell R. McConnell

Reviewers

Rashid Al-Hmoud, *Texas Tech University*
Jeff Ankrom, *Wittenberg University*
Deborah Bridges, *University of Nebraska, Kearney*
Gary Campbell, *Michigan Technological University*
Porchiung Chou, *New Jersey Institute of Technology*
Norman Cloutier, *University of Wisconsin, Parkside*
Linda Corrin, *New Jersey Institute of Technology*
Carole Endres, *Wright State University*
S.N. Gajanan, *University of Pittsburgh*
James R. Gale, *Michigan Technological University*
David Gordon, *Illinois Valley Community College*
Ali Hekmat, *College of Eastern Utah*
John Heywood, *University of Wisconsin, Milwaukee*
Robert Kennison, *Webster University, San Antonio Campus*
Marie Kratochvil, *Nassau Community College*
Herb Kretz, *Webster University*
Donald Leet, *CSU Fresno*
Zachary Machunda, *Minnesota State University, Moorhead*
Robert Moden, *Virginia Community College*
Dr. Jamal Nahavandi, *Pfeiffer University*
Jack Osman, *San Francisco State University*
Michael Ryan, *Gainesville College*
Rolando Santos, *Lakeland Community College*
James Ross Thomas, *Albuquerque Technical-Vocational Institute*

PART ONE

Introduction

1 Limits, Alternatives, and Choices

2 The Market System and the Circular Flow

To the Student

This book and its ancillaries contain several features designed to help you learn economics:

- ***Icons in the margins*** A glance through the book reveals many pages with symbols in the margins. These icons are designed to alert you to helpful learning aids available with the book. The graph icon denotes "Interactive Graphs" found at the text's Website, www.brueonline.com. Brief exercises have you interact with the graphs, for example, by clicking on a specific curve and dragging it to a new location. These exercises will enhance your understanding of the underlying concepts. The light-bulb icon, in contrast, stands for "Origin of the Idea." Each of these pieces traces a particular idea to the person or persons who first developed it.

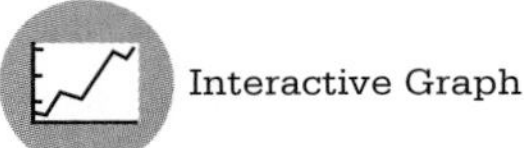

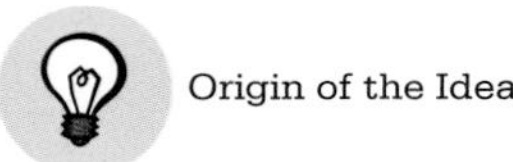

- ***Other Internet aids*** Our Internet site contains many other aids. In the student section at the Online Learning Center, you will find self-testing multiple-choice quizzes, links to relevant news articles, and much more.
- ***Appendix on graphs*** To understand the content in this book, you will need to be comfortable with basic graphical analysis and a few quantitative concepts. The appendix (pages 438–444) near the end of the book reviews graphing and slopes of curves. Be sure not to skip it.
- ***Key terms*** Key terms are set in boldface type within the chapters, defined in the margins, listed at the end of each chapter, and again defined in the Glossary toward the end of the book.
- ***"Illustrating the Idea" and "Applying the Analysis"*** These sections flow logically and smoothly from the content that precedes them. They are part and parcel of the development of the ideas and cannot be skipped.
- ***Questions*** Each "Illustrating the Idea" and "Applying the Analysis" section is followed by a question. A comprehensive list of study questions is located at the end of each chapter. At the Internet site, there are multiple-choice quizzes and one or more Web-based questions that require you to find information at specified Websites to formulate answers.
- **Study Guide** We enthusiastically recommend the *Study Guide* accompanying this text. This "portable tutor" contains not only a broad sampling of various kinds of questions but a host of useful learning aids.

Our two main goals are to help you understand and apply economics and help you improve your analytical skills. An understanding of economics will enable you to comprehend a whole range of economic, social, and political problems that otherwise would seem puzzling and perplexing. Also, your study will enhance reasoning skills that are highly prized in the workplace.

Good luck with your study. We think it will be well worth your effort.

CHAPTER ONE

Limits, Alternatives, and Choices

In this chapter you will learn:

- The definition of economics and the features of the economic perspective.
- The role of economic theory in economics.
- The distinction between microeconomics and macroeconomics.
- The categories of scarce resources and the nature of the economic problem.
- About production possibilities analysis, increasing opportunity costs, and economic growth.

Economics is about wants and means. Biologically, people need only air, water, food, clothing, and shelter. But in modern society people also desire goods and services that provide a more comfortable or affluent standard of living. We want bottled water, soft drinks, and fruit juices, not just water from the creek. We want salads, burgers, and pizzas, not just berries and nuts. We want jeans, suits, and coats, not just woven reeds. We want apartments, condominiums, or houses, not just mud huts. And, as the saying goes, "that is not the half of it." We also want DVD players, Internet service, education, homeland security, cell phones, and much more.

Fortunately, society possesses productive resources, such as labor and managerial talent, tools and machinery, and land and mineral deposits. These resources, employed in the economic system (or simply the economy), help us produce goods and services that satisfy many of our economic wants. But the blunt reality is that our economic wants far exceed the productive capacity of our scarce (limited) resources. We are forced to make choices. This unyielding truth underlies the definition of **economics:** It is the study of how people, institutions, and society make choices under conditions of scarcity.

1.1 Origin of the term "economics"

economics The study of how people, institutions, and society make economic choices under conditions of scarcity.

economic perspective A viewpoint that envisions individuals and institutions making rational decisions by comparing the marginal benefits and marginal costs of their actions.

opportunity cost The value of the good, service, or time forgone to obtain something else.

The Economic Perspective

Economists view things through a particular perspective. This **economic perspective,** or economic way of thinking, has several critical and closely interrelated features.

Scarcity and Choice

From our definition of economics, it is easy to see why economists view the world through the lens of scarcity. Scarce economic resources mean limited goods and services. Scarcity restricts options and demands choices. Because we "can't have it all," we must decide what we will have and what we must forgo.

At the core of economics is the idea that "there is no free lunch." You may be treated to lunch, making it "free" to you, but someone bears a cost—ultimately, society. Scarce inputs of land, equipment, farm labor, the labor of cooks and waiters, and managerial talent are required. Because these resources could have been used to produce something else, society sacrifices those other goods and services in making the lunch available. Economists call such sacrifices **opportunity costs:** the value of what is given up to obtain something else. To get more of one thing, society forgoes the opportunity of getting something else. So the cost of that obtained is the value of that sacrificed to get it.

Did Gates, Winfrey, and Rodriguez Make Bad Choices?

The importance of opportunity costs in decision making is illustrated by different choices people make with respect to college. College graduates usually earn about 50% more during their lifetimes than persons with just high school diplomas. For most capable students, "Go to college, stay in college, and earn a degree" is very sound advice.

Yet Microsoft cofounder Bill Gates and talk-show host Oprah Winfrey* both dropped out of college, and baseball star Alex Rodriguez ("A-Rod") never even bothered to enroll. What were they thinking? Unlike most students, Gates faced enormous opportunity costs for staying in college. He had a vision for his company, and his starting work young helped ensure Microsoft's success. Similarly, Winfrey landed a spot in local television news when she was a teenager, eventually producing and starring in the *Oprah Winfrey Show* when she was 32 years old. Getting a degree in her twenties might have interrupted the string of successes that made her famous talk show possible. And Rodriguez knew that professional athletes have short careers. Therefore, going to college directly after high school would have taken away 4 years of his peak earning potential.

So Gates, Winfrey, and Rodriguez understood opportunity costs and made their choices accordingly. The size of opportunity costs greatly matters in making individual decisions.

Question:
Professional athletes sometimes return to college after they retire from professional sports. How does that college decision relate to opportunity costs?

* Winfrey eventually went back to school and earned a degree from Tennessee State University when she was in her thirties.

Purposeful Behavior

Economics assumes that human behavior reflects "rational self-interest." Individuals look for and pursue opportunities to increase their **utility:** pleasure, happiness, or satisfaction. They allocate their time, energy, and money to maximize their satisfaction. Because they weigh costs and benefits, their decisions are "purposeful" or "rational," not "random" or "chaotic."

utility The satisfaction obtained from consuming a good or service.

Consumers are purposeful in deciding what goods and services to buy. Business firms are purposeful in deciding what products to produce and how to produce them. Government entities are purposeful in deciding what public services to provide and how to finance them.

1.2 Utility

Purposeful behavior does not assume that people and institutions are immune from faulty logic and therefore are perfect decision makers. They sometimes make mistakes. Nor does it mean that people's decision are unaffected by emotion or the decisions of those around them. Purposeful behavior simply means that people make decisions with some desired outcome in mind.

Nor is rational self-interest the same as selfishness. People make personal sacrifices to others. They contribute time and money to charities because they derive pleasure from doing so. Parents help pay for their children's education for the same reason. These self-interest, but unselfish, acts help maximize the givers' satisfaction as much as any personal purchase of goods or services. Self-interest behavior is simply behavior designed to increase personal satisfaction, however it may be derived.

Marginalism: Benefits and Costs

The economic perspective focuses largely on **marginal analysis**—comparisons of marginal benefits and marginal costs. To economists, "marginal" means "extra," "additional," or "a change in." Most choices or decisions involve changes in the status quo, meaning the existing state of affairs.

marginal analysis The comparison of marginal ("extra" or "additional") benefits and marginal costs, usually for decision making.

Should you attend school for another year? Should you study an extra hour for an exam? Should you supersize your fries? Similarly, should a business expand or reduce its output? Should government increase or decrease its funding for a missile defense system?

1.3 Marginal analysis

Each option involves marginal benefits and, because of scarce resources, marginal costs. In making choices rationally, the decision maker must compare those two amounts. Example: You and your fiancée are shopping for an engagement ring. Should you buy a 1/2-carat diamond, a 5/8-carat diamond, a 3/4-carat diamond, a 1-carat diamond, or something even larger? The marginal cost of a larger-size diamond is the added expense beyond the cost of the smaller-size diamond. The marginal benefit is the perceived greater lifetime pleasure (utility) from the larger-size stone. If the marginal benefit of the larger diamond exceeds its marginal cost (and you can afford it), buy the larger stone. But if the marginal cost is more than the marginal benefit, buy the smaller diamond instead, even if you can afford the larger stone!

In a world of scarcity, the decision to obtain the marginal benefit associated with some specific option always includes the marginal cost of forgoing something else. The money spent on the larger-size diamond means forgoing some other product. Opportunity costs are present whenever a decision is made.

Fast-Food Lines

The economic perspective is useful in analyzing all sorts of behaviors. Consider an everyday example: the behavior of fast-food customers. When customers enter the restaurant, they go to the shortest line, believing that line will minimize their time cost of obtaining food. They are acting purposefully; time is limited, and people prefer using it in some way other than standing in a long line.

If one fast-food line is temporarily shorter than other lines, some people will move to that line. These movers apparently view the time saving from the shorter line (marginal benefit) as exceeding the cost of moving from their present line (marginal cost). The line switching tends to equalize line lengths. No further movement of customers between lines occurs once all lines are about equal.

Fast-food customers face another cost-benefit decision when a clerk opens a new station at the counter. Should they move to the new station or stay put? Those who shift to the new line decide that the time saving from the move exceeds the extra cost of physically moving. In so deciding, customers must also consider just how quickly they can get to the new station compared with others who may be contemplating the same move. (Those who hesitate in this situation are lost!)

Customers at the fast-food establishment do not have perfect information when they select lines. Thus, not all decisions turn out as expected. For example, you might enter a short line and find someone in front of you is ordering hamburgers and fries for 40 people in the Greyhound bus parked out back (and the employee is a trainee)! Nevertheless, at the time you made your decision, you thought it was optimal.

Finally, customers must decide what food to order when they arrive at the counter. In making their choices, they again compare marginal costs and marginal benefits in attempting to obtain the greatest personal satisfaction for their expenditure.

Economists believe that what is true for the behavior of customers at fast-food restaurants is true for economic behavior in general. Faced with an array of choices, consumers, workers, and businesses rationally compare marginal costs and marginal benefits in making decisions.

Question:
Have you ever gone to a fast-food restaurant only to observe long lines and then leave? Use the economic perspective to explain your behavior.

Theories, Principles, and Models

scientific method The systematic pursuit of knowledge by observing facts and formulating and testing hypotheses to obtain theories, principles, and laws.

Like the physical and life sciences, as well as other social sciences, economics relies on the **scientific method.** That procedure consists of several elements:

- The observation of real-world behavior and outcomes.

- Based on those observations, the formulation of a possible explanation of cause and effect (hypothesis).
- The testing of this explanation by comparing the outcomes of specific events to the outcome predicted by the hypothesis.
- The acceptance, rejection, or modification of the hypothesis, based on these comparisons.
- The continued testing of the hypothesis against the facts. As favorable results accumulate, the hypothesis evolves into a *theory*. A very well tested and widely accepted theory is referred to as a *law* or *principle*. Combinations of such laws or principles are incorporated into *models*, which are simplified representations of how something works, such as a market or segment of the economy.

Economists develop theories of the behavior of individuals (consumers, workers) and institutions (businesses, governments) engaged in the production, exchange, and consumption of goods and services. Economic theories and **principles** are statements about economic behavior or the economy that enable prediction of the probable effects of certain actions. They are "purposeful simplifications." The full scope of economic reality itself is too complex and bewildering to be understood as a whole. In developing theories and principles, economists remove the clutter and simplify.

principles
Statements about economic behavior that enable prediction of the probable effects of certain actions.

Economic principles and models are highly useful in analyzing economic behavior and understanding how the economy operates. They are the tools for ascertaining cause and effect (or action and outcome) within the economic system. Good theories do a good job of explaining and predicting. They are supported by facts concerning how individuals and institutions actually behave in producing, exchanging, and consuming goods and services.

There are some other things you should know about economic principles:

- ***Generalizations*** Economic principles are *generalizations* relating to economic behavior or to the economy itself. Economic principles are expressed as the tendencies of typical or average consumers, workers, or business firms. For example, economists say that consumers buy more of a particular product when its price falls. Economists recognize that some consumers may increase their purchases by a large amount, others by a small amount, and a few not at all. This "price-quantity" principle, however, holds for the typical consumer and for consumers as a group.
- ***Other-things-equal assumption*** Like other scientists, economists use the *ceteris paribus* or **other-things-equal assumption** to construct their theories. They assume that all variables except those under immediate consideration are held constant for a particular analysis. For example, consider the relationship between the price of Pepsi and the amount of it purchased. It helps to assume that, of all the factors that might influence the amount of Pepsi purchased (for example, the price of Pepsi, the price of Coca-Cola, and consumer incomes and preferences), only the price of Pepsi varies. The economist can then focus on the "price of Pepsi–purchases of Pepsi" relationship without being confused by changes in other variables.

1.4
Ceteris paribus

other-things-equal assumption
The assumption that factors other than those being considered do not change.

- ***Graphical expression*** Many economic models are expressed graphically. Be sure to read the special appendix at the end of this book as a review of graphs.

Microeconomics and Macroeconomics

Economists develop economic principles and models at two levels.

Microeconomics

microeconomics The part of economics concerned with individual units such as a household, a firm, or an industry.

Microeconomics looks at specific economic units. At this level of analysis, the economist observes the details of an economic unit, or very small segment of the economy, under a figurative microscope. In microeconomics we talk of an individual household, firm, or industry. We measure the price of a specific product, the number of workers employed by a single firm, the revenue or income of a particular firm or household, or the expenditures of a specific firm, government entity, or family.

Macroeconomics

macroeconomics The part of economics concerned with the economy as a whole or major components of the economy.

aggregate A collection of specific economic units treated as if they were one unit.

Macroeconomics examines either the economy as a whole or its basic subdivisions or aggregates, such as the government, household, and business sectors. An **aggregate** is a collection of specific economic units treated as if they were one unit. Therefore, we might lump together the millions of consumers in the U.S. economy and treat them as if they were one huge unit called "consumers."

In using aggregates, macroeconomics seeks to obtain an overview, or general outline, of the structure of the economy and the relationships of its major aggregates. Macroeconomics speaks of such economic measures as total output, total employment, total income, aggregate expenditures, and the general level of prices in analyzing various economic problems. No or very little attention is given to specific units making up the various aggregates.

© Robert Holmes/CORBIS

© C. Lee/PhotoLink/Getty Images/DIL

Photo Op Micro versus Macro

Figuratively, microeconomics examines the sand, rock, and shells, not the beach; in contrast, macroeconomics examines the beach, not the sand, rocks, and shells.

Individual's Economic Problem

It is clear from our previous discussion that both individuals and society face an **economic problem:** They need to make choices because economic wants are unlimited but the means (income, time, resources) for satisfying those wants are limited. Let's first look at the economic problem faced by individuals. To explain the idea, we will construct a very simple microeconomic model.

economic problem The need for individuals and society to make choices because wants exceed means.

Limited Income

We all have a finite amount of income, even the wealthiest among us. Sure Bill Gates earns a bit more than the rest of us, but he still has to decide how to spend his money! And the majority of us have much more limited means. Our income comes to us in the form of wages, interest, rent, and profit, although we may also receive money from government programs or family members. As Global Snapshot 1.1 shows, the average income of Americans in 2004 was $41,400. In the poorest nations, it was less than $500.

Global Snapshot 1.1

Average Income, Selected Nations

Average income (total income/population) and therefore typical budget constraints vary greatly among nations.

Country	Per Capita Income, 2004*
Switzerland	$48,230
United States	41,400
Japan	37,180
France	30,090
South Korea	13,980
Mexico	6,770
Brazil	3,090
China	1,290
Pakistan	600
Nigeria	390
Rwanda	220
Liberia	110

* U.S. dollars.

Source: World Bank, www.worldbank.org.

Unlimited Wants

For better or worse, most people have virtually unlimited wants. We desire various goods and services that provide utility. Our wants extend over a wide range of products, from *necessities* (food, shelter, clothing) to *luxuries* (perfumes, yachts, sports cars). Some wants such as basic food, clothing, and shelter have biological roots. Other wants, for example, specific kinds of food, clothing, and shelter, arise from the conventions and customs of society.

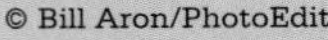

© Bill Aron/PhotoEdit

© F. Schussler/PhotoLink/Getty Images/DIL

Photo Op Necessities versus Luxuries

Economic wants include both necessities and luxuries. Each type of item provides utility to the buyer.

Over time, economic wants tend to change and multiply, fueled by new products. Only recently have people wanted MP3 players, Internet service, digital cameras, or camera phones because those products did not exist a few decades ago. Also, the satisfaction of certain wants may trigger others: The acquisition of a Neon or a Civic has been known to whet the appetite for a Porsche or a Mercedes.

Services, as well as goods, satisfy our wants. Car repair work, the removal of an inflamed appendix, legal and accounting advice, and haircuts all satisfy human wants. Actually, we buy many goods, such as automobiles and washing machines, for the services they render. The differences between goods and services are often smaller than they appear to be.

For most people, the desires for goods and services cannot be fully satisfied. Bill Gates may have all that he wants for himself, but it is clear from his massive charitable giving that he keenly wants better health care for the world's poor. Our desires for a *particular* good or service can be satisfied; over a short period of time we can surely obtain enough toothpaste or pasta. And one appendectomy is plenty. But goods and services *in general* seem to be another story.

Because we have only limited income but seemingly insatiable wants, it is in our self-interest to economize: to pick and choose goods and services that create maximum utility.

A Budget Line

The economic problem facing individuals can be depicted as a **budget line** (or, more technically, *budget constraint*). It is a schedule or curve that shows various combinations of two products a consumer can purchase with a specific money income.

budget line
A line that shows various combinations of two products a consumer can purchase with a specific money income, given the products' prices.

To understand this idea, suppose that you received a Barnes & Noble (or Borders) gift card as a birthday present. The $120 card is soon to expire. You take the card to the store and confine your purchase decisions to two alternatives: DVDs and paperback books. DVDs are $20 each and paperback books are $10 each. Your purchase options are shown in the table in Figure 1.1.

At one extreme, you might spend all of your $120 "income" on 6 DVDs at $20 each and have nothing left to spend on books. Or, by giving up 2 DVDs and thereby gaining $40, you can have 4 DVDs at $20 each and 4 books at $10 each. And so on to the other extreme, at which you could buy 12 books at $10 each, spending your entire gift card on books with nothing left to spend on DVDs.

The graph in Figure 1.1 shows the budget line. Note that the graph is not restricted to whole units of DVDs and books as is the table. Every point on the graph represents a possible combination of DVDs and books, including fractional quantities. The slope of the graphed budget line measures the ratio of the price of books (P_b) to the price of DVDs (P_{dvd}); more precisely, the slope is $P_b/P_{dvd} = \$ -10/\$ +20 = -1/2$ or $-.5$. So you must forgo 1 DVD (measured on the vertical axis) to buy 2 books (measured on the horizontal axis). This yields a slope of $-1/2$ or $-.5$.

The budget line illustrates several ideas.

FIGURE 1.1
A consumer's budget line. The budget line (or budget constraint) shows all the combinations of any two products that can be purchased, given the prices of the products and the consumer's money income.

The Budget Line: Whole-Unit Combinations of DVDs and Paperback Books Attainable with an Income of $120

Units of DVDs (Price = $20)	Units of Books (Price = $10)	Total Expenditure
6	0	($120 = $120 + $0)
5	2	($120 = $100 + $20)
4	4	($120 = $80 + $40)
3	6	($120 = $60 + $60)
2	8	($120 = $40 + $80)
1	10	($120 = $20 + $100)
0	12	($120 = $0 + $120)

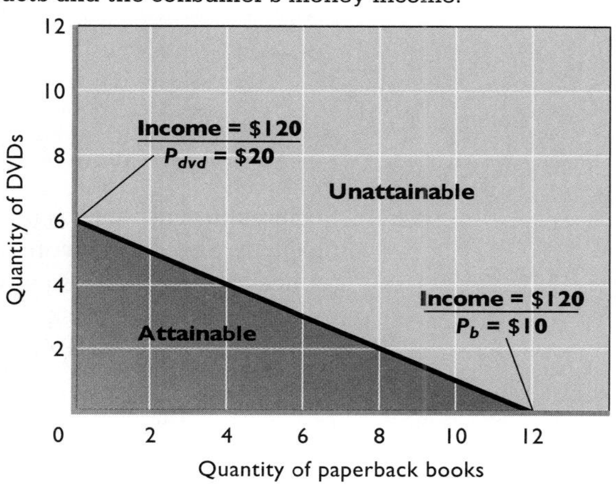

Attainable and Unattainable Combinations All the combinations of DVDs and books on or inside the budget line are *attainable* from the $120 of money income. You can afford to buy, for example, 3 DVDs at $20 each and 6 books at $10 each. You also can obviously afford to buy 2 DVDs and 5 books, if so desired, and not use up the value on the gift card. But to achieve maximum utility you will want to spend the full $120.

In contrast, all combinations beyond the budget line are *unattainable*. The $120 limit simply does not allow you to purchase, for example, 5 DVDs at $20 each and 5 books at $10 each. That $150 expenditure would clearly exceed the $120 limit. In Figure 1.1 the attainable combinations are on and within the budget line; the unattainable combinations are beyond the budget line.

1.5 Opportunity cost

Tradeoffs and Opportunity Costs The budget line in Figure 1.1 illustrates the idea of tradeoffs arising from limited income. To obtain more DVDs, you have to give up some books. For example, to acquire the first DVD, you trade off 2 books. So the opportunity cost of the first DVD is 2 books. To obtain the second DVD the opportunity cost is also 2 books. The straight-line budget constraint, with its constant slope, indicates **constant opportunity cost.** That is, the opportunity cost of 1 extra DVD remains the same (= 2 books) as more DVDs are purchased. And, in reverse, the opportunity cost of 1 extra book does not change (= 1/2 DVD) as more books are bought.

constant opportunity cost An opportunity cost that remains the same as consumers shift purchases from one product to another along a straight-line budget line.

Choice Limited income forces people to choose what to buy and what to forgo to fulfill wants. You will select the combination of DVDs and paperback books that you think is "best." That is, you will evaluate your marginal benefits and your marginal costs (here, product price) to make choices that maximize your satisfaction. Other people, with the same $120 gift card, would undoubtedly make different choices.

Income Changes The location of the budget line varies with money income. An increase in money income shifts the budget line to the right; a decrease in money income shifts it to the left. To verify this, recalculate the table in Figure 1.1, assuming the card value (income) is (a) $240 and (b) $60, and plot the new budget lines in the graph. No wonder people like to have more income: That shifts their budget lines outward and enables them to buy more goods and services. But even with more income, people will still face spending tradeoffs, choices, and opportunity costs.

Society's Economic Problem

Society must also make choices under conditions of scarcity. It, too, faces an economic problem. Should it devote more of its limited resources to the criminal justice system (police, courts, and prisons) or to education (teachers, books, and schools)? If it decides to devote more resources to both, what other goods and services does it forgo? Health care? Homeland defense?

economic resources The land, labor, capital, and entrepreneurial ability used in the production of goods and services.

Scarce Resources

Society's economic resources are limited or scarce. By **economic resources** we mean all natural, human, and manufactured resources that go into the production of goods and services. That includes the entire set of factory and farm buildings and all the equipment, tools, and machinery used to produce manufactured goods and agricultural products; all transportation and communication facilities; all types of labor; and land and mineral resources.

Resource Categories

Economists classify economic resources into four general categories.

Land

Land means much more to the economist than it does to most people. To the economist **land** includes all natural resources ("gifts of nature") used in the production process, such as arable land, forests, mineral and oil deposits, and water resources.

land
Natural resources ("gifts of nature") used to produce goods and services.

Labor

The resource **labor** consists of the physical and mental talents of individuals used in producing goods and services. The services of a logger, retail clerk, machinist, teacher, professional football player, and nuclear physicist all fall under the general heading "labor."

labor
The physical and mental talents and efforts of people used to produce goods and services.

Capital

For economists, **capital** (or *capital goods*) includes all manufactured aids used in producing consumer goods and services. Included are all factory, storage, transportation, and distribution facilities, as well as all tools and machinery. Economists refer to the purchase of capital goods as **investment.**

Capital goods differ from consumer goods because consumer goods satisfy wants directly, while capital goods do so indirectly by aiding the production of consumer goods. Note that the term "capital" as used by economists refers not to money but to tools, machinery, and other productive equipment. Because money produces nothing, economists do not include it as an economic resource. Money (or money capital or financial capital) is simply a means for purchasing real capital.

capital
Human-made resources (buildings, machinery, and equipment) used to produce goods and services.

investment
The purchase of capital resources.

Entrepreneurial Ability

Finally, there is the special human resource, distinct from labor, called **entrepreneurial ability.** The entrepreneur performs several functions:

entrepreneurial ability
The human talent that combines the other resources to produce a product, make strategic decisions, and bear risks.

- The entrepreneur takes the initiative in combining the resources of land, labor, and capital to produce a good or a service. Both a spark plug and a catalyst, the entrepreneur is the driving force behind production and the agent who combines the other resources in what is hoped will be a successful business venture.
- The entrepreneur makes the strategic business decisions that set the course of an enterprise.
- The entrepreneur is an innovator. He or she commercializes new products, new production techniques, or even new forms of business organization.
- The entrepreneur is a risk bearer. The entrepreneur has no guarantee of profit. The reward for the entrepreneur's time, efforts, and abilities may be profits or losses. The entrepreneur risks not only his or her invested funds but those of associates and stockholders as well.

© Lester Lefkowitz/ CORBIS

© L. Nelson/Stock Photos/zefa/CORBIS

© Creatas/PunchStock/DIL

© Neville Elder/CORBIS/DIL

Photo Op Economic Resources

Land, labor, capital, and entrepreneurial ability all contribute to producing goods and services.

Because land, labor, capital, and entrepreneurial ability are combined to produce goods and services, they are called the **factors of production** or simply inputs.

factors of production Economic resources: land, labor, capital, and entrepreneurial ability.

Production Possibilities Model

Society uses its scarce resources to produce goods and services. The alternatives and choices it faces can best be understood through a macroeconomic model of production possibilities. To keep things simple, we assume:

- ***Full employment*** The economy is employing all its available resources.
- ***Fixed resources*** The quantity and quality of the factors of production are fixed.
- ***Fixed technology*** The state of technology (the methods used to produce output) is constant.
- ***Two goods*** The economy is producing only two goods: food products and manufacturing equipment. Food products symbolize **consumer goods,** products that satisfy our wants directly; manufacturing equipment symbolizes **capital goods,** products that satisfy our wants indirectly by making possible more efficient production of consumer goods.

consumer goods Products and services that directly satisfy consumer wants.

capital goods Items that are used to produce other goods and therefore do not directly satisfy consumer wants.

Production Possibilities Table

A production possibilities table lists the different combinations of two products that can be produced with a specific set of resources, assuming full employment. Figure 1.2 contains such a table for a simple economy that is producing food products and manufacturing equipment; the data are, of course, hypothetical. At alternative A, this economy would be devoting all its available resources to the production of manufacturing equipment (capital goods); at alternative E, all resources would go to food-product production (consumer goods). Those alternatives are unrealistic extremes; an economy typically produces both capital goods and consumer goods, as in B, C, and D. As we move from alternative A to E, we increase the production of food products at the expense of the production of manufacturing equipment.

FIGURE 1.2
The production possibilities curve. Each point on the production possibilities curve represents some maximum combination of two products that can be produced if resources are fully and efficiently employed. When an economy is operating on the curve, more manufacturing equipment means less food products, and vice versa. Limited resources and a fixed technology make any combination of manufacturing equipment and food products lying outside the curve (such as at *W*) unattainable. Points inside the curve are attainable, but they indicate that full employment is not being realized.

	Production Alternatives				
Type of Product	**A**	**B**	**C**	**D**	**E**
Food products (hundred thousands)	0	1	2	3	4
Manufacturing equipment (thousands)	10	9	7	4	0

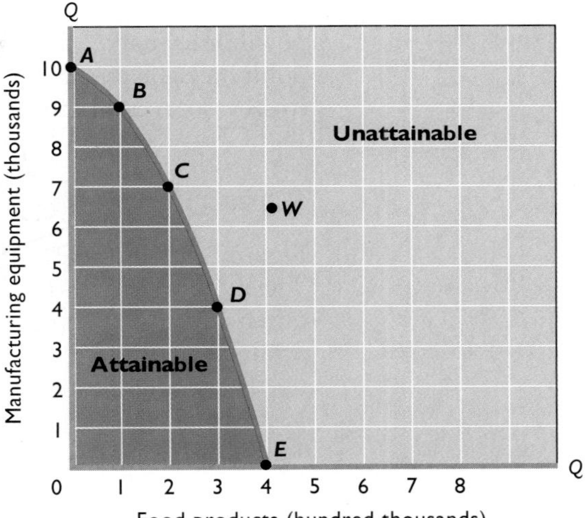

Because consumer goods satisfy our wants directly, any movement toward E looks tempting. In producing more food products, society increases the current satisfaction of its wants. But there is a cost: More food products mean less manufacturing equipment. This shift of resources to consumer goods catches up with society over time because the stock of capital goods does not expand at the current rate, with the result that some potential for greater future production is lost. By moving toward alternative E, society chooses "more now" at the expense of "much more later."

By moving toward A, society chooses to forgo current consumption, thereby freeing up resources that can be used to increase the production of capital goods. By building up its stock of capital this way, society will have greater future production and, therefore, greater future consumption. By moving toward A, society is choosing "more later" at the cost of "less now."

Generalization: At any point in time, a fully employed economy must sacrifice some of one good to obtain more of another good. Scarce resources prohibit such an economy from having more of both goods. Society must choose among alternatives. There is no such thing as a free bag of groceries or a free manufacturing machine.

Production Possibilities Curve

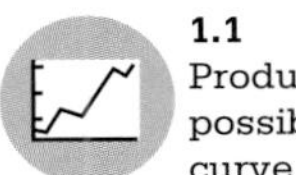

1.1 Production possibilities curve

The data presented in a production possibilities table can also be shown graphically. We arbitrarily represent the economy's output of capital goods (here, manufacturing equipment) on the vertical axis and the output of consumer goods (here, food products) on the horizontal axis, as shown in Figure 1.2.

production possibilities curve
A curve showing the different combinations of goods and services that can be produced in a fully employed economy, assuming the available supplies of resources and technology are fixed.

Each point on the **production possibilities curve** represents some maximum output of the two products. The curve is a "constraint" because it shows the limit of attainable outputs. Points on the curve are attainable as long as the economy uses all its available resources. Points lying inside the curve are also attainable, but they reflect less total output and therefore are not as desirable as points on the curve. Points inside the curve imply that the economy could have more of both manufacturing equipment and food products if it achieved full employment. Points lying beyond the production possibilities curve, like *W*, would represent a greater output than the output at any point on the curve. Such points, however, are unattainable with the current availability of resources and technology.

Law of Increasing Opportunity Cost

Figure 1.2 clearly shows that more food products mean less manufacturing equipment. The number of units of manufacturing equipment that must be given up to obtain another unit of food products, of course, is the opportunity cost of that unit of food products.

In moving from alternative A to alternative B in the table in Figure 1.2, the cost of 1 additional unit of food products is 1 less unit of manufacturing equipment. But when additional units are considered—B to C, C to D, and D to E—an important economic principle is revealed: The opportunity cost of each additional unit of food products is greater than the opportunity cost of the preceding one. When we move from A to B, just 1 unit of manufacturing equipment is sacrificed for 1 more unit of food products; but in going from B to C, we sacrifice 2 additional units of manufacturing equipment for 1 more unit of food products; then 3 more of manufacturing equipment for 1 more of food products; and finally 4 for 1. Conversely, confirm that as we move from E to A, the cost of an additional unit of manufacturing equipment (on average) is 1/4, 1/3, 1/2, and 1 unit of food products, respectively, for the four successive moves.

law of increasing opportunity costs
The principle that as the production of a good increases, the opportunity cost of producing an additional unit rises.

Our example illustrates the **law of increasing opportunity costs:** The more of a product that society produces, the greater is the opportunity cost of obtaining an extra unit.

Shape of the Curve

The law of increasing opportunity costs is reflected in the shape of the production possibilities curve: The curve is bowed out from the origin of the graph. Figure 1.2 shows that when the economy moves from *A* to *E*, it must give up successively larger amounts of manufacturing equipment (1, 2, 3, and 4) to acquire equal increments of food products (1, 1, 1, and 1). This is shown in the slope of the production possibilities curve, which becomes steeper as we move from *A* to *E*.

Economic Rationale

The economic rationale for the law of increasing opportunity costs is that economic resources are not completely adaptable to alternative uses. Many resources are better at producing one type of good than at producing others. Farms and ranches are highly suited to producing the ingredients needed to make food products, while lands rich in mineral deposits are more suited to producing the materials needed to make manufacturing equipment. As society steps up the production of food products, it must push resources that are less and less adaptable to making them into their production.

If we start at *A* and move to *B* in Figure 1.2, we can shift resources whose productivity is relatively high in food production and low in manufacturing equipment. But as we move from *B* to *C*, *C* to *D*, and so on, resources highly productive of food products become increasingly scarce. To get more food products, resources whose productivity in manufacturing equipment is relatively great will be needed. It will take increasingly more of such resources, and hence greater sacrifices of manufacturing equipment, to achieve each 1-unit increase in food products. This lack of perfect flexibility, or interchangeability, on the part of resources is the cause of increasing opportunity costs for society.

Optimal Allocation

Of all the attainable combinations of food products and manufacturing equipment on the curve in Figure 1.2, which is optimal? That is, what specific quantities of resources should be allocated to food products and what specific quantities to manufacturing equipment in order to maximize satisfaction?

Recall that economic decisions center on comparisons of marginal benefits (MB) and marginal costs (MC). Any economic activity should be expanded as long as marginal benefit exceeds marginal cost and should be reduced if marginal cost exceeds marginal benefit. The optimal amount of the activity occurs where MB = MC. Society needs to make a similar assessment about its production decision.

Consider food products. We already know from the law of increasing opportunity costs that the marginal costs of additional units of food products will rise as more units are produced. We also know that we obtain extra or marginal benefits from additional units of food products. However, although economic wants in the aggregate are insatiable, it is reasonable to assume that successive units of a particular product yield less additional benefits to society than prior units.

The optimal quantity of food production is indicated by the intersection of the MB and MC curves: 200,000 units in Figure 1.3. Why is this amount the optimal quantity? If only 100,000 units of food products were produced, the marginal benefit of an extra unit of them would exceed its marginal cost. In money terms, MB is $15, while MC is only $5. When society gains something worth $15 at a marginal cost of

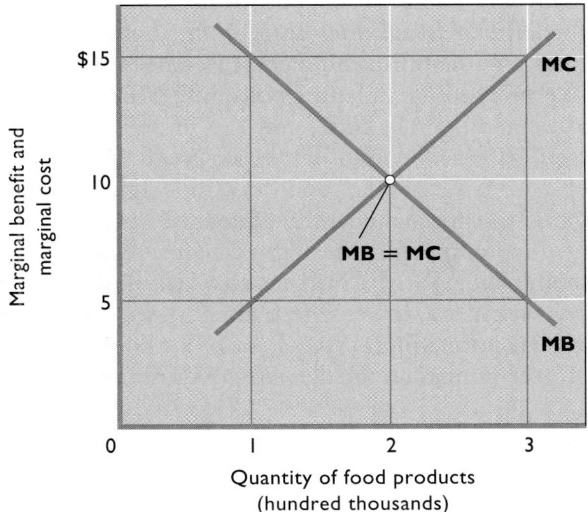

FIGURE 1.3
Optimal output: MB = MC. Achieving the optimal output requires the expansion of a good's output until its marginal benefit (MB) and marginal cost (MC) are equal. No resources beyond that point should be allocated to the product. Here, optimal output occurs when 200,000 units of food products are produced.

only \$5, it is better off. In Figure 1.3, net gains of decreasing amounts can be realized until food-product production has been increased to 200,000.

In contrast, the production of 300,000 units of food products is excessive. There the MC of an added unit is \$15 and its MB is only \$5. This means that 1 unit of food products is worth only \$5 to society but costs it \$15 to obtain. This is a losing proposition for society!

So resources are being efficiently allocated to any product when the marginal benefit and marginal cost of its output are equal (MB = MC). Suppose that by applying the above analysis to manufacturing equipment, we find its optimal (MB = MC) output is 7000. This would mean that alternative *C* (200,000 units of food products and 7000 units of manufacturing equipment) on the production possibilities curve in Figure 1.2 would be optimal for this economy.

Applying the Analysis

The War on Terrorism

Production possibilities analysis is helpful in assessing the costs and benefits of waging the war on terrorism, including the wars in Afghanistan and Iraq. The Defense Department estimated that the costs of homeland security and the war on terrorism in Afghanistan were \$30 billion in 2002. First estimates of the cost of the war in Iraq are \$174 billion, and further conflict and reconstruction may cost even more.

If we categorize all of U.S. production as either "defense goods" or "civilian goods," we can measure them on the axes of a production possibilities diagram such as that shown in Figure 1.2. The opportunity cost of using more resources for defense goods is the civilian goods sacrificed. In a fully employed economy, more defense goods are achieved at the opportunity cost of fewer civilian goods—health care, education, pollution control, personal computers, houses, and so on. The cost of waging war is the other goods forgone. The benefits are numerous and diverse but clearly include the gains from protecting against future loss of American lives, assets, income, and well-being.

Society must assess the marginal benefit (MB) and marginal cost (MC) of additional defense goods to determine their optimal amounts—where to locate on the defense goods–civilian goods production possibilities curve. Although estimating marginal benefits and marginal costs is an imprecise art, the MB-MC framework is a useful way of approaching choices. Allocative efficiency requires that society expand production of defense goods until MB = MC.

The events of September 11, 2001, and the future threats they posed increased the perceived marginal benefits of defense goods. If we label the horizontal axis in Figure 1.3 "defense goods," and draw in a rightward shift of the MB curve, you will see that the optimal quantity of defense goods rises. In view of the concerns relating to September 11, the United States allocated more of its resources to defense. But the MB-MC analysis also reminds us we can spend too much on defense, as well as too little. The United States should not expand defense goods beyond the point where MB = MC. If it does, it will be sacrificing civilian goods of greater value than the defense goods obtained.

Question:
Would society's costs of war be lower if it drafted soldiers at low pay rather than attracted them voluntarily to the military through market pay?

Unemployment, Growth, and the Future

In the depths of the Great Depression of the 1930s, one-quarter of U.S. workers were unemployed and one-third of U.S. production capacity was idle. The United States has suffered a number of much milder downturns since then, the latest occurring in 2001. In that year total production fell and unemployment increased.

Almost all nations have experienced widespread unemployment and unused production capacity from business downturns at one time or another. Since 1995, for example, several nations—including Argentina, Japan, Mexico, Germany, and South Korea—have had economic downturns and unemployment.

How do these realities relate to the production possibilities model? Our analysis and conclusions change if we relax the assumption that all available resources are fully employed. The five alternatives in the table of Figure 1.2 represent maximum outputs; they illustrate the combinations of food products and manufacturing equipment that can be produced when the economy is operating at full employment. With unemployment, this economy would produce less than each alternative shown in the table.

Graphically, we represent situations of unemployment by points inside the original production possibilities curve (reproduced in Figure 1.4). Point *U* is one such point. Here the economy is falling short of the various maximum combinations of food products and manufacturing equipment represented by the points on the production possibilities curve. The arrows in Figure 1.4 indicate three possible paths back to full employment. A move toward full employment would yield a greater output of one or both products.

A Growing Economy

When we drop the assumptions that the quantity and quality of resources and technology are fixed, the production possibilities curve shifts positions and the potential maximum output of the economy changes.

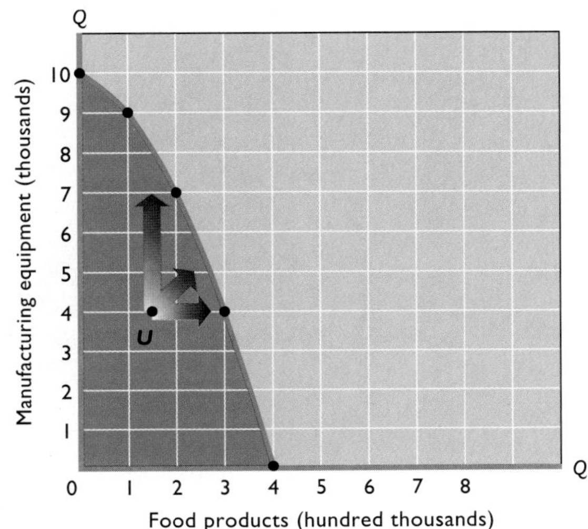

FIGURE 1.4
Unemployment and the production possibilities curve. Any point inside the production possibilities curve, such as *U*, represents unemployment or a failure to achieve full employment. The arrows indicate that, by realizing full employment, the economy could operate on the curve. This means it could produce more of one or both products than it is producing at point *U*.

Increases in Resource Supplies Although resource supplies are fixed at any specific moment, they change over time. For example, a nation's growing population brings about increases in the supplies of labor and entrepreneurial ability. Also, labor quality usually improves over time. Historically, the economy's stock of capital has increased at a significant, though unsteady, rate. And although some of our energy and mineral resources are being depleted, new sources are also being discovered. The development of irrigation programs, for example, adds to the supply of arable land.

The net result of these increased supplies of the factors of production is the ability to produce more of both consumer goods and capital goods. Thus 20 years from now, the production possibilities in Figure 1.5 may supersede those shown in Figure 1.2. The greater abundance of resources will result in a greater potential output of one or both products at each alternative. The economy will have achieved economic growth in the form of expanded potential output. Thus, when an increase in the quantity or quality of resources occurs, the production possibilities curve shifts outward and to the right, as illustrated by the move from the inner curve to curve *A′B′C′D′E′* in Figure 1.5. This sort of shift represents growth of economic capacity, which, when used, means **economic growth:** a larger total output.

economic growth An outward shift of the production possibilities curve that results from an increase in resource supplies or quality or an improvement in technology.

Advances in Technology An advancing technology brings both new and better goods and improved ways of producing them. For now, let's think of technological advance as being only improvements in the methods of production, for example, the introduction of computerized systems to manage inventories and schedule pro-

FIGURE 1.5
Economic growth and the production possibilities curve. The increase in supplies of resources, the improvements in resource quality, and the technological advances that occur in a dynamic economy move the production possibilities curve outward and to the right, allowing the economy to have larger quantities of both types of goods.

	Production Alternatives				
Type of Product	**A′**	**B′**	**C′**	**D′**	**E′**
Food products (hundred thousands)	0	2	4	6	8
Manufacturing equipment (thousands)	14	12	9	5	0

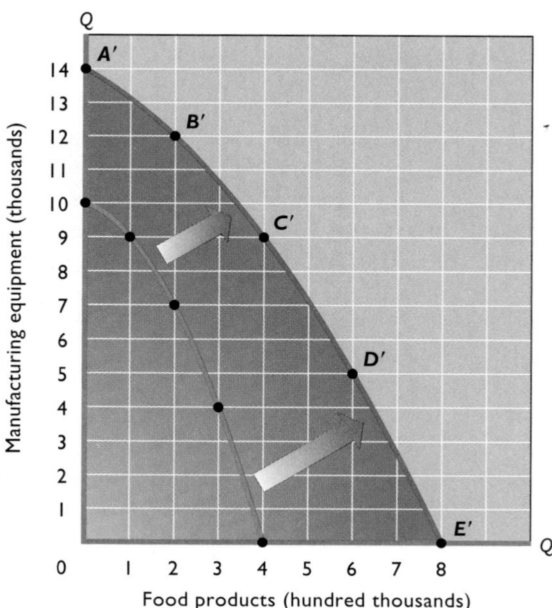

duction. These advances alter our previous discussion of the economic problem by allowing society to produce more goods with available resources. As with increases in resource supplies, technological advances make possible the production of more manufacturing equipment and more food products.

Applying the Analysis

Information Technology and Biotechnology

A real-world example of improved technology is the recent surge of new technologies relating to computers, communications, and biotechnology. Technological advances have dropped the prices of computers and greatly increased their speed. Improved software has greatly increased the everyday usefulness of computers. Cellular phones and the Internet have increased communications capacity, enhancing production and improving the efficiency of markets. Advances in biotechnology have resulted in important agricultural and medical discoveries. The sum of these new technologies is so significant that they may be contributing to greater-than-normal U.S. economic growth (larger rightward shifts of the nation's production possibilities curve).

Question:
How have technological advances in medicine helped expand production possibilities in the United States?

Conclusion: Economic growth is the result of (1) increases in supplies of resources, (2) improvements in resource quality, and (3) technological advances. The consequence of growth is that a full-employment economy can enjoy a greater output of both consumption goods and capital goods. While static, no-growth economies must sacrifice some of one good to obtain more of another, dynamic, growing economies can have larger quantities of both goods.

Present Choices and Future Possibilities

An economy's current choice of positions on its production possibilities curve helps determine the future location of that curve. Let's designate the two axes of the production possibilities curve as "goods for the future" and "goods for the present," as in Figure 1.6. Goods for the future are such things as capital goods, research and education, and preventive medicine. They increase the quantity and quality of property resources, enlarge the stock of technological information, and improve the quality of human resources. As we have already seen, goods for the future, such as capital goods, are the ingredients of economic growth. Goods for the present are consumer goods, such as food, clothing, and entertainment.

Now suppose there are two hypothetical economies, Presentville and Futureville, which are initially identical in every respect except one: Presentville's current choice of positions on its production possibilities curve strongly favors present goods over future goods. Point P in Figure 1.6a indicates that choice. It is located quite far down the curve to the right, indicating a high priority for goods for the present, at the expense of fewer goods for the future. Futureville, in contrast, makes a current choice that stresses larger amounts of future goods and smaller amounts of present goods, as shown by point F in Figure 1.6b.

FIGURE 1.6
Present choices and future locations of production possibilities curves. A nation's current choice favoring "present goods," as made by Presentville in (a), will cause a modest outward shift of the production possibilities curve in the future. A nation's current choice favoring "future goods," as made by Futureville in (b), will result in a greater outward shift of the curve in the future.

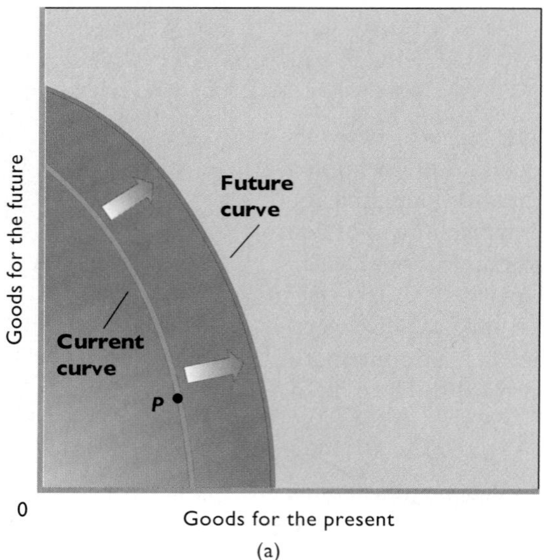

(a)
Presentville

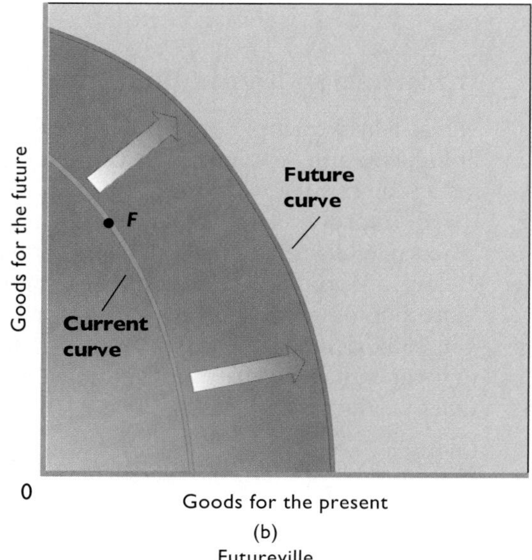

(b)
Futureville

Now, other things equal, we can expect the future production possibilities curve of Futureville to be farther to the right than Presentville's curve. By currently choosing an output more favorable to technological advances and to increases in the quantity and quality of resources, Futureville will achieve greater economic growth than Presentville. In terms of capital goods, Futureville is choosing to make larger current additions to its "national factory" by devoting more of its current output to capital than Presentville. The payoff from this choice for Futureville is greater future production capacity and economic growth. The opportunity cost is fewer consumer goods in the present for Futureville to enjoy.

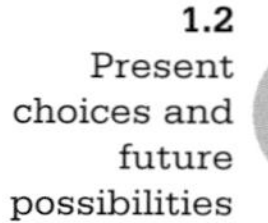
1.2 Present choices and future possibilities

Is Futureville's choice thus necessarily "better" than Presentville's? That, we cannot say. The different outcomes simply reflect different preferences and priorities in the two countries. But each country will have to live with the consequences of its choice.

Summary

1. Economics is the study of how people, institutions, and society make choices under conditions of scarcity.
2. The economic perspective includes three elements: scarcity and choice, purposeful behavior, and marginalism. It sees individuals and institutions making rational decisions based on comparisons of marginal costs and marginal benefits.
3. Economists employ the scientific method, in which they form and test hypotheses of cause-and-effect relationships to generate theories, laws, and principles. Economists often combine theories into representations called models.

4. Microeconomics examines specific economic units or institutions. Macroeconomics looks at the economy as a whole or its major aggregates.
5. Individuals face an economic problem. Because their wants exceed their income, they must decide what to purchase and what to forgo. Society also faces an economic problem. Societal wants exceed the available resources necessary to fulfill them. Society therefore must decide what to produce and what to forgo.
6. Graphically, a budget line (or budget constraint) illustrates the economic problem for individuals. The line shows the various combinations of two products that a consumer can purchase with a specific money income, given the prices of the two products.
7. Economic resources are inputs into the production process and can be classified as land, labor, capital, and entrepreneurial ability. Economic resources are also known as factors of production or inputs.
8. Society's economic problem can be illustrated through production possibilities analysis. Production possibilities tables and curves show the different combinations of goods and services that can be produced in a fully employed economy, assuming that resource quantity, resource quality, and technology are fixed.
9. An economy that is fully employed and thus operating on its production possibilities curve must sacrifice the output of some types of goods and services to increase the production of others. The gain of one type of good or service is always accompanied by an opportunity cost in the form of the loss of some of the other type.
10. Because resources are not equally productive in all possible uses, shifting resources from one use to another results in increasing opportunity costs. The production of additional units of one product requires the sacrifice of increasing amounts of the other product.
11. The optimal point on the production possibilities curve represents the most desirable mix of goods and is determined by expanding the production of each good until its marginal benefit (MB) equals its marginal cost (MC).
12. Over time, technological advances and increases in the quantity and quality of resources enable the economy to produce more of all goods and services, that is, to experience economic growth. Society's choice as to the mix of consumer goods and capital goods in current output is a major determinant of the future location of the production possibilities curve and thus of the extent of economic growth.

Terms and Concepts

economics
economic perspective
opportunity cost
utility
marginal analysis
scientific method
principles
other-things-equal assumption
microeconomics
macroeconomics
aggregate
economic problem
budget line
constant opportunity cost
economic resources
land
labor
capital
investment
entrepreneurial ability
factors of production
consumer goods
capital goods
production possibilities curve
law of increasing opportunity costs
economic growth

Study Questions

1. Ralph Waldo Emerson once wrote: "Want is a growing giant whom the coat of have was never large enough to cover." How does this statement relate to the definition of economics?
2. "Buy 2, get 1 free." Explain why the "1 free" is free to the buyer but not to society.
3. Which of the following decisions would entail the largest opportunity cost: allocating a

square block in the heart of New York City for a surface parking lot or allocating a square block at the edge of a typical suburb for such a lot? Explain.

4. What is meant by the term "utility," and how does it relate to purposeful behavior?

5. Cite three examples of recent decisions that you made in which you, at least implicitly, weighed marginal cost and marginal benefit.

6. Indicate whether each of the following statements applies to microeconomics or macroeconomics:

a. The unemployment rate in the United States was 5.2% in January 2005.

b. A U.S. software firm discharged 15 workers last month and transferred the work to India.

c. An unexpected freeze in central Florida reduced the citrus crop and caused the price of oranges to rise.

d. U.S. output, adjusted for inflation, grew by 4.4% in 2004.

e. Last week Wells Fargo Bank lowered its interest rate on business loans by one-half of 1 percentage point.

f. The consumer price index rose by 2.7% in 2004.

7. Suppose you won \$15 on a lotto ticket at the local 7-Eleven and decided to spend all the winnings on candy bars and bags of peanuts. The price of candy bars is \$.75 and the price of peanuts is \$1.50.

a. Construct a table showing the alternative combinations of the two products that are available.

b. Plot the data in your table as a budget line in a graph. What is the slope of the budget line? What is the opportunity cost of one more candy bar? Of one more bag of peanuts? Do these opportunity costs rise, fall, or remain constant as each additional unit of the product is purchased?

c. How, in general, would you decide which of the available combinations of candy bars and bags of peanuts to buy?

d. Suppose that you had won \$30 on your ticket, not \$15. Show the \$30 budget line in your diagram. Why would this budget line be preferable to the old one?

8. What are economic resources? What categories do economists use to classify them? Why are resources also called factors of production? Why are they called inputs?

9. Why isn't money considered a capital resource in economics? Why is entrepreneurial ability considered a category of economic resource, distinct from labor? What are the major functions of the entrepreneur?

10. Below is a production possibilities table for consumer goods (automobiles) and capital goods (forklifts):

	Production Alternatives				
Type of Production	**A**	**B**	**C**	**D**	**E**
Automobiles	0	2	4	6	8
Forklifts	30	27	21	12	0

a. Show these data graphically. Upon what specific assumptions is this production possibilities curve based?

b. If the economy is at point *C*, what is the cost of one more automobile? Of one more forklift? Explain how the production possibilities curve reflects the law of increasing opportunity costs.

c. If the economy characterized by this production possibilities table and curve were producing 3 automobiles and 20 forklifts, what could you conclude about its use of its available resources?

d. What would production at a point outside the production possibilities curve indicate? What must occur before the economy can attain such a level of production?

e. Suppose improvement occurs in the technology of producing forklifts but not in the technology of producing automobiles. Draw the new production possibilities curve. Now assume that a technological advance occurs in producing automobiles but not in producing forklifts. Draw the new production possibilities curve. Now draw a production possibilities curve that reflects technological improvement in the production of both goods.

11. Specify and explain the typical shapes of marginal-benefit and marginal-cost curves. How are these curves used to determine the optimal allocation of resources to a particular product? If current output is such that marginal cost exceeds marginal benefit, should more or fewer resources be allocated to this product? Explain.

12. Explain how (if at all) each of the following events affects the location of a country's production possibilities curve:
   a. The quality of education increases.
   b. The number of unemployed workers increases.
   c. A new technique improves the efficiency of extracting copper from ore.
   d. A devastating earthquake destroys numerous production facilities.

Website Questions

At the text's Website, www.brueonline.com, you will find three multiple-choice quizzes on this chapter's content. We encourage you to take the quizzes to see how you do. Also, you will find one or more Web-based questions that require information from the Internet to answer.

REMINDER: An appendix on understanding graphs is near the end of this book. We highly recommend it for anyone who needs a quick review of this mathematical tool.

In *pure* capitalism—or *laissez-faire* capitalism—government's role would be limited to protecting private property and establishing an environment appropriate to the operation of the market system. The term "laissez-faire" means "let it be," that is, keep government from interfering with the economy. The idea is that such interference will disturb the efficient working of the market system.

But in the capitalism practiced in the United States and most other countries, government plays a substantial role in the economy. It not only provides the rules for economic activity but also promotes economic stability and growth, provides certain goods and services that would otherwise be underproduced or not produced at all, and modifies the distribution of income. The government, however, is not the dominant economic force in deciding what to produce, how to produce it, and who will get it. That force is the market.

Characteristics of the Market System

It will be very instructive to examine some of the key features of the market system in more detail.

Private Property

private property The right of persons and firms to obtain, own, control, employ, dispose of, and bequeath land, capital, and other property.

In a market system, private individuals and firms, not the government, own most of the property resources (land and capital). It is this extensive private ownership of capital that gives capitalism its name. This right of **private property,** coupled with the freedom to negotiate binding legal contracts, enables individuals and businesses to obtain, use, and dispose of property resources as they see fit. The right of property owners to designate who will receive their property when they die sustains the institution of private property.

Property rights encourage investment, innovation, exchange, maintenance of property, and economic growth. Why would anyone stock a store, build a factory, or clear land for farming if someone else, or the government itself, could take that property for his or her own benefit?

Property rights also extend to intellectual property through patents, copyrights, and trademarks. Such long-term protection encourages people to write books, music, and computer programs and to invent new products and production processes without fear that others will steal them and the rewards they may bring.

Moreover, property rights facilitate exchange. The title to an automobile or the deed to a cattle ranch assures the buyer that the seller is the legitimate owner. Also, property rights encourage owners to maintain or improve their property so as to preserve or increase its value. Finally, property rights enable people to use their time and resources to produce more goods and services, rather than using them to protect and retain the property they have already produced or acquired.

Freedom of Enterprise and Choice

freedom of enterprise The freedom of firms to obtain economic resources, to use those resources to produce products of the firms' own choosing, and to sell their products in markets of their choice.

Closely related to private ownership of property is freedom of enterprise and choice. The market system requires that various economic units make certain choices, which are expressed and implemented in the economy's markets:

- **Freedom of enterprise** ensures that entrepreneurs and private businesses are free to obtain and use economic resources to produce their choice of goods and services and to sell them in their chosen markets.

- **Freedom of choice** enables owners to employ or dispose of their property and money as they see fit. It also allows workers to enter any line of work for which they are qualified. Finally, it ensures that consumers are free to buy the goods and services that best satisfy their wants.

freedom of choice The freedom of owners of resources to employ or dispose of them as they see fit, and the freedom of consumers to spend their incomes in a manner they think is appropriate.

These choices are free only within broad legal limitations, of course. Illegal choices such as selling human organs or buying illicit drugs are punished through fines and imprisonment. (Global Snapshot 2.1 reveals that the degree of economic freedom varies greatly from nation to nation.)

Global Snapshot 2.1

Index of Economic Freedom, Selected Economies

The Index of Economic Freedom measures economic freedom using 10 broad categories such as trade policy, property rights, and government intervention, with each category containing more than 50 specific criteria. The index then ranks 156 economies according to their degree of economic freedom. A few selected rankings for 2005 are listed below.

FREE

1 Hong Kong
5 New Zealand
12 United States

MOSTLY FREE

18 Germany
31 Spain
44 France

MOSTLY UNFREE

90 Brazil
112 China
124 Russia

REPRESSED

148 Iran
149 Cuba
155 North Korea

Source: Heritage Foundation (www.heritage.org) and *The Wall Street Journal*.

Self-Interest

In the market system, **self-interest** is the motivating force of the various economic units as they express their free choices. Self-interest simply means that each economic unit tries to achieve its own particular goal, which usually requires delivering something of value to others. Entrepreneurs try to maximize profit or minimize loss. Property owners try to get the highest price for the sale or rent of

self-interest The most-advantageous outcome as viewed by each firm, property owner, worker, or consumer.

their resources. Workers try to maximize their utility (satisfaction) by finding jobs that offer the best combination of wages, hours, fringe benefits, and working conditions. Consumers try to obtain the products they want at the lowest possible price and apportion their expenditures to maximize their utility. The motive of self-interest gives direction and consistency to what might otherwise be a chaotic economy.

Competition

competition The presence in a market of independent buyers and sellers vying with one another, and the freedom of buyers and sellers to enter and leave the market.

The market system depends on **competition** among economic units. The basis of this competition is freedom of choice exercised in pursuit of a monetary return. Very broadly defined, competition requires:

- Independently acting sellers and buyers operating in a particular product or resource market.
- Freedom of sellers and buyers to enter or leave markets, on the basis of their economic self-interest.

2.1 Self-interest 

Competition diffuses economic power within the businesses and households that make up the economy. When there are independently acting sellers and buyers in a market, no one buyer or seller is able to dictate the price of the product or resource because others can undercut that price.

Competition also implies that producers can enter or leave an industry; there are no insurmountable barriers to an industry's expanding or contracting. This freedom of an industry to expand or contract provides the economy with the flexibility needed to remain efficient over time. Freedom of entry and exit enables the economy to adjust to changes in consumer tastes, technology, and resource availability.

The diffusion of economic power inherent in competition limits the potential abuse of that power. A producer that charges more than the competitive market price will lose sales to other producers. An employer who pays less than the competitive market wage rate will lose workers to other employers. A firm that fails to exploit new technology will lose profits to firms that do. Competition is the basic regulatory force in the market system.

Markets and Prices

market An institution or mechanism that brings buyers and sellers together.

Markets and prices are key components of the market system. They give the system its ability to coordinate millions of daily economic decisions. A **market** is an institution or mechanism that brings buyers ("demanders") and sellers ("suppliers") into contact. A market system conveys the decisions made by buyers and sellers of products and resources. The decisions made on each side of the market determine a set of product and resource prices that guide resource owners, entrepreneurs, and consumers as they make and revise their choices and pursue their self-interest.

Just as competition is the regulatory mechanism of the market system, the market system itself is the organizing mechanism. It is an elaborate communication network through which innumerable individual free choices are recorded, summarized, and balanced. Those who respond to market signals and heed market dictates are rewarded with greater profit and income; those who do not respond to those signals and choose to ignore market dictates are penalized. Through this mechanism society decides what the economy should produce, how production can be organized efficiently, and how the fruits of production are to be distributed among the various units that make up the economy.

Technology and Capital Goods

In the market system, competition, freedom of choice, self-interest, and personal reward provide the opportunity and motivation for technological advance. The monetary rewards for new products or production techniques accrue directly to the innovator. The market system therefore encourages extensive use and rapid development of complex capital goods: tools, machinery, large-scale factories, and facilities for storage, communication, transportation, and marketing.

Advanced technology and capital goods are important because the most direct methods of production are often the least efficient. The only way to avoid that inefficiency is to rely on capital goods. It would be ridiculous for a farmer to go at production with bare hands. There are huge benefits to be derived from creating and using such capital equipment as plows, tractors, storage bins, and so on. The more efficient production means much more abundant outputs.

Specialization

The extent to which market economies rely on **specialization** is extraordinary. Specialization is the use of resources of an individual, region, or nation to produce one or a few goods or services rather than the entire range of goods and services. Those goods and services are then exchanged for a full range of desired products. The majority of consumers produce virtually none of the goods and services they consume, and they consume little or nothing of the items they produce. The person working nine to five installing windows in Fords may own a Honda. Many farmers sell their milk to the local dairy and then buy butter at the local grocery store. Society learned long ago that self-sufficiency breeds inefficiency. The jack-of-all-trades may be a very colorful individual but is certainly not an efficient producer.

specialization The use of resources of an individual, region, or nation to produce one or a few goods and services rather than the entire range of goods and services.

Division of Labor

Human specialization—called the **division of labor**—contributes to a society's output in several ways:

division of labor The separation of the work required to produce a product into a number of different tasks that are performed by different workers.

2.2 Specialization/division of labor

- ***Specialization makes use of differences in ability*** Specialization enables individuals to take advantage of existing differences in their abilities and skills. If Peyton is strong, athletic, and good at throwing a football and Beyonce is beautiful, agile, and can sing, their distribution of talents can be most efficiently used if Peyton plays professional football and Beyonce records songs and gives concerts.
- ***Specialization fosters learning by doing*** Even if the abilities of two people are identical, specialization may still be advantageous. By devoting time to a single task, a person is more likely to develop the skills required and to improve techniques than by working at a number of different tasks. You learn to be a good lawyer by studying and practicing law.
- ***Specialization saves time*** By devoting time to a single task, a person avoids the loss of time incurred in shifting from one job to another.

For all these reasons, specialization increases the total output society derives from limited resources.

© Brent Smith/Reuters/CORBIS

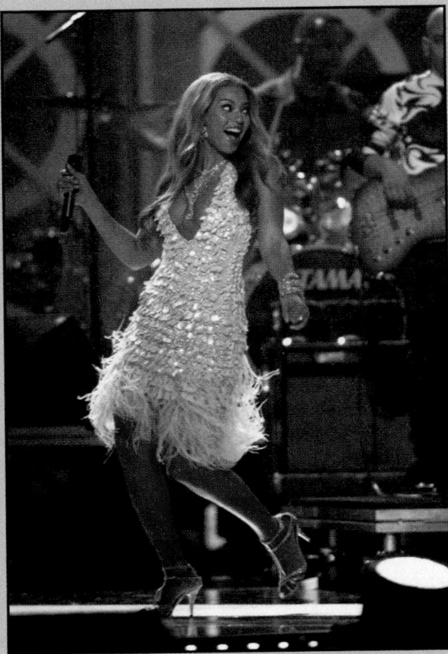

© Chris Farina/CORBIS

Photo Op Peyton Manning and Beyonce Knowles

It makes economic sense for Peyton Manning and Beyonce Knowles to specialize in what they do best.

Geographic Specialization Specialization also works on a regional and international basis. It is conceivable that oranges could be grown in Nebraska, but because of the unsuitability of the land, rainfall, and temperature, the costs would be very high. And it is conceivable that wheat could be grown in Florida but such production would be costly for similar geographical reasons. So Nebraskans produce products—wheat in particular—for which their resources are best suited, and Floridians do the same, producing oranges and other citrus fruits. By specializing, both economies produce more than is needed locally. Then, very sensibly, Nebraskans and Floridians swap some of their surpluses—wheat for oranges, oranges for wheat.

Similarly, on an international scale, the United States specializes in producing such items as commercial aircraft and computers, which it sells abroad in exchange for video recorders from Japan, bananas from Honduras, and woven baskets from Thailand. Both human specialization and geographic specialization are needed to achieve efficiency in the use of limited resources.

Use of Money

medium of exchange Any item sellers generally accept and buyers generally use to pay for goods and services.

A rather obvious characteristic of any economic system is the extensive use of money. Money performs several functions, but first and foremost it is a **medium of exchange.** It makes trade easier.

Specialization requires exchange. Exchange can, and sometimes does, occur through **barter**—swapping goods for goods, say, wheat for oranges. But barter poses serious problems because it requires a *coincidence of wants* between the buyer and the seller. In our example, we assumed that Nebraskans had excess wheat to trade and wanted oranges. And we assumed that Floridians had excess oranges to trade and wanted wheat. So an exchange occurred. But if such a coincidence of wants is missing, trade is stymied.

barter
The exchange of one good or service for another good or service.

Suppose that Nebraska has no interest in Florida's oranges but wants potatoes from Idaho. And suppose that Idaho wants Florida's oranges but not Nebraska's wheat. And, to complicate matters, suppose that Florida wants some of Nebraska's wheat but none of Idaho's potatoes. We summarize the situation in Figure 2.1.

In none of the cases shown in the figure is there a coincidence of wants. Trade by barter clearly would be difficult. Instead, people in each state use **money,** which is simply a convenient social invention to facilitate exchanges of goods and services. Historically, people have used cattle, cigarettes, shells, stones, pieces of metal, and many other commodities, with varying degrees of success, as a medium of exchange. But to serve as money, an item needs to pass only one test: It must be generally acceptable to sellers in exchange for their goods and services. Money is socially defined; whatever society accepts as a medium of exchange *is* money.

money
Any item that is generally acceptable to sellers in exchange for goods and services.

Most economies use pieces of paper as money. The use of paper dollars (currency) as a medium of exchange is what enables Nebraska, Florida, and Idaho to overcome their trade stalemate, as demonstrated in Figure 2.1.

On a global basis different nations have different currencies, and that complicates specialization and exchange. But markets in which currencies are bought and sold make it possible for U.S. residents, Japanese, Germans, Britons, and Mexicans, through the swapping of dollars, yen, euros, pounds, and pesos, one for another, to exchange goods and services.

FIGURE 2.1
Money facilitates trade when wants do not coincide. The use of money as a medium of exchange permits trade to be accomplished despite a noncoincidence of wants. (1) Nebraska trades the wheat that Florida wants for money from Floridians; (2) Nebraska trades the money it receives from Florida for the potatoes it wants from Idaho; (3) Idaho trades the money it receives from Nebraska for the oranges it wants from Florida.

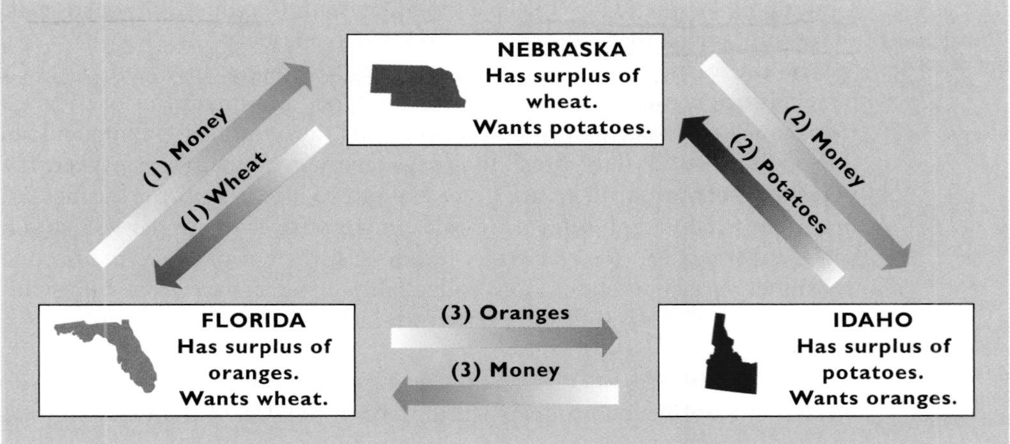

Active, but Limited, Government

An active, but limited, government is the final characteristic of market systems in real-life advanced industrial economies. Although a market system promotes a high degree of efficiency in the use of its resources, it has certain inherent shortcomings. We will discover in Chapter 5 that government can increase the overall effectiveness of the economic system in several ways.

Four Fundamental Questions

The key features of the market system help explain how market economies respond to four fundamental questions:

- What goods and services will be produced?
- How will the goods and services be produced?
- Who will get the goods and services?
- How will the system promote progress?

These four questions highlight the economic choices underlying the production possibilities curve discussed in Chapter 1. They reflect the reality of scarce resources in a world of unlimited wants. All economies, whether market or command, must address these four questions.

What Will Be Produced?

How will a market system decide on the specific types and quantities of goods to be produced? The simple answer is this: The goods and services produced at a continuing profit will be produced, and those produced at a continuing loss will not. Profits and losses are the difference between the total revenue (TR) a firm receives from the sale of its products and the total cost (TC) of producing those products. (For economists, economic costs include not only wage and salary payments to labor, and interest and rental payments for capital and land, but also payments to the entrepreneur for organizing and combining the other resources to produce a commodity.)

Continuing economic profit (TR > TC) in an industry results in expanded production and the movement of resources toward that industry. The industry expands. Continuing losses (TC > TR) in an industry leads to reduced production and the exit of resources from that industry. The industry contracts.

consumer sovereignty Determination by consumers of the types and quantities of goods and services that will be produced with the economy's scarce resources.

In the market system, consumers are sovereign (in command). **Consumer sovereignty** is crucial in determining the types and quantities of goods produced. Consumers spend their income on the goods they are most willing and able to buy. Through these **"dollar votes"** they register their wants in the market. If the dollar votes for a certain product are great enough to create a profit, businesses will produce that product and offer it for sale. In contrast, if the dollar votes do not create sufficient revenues to cover costs, businesses will not produce the product. So the consumers are sovereign. They collectively direct resources to industries that are meeting consumer wants and away from industries that are not meeting consumer wants.

dollar votes The "votes" that consumers and entrepreneurs cast for the production of consumer and capital goods when they purchase them in product and resource markets.

The dollar votes of consumers determine not only which industries will continue to exist but also which products will survive or fail. Only profitable industries, firms, and products survive.

McHits and McMisses

McDonald's has introduced several new menu items over the decades. Some have been profitable "hits," while others have been "misses." Ultimately, consumers decide whether a menu item is profitable and therefore whether it stays on the McDonald's menu.

- Hulaburger (1962)—McMiss
- Filet-O-Fish (1963)—McHit
- Strawberry shortcake (1966)—McMiss
- Big Mac (1968)—McHit
- Hot apple pie (1968)—McHit
- Egg McMuffin (1975)—McHit
- Drive-thru (1975)—McHit
- Chicken McNuggets (1983)—McHit
- Extra Value Meal (1991)—McHit
- McLean Deluxe (1991)—McMiss
- Arch Deluxe (1996)—McMiss
- 55-cent special (1997)—McMiss
- Big Xtra (1999)—McHit

Question:
Do you think McDonald's premium salads will be a lasting McHit, or do you think they eventually will become a McMiss?

Source: "Polishing the Golden Arches," *Forbes,* June 15, 1998, pp. 42–43, updated.

How Will the Goods and Services Be Produced?

What combinations of resources and technologies will be used to produce goods and services? How will the production be organized? The answer: In combinations and ways that minimize the cost per unit of output. Because competition eliminates high-cost producers, profitability requires that firms produce their output at minimum cost per unit. Achieving this least-cost production necessitates, for example, that firms use the right mix of labor and capital, given the prices and productivity of those resources. It also means locating production facilities optimally to hold down production and transportation expenses. Finally, it means using the most appropriate technology in producing and distributing output. In a competitive market economy, high-cost producers lose business to low-cost producers of equal-quality products.

Who Will Get the Output?

The market system enters the picture in two ways when determining the distribution of total output. Generally, any product will be distributed to consumers on the basis of their ability and willingness to pay its existing market price. If the price of some product, say, a small sailboat, is $3000, then buyers who are willing and able to pay that price will "sail, sail away." Consumers who are unwilling or unable to pay the price will "sit on the dock of the bay."

The ability to pay the prices for sailboats and other products depends on the amount of income that consumers have, along with the prices of, and preferences for, various goods. If consumers have sufficient income and want to spend their money on a particular good, they can have it. And the amount of income they have depends on (1) the quantities of the property and human resources they supply and (2) the prices those resources command in the resource market. Resource prices (wages, interest, rent, profit) are key in determining the size of each household's income and therefore each household's ability to buy part of the economy's output.

How Will the System Promote Progress?

Society desires economic growth (greater output) and higher standards of living (greater income per person). How does the market system promote technological improvements and capital accumulation, both of which contribute to a higher standard of living for society?

Technological Advance The market system provides a strong incentive for technological advance and enables better products and processes to supplant inferior ones. An entrepreneur or firm that introduces a popular new product will gain revenue and economic profit at the expense of rivals. Firms that are highly profitable one year may find they are in financial trouble just a few years later.

Technological advance also includes new and improved methods that reduce production or distribution costs. By passing part of its cost reduction on to the consumer through a lower product price, the firm can increase sales and obtain economic profit at the expense of rival firms.

Moreover, the market system promotes the *rapid spread* of technological advance throughout an industry. Rival firms must follow the lead of the most innovative firm or else suffer immediate losses and eventual failure. In some cases, the result is **creative destruction:** The creation of new products and production methods completely destroys the market positions of firms that are wedded to existing products and older ways of doing business. Example: The advent of compact discs largely demolished long-play vinyl records, and MP3 and other digital technologies may some day supplant CDs.

creative destruction The idea that the creation of new products and production methods may simultaneously destroy the market power of existing firms.

Capital Accumulation Most technological advances require additional capital goods. The market system provides the resources necessary to produce those goods through increased dollar votes for capital goods. That is, the market system acknowledges dollar voting for capital goods as well as for consumer goods.

But who will register votes for capital goods? Answer: Entrepreneurs and owners of businesses. As receivers of profit income, they often use part of that income to purchase capital goods. Doing so yields even greater profit income in the future if the technological innovation is successful. Also, by paying interest or selling ownership shares, the entrepreneur and firm can attract some of the income of households to cast dollar votes for the production of more capital goods.

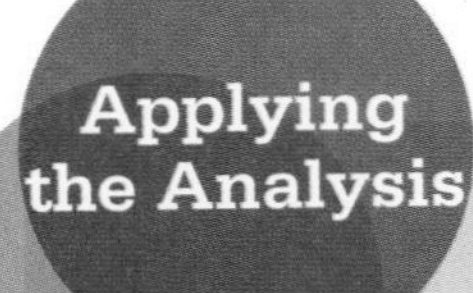

The "Invisible Hand"

In his 1776 book *The Wealth of Nations*, Adam Smith first noted that the operation of a market system creates a curious unity between private interests and social interests. Firms and resource suppliers, seeking to further their own self-interest and operating within the framework of a highly competitive market system, will simultaneously, as though guided by an **"invisible hand,"** promote the public or social interest. For example, we have seen that in a competitive environment, businesses seek to build new and improved products to increase profits. Those enhanced products increase society's well-being. Businesses also use the least costly combination of resources to produce a specific output because it is in their self-interest to do so. To act otherwise would be to forgo profit or even to risk business failure. But, at the same time, to use scarce resources in the least costly way is clearly in the social interest as well. It "frees up" resources to produce something else that society desires.

"invisible hand" The tendency of firms and resource suppliers that are seeking to further their own self-interest in competitive markets to also promote the interest of society as a whole.

Self-interest, awakened and guided by the competitive market system, is what induces responses appropriate to the changes in society's wants. Businesses seeking to make higher profits and to avoid losses, and resource suppliers pursuing greater monetary rewards, negotiate changes in the allocation of resources and end up with the output that society wants. Competition controls or guides self-interest such that self-interest automatically and quite unintentionally furthers the best interest of society. The invisible hand ensures that when firms maximize their profits and resource suppliers maximize their incomes, these groups also help maximize society's output and income.

Question:
Are "doing good for others" and "doing well for oneself" conflicting ideas, according to Adam Smith?

The Demise of the Command Systems

Now that you know how the market system answers the four fundamental questions, you can easily understand why command systems of the Soviet Union, eastern Europe, and prereform China failed. Those systems encountered two insurmountable problems.

The first difficulty was the *coordination problem*. The central planners had to coordinate the millions of individual decisions by consumers, resource suppliers, and businesses. Consider the setting up of a factory to produce tractors. The central planners had to establish a realistic annual production target, for example, 1000 tractors. They then had to make available all the necessary inputs—labor, machinery, electric power, steel, tires, glass, paint, transportation—for the production and delivery of those 1000 tractors.

Because the outputs of many industries serve as inputs to other industries, the failure of any single industry to achieve its output target caused a chain reaction of repercussions. For example, if iron mines, for want of machinery or labor or transportation, did not supply the steel industry with the required inputs of iron ore, the steel mills were unable to fulfill the input needs of the many industries that depended on steel. Those steel-using industries (such as tractor, automobile, and transportation) were unable to fulfill their planned production goals. Eventually the chain reaction spread to all firms that used steel as an input and from there to other input buyers or final consumers.

The coordination problem became more difficult as the economies expanded. Products and production processes grew more sophisticated, and the number of industries requiring planning increased. Planning techniques that worked for the simpler economy proved highly inadequate and inefficient for the larger economy. Bottlenecks and production stoppages became the norm, not the exception.

A lack of a reliable success indicator added to the coordination problem in the Soviet Union and prereform China. We have seen that market economies rely on profit as a success indicator. Profit depends on consumer demand, production efficiency, and product quality. In contrast, the major success indicator for the command economies usually was a quantitative production target that the central planners assigned. Production costs, product quality, and product mix were secondary considerations. Managers and workers often sacrificed product quality because they were being awarded bonuses for meeting quantitative, not qualitative, targets. If meeting production goals meant sloppy assembly work, so be it.

It was difficult at best for planners to assign quantitative production targets without unintentionally producing distortions in output. If the production target for an enterprise manufacturing nails was specified in terms of *weight* (tons of nails), the producer made only large nails. But if its target was specified as a *quantity* (thousands of nails), the producer made all small nails, and lots of them!

The command economies also faced an *incentive problem*. Central planners determined the output mix. When they misjudged how many automobiles, shoes, shirts, and chickens were wanted at the government-determined prices, persistent shortages and surpluses of those products arose. But as long as the managers who oversaw the production of those goods were rewarded for meeting their assigned production goals, they had no incentive to adjust production in response to the shortages and surpluses. And there were no fluctuations in prices and profitability to signal that more or less of certain products was desired. Thus, many products were unavailable or in short supply, while other products were overproduced and sat for months or years in warehouses.

The command systems of the Soviet Union and prereform China also lacked entrepreneurship. Central planning did not trigger the profit motive, nor did it reward innovation and enterprise. The route for getting ahead was through participation in the political hierarchy of the Communist Party. Moving up the hierarchy meant better housing, better access to health care, and the right to shop in special stores. Meeting production targets and maneuvering through the minefields of party politics were measures of success in "business." But a definition of business success based solely on political savvy is not conducive to technological advance, which is often disruptive to existing products, production methods, and organizational structures.

Question:

In market economies, firms rarely worry about the availability of inputs to produce their products, whereas in command economies input availability was a constant concern. Why the difference?

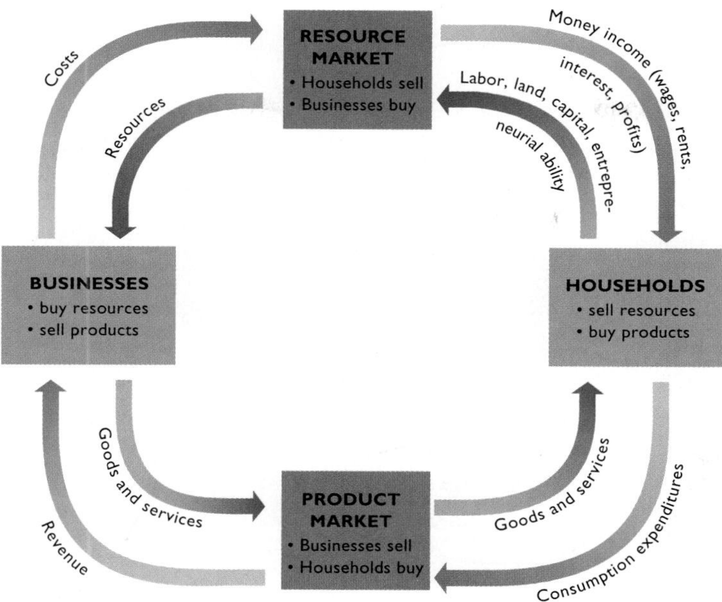

FIGURE 2.2
The circular flow diagram. Products flow from businesses to households through the product market, and resources flow from households to businesses through the resource market. Opposite those real flows are monetary flows. Households receive income from businesses (their costs) through the resource market, and businesses receive revenue from households (their expenditures) through the product market.

The Circular Flow Model

The dynamic market economy creates continuous, repetitive flows of goods and services, resources, and money. The **circular flow diagram,** shown in Figure 2.2, illustrates those flows. Observe that in the diagram we group private decision makers into *businesses* and *households* and group markets into the *resource market* and the *product market*.

circular flow diagram
The flow of resources from households to firms and of products from firms to households.

Resource Market

The upper half of the circular flow diagram represents the **resource market:** the place where resources or the services of resource suppliers are bought and sold. In the resource market, households sell resources and businesses buy them. Households (that is, people) own all economic resources either directly as workers or entrepreneurs or indirectly through their ownership of business corporations. They sell their resources to businesses, which buy them because they are necessary for producing goods and services. The funds that businesses pay for resources are costs to businesses but are flows of wage, rent, interest, and profit income to the households. Productive resources therefore flow from households to businesses, and money flows from businesses to households.

resource market
A market in which households sell and firms buy economic resources.

Product Market

Next consider the lower part of the diagram, which represents the **product market:** the place where goods and services produced by businesses are bought and sold. In the product market, businesses combine resources to produce and sell goods and services. Households use the (limited) income they have received from the sale of resources to buy goods and services. The monetary flow of consumer spending on goods and services yields sales revenues for businesses. Businesses compare those revenues to their costs in determining profitability and whether or not a particular good or service should continue to be produced.

product market
A market in which goods and services (products) are sold by firms and bought by households.

© T. O'Keefe/PhotoLink/Getty Images/DIL

© Royalty-Free/CORBIS

Photo Op Resource Markets and Product Markets

The sale of a grove of orange trees would be a transaction in the resource market; the sale of oranges to final consumers would be a transaction in the product market.

The circular flow model depicts a complex, interrelated web of decision making and economic activity involving businesses and households. For the economy, it is the circle of life. Businesses and households are both buyers and sellers. Businesses buy resources and sell products. Households buy products and sell resources. As shown in Figure 2.2, there is a counterclockwise *real flow* of economic resources and finished goods and services and a clockwise *money flow* of income and consumption expenditures.

Applying the Analysis

Some Facts about U.S. Businesses

Businesses constitute one part of the private sector. The business population is extremely diverse, ranging from giant corporations such as General Motors, with 2004 sales of $193 billion and 324,000 employees, to neighborhood specialty shops with one or two employees and sales of only $200 to $300 per day. There are three major legal forms of businesses: sole proprietorships, partnerships, and corporations.

A *sole proprietorship* is a business owned and operated by one person. Usually, the proprietor (the owner) personally supervises its operation. In a *partnership*, two or more individuals (the partners) agree to own and operate a business together.

A *corporation* is a legal creation that can acquire resources, own assets, produce and sell products, incur debts, extend credit, sue and be sued, and perform the functions of any other type of enterprise. A corporation sells stocks (ownership shares) to raise funds but is legally distinct and separate from the individual stockholders. The stockholders' legal and financial liability is limited to the loss of the value of their shares. Hired executives and managers operate corporations on a day-to-day basis.

Figure 2.3a shows how the business population is distributed among the three major legal forms. About 72% of firms are sole proprietorships, whereas only 20%

FIGURE 2.3

The business population and shares of total revenue. (a) Sole proprietorships dominate the business population numerically, but (b) corporations dominate total sales revenue (total output).

Source: U.S. Census Bureau, www.census.gov.

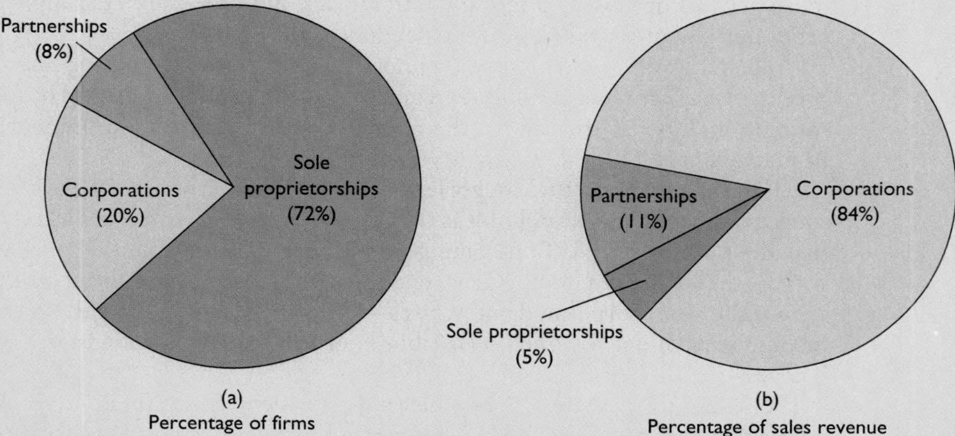

are corporations. But as Figure 2.3b indicates, corporations account for 84% of total sales revenue (and therefore total output) in the United States. Virtually all the nation's largest business enterprises are corporations. Global Snapshot 2.2 lists the world's largest corporations.

Question:
Why do you think sole proprietorships and partnerships typically incorporate (become corporations) when they experience rapid and sizable increases in their production, sales, and profits?

The World's 10 Largest Corporations

Six of the word's ten largest corporations, based on dollar revenue in 2004, were headquartered in the United States.

Wal-Mart (USA) $285 billion
BP (Britain) $285 billion
Shell (Britain/Netherlands) $265 billion
ExxonMobil (USA) $264 billion
General Motors (USA) $193 billion
DaimlerChrysler (Germany) $193 billion
Ford Motor (USA) $171 billion
Toyota (Japan) $166 billion
General Electric (USA) $152 billion
ChevronTexaco (USA) $143 billion

Source: *Fortune*, www.fortune.com.

Some Facts about U.S. Households

Households constitute the second part of the private sector. The U.S. economy currently has about 113 million households. These households consist of one or more persons occupying a housing unit and are both the ultimate suppliers of all economic resources *and* the major spenders in the economy.

The nation's earned income is apportioned among wages, rents, interest, and profits. *Wages* are paid to labor; *rents* and *interest* are paid to owners of property resources; and *profits* are paid to the owners of corporations and unincorporated businesses.

Figure 2.4a shows the categories of U.S. income earned in 2004. The largest source of income for households is the wages and salaries paid to workers. Notice that the bulk of total U.S. income goes to labor, not to capital. Proprietors' income—the income of doctors, lawyers, small-business owners, farmers, and owners of other unincorporated enterprises—also has a "wage" element. Some of this income is payment for one's own labor, and some of it is profit from one's own business.

The other three types of income are self-evident: Some households own corporate stock and receive dividend incomes as their share of corporate profits. Many

FIGURE 2.4

Sources of U.S. income and the composition of spending. (a) Seventy percent of U.S. income is received as wages and salaries. Income to property owners—corporate profit, interest, and rents—accounts for about 20% of total income. (b) Consumers divide their spending among durable goods, nondurable goods, and services. Nearly 60% of consumer spending is for services; the rest is for goods.

Source: Bureau of Economic Analysis, www.bea.gov.

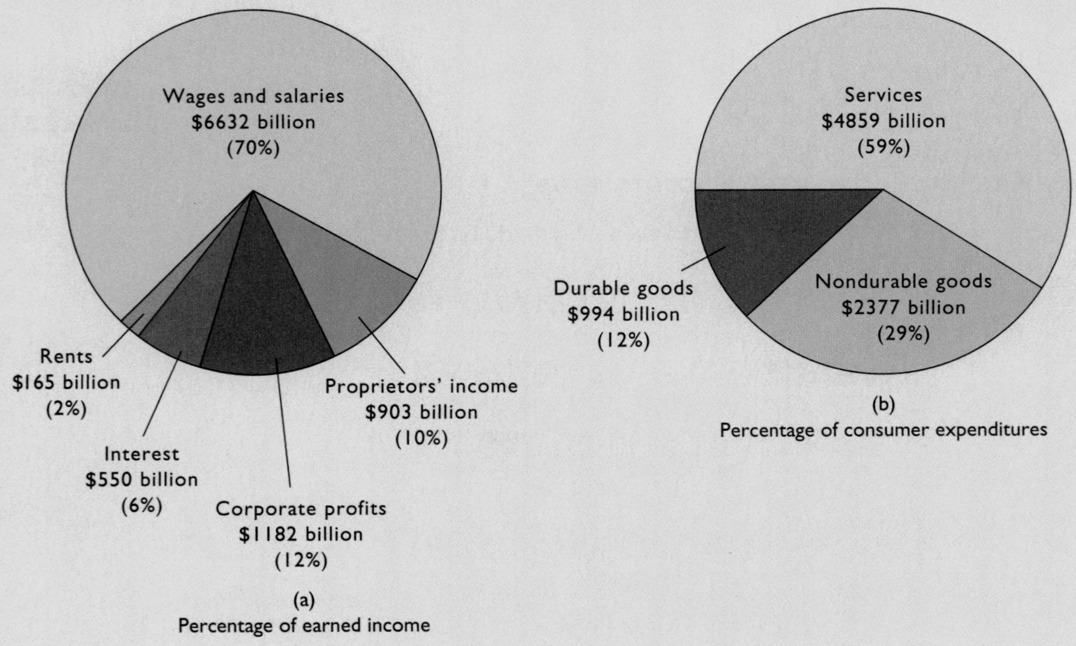

households also own bonds and savings accounts that yield interest income. And some households receive rental income by providing buildings and natural resources (including land) to businesses and other individuals.

U.S. households use their income to buy (spend), save, and pay taxes. Figure 2.4b shows how households divide their spending among three broad categories of goods and services: *consumer durables* (goods such as cars, refrigerators, and personal computers that have expected lives of 3 years or longer), *nondurables* (goods such as food, clothing, and gasoline that have lives of less than 3 years), and *services* (the work done by people such as lawyers, physicians, and recreational workers). Observe that nearly 60% of consumer spending is on services. For this reason, the United States is known as a *service-oriented economy*.

Question:
Over the past several decades, the service share of spending in the United States has increased relative to the goods share. Why do you think that trend has occurred?

Courtesy of Maytag Corporation.

© Ed Carey/Cole Group/Getty Images/DIL

© Royalty-Free/CORBIS

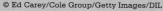

Photo Op Durable Goods, Nondurable Goods, and Services

Consumers collectively spend their income on durable goods (such as the washer-dryer combo), nondurable goods (such as the pizza), and services (such as hair care).

Summary

1. The market system and the command system are the two broad types of economic systems used to address the economic problem. In the market system (or capitalism), private individuals own most resources, and markets coordinate most economic activity. In the command system (or socialism or communism), government owns most resources, and central planners coordinate most economic activity.
2. The market system is characterized by the private ownership of resources, including capital, and the freedom of individuals to engage in economic activities of their choice to advance their material well-being. Self-interest is the driving force of such an economy, and competition functions as a regulatory or control mechanism.
3. In the market system, markets, prices, and profits organize and make effective the many millions of individual economic decisions that occur daily.
4. Specialization, use of advanced technology, and the extensive use of capital goods are common features of market systems. Functioning as a medium of exchange, money eliminates the problems of bartering and permits easy trade and greater specialization, both domestically and internationally.
5. Every economy faces four fundamental questions: (a) What goods and services will be produced? (b) How will the goods and services be produced? (c) Who will get the goods and services? (d) How will the system promote progress?
6. The market system produces products whose production and sale yield total revenue sufficient to cover total cost. It does not produce products for which total revenue continuously falls short of total cost. Competition forces firms to use the lowest-cost production techniques.
7. Economic profit (total revenue minus total cost) indicates that an industry is prosperous and promotes its expansion. Losses signify that an industry is not prosperous and hasten its contraction.
8. Consumer sovereignty means that both businesses and resource suppliers are subject to the wants of consumers. Through their dollar votes, consumers decide on the composition of output.
9. The prices that a household receives for the resources it supplies to the economy determine that household's income. This income determines the household's claim on the economy's output. Those who have income to spend get the products produced in the market system.
10. The market system encourages technological advance and capital accumulation, both of which raise a nation's standard of living.
11. Competition, the primary mechanism of control in the market economy, promotes a unity of self-interest and social interests. As directed by an invisible hand, competition harnesses the self-interest motives of businesses and resource suppliers to further the social interest.
12. The circular flow model illustrates the flows of resources and products from households to businesses and from businesses to households, along with the corresponding monetary flows. Businesses are on the buying side of the resource market and the selling side of the product market. Households are on the selling side of the resource market and the buying side of the product market.

Terms and Concepts

economic system
command system
market system
private property
freedom of enterprise
freedom of choice
self-interest
competition
market
specialization
division of labor
medium of exchange
barter
money
consumer sovereignty
dollar votes
creative destruction
"invisible hand"
circular flow diagram
resource market
product market

Study Questions

1. Contrast how a market system and a command economy try to cope with economic scarcity.
2. How does self-interest help achieve society's economic goals? Why is there such a wide variety of desired goods and services in a market system? In what way are entrepreneurs and businesses at the helm of the economy but commanded by consumers?

Demand

Demand is a schedule or a curve that shows the various amounts of a product that consumers will purchase at each of several possible prices during a specified period of time.[1] The table in Figure 3.1 is a hypothetical demand schedule for a *single consumer* purchasing a particular product, in this case, lattes. (For simplicity, we will categorize all espresso drinks as "lattes" and assume a highly competitive market.)

The table reveals that, if the price of lattes were $5 each, Joe Java would buy 10 lattes per month; if it were $4, he would buy 20 lattes per month; and so forth.

The table does not tell us which of the five possible prices will actually exist in the market. That depends on demand and supply. Demand is simply a statement of a buyer's plans, or intentions, with respect to the purchase of a product.

To be meaningful, the quantities demanded at each price must relate to a specific period—a day, a week, a month. Here that period is 1 month.

demand
A schedule or curve that shows the various amounts of a product that consumers will buy at each of a series of possible prices during a specific period.

Law of Demand

3.2
Law of demand

A fundamental characteristic of demand is this: All else equal, as price falls, the quantity demanded rises, and as price rises, the quantity demanded falls. In short, there is an *inverse* relationship between price and quantity demanded. Economists call this inverse relationship the **law of demand.**

law of demand
The principle that, all else equal, as price falls, the quantity demanded rises, and as price rises, the quantity demanded falls.

[1] This definition obviously is worded to apply to product markets. To adjust it to apply to resource markets, substitute the word "resource" for "product" and the word "businesses" for "consumers."

FIGURE 3.1
Joe Java's demand for lattes. Because price and quantity demanded are inversely related, an individual's demand schedule graphs as a downsloping curve such as *D*. Other things equal, consumers will buy more of a product as its price declines and less of the product as its price rises. (Here and in later figures, *P* stands for price, and *Q* stands for quantity demanded or supplied.)

Joe Java's Demand for Lattes

Price per Latte	Quantity Demanded per Month
$5	10
4	20
3	35
2	55
1	80

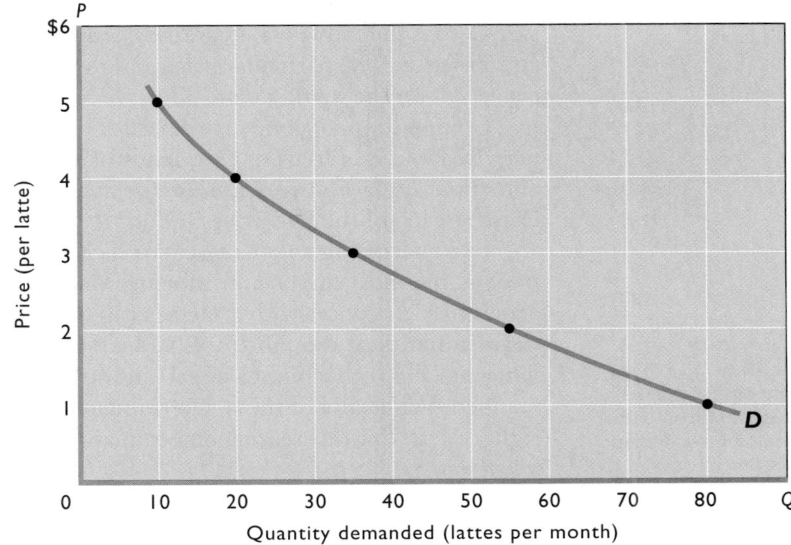

The other-things-equal assumption is critical here. Many factors other than the price of the product being considered affect the amount purchased. The quantity of lattes purchased will depend not only on the price of lattes but also on the prices of such substitutes as tea, soda, fruit juice, and bottled water. The law of demand in this case says that fewer lattes will be purchased if the price of lattes rises while the prices of tea, soda, fruit juice, and bottled water all remain constant.

The law of demand is consistent with both common sense and observation. People ordinarily *do* buy more of a product at a low price than at a high price. Price is an obstacle that deters consumers from buying. The higher that obstacle, the less of a product they will buy; the lower the obstacle, the more they will buy. The fact that businesses reduce prices to clear unsold goods is evidence of their belief in the law of demand.

The Demand Curve

The inverse relationship between price and quantity demanded for any product can be represented on a simple graph, in which, by convention, we measure *quantity demanded* on the horizontal axis and *price* on the vertical axis. In Figure 3.1 we have plotted the five price-quantity data points listed in the table and connected the points with a smooth curve, labeled *D*. This is a **demand curve.** Its downward slope reflects the law of demand: People buy more of a product, service, or resource as its price falls. They buy less as its price rises. There is an inverse relationship between price and quantity demanded.

demand curve
A curve illustrating the inverse relationship between the price of a product and the quantity of it demanded, other things equal.

The table and graph in Figure 3.1 contain exactly the same data and reflect the same inverse relationship between price and quantity demanded.

Market Demand

So far, we have concentrated on just one consumer, Joe Java. But competition requires that more than one buyer be present in each market. By adding the quantities demanded by all consumers at each of the various possible prices, we can get from *individual* demand to *market* demand. If there are just three buyers in the market (Joe Java, Sarah Coffee, and Mike Cappuccino), as represented by the table and graph in Figure 3.2, it is relatively easy to determine the total quantity demanded at each price. We simply sum the individual quantities demanded to obtain the total quantity demanded at each price. The particular price and the total quantity demanded are then plotted as one point on the market demand curve in Figure 3.2.

Competition, of course, ordinarily entails many more than three buyers of a product. To avoid hundreds or thousands of additions, let's simply suppose that the table and curve D_1 in Figure 3.3 show the amounts all the buyers in this market will purchase at each of the five prices.

In constructing a demand curve such as D_1 in Figure 3.3, economists assume that price is the most important influence on the amount of any product purchased. But economists know that other factors can and do affect purchases. These factors, called **determinants of demand,** are held constant when a demand curve like D_1 is drawn. They are the "other things equal" in the relationship between price and quantity demanded. When any of these determinants changes, the demand curve will shift to the right or left. For this reason, determinants of demand are sometimes referred to as *demand shifters*.

determinants of demand
Factors other than price that locate the position of a demand curve.

The basic determinants of demand are (1) consumers' tastes (preferences), (2) the number of consumers in the market, (3) consumers' incomes, (4) the prices of related goods, and (5) expected prices.

FIGURE 3.2

Market demand for lattes, three buyers. We establish the market demand curve *D* by adding horizontally the individual demand curves (D_1, D_2, and D_3) of all the consumers in the market. At the price of $3, for example, the three individual curves yield a total quantity demanded of 100 lattes.

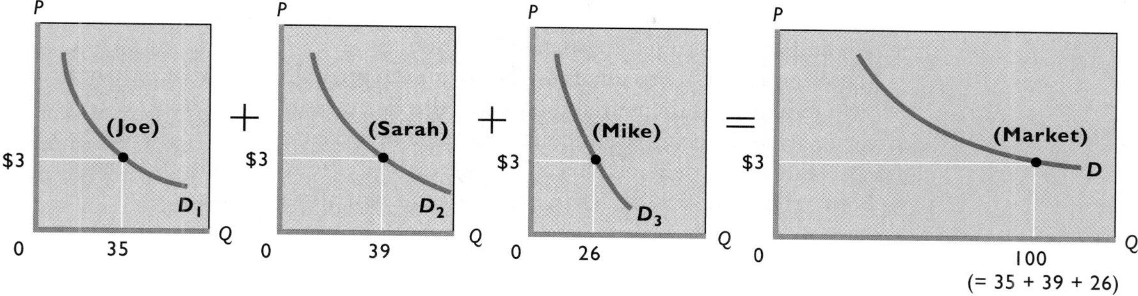

Market Demand for Lattes, Three Buyers

Price per Latte	Quantity Demanded: Joe Java		Quantity Demanded: Sarah Coffee		Quantity Demanded: Mike Cappuccino		Total Quantity Demanded per Month
$5	10	+	12	+	8	=	30
4	20	+	23	+	17	=	60
3	35	+	39	+	26	=	100
2	55	+	60	+	39	=	154
1	80	+	87	+	54	=	221

FIGURE 3.3

Changes in the demand for lattes. A change in one or more of the determinants of demand causes a change in demand. An increase in demand is shown as a shift of the demand curve to the right, as from D_1 to D_2. A decrease in demand is shown as a shift of the demand curve to the left, as from D_1 to D_3. These changes in demand are to be distinguished from a change in *quantity demanded,* which is caused by a change in the price of the product, as shown by a movement from, say, point *a* to point *b* on fixed demand curve D_1.

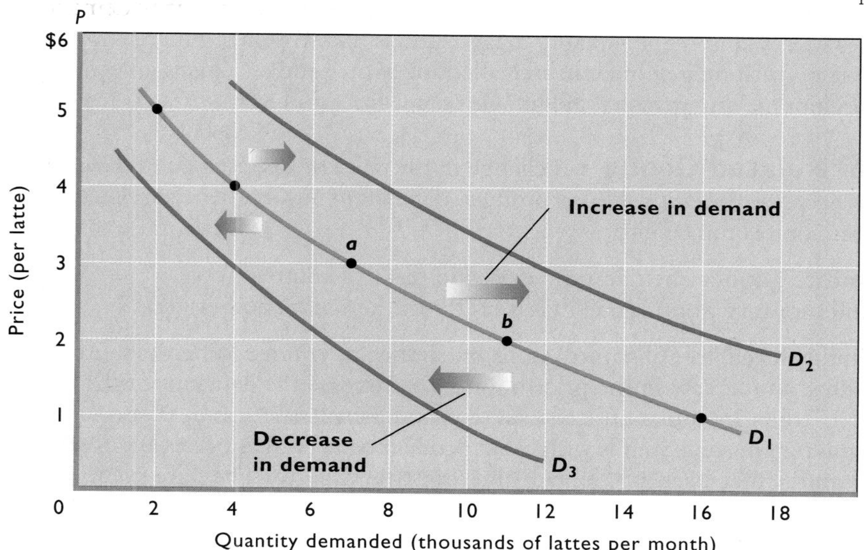

Market Demand for Lattes (D_1)

(1) Price per Latte	(2) Total Quantity Demanded per Month
$5	2,000
4	4,000
3	7,000
2	11,000
1	16,000

Changes in Demand

A change in one or more of the determinants of demand will change the underlying demand data (the demand schedule in the table) and therefore the location of the demand curve in Figure 3.3. A change in the demand schedule or, graphically, a shift in the demand curve is called a *change in demand.*

If consumers desire to buy more lattes at each possible price, that *increase in demand* is shown as a shift of the demand curve to the right, say, from D_1 to D_2. Conversely, a *decrease in demand* occurs when consumers buy fewer lattes at each possible price. The leftward shift of the demand curve from D_1 to D_3 in Figure 3.3 shows that situation.

Now let's see how changes in each determinant affect demand.

Tastes A favorable change in consumer tastes (preferences) for a product means more of it will be demanded at each price. Demand will increase; the demand curve will shift rightward. For example, the rise in patriotism after September 11, 2001, has increased the demand for American flags. An unfavorable change in consumer preferences will decrease demand, shifting the demand curve to the left. For example, the recent popularity of low-carbohydrate diets has reduced the demand for bread and pasta.

Number of Buyers An increase in the number of buyers in a market increases product demand. For example, the rising number of older persons in the United States in recent years has increased the demand for motor homes and retirement communities. In contrast, the migration of people away from many small rural communities has reduced the demand for housing, home appliances, and auto repair in those towns.

normal good
A good (or service) whose consumption rises when income increases and falls when income decreases.

Income The effect of changes in income on demand is more complex. For most products, a rise in income increases demand. Consumers collectively buy more airplane tickets, projection TVs, and gas grills as their incomes rise. Products whose demand increases or decreases *directly* with changes in income are called *superior goods*, or **normal goods.**

inferior good
A good (or service) whose consumption declines as income rises and rises as income decreases.

Although most products are normal goods, there are a few exceptions. As incomes increase beyond some point, the demand for used clothing, retread tires, and soy-enhanced hamburger may decline. Higher incomes enable consumers to buy new clothing, new tires, and higher-quality meats. Goods whose demand increases or decreases *inversely* with money income are called **inferior goods.** (This is an economic term; we are not making personal judgments on specific products.)

substitute good
A good (or service) that can be used in place of some other good (or service).

complementary good
A good (or service) that is used in conjunction with some other good (or service).

Prices of Related Goods A change in the price of a related good may either increase or decrease the demand for a product, depending on whether the related good is a substitute or a complement:

- A **substitute good** is one that can be used in place of another good.
- A **complementary good** is one that is used together with another good.

Beef and chicken are substitute goods or, simply, *substitutes.* When two products are substitutes, an increase in the price of one will increase the demand for the other. For example, when the price of beef rises, consumers will buy less beef and increase their demand for chicken. So it is with other product pairs such as Nikes and Reeboks, Budweiser and Miller beer, or Colgate and Crest toothpaste. They are *substitutes in consumption.*

© Trinette Reed/CORBIS

© Doug Menuez/Getty Images/DIL

Photo Op Normal versus Inferior Goods

New television sets are normal goods. People buy more of them as their incomes rise. Hand-pushed lawn mowers are inferior goods. As incomes rise, people purchase gas-powered mowers instead.

Complementary goods (or, simply, *complements*) are products that are used together and thus are typically demanded jointly. Examples include computers and software, cell phones and cellular service, and snowboards and lift tickets. If the price of a complement (for example, lettuce) goes up, the demand for the related good (salad dressing) will decline. Conversely, if the price of a complement (for example, tuition) falls, the demand for a related good (textbooks) will increase.

The vast majority of goods that are unrelated to one another are called *independent goods*. There is virtually no demand relationship between bacon and golf balls or pickles and ice cream. A change in the price of one will have virtually no effect on the demand for the other.

Expected Prices Changes in expected prices may shift demand. A newly formed expectation of a higher price in the future may cause consumers to buy now in order to "beat" the anticipated price rise, thus increasing current demand. For example, when freezing weather destroys much of Brazil's coffee crop, buyers may conclude that the price of coffee beans will rise. They may purchase large quantities now to stock up on beans. In contrast, a newly formed expectation of falling prices may decrease current demand for products.

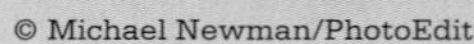
© Michael Newman/PhotoEdit

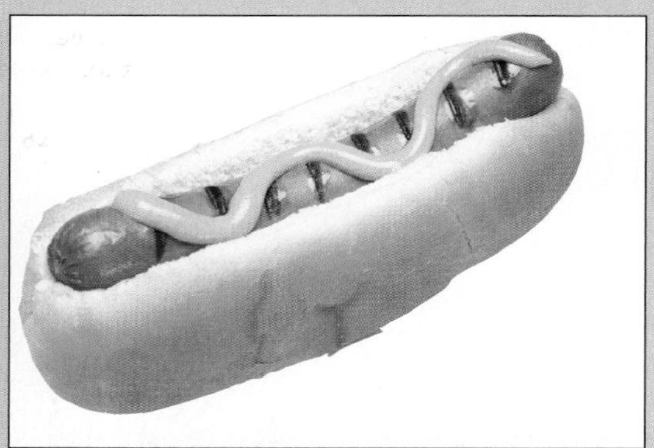
© John A. Rizzo/Getty Images/DIL

Photo Op Substitutes versus Complements

Different brands of soft drinks are substitute goods; goods consumed jointly such as hot dogs and mustard are complementary goods.

Changes in Quantity Demanded

change in demand A change in the quantity demanded of a product at every price.

Be sure not to confuse a *change in demand* with a *change in quantity demanded.* A **change in demand** is a shift of the demand curve to the right (an increase in demand) or to the left (a decrease in demand). It occurs because the consumer's state of mind about purchasing the product has been altered in response to a change in one or more of the determinants of demand. Recall that "demand" is a schedule or a curve; therefore, a "change in demand" means a change in the schedule and a shift of the curve.

change in quantity demanded A movement from one point to another on a demand curve.

In contrast, a **change in quantity demanded** is a movement from one point to another point—from one price-quantity combination to another—on a fixed demand schedule or demand curve. The cause of such a change is an increase or decrease in the price of the product under consideration. In the table in Figure 3.3, for example, a decline in the price of lattes from $5 to $4 will increase the quantity of lattes demanded from 2000 to 4000.

In the graph in Figure 3.3, the shift of the demand curve D_1 to either D_2 or D_3 is a change in demand. But the movement from point *a* to point *b* on curve D_1 represents a change in quantity demanded*:* Demand has not changed; it is the entire curve, and it remains fixed in place.

Supply

supply A schedule or curve that shows the amounts of a product that producers are willing to make available for sale at each of a series of possible prices during a specific period.

Supply is a schedule or curve showing the amounts of a product that producers will make available for sale at each of a series of possible prices during a specific period.[2] The table in Figure 3.4 is a hypothetical supply schedule for Star Buck, a single supplier of lattes. Curve *S* incorporates the data in the table and is called a *supply curve.* The schedule and curve show the quantities of lattes that will be supplied at various prices, other things equal.

[2] This definition is worded to apply to product markets. To adjust it to apply to resource markets, substitute "resource" for "product" and "owners" for "producers."

FIGURE 3.4

Star Buck's supply of lattes. Because price and quantity supplied are directly related, the supply curve for an individual producer graphs as an upsloping curve. Other things equal, producers will offer more of a product for sale as its price rises and less of the product for sale as its price falls.

Star Buck's Supply of Lattes	
Price per Latte	**Quantity Supplied per Month**
$5	60
4	50
3	35
2	20
1	5

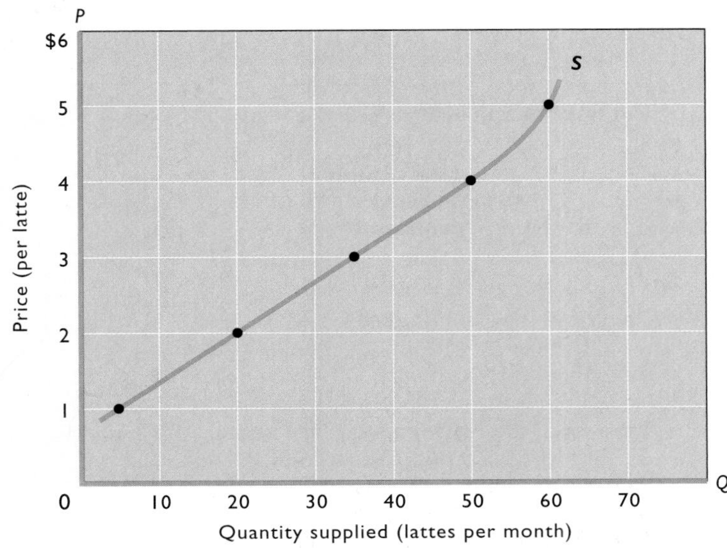

Law of Supply

Figure 3.4 shows a positive or direct relationship that prevails between price and quantity supplied. As price rises, the quantity supplied rises; as price falls, the quantity supplied falls. This relationship is called the **law of supply.** A supply schedule or curve reveals that firms will offer for sale more of their product at a high price than at a low price. This, again, is basically common sense.

law of supply The principle that, other things equal, an increase in the price of a product will increase the quantity of it supplied; and conversely for a price decrease.

Price is an obstacle from the standpoint of the consumer (for example, Joe Java), who is on the paying end. The higher the price, the less the consumer will buy. But the supplier (for example, Star Buck) is on the receiving end of the product's price. To a supplier, price represents *revenue,* which is needed to cover costs and earn a profit. Higher prices therefore create a profit incentive to produce and sell more of a product. The higher the price, the greater this incentive and the greater the quantity supplied.

Market Supply

Market supply is derived from individual supply in exactly the same way that market demand is derived from individual demand (Figure 3.2). We sum (not shown) the quantities supplied by each producer at each price. That is, we obtain the market **supply curve** by "horizontally adding" (also not shown) the supply curves of the individual producers. The price and quantity-supplied data in the table in Figure 3.5 are for the many suppliers in the market, each willing to supply lattes. Curve S_1 is a graph of the market supply data. Note that the axes in Figure 3.5 are the same as those used in our graph of market demand (Figure 3.3), except for the change from "quantity demanded" to "quantity supplied" on the horizontal axis.

supply curve Curve illustrating the direct relationship between the quantity supplied of a product and its price, other things equal.

Determinants of Supply

In constructing a supply curve, we assume that price is the most significant influence on the quantity supplied of any product. But other factors (the "other things equal")

FIGURE 3.5
Changes in the supply of lattes. A change in one or more of the determinants of supply causes a change in supply. An increase in supply is shown as a rightward shift of the supply curve, as from S_1 to S_2. A decrease in supply is depicted as a leftward shift of the curve, as from S_1 to S_3. In contrast, a change in the *quantity supplied* is caused by a change in the product's price and is shown by a movement from one point to another, as from *a* to *b*, on fixed supply curve S_1.

Market Supply of Lattes (S_1)	
(1) Price per Latte	(2) Total Quantity Supplied per Month
$5	12,000
4	10,000
3	7,000
2	4,000
1	1,000

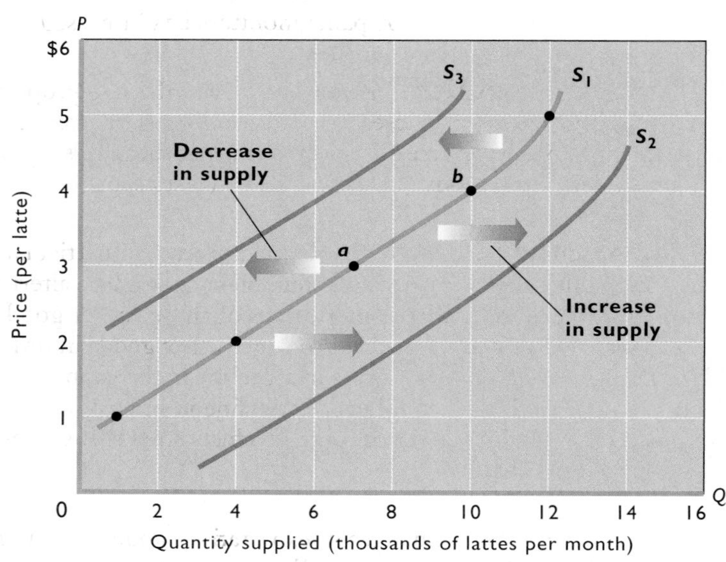

can and do affect supply. The supply curve is drawn on the assumption that these other things are fixed and do not change. If one of them does change, a *change in supply* will occur, meaning that the entire supply curve will shift.

determinants of supply
Factors other than price that determine the quantities supplied of products.

The basic **determinants of supply** are (1) resource prices, (2) technology, (3) taxes and subsidies, (4) prices of other goods, (5) expected price, and (6) the number of sellers in the market. A change in any one or more of these determinants of supply, or *supply shifters*, will move the supply curve for a product either right or left. A shift to the *right*, as from S_1 to S_2 in Figure 3.5, signifies an *increase* in supply: Producers supply larger quantities of the product at each possible price. A shift to the *left*, as from S_1 to S_3, indicates a *decrease* in supply: Producers offer less output at each price.

Changes in Supply

Let's consider how changes in each of the determinants affect supply. The key idea is that costs are a major factor underlying supply curves; anything that affects costs (other than changes in output itself) usually shifts the supply curve.

Resource Prices The prices of the resources used in the production process help determine the costs of production incurred by firms. Higher *resource* prices raise production costs and, assuming a particular *product* price, squeeze profits. That reduction in profits reduces the incentive for firms to supply output at each product price. For example, an increase in the prices of coffee beans and milk will increase the cost of making lattes and therefore reduce their supply.

In contrast, lower *resource* prices reduce production costs and increase profits. So when resource prices fall, firms supply greater output at each product price. For example, a decrease in the prices of sand, gravel, and limestone will increase the supply of concrete.

Technology Improvements in technology (techniques of production) enable firms to produce units of output with fewer resources. Because resources are costly, using fewer of them lowers production costs and increases supply. Example: Technological advances in producing flat-panel computer monitors have greatly reduced their cost. Thus, manufacturers will now offer more such monitors than previously at the various prices; the supply of flat-panel monitors has increased.

Taxes and Subsidies Businesses treat sales and property taxes as costs. Increases in those taxes will increase production costs and reduce supply. In contrast, subsidies are "taxes in reverse." If the government subsidizes the production of a good, it in effect lowers the producers' costs and increases supply.

Prices of Other Goods Firms that produce a particular product, say, soccer balls, can usually use their plant and equipment to produce alternative goods, say, basketballs and volleyballs. The higher prices of these "other goods" may entice soccer ball producers to switch production to those other goods in order to increase profits. This *substitution in production* results in a decline in the supply of soccer balls. Alternatively, when basketballs and volleyballs decline in price relative to the price of soccer balls, firms will produce fewer of those products and more soccer balls, increasing the supply of soccer balls.

Expected Prices Changes in expectations about the future price of a product may affect the producer's current willingness to supply that product. It is difficult, however, to generalize about how a new expectation of higher prices affects the present supply of a product. Farmers anticipating a higher wheat price in the future might withhold some of their current wheat harvest from the market, thereby causing a decrease in the current supply of wheat. In contrast, in many types of manufacturing industries, newly formed expectations that price will increase may induce firms to add another shift of workers or to expand their production facilities, causing current supply to increase.

Number of Sellers Other things equal, the larger the number of suppliers, the greater the market supply. As more firms enter an industry, the supply curve shifts to the right. Conversely, the smaller the number of firms in the industry, the less the market supply. This means that as firms leave an industry, the supply curve shifts to the left. Example: The United States and Canada have imposed restrictions on haddock fishing to replenish dwindling stocks. As part of that policy, the Federal government has bought the boats of some of the haddock fishers as a way of putting them out of business and decreasing the catch. The result has been a decline in the market supply of haddock.

Changes in Quantity Supplied

The distinction between a *change in supply* and a *change in quantity supplied* parallels the distinction between a change in demand and a change in quantity demanded. Because supply is a schedule or curve, a **change in supply** means a change in the schedule and a shift of the curve. An increase in supply shifts the curve to the right; a decrease in supply shifts it to the left. The cause of a change in supply is a change in one or more of the determinants of supply.

change in supply A change in the quantity supplied of a product at every price; a shift of the supply curve to the left or right.

change in quantity supplied
A movement from one point to another on a fixed supply curve.

In contrast, a **change in quantity supplied** is a movement from one point to another on a fixed supply curve. The cause of such a movement is a change in the price of the specific product being considered. In Figure 3.5, a decline in the price of lattes from $4 to $3 decreases the quantity of lattes supplied per month from 10,000 to 7000. This movement from point *b* to point *a* along S_1 is a change in quantity supplied, not a change in supply. Supply is the full schedule of prices and quantities shown, and this schedule does not change when the price of lattes changes.

Market Equilibrium

With our understanding of demand and supply, we can now show how the decisions of Joe Java and other buyers of lattes interact with the decisions of Star Buck and other sellers to determine the price and quantity of lattes. In the table in Figure 3.6, columns 1 and 2 repeat the market supply of lattes (from Figure 3.5), and columns 2 and 3

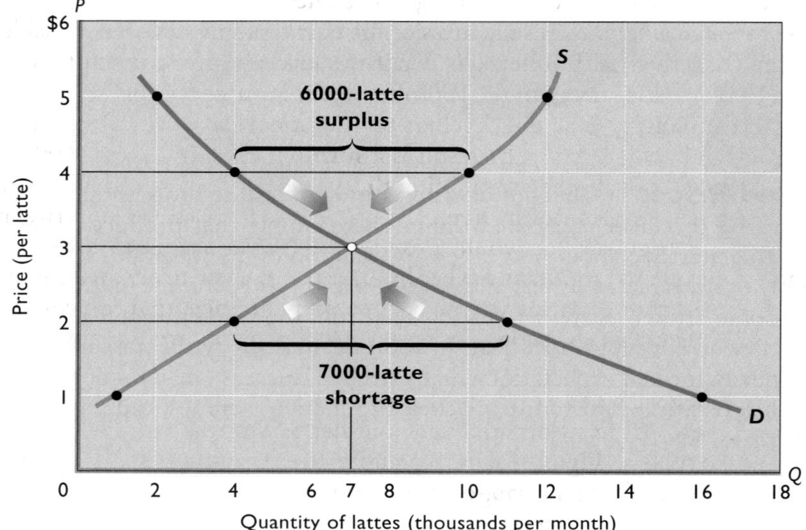

FIGURE 3.6
Equilibrium price and quantity. The intersection of the downsloping demand curve *D* and the upsloping supply curve *S* indicates the equilibrium price and quantity, here $3 and 7000 lattes. The shortages of lattes at below-equilibrium prices (for example, 7000 at $2) drive up price. The higher prices increase the quantity supplied and reduce the quantity demanded until equilibrium is achieved. The surpluses caused by above-equilibrium prices (for example, 6000 lattes at $4) push price down. As price drops, the quantity demanded rises and the quantity supplied falls until equilibrium is established. At the equilibrium price and quantity, there are neither shortages nor surpluses of lattes.

Market Supply of and Demand for Lattes

(1) Total Quantity Supplied per Month	(2) Price per Latte	(3) Total Quantity Demanded per Month	(4) Surplus (+) or Shortage (−)*
12,000	$5	2,000	+10,000 ↓
10,000	4	4,000	+6,000 ↓
7,000	***3***	***7,000***	***0***
4,000	2	11,000	−7,000 ↑
1,000	1	16,000	−15,000 ↑

* Arrows indicate the effect on price.

repeat the market demand for lattes (from Figure 3.3). We assume this is a competitive market, so neither buyers nor sellers can set the price.

Equilibrium Price and Quantity

We are looking for the equilibrium price and equilibrium quantity. The **equilibrium price** (or *market-clearing price*) is the price at which the intentions of buyers and sellers match. It is the price at which quantity demanded equals quantity supplied. The table in Figure 3.6 reveals that at $3, *and only at that price*, the number of lattes that sellers wish to sell (7000) is identical to the number that consumers want to buy (also 7000). At $3 and 7000 lattes, there is neither a shortage nor a surplus of lattes. So seven thousand lattes is the **equilibrium quantity:** the quantity demanded and quantity supplied that occur at the equilibrium price in a competitive market.

equilibrium price The price in a competitive market at which the quantity demanded and quantity supplied of a product are equal.

equilibrium quantity The quantity demanded and quantity supplied that occur at the equilibrium price in a competitive market.

Graphically, the equilibrium price is indicated by the intersection of the supply curve and the demand curve in Figure 3.6. (The horizontal axis now measures both quantity demanded and quantity supplied.) With neither a shortage nor a surplus at $3, the market is in equilibrium, meaning "in balance" or "at rest."

To better understand the uniqueness of the equilibrium price, let's consider other prices. At any above-equilibrium price, quantity supplied exceeds quantity demanded. For example, at the $4 price, sellers will offer 10,000 lattes, but buyers will purchase only 4000. The $4 price encourages sellers to offer lots of lattes but discourages many consumers from buying them. The result is a **surplus** or *excess supply* of 6000 lattes. If latte sellers made them all, they would find themselves with 6000 unsold lattes.

surplus The amount by which the quantity supplied of a product exceeds the quantity demanded at a specific (above-equilibrium) price.

Surpluses drive prices down. Even if the $4 price existed temporarily, it could not persist. The large surplus would prompt competing sellers to lower the price to encourage buyers to stop in and take the surplus off their hands. As the price fell, the incentive to produce lattes would decline and the incentive for consumers to buy lattes would increase. As shown in Figure 3.6, the market would move to its equilibrium at $3.

Any price below the $3 equilibrium price would create a shortage; quantity demanded would exceed quantity supplied. Consider a $2 price, for example. We see in column 4 of the table in Figure 3.6 that quantity demanded exceeds quantity supplied at that price. The result is a **shortage** or *excess demand* of 7000 lattes. The $2 price discourages sellers from devoting resources to lattes and encourages consumers to desire more lattes than are available. The $2 price cannot persist as the equilibrium price. Many consumers who want to buy lattes at this price will not obtain them. They will express a willingness to pay more than $2 to get them. Competition among these buyers will drive up the price, eventually to the $3 equilibrium level. Unless disrupted by supply or demand changes, this $3 price of lattes will continue.

shortage The amount by which the quantity demanded of a product exceeds the quantity supplied at a specific (below-equilibrium) price.

Rationing Function of Prices

3.1 Supply and demand

The ability of the competitive forces of supply and demand to establish a price at which selling and buying decisions are consistent is called the *rationing function of prices*. In our case, the equilibrium price of $3 clears the market, leaving no burdensome surplus for sellers and no inconvenient shortage for potential buyers. And it is the combination of freely made individual decisions that sets this market-clearing price. In effect, the market outcome says that all buyers who are willing and able to pay $3 for a latte will obtain one; all buyers who cannot or will not pay $3 will go without one. Similarly, all producers who are willing and able to offer a latte for sale at $3 will sell it; all producers who cannot or will not sell for $3 will not sell their product.

Ticket Scalping

Ticket prices for athletic events and musical concerts are usually set far in advance of the events. Sometimes the original ticket price is too low to be the equilibrium price. Lines form at the ticket window, and a severe shortage of tickets occurs at the printed price. What happens next? Buyers who are willing to pay more than the original price bid up the equilibrium price in resale ticket markets. The price rockets upward.

Tickets sometimes get resold for much greater amounts than the original price—market transactions known as "scalping." For example, an original buyer may resell a $75 ticket to a concert for $200, $250, or more. The media sometimes denounce scalpers for "ripping off" buyers by charging "exorbitant" prices.

But is scalping really a rip-off? We must first recognize that such ticket resales are voluntary transactions. If both buyer and seller did not expect to gain from the exchange, it would not occur! The seller must value the $200 more than seeing the event, and the buyer must value seeing the event at $200 or more. So there are no losers or victims here: Both buyer and seller benefit from the transaction. The "scalping" market simply redistributes assets (game or concert tickets) from those who would rather have the money (other things) to those who would rather have the tickets.

Does scalping impose losses or injury on the sponsors of the event? If the sponsors are injured, it is because they initially priced tickets below the equilibrium level. Perhaps they did this to create a long waiting line and the attendant media publicity. Alternatively, they may have had a genuine desire to keep tickets affordable for lower-income, ardent fans. In either case, the event sponsors suffer an opportunity cost in the form of less ticket revenue than they might have otherwise received. But such losses are self-inflicted and quite separate and distinct from the fact that some tickets are later resold at a higher price.

So is ticket scalping undesirable? Not on economic grounds! It is an entirely voluntary activity that benefits both sellers and buyers.

Question:
Why do you suppose some professional sports teams are setting up legal "ticket exchanges" (at buyer-and-seller-determined prices) at their Internet sites? (*Hint:* For the service, the teams charge a percentage of the transaction price of each resold ticket.)

Changes in Demand, Supply, and Equilibrium

We know that prices can and do change in markets. For example, demand might change because of fluctuations in consumer tastes or incomes, changes in expected price, or variations in the prices of related goods. Supply might change in response to changes in resource prices, technology, or taxes. How will such changes in demand and supply affect equilibrium price and quantity?

Changes in Demand

Suppose that the supply of some good (for example, beef) is constant and the demand for the good increases, as shown in Figure 3.7a. As a result, the new intersection of the supply and demand curves is at higher values on both the price and the quantity axes. Clearly, an increase in demand raises both equilibrium price and equilibrium quantity. Conversely, a decrease in demand, such as that shown in Figure 3.7b, reduces both equilibrium price and equilibrium quantity.

FIGURE 3.7

Changes in demand and supply and the effects on price and quantity. The increase in demand from D_1 to D_2 in (a) increases both equilibrium price and equilibrium quantity. The decrease in demand from D_1 to D_2 in (b) decreases both equilibrium price and equilibrium quantity. The increase in supply from S_1 to S_2 in (c) decreases equilibrium price and increases equilibrium quantity. The decline in supply from S_1 to S_2 in (d) increases equilibrium price and decreases equilibrium quantity. The boxes in the top right summarize the respective changes and outcomes. The upward arrows in the boxes signify increases in demand (D), supply (S), equilibrium price (P), and equilibrium quantity (Q); the downward arrows signify decreases in these items.

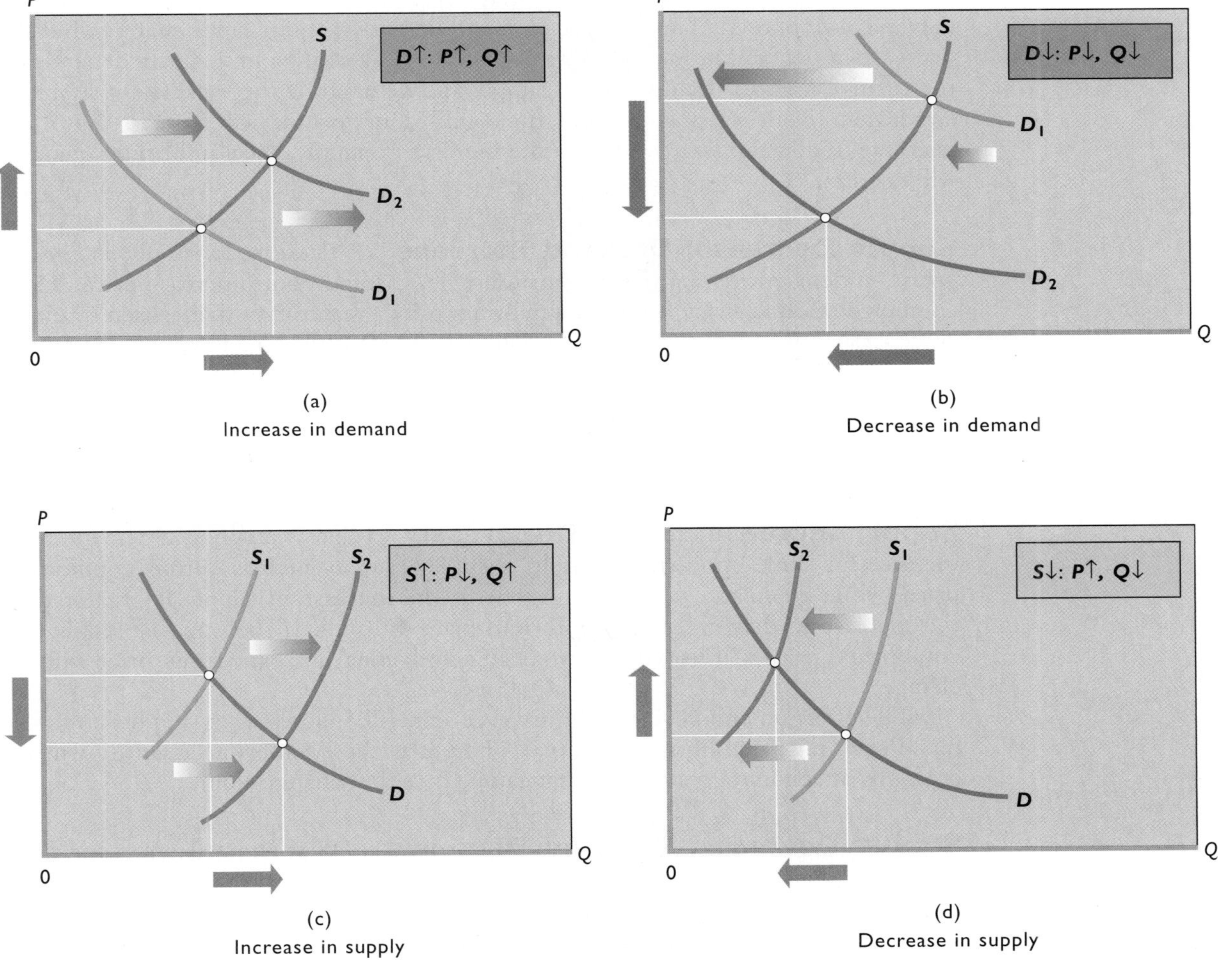

Changes in Supply

What happens if the demand for some good (for example, lettuce) is constant but the supply increases, as in Figure 3.7c. The new intersection of supply and demand is located at a lower equilibrium price but at a higher equilibrium quantity. An increase in supply reduces equilibrium price but increases equilibrium quantity. In contrast, if supply decreases, as in Figure 3.7d, the equilibrium price rises while the equilibrium quantity declines.

Complex Cases

When both supply and demand change, the effect is a combination of the individual effects.

Supply Increase; Demand Decrease What effect will a supply increase for some good (for example, apples) and a demand decrease have on equilibrium price? Both changes decrease price, so the net result is a price drop greater than that resulting from either change alone.

What about equilibrium quantity? Here the effects of the changes in supply and demand are opposed: The increase in supply increases equilibrium quantity, but the decrease in demand reduces it. The direction of the change in quantity depends on the relative sizes of the changes in supply and demand. If the increase in supply is larger than the decrease in demand, the equilibrium quantity will increase. But if the decrease in demand is greater than the increase in supply, the equilibrium quantity will decrease.

Supply Decrease; Demand Increase A decrease in supply and an increase in demand for some good (for example, gasoline) both increase price. Their combined effect is an increase in equilibrium price greater than that caused by either change separately. But their effect on equilibrium quantity is again indeterminate, depending on the relative sizes of the changes in supply and demand. If the decrease in supply is larger than the increase in demand, the equilibrium quantity will decrease. In contrast, if the increase in demand is greater than the decrease in supply, the equilibrium quantity will increase.

Supply Increase; Demand Increase What if supply and demand both increase for some good (for example, sushi)? A supply increase drops equilibrium price, while a demand increase boosts it. If the increase in supply is greater than the increase in demand, the equilibrium price will fall. If the opposite holds, the equilibrium price will rise. If the two changes are equal and cancel out, price will not change.

The effect on equilibrium quantity is certain: The increases in supply and in demand each raise equilibrium quantity. Therefore, the equilibrium quantity will increase by an amount greater than that caused by either change alone.

Supply Decrease; Demand Decrease What about decreases in both supply and demand for some good (for example, cedar logs)? If the decrease in supply is greater than the decrease in demand, equilibrium price will rise. If the reverse is true, equilibrium price will fall. If the two changes are of the same size and cancel out, price will not change. Because decreases in supply and in demand each reduce equilibrium quantity, we can be sure that equilibrium quantity will fall.

Government-Set Prices

In most markets, prices are free to rise or fall with changes in supply or demand, no matter how high or low those prices might be. However, government occasionally concludes that changes in supply and demand have created prices that are unfairly high to buyers or unfairly low to sellers. Government may then place legal limits on how high or low a price or prices may go. Our previous analysis of shortages and surpluses helps us evaluate the wisdom of government-set prices.

Price Ceilings on Gasoline

A **price ceiling** sets the maximum legal price a seller may charge for a product or service. A price at or below the ceiling is legal; a price above it is not. The rationale for establishing price ceilings (or ceiling prices) on specific products is that they purportedly enable consumers to obtain some "essential" good or service that they could not afford at the equilibrium price.

price ceiling A legally established maximum (below-equilibrium) price for a product.

Figure 3.8 shows the effects of price ceilings graphically. Suppose that rapidly rising world income boosts the purchase of automobiles and increases the demand for gasoline so that the equilibrium or market price reaches $2.50 per gallon. The rapidly rising price of gasoline greatly burdens low- and moderate-income households, which pressure government to "do something." To keep gasoline affordable for these households, the government imposes a ceiling price of $2 per gallon. To impact the market, a price ceiling must be below the equilibrium price. A ceiling price of $3, for example, would have had no immediate effect on the gasoline market.

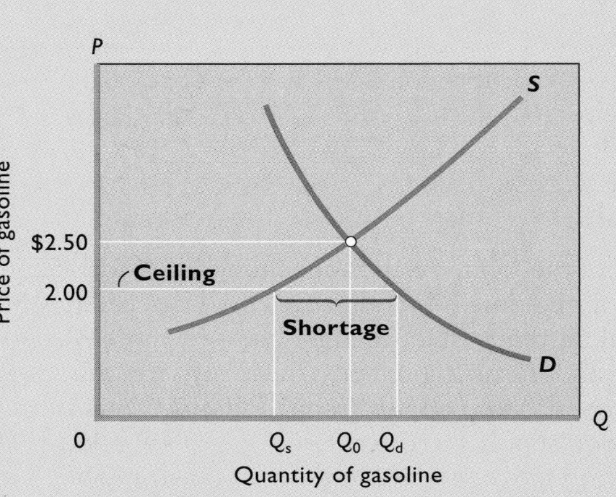

FIGURE 3.8
A price ceiling. A price ceiling is a maximum legal price, such as $2, that is below the equilibrium price. It results in a persistent product shortage, here shown by the distance between Q_d and Q_s.

What are the effects of this \$2 ceiling price? The rationing ability of the free market is rendered ineffective. Because the \$2 ceiling price is below the \$2.50 market-clearing price, there is a lasting shortage of gasoline. The quantity of gasoline demanded at \$2 is Q_d, and the quantity supplied is only Q_s; a persistent excess demand or shortage of amount $Q_d - Q_s$ occurs.

The \$2 price ceiling prevents the usual market adjustment in which competition among buyers bids up price, inducing more production and rationing some buyers out of the market. That process would continue until the shortage disappeared at the equilibrium price and quantity, \$2.50 and Q_0.

How will sellers apportion the available supply Q_s among buyers, who want the greater amount Q_d? Should they distribute gasoline on a first-come, first-served basis, that is, to those willing and able to get in line the soonest and stay in line? Or should gas stations distribute it on the basis of favoritism? Since an unregulated shortage does not lead to an equitable distribution of gasoline, the government must establish some formal system for rationing it to consumers. One option is to issue ration coupons, which authorize bearers to purchase a fixed amount of gasoline per month. The rationing system would entail first the printing of coupons for *Qs* gallons of gasoline and then the equitable distribution of the coupons among consumers so that the wealthy family of four and the poor family of four both receive the same number of coupons.

But ration coupons would not prevent a second problem from arising. The demand curve in Figure 3.8 reveals that many buyers are willing to pay more than the \$2 ceiling price. And, of course, it is more profitable for gasoline stations to sell at prices above the ceiling. Thus, despite a sizable enforcement bureaucracy that would have to accompany the price controls, *black markets* in which gasoline is illegally bought and sold at prices above the legal limits will flourish. Counterfeiting of ration coupons will also be a problem. And since the price of gasoline is now "set by government," there might be political pressure on government to set the price even lower.

Question:
Why is it typically difficult to end price ceilings once they have been in place for a long time?

Rent Controls

About 200 cities in the United States, including New York City, Boston, and San Francisco, have at one time or another enacted price ceilings in the form of rent controls—maximum rents established by law—or, more recently, have set maximum rent increases for existing tenants: Such laws are well intended. Their goals are to protect low-income families from escalating rents caused by demand increases that outstrip supply increases. Rent controls are designed to alleviate perceived housing shortages and make housing more affordable.

What have been the actual economic effects? On the demand side, it is true that as long as rents are below equilibrium, more families are willing to consume rental housing; the quantity of rental housing demanded increases at the lower price. But a large problem occurs on the supply side. Price controls make it less attractive for landlords to offer housing on the rental market. In the short run, owners may sell their rental units or convert them to condominiums. In the long run, low rents make it unprofitable for owners to repair or renovate their rental units. (Rent controls are one cause of the many abandoned apartment buildings found in some larger cities.) Also, insurance companies, pension funds, and other potential new investors in housing will find it more profitable to invest in office buildings, shopping malls, or motels, where rents are not controlled.

In brief, rent controls distort market signals, and thus resources are misallocated: Too few resources are allocated to rental housing, and too many to alternative uses. Ironically, although rent controls are often legislated to lessen the effects of perceived shortages, controls in fact are a primary cause of such shortages. For that reason, most American cities either have abandoned rent controls or are gradually phasing them out.

Question:
Why does maintenance tend to diminish in rent-controlled apartment buildings relative to maintenance in buildings where owners can charge market-determined rents?

Price Floors on Wheat

A **price floor** is a minimum price fixed by the government. A price at or above the price floor is legal; a price below it is not. Price floors above equilibrium prices are usually invoked when society feels that the free functioning of the market system has not provided a sufficient income for certain groups of resource suppliers or producers. Supported prices for agricultural products and current minimum wages are two examples of price (or wage) floors. Let's look at the former.

price floor
A legally established minimum (above-equilibrium) price for a product.

Suppose the demand for wheat declines relative to supply, pushing down the equilibrium price of wheat to \$2 per bushel. Because of that low price, many farmers have extremely low incomes. The government decides to help out by establishing a legal price floor (or "price support") of \$3 per bushel.

What will be the effects? At any price above the equilibrium price, quantity supplied will exceed quantity demanded—that is, there will be a persistent surplus of the product. Farmers will be willing to produce and offer for sale more wheat than private buyers are willing to buy at the \$3 price floor. As we saw with a price ceiling, an imposed legal price disrupts the rationing ability of the free market.

Figure 3.9 illustrates the effect of a price floor graphically. Suppose that *S* and *D* are the supply and demand curves for wheat. Equilibrium price and quantity are \$2 and Q_0, respectively. If the government imposes a price floor of \$3, farmers will produce Q_s but private buyers will purchase only Q_d. The surplus is the excess of Q_s over Q_d.

FIGURE 3.9
A price floor.
A price floor is a minimum legal price, such as $3, that results in a persistent product surplus, here shown by the distance between Q_s and Q_d.

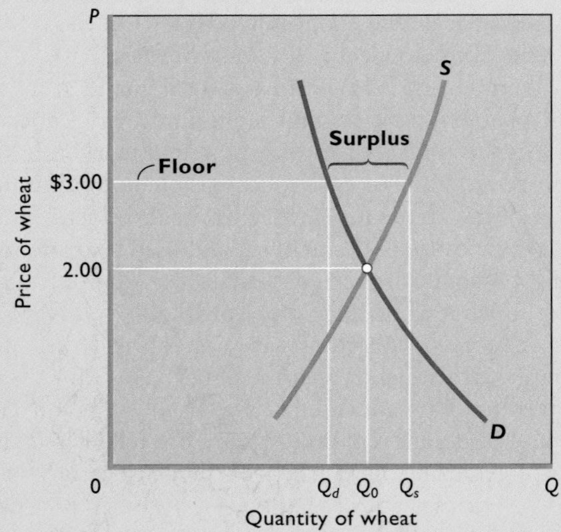

The government may cope with the surplus resulting from a price floor in two ways:

- It can restrict supply (for example, by instituting acreage allotments by which farmers agree to take a certain amount of land out of production) or increase demand (for example, by researching new uses for the product involved). These actions may reduce the difference between the equilibrium price and the price floor and that way reduce the size of the resulting surplus.
- If these efforts are not wholly successful, then the government must purchase the surplus output at the $3 price (thereby subsidizing farmers) and store or otherwise dispose of it.

Price floors such as $3 in Figure 3.9 not only disrupt the rationing ability of prices but also distort resource allocation. Without the price floor, the $2 equilibrium price of wheat would cause financial losses and force high-cost wheat producers to plant other crops or abandon farming altogether. But the $3 price floor allows them to continue to grow wheat and remain farmers. So society devotes too many scarce resources to wheat production and too few to producing other, more valuable, goods and services. It fails to achieve an optimal allocation of resources.

That's not all. Consumers of wheat-based products pay higher prices because of the price floor. Taxpayers pay higher taxes to finance the government's purchase of the surplus. Also, the price floor causes potential environmental damage by encouraging wheat farmers to bring hilly, erosion-prone "marginal land" into production. The higher price also prompts imports of wheat. But, since such imports would increase the quantity of wheat supplied and thus undermine the price floor, the government needs to erect tariffs (taxes on imports) to keep the foreign wheat out. Such tariffs usually prompt other countries to retaliate with their own tariffs against U.S. agricultural or manufacturing exports.

Question:
To maintain price floors on milk, the U.S. government has at times bought out and destroyed entire dairy herds from dairy farmers. What's the economic logic of these actions?

It is easy to see why economists "sound the alarm" when politicians advocate imposing price ceilings or price floors such as price controls, rent controls, interest-rate lids, or agricultural price supports. In all these cases, good intentions lead to bad economic outcomes. Government-controlled prices lead to shortages or surpluses, distort resource allocations, and cause negative side effects.

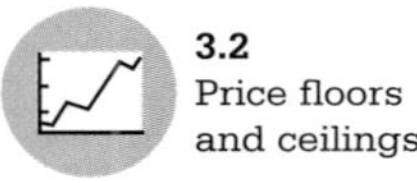
3.2
Price floors and ceilings

Summary

1. Demand is a schedule or curve representing the willingness of buyers in a specific period to purchase a particular product at each of various prices. The law of demand implies that consumers will buy more of a product at a low price than at a high price. So, other things equal, the relationship between price and quantity demanded is inverse and is graphed as a downsloping curve.
2. Market demand curves are found by adding horizontally the demand curves of the many individual consumers in the market.
3. Changes in one or more of the determinants of demand (consumer tastes, the number of buyers in the market, the money incomes of consumers, the prices of related goods, and expected prices) shift the market demand curve. A shift to the right is an increase in demand; a shift to the left is a decrease in demand. A change in demand is different from a change in the quantity demanded, the latter being a movement from one point to another point on a fixed demand curve because of a change in the product's price.
4. Supply is a schedule or curve showing the amounts of a product that producers are willing to offer in the market at each possible price during a specific period. The law of supply states that, other things equal, producers will offer more of a product at a high price than at a low price. Thus, the relationship between price and quantity supplied is positive or direct, and supply is graphed as an upsloping curve.
5. The market supply curve is the horizontal summation of the supply curves of the individual producers of the product.
6. Changes in one or more of the determinants of supply (resource prices, production techniques, taxes or subsidies, the prices of other goods, expected prices, or the number of suppliers in the market) shift the supply curve of a product. A shift to the right is an increase in supply; a shift to the left is a decrease in supply. In contrast, a change in the price of the product being considered causes a change in the quantity supplied, which is shown as a movement from one point to another point on a fixed supply curve.
7. The equilibrium price and quantity are established at the intersection of the supply and demand curves. The interaction of market demand and market supply adjusts the price to the point at which the quantities demanded and supplied are equal. This is the equilibrium price. The corresponding quantity is the equilibrium quantity.
8. A change in either demand or supply changes the equilibrium price and quantity. Increases in demand raise both equilibrium price and equilibrium quantity; decreases in demand lower both equilibrium price and equilibrium quantity. Increases in supply lower equilibrium price and raise equilibrium quantity; decreases in supply raise equilibrium price and lower equilibrium quantity.
9. Simultaneous changes in demand and supply affect equilibrium price and quantity in various ways, depending on their direction and relative magnitudes.
10. A price ceiling is a maximum price set by government and is designed to help consumers. Effective price ceilings produce persistent product shortages, and if an equitable distribution of the product is sought, government must ration the product to consumers.
11. A price floor is a minimum price set by government and is designed to aid producers. Price floors lead to persistent product surpluses; the government must either purchase the product or eliminate the surplus by imposing restrictions on production or increasing private demand.
12. Legally fixed prices stifle the rationing function of prices and distort the allocation of resources.

solution eliminates the "up versus down" problem. All the elasticity coefficients that follow are calculated using this *midpoints approach*.

Elimination of Minus Sign Because demand curves slope downward, the price-elasticity coefficient of demand E_d will always be a negative number. As an example, if price declines, quantity demanded will increase. This means that the numerator in our formula will be positive and the denominator negative, yielding a negative E_d. For an increase in price, the numerator will be negative but the denominator positive, again producing a negative E_d.

Economists usually ignore the minus sign and simply present the absolute value of the elasticity coefficient to avoid an ambiguity that might otherwise arise. It can be confusing to say that an E_d of -4 is greater than one of -2. This possible confusion is avoided when we say an E_d of 4 reveals greater elasticity than an E_d of 2. In what follows, we ignore the minus sign in the coefficient of price elasticity of demand and show only the absolute value.

Interpretations of E_d

We can interpret the coefficient of price elasticity of demand as follows.

elastic demand Product demand for which price changes cause relatively larger changes in quantity demanded.

Elastic Demand Demand is **elastic** if a specific percentage change in price results in a larger percentage change in quantity demanded. Then E_d will be greater than 1. Example: Suppose that a 2 percent decline in the price of cut flowers results in a 4 percent increase in quantity demanded. Then demand for cut flowers is elastic and

$$E_d = \frac{.04}{.02} = 2$$

inelastic demand Product demand for which price changes cause relatively smaller changes in quantity demanded.

Inelastic Demand If a specific percentage change in price produces a smaller percentage change in quantity demanded, demand is **inelastic.** Then E_d will be less than 1. Example: Suppose that a 2 percent decline in the price of tea leads to only a 1 percent increase in quantity demanded. Then demand is inelastic and

$$E_d = \frac{.01}{.02} = .5$$

unit elasticity Product demand for which relative price changes and changes in quantity demanded are equal.

Unit Elasticity The case separating elastic and inelastic demands occurs where a percentage change in price and the resulting percentage change in quantity demanded are the same. Example: Suppose that a 2 percent drop in the price of chocolate causes a 2 percent increase in quantity demanded. This special case is termed **unit elasticity** because E_d is exactly 1, or unity. In this example,

$$E_d = \frac{.02}{.02} = 1$$

perfectly inelastic demand Product demand for which quantity demanded does not respond to a change in price.

Extreme Cases When we say demand is "inelastic," we do not mean that consumers are completely unresponsive to a price change. In that extreme situation, where a price change results in no change whatsoever in the quantity demanded, economists say that demand is **perfectly inelastic.** The price-elasticity coefficient is zero because there is no response to a change in price. Approximate examples include an acute diabetic's demand for insulin or an addict's demand for heroin. A line parallel to the vertical axis, such as D_1 in Figure 4.1a, shows perfectly inelastic demand graphically.

© Nik Wheeler/CORBIS

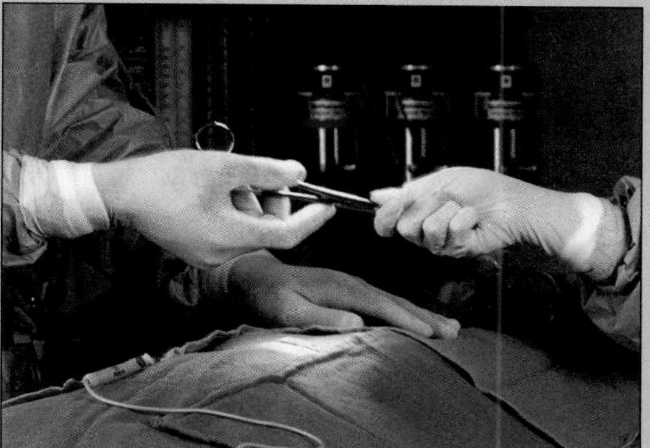

© PhotoLink/Getty Images/DIL

Photo Op Elastic versus Inelastic Demand

The demand for expensive vacation activities such as cruise vacations is elastic; the demand for surgery or other nonelective medical care is inelastic.

Conversely, when we say demand is "elastic," we do not mean that consumers are completely responsive to a price change. In that extreme situation, where a small price reduction causes buyers to increase their purchases from zero to all they can obtain, the elasticity coefficient is infinite (∞) and economists say demand is **perfectly elastic.** A line parallel to the horizontal axis, such as D_2 in Figure 4.1b, shows perfectly elastic demand. Such a demand curve, for example, faces wheat growers who can sell all or none of their wheat at the equilibrium market price.

perfectly elastic demand
Product demand for which quantity demanded can be any amount at a particular price.

The Total-Revenue Test

The importance of elasticity for firms relates to the effect of price changes on total revenue and thus on profits (total revenue minus total costs).

FIGURE 4.1
Perfectly inelastic and elastic demands. Demand curve D_1 in (a) represents perfectly inelastic demand ($E_d = 0$). A price increase will result in no change in quantity demanded. Demand curve D_2 in (b) represents perfectly elastic demand. A price increase will cause quantity demanded to decline from an infinite amount to zero ($E_d = \infty$).

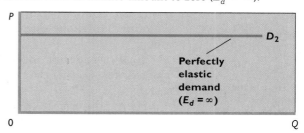

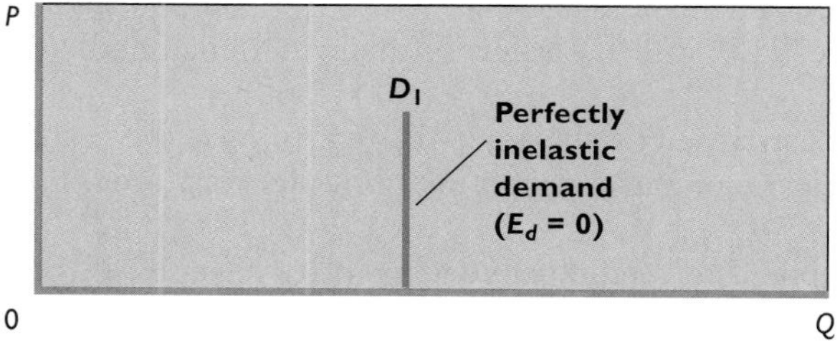

(a)
Perfectly inelastic demand

P
D_2
Perfectly elastic demand ($E_d = \infty$)
0
Q

(b)
Perfectly elastic demand

A Bit of a Stretch

The following analogy might help you remember the distinction between "elastic" and "inelastic." Imagine two objects: (1) an Ace elastic bandage used to wrap injured joints and (2) a relatively firm rubber tie-down used for securing items for transport. The Ace bandage stretches a great deal when pulled with a particular force; the rubber tie-down stretches some, but not a lot.

Similar differences occur for the quantity demanded of various products when their prices change. For some products, a price change causes a substantial "stretch" of quantity demanded. When this stretch in percentage terms exceeds the percentage change in price, demand is elastic. For other products, quantity demanded stretches very little in response to the price change. When this stretch in percentage terms is less than the percentage change in price, demand is inelastic.

In summary:

- Elastic demand displays considerable "quantity stretch" (as with the Ace bandage).
- Inelastic demand displays relatively little "quantity stretch" (as with the rubber tie-down).

And through extension:

- Perfectly elastic demand has infinite quantity stretch.
- Perfectly inelastic demand has zero quantity stretch.

Question:
Which do you think has the most quantity stretch, given an equal percentage increase in price—toothpaste or townhouses?

total revenue (TR) The total number of dollars received by a firm from the sale of a product in a particular period.

Total revenue (TR) is the total amount the seller receives from the sale of a product in a particular time period; it is calculated by multiplying the product price (P) by the quantity demanded and sold (Q). In equation form:

$$\text{TR} = P \times Q$$

Graphically, total revenue is represented by the $P \times Q$ rectangle lying below a point on a demand curve. At point a in Figure 4.2a, for example, price is \$2 and quantity demanded is 10 units. So total revenue is \$20 (=\$2 × 10), shown by the rectangle composed of the blue and gold areas under the demand curve. We know from basic geometry that the area of a rectangle is found by multiplying one side by the other. Here, one side is "price" (\$2) and the other is "quantity demanded" (10 units).

total-revenue test A test that determines elasticity by examining what happens to total revenue when price changes.

Total revenue and the price elasticity of demand are related. In fact, the easiest way to infer whether demand is elastic or inelastic is to employ the **total-revenue test.**

Here is the test: Note what happens to total revenue when price changes. If total revenue changes in the opposite direction from price, demand is elastic. If total revenue changes in the same direction as price, demand is inelastic. If total revenue does not change when price changes, demand is unit-elastic.

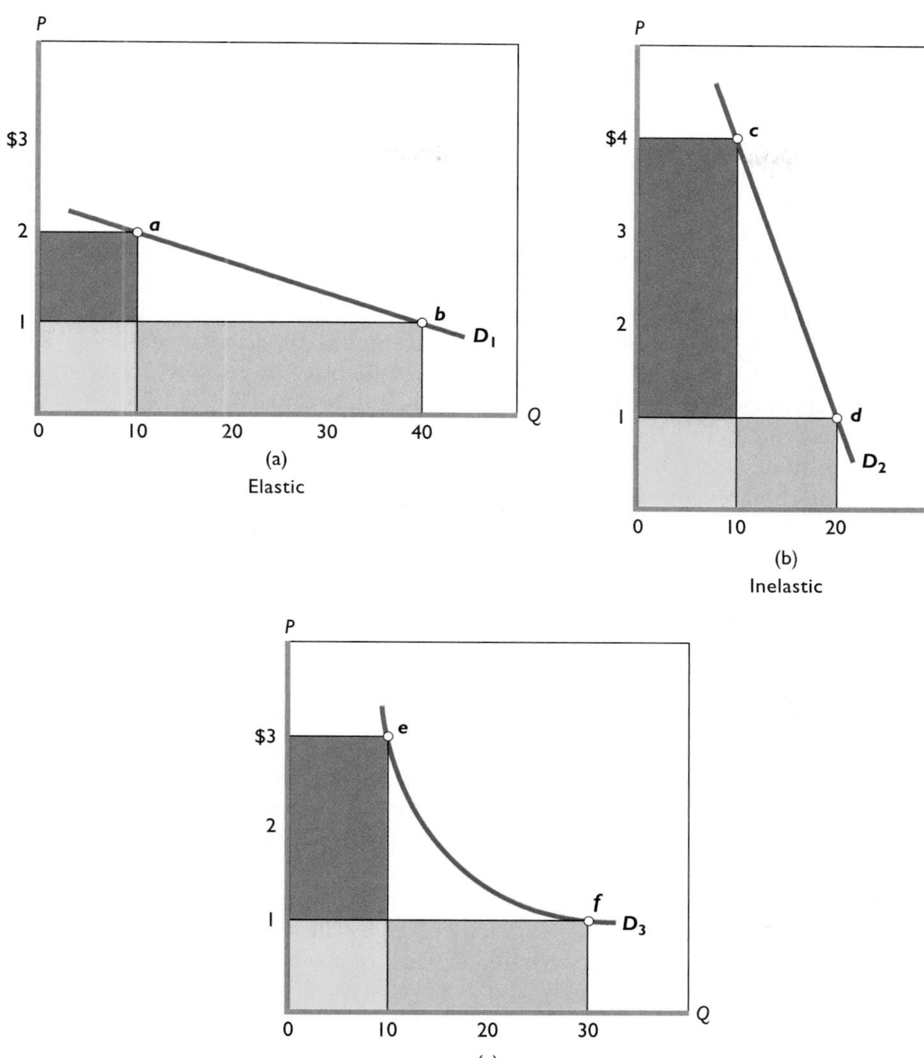

FIGURE 4.2
The total-revenue test for price elasticity. (a) Price declines from $2 to $1, and total revenue increases from $20 to $40. So demand is elastic. The gain in revenue (tan area) exceeds the loss of revenue (blue area). (b) Price declines from $4 to $1, and total revenue falls from $40 to $20. So demand is inelastic. The gain in revenue (tan area) is less than the loss of revenue (blue area). (c) Price declines from $3 to $1, and total revenue does not change. Demand is unit-elastic. The gain in revenue (tan area) equals the loss of revenue (blue area).

Elastic Demand If demand is elastic, a decrease in price will increase total revenue. Even though a lesser price is received per unit, enough additional units are sold to more than make up for the lower price. For an example, look at demand curve D_1 in Figure 4.2a. We have already established that at point *a*, total revenue is $20 (=$2 × 10), shown as the blue plus gold area.

If the price declines from $2 to $1 (point *b*), the quantity demanded becomes 40 units and total revenue is $40 (=$1 × 40). As a result of the price decline, total revenue has increased from $20 to $40. Total revenue has increased in this case because the $1 decline in price applies to 10 units, with a consequent revenue loss of $10 (the blue area). But 30 more units are sold at $1 each, resulting in a revenue gain of $30 (the tan area). Visually, it is apparent that the gain of the tan area exceeds the loss of the blue area. As indicated, the overall result is a net increase in total revenue of $20 (=$30 − $10).

The analysis is reversible: If demand is elastic, a price increase will reduce total revenue. The revenue gained on the higher-priced units will be more than offset by the revenue lost from the lower quantity sold. Bottom line: Other things equal, when price and total revenue move in opposite directions, demand is elastic. E_d is greater than 1, meaning the percentage change in quantity demanded is greater than the percentage change in price.

Inelastic Demand If demand is inelastic, a price decrease will reduce total revenue. The increase in sales will not fully offset the decline in revenue per unit, and total revenue will decline. To see this, look at demand curve D_2 in Figure 4.2b. At point *c* on the curve, price is $4 and quantity demanded is 10. So total revenue is $40, shown by the combined blue and gold rectangle. If the price drops to $1 (point *d*), total revenue declines to $20, which obviously is less than $40. Total revenue has declined because the loss of revenue (the blue area) from the lower unit price is larger than the gain in revenue (the tan area) from the accompanying increase in sales. Price has fallen, and total revenue has also declined.

Our analysis is again reversible: If demand is inelastic, a price increase will increase total revenue. So, other things equal, when price and total revenue move in the same direction, demand is inelastic. E_d is less than 1, meaning the percentage change in quantity demanded is less than the percentage change in price.

Unit Elasticity In the special case of unit elasticity, an increase or a decrease in price leaves total revenue unchanged. The loss in revenue from a lower unit price is exactly offset by the gain in revenue from the accompanying increase in sales. Conversely, the gain in revenue from a higher unit price is exactly offset by the revenue loss associated with the accompanying decline in the amount demanded.

In Figure 4.2c (demand curve D_3) we find that at the $3 price, 10 units will be sold, yielding total revenue of $30. At the lower $1 price, a total of 30 units will be sold, again resulting in $30 of total revenue. The $2 price reduction causes the loss of revenue shown by the blue area, but this is exactly offset by the revenue gain shown by the tan area. Total revenue does not change. In fact, that would be true for all price changes along this particular curve.

Other things equal, when price changes and total revenue remains constant, demand is unit-elastic (or unitary). E_d is 1, meaning the percentage change in quantity equals the percentage change in price.

Price Elasticity along a Linear Demand Curve

Now a major confession! Although the demand curves depicted in Figure 4.2 nicely illustrate the total-revenue test for elasticity, two of the graphs involve specific movements along linear (straight-line) demand curves. That presents no problem for explaining the total-revenue test. However, you need to know that elasticity typically varies over the different price ranges of the same demand curve. (The exception is the curve in Figure 4.2c. Elasticity is 1 along the entire curve.)

Consider columns 1 and 2 of the table in Figure 4.3, which shows hypothetical data for movie tickets. We plot these data as demand curve *D* in the accompanying graph. The notation above the curve correctly suggests that demand is more price-elastic toward the upper left (the $5–$8 price range of *D*) than toward the lower right (the $4–$1 price range of *D*). This fact is confirmed by the elasticity coefficients in column (3) of the table: The coefficients decline as price falls. Also, note from column

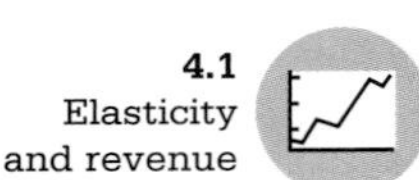

(1) Total Quantity of Tickets Demanded per Week, Thousands	(2) Price per Ticket	(3) Elasticity Coefficient (E_d)	(4) Total Revenue, (1) × (2)	(5) Total-Revenue Test
1	$8		$ 8,000	
		5.00		Elastic
2	7		14,000	
		2.60		Elastic
3	6		18,000	
		1.57		Elastic
4	5		20,000	
		1.00		Unit elastic
5	4		20,000	
		0.64		Inelastic
6	3		18,000	
		0.38		Inelastic
7	2		14,000	
		0.20		Inelastic
8	1		8,000	

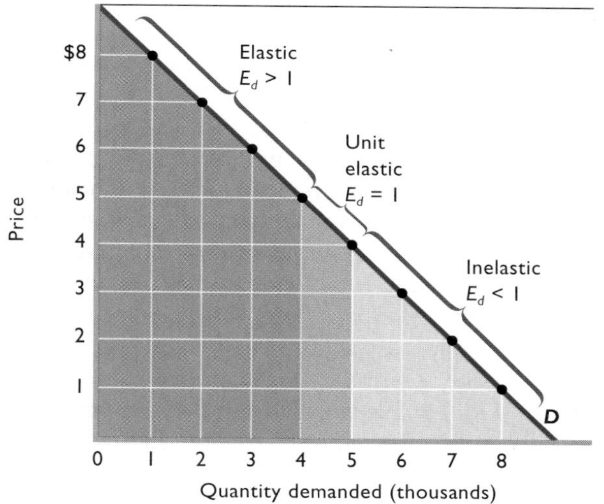

FIGURE 4.3
Price elasticity of demand along a linear demand curve as measured by the elasticity coefficient and the total-revenue test. Demand curve *D* is based on columns (1) and (2) of the table and is labeled to show that the hypothetical weekly demand for movie tickets is elastic at higher price ranges and inelastic at lower price ranges. That fact is confirmed by the elasticity coefficients (column 3) as well as the total-revenue test (columns 4 and 5) in the table.

(4) that total revenue first rises as price falls and then eventually declines as price falls further. Column (5) employs the total-revenue test to show that elasticity declines as price falls along a linear demand curve.

The demand curve in Figure 4.3 illustrates that the slope of a demand curve (its flatness or steepness) is an unreliable basis for judging elasticity. The slope of the curve is computed from *absolute* changes in price and quantity, while elasticity involves *relative* or *percentage* changes in price and quantity. The demand curve in Figure 4.3 is linear, which means its slope is constant throughout. But this linear curve is elastic in its high-price ($8–$5) range and inelastic in its low-price ($4–$1) range.

Determinants of Price Elasticity of Demand

We cannot say what will determine the price elasticity of demand in each individual situation, but the following generalizations are often helpful.

Substitutability Generally, the larger the number of substitute goods that are available, the greater is the price elasticity of demand. Mercedes, BMWs, and Lincolns are effective substitutes for Cadillacs, making the demand for Cadillacs elastic. At the other extreme, we saw earlier that the diabetic's demand for insulin is highly inelastic because there simply are no close substitutes.

The elasticity of demand for a product depends on how narrowly the product is defined. Demand for Reebok sneakers is more elastic than is the overall demand for shoes. Many other brands are readily substitutable for Reebok sneakers, but there are few, if any, good substitutes for shoes.

Proportion of Income Other things equal, the higher the price of a product relative to one's income, the greater the price elasticity of demand for it. A 10 percent increase in the price of low-priced pencils or chewing gum amounts to a very small portion of most people's incomes, and quantity demanded will probably decline only slightly. Thus, price elasticity for such low-priced items tends to be low. But a 10 percent increase in the price of relatively high-priced automobiles or houses means additional expenditures of perhaps \$3000 or \$20,000. That price increase is a significant fraction of the incomes and budgets of most families, and the number of units demanded will likely diminish significantly. Price elasticity for such items tends to be high.

Luxuries versus Necessities In general, the more that a good is considered to be a "luxury" rather than a "necessity," the greater is the price elasticity of demand. Electricity is generally regarded as a necessity; it is difficult to get along without it. A price increase will not significantly reduce the amount of lighting and power used in a household. (Note the very low price-elasticity coefficient of these goods in Table 4.1.) An extreme case: A person does not decline emergency heart bypass surgery because the physician's fee has just gone up by 10 percent.

TABLE 4.1

Selected Price Elasticities of Demand

Product or Service	Coefficient of Price Elasticity of Demand (E_d)	Product or Service	Coefficient of Price Elasticity of Demand (E_d)
Newspapers	.10	Milk	.63
Electricity (household)	.13	Household appliances	.63
Bread	.15	Movies	.87
Major-league baseball tickets	.23	Beer	.90
Telephone service	.26	Shoes	.91
Sugar	.30	Motor vehicles	1.14
Medical care	.31	Beef	1.27
Eggs	.32	China, glassware, tableware	1.54
Legal services	.37	Residential land	1.60
Automobile repair	.40	Restaurant meals	2.27
Clothing	.49	Lamb and mutton	2.65
Gasoline	.60	Fresh peas	2.83

Source: Compiled from numerous studies and sources reporting price elasticity of demand.

On the other hand, vacation travel and jewelry are luxuries that can easily be forgone. If the prices of vacation travel and jewelry rise, a consumer need not buy them and will suffer no great hardship without them.

What about the demand for a common product like salt? It is highly inelastic on three counts: There are few good substitutes available; salt is a negligible item in the family budget; and it is a "necessity" rather than a luxury.

Time Generally, product demand is more elastic the longer the time period under consideration. Consumers often need time to adjust to changes in prices. For example, consumers may not immediately reduce their purchases very much when the price of beef rises by 10 percent, but in time they may shift to chicken, pork, or fish.

Another consideration is product durability. Studies show that "short-run" demand for gasoline is more inelastic ($E_d = .2$) than is "long-run" demand ($E_d = .7$). In the short run, people are "stuck" with their present cars and trucks, but with rising gasoline prices they eventually replace them with smaller, more fuel-efficient vehicles.

Table 4.1 shows estimated price-elasticity coefficients for a number of products. Each reflects some combination of the elasticity determinants just discussed.

Applying the Analysis

Fluctuating Farm Income

Inelastic demand for farm products and year-to-year changes in farm output combine to produce highly volatile farm prices and incomes. Let's see why.

In industrially advanced economies, the price elasticity of demand for agricultural products is low. For farm products in the aggregate, the elasticity coefficient is between .20 and .25. These figures suggest that the prices of agricultural products would have to fall by 40 to 50 percent for consumers to increase their purchases by a mere 10 percent. Consumers apparently put a low value on additional farm output compared with the value they put on additional units of alternative goods.

Why is this so? Recall that a basic determinant of elasticity of demand is substitutability. When the price of one product falls, the consumer tends to substitute that product for other products whose prices have not fallen. But in relatively wealthy societies this substitution is very modest for food. Although people may eat more, they do not switch from three meals a day to, say, five or six meals a day in response to a decline in the relative prices of farm products. Real biological factors constrain an individual's capacity to substitute food for other products.

Farm output tends to fluctuate from year to year, mainly because farmers have limited control over their output. Floods, droughts, unexpected frost, insect damage, and similar disasters can mean poor crops, while an excellent growing season means bumper crops (extraordinarily large crops). Such natural phenomena are beyond the control of farmers, yet those phenomena exert an important influence on output.

In addition to natural phenomena, the highly competitive nature of agriculture makes it difficult for farmers to form huge combinations to control production. If the thousands of widely scattered and independent producers happened to plant an unusually large or an abnormally small portion of their land one year, an extra-large or a very small farm output would result even if the growing season were normal.

Combining inelastic demand with the instability of output, we can see why farm prices and incomes are unstable. Even if the market demand for some crop such as barley remains fixed, its price inelasticity will magnify small changes in output into relatively large changes in farm prices and income. For example, suppose that a "normal" barley crop of 100 million bushels results in a "normal" price per bushel of $3 and a "normal" farm income of $300 million (=$3 × 100 million).

A bumper crop of barley will cause large deviations from these normal prices and incomes because of the inelasticity of demand. Suppose that a good growing season occurs and that the result is a large crop of 110 million bushels. As farmers watch their individual crops mature, little will they realize that their collectively large crop, when harvested, will drive the price per bushel down to, say, $2.50. Their revenue will fall from $300 million in the normal year to $275 million (=$2.50 × 110 million bushels) this year. When demand is inelastic, an increase in the quantity sold will be accompanied by a more-than-proportionate decline in price. The net result is that total revenue, that is, total farm income, will decline disproportionately.

Similarly, a small crop of 90 million bushels, perhaps caused by drought, might boost the price to $3.50. Total farm income will rise to $315 million (=$3.50 × 90 million bushels) from the normal level of $300 million. A decline in output will cause a more-than-proportionate increase in price and in income when demand is inelastic. Ironically, for farmers as a group, a poor crop may be a blessing, and a bumper crop a hardship.

Question:
How might government programs to pay farmers to take land out of production in order to achieve conservation goals (such as erosion control and wildlife protection) increase crop prices and farm income?

Excise Taxes and Tax Revenue

The government pays attention to elasticity of demand when it selects goods and services on which to levy *excise taxes* (taxes levied on the production of a product or on the quantity of the product purchased). If a $1 tax is levied on a product and 10,000 units are sold, tax revenue will be $10,000 (=$1 × 10,000 units sold). If the government raises the tax to $1.50 but the higher price that results reduces sales (quantity demanded) to 4000 because demand is elastic, tax revenue will decline to $6000 (=$1.50 × 4000 units sold). So a higher tax on a product that has an elastic demand will bring in less tax revenue.

In contrast, if demand is inelastic, the tax increase from $1 to $1.50 will boost tax revenue. For example, if sales fall from 10,000 to 9000, tax revenue will rise from $10,000 to $13,500 (=$1.50 × 9000 units). Little wonder that legislatures tend to seek out products such as liquor, gasoline, cigarettes, and phone service when levying and raising taxes. Those taxes yield high tax revenues.

Question:
Under what circumstance might a reduction of an excise tax actually produce more tax revenue?

Applying the Analysis

Decriminalization of Illegal Drugs

In recent years proposals to legalize drugs have been widely debated. Proponents contend that drugs should be treated like alcohol; they should be made legal for adults and regulated for purity and potency. The current war on drugs, it is argued, has been unsuccessful, and the associated costs—including enlarged police forces, the construction of more prisons, an overburdened court system, and untold human costs—have increased markedly. Legalization would allegedly reduce drug trafficking significantly by taking the profit out of it. Crack cocaine and heroin, for example, are cheap to produce and could be sold at low prices in legal markets. Because the demand of addicts is highly inelastic, the amounts consumed at the lower prices would increase only modestly. Addicts' total expenditures for cocaine and heroin would decline, and so would the street crime that finances those expenditures.

Opponents of legalization say that the overall demand for cocaine and heroin is far more elastic than proponents think. In addition to the inelastic demand of addicts, there is another market segment whose demand is relatively elastic. This segment consists of the occasional users or "dabblers," who use hard drugs when their prices are low but who abstain or substitute, say, alcohol when their prices are high. Thus, the lower prices associated with the legalization of hard drugs would increase consumption by dabblers. Also, removal of the legal prohibitions against using drugs might make drug use more socially acceptable, increasing the demand for cocaine and heroin.

Many economists predict that the legalization of cocaine and heroin would reduce street prices by up to 60 percent, depending on if and how much they were taxed. According to one study, price declines of that size would increase the number of occasional users of heroin by 54 percent and the number of occasional users of cocaine by 33 percent. The total quantity of heroin demanded would rise by an estimated 100 percent, and the quantity of cocaine demanded would rise by 50 percent.* Moreover, many existing and first-time dabblers might in time become addicts. The overall result, say the opponents of legalization, would be higher social costs, possibly including an increase in street crime.

Question:
In what ways do drug rehabilitation programs increase the elasticity of demand for illegal drugs?

* Henry Saffer and Frank Chaloupka, "The Demand for Illegal Drugs," *Economic Inquiry*, July 1999, pp. 401–411.

Price Elasticity of Demand and College Tuition

For some goods and services, for-profit firms or not-for-profit institutions may find it advantageous to determine differences in price elasticity of demand for different groups of customers and then charge different prices to the different groups. Price increases for groups that have inelastic demand will increase total revenue, as will price decreases for groups that have elastic demand.

It is relatively easy to observe differences between group elasticities. Consider tuition pricing by colleges and universities. Prospective students from low-income families generally have more elastic demands for higher education than similar students from high-income families. This is true because tuition is a much larger proportion of household income for a low-income student or family than for his or her high-income counterpart. Desiring a diverse student body, colleges charge different *net* prices (=tuition *minus* financial aid) to the two groups on the basis of elasticity of demand. High-income students pay full tuition, unless they receive merit-based scholarships. Low-income students receive considerable financial aid in addition to merit-based scholarships and, in effect, pay a lower *net* price.

It is common for colleges to announce a large tuition increase and immediately cushion the news by emphasizing that they also are increasing financial aid. In effect, the college is increasing the tuition for students who have inelastic demand by the full amount and raising the *net* tuition of those with elastic demand by some lesser amount or not at all. Through this strategy, colleges boost revenue to cover rising costs while maintaining affordability for a wide range of students.

Question:
What are some other examples of charging different prices to different groups of customers on the basis of differences in elasticity of demand? (*Hint:* Think of price discounts based on age or time of purchase.)

Price Elasticity of Supply

4.2 Price elasticity of supply

The concept of price elasticity also applies to supply. If producers are relatively responsive to price changes, supply is elastic. If they are relatively insensitive to price changes, supply is inelastic.

We measure the degree of price elasticity or inelasticity of supply with the coefficient E_s, defined almost like E_d except that we substitute "percentage change in quantity supplied" for "percentage change in quantity demanded":

$$E_s = \frac{\text{percentage change in quantity supplied of X}}{\text{percentage change in price of X}}$$

For reasons explained earlier, the averages, or midpoints, of the before and after quantities supplied and the before and after prices are used as reference points for the percentage changes. Suppose an increase in the price of a good from \$4 to \$6 increases the quantity supplied from 10 units to 14 units. The percentage change in price would be 2/5, or 40 percent, and the percentage change in quantity would be 4/12, or 33 percent:

$$E_s = \frac{.33}{.40} = .83$$

In this case, supply is inelastic, since the price-elasticity coefficient is less than 1. If E_s is greater than 1, supply is elastic. If it is equal to 1, supply is unit-elastic. Also, E_s is never negative, since price and quantity supplied are directly related. Thus, there are no minus signs to drop, as was necessary with elasticity of demand.

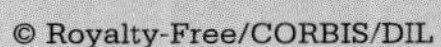

Photo Op Elastic versus Inelastic Supply

The supply of automobiles is elastic, whereas the supply of Monet paintings is inelastic.

The degree of **price elasticity of supply** depends mainly on how easily and quickly producers can shift resources between alternative uses to alter production of a good. The easier and more rapid the transfers of resources, the greater is the price elasticity of supply. Take the case of a producer of surfboards. The producer's response to an increase in the price of surfboards depends on its ability to shift resources from the production of other products such as wakeboards, skateboards, and snowboards (whose prices we assume remain constant) to the production of surfboards. And shifting resources takes time: The longer the time, the greater the transferability of resources. So there will be a greater production response, and therefore greater elasticity of supply, the longer a firm has to adjust to a price change.

price elasticity of supply
A measure of the responsiveness of sellers to a change in the price of a product.

In analyzing the impact of time on elasticity, economists distinguish among the immediate market period, the short run, and the long run.

Price Elasticity of Supply: The Market Period

The **market period** is the period that occurs when the time immediately after a change in market price is too short for producers to respond with a change in the amount they supply. Suppose a farmer brings to market one truckload of tomatoes that is the entire season's output. The supply curve for the tomatoes is perfectly inelastic (vertical); the farmer will sell the truckload whether the price is high or low. Why? Because the farmer can offer only one truckload of tomatoes even if the price of tomatoes is much higher than anticipated. He or she might like to offer more tomatoes, but tomatoes cannot be produced overnight. Another full growing season is needed to respond to a higher-than-expected price by producing more than one truckload. Similarly, because the product is perishable, the farmer cannot withhold it from the market. If the price is lower than anticipated, he or she will still sell the entire truckload.

market period
A period in which producers of a product are unable to change the quantity produced in response to a change in price.

FIGURE 4.4

Time and the elasticity of supply. The greater the amount of time producers have to adjust to a change in demand, here from D_1 to D_2, the greater will be their output response. In the immediate market period (a) there is insufficient time to change output, and so supply is perfectly inelastic. In the short run (b) plant capacity is fixed, but changing the intensity of its use can alter output; supply is therefore more elastic. In the long run (c) all desired adjustments, including changes in plant capacity, can be made, and supply becomes still more elastic.

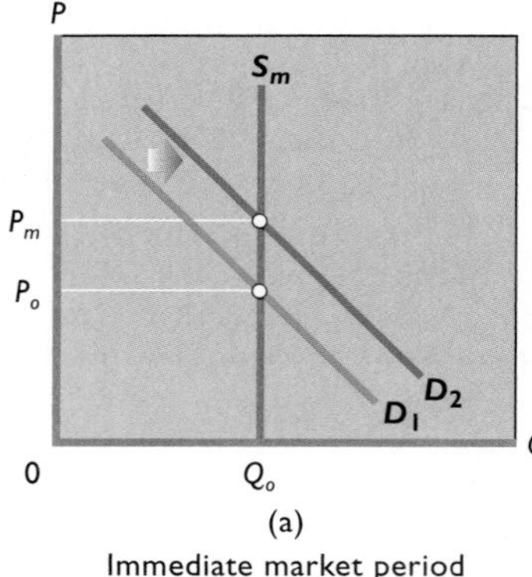

(a)
Immediate market period

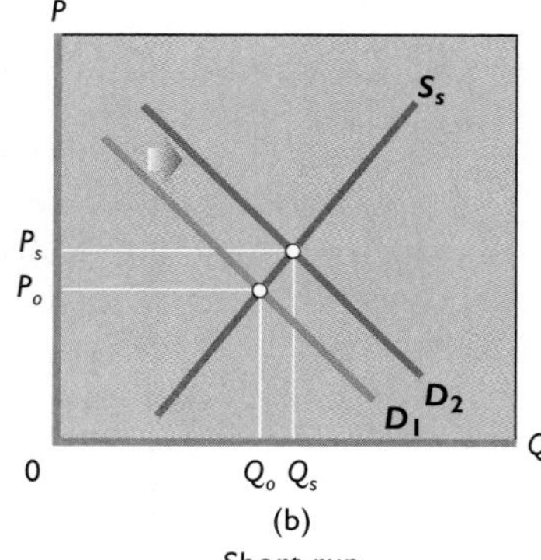

(b)
Short run

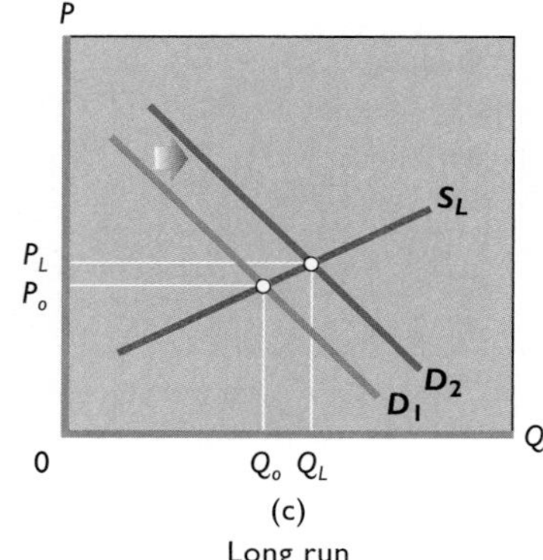

(c)
Long run

The farmer's costs of production, incidentally, will not enter into this decision to sell. Though the price of tomatoes may fall far short of production costs, the farmer will nevertheless sell out to avoid a total loss through spoilage. During the market period, our farmer's supply of tomatoes is fixed: Only one truckload is offered no matter how high or low the price.

Figure 4.4a shows the farmer's vertical supply curve during the market period. Supply is perfectly inelastic because the farmer does not have time to respond to a change in demand, say, from D_1 to D_2. The resulting price increase from P_0 to P_m simply determines which buyers get the fixed quantity supplied; it elicits no increase in output.

However, not all supply curves need be perfectly inelastic immediately after a price change. If the product is not perishable and the price rises, producers may choose to increase quantity supplied by drawing down their inventories of unsold, stored goods. This will cause the market supply curve to attain some positive slope. For our tomato farmer, the market period may be a full growing season; for producers of goods that can be inexpensively stored, there may be no market period at all.

Price Elasticity of Supply: The Short Run

short run
A period in which producers are able to change the quantities of some but not all the resources they employ.

The **short run** in microeconomics is a period of time too short to change plant capacity but long enough to use fixed plant more or less intensively. In the short run, our farmer's plant (land and farm machinery) is fixed. But he does have time in the short run to cultivate tomatoes more intensively by applying more labor and more fertilizer and pesticides to the crop. The result is a somewhat greater output in response to a presumed increase in demand; this greater output is reflected in a more elastic supply of tomatoes, as shown by S_s in Figure 4.4b. Note now that the increase in demand from D_1 to D_2 is met by an increase in quantity (from Q_0 to Q_s), so there is a smaller price adjustment (from P_0 to P_s) than would be the case in the market period. The equilibrium price is therefore lower in the short run than in the market period.

Price Elasticity of Supply: The Long Run

The **long run** in microeconomics is a time period long enough for firms to adjust their plant sizes and for new firms to enter (or existing firms to leave) the industry. In the "tomato industry," for example, our farmer has time to acquire additional land and buy more machinery and equipment. Furthermore, other farmers may, over time, be attracted to tomato farming by the increased demand and higher price. Such adjustments create a larger supply response, as represented by the more elastic supply curve S_L in Figure 4.4c. The outcome is a smaller price rise (P_0 to P_L) and a larger output increase (Q_0 to Q_L) in response to the increase in demand from D_1 to D_2.

long run
A period long enough to enable producers of a product to change all the resources they employ.

There is no total-revenue test for elasticity of supply. Supply shows a positive or direct relationship between price and amount supplied; the supply curve is upsloping. Regardless of the degree of elasticity or inelasticity, price and total revenue always move together.

Antiques and Reproductions

The *Antiques Road Show* is a popular PBS television program in which people bring antiques to a central location for appraisal by experts. Some people are pleased to learn that their old piece of furniture or funky folk art is worth a large amount, say, $30,000 or more.

The high price of a particular antique is due to strong demand and limited, highly inelastic supply. Because a genuine antique can no longer be reproduced, its quantity supplied either does not rise or rises only slightly as its price goes up. The higher price might prompt the discovery of a few more of the remaining originals and thus add to the quantity available for sale, but this quantity response is usually quite small. So the supply of antiques and other collectibles tends to be inelastic. For one-of-a-kind antiques, the supply is perfectly inelastic.

Factors such as increased population, higher income, and greater enthusiasm for collecting antiques have increased the demand for antiques over time. Because the supply of antiques is limited and inelastic, those increases in demand have greatly boosted the prices of antiques.

Contrast the inelastic supply of original antiques with the elastic supply of modern "made-to-look-old" reproductions. Such faux antiques are quite popular and widely available at furniture stores and knickknack shops. When the demand for reproductions increases, the firms making them simply boost production. Because the supply of reproductions is highly elastic, increased demand raises their prices only slightly.

Question:
How does the reluctance to sell antiques add to their inelastic supply?

Volatile Gold Prices

The price of gold is quite volatile, sometimes rocketing upward one period and plummeting downward the next. The main sources of these fluctuations are shifts in demand and highly inelastic supply. Gold production is a costly and time-consuming process of exploration, mining, and refining. Moreover, the physical availability of gold is highly limited. For both reasons, increases in gold prices do not elicit substantial increases in quantity supplied. Conversely, gold mining is costly to shut down, and existing gold bars are expensive to store. Price decreases therefore do not produce large drops in the quantity of gold supplied. In short, the supply of gold is inelastic.

The demand for gold is partly derived from the demand for its uses, such as for jewelry, dental fillings, and coins. But people also demand gold as a speculative financial investment. They increase their demand for gold when they fear general inflation or domestic or international turmoil that might undermine the value of currency and more traditional investments. They reduce their demand when events settle down. Because of the inelastic supply of gold, even relatively small changes in demand produce relatively large changes in price.

Question:
What is the current price of gold? (See www.goldprices.com.) What were the highest and the lowest prices over the last 12 months?

Income Elasticity of Demand

income elasticity of demand A measure of the responsiveness of consumer purchases to changes in consumer income.

Income elasticity of demand measures the degree to which consumers respond to a change in their incomes by buying more or less of a particular good. The coefficient of income elasticity of demand E_i is determined with the formula

$$E_i = \frac{\text{percentage change in quantity demanded}}{\text{percentage change in income}}$$

Normal Goods

For most goods, the income-elasticity coefficient E_i is positive, meaning that more of them are demanded as income rises. Such goods are called *normal* or *superior goods*, which we first described in Chapter 3. But the value of E_i varies greatly among normal goods. For example, income elasticity of demand for automobiles is about +3, while income elasticity for most farm products is only about +.20.

Inferior Goods

A negative income-elasticity coefficient designates an inferior good. Used mattresses, long-distance bus tickets, used clothing, and some frozen meals are likely candidates. Consumers decrease their purchases of inferior goods as their incomes rise.

Applying the Analysis

Income Elasticity and Insights about the Economy

Coefficients of income elasticity of demand provide insights into the economy. For example, income elasticity helps explain the expansion and contraction of industries in the United States. On average, total income in the economy has grown 2 to 3 percent annually. As income has expanded, industries producing products for which demand is quite income-elastic have expanded their outputs. Thus automobiles ($E_i = +3$), housing ($E_i = +1.5$), books ($E_i = +1.4$), and restaurant meals ($E_i = +1.4$) have all experienced strong growth of output. Meanwhile, industries producing products for which income elasticity is low or negative have tended to grow less rapidly or to decline. For example, agriculture ($E_i = +.20$) has grown far more slowly than has the economy's total output. We do not eat twice as much when our incomes double.

As another example, when recessions occur and people's incomes decline, grocery stores do relatively better than stores selling electronic equipment. People do not substantially cut back on their purchases of food when their incomes fall; income elasticity of demand for food is relatively low. But they do substantially cut back on their purchases of electronic equipment; income elasticity on such equipment is relatively high.

Question:
Why did discount clothing stores (such as Kohls) suffer less than high-end clothing stores (such as Nordstrom) when income declined during the 2001 U.S. recession?

Summary

1. Price elasticity of demand measures consumer response to price changes. If consumers are relatively sensitive to price changes, demand is elastic. If they are relatively unresponsive to price changes, demand is inelastic.
2. The price-elasticity coefficient E_d measures the degree of elasticity or inelasticity of demand. The coefficient is found by the formula

$$E_d = \frac{\text{percentage change in quantity demanded of X}}{\text{percentage change in price of X}}$$

   Economists use the averages of prices and quantities under consideration as reference points in determining percentage changes in price and quantity. If E_d is greater than 1, demand is elastic. If E_d is less than 1, demand is inelastic. Unit elasticity is the special case in which E_d equals 1.
3. Perfectly inelastic demand is graphed as a line parallel to the vertical axis; perfectly elastic demand is shown by a line above and parallel to the horizontal axis.
4. Total revenue (TR) is the total number of dollars received by a firm from the sale of a product in a particular period. It is found by multiplying price times quantity. Graphically, TR is shown as the $P \times Q$ rectangle under a point on a demand curve.
5. If total revenue changes in the opposite direction from prices, demand is elastic. If price and total revenue change in the same direction, demand is inelastic. Where demand is of unit elasticity, a change in price leaves total revenue unchanged.
6. Elasticity varies at different price ranges on a demand curve, tending to be elastic in the upper left segment and inelastic in the lower right segment. Elasticity cannot be judged by the steepness or flatness of a demand curve.
7. The number of available substitutes, the size of an item's price relative to one's budget, whether the product is a luxury or a necessity, and the length of time to adjust are all determinants of elasticity of demand.

produce other goods. This is clearly better than producing the bottle of water for $5 and having only $95 of resources available for alternative uses.

allocative efficiency The production of the "right" mix of goods and services (minimum-cost production assumed).

Competitive markets also produce **allocative efficiency:** the *particular mix* of goods and services most highly valued by society (minimum-cost production assumed). For example, society wants high-quality mineral water to be used for bottled water, not for gigantic blocks of refrigeration ice. It wants MP3 players (such as iPods), not phonographs and 45-rpm records. Moreover, society does not want to devote all its resources to bottled water and MP3 players. It wants to assign some resources to automobiles and personal computers. Competitive markets make those proper assignments.

The equilibrium price and quantity in competitive markets usually produce an assignment of resources that is "right" from an economic perspective. Demand reflects the marginal benefit (MB) of the good, and supply reflects its marginal cost (MC). The market ensures that firms produce all units of goods for which MB exceeds MC and no units for which MC exceeds MB. At the intersection of the demand and supply curves, MB equals MC and allocative efficiency results. There is neither underproduction nor overproduction of the product.

Public Goods

public goods Goods that everyone can simultaneously consume and from which no one can be excluded, even if they do not pay.

Certain other goods and services called **public goods** have the opposite characteristics of private goods. Public goods are distinguished by nonrivalry and nonexcludability.

- *Nonrivalry* (in consumption) means that one person's consumption of a good does not preclude consumption of the good by others. Everyone can simultaneously obtain the benefit from a public good such as a global positioning system, national defense, street lighting, and environmental protection.
- *Nonexcludability* means there is no effective way of excluding individuals from the benefit of the good once it comes into existence.

free-rider problem The inability of a firm to provide a good profitably because everyone, including nonpayers, can obtain the benefit.

These two characteristics create a **free-rider problem.** Once a producer has provided a public good, everyone including nonpayers can obtain the benefit. Most people do not voluntarily pay for something they can obtain for free!

With only free riders, the demand for a public good does not get expressed in the market. With no market demand, there is no potential for firms to "tap the demand" for revenues and profits. The free-rider problem makes it impossible for firms to gather together resources and profitably provide the good. If society wants a public good, society will have to direct government to provide it. We will soon see that government can finance the provision of such goods through taxation.

A significant example of a public good is homeland defense. The vast majority of Americans think this public good is economically justified because they perceive the benefits as exceeding the costs. Once homeland defense efforts are undertaken, however, the benefits accrue to all Americans (nonrivalry). And there is no practical way to exclude any American from receiving those benefits (nonexcludability).

No private firm will undertake overall homeland defense because the free-rider problem means that benefits cannot be profitably sold. So here we have a service that yields substantial net benefits but to which the market system will not allocate sufficient resources. Like national defense in general, homeland defense is a public good. Society signals its desire for such goods by voting for particular political candidates who support their provision. Because of the free-rider problem, government provides these goods and finances them through compulsory charges in the form of taxes.

© David Samuel Robbins/CORBIS

© S. Solum/PhotoLink/Getty Images/DIL

Photo Op Private versus Public Goods

Apples, distinguished by rivalry (in consumption) and excludability, are examples of private goods. In contrast, streetlights, distinguished by nonrivalry (in consumption) and nonexcludability, are examples of public goods.

Illustrating the Idea

Art for Art's Sake

Suppose an enterprising sculptor creates a piece of art costing $600 and, with permission, places it in the town square. Also suppose that Jack gets $300 of enjoyment from the art and Diane gets $400. Sensing this enjoyment and hoping to make a profit, the sculptor approaches Jack for a donation equal to his satisfaction. Jack falsely says that, unfortunately, he does not particularly like the piece. The sculptor then tries Diane, hoping to get $400 or so. Same deal: Diane professes not to like the piece either. Jack and Diane have become free riders. Although feeling a bit guilty, both reason that it makes no sense to pay for something when anyone can receive the benefits without paying for them. The artist is a quick learner; he vows never to try anything like that again.

Question:
What is the rationale for government funding for art placed in town squares and other public spaces?

Optimal Quantity of a Public Good

If consumers need not reveal their true demand for a public good in the marketplace, how can society determine the optimal amount of that good? The answer is that the government has to try to estimate the demand for a public good through surveys or public votes. It can then compare the marginal benefit of an added unit of the good against the government's marginal cost of providing it. Adhering to the MB = MC rule, it can provide the "right" amount of the public good.

Measuring Demand

Suppose that Adams and Benson are the only two people in the society and that their willingness to pay for a public good, this time the war on terrorism, is as shown in columns 1 and 2 and columns 1 and 3 in Table 5.1. Economists might have discovered these schedules through a survey asking hypothetical questions about how much each citizen was willing to pay for various types and amounts of public goods rather than go without them.

Notice that the schedules in the first four columns of Table 5.1 are price-quantity schedules, meaning they are demand schedules. Rather than depicting demand in the usual way—the quantity of a product someone is willing to buy at each possible price—these schedules show the price someone is willing to pay for the extra unit of each possible quantity. That is, Adams is willing to pay $4 for the first unit of the public good, $3 for the second, $2 for the third, and so on.

Suppose the government produces 1 unit of this public good. Because of nonrivalry, Adams' consumption of the good does not preclude Benson from also consuming it, and vice versa. So both people consume the good, and neither volunteers to pay for it. But from Table 5.1 we can find the amount these two people would be willing to pay, together, rather than do without this 1 unit of the good. Columns 1 and 2 show that Adams would be willing to pay $4 for the first unit of the public good, whereas columns 1 and 3 reveal that Benson would be willing to pay $5 for it. Adams and Benson therefore are jointly willing to pay $9 (=$4 + $5) for this first unit.

For the second unit of the public good, the collective price they are willing to pay is $7 (=$3 from Adams + $4 from Benson); for the third unit they will pay $5 (=$2 + $3); and so on. By finding the collective willingness to pay for each additional unit (column 4), we can construct a collective demand schedule (a willingness-to-pay schedule) for the public good. Here we are *not* adding the quantities demanded at each possible price, as with the market demand for a private good. Instead, we are adding the prices

TABLE 5.1
Optimal Quantity of a Public Good, Two Individuals

(1) Quantity of Public Good	(2) Adams' Willingness to Pay (Price)		(3) Benson's Willingness to Pay (Price)		(4) Collective Willingness to Pay (Price)	(5) Marginal Cost
1	$4	+	$5	=	$9	$3
2	3	+	4	=	7	4
3	***2***	+	***3***	=	***5***	***5***
4	1	+	2	=	3	6
5	0	+	1	=	1	7

that people are willing to pay for the last unit of the public good at each possible quantity demanded.

What does it mean in columns 1 and 4 of Table 5.1 that, for example, Adams and Benson are collectively willing to pay $7 for the second unit of the public good? It means that they jointly expect to receive $7 of extra benefit or utility from that unit. Column 4, in effect, reveals the collective marginal benefit of each unit of the public good.

Comparing Marginal Benefit and Marginal Cost

Now let's suppose the marginal cost of providing the public good is as shown in column 5 of Table 5.1. As explained in Chapter 2, marginal cost tends to rise as more of a good is produced. In view of the marginal-cost data shown, how much of the good should government provide? The optimal amount occurs at the quantity where marginal benefit equals marginal cost. In Table 5.1 that quantity is 3 units, where the collective willingness to pay for the third unit—the $5 marginal benefit—just matches that unit's $5 marginal cost. As we saw in Chapter 2, equating marginal benefit and marginal cost efficiently allocates society's scarce resources.

Applying the Analysis

Cost-Benefit Analysis

The above example suggests a practical means, called **cost-benefit analysis,** for deciding whether to provide a particular public good and how much of it to provide. Like our example, cost-benefit analysis (or marginal-benefit–marginal-cost analysis) involves a comparison of marginal costs and marginal benefits.

cost-benefit analysis The formal comparison of marginal costs and marginal benefits of a government project to decide whether it is worth doing and to what extent resources should be devoted to it.

Suppose the Federal government is contemplating a highway construction plan. Because the economy's resources are limited, any decision to use more resources in the public sector will mean fewer resources for the private sector. There will be both a cost and a benefit. The cost is the loss of satisfaction resulting from the accompanying decline in the production of private goods; the benefit is the extra satisfaction resulting from the output of more public goods. Should the needed resources be shifted from the private to the public sector? The answer is yes if the benefit from the extra public goods exceeds the cost that results from having fewer private goods. The answer is no if the cost of the forgone private goods is greater than the benefit associated with the extra public goods.

Cost-benefit analysis, however, can indicate more than whether a public program is worth doing. It can also help the government decide on the extent to which a project should be pursued. Real economic questions cannot usually be answered simply by "yes" or "no" but, rather, involve questions such as "how much" or "how little."

Although private toll roads exist, highways clearly have public goods characteristics because the benefits are widely diffused and highway use is relatively difficult to price. Should the Federal government expand the Federal highway system? If so, what is the proper size or scope for the overall project?

Table 5.2 lists a series of increasingly ambitious and increasingly costly highway projects: widening existing two-lane highways; building new two-lane highways; building new four-lane highways; building new six-lane highways. The extent to which government should undertake highway construction depends on the costs and benefits. The costs are largely the costs of constructing and maintaining the highways; the benefits are improved flows of people and goods throughout the nation.

TABLE 5.2

Cost-Benefit Analysis for a National Highway Construction Project (in Billions)

(1) Plan	(2) Total Cost of Project	(3) Marginal Cost	(4) Total Benefit	(5) Marginal Benefit	(6) Net Benefit (4) − (2)
No new construction	$ 0		$ 0		$ 0
		$ 4		$ 5	
A: Widen existing highways	4		5		1
		6		8	
B: New 2-lane highways	10		13		3
		8		***10***	
C: New 4-lane highways	***18***		***23***		***5***
		10		3	
D: New 6-lane highways	28		26		−2

The table shows that total annual benefit (column 4) exceeds total annual cost (column 2) for plans A, B, and C, indicating that some highway construction is economically justifiable. We see this directly in column 6, where total costs (column 2) are subtracted from total annual benefits (column 4). Net benefits are positive for plans A, B, and C. Plan D is not economically justifiable because net benefits are negative.

But the question of optimal size or scope for this project remains. Comparing the additional, or marginal, cost and the additional, or marginal, benefit relating to each plan determines the answer. The guideline is well known to you from previous discussions: Increase an activity, project, or output as long as the marginal benefit (column 5) exceeds the marginal cost (column 3). Stop the activity at, or as close as possible to, the point at which the marginal benefit equals the marginal cost. Do not undertake a project for which marginal cost exceeds marginal benefit.

In this case plan C (building new four-lane highways) is the best plan. Plans A and B are too modest; the marginal benefits exceed the marginal costs. Plan D's marginal cost ($10 billion) exceeds the marginal benefit ($3 billion) and therefore cannot be justified; it overallocates resources to the project. Plan C is closest to the theoretical optimum because its marginal benefit ($10 billion) still exceeds marginal cost ($8 billion) but approaches the MB = MC (or MC = MB) ideal.

This marginal-cost–marginal-benefit rule tells government which plan provides the maximum excess of total benefits over total costs or, in other words, the plan that provides society with the maximum net benefit. You can confirm directly in column 6 that the maximum net benefit ($5 billion) is associated with plan C.

Question:

Do you think it is generally easier to measure the costs of public goods or their benefits? Explain your reasoning.

Externalities

When we say that competitive markets automatically bring about allocative efficiency, we assume that all the benefits and costs for each product are fully reflected in the market demand and supply curves. That is not always the case. In some markets certain benefits or costs may escape the buyer or seller.

An *externality* occurs when some of the costs or the benefits of a good are passed on to or "spill over to" someone other than the immediate buyer or seller. Externalities are benefits or costs that accrue to some third party that is external to the market transaction.

Negative Externalities

Production or consumption costs inflicted on a third party without compensation are called **negative externalities** or *spillover costs*. Environmental pollution is an example. When a chemical manufacturer or a meatpacking plant dumps its wastes into a lake or river, water users such as swimmers, fishers, and boaters suffer negative externalities. When a petroleum refinery pollutes the air with smoke or a paper mill creates obnoxious odors, the community experiences negative externalities for which it is not compensated.

negative externalities Spillover production or consumption costs imposed on third parties without compensation to them.

Figure 5.1a illustrates how negative externalities affect the allocation of resources. When producers shift some of their costs onto the community as spillover costs, producers' marginal costs are lower than otherwise. So their supply curves do not include or "capture" all the costs legitimately associated with the production of their goods. A supply curve such as *S* in Figure 5.1a therefore understates the total cost of production for a polluting firm. Its supply curve lies to the right of (or below) the full-cost supply curve S_t, which would include the negative externality. Through polluting and thus transferring cost to society, the firm enjoys lower production costs and has the supply curve *S*.

The resource allocation outcome is shown in Figure 5.1a, where equilibrium output Q_e is larger than the optimal output Q_o. This is a market failure because resources are *overallocated* to the production of this commodity; too many units of it are produced.

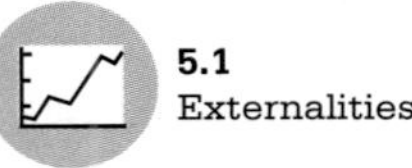
5.1 Externalities

Positive Externalities

Sometimes spillovers appear as external benefits. The production or consumption of certain goods and services may confer spillover or external benefits on third parties or

FIGURE 5.1
Negative externalities and positive externalities. (a) With negative externalities (spillover costs) borne by society, the producers' supply curve *S* is to the right of (below) the full-cost curve S_t. Consequently, the equilibrium output Q_e is greater than the optimal output Q_o. (b) When positive externalities (spillover benefits) accrue to society, the market demand curve *D* is to the left of (below) the full-benefit demand curve D_t. As a result, the equilibrium output Q_e is less than the optimal output Q_o.

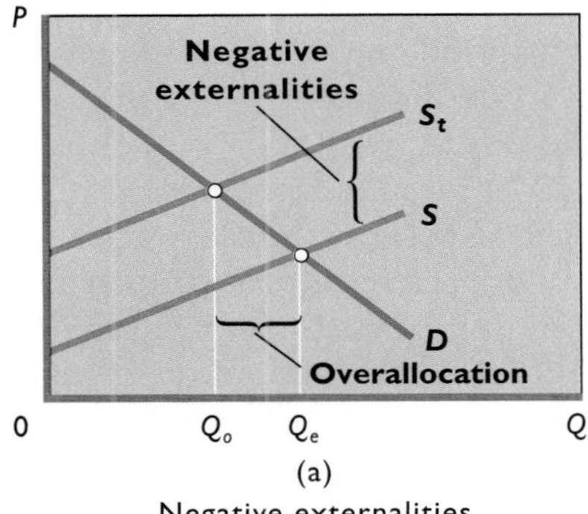

(a) Negative externalities

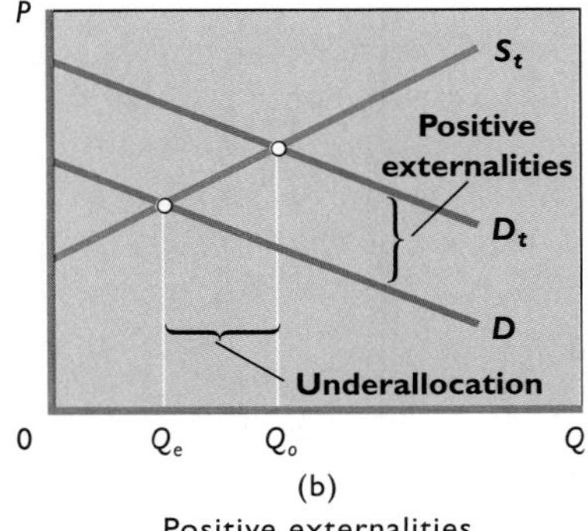

(b) Positive externalities

on the community at large without compensating payment. Immunization against measles and polio results in direct benefits to the immediate consumer of those vaccines. But it also results in widespread substantial positive externalities to the entire community.

positive externalities Spillover production or consumption benefits conferred on third parties without compensation from them.

Education is another example of **positive externalities.** Education benefits individual consumers: Better-educated people generally achieve higher incomes than less well educated people. But education also benefits society through a more versatile and more productive labor force, on the one hand, and smaller outlays for crime prevention, law enforcement, and welfare programs, on the other.

Figure 5.1b shows the impact of positive externalities on resource allocation. When positive externalities occur, the market demand curve D lies to the left of (or below) the full-benefits demand curve. That is, D does not include the positive externalities of the product, whereas D_t does. Consider inoculations against a communicable disease. Alvarez and Anderson benefit when they get vaccinated, but so do their associates Bronson and Berkshire, who are less likely to contract the disease from them. The market demand curve reflects only the direct, private benefits to Alvarez and Anderson. It does not reflect the positive externalities—the spillover benefits—to Bronson and Berkshire, which are included in D_t.

The outcome, as shown in Figure 5.1b, is that the equilibrium output Q_e is less than the optimal output Q_o. The market fails to produce enough vaccinations, and resources are *underallocated* to this product.

5.1 Externalities

Economists have explored several approaches to the problems of negative and positive externalities. Let's first look at situations where government intervention is not needed and then at some possible government solutions.

Coase theorem The idea that externality problems can be resolved through private negotiations by the affected parties when property rights are clearly established.

Individual Bargaining: Coase Theorem

In the **Coase theorem,** conceived decades ago by economist Ronald Coase at the University of Chicago, government is not needed to remedy negative or positive externalities where (1) property ownership is clearly defined, (2) the number of people involved is small, and (3) bargaining costs are negligible. Under these circumstances the government should confine its role to encouraging bargaining between affected individuals or groups. Property rights place a price tag on an externality, creating opportunity costs for all parties. Because the economic self-interests of the parties are at stake, bargaining will enable them to find a mutually acceptable solution to the externality problem.

A Forest Tale

Suppose the owner of a large parcel of forestland is considering a plan to clear-cut (totally level) thousands of acres of mature fir trees. The complication is that the forest surrounds a lake with a popular resort on its shore. The resort is on land owned by the resort. The unspoiled beauty of the general area attracts vacationers from all over the nation to the resort, and the resort owner is against the clear-cutting. Should state or local government intervene to allow or prevent the tree cutting?

According to the Coase theorem, the forest owner and the resort owner can resolve this situation without government intervention. As long as one of the parties to the dispute has property rights to what is at issue, an incentive will exist for both parties to negotiate a solution acceptable to each. In our example, the owner of the timberland holds the property rights to the land to be logged and thus has the right to clear-cut it. The owner of the resort therefore has an economic incentive to negotiate with the forest owner to reduce the logging impact. Excessive logging of the forest surrounding the resort will reduce tourism and revenues to the resort owner.

But less clear is the reason why the forest owner has an incentive to negotiate with the resort owner. The rationale draws directly on the idea of opportunity cost. One cost to the forest owner incurred in logging the forest is the forgone payment that he or she could obtain from the resort owner for agreeing not to clear-cut the fir trees. The resort owner might be willing to make a lump-sum or annual payment to the owner of the forest to avoid or minimize the negative externality. Or perhaps the resort owner might be willing to buy the forested land to prevent the logging. As viewed by the forest owner, a payment for not clear-cutting or a purchase price above the prior market value of the land is an opportunity cost of logging the land.

Both parties would probably regard a negotiated agreement as better than clear-cutting the firs.

Question:
Suppose the resort, not the timber company, owned the surrounding forest. Why would there still be an incentive for both to negotiate about the type and degree of logging in the forest?

Unfortunately, many externalities involve huge numbers of affected parties, high bargaining costs, and community property such as air and water. In such situations private bargaining cannot be used as a remedy. As an example, the global-warming problem affects millions of people in many nations. The vast number of affected parties could not individually negotiate an agreement to remedy this problem. Instead, they must rely on their governments to represent the millions of affected parties and find an acceptable solution.

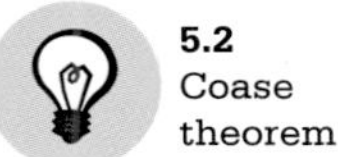
5.2 Coase theorem

Liability Rules and Lawsuits

Although private negotiation may not be a realistic solution to many externality problems, clearly established property rights may help in another way. The government has erected a framework of laws that define private property and protect it from damage done by other parties. Those laws, and the damage recovery system to which they give rise, permit parties suffering negative externalities to sue for compensation.

Suppose the Ajax Degreaser Company regularly dumps leaky barrels containing solvents into a nearby canyon owned by Bar Q Ranch. Bar Q eventually discovers this dump site and, after tracing the drums to Ajax, immediately contacts its lawyer. Soon after, Bar Q sues Ajax. If Ajax loses the case, it will have to pay for the cleanup and may also have to pay Bar Q additional damages for ruining its property.

Clearly defined property rights and government liability laws thus help remedy some externality problems. They do so directly by forcing the perpetrator of the harmful externality to pay damages to those injured. They do so indirectly by discouraging firms and individuals from generating negative externalities for fear of being sued. It is not surprising, then, that many spillovers do not involve private property but rather property held in common by society. It is the public bodies of water, the public lands, and the public air, where ownership is less clear, that often bear the brunt of spillovers.

Caveat: Like private negotiations, private lawsuits to resolve externalities have their own limitations. Large legal fees and major time delays in the court system are commonplace. Also, the uncertainty associated with the court outcome reduces the

demand curve for inoculations from too low D to the appropriate D_t. The number of inoculations would rise from Q_e to the economically optimal Q_o, eliminating the underallocation of resources shown in Figure 5.3a.

- ***Subsidies to producers*** A subsidy to producers is a specific tax in reverse. Taxes impose an extra cost on producers, while subsidies reduce producers' costs. As shown in Figure 5.3c, a subsidy of U per inoculation to physicians and medical clinics would reduce their marginal costs and shift their supply curve rightward from S_t to S_t'. The output of inoculations would increase from Q_e to the optimal level Q_o, correcting the underallocation of resources shown in Figure 5.3a.
- ***Government provision*** Finally, where positive externalities are extremely large, the government may decide to provide the product for free or for a minimal charge. Government provides many goods that could be produced and delivered in such a way that exclusion would be possible. Such goods, called **quasi-public goods,** include education, streets and highways, police and fire protection, libraries and museums, preventive medicine, and sewage disposal. They could all be priced and provided by private firms through the market system because the free-rider problem would be minimal. But, because spillover benefits extend well beyond the individual buyer, the market system may underproduce them. Therefore, government often provides quasi-public goods.

quasi-public goods Goods for which exclusion could occur but which government provides because of perceived widespread and diffuse benefits.

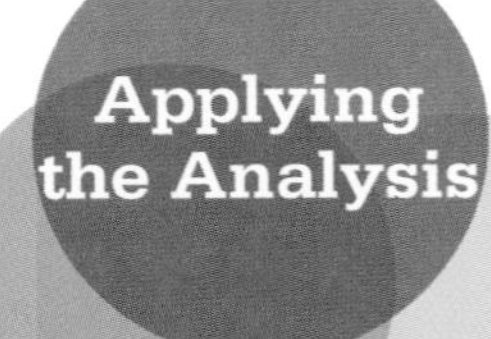

Lojack: A Case of Positive Externalities

Economists Ayres and Levitt point out that some forms of private crime prevention simply redistribute crime rather than reduce it. For example, car alarm systems that have red blinking warning lights may simply divert professional auto thieves to vehicles that do not have such lights and alarms. The owner of a car with such an alarm system benefits through reduced likelihood of theft but imposes a cost on other car owners who do not have such alarms. Their cars are more likely to be targeted for theft by thieves because other cars have visible security systems.

In contrast, some private crime prevention measures actually reduce crime, rather than simply redistribute it. One such measure is installation of a Lojack (or some similar) car retrieval system. Lojack is a tiny radio transmitter that is hidden in one of many possible places within the car. When an owner reports a stolen car, the police can remotely activate the transmitter. Police then can determine the car's precise location and track its subsequent movements.

The owner of the car benefits because the 95 percent retrieval rate on cars with the Lojack system is higher than the 60 percent retrieval rate for cars without the system. But, according to a study by Ayres and Levitt, the benefit to the car owner is only 10 percent of the total benefit. Ninety percent of the total benefit is external; it is a spillover benefit to other car owners in the community.

There are two sources of this positive externality. First, the presence of the Lojack device sometimes enables police to intercept the car while the thief is still driving it. For example, in California the arrest rate for cars with Lojack was three times greater than that for cars without it. The arrest puts the car thief out of commission for a time and thus reduces subsequent car thefts in the community.

Second, and far more important, the device enables police to trace cars to "chop shops," where crooks disassemble cars for resale of the parts. When police raid the chop shop, they put the entire theft ring out of business. In Los Angeles alone, Lojack has eliminated 45 chop shops in just a few years. The purging of the chop shop and theft ring reduces auto theft in the community. So auto owners who do not have Lojack devices in their cars benefit from car owners who do. Ayres and Levitt estimate the *marginal social benefit* of Lojack—the marginal benefit to the Lojack car owner *plus* the spillover benefit to other car owners—is 15 times greater than the marginal cost of the device.

We saw in Figure 5.3a that the existence of positive externalities causes an insufficient quantity of a product and thus an underallocation of scarce resources to its production. The two general ways to correct the outcome are to subsidize the consumer, as shown in Figure 5.3b, or to subsidize the producer, as shown in Figure 5.3c. Currently, there is only one form of government intervention in place: state-mandated insurance discounts for people who install auto retrieval systems such as Lojack. In effect, those discounts on insurance premiums subsidize the consumer by lowering the "price" of the system to consumers. The lower price raises the number of systems installed. But, on the basis of their research, Ayres and Levitt contend that the current levels of insurance discounts are far too small to correct the underallocation that results from the positive externalities created by Lojack.

Question:
Other than mandating lower insurance premiums for Lojack users, what might government do to increase the use of Lojack devices in automobiles?

Source: Based on Ian Ayres and Steven D. Levitt, "Measuring Positive Externalities from Unobservable Victim Precaution: An Empirical Analysis of Lojack," *Quarterly Journal of Economics,* February 1998, pp. 43–77. The authors point out that Lojack did not fund their work; nor do they have any financial stake in Lojack.

A Market-Based Approach

One novel approach to negative externalities involves only limited government action. The idea is to create a market for externality rights.

Operation of the Market In this market approach, an appropriate pollution-control agency determines the amount of pollutants that firms can discharge into the water or air of a specific region annually while maintaining the water or air quality at some acceptable level. Suppose the agency ascertains that 500 tons of pollutants can be discharged into Metropolitan Lake and "recycled" by nature each year. Then 500 pollution rights, each entitling the owner to dump 1 ton of pollutants into the lake in 1 year, are made available for sale to producers each year. The supply of these pollution rights is fixed and therefore perfectly inelastic, as shown in Figure 5.4.

The demand for pollution rights, represented by D_{2006} in the figure, takes the same downsloping form as the demand for any other input. At higher prices there is less pollution, as polluters either stop polluting or pollute less by acquiring pollution-abatement equipment. An equilibrium market price for pollution rights, here \$100, will be determined at which the environment-preserving quantity of pollution rights is rationed to polluters. Figure 5.4 shows that if the use of the lake as a dump site for

FIGURE 5.4

A market for pollution rights. The supply of pollution rights S is set by the government, which determines that a specific body of water can safely recycle 500 tons of waste. In 2006, the demand for pollution rights is D_{2006} and the 1-ton price is \$100. The quantity of pollution is 500 tons, not the 750 tons it would have been without the pollution rights. Over time, the demand for pollution rights increases to D_{2016} and the 1-ton price rises to \$200. But the amount of pollution stays at 500 tons, rather than rising to 1000 tons.

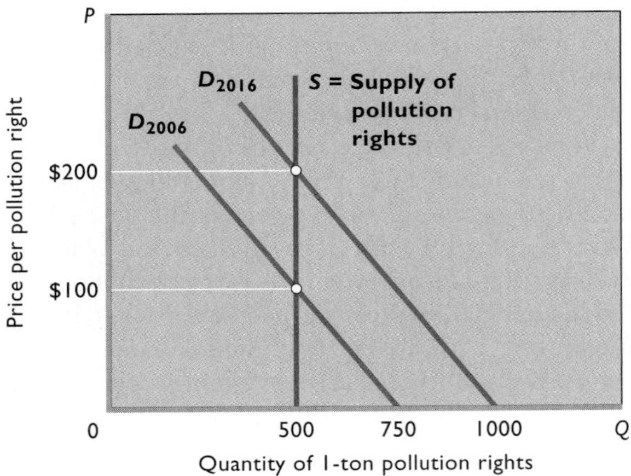

pollutants were instead free, 750 tons of pollutants would be discharged into the lake; it would be "overconsumed," or polluted, in the amount of 250 tons.

Over time, as human and business populations expand, demand will increase, as from D_{2006} to D_{2016}. Without a market for pollution rights, pollution in 2016 would be 1000 tons, 500 tons beyond what can be assimilated by nature. With the market for pollution rights, the price would rise from \$100 to \$200, and the amount of pollutants would remain at 500 tons—the amount that the lake can recycle.

Advantages This scheme has several advantages over direct controls. Most important, it reduces society's costs by allowing pollution rights to be bought and sold. Suppose it costs Acme Pulp Mill \$20 a year to reduce a specific noxious discharge by 1 ton while it costs Zemo Chemicals \$8000 a year to accomplish the same 1-ton reduction. Also assume that Zemo wants to expand production but doing so will increase its pollution discharge by 1 ton.

Without a market for pollution rights, Zemo would have to use \$8000 of society's scarce resources to keep the 1-ton pollution discharge from occurring. But with a market for pollution rights, Zemo has a better option: It buys 1 ton of pollution rights for the \$100 price shown in Figure 5.4. Acme is willing to sell Zemo 1 ton of pollution rights for \$100 because that amount is more than Acme's \$20 cost of reducing its pollution by 1 ton. Zemo increases its discharge by 1 ton; Acme reduces its discharge by 1 ton. Zemo benefits by paying \$100 for something that would otherwise cost \$8000. Acme benefits by selling something for \$100 that costs only \$20 to "produce." Society saves \$7980. Rather than using \$8000 of its scarce resources to hold the discharge at the specified level, society uses only \$20 of those resources.

Market-based plans have other advantages. Potential polluters have a monetary incentive not to pollute, because they must pay for the right to discharge effluent. Conservation groups can fight pollution by buying up and withholding pollution rights, thereby reducing pollution below governmentally determined standards. As the demand for pollution rights increases over time, the growing revenue from the sale of a fixed quantity of pollution rights could be devoted to environmental improvement. At the same time, the rising price of pollution rights should stimulate the search for improved pollution-control techniques.

Tradable Emission Allowances

Administrative and political problems have kept the government from replacing direct controls—such as uniform emission limits—with a full-scale market for pollution rights. But in the 1980s the Environmental Protection Agency (EPA) established a system of pollution rights, or tradable emission allowances, as part of a plan to reduce the sulfur dioxide emitted by coal-burning public utilities. Those emissions are the major source of acid rain.

In the 1990s the Federal government greatly expanded the market for such rights through legislation. The Clean Air Act of 1990 established a limited market for pollution rights, similar to that shown in Figure 5.4, by allowing utilities to trade emission credits provided by government. Utilities can obtain credits by reducing sulfur-dioxide emissions by more than the specified amount. They can then sell their credits to other utilities that find it less costly to buy the credits than to install additional pollution-control equipment.

This market for sulfur-dioxide-emission credits complements other air pollution policies that also permit the internal exchange of pollution rights. The EPA now allows firms to transfer air pollution between individual sources within their plants. That is, as long as it meets the overall pollution standard assigned to it, a firm may increase one source of pollution by offsetting it with reduced pollution from another part of its operations.

The EPA also permits external trading of pollution rights. It has set targets for reducing air pollution in regions where the minimum standards are not being met. Previously, new pollution sources could not enter these regions unless existing polluters went out of business. But under the system of external trading rights, the EPA allows firms that reduce their pollution below set standards to sell their pollution rights to other firms. A new firm that wants to locate in the Los Angeles area, for example, might be able to buy rights to emit 20 tons of nitrous oxide annually from an existing firm that has reduced its emissions below its allowable limit. The price of emission rights depends on their supply and demand.

Finally, in 2003 the EPA extended the market-based approach to the Clean Water Act. Industry, agriculture, and municipalities within a defined watershed can meet their EPA-approved maximum daily discharge limits through trading "water quality credits." Entities that find it extremely expensive to reduce water pollution can buy credits from entities that can reduce pollution relatively inexpensively. Therefore, society incurs less total cost in improving water quality.

Question:
Why would rising prices of pollution credits increase the incentive for firms to use cleaner production methods?

Financing the Public Sector: Taxation

How are resources reallocated from the production of private goods to the production of public goods (and quasi-public goods)? How are government programs to deal with externalities funded? If the resources of the economy are fully employed, government must free up resources from the production of private goods and make them available for producing public and quasi-public goods. It does so by reducing the demand for private goods. And it does that by levying taxes on households and businesses, taking some of their income out of the circular flow. With lower incomes and therefore reduced purchasing power, households and businesses must curtail their spending.

As a result, the private demand for goods and services declines, as does the private demand for resources. So by diverting purchasing power from private spenders to government, taxes remove resources from private use.

Government then spends the tax proceeds to provide public and quasi-public goods and services. Taxation releases resources from the production of private consumer goods (food, clothing, television sets) and private investment goods (printing presses, boxcars, warehouses). Government shifts those resources to the production of public and quasi-public goods (post offices, submarines, parks), changing the composition of the economy's total output.

Apportioning the Tax Burden

Once government has decided on the total tax revenue it needs to finance its activities, including the provision of public and quasi-public goods, it must determine how to apportion the tax burden among the citizens. (By "tax burden" we mean the total cost of taxes imposed on society.) This apportionment question affects each of us. The overall level of taxes is important, but the average citizen is much more concerned with his or her share of taxes.

Benefits Received versus Ability to Pay

There are two basic philosophies on how the economy's tax burden should be assigned.

benefits-received principle
The idea that people who receive the benefits from government-provided goods and services should pay the taxes required to finance them.

Benefits-Received The **benefits-received principle** of taxation states that households and businesses should purchase the goods and services of government in the same way they buy other commodities. Those who benefit most from government-supplied goods or services should pay the taxes necessary to finance them. A few public goods are now financed on this basis. For example, money collected as gasoline taxes is typically used to finance highway construction and repairs. Thus people who benefit from good roads pay the cost of those roads. Difficulties immediately arise, however, when we consider widespread application of the benefits-received principle:

- How will the government determine the benefits that individual households and businesses receive from national defense, education, the court system, and police and fire protection? Recall that public goods are characterized by nonrivalry and nonexcludability. So benefits from public goods are especially widespread and diffuse. Even in the seemingly straightforward case of highway financing it is difficult to measure benefits. Good roads benefit the owners of cars in different degrees. But others also benefit. For example, businesses benefit because good roads bring them customers.

- Government cannot logically apply the benefits-received principle to some government programs such as "safety net" programs. It would be absurd to ask poor families to pay the taxes needed to finance their welfare payments. It would be ridiculous to think of taxing only unemployed workers to finance the unemployment compensation payments they receive.

Ability to Pay The **ability-to-pay principle** of taxation states that government should apportion the tax burden according to taxpayers' income. In the United States this means that individuals and businesses with larger incomes should pay more taxes in both absolute and relative terms than those with smaller incomes.

ability-to-pay principle The idea that people who have greater income should pay a greater proportion of it as taxes than those who have less income.

The rationale of ability-to-pay taxation is the proposition that each additional dollar of income received by a household yields a smaller amount of satisfaction or marginal utility when it is spent. Because consumers act rationally, the first dollars of income received in any time period will be spent on high-urgency goods that yield the greatest marginal utility. Successive dollars of income will go for less urgently needed goods and finally for trivial goods and services. This means that a dollar taken through taxes from a poor person who has few dollars represents a greater utility sacrifice than a dollar taken through taxes from a rich person who has many dollars. To balance the sacrifices that taxes impose on income receivers, taxes should be apportioned according to the amount of income a taxpayer receives.

This argument is appealing, but application problems arise here too. Although we might agree that the household earning $100,000 per year has a greater ability to pay taxes than a household receiving $10,000, we don't know exactly how much more ability to pay the first family has. Should the wealthier family pay the same percentage of its larger income, and hence a larger absolute amount, as taxes? Or should it be made to pay a larger fraction of its income as taxes? And how much larger should that fraction be?

There is no scientific way of making utility comparisons among individuals and thus of measuring someone's relative ability to pay taxes. That is the main problem. In practice, the solution hinges on guesswork, expediency, the tax views of the political party in power, and how urgently the government needs revenue.

marginal tax rate The tax rate paid on each additional dollar of income.

average tax rate The total tax paid divided by total taxable income, as a percentage.

Progressive, Proportional, and Regressive Taxes

Any discussion of taxation leads ultimately to the question of tax rates. The **marginal tax rate** is the rate paid on each additional dollar of income (or purchases). The **average tax rate** is the total tax paid as a percentage of income.

Taxes are classified as progressive, regressive, or proportional taxes, depending on the relationship between average tax rates and taxpayer incomes. We focus on incomes because all taxes, whether on income or on a product or a building or a parcel of land, are ultimately paid out of someone's income.

- A tax is **progressive** if its average rate increases as income increases. Such a tax claims not only a larger absolute (dollar) amount but also a larger percentage of income as income increases.
- A tax is **regressive** if its average rate declines as income increases. Such a tax takes a smaller proportion of income as income increases. A regressive tax may or may not take a larger absolute amount of income as income increases. (You may want to derive an example to substantiate this conclusion.)
- A tax is **proportional** if its average rate remains the same regardless of the size of income.

progressive tax A tax whose average tax rate increases as the taxpayer's income increases.

regressive tax A tax whose average tax rate decreases as the taxpayer's income increases.

proportional tax A tax whose average tax rate remains constant as the taxpayer's income increases.

We can illustrate these ideas with the personal income tax. Suppose tax rates are such that a household pays 10 percent of its income in taxes regardless of the size of its income. This is a proportional income tax. Now suppose the rate structure is such that a household with an annual taxable income of less than $10,000 pays 5 percent in income taxes; a household with an income of $10,000 to $20,000 pays 10 percent; one with a $20,000 to $30,000 income pays 15 percent; and so forth. This is a progressive income tax. Finally, suppose the rate declines as taxable income rises: You pay 15 percent if you earn less than $10,000; 10 percent if you earn $10,000 to $20,000; 5 percent if you earn $20,000 to $30,000; and so forth. This is a regressive income tax.

In general, progressive taxes are those that fall relatively more heavily on people with high incomes; regressive taxes are those that fall relatively more heavily on the poor.

Tax Progressivity in the United States

The progressivity or regressivity of taxes varies by type of tax in the United States. As shown in Table 5.3, the Federal *personal income tax* is progressive. Marginal tax rates (column 2)—those assessed on additional income—ranged from 10 to 35 percent in 2005. Rules that allow individuals to deduct from income interest on home mortgages and property taxes and that exempt interest on state and local bonds from taxation tend to make the tax less progressive than these marginal rates suggest. Nevertheless, average tax rates (column 4) rise with income.

At first thought, a *general sales tax* with, for example, a 5 percent rate would seem to be proportional. But in fact it is regressive with respect to income (rather than purchases). A larger portion of a low-income person's income is exposed to the tax than is the case for a high-income person; the rich pay no tax on the part of income that is saved, whereas the poor are unable to save. Example: "Low-income" Smith has an income of $15,000 and spends it all. "High-income" Jones has an income of $300,000 but spends only $200,000 and saves the rest. Assuming a 5 percent sales tax applies to all expenditures of each individual, we find that Smith pays $750 (=5 percent of $15,000) in sales taxes and Jones pays $10,000 (=5 percent of $200,000). But Smith pays $750/$15,000, or 5 percent of income, as sales taxes, while Jones pays $10,000/$300,000, or 3.3 percent of income. The general sales tax therefore is regressive.

TABLE 5.3
Federal Personal Income Tax Rates, 2005*

(1) Total Taxable Income	(2) Marginal Tax Rate, %	(3) Total Tax on Highest Income in Bracket	(4) Average Tax Rate on Highest Income in Bracket, % (3) ÷ (1)
$1–$14,600	10.0	$ 1,460.00	10.0
$14,601–$59,400	15.0	8,180.00	13.8
$59,401–$119,950	25.0	23,317.50	19.4
$119,951–$182,800	28.0	40,915.50	22.4
$182,801–$326,450	33.0	88,320.00	27.1
Over $326,450	35.0		

* For a married couple filing a joint return.

The Federal *corporate income tax* is essentially a proportional tax with a flat 35 percent tax rate. But this assumes that corporation owners (shareholders) bear the tax. Some tax experts argue that at least part of the tax is passed through to consumers in the form of higher product prices. To the extent that this occurs, the tax is like a sales tax and is thus regressive.

Payroll taxes (Social Security and Medicare) are regressive because the Social Security tax applies to only a fixed amount of income. For example, in 2005 the Social Security tax rate was 6.2 percent, but only of the first $90,000 of a person's wage income. The Medicare tax was 1.45 percent of all wage income. Someone earning exactly $90,000 would pay $6885, or 7.65 percent (6.2 percent + 1.45 percent) of his or her income. Someone with twice that wage income, or $180,000, would pay $8190 (=$6885 on the first $90,000 + $1305 on the second $90,000), which is only 4.55 percent of his or her wage income. So the average payroll tax falls as income rises, confirming that the payroll tax is regressive.

Most economists conclude that *property taxes* on buildings are regressive for the same reasons as are sales taxes. First, property owners add the tax to the rents they charge tenants. Second, property taxes, as a percentage of income, are higher for low-income families than for high-income families because the poor must spend a larger proportion of their incomes for housing. This alleged regressivity of property taxes may be increased by differences in property-tax rates from locality to locality. In general, property-tax rates are higher in poorer areas, to make up for lower property values.

Is the overall U.S. tax structure—Federal, state, and local taxes combined—progressive, proportional, or regressive? This question is difficult to answer. Estimates of the distribution of the total tax burden depend on the extent to which the various taxes are shifted to others, and who bears the ultimate burden is subject to dispute. But the majority view of economists is as follows:

- The Federal tax system is progressive. In 2004, the 20 percent of families with the lowest income paid an average Federal tax rate (on Federal income, payroll, and excise taxes) of 5.2 percent. The 20 percent with the highest income paid a 23.8 percent average rate; the top 10 percent paid 24.9 percent; and the top 1 percent paid 26.7 percent.[1]
- The state and local tax structures are largely regressive. As a percentage of income, property taxes and sales taxes fall as income rises. Also, state income taxes are generally less progressive than the Federal income tax.
- The overall U.S. tax system is slightly progressive. Higher-income people carry a slightly larger tax burden, as a percentage of their income, than do lower-income people.

Government's Role: A Qualification

Along with providing public goods and correcting externalities, government's economic role includes setting the rules and regulations for the economy, redistributing income when desirable, and taking macroeconomic actions to stabilize the economy.

Government does not have an easy task in performing its economic functions. In a democracy, government undertakes its economic role in the context of politics. To

[1] *Effective Federal Tax Rates under Current Law, 2001–2014*, Congressional Budget Office, August 2004.

serve the public, politicians need to get elected. To stay elected, officials (presidents, senators, representatives, mayors, council members, school board members) need to satisfy their particular constituencies. At best, the political realities complicate government's role in the economy; at worst, they sometimes produce undesirable economic outcomes.

In the political context, some public goods and quasi-public goods may get produced not because their benefits exceed their costs but because their benefits accrue to firms located in states served by powerful elected officials. Inefficiency can easily creep into government activities because of the lack of a profit incentive to hold down costs. Indeed, the failure of programs to achieve their goals may simply lead to calls for more funding for the failed programs. Policies to correct negative externalities can be politically blocked by the very parties that are producing the spillovers. Overregulation can occur in some cases; underregulation, in others. Income can be redistributed to such an extent that incentives to work, save, and invest suffer. In short, the economic role of government, although critical to a well-functioning economy, is not always perfectly carried out.

Summary

1. Private goods are distinguished by rivalry (in consumption) and excludability. One person's purchase and consumption of a private good precludes others from also buying and consuming it. Producers can exclude nonpayers (free riders) from receiving the benefits. Competitive markets usually ensure that private goods are (a) available, (b) produced at minimum average cost, and (c) produced and sold in the "right" amounts.
2. Public goods are distinguished by nonrivalry (in consumption) and nonexcludability. Public goods are not profitable to private firms because nonpayers (free riders) can obtain and consume those goods. Only government is willing to provide desirable public goods.
3. The collective demand schedule for a particular public good is found by summing the prices that each individual is willing to pay for an additional unit. The optimal quantity of a public good occurs where the society's willingness to pay for the last unit—the marginal benefit of the good—equals the marginal cost of the good.
4. Cost-benefit analysis can provide guidance as to the economic desirability and optimal scope of public goods output.
5. Externalities cause the equilibrium output of certain goods to vary from their optimal output. Negative externalities (spillover costs) result in an overallocation of resources, which society can correct through private bargaining, legislation, or specific taxes. Positive externalities (spillover benefits) are accompanied by an underallocation of resources, which society can correct through private bargaining, subsidies to consumers, subsidies to producers, or government provision.
6. The Coase theorem holds that private bargaining is capable of solving potential externality problems where (a) the property rights are clearly defined, (b) the number of people involved is small, and (c) bargaining costs are negligible.
7. Clearly established property rights and liability rules enable private lawsuits that can prevent or remedy some negative externalities. Lawsuits, however, can be costly, time-consuming, and of uncertain result.
8. Direct controls and specific taxes can improve resource allocation in situations where negative externalities affect many people and community resources. Both direct controls (for example, smokestack emission standards) and specific taxes (for example, taxes on firms producing toxic chemicals) increase production costs and raise product price. As product price rises, the externality declines because less of the output is produce and purchased.
9. Markets for pollution rights, where firms can buy and sell the right to discharge a fixed amount of pollution, put a price on pollution and encourage firms to reduce or eliminate it.

Markets for such rights (or "tradable credits") currently exist under terms of U.S. antipollution laws.

10. Government reallocates resources from the private sector to the public sector through taxation, which decreases after-tax income and therefore reduces the demand for private goods. Government then uses the tax revenues to finance the provision of public goods and quasi-public goods.
11. The benefits-received principle of taxation states that those who receive the benefits of goods and services provided by government should pay the taxes required to finance them. The ability-to-pay principle states that those who have greater income should be taxed more, absolutely and relatively, than those who have less income.
12. The Federal income tax is progressive (average tax rate rises as income rises). The corporate income tax is roughly proportional (average tax rate remains constant as income rises). General sales, excise, payroll, and property taxes are regressive (average tax rate falls as income rises). Overall, the U.S. tax system is slightly progressive.

Terms and Concepts

market failure

private goods

productive efficiency

allocative efficiency

public goods

free-rider problem

cost-benefit analysis

negative externalities

positive externalities

Coase theorem

quasi-public goods

benefits-received principle

ability-to-pay principle

marginal tax rate

average tax rate

progressive tax

regressive tax

proportional tax

Study Questions

1. Use the characteristics of private goods to explain why firms can profitably offer them for sale. Why do competitive firms tend to produce private goods at minimum average cost? What do economists mean when they say that private goods tend to be produced in the "right" amounts?
2. Contrast the characteristics of public goods with those of private goods. Why won't private firms produce public goods?
3. The accompanying table relating to a public good provides information on the prices Young and Zorn are willing to pay for various quantities of that public good. These two people are the only members of society. Determine the price that society is willing to pay for the public good at each quantity of output. If the government's marginal cost of providing this public good is constant at $7, how many units of the public good should government provide? Why not less? Why not more?

Young		Zorn		Society	
P	Q_d	P	Q_d	P	Q_d
$8	0	$8	1	$___	1
7	0	7	2	___	2
6	0	6	3	___	3
5	1	5	4	___	4
4	2	4	5	___	5
3	3	3	6	___	6
2	4	2	7	___	7
1	5	1	8	___	8

4. The table on page 112 shows the total costs and total benefits in billions for four different antipollution programs of increasing scope. Use cost-benefit analysis to determine which program should be undertaken. Explain.

you a $50 interest payment for each of the next 10 years and then repays your $1000 principal at the end of that period.

Financing through sales of stocks and bonds also provides other advantages to those who purchase these *corporate securities.* An individual investor can spread risks by buying the securities of several corporations. And it is usually easy for holders of corporate securities to sell their holdings. Organized stock exchanges and bond markets simplify the transfer of securities from sellers to buyers. This "ease of sale" increases the willingness of savers to make financial investments in corporate securities. Besides, corporations have easier access to bank credit than do other types of business organizations. Corporations are better risks and are more likely to become profitable clients of banks.

limited liability Restriction of the maximum loss to a shareholder to the amount paid for the stock.

Corporations provide **limited liability** to owners (stockholders), who risk only what they paid for their stock. Their personal assets are not at stake if the corporation defaults on its debts. Creditors can sue the corporation as a legal entity but cannot sue the owners of the corporation as individuals.

Because of their ability to attract financial capital, successful corporations can easily expand the scope of their operations and realize the benefits of expansion. For example, they can take advantage of mass-production technologies and division of labor. A corporation can hire specialists in production, accounting, and marketing functions and thus improve efficiency.

As a legal entity, the corporation has a life independent of its owners and its officers. Legally, at least, corporations are immortal. The transfer of corporate ownership through inheritance or the sale of stock does not disrupt the continuity of the corporation. Corporations have permanence that lends itself to long-range planning and growth.

The Principal-Agent Problem

Many of the world's corporations are extremely large. In 2004, 256 of the world's corporations had annual sales of more than $20 billion, and 563 firms had sales of more than $10 billion. U.S.-based Wal-Mart alone sold $288 billion of goods in 2004.

6.1 Principal-agent problem 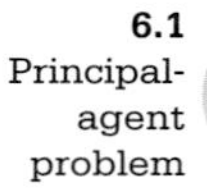

But large size creates a potential problem. In sole proprietorships and partnerships, the owners of the real and financial assets of the firm enjoy direct control of those assets. But ownership of large corporations is spread over tens or hundreds of thousands of stockholders. The owners of a corporation usually do not manage it—they hire others to do so.

principal-agent problem A conflict of interest that occurs when agents (managers) pursue their own objectives to the detriment of the principals' (stockholders') goals.

That practice can create a **principal-agent problem.** The *principals* are the stockholders who own the corporation and who hire executives as their *agents* to run the business on their behalf. But the interests of these managers (the agents) and the wishes of the owners (the principals) do not always coincide. The owners typically want maximum company profit and stock price. However, the agents may want the power, prestige, and pay that often accompany control over a large enterprise, independent of its profitability and stock price.

So a conflict of interest may develop. For example, executives may build expensive office buildings, enjoy excessive perks such as corporate jets, and pay too much to acquire other corporations. Consequently, the firm's costs will be excessive, and the firm will fail to maximize profits and stock prices for its owners.

Applying the Analysis

Unprincipled Agents

In the 1990s many corporations addressed the principal-agent problem by providing a substantial part of executive pay either as shares of the firm's stock or as stock options. *Stock options* are contracts that allow executives or other key employees to buy shares of their employers' stock at fixed, lower prices when the stock prices rise. The idea was to align the interest of the executives and other key employees more closely with those of the broader corporate owners. By pursuing high profits and share prices, the executives would enhance their own wealth as well as that of all the stockholders.

This "solution" to the principal-agent problem had an unexpected negative side effect. It prompted a few unscrupulous executives to inflate their firm's share prices by hiding costs, overstating revenues, engaging in deceptive transactions, and, in general, exaggerating profits. These executives then sold large quantities of their inflated stock, making quick personal fortunes. In some cases, "independent" outside auditing firms turned out to be "not so independent" because they held valuable consulting contracts with the firms being audited.

When the stock market bubble of the late 1990s burst, many instances of business manipulations and fraudulent accounting were exposed. Several executives of large U.S. firms were indicted, and a few large firms collapsed, among them Enron (energy trading), WorldCom (communications), and Arthur Andersen (business consulting). General stockholders of those firms were left holding severely depressed or even worthless stock.

In 2002 Congress strengthened the laws and penalties against executive misconduct. Also, corporations have improved their accounting and auditing procedures. But the revelations of recent wrongdoings make it clear that the principal-agent problem is not an easy problem to solve.

Question:
Why are accurate accounting and independent auditing so crucial in reducing the principal-agent problem?

Economic Costs

Costs exist because resources are scarce and productive and have alternative uses. When society uses a specific combination of resources to produce some product, it forgoes all alternative opportunities to use those resources for other purposes. The measure of the economic cost, or opportunity cost, of any resource is the value or worth it would have in its best alternative use. We stressed this view of costs in our analysis of production possibilities in Chapter 1, where we found that the opportunity cost of producing more food products is the manufacturing equipment that must be forgone. Similarly, the paper used for printing economics textbooks is not available for printing encyclopedias or romance novels. And if an assembly-line worker is capable of assembling personal computers or washing machines, then the cost to society of employing that worker in a computer plant is the contribution he or she would otherwise have made in producing washing machines.

Explicit and Implicit Costs

Now let's consider costs from the viewpoint of a typical firm. Keeping opportunity costs in mind, we can say that *economic costs are the payments a firm must make, or the incomes it must provide, to attract the resources it needs away from alternative production opportunities.* Those payments to resource suppliers are explicit (revealed and expressed) or implicit (present but not obvious). So in producing products firms incur explicit costs and implicit costs.

explicit costs The monetary payments a firm must make to an outsider to obtain a resource.

implicit costs The monetary income a firm sacrifices when it uses a resource it owns rather than supplying the resource in the market.

- A firm's **explicit costs** are the monetary payments (or cash expenditures) it makes to those who supply labor services, materials, fuel, transportation services, and the like. Such money payments are for the use of resources owned by others.
- A firm's **implicit costs** are the opportunity costs of using its self-owned, self-employed resources. To the firm, implicit costs are the money payments that self-employed resources could have earned in their best alternative use.

Example: Suppose you are earning $22,000 a year as a sales representative for a T-shirt manufacturer. At some point you decide to open a retail store of your own to sell T-shirts. You invest $20,000 of savings that have been earning you $1000 per year. And you decide that your new firm will occupy a small store that you own and have been renting out for $5000 per year. You hire one clerk to help you in the store, paying her $18,000 annually.

A year after you open the store, you total up your accounts and find the following:

Total sales revenue		$120,000
Cost of T-shirts	$40,000	
Clerk's salary	18,000	
Utilities	5,000	
Total (explicit) costs		63,000
Accounting profit		$ 57,000

It looks good. But unfortunately your accounting profit of $57,000 ignores your implicit costs and thus overstates the economic success of your venture. By providing your own financial capital, building, and labor, you incur implicit costs (forgone incomes) of $1000 of interest, $5000 of rent, and $22,000 of wages. If your entrepreneurial talent is worth, say, $5000 annually in other business endeavors of similar scope, you have also ignored that implicit cost. So:

Accounting profit		$57,000
Forgone interest	$ 1,000	
Forgone rent	5,000	
Forgone wages	22,000	
Forgone entrepreneurial income	5,000	
Total implicit costs		33,000
Economic profit		$24,000

Normal Profit as a Cost

normal profit A payment that must be made by a firm to obtain and retain entrepreneurial ability.

The $5000 implicit cost of your entrepreneurial talent in the above example is a **normal profit.** As is true of the forgone rent and forgone wages, the payment you could otherwise receive for performing entrepreneurial functions is indeed an implicit cost. If you did not realize at least this minimum, or normal, payment for your effort, you could withdraw from this line of business and shift to a more attractive endeavor. So a normal profit is a cost of doing business.

The economist includes as costs of production all the costs—explicit and implicit, including a normal profit—required to attract and retain resources in a specific line of production. For economists, a firm's economic costs are the opportunity costs of the resources used, whether those resources are owned by others or by the firm. In our example, economic costs are $96,000 (=$63,000 of explicit costs + $33,000 of implicit costs).

Economic Profit (or Pure Profit)

Obviously, then, economists use the term "profit" differently from the way accountants use it. To the accountant, profit is the firm's total revenue less its explicit costs (or accounting costs). To the economist, **economic profit** is total revenue less economic costs (explicit and implicit costs, the latter including a normal profit to the entrepreneur). So when an economist says a certain firm is earning only enough revenue to cover its costs, this means it is meeting all explicit and implicit costs and the entrepreneur is receiving a payment just large enough to retain his or her talents in the present line of production.

economic profit
A firm's total revenue less its total cost (=explicit cost + implicit cost).

If a firm's total revenue exceeds all its economic costs (explicit + implicit), any residual goes to the entrepreneur. That residual is called an *economic*, or *pure, profit.* In short:

$$\text{Economic profit} = \text{total revenue} - \text{economic cost}$$

In our example, economic profit is $24,000, found by subtracting the $96,000 of economic cost from the $120,000 of revenue. An *economic* profit is not a cost, because it is a return in excess of the normal profit that is required to retain the entrepreneur in this particular line of production. Even if the economic profit is zero, the entrepreneur is still covering all explicit and implicit costs, including a normal profit. In our example, as long as accounting profit is $33,000 or more (so economic profit is zero or more), you will be earning a $5000 normal profit and will therefore continue to operate your T-shirt store.

Figure 6.1 shows the relationship among the various cost and profit concepts that we have just discussed. To test yourself, you might want to enter cost data from our example in the appropriate blocks.

FIGURE 6.1
Economic profit versus accounting profit. Economic profit is equal to total revenue less economic costs. Economic costs are the sum of explicit and implicit costs and include a normal profit to the entrepreneur. Accounting profit is equal to total revenue less accounting (explicit) costs.

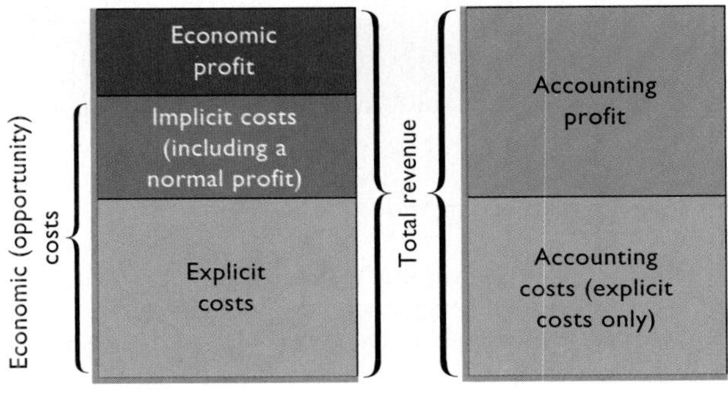

Short Run and Long Run

When the demand for a firm's product changes, the firm's profitability may depend on how quickly it can adjust the amounts of the various resources it employs. It can easily and quickly adjust the quantities employed of many resources such as hourly labor, raw materials, fuel, and power. It needs much more time, however, to adjust its *plant capacity*—the size of the factory building, the amount of machinery and equipment, and other capital resources. In some heavy industries such as aircraft manufacturing, a firm may need several years to alter plant capacity. Because of these differences in adjustment time, economists find it useful to distinguish between two conceptual periods: the short run and the long run. We will discover that costs differ in these two time periods.

short run
A time period in which producers are able to change the quantities of some but not all of the resources they employ.

Short Run: Fixed Plant

The **short run** is a period too brief for a firm to alter its plant capacity yet long enough to permit a change in the degree to which the fixed plant is used. The firm's plant capacity is fixed in the short run. However, the firm can vary its output by applying larger or smaller amounts of labor, materials, and other resources to that plant. It can use its existing plant capacity more or less intensively in the short run.

If Boeing hires 1000 extra workers for one of its commercial airline plants or adds an entire shift of workers, we are speaking of the short run. Both are *short-run adjustments.*

long run
A time period sufficiently long to enable producers to change the quantities of all the resources they employ.

Long Run: Variable Plant

From the viewpoint of an existing firm, the **long run** is a period long enough for it to adjust the quantities of all the resources that it employs, including plant capacity. From the industry's viewpoint, the long run also includes enough time for existing firms to dissolve and leave the industry or for new firms to be created and enter the industry. While the short run is a "fixed-plant" period, the long run is a "variable-plant" period. If Boeing adds a new production facility or merges with a supplier, we are referring to the long run. Both are *long-run adjustments.*

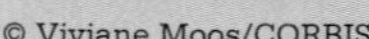

© Viviane Moos/CORBIS

© Richard Klune/CORBIS

Photo Op Long-Run Adjustments by Firms

An apparel manufacturer can make long-run adjustments to add production capacity in a matter of days by leasing another building and ordering and installing extra sewing machines. In contrast, an oil firm may need 2 to 3 years to construct a new refinery to increase its production capacity.

The short run and the long run are conceptual periods rather than calendar time periods. As indicated in the Photo Op, light-manufacturing industries can accomplish changes in plant capacity almost overnight. But for heavy industry the long run is a different matter. A firm may require several years to construct a new facility.

Short-Run Production Relationships

A firm's costs of producing a specific output depend on the prices of the needed resources and the quantities of those resources (inputs) needed to produce that output. Resource supply and demand determine resource prices. The technological aspects of production, specifically the relationships between inputs and output, determine the quantities of resources needed. Our focus will be on the *labor*-output relationship, given a fixed plant capacity. But before examining that relationship, we need to define three terms:

- **Total product (TP)** is the total quantity, or total output, of a particular good or service produced.
- **Marginal product (MP)** is the extra output or added product associated with adding a unit of a variable resource, in this case labor, to the production process. Thus,

$$\text{Marginal product} = \frac{\text{change in total product}}{\text{change in labor input}}$$

- **Average product (AP),** also called *labor productivity*, is output per unit of labor input:

$$\text{Average product} = \frac{\text{total product}}{\text{units of labor}}$$

total product (TP) The total output of a particular good or service produced by a firm.

marginal product (MP) The extra output or added product associated with adding a unit of a variable resource (labor) to the production process.

average product (AP) The total output divided by the quantity of the resource employed (labor).

In the short run, a firm for a time can increase its output by adding units of labor to its fixed plant. But by how much will output rise when it adds the labor? Why do we say "for a time"?

Law of Diminishing Returns

The answers are provided in general terms by the **law of diminishing returns.** This law assumes that technology is fixed and thus the techniques of production do not change. It states that as successive units of a variable resource (say, labor) are added to a fixed resource (say, capital or land), beyond some point the extra, or marginal, product that can be attributed to each additional unit of the variable resource will decline. For example, if additional workers are hired to work with a constant amount of capital equipment, output will eventually rise by smaller and smaller amounts as more workers are hired. Diminishing returns will eventually occur.

law of diminishing returns The principle that as successive units of a variable resource are added to a fixed resource, the marginal product of the variable resource will eventually decline.

Relevancy for Firms

6.2 Law of diminishing returns

The law of diminishing returns is highly relevant for production within firms. As producers add successive units of a variable input such as labor to a fixed input such as capital, the marginal product of labor eventually declines. Diminishing returns will occur sooner or later. Total product eventually will rise at a diminishing rate, then reach a maximum, and finally decline.

Diminishing Returns from Study

The following noneconomic example of a relationship between "inputs" and "output" may help you better understand the idea. Suppose for an individual that

Total course learning = f(intelligence, quality of course materials, instructor effectiveness, class time, and study time)

where f means "function of" or "depends on." So this relationship supposes that total course learning depends on intelligence (however defined), the quality of course materials such as the textbook, the effectiveness of the instructor, the amount of class time, and the amount of personal study time outside the class.

For analytical purposes, let's assume that one's intelligence, the quality of course materials, the effectiveness of the instructor, and the amount of class time are *fixed*—meaning they do not change over the length of the course. Now let's add units of study time per day over the length of the course to "produce" greater course learning. The first hour of study time per day increases total course learning. Will the second hour enhance course learning by as much as the first? By how much will the third, fourth, fifth, . . . or fifteenth hour of study per day contribute to total course learning relative to the *immediate previous hour?*

We think you will agree that eventually diminishing returns to course learning will set in as successive hours of study are added each day. At some point the marginal product of an extra hour of study time will decline and, at some further point, become zero.

Question:
Given diminishing returns to study time, why devote any extra time to study?

What is true for study time is true for producers. Suppose a farmer has a fixed resource of 80 acres planted in corn. If the farmer does not cultivate the cornfields (clear the weeds) at all, the yield will be 40 bushels per acre. If he cultivates the land once, output may rise to 50 bushels per acre. A second cultivation may increase output to 57 bushels per acre, a third to 61, and a fourth to 63. Succeeding cultivations will add less and less to the land's yield. If this were not so, the world's needs for corn could be fulfilled by extremely intense cultivation of this single 80-acre plot of land. Indeed, if diminishing returns did not occur, the world could be fed out of a flowerpot. Why not? Just keep adding more seed, fertilizer, and harvesters!

The law of diminishing returns also holds true in nonagricultural industries. Assume a wood shop is manufacturing furniture frames. It has a specific amount of equipment such as lathes, planers, saws, and sanders. If this shop hired just one or two workers, total output and productivity (output per worker) would be very low. The workers would have to perform many different jobs, and the advantages of specialization would not be realized. Time would be lost in switching from one job to another, and machines would stand idle much of the time. In short, the plant would be understaffed, and production would be inefficient because there would be too much capital relative to the amount of labor.

The shop could eliminate those difficulties by hiring more workers. Then the equipment would be more fully used, and workers could specialize in doing a single job. Time would no longer be lost switching from job to job. As more workers were added, production would become more efficient and the marginal product of each succeeding worker would rise.

But the rise could not go on indefinitely. If still more workers were added, beyond a certain point, overcrowding would set in. Since workers would then have to wait in line to use the machinery, they would be underused. Total output would increase at a diminishing rate, because, given the fixed size of the plant, each worker would have less capital equipment to work with as more and more labor was hired. The marginal product of additional workers would decline, because there would be more labor in proportion to the fixed amount of capital. Eventually, adding still more workers would cause so much congestion that marginal product would become negative and total product would decline. At the extreme, the addition of more and more labor would exhaust all the standing room, and total product would fall to zero.

Note that the law of diminishing returns assumes that all units of labor are of equal quality. Each successive worker is presumed to have the same innate ability, motor coordination, education, training, and work experience. Less-skilled or less-energetic workers are not the cause of diminishing returns. Rather, marginal product ultimately diminishes because more workers are being used relative to the amount of plant and equipment available.

Tabular and Graphical Representations

The table at the top of Figure 6.2 is a numerical illustration of the law of diminishing returns. Column 2 shows the total product, or total output, resulting from combining each level of a variable input (labor) in column 1 with a fixed amount of capital, using the existing technology.

Column 3 shows the marginal product (MP), the change in total product associated with each additional unit of labor. Note that with no labor input, total product is zero; a plant with no workers will produce no output. The first 3 units of labor reflect increasing marginal returns, with marginal products of 10, 15, and 20 units, respectively. But beginning with the fourth unit of labor, marginal product diminishes continuously, becoming zero with the seventh unit of labor and negative with the eighth.

Average product, or output per labor unit, is shown in column 4. It is calculated by dividing total product (column 2) by the number of labor units needed to produce it (column 1). At 5 units of labor, for example, AP is 14 (=70/5).

Figure 6.2 also shows the diminishing-returns data graphically and further clarifies the relationships between total, marginal, and average products. (Marginal product in Figure 6.2b is plotted halfway between the units of labor, since it applies to the addition of each labor unit.)

Note first in Figure 6.2a that total product, TP, goes through three phases: It rises initially at an increasing rate; then it increases, but at a diminishing rate; finally, after reaching a maximum, it declines.

Geometrically, marginal product—shown by the MP curve in Figure 6.2b—is the slope of the total-product curve. Marginal product measures the change in total product associated with each succeeding unit of labor. Thus, the three phases of total product are also reflected in marginal product. Where total product is increasing at an increasing rate, marginal product is rising. Here, extra units of labor are adding larger and larger amounts to total product. Similarly, where total product is increasing but at a decreasing rate, marginal product is positive but falling. Each additional unit of labor adds less to total product than did the previous unit. When total product is at a

FIGURE 6.2
The law of diminishing returns. (a) As a variable resource (labor) is added to fixed amounts of other resources (land or capital), the total product that results will eventually increase by diminishing amounts, reach a maximum, and then decline. (b) Marginal product is the change in total product associated with each new unit of labor. Average product is simply output per labor unit. Note that marginal product intersects average product at the maximum average product.

(1) Units of the Variable Resource (Labor)	(2) Total Product (TP)	(3) Marginal Product (MP), Change in (2)/ Change in (1)		(4) Average Product (AP), (2)/(1)
0	0			—
1	10	10	Increasing marginal returns	10.00
2	25	15		12.50
3	45	20		15.00
4	60	15	Diminishing marginal returns	15.00
5	70	10		14.00
6	75	5		12.50
7	75	0	Negative marginal returns	10.71
8	70	−5		8.75

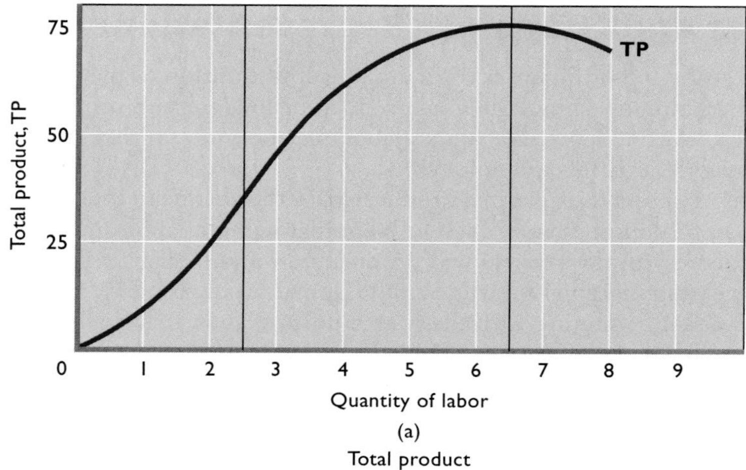

(a)
Total product

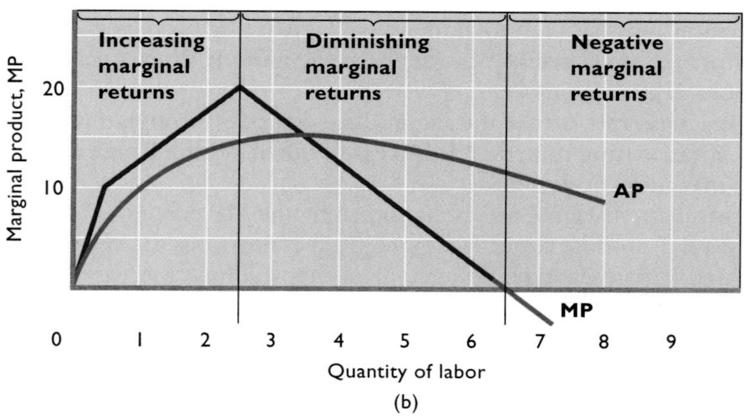

(b)
Marginal and average products

maximum, marginal product is zero. When total product declines, marginal product becomes negative.

Average product, AP (Figure 6.2b), displays the same tendencies as marginal product. It increases, reaches a maximum, and then decreases as more and more units of labor are added to the fixed plant. But note the relationship between marginal product and average product: Where marginal product exceeds average product, average product rises. And where marginal product is less than average product, average product declines. It follows that marginal product intersects average product where average product is at a maximum.

6.3
Production relationships

Exam Scores

The relationship between "marginal" and "average" shown in Figure 6.2b is a mathematical necessity. If you add a larger number to a total than the current average of that total, the average must rise. And if you add a smaller number to a total than the current average of that total, the average must fall. You raise your average examination grade only when your score on an additional (marginal) examination is greater than the average of all your past scores. You lower your average when your grade on an additional exam is below your current average. In our production example, when the amount an extra worker adds to total product exceeds the average product of all workers currently employed, average product will rise. Conversely, when an extra worker adds to total product an amount that is less than the current average product, then average product will decrease.

Question:
Suppose your average exam score for the first three exams is 80 and you receive a 92 on your fourth exam. What is your marginal score? What is your new average score? Why did your average go up?

Short-Run Production Costs

Production information such as that in Figure 6.2 must be coupled with resource prices to determine the total and per-unit costs of producing various levels of output. We know that in the short run some resources, those associated with the firm's plant, are fixed. Other resources, however, are variable. So short-run costs are either fixed or variable.

Fixed, Variable, and Total Costs

Let's see what distinguishes fixed costs, variable costs, and total costs from one another.

fixed costs
Costs that do not change in total when the firm changes its output.

Fixed Costs **Fixed costs** are costs that do not vary with changes in output. Fixed costs are associated with the very existence of a firm's plant and therefore must be paid even if its output is zero. Such costs as rental payments, interest on a firm's debts, a portion of depreciation on equipment and buildings, and insurance premiums are generally fixed costs; they do not increase even if a firm produces more. In column 2 of Figure 6.3's table, we assume that the firm's total fixed cost is $100. By definition, this fixed cost is incurred at all levels of output, including zero. The firm cannot avoid paying fixed costs in the short run.

FIGURE 6.3

A firm's cost curves. AFC falls as a given amount of fixed costs is apportioned over a larger and larger output. AVC initially falls because of increasing marginal returns but then rises because of diminishing marginal returns. The marginal-cost (MC) curve eventually rises because of diminishing returns and cuts through the average-total-cost (ATC) curve and the average-variable-cost (AVC) curve at their minimum points.

Total-Cost Data				Average-Cost Data			Marginal Cost
(1) Total Product (*Q*)	(2) Total Fixed Cost (TFC)	(3) Total Variable Cost (TVC)	(4) Total Cost (TC) TC = TFC + TVC	(5) Average Fixed Cost (AFC) $AFC = \frac{TFC}{Q}$	(6) Average Variable Cost (AVC) $AVC = \frac{TVC}{Q}$	(7) Average Total Cost (ATC) $ATC = \frac{TC}{Q}$	(8) Marginal Cost (MC) $MC = \frac{\text{change in TC}}{\text{change in } Q}$
0	$100	$ 0	$ 100				
							$ 90
1	100	90	190	$100.00	$90.00	$190.00	
							80
2	100	170	270	50.00	85.00	135.00	
							70
3	100	240	340	33.33	80.00	113.33	
							60
4	100	300	400	25.00	75.00	100.00	
							70
5	100	370	470	20.00	74.00	94.00	
							80
6	100	450	550	16.67	75.00	91.67	
							90
7	100	540	640	14.29	77.14	91.43	
							110
8	100	650	750	12.50	81.25	93.75	
							130
9	100	780	880	11.11	86.67	97.78	
							150
10	100	930	1030	10.00	93.00	103.00	

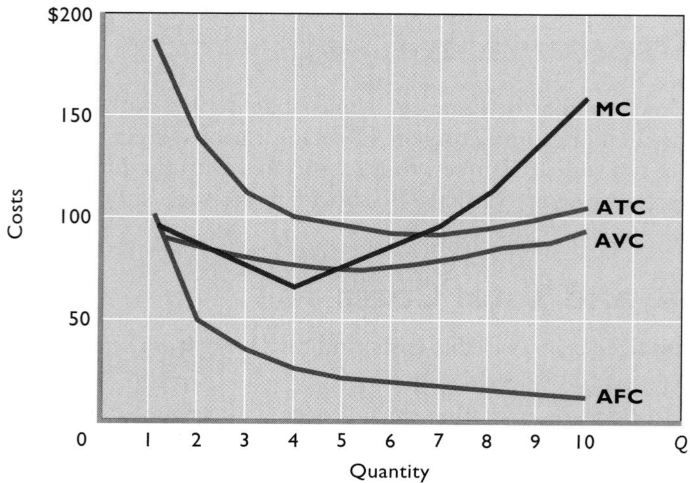

Applying the Analysis

Sunk Costs

Some of a firm's costs are not only *fixed* (recurring, but unrelated to the level of output) but *sunk* (unrecoverable). Such costs are like sunken ships on the ocean floor: Once these costs are incurred, they cannot be recovered. For example, suppose a firm spends $1 million on R&D to bring out a new product, only to discover that the product sells very poorly. Should the firm continue to produce the product at a loss even when there is no realistic hope for future success? Obviously, it should not. In making this decision, the firm realizes that the amount it has spent in developing the product is irrelevant; it should stop production of the product and cut its losses. In fact, many firms have dropped products after spending millions of dollars on their development. Examples are the quick decision by Coca-Cola to drop its New Coke and the eventual decision by McDonald's to drop its McLean Burger.

In short, a firm should ignore any cost that it cannot partly or fully recoup through a subsequent choice. Such costs are sunk costs. They are irrelevant in making future-oriented business decisions. Or, as the saying goes, don't cry over spilt milk.

Question:
Which is a sunk cost, rather than simply a recurring fixed cost: (1) a prior expenditure on a business computer that is now outdated or (2) a current monthly payment on an equipment lease that runs for 6 more months? Explain.

Variable Costs Unlike fixed costs, **variable costs** are costs that change with the level of output. They include payments for materials, fuel, power, transportation services, most labor, and similar variable resources. In column 3 of the table in Figure 6.3, we find that the total of variable costs changes directly with output.

variable costs
Costs that increase or decrease with a firm's output.

Total Cost **Total cost** is the sum of fixed cost and variable cost at each level of output. It is shown in column 4 of the table in Figure 6.3. At zero units of output, total cost is equal to the firm's fixed cost. Then for each unit of the 10 units of production, total cost increases by the same amount as variable cost.

total cost
The sum of fixed cost and variable cost.

The distinction between fixed and variable costs is significant to the business manager. Variable costs can be controlled or altered in the short run by changing production levels. Fixed costs are beyond the business manager's current control; they are incurred in the short run and must be paid regardless of output level.

Per-Unit, or Average, Costs

Producers are certainly interested in their total costs, but they are equally concerned with per-unit, or average, costs. In particular, average-cost data are more meaningful for making comparisons with product price, which is always stated on a per-unit basis. Average fixed cost, average variable cost, and average total cost are shown in columns 5 to 7 of the table in Figure 6.3.

average fixed cost (AFC)
A firm's total fixed cost divided by output.

AFC **Average fixed cost (AFC)** for any output level is found by dividing total fixed cost (TFC) by that output (Q). That is,

$$AFC = \frac{TFC}{Q}$$

Because the total fixed cost is, by definition, the same regardless of output, AFC must decline as output increases. As output rises, the total fixed cost is spread over a larger and larger output. When output is just 1 unit in Figure 6.3's table, TFC and AFC are the same at $100. But at 2 units of output, the total fixed cost of $100 becomes $50 of AFC or fixed cost per unit; then it becomes $33.33 per unit as $100 is spread over 3 units, and $25 per unit when spread over 4 units. This process is sometimes referred to as "spreading the overhead." Figure 6.3 shows that AFC graphs as a continuously declining curve as total output is increased.

average variable cost (AVC)
A firm's total variable cost divided by output.

AVC **Average variable cost (AVC)** for any output level is calculated by dividing total variable cost (TVC) by that output (Q):

$$AVC = \frac{TVC}{Q}$$

As added variable resources increase output, AVC declines initially, reaches a minimum, and then increases again. A graph of AVC is a U-shaped or saucer-shaped curve, as shown in Figure 6.3.

Because total variable cost reflects the law of diminishing returns, so must AVC, which is derived from total variable cost. Because marginal returns increase initially, it takes fewer and fewer additional variable resources to produce each of the first 4 units of output. As a result, variable cost per unit declines. AVC hits a minimum with the fifth unit of output, and beyond that point AVC rises, because diminishing returns require more and more variable resources to produce each additional unit of output.

You can verify the U or saucer shape of the AVC curve by returning to the production table in Figure 6.2. Assume the price of labor is $10 per unit. By dividing average product (output per labor unit) into $10 (price per labor unit), we determine the labor cost per unit of output. Because we have assumed labor to be the only variable input, the labor cost per unit of output is the variable cost per unit of output, or AVC. When average product is initially low, AVC is high. As workers are added, average product rises and AVC falls. When average product is at its maximum, AVC is at its minimum. Then, as still more workers are added and average product declines, AVC rises. The "hump" of the average-product curve is reflected in the saucer or U shape of the AVC curve.

average total cost (ATC)
A firm's total cost (=explicit cost + implicit cost) divided by output.

ATC **Average total cost (ATC)** for any output level is found by dividing total cost (TC) by that output (Q) or by adding AFC and AVC at that output:

$$ATC = \frac{TC}{Q} = \frac{TFC}{Q} + \frac{TVC}{Q} = AFC + AVC$$

Graphically, we can find ATC by adding vertically the AFC and AVC curves, as in Figure 6.3. Thus the vertical distance between the ATC and AVC curves measures AFC at any level of output.

Marginal Cost

One final and very crucial cost concept remains: **Marginal cost (MC)** is *the extra, or additional, cost of producing 1 more unit of output.* MC can be determined for each added unit of output by noting the change in total cost which that unit's production entails:

marginal cost (MC) The extra or additional cost of producing 1 more unit of output.

$$MC = \frac{\text{change in TC}}{\text{change in } Q}$$

Calculations In column 4 of Figure 6.3's table, production of the first unit of output increases total cost from \$100 to \$190. Therefore, the additional, or marginal, cost of that first unit is \$90 (column 8). The marginal cost of the second unit is \$80 (=\$270 − \$190); the MC of the third is \$70 (=\$340 − \$270); and so forth. The MC for each of the 10 units of output is shown in column 8.

MC can also be calculated from the total-variable-cost column, because the only difference between total cost and total variable cost is the constant amount of fixed costs (\$100). Thus, the change in total cost and the change in total variable cost accompanying each additional unit of output are always the same.

Marginal Decisions Marginal costs are costs the firm can control directly and immediately. Specifically, MC designates all the cost incurred in producing the last unit of output. Thus, it also designates the cost that can be "saved" by not producing that last unit. Average-cost figures do not provide this information. For example, suppose the firm is undecided whether to produce 3 or 4 units of output. At 4 units the table in Figure 6.3 indicates that ATC is \$100. But the firm does not increase its total costs by \$100 by producing the fourth unit, nor does it save \$100 by not producing that unit. Rather, the change in costs involved here is only \$60, as the MC column in the table reveals.

A firm's decisions as to what output level to produce are typically marginal decisions, that is, decisions to produce a few more or a few less units. Marginal cost is the change in costs when 1 more or 1 less unit of output is produced. When coupled with marginal revenue (which, as you will see in Chapter 7, indicates the change in revenue from 1 more or 1 less unit of output), marginal cost allows a firm to determine if it is profitable to expand or contract its production. The analysis in the next three chapters focuses on those marginal calculations.

Graphical Portrayal Marginal cost is shown graphically in Figure 6.3. Marginal cost at first declines sharply, reaches a minimum, and then rises rather abruptly. This reflects the fact that variable costs, and therefore total cost, increase first by decreasing amounts and then by increasing amounts.

6.1 Production and costs

Relation of MC to AVC and ATC Figure 6.3 shows that the marginal-cost curve MC intersects both the AVC and the ATC curves at their minimum points. As noted earlier, this marginal-average relationship is a mathematical necessity. When the amount (the marginal cost) added to total cost is less than the current average total cost, ATC will fall. Conversely, when the marginal cost exceeds ATC, ATC will rise. This means in Figure 6.3 that as long as MC lies below ATC, ATC will fall, and whenever MC lies above ATC, ATC will rise. Therefore, at the point of intersection where MC equals ATC, ATC has just ceased to fall but has not yet begun to rise. This, by definition, is the minimum point on the ATC curve. The marginal-cost curve intersects the average-total-cost curve at the ATC curve's minimum point.

Marginal cost can be defined as the addition either to total cost or to total variable cost resulting from 1 more unit of output; thus this same rationale explains why the MC curve also crosses the AVC curve at the AVC curve's minimum point. No such relationship exists between the MC curve and the average-fixed-cost curve, because the two are not related; marginal cost includes only those costs that change with output, and fixed costs by definition are those that are independent of output.

Applying the Analysis

Rising Cost of Insurance and Security

Following the terrorist attacks of September 11, 2001, and the threat of additional attacks, insurance premiums rose for many American businesses. In the short run, insurance premiums are fixed costs because they are independent of the level of production. The terrorist attacks also increased security costs, some of which are fixed (for example, video cameras) and others of which are variable (security workers). Together, higher insurance premiums and added security costs increased average fixed cost, variable cost, and average total cost for many firms. In terms of Figure 6.3, their short-run ATC curves shifted upward.

Question:
What is an example of higher security costs incurred by airlines following the terrorist attacks?

Long-Run Production Costs

In the long run an industry and the individual firms it comprises can undertake all desired resource adjustments. That is, they can change the amount of all inputs used. The firm can alter its plant capacity; it can build a larger plant or revert to a smaller plant than that assumed in Figures 6.2 and 6.3. The industry also can change its plant size; the long run allows sufficient time for new firms to enter or for existing firms to leave an industry. We will discuss the impact of the entry and exit of firms to and from an industry in the next chapter; here we are concerned only with changes in plant capacity made by a single firm. Let's couch our analysis in terms of average total cost (ATC), making no distinction between fixed and variable costs because all resources, and therefore all costs, are variable in the long run.

Firm Size and Costs

Suppose a single-plant manufacturer begins on a small scale and, as the result of successful operations, expands to successively larger plant sizes with larger output capacities. What happens to average total cost as this occurs? For a time, successively larger plants will lower average total cost. However, eventually the building of a still larger plant may cause ATC to rise.

Figure 6.4 illustrates this situation for five possible plant sizes. ATC-1 is the short-run average-total-cost curve for the smallest of the five plants, and ATC-5 the curve for the largest. Constructing larger plants will lower the minimum average total costs through plant size 3. But then larger plants will mean higher minimum average total costs.

FIGURE 6.4

The long-run average-total-cost curve: five possible plant sizes. The long-run average-total-cost curve is made up of segments of the short-run cost curves (ATC-1, ATC-2, etc.) of the various-size plants from which the firm might choose. Each point on the bumpy planning curve shows the lowest unit cost attainable for any output when the firm has had time to make all desired changes in its plant size.

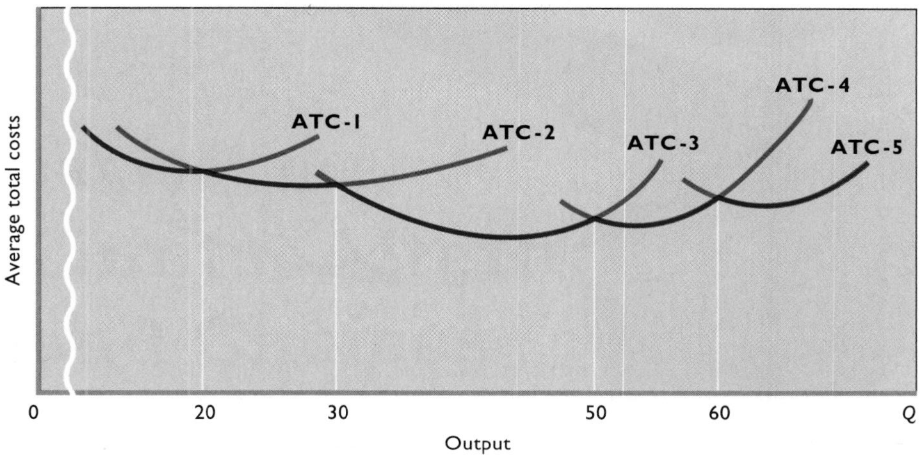

The Long-Run Cost Curve

The vertical lines perpendicular to the output axis in Figure 6.4 indicate the outputs at which the firm should change plant size to realize the lowest attainable average total costs of production. These are the outputs at which the per-unit costs for a larger plant drop below those for the current, smaller plant. For all outputs up to 20 units, the lowest average total costs are attainable with plant size 1. However, if the firm's volume of sales expands beyond 20 units but less than 30, it can achieve lower per-unit costs by constructing a larger plant, size 2. Although total cost will be higher at the expanded levels of production, the cost per unit of output will be less. For any output between 30 and 50 units, plant size 3 will yield the lowest average total costs. From 50 to 60 units of output, the firm must build the size-4 plant to achieve the lowest unit costs. Lowest average total costs for any output over 60 units require construction of the still larger plant, size 5.

Tracing these adjustments, we find that the long-run ATC curve for the enterprise is made up of segments of the short-run ATC curves for the various plant sizes that can be constructed. The long-run ATC curve shows the lowest average total cost at which *any output level* can be produced after the firm has had time to make all appropriate adjustments in its plant size. In Figure 6.4 the red, bumpy curve is the firm's long-run ATC curve or, as it is often called, the firm's *planning curve.*

In most lines of production the choice of plant size is much wider than in our illustration. In many industries the number of possible plant sizes is virtually unlimited, and in time quite small changes in the volume of output will lead to changes in plant size. Graphically, this implies an unlimited number of short-run ATC curves, one for each output level, as suggested by Figure 6.5. Then, rather than being made up of segments of short-run ATC curves as in Figure 6.4, the long-run ATC curve is made up of all the points of tangency of the unlimited number of short-run ATC curves from which the long-run ATC curve is derived. Therefore, the planning curve is smooth

FIGURE 6.5

The long-run average-total-cost curve: unlimited number of plant sizes. If the number of possible plant sizes is very large, the long-run average-total-cost curve approximates a smooth curve. Economies of scale, followed by diseconomies of scale, cause the curve to be U-shaped.

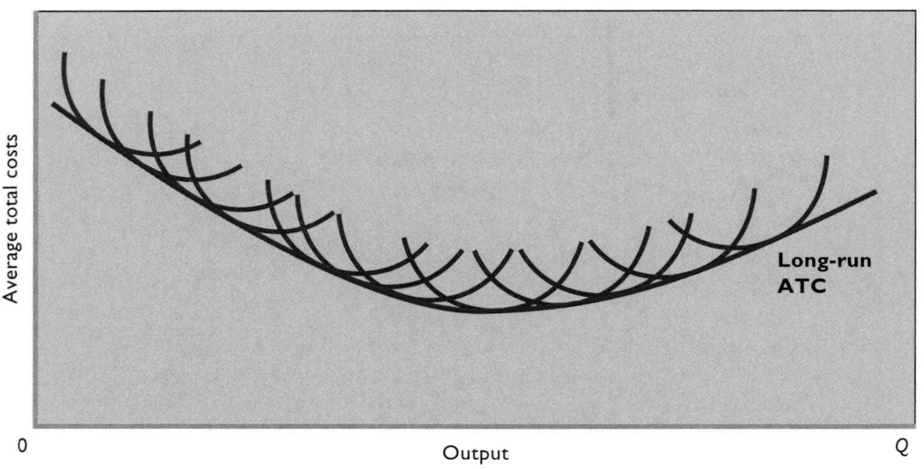

rather than bumpy. Each point on it tells us the minimum ATC of producing the corresponding level of output.

Economies and Diseconomies of Scale

We have assumed that for a time larger and larger plant sizes will lead to lower unit costs but that beyond some point successively larger plants will mean higher average total costs. That is, we have assumed the long-run ATC curve is U-shaped. But why should this be? Note, first, that the law of diminishing returns does not apply in the long run. That's because diminishing returns presume one resource is fixed in supply while the long run means all resources are variable. Also, our discussion assumes resource prices are constant. We can explain the U-shaped long-run average-total-cost curve in terms of economies and diseconomies of large-scale production.

economies of scale Reductions in the average total cost of producing a product as the firm expands the size of its operations (output) in the long run.

Economies of Scale

Economies of scale, or *economies of mass production,* explain the downsloping part of the long-run ATC curve, as indicated in Figure 6.6, graphs (a), (b), and (c). As plant size increases, a number of factors will for a time lead to lower average costs of production.

Labor Specialization Increased specialization in the use of labor becomes more achievable as a plant increases in size. Hiring more workers means jobs can be divided and subdivided. Each worker may now have just one task to perform instead of five or six. Workers can work full-time on the tasks for which they have special skills. In a small plant, skilled machinists may spend half their time performing unskilled tasks, leading to higher production costs.

Further, by working at fewer tasks, workers become even more proficient at those tasks. The jack-of-all-trades doing five or six jobs is not likely to be efficient in any of them. Concentrating on one task, the same worker may become highly efficient.

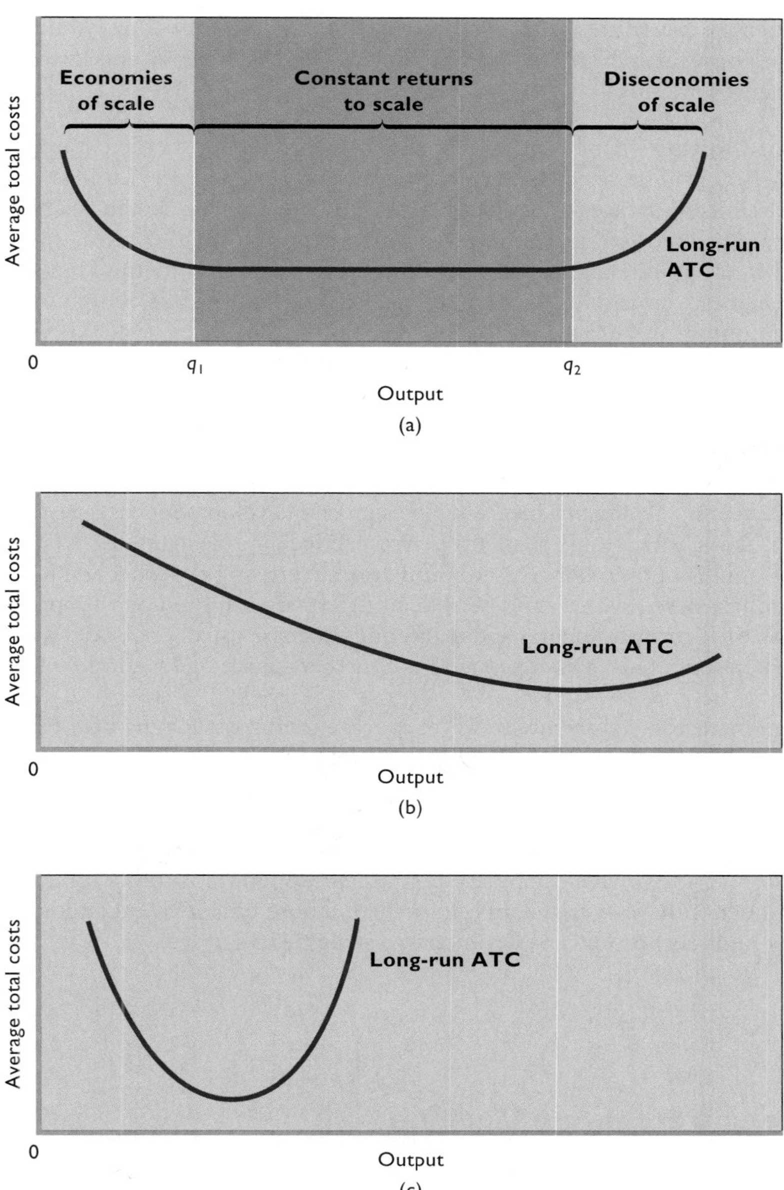

FIGURE 6.6
Various possible long-run average-total-cost curves. In (a), economies of scale are rather rapidly obtained as plant size rises, and diseconomies of scale are not encountered until a considerably large scale of output has been achieved. Thus, long-run average total cost is constant over a wide range of output. In (b), economies of scale are extensive, and diseconomies of scale occur only at very large outputs. Average total cost therefore declines over a broad range of output. In (c), economies of scale are exhausted quickly, followed immediately by diseconomies of scale. Minimum ATC thus occurs at a relatively low output.

Finally, greater labor specialization eliminates the loss of time that accompanies each shift of a worker from one task to another.

Managerial Specialization Large-scale production also means better use of, and greater specialization in, management. A supervisor who can handle 20 workers is underused in a small plant that employs only 10 people. The production staff could be doubled with no increase in supervisory costs.

Small firms cannot use management specialists to best advantage. In a small plant a sales specialist may have to divide his or her time between several executive functions, for example, marketing, personnel, and finance. A larger scale of operations means that the marketing expert can supervise marketing full-time, while other specialists perform further managerial functions. Greater efficiency and lower unit costs are the net result.

Efficient Capital Small firms often cannot afford the most efficient equipment. In many lines of production such machinery is available only in very large and extremely expensive units. Furthermore, effective use of the equipment demands a high volume of production, and that again requires large-scale producers.

In the automobile industry the most efficient fabrication method employs robotics and elaborate assembly-line equipment. Effective use of this equipment demands an annual output of perhaps 200,000 to 400,000 automobiles. Only very large-scale producers can afford to purchase and use this equipment efficiently. The small-scale producer is faced with a dilemma. To fabricate automobiles using other equipment is inefficient and therefore more costly per unit. The alternative of purchasing the efficient equipment and underusing it at low levels of output is also inefficient and costly.

Other Factors Many products entail design and development costs, as well as other "start-up" costs, which must be incurred irrespective of projected sales. These costs decline per unit as output is increased. Similarly, advertising costs decline per auto, per computer, per stereo system, and per box of detergent as more units are produced and sold. Also, the firm's production and marketing expertise usually rises as it produces and sells more output. This *learning by doing* is a further source of economies of scale.

All these factors contribute to lower average total costs for the firm that is able to expand its scale of operations. Where economies of scale are possible, an increase in all resources of, say, 10 percent will cause a more-than-proportionate increase in output of, say, 20 percent. The result will be a decline in ATC.

In many U.S. manufacturing industries economies of scale have been of great significance. Firms that have expanded their scale of operations to obtain economies of mass production have survived and flourished. Those unable to expand have become relatively high-cost producers, doomed to a struggle to survive.

Applying the Analysis

The Verson Stamping Machine

In 1996 Verson (a U.S. firm located in Chicago) introduced a 49-foot-tall metal-stamping machine that is the size of a house and weighs as much as 12 locomotives. This $30 million machine, which cuts and sculpts raw sheets of steel into automobile hoods and fenders, enables automakers to make new parts in just 5 minutes compared with 8 hours for older stamping presses. A single machine is designed to make 5 million auto parts per year. So, to achieve the cost saving from the machine, an auto manufacturer must have sufficient auto production to use all these parts. By allowing the use of this cost-saving piece of equipment, large firm size achieves economies of scale.

Question:
Do you see any potential problems for a company that relies too heavily on just a few large machines for fabricating millions of its critical product parts?

Diseconomies of Scale In time the expansion of a firm may lead to diseconomies and therefore higher average total costs.

The main factor causing **diseconomies of scale** is the difficulty of efficiently controlling and coordinating a firm's operations as it becomes a large-scale producer. In a small plant a single key executive may make all the basic decisions for the plant's operation. Because of the firm's small size, the executive is close to the production line, understands the firm's operations, and can digest information and make efficient decisions.

diseconomies of scale
Increases in the average total cost of producing a product as the firm expands the size of its operations (output) in the long run.

This neat picture changes as a firm grows. There are now many management levels between the executive suite and the assembly line; top management is far removed from the actual production operations of the plant. One person cannot assemble, digest, and understand all the information essential to decision making on a large scale. Authority must be delegated to many vice-presidents, second vice-presidents, and so forth. This expansion of the management hierarchy leads to problems of communication and cooperation, bureaucratic red tape, and the possibility that decisions will not be coordinated. Similarly, decision making may be slowed down to the point that decisions fail to reflect changes in consumer tastes or technology quickly enough. The result is impaired efficiency and rising average total costs.

Also, in massive production facilities workers may feel alienated from their employers and care little about working efficiently. Opportunities to shirk, by avoiding work in favor of on-the-job leisure, may be greater in large plants than in small ones. Countering worker alienation and shirking may require additional worker supervision, which increases costs.

Where diseconomies of scale are operative, an increase in all inputs of, say, 10 percent will cause a less-than-proportionate increase in output of, say, 5 percent. As a consequence, ATC will increase. The rising portion of the long-run cost curves in Figure 6.6 illustrates diseconomies of scale.

Constant Returns to Scale In some industries there may exist a rather wide range of output between the output at which economies of scale end and the output at which diseconomies of scale begin. That is, there may be a range of **constant returns to scale** over which long-run average cost does not change. The q_1q_2 output range of Figure 6.6a is an example. Here a given percentage increase in all inputs of, say, 10 percent will cause a proportionate 10 percent increase in output. Thus, in this range ATC is constant.

constant returns to scale
No changes in the average total cost of producing a product as the firm expands the size of its operations (output) in the long run.

Minimum Efficient Scale and Industry Structure

Economies and diseconomies of scale are an important determinant of an industry's structure. Here we introduce the concept of **minimum efficient scale (MES),** which is the lowest level of output at which a firm can minimize long-run average costs. In Figure 6.6a that level occurs at q_1 units of output. Because of the extended range of constant returns to scale, firms producing substantially greater outputs could also realize the minimum attainable average costs. Specifically, firms within the q_1q_2 range would be equally efficient. So we would not be surprised to find an industry with such cost conditions to be populated by firms of quite different sizes. The apparel, banking, furniture, snowboard, wood products, food processing, and small-appliance industries are examples. With an extended range of constant returns to scale, relatively large and relatively small firms can coexist in an industry and be equally successful.

minimum efficient scale (MES)
The lowest level of output at which a firm can minimize long-run average total cost.

Compare this with Figure 6.6b, where economies of scale continue over a wide range of outputs and diseconomies of scale appear only at very high levels of output. This pattern of declining long-run average total cost occurs in the automobile, aluminum, steel, and other heavy industries. The same pattern holds in several of the new industries related to information technology, for example, computer microchips, operating system software, and Internet service provision. Given consumer demand, efficient production will be achieved with a few large-scale producers. Small firms cannot realize the minimum efficient scale and will not be able to compete.

Where economies of scale are few and diseconomies come into play quickly, the minimum efficient size occurs at a low level of output, as shown in Figure 6.6c. In such industries a particular level of consumer demand will support a large number of relatively small producers. Many retail trades and some types of farming fall into this category. So do certain kinds of light manufacturing, such as the baking, clothing, and shoe industries. Fairly small firms are more efficient than larger-scale producers would be if they were present in such industries.

Our point here is that the shape of the long-run average-total-cost curve is determined by technology and the economies and diseconomies of scale that result. The shape of the long-run ATC curve, in turn, can be significant in determining whether an industry is populated by a relatively large number of small firms or is dominated by a few large producers, or lies somewhere in between.

6.4 Minimum efficient scale

But we must be cautious in our assessment because industry structure does not depend on cost conditions alone. Government policies, the geographic size of markets, managerial strategy and skill, and other factors must be considered in explaining the structure of a particular industry.

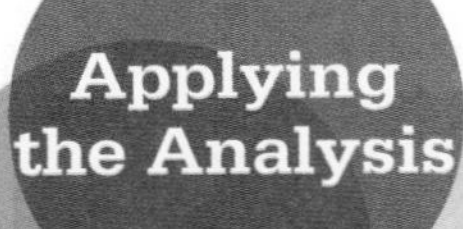

Aircraft Assembly Plants versus Concrete Plants

Why are there only three plants in the United States (all operated by Boeing) that produce large commercial aircraft and thousands of plants (owned by hundreds of firms) that produce ready-mixed concrete? The simple answer is that MES is radically different in the two industries. Why is that? First, economies of scale are extensive in assembling large commercial aircraft and very modest in mixing concrete. Manufacturing airplanes is a complex process that requires huge facilities, thousands of workers, and very expensive, specialized machinery. Economies of scale extend to huge plant sizes. But mixing Portland cement, sand, gravel, and water efficiently to produce concrete requires only a handful of workers and relatively inexpensive equipment. Economies of scale are exhausted at relatively small size.

The differing MES also derives from the vastly different sizes of the geographic markets. The market for commercial airplanes is global, and aircraft manufacturers can deliver new airplanes anywhere in the world by flying them there. In contrast, the geographic market for a concrete plant is roughly the 50-mile radius that enables the concrete to be delivered before it "sets up." So in the ready-mix concrete industry, thousands of small concrete plants are positioned close to their customers in hundreds of small and large cities.

Question:
Speculate as to why the MES of firms in the Portland cement industry is considerably larger than the MES of single ready-mix concrete plants.

Summary

1. Corporations—the dominant form of business organizations—are legal entities, distinct and separate from the individuals who own them. They often have thousands, or even millions, of stockholders who jointly own them. They finance their operations and purchases of new plant and equipment partly through the issuance of stocks and bonds. Stocks are ownership shares of a corporation, and bonds are promises to repay a loan, usually at a set rate of interest.
2. A principal-agent problem may occur in corporations when the agents (managers) hired to represent the interest of the principals (stockholders) pursue their own objectives to the detriment of the objectives of the principals.
3. Economic costs include all payments that must be received by resource owners to ensure a continued supply of needed resources to a particular line of production. Economic costs include explicit costs, which flow to resources owned and supplied by others, and implicit costs, which are payments for the use of self-owned and self-employed resources. One implicit cost is a normal profit to the entrepreneur. Economic profit occurs when total revenue exceeds total cost (=explicit costs + implicit costs, including a normal profit).
4. In the short run a firm's plant capacity is fixed. The firm can use its plant more or less intensively by adding or subtracting units of variable resources, but it does not have sufficient time in the short run to alter plant size.
5. The law of diminishing returns describes what happens to output as a fixed plant is used more intensively. As successive units of a variable resource, such as labor, are added to a fixed plant, beyond some point the marginal product associated with each additional unit of a resource declines.
6. Because some resources are variable and others are fixed, costs can be classified as variable or fixed in the short run. Fixed costs are independent of the level of output; variable costs vary with output. The total cost of any output is the sum of fixed and variable costs at that output.
7. Average fixed, average variable, and average total costs are fixed, variable, and total costs per unit of output. Average fixed cost declines continuously as output increases because a fixed sum is being spread over a larger and larger number of units of production. A graph of average variable cost is U-shaped, reflecting the law of diminishing returns. Average total cost is the sum of average fixed and average variable costs; its graph is also U-shaped.
8. Marginal cost is the extra, or additional, cost of producing 1 more unit of output. It is the amount by which total cost and total variable cost change when 1 more or 1 less unit of output is produced. Graphically, the marginal-cost curve intersects the ATC and AVC curves at their minimum points.
9. The long run is a period of time sufficiently long for a firm to vary the amounts of all resources used, including plant size. In the long run all costs are variable. The long-run ATC, or planning, curve is composed of segments of the short-run ATC curves, and it represents the various plant sizes a firm can construct in the long run.
10. The long-run ATC curve is generally U-shaped. Economies of scale are first encountered as a small firm expands. Greater specialization in the use of labor and management, the ability to use the most efficient equipment, and the spreading of start-up costs among more units of output all contribute to economies of scale. As the firm continues to grow, it will encounter diseconomies of scale stemming from the managerial complexities that accompany large-scale production. The ranges of output over which economies and diseconomies of scale occur in an industry are often an important determinant of the structure of that industry.

Terms and Concepts

stocks
bonds
limited liability
principal-agent problem
explicit costs
implicit costs
normal profit
economic profit
short run
long run
total product (TP)
marginal product (MP)
average product (AP)
law of diminishing returns
fixed costs

variable costs
total cost
average fixed cost (AFC)
average variable cost (AVC)
average total cost (ATC)
marginal cost (MC)
economies of scale
diseconomies of scale
constant returns to scale
minimum efficient scale (MES)

Study Questions

1. Distinguish between a plant, a firm, and an industry. Contrast a vertically integrated firm, a horizontally integrated firm, and a conglomerate. Cite an example of a horizontally integrated firm from which you have recently made a purchase.
2. What major advantages of corporations have given rise to their dominance as a form of business organization?
3. What is the principal-agent problem as it relates to corporate managers and stockholders? How did firms try to solve this problem in the 1990s? In what way did the "solution" backfire on some firms?
4. Distinguish between explicit and implicit costs, giving examples of each. Why does the economist classify normal profit as a cost? Is economic profit a cost of production? Explain why or why not.
5. Gomez runs a small pottery firm. He hires one helper at $12,000 per year, pays annual rent of $5000 for his shop, and spends $20,000 per year on materials. He has $40,000 of his own funds invested in equipment (pottery wheels, kilns, and so forth) that could earn him $4000 per year if alternatively invested. He has been offered $15,000 per year to work as a potter for a competitor. He estimates his entrepreneurial talents are worth $3000 per year. Total annual revenue from pottery sales is $72,000. Calculate the accounting profit and the economic profit for Gomez's pottery firm.
6. Which of the following are short-run and which are long-run adjustments?
   a. Wendy's builds a new restaurant.
   b. IBM hires 200 more software engineers.
   c. A farmer increases the amount of fertilizer used on his corn crop.
   d. An Alcoa aluminum plant adds a third shift of workers.
7. Complete the following table by calculating marginal product and average product from the data given:

Inputs of Labor	Total Product	Marginal Product	Average Product
0	0		
1	15	_____	_____
2	34	_____	_____
3	51	_____	_____
4	65	_____	_____
5	74	_____	_____
6	80	_____	_____
7	83	_____	_____
8	82	_____	_____

   Explain why marginal product eventually declines and ultimately becomes negative. What bearing does the law of diminishing returns have on marginal costs? Be specific.
8. Why can the distinction between fixed costs and variable costs be made in the short run? Classify the following as fixed or variable costs: advertising expenditures, fuel, interest on company-issued bonds, shipping charges, payments for raw materials, real estate taxes, executive salaries, insurance premiums, wage payments, sales taxes, and rental payments on leased office machinery.
9. A firm has fixed costs of $60 and variable costs as indicated in the table on page 139.

   Complete the table and check your calculations by referring to question 3 at the end of Chapter 7.
   a. Graph the AFC, ATC, and MC curves. Why does the AFC curve slope continuously downward? Why does the MC curve eventually slope upward? Why does the MC curve intersect the ATC curve at its minimum point?

Total Product	Total Fixed Cost	Total Variable Cost	Total Cost	Average Fixed Cost	Average Variable Cost	Average Total Cost	Marginal Cost
							$____
0	$____	$ 0	$____	$____	$____	$____	
1	____	45	____	____	____	____	____
2	____	85	____	____	____	____	____
3	____	120	____	____	____	____	____
4	____	150	____	____	____	____	____
5	____	185	____	____	____	____	____
6	____	225	____	____	____	____	____
7	____	270	____	____	____	____	____
8	____	325	____	____	____	____	____
9	____	390	____	____	____	____	____
10	____	465	____	____	____	____	____

b. Explain how the location of each curve graphed in question 9a would be altered if (1) total fixed cost had been $100 rather than $60 and (2) total variable cost had been $10 less at each level of output.

10. Indicate how each of the following would shift the (1) marginal-cost curve, (2) average-variable-cost curve, (3) average-fixed-cost curve, and (4) average-total-cost curve of a manufacturing firm. In each case specify the direction of the shift.

a. A reduction in business property taxes.

b. An increase in the hourly wage rates of production workers.

c. A decrease in the price of electricity.

d. An increase in transportation costs.

11. Suppose a firm has only three possible plant-size options, represented by the ATC curves shown in the accompanying figure. What plant size will the firm choose in producing (a) 50, (b) 130, (c) 160, and (d) 250 units of output? Draw the firm's long-run average-cost curve on the diagram and describe this curve.

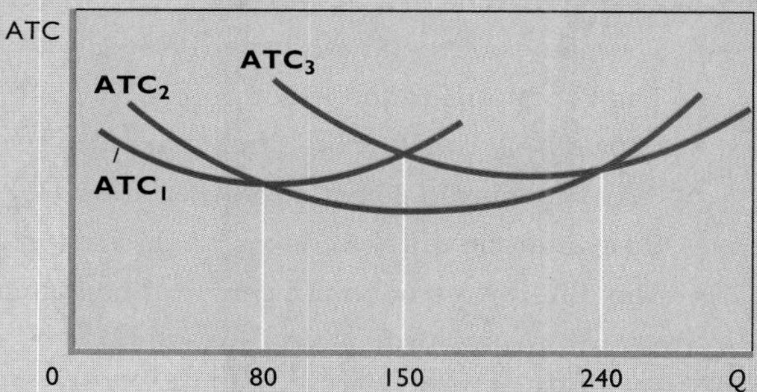

12. Use the concepts of economies and diseconomies of scale to explain the shape of a firm's long-run ATC curve. What is the concept of minimum efficient scale? What bearing can the shape of the long-run ATC curve have on the structure of an industry?

Website Questions

At the text's Website, www.brueonline.com, you will find three multiple-choice quizzes on this chapter's content. We encourage you to take the quizzes to see how you do. Also, you will find one or more Web-based questions that require information from the Internet to answer.

CHAPTER SEVEN

Pure Competition

In this chapter you will learn:

- The names of the four basic market models.
- The conditions required for purely competitive markets.
- How purely competitive firms maximize profits or minimize losses.
- Why the marginal-cost curve and supply curve of competitive firms are identical.
- How industry entry and exit produce economic efficiency.
- The differences between constant-cost, increasing-cost, and decreasing-cost industries.

In Chapter 5 we examined the relationship between product demand and total revenue, and in Chapter 6 we discussed businesses and their costs of production. Now we want to put revenues and costs together to see how a business decides what price to charge and how much output to produce. But a firm's decisions concerning price and production depend greatly on the character of the industry in which it is operating. There is no "average" or "typical" industry. At one extreme is a single producer that dominates the market; at the other extreme are industries in which thousands of firms each produce a tiny fraction of market supply. Between these extremes are many other industries.

Since we cannot examine each industry individually, our approach will be to look at several basic *models* of market structure. Together, these models will help you understand how price, output, and profit are determined in the many product markets in the economy. They will also help you evaluate the efficiency or inefficiency of those markets.

Four Market Models

Economists group industries into four distinct market structures: pure competition, pure monopoly, monopolistic competition, and oligopoly. These four market models differ in several respects: the number of firms in the industry, whether those firms produce a standardized product or try to distinguish their products from those of other firms, and how easy or how difficult it is for firms to enter the industry.

The four models are as follows, presented in order of degree of competition (most to least):

- *Pure competition* involves a very large number of firms producing a standardized product (that is, a product identical to that of other producers, such as corn or cucumbers). New firms can enter or exit the industry very easily.
- *Monopolistic competition* is characterized by a relatively large number of sellers producing differentiated products (clothing, furniture, books). There is widespread *nonprice competition*, a selling strategy in which one firm tries to distinguish its product or service from all competing products on the basis of attributes such as design and workmanship (an approach called product differentiation). Either entry to or exit from monopolistically competitive industries is quite easy.
- *Oligopoly* involves only a few sellers of a standardized or differentiated product, so each firm is affected by the decisions of its rivals and must take those decisions into account in determining its own price and output.

© Getty Images/DIL

© Amy Etra/PhotoEdit

Photo Op Standardized versus Differentiated Products

Wheat is an example of a standardized product, whereas Pert shampoo is an example of a differentiated product.

- *Pure monopoly* is a market structure in which one firm is the sole seller of a product or service for which there is no good substitute (for example, a local electric utility or patented medical device). Since the entry of additional firms is blocked, one firm constitutes the entire industry. Because the monopolist produces a unique product, it makes no effort to differentiate its product.

Pure Competition: Characteristics and Occurrence

pure competition A market structure in which a very large number of firms produce a standardized product and there are no restrictions on entry.

Let's take a fuller look at **pure competition**, the focus of the remainder of this chapter:

- ***Very large numbers*** A basic feature of a purely competitive market is the presence of a large number of independently acting sellers, often offering their products in large national or international markets. Examples: markets for farm commodities, the stock market, and the foreign exchange market.
- ***Standardized product*** Purely competitive firms produce a standardized (identical or homogeneous) product. As long as the price is the same, consumers will be indifferent about which seller to buy the product from. Buyers view the products of firms B, C, D, and E as perfect substitutes for the product of firm A. Because purely competitive firms sell standardized products, they make no attempt to differentiate their products and do not engage in other forms of nonprice competition.
- "***Price takers***" In a purely competitive market, individual firms exert no significant control over product price. Each firm produces such a small fraction of total output that increasing or decreasing its output will not perceptibly influence total supply or, therefore, product price. In short, the competitive firm is a **price taker:** It cannot change market price; it can only adjust to it. That means that the individual competitive producer is at the mercy of the market. Asking a price higher than the market price would be futile. Consumers will not buy from firm A at $2.05 when its 9999 competitors are selling an identical product, and therefore a perfect substitute, at $2 per unit. Conversely, because firm A can sell as much as it chooses at $2 per unit, there is no reason for it to charge a lower price, say, $1.95, for to do so would shrink its profit.
- ***Free entry and exit*** New firms can freely enter and existing firms can freely leave purely competitive industries. No significant legal, technological, financial, or other obstacles prohibit new firms from selling their output in any competitive market.

price taker A competitive firm that cannot change the market price, but can only accept it as "given" and adjust to it.

Although pure competition is somewhat rare in the real world, this market model is highly relevant. A few industries more closely approximate pure competition than any other market structure. In particular, we can learn much about markets for agricultural goods, fish products, foreign exchange, basic metals, and stock shares by studying the pure-competition model. Also, pure competition is a meaningful starting point for any discussion of how prices and output are determined. Moreover, the operation of a purely competitive economy provides a norm for evaluating the efficiency of the real-world economy.

Demand as Seen by a Purely Competitive Seller

To develop a model of pure competition, we first examine demand from a competitive seller's viewpoint and see how it affects revenue. This seller might be a wheat farmer, a strawberry grower, a sheep rancher, a catfish raiser, or the like. Because each purely competitive firm offers only a negligible fraction of total market supply, it must accept the price predetermined by the market. Pure competitors are price takers, not price makers.

Perfectly Elastic Demand

The demand schedule faced by the *individual firm* in a purely competitive industry is perfectly elastic at the market price, as demonstrated in Figure 7.1. As shown in column 1 of the table in Figure 7.1, the market price is $131. The firm represented cannot obtain a higher price by restricting its output, nor does it need to lower its price to increase its sales volume. Columns 1 and 2 show that the firm can produce as little or much as it wants and sell all the units at $131 each.

We are *not* saying that *market* demand is perfectly elastic in a competitive market. Rather, market demand graphs as a downsloping curve. An entire industry (all firms producing a particular product) can affect price by changing industry output. For example, all firms, acting independently but simultaneously, can increase price by reducing output. But the individual competitive firm cannot do that. Its demand curve will plot as a straight, horizontal line such as *D* in Figure 7.1

Average, Total, and Marginal Revenue

The firm's demand schedule is also its average-revenue schedule. Price per unit to the purchaser is also revenue per unit, or average revenue, to the seller. To say that all buyers must pay $131 per unit is to say that the revenue per unit, or **average revenue,** received by the seller is $131. Price and average revenue are the same thing from different viewpoints.

average revenue
Total revenue from the sale of a product divided by the quantity of the product sold.

The **total revenue** for each sales level is found by multiplying price by the corresponding quantity the firm can sell. (Column 1 multiplied by column 2 in the table in Figure 7.1 yields column 3.) In this case, total revenue increases by a constant amount, $131, for each additional unit of sales. Each unit sold adds exactly its constant price to total revenue.

total revenue
The total number of dollars received by a firm from the sale of a product.

When a firm is pondering a change in its output, it will consider how its total revenue will change as a result. **Marginal revenue** is the change in total revenue (or the extra revenue) that results from selling 1 more unit of output. In column 3 of the table in Figure 7.1, total revenue is zero when zero units are sold. The first unit of output sold increases total revenue from zero to $131, so marginal revenue for that unit is $131. The second unit sold increases total revenue from $131 to $262, and marginal revenue is again $131. Note in column 4 that marginal revenue is a constant $131, as is price. In pure competition, marginal revenue and price are equal.

marginal revenue
The change in total revenue that results from selling 1 more unit of a firm's product.

Figure 7.1 shows the purely competitive firm's total-revenue, demand, marginal-revenue, and average-revenue curves. Total revenue (TR) is a straight line that slopes

FIGURE 7.1
A purely competitive firm's demand and revenue curves. The demand curve (*D*) of a purely competitive firm is a horizontal line (perfectly elastic) because the firm can sell as much output as it wants at the market price (here, $131). Because each additional unit sold increases total revenue by the amount of the price, the firm's total-revenue curve (TR) is a straight upward-sloping line and its marginal-revenue curve (MR) coincides with the firm's demand curve. The average-revenue curve (AR) also coincides with the demand curve.

Firm's Demand Schedule		Firm's Revenue Data	
(1) Product Price (*P*) (Average Revenue)	(2) Quantity Demanded (*Q*)	(3) Total Revenue (TR), (1) × (2)	(4) Marginal Revenue (MR)
$131	0	$ 0	
			$131
131	1	131	
			131
131	2	262	
			131
131	3	393	
			131
131	4	524	
			131
131	5	655	
			131
131	6	786	
			131
131	7	917	
			131
131	8	1048	
			131
131	9	1179	
			131
131	10	1310	

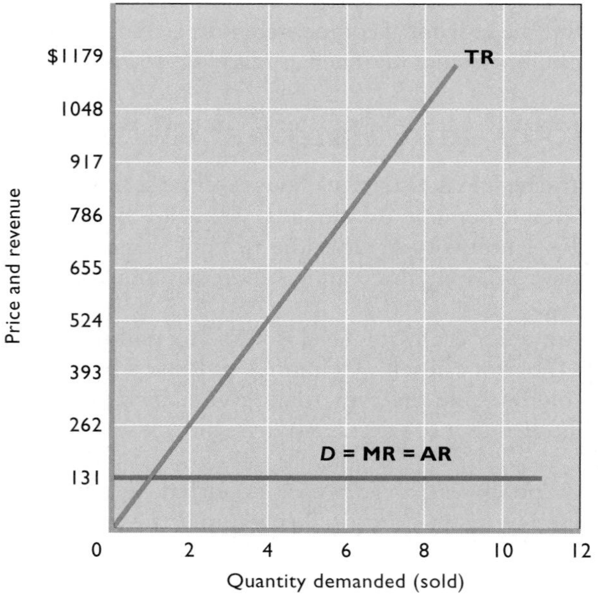

upward to the right. Its slope is constant because each extra unit of sales increases TR by $131. The demand curve (*D*) is horizontal, indicating perfect price elasticity. The marginal-revenue curve (MR) coincides with the demand curve because the product price (and hence MR) is constant. The average revenue equals price and therefore also coincides with the demand curve.

Profit Maximization in the Short Run

Because the purely competitive firm is a price taker, it can maximize its economic profit (or minimize its loss) only by adjusting its *output*. And, in the short run, the firm has a fixed plant. Thus it can adjust its output only through changes in the amount of variable resources (materials, labor) it uses. It adjusts its variable resources to achieve the output level that maximizes its profit.

More specifically, the firm compares the amounts that each *additional* unit of output would add to total revenue and to total cost. In other words, the firm compares the *marginal revenue* (MR) and the *marginal cost* (MC) of each successive unit of output. Assuming that producing is preferable to shutting down, the firm should produce any unit of output whose marginal revenue exceeds its marginal cost because the firm would gain more in revenue from selling that unit than it would add to its costs by producing it. Conversely, if the marginal cost of a unit of output exceeds its marginal revenue, the firm should not produce that unit. Producing it would add more to costs than to revenue, and profit would decline or loss would increase.

In the initial stages of production, where output is relatively low, marginal revenue will usually (but not always) exceed marginal cost. So it is profitable to produce through this range of output. But at later stages of production, where output is relatively high, rising marginal costs will exceed marginal revenue. Obviously, a profit-maximizing firm will want to avoid output levels in that range. Separating these two production ranges is a unique point at which marginal revenue equals marginal cost. This point is the key to the output-determining rule: *In the short run, the firm will maximize profit or minimize loss by producing the output at which marginal revenue equals marginal cost (as long as producing is preferable to shutting down).* This profit-maximizing guide is known as the **MR = MC rule.** (For most sets of MR and MC data, MR and MC will be precisely equal at a fractional level of output. In such instances the firm should produce the last complete unit of output for which MR exceeds MC.)

MR = MC rule
A method of determining the total output at which economic profit is at a maximum (or losses at a minimum).

Keep in mind these three features of the MR = MC rule:

- As noted, the rule applies only if producing is preferable to shutting down. We will show shortly that if marginal revenue does not equal or exceed average variable cost, the firm will shut down rather than produce the MR = MC output.
- The rule is an accurate guide to profit maximization for all firms whether they are purely competitive, monopolistic, monopolistically competitive, or oligopolistic.
- We can restate the rule as P = MC when applied to a purely competitive firm. Because the demand schedule faced by a competitive seller is perfectly elastic at the going market price, product price and marginal revenue are equal. So under pure competition (and only under pure competition) we may substitute P for MR in the rule: *When producing is preferable to shutting down, the competitive firm that wants to maximize its profit or minimize its loss should produce at that point where price equals marginal cost* (P = *MC*).

Now let's apply the MR = MC rule or, because we are considering pure competition, the P = MC rule.

Profit Maximization

The first five columns in the table in Figure 7.2 reproduce the AFC, AVC, ATC, and MC data derived for our product in Chapter 6. Here, we will compare the marginal-cost data of column 5 with price (equals marginal revenue) for each unit of output.

Suppose first that the market price, and therefore marginal revenue, is $131, as shown in column 6.

What is the profit-maximizing output? Every unit of output up to and including the ninth unit represents greater marginal revenue than marginal cost of output. Each of the first 9 units therefore adds to the firm's profit and should be produced. The firm, however, should not produce the tenth unit. It would add more to cost ($150) than to revenue ($131).

FIGURE 7.2

Short-run profit maximizing for a purely competitive firm. The MR = MC output enables the purely competitive firm to maximize profits or to minimize losses. In this case MR (=P in pure competition) and MC are equal at 9 units of output, Q. There P exceeds the average total cost A = $97.78, so the firm realizes an economic profit of $P - A$ per unit. The total economic profit is represented by the gray rectangle and is $9 \times (P - A)$.

(1) Total Product (Output)	(2) Average Fixed Cost (AFC)	(3) Average Variable Cost (AVC)	(4) Average Total Cost (ATC)	(5) Marginal Cost (MC)	(6) Price = Marginal Revenue (MR)	(7) Total Economic Profit (+) or Loss (−)
0						$−100
				$ 90	$131	
1	$100.00	$90.00	$190.00			− 59
				80	131	
2	50.00	85.00	135.00			− 8
				70	131	
3	33.33	80.00	113.33			+ 53
				60	131	
4	25.00	75.00	100.00			+124
				70	131	
5	20.00	74.00	94.00			+185
				80	131	
6	16.67	75.00	91.67			+236
				90	131	
7	14.29	77.14	91.43			+277
				110	131	
8	12.50	81.25	93.75			+298
				130	***131***	
9	***11.11***	***86.67***	***97.78***			***+299***
				150	131	
10	10.00	93.00	103.00			+280

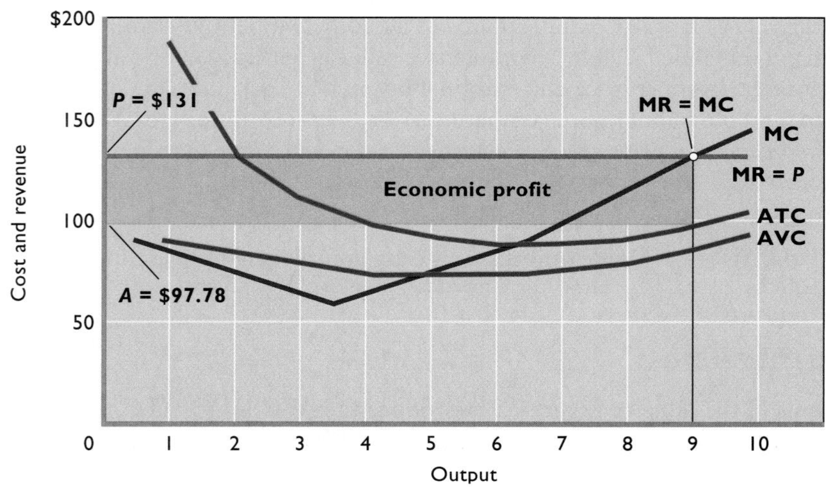

We can calculate the economic profit realized by producing 9 units from the average-total-cost data. Price ($131) multiplied by output (9) yields total revenue of $1179. Multiplying average total cost ($97.78) by output (9) gives us total cost of $880.[1] The difference of $299 (=$1179 − $880) is the economic profit. Clearly, this firm will prefer to operate rather than shut down.

An alternative, and perhaps easier, way to calculate the economic profit is to determine the profit per unit by subtracting the average total cost ($97.78) from the product price ($131). Then multiply the difference (a per-unit profit of $33.22) by output (9). Take some time now to verify the numbers in column 7 in the table in Figure 7.2. You will find that any output other than that which adheres to the MR = MC rule will yield either profits below $299 or losses.

Figure 7.2 also shows price (=MR) and marginal cost graphically. Price equals marginal cost at the profit-maximizing output of 9 units. There the per-unit economic profit is $P - A$, where P is the market price and A is the average total cost of 9 units of output. The total economic profit is $9 \times (P - A)$, shown by the gray rectangular area.

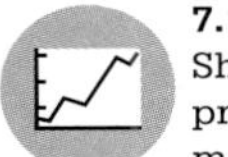

7.1
Short-run profit maximization

Loss Minimization and Shutdown

Now let's assume that the market price is $81 rather than $131. Should the firm still produce? If so, how much? And what will be the resulting profit or loss? The answers, respectively, are "Yes," "Six units," and "A loss of $64."

The first five columns in the table in Figure 7.3 are the same as those in Figure 7.2. Column 6, however, shows the new price (equal to MR) of $81. Looking at columns 5 and 6, notice that the first unit of output adds $90 to total cost but only $81 to total revenue. One might conclude: "Don't produce—close down!" But that would be hasty. Remember that in the very early stages of production, marginal product is low, making marginal cost unusually high. The price–marginal cost relationship improves with increased production. For units 2 through 6, price exceeds marginal cost. Each of these 5 units adds more to revenue than to cost, and as shown in column 7, they decrease the total loss. Together they more than compensate for the "loss" taken on the first unit. Beyond 6 units, however, MC exceeds MR (=P). The firm should therefore produce 6 units. In general, the profit-seeking producer should always compare marginal revenue (or price under pure competition) with the rising portion of the marginal-cost schedule or curve.

Loss Minimization Will production be profitable? No, because at 6 units of output the average total cost of $91.67 exceeds the price of $81 by $10.67 per unit. If we multiply that by the 6 units of output, we find the firm's total loss is $64. Alternatively, comparing the total revenue of $486 (=6 × $81) with the total cost of $550 (=6 × $91.67), we see again that the firm's loss is $64.

Then why produce? Because this loss is less than the firm's $100 of fixed costs, which is the $100 loss the firm would incur in the short run by closing down. The firm receives enough revenue per unit ($81) to cover its average variable costs of $75 and also provide $6 per unit, or a total of $36, to apply against fixed costs. Therefore, the firm's loss is only $64 (=$100 − $36), not $100.

[1] Most of the unit-cost data are rounded figures from the total-cost figures presented in the previous chapter. Therefore, economic profits calculated from the unit-cost figures will typically vary by a few cents from the profits determined by subtracting actual total cost from total revenue. Here we simply ignore the few-cents differentials.

FIGURE 7.3

Short-run loss minimization for a purely competitive firm. If price P exceeds the minimum AVC (here, \$74 at $Q = 5$) but is less than ATC, the MR = MC output (here, 6 units) will permit the firm to minimize its losses. In this instance the loss is $A - P$ per unit, where A is the average total cost at 6 units of output. The total loss is shown by the red area and is equal to $6 \times (A - P)$.

(1) Total Product (Output)	(2) Average Fixed Cost (AFC)	(3) Average Variable Cost (AVC)	(4) Average Total Cost (ATC)	(5) Marginal Cost (MC)	(6) \$81 Price = Marginal Revenue (MR)	(7) Profit (+) or Loss (−), \$81 Price
0						\$−100
1	\$100.00	\$90.00	\$190.00	\$ 90	\$81	−109
2	50.00	85.00	135.00	80	81	−108
3	33.33	80.00	113.33	70	81	− 97
4	25.00	75.00	100.00	60	81	− 76
5	20.00	74.00	94.00	70	81	− 65
6	***16.67***	***75.00***	***91.67***	***80***	***81***	− ***64***
7	14.29	77.14	91.43	90	81	− 73
8	12.50	81.25	93.75	110	81	−102
9	11.11	86.67	97.78	130	81	−151
10	10.00	93.00	103.00	150	81	−220

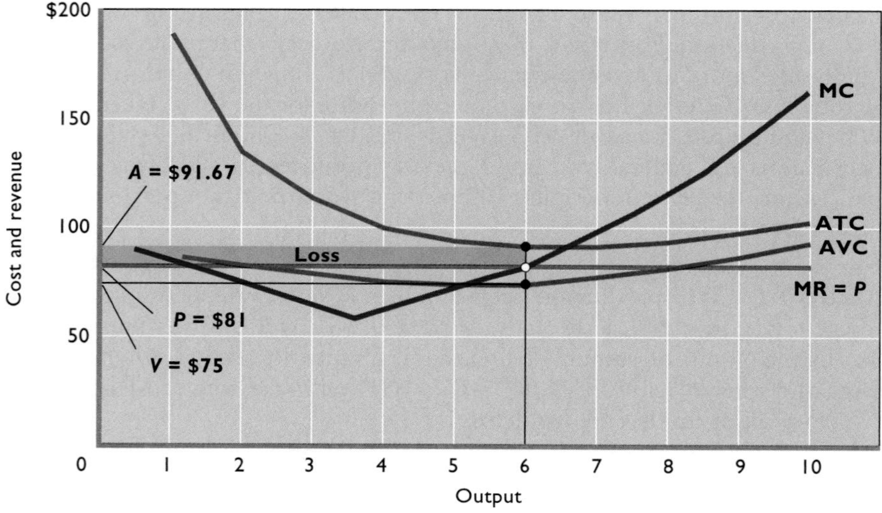

This loss-minimizing case is shown graphically in Figure 7.3. Wherever price P exceeds average variable cost AVC but is less than ATC, the firm can pay part, but not all, of its fixed costs by producing. The firm minimizes its loss by producing the output at which MC = MR (here, 6 units). At that output, each unit contributes $P - V$ to covering fixed cost, where V is the AVC at 6 units of output. The per-unit loss is $A - P = \$10.67$, and the total loss is $6 \times (A - P)$, or \$64, as shown by the red area.

Shutdown Suppose now that the market yields a price of only $71. Should the firm produce? No, because at every output the firm's average variable cost is greater than the price (compare columns 3 and 6 in the table in Figure 7.4). The smallest loss the firm can incur by producing is greater than the $100 fixed cost it will lose by shutting down (as shown by column 7). The best action is to shut down.

You can see this shutdown situation in the graph in Figure 7.4, where the MR = *P* line lies below AVC at all points. The $71 price comes closest to covering average

FIGURE 7.4

The short-run shutdown case for a purely competitive firm. If price *P* (here, $71) falls below the minimum AVC (here, $74 at Q = 5), the competitive firm will minimize its losses in the short run by shutting down. There is no level of output at which the firm can produce and realize a loss smaller than its total fixed cost.

(1) Total Product (Output)	(2) Average Fixed Cost (AFC)	(3) Average Variable Cost (AVC)	(4) Average Total Cost (ATC)	(5) Marginal Cost (MC)	(6) $71 Price = Marginal Revenue (MR)	(7) Profit (+) or Loss (−), $71 Price
0						*$−100*
				$90	$71	
1	$100.00	$90.00	$190.00			−119
				80	71	
2	50.00	85.00	135.00			−128
				70	71	
3	33.33	80.00	113.33			−127
				60	71	
4	25.00	75.00	100.00			−116
				70	71	
5	20.00	74.00	94.00			−115
				80	71	
6	16.67	75.00	91.67			−124
				90	71	
7	14.29	77.14	91.43			−143
				110	71	
8	12.50	81.25	93.75			−182
				130	71	
9	11.11	86.67	97.78			−241
				150		
10	10.00	93.00	103.00			−320

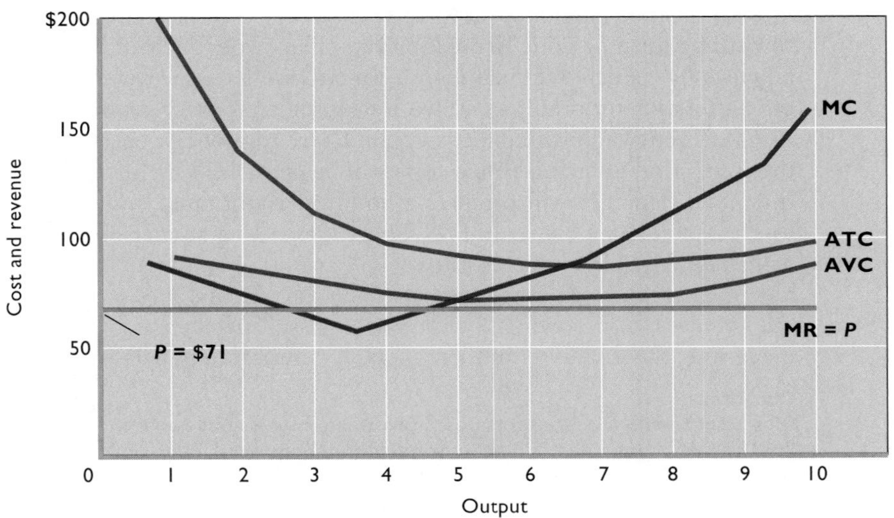

variable costs at the MR (=*P*) = MC output of 5 units. But even here, the table reveals that price or revenue per unit would fall short of average variable cost by \$3 (=\$74 − \$71). By producing at the MR (=*P*) = MC output, the firm would lose its \$100 worth of fixed cost plus \$15 (=\$3 of variable cost on each of the 5 units), for a total loss of \$115. This compares unfavorably with the \$100 fixed-cost loss the firm would incur by shutting down and producing no output. So it will make sense for the firm to shut down rather than produce at a \$71 price—or at any price less than the minimum average variable cost of \$74.

The shutdown case reminds us of the qualifier to our MR (=*P*) = MC rule. A competitive firm will maximize profit or minimize loss in the short run by producing that output at which MR (=*P*) = MC, *provided that market price exceeds minimum average variable cost.*

Applying the Analysis

The Still There Motel

Have you ever driven by a poorly maintained business facility and wondered why the owner does not either fix up the property or go out of business? The somewhat surprising reason is that it may be unprofitable to improve the facility yet profitable to continue for a time to operate the business as it deteriorates. Seeing why will aid your understanding of the "stay open or shut down" decision facing firms experiencing declining demand.

Consider the Still There Motel on Old Highway North, Anytown, USA. The owner built the motel on the basis of traffic patterns and competition existing several decades ago. But as interstate highways were built, the motel found itself located on a relatively vacant stretch of road. Also, it faced severe competition from "chain" motels located much closer to the interstate highway.

As demand and revenue fell, Still There moved from profitability to loss. But at first its room rates and annual revenue were sufficient to cover its total variable costs and contribute some to the payment of fixed costs (or $P >$ AVC; $P <$ ATC). By staying open, Still There lost less than it would have if it shut down. But since its total revenue did not cover its total costs (or $P <$ ATC), the owner realized that something must be done in the long run. The owner decided to lower average total costs by reducing annual maintenance. In effect, the owner decided to allow the motel to deteriorate as a way of regaining temporary profitability.

This renewed profitability of Still There cannot last because in time no further reduction in maintenance costs will be possible. The further deterioration of the motel structure will produce even lower room rates, and therefore even less total revenue. The owner of Still There knows that sooner or later total revenue will again fall below total cost (or *P* will again fall below ATC), even with an annual maintenance expense of zero. When that occurs, the owner will close down the business, tear down the structure, and sell the vacant property. But, in the meantime, the motel is still there—open, deteriorating, and profitable.

Question:
Why might even a well-maintained, profitable motel shut down in the long run if the land on which it is located becomes extremely valuable due to surrounding economic development?

Marginal Cost and Short-Run Supply

In the preceding section we simply selected three different prices and asked what quantity the profit-seeking competitive firm, faced with certain costs, would choose to offer in the market at each price. This set of product prices and corresponding quantities supplied constitutes part of the supply schedule for the competitive firm.

Table 7.1 summarizes the supply schedule data for those three prices ($131, $81, and $71) and four others. This table confirms the direct relationship between product price and quantity supplied that we identified in Chapter 3. Note first that the firm will not produce at price $61 or $71, because both are less than the $74 minimum AVC. Then note that quantity supplied increases as price increases. Observe finally that economic profit is higher at higher prices.

Generalized Depiction

Figure 7.5 generalizes the MR = MC rule and the relationship between short-run production costs and the firm's supply behavior. The ATC, AVC, and MC curves are shown, along with several marginal-revenue lines drawn at possible market prices. Let's observe quantity supplied at each of these prices:

- Price P_1 is below the firm's minimum average variable cost, so at this price the firm won't operate at all. Quantity supplied will be zero, as it will be at all other prices below P_2.
- Price P_2 is just equal to the minimum average variable cost. The firm will supply Q_2 units of output (where $MR_2 = MC$) and just cover its total variable cost. Its loss will equal its total fixed cost. (Actually, the firm would be indifferent as to shutting down or supplying Q_2 units of output, but we assume it produces.)
- At price P_3 the firm will supply Q_3 units of output to minimize its short-run losses. At any other price between P_2 and P_4 the firm will minimize its losses by producing and supplying the MR = MC quantity.
- The firm will just break even at price P_4. There it will supply Q_4 units of output (where $MR_4 = MC$), earning a normal profit but not an economic profit. (Recall that a normal profit is a cost and included in the cost curves.) Total revenue will just cover total cost, including a normal profit, because the revenue per unit ($MR_4 = P_4$) and the total cost per unit (ATC) are the same.

TABLE 7.1
The Supply Schedule of a Competitive Firm Confronted with the Cost Data in Figure 7.2

Price	Quantity Supplied	Maximum Profit (+) or Minimum Loss (−)
$151	10	$ +480
131	9	+299
111	8	+138
91	7	− 3
81	6	− 64
71	0	−100
61	0	−100

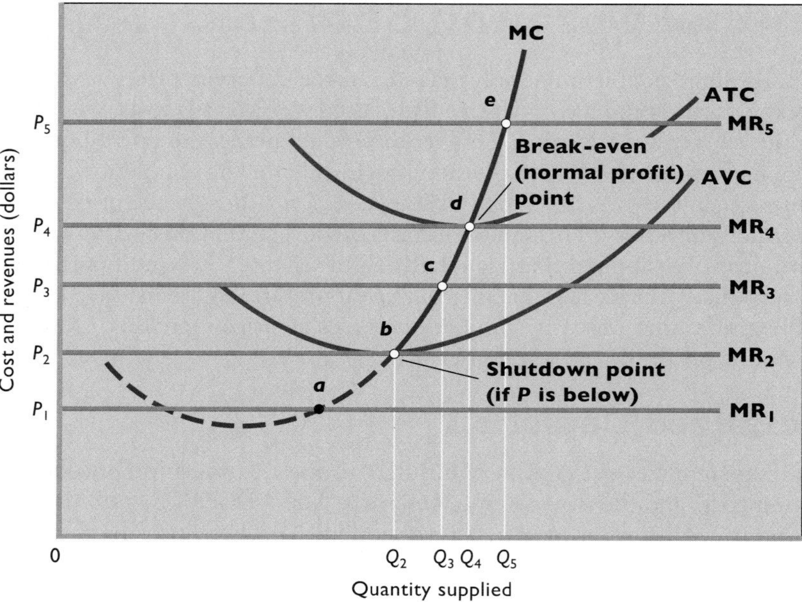

FIGURE 7.5
The P = MC rule and the competitive firm's short-run supply curve. Application of the P = MC rule, as modified by the shutdown case, reveals that the (solid) segment of the firm's MC curve that lies above AVC is the firm's short-run supply curve.

- At price P_5 the firm will realize an economic profit by producing and supplying Q_5 units of output. In fact, at any price above P_4 the firm will obtain economic profit by producing to the point where MR (=P) = MC.

Note that each of the MR (=P) = MC intersection points labeled *b*, *c*, *d* and *e* in Figure 7.5 indicates a possible product price (on the vertical axis) and the corresponding quantity that the firm would supply at that price (on the horizontal axis). Thus, points such as these are on the upsloping supply curve of the competitive firm. Note too that quantity supplied would be zero at any price below the minimum average variable cost (AVC). We can conclude that the portion of the firm's marginal-cost curve lying above its average-variable-cost curve is its short-run supply curve. In Figure 7.5, the solid segment of the marginal-cost curve MC *is* this firm's **short-run supply curve.** It tells us the amount of output the firm will supply at each price in a series of prices. It slopes upward because of the law of diminishing returns.

short-run supply curve
A curve that shows the quantity of a product a firm in a purely competitive industry will offer to sell at various prices in the short run.

Firm and Industry: Equilibrium Price

In the preceding section we developed the competitive firm's short-run supply curve by applying the MR (=P) = MC rule. We now determine which of the various possible prices will actually be the market equilibrium price.

From Chapter 3 we know that in a purely competitive market, equilibrium price is determined by total, or market, supply and total demand. To derive total supply, we must sum the supply schedules or curves of the individual competitive sellers. Columns 1 and 3 in Table 7.2 repeat the supply schedule for the individual competitive firm, as derived in Table 7.1. We now assume that there are 1000 competitive firms in this industry, all having the same total and unit costs as the single firm we discussed. This lets us calculate the market supply schedule (columns 2 and 3) by multiplying the quantity-supplied figures of the single firm (column 1) by 1000.

Market Price and Profits To determine the equilibrium price and output, we must compare these total-supply data with total-demand data. Let's assume that total

TABLE 7.2
Firm and Market Supply and Market Demand

(1) Quantity Supplied, Single Firm	(2) Total Quantity Supplied, 1000 Firms	(3) Product Price	(4) Total Quantity Demanded
10	10,000	$151	4,000
9	9,000	131	6,000
8	***8,000***	***111***	***8,000***
7	7,000	91	9,000
6	6,000	81	11,000
0	0	71	13,000
0	0	61	16,000

demand is as shown in columns 3 and 4 in Table 7.2. By comparing the total quantity supplied and the total quantity demanded at the seven possible prices, we determine that the equilibrium price is $111 and the equilibrium quantity is 8000 units for the industry—8 units for each of the 1000 identical firms.

Will these conditions of market supply and demand make this a profitable or unprofitable industry? Multiplying product price ($111) by output (8 units), we find that the total revenue of each firm is $888. The total cost is $750, found by looking at column 4 in the table in Figure 6.3. The $138 difference is the economic profit of each firm. For the industry, total economic profit is $138,000. This, then, is a profitable industry.

Another way of calculating economic profit is to determine per-unit profit by subtracting average total cost ($93.75) from product price ($111) and multiplying the difference (per-unit profit of $17.25) by the firm's equilibrium level of output (8). Again we obtain an economic profit of $138 per firm and $138,000 for the industry.

Figure 7.6 shows this analysis graphically. The individual supply curves of each of the 1000 identical firms—one of which is shown as s = MC in Figure 7.6a—are summed horizontally to get the total-supply curve S = ΣMC's of Figure 7.6b. With total-demand curve D, it yields the equilibrium price $111 and equilibrium quantity (for the industry) 8000 units. This equilibrium price is given and unalterable to the individual firm; that is, each firm's demand curve is perfectly elastic at the equilibrium price, as indicated by d in Figure 7.6a. Because the individual firm is a price taker, the marginal-revenue curve coincides with the firm's demand curve d. This $111 price exceeds the average total cost at the firm's equilibrium MR = MC output of 8 units, so the firm earns an economic profit represented by the gray area in Figure 7.6a.

Assuming no changes in costs or market demand, these diagrams reveal a genuine equilibrium in the short run. There are no shortages or surpluses in the market to cause price or total quantity to change. Nor can any firm in the industry increase its profit by altering its output. Note, however, that weaker market demand or stronger market supply (and therefore lower prices) could shift the line d downward and change the situation to losses ($P <$ ATC) or even to shutdown ($P <$ AVC).

Firm versus Industry Figure 7.6 underscores a point made earlier: Product price is a given fact to the individual competitive firm, but the supply plans of all competitive producers as a group are a basic determinant of product price. There is no inconsistency here. One firm, supplying a negligible fraction of total supply, cannot affect price. But the sum of the supply curves of all the firms in the industry constitutes

FIGURE 7.6
Short-run competitive equilibrium for (a) a firm and (b) the industry. The horizontal sum of the 1000 firms' individual supply curves (*s*) determines the industry (market) supply curve (*S*). Given industry (market) demand (*D*), the short-run equilibrium price and output for the industry are $111 and 8000 units. Taking the equilibrium price as given, the individual firm establishes its profit-maximizing output at 8 units and, in this case, realizes the economic profit represented by the gray area.

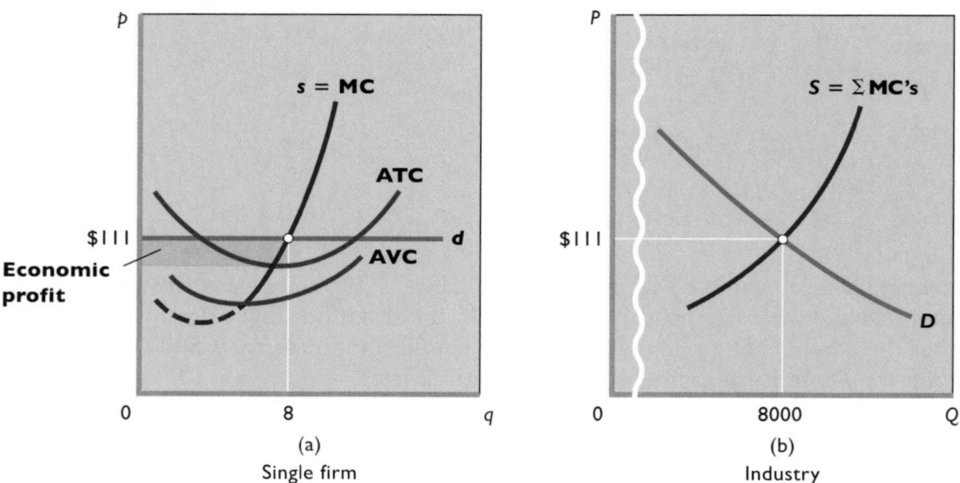

the market supply curve, and that curve (along with demand) does have an important bearing on equilibrium price.

Profit Maximization in the Long Run

In the short run the industry is composed of a specific number of firms, each with a fixed, unalterable plant. Firms may shut down in the sense that they can produce zero units of output in the short run, but they do not have sufficient time to liquidate their assets and go out of business. By contrast, in the long run firms already in an industry have sufficient time either to expand or to contract their plant capacities. More important, the number of firms in the industry may either increase or decrease as new firms enter or existing firms leave. We now examine how these long-run adjustments modify our conclusions concerning short-run output and price determination.

Assumptions

We make three simplifying assumptions, none of which alters our conclusions:

- ***Entry and exit only*** The only long-run adjustment is the entry or exit of firms. Moreover, we ignore all short-run adjustments in order to concentrate on the effects of the long-run adjustments.
- ***Identical costs*** All firms in the industry have identical cost curves. This assumption lets us discuss an "average," or "representative," firm, knowing that all other firms in the industry are similarly affected by any long-run adjustments that occur.
- ***Constant-cost industry*** The industry is a constant-cost industry. This means that the entry and exit of firms does not affect resource prices or, consequently, the locations of the average-total-cost curves of individual firms.

Goal of Our Analysis

The basic conclusion we seek to explain is this: After all long-run adjustments are completed, product price will be exactly equal to, and production will occur at, each firm's minimum average total cost.

This conclusion follows from two basic facts: (1) Firms seek profits and shun losses, and (2) under pure competition, firms are free to enter and leave an industry. If market price initially exceeds average total costs, the resulting economic profits will attract new firms to the industry. But this industry expansion will increase supply until price is brought back down to equality with minimum average total cost. Conversely, if price is initially less than average total cost, resulting losses will cause firms to leave the industry. As they leave, total supply will decline, bringing the price back up to equality with minimum average total cost.

Long-Run Equilibrium

Consider the average firm in a purely competitive industry that is initially in long-run equilibrium. This firm is represented in Figure 7.7a, where MR = MC and price and minimum average total cost are equal at $50. Economic profit here is zero; the industry is in equilibrium or "at rest" because there is no tendency for firms to enter or to leave. The existing firms are earning normal profits, which, recall, are included in their cost curves. The $50 market price is determined in Figure 7.7b by market or industry demand D_1 and supply S_1. (S_1 is a short-run supply curve; we will develop the long-run industry supply curve in our discussion.)

As shown on the quantity axes of the two graphs, equilibrium output in the industry is 100,000 while equilibrium output for the single firm is 100. If all firms in the industry are identical, there must be 1000 firms (=100,000/100).

FIGURE 7.7
Temporary profits and the reestablishment of long-run equilibrium in (a) a representative firm and (b) the industry. A favorable shift in demand (D_1 to D_2) will upset the original industry equilibrium and produce economic profits. But those profits will cause new firms to enter the industry, increasing supply (S_1 to S_2) and lowering product price until economic profits are once again zero.

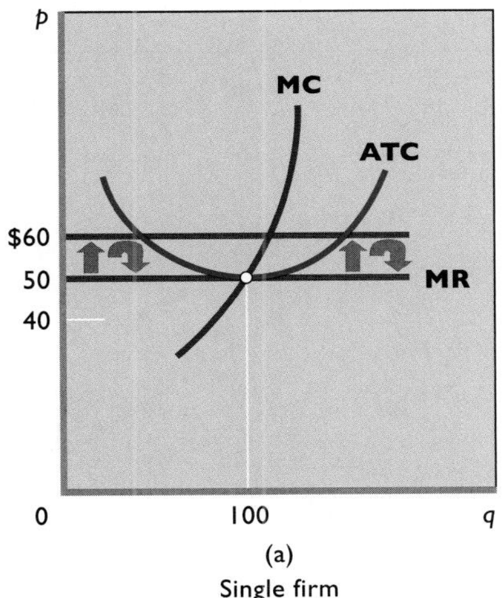

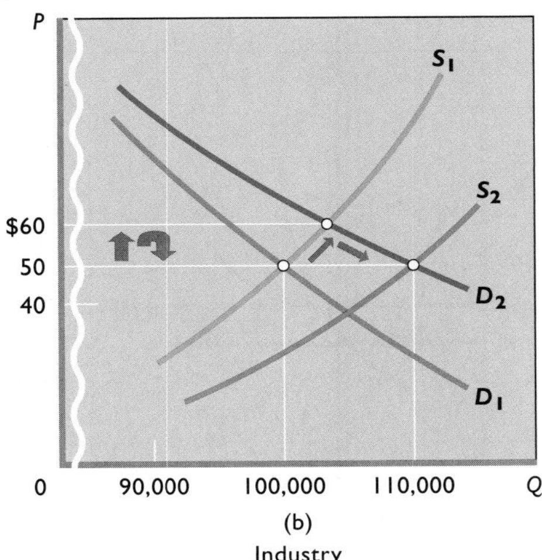

Entry Eliminates Economic Profits Let's upset the long-run equilibrium in Figure 7.7 and see what happens. Suppose a change in consumer tastes increases product demand from D_1 to D_2. Price will rise to \$60, as determined at the intersection of D_2 and S_1, and the firm's marginal-revenue curve will shift upward to \$60. This \$60 price exceeds the firm's average total cost of \$50 at output 100, creating an economic profit of \$10 per unit. This economic profit will lure new firms into the industry. Some entrants will be newly created firms; others will shift from less prosperous industries.

As firms enter, the market supply of the product increases and the product price falls below \$60. Economic profits persist, and entry continues until short-run supply increases to S_2. Market price falls to \$50, as does marginal revenue for the firm. Price and minimum average total cost are again equal at \$50. The economic profits caused by the boost in demand have been eliminated, and, as a result, the previous incentive for more firms to enter the industry has disappeared. Long-run equilibrium has been restored.

Observe in Figure 7.7a and 7.7b that total quantity supplied is now 110,000 units and each firm is producing 100 units. Now 1100 firms rather than the original 1000 populate the industry. Economic profits have attracted 100 more firms.

Exit Eliminates Losses Now let's consider a shift in the opposite direction. We begin in Figure 7.8b with curves S_1 and D_1 setting the same initial long-run equilibrium situation as in our previous analysis, including the \$50 price.

Suppose consumer demand declines from D_1 to D_3. This forces the market price and marginal revenue down to \$40, making production unprofitable at the minimum ATC of \$50. In time the resulting losses will induce firms to leave the industry. Their owners will seek a normal profit elsewhere rather than accept the below-normal profits (loss) now confronting them. And as capital equipment wears out, some firms will simply go out of business. As this exodus of firms proceeds, however, industry supply decreases, pushing the price up from \$40 toward \$50. Losses continue and more firms

FIGURE 7.8

Temporary losses and the reestablishment of long-run equilibrium in (a) a representative firm and (b) the industry. An unfavorable shift in demand (D_1 to D_3) will upset the original industry equilibrium and produce losses. But those losses will cause firms to leave the industry, decreasing supply (S_1 to S_3) and increasing product price until all losses have disappeared.

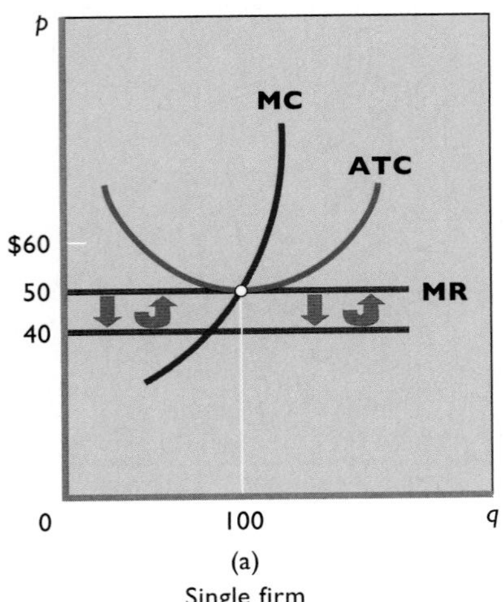

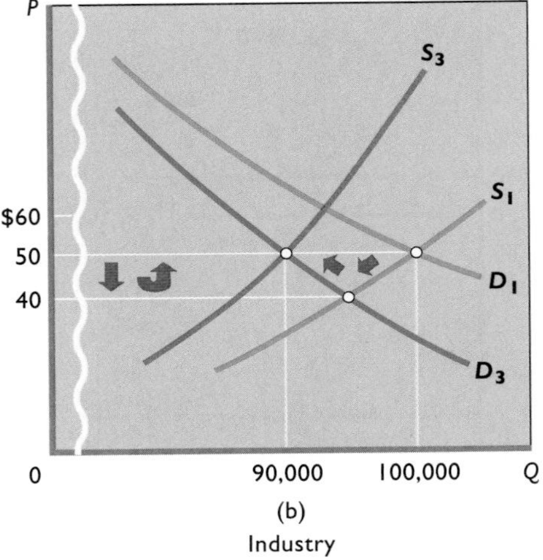

leave the industry until the supply curve shifts to S_3. Once this happens, price is again \$50, just equal to the minimum average total cost. Losses have been eliminated and long-run equilibrium is restored.

In Figure 7.8a and 7.8b, total quantity supplied is now 90,000 units and each firm is producing 100 units. Only 900 firms, not the original 1000, populate the industry. Losses have forced 100 firms out.

You may have noted that we have sidestepped the question of which firms will leave the industry when losses occur by assuming that all firms have identical cost curves. In the "real world," of course, entrepreneurial talents differ. Even if resource prices and technology are the same for all firms, inferior entrepreneurs tend to incur higher costs and therefore are the first to leave an industry when demand declines. Similarly, firms with less productive labor forces will be higher-cost producers and likely candidates to quit an industry when demand decreases.

Applying the Analysis

The Exit of Farmers from U.S. Agriculture

The U.S. agricultural industry serves as a good example of how losses resulting from declining prices received by individual producers create an exit of producers from an industry.

A rapid rate of technological advance has significantly increased the *supply* of U.S. agricultural products over time. This technological progress has many roots: the mechanization of farms, improved techniques of land management, soil conservation, irrigation, development of hybrid crops, availability of improved fertilizers and insecticides, polymer-coated seeds, and improvements in the breeding and care of livestock. In 1950 each farmworker produced enough food and fiber to support about a dozen people. By 2005 that figure had increased to more than 100 people!

Increases in *demand* for agricultural products, however, have failed to keep pace with technologically created increases in the supply of the products. The demand for farm products in the United States is *income-inelastic*. Estimates indicate that a 10 percent increase in real per capita after-tax income produces about a 2 percent increase in consumption of farm products. Once consumers' stomachs are filled, they turn to the amenities of life that manufacturing and services, not agriculture, provide. So, as the incomes of Americans rise, the demand for farm products increases far less rapidly than the demand for products in general.

The consequences of the long-run supply and demand conditions just outlined have been those predicted by the long-run pure-competition model. Financial losses in agriculture have triggered a large decline in the number of farms and a massive exit of workers to other sectors of the economy. In 1950 there were 5400 farms in the United States employing 10 million people. Today there are 2200 farms employing 3 million people. Since 1950, farm employment has declined from 17 percent of the U.S. work force to just 2 percent. Moreover, the exodus of farmers would have been even larger in the absence of government subsidies that have enabled many farmers to remain in agriculture. Such subsidies were traditionally in the form of government price supports (price floors) but have more recently evolved to direct subsidy payments to farmers. Such payments have averaged more than \$20 billion annually over the last decade.

Question:
Why is the exit of farmers from U.S. agriculture bad for the farmers who must leave but good for the farmers who remain?

Long-Run Supply for a Constant-Cost Industry

long-run supply curve
A curve that shows the prices at which a purely competitive industry will make various quantities of the product available in the long run.

constant-cost industry
An industry in which the entry of new firms has no effect on resource prices and thus no effect on production costs.

We have established that changes in market supply through entry and exit create a long-run equilibrium in purely competitive markets. Although our analysis has dealt with the long run, we have noted that the market supply curves in Figures 7.7b and 7.8b are short-run curves. What then is the character of the **long-run supply curve** of a competitive industry? The analysis points us toward an answer. The crucial factor here is the effect, if any, that changes in the number of firms in the industry will have on costs of the individual firms in the industry.

In our discussion of long-run competitive equilibrium we assumed that the industry under discussion was a **constant-cost industry.** This means that industry expansion or contraction will not affect resource prices and therefore production costs. Graphically, it means that the entry or exit of firms does not shift the long-run ATC curves of individual firms. This is the case when the industry's demand for resources is small in relation to the total demand for those resources. Then the industry can expand or contract without significantly affecting resource prices and costs.

What does the long-run supply curve of a constant-cost industry look like? The answer is contained in our previous analysis. There we saw that the entry and exit of firms changes industry output but always brings the product price back to its original level, where it is just equal to the constant minimum ATC. Specifically, we discovered that the industry would supply 90,000, 100,000, or 110,000 units of output, all at a price of $50 per unit. In other words, the long-run supply curve of a constant-cost industry is perfectly elastic.

Figure 7.9a demonstrates this graphically. Suppose industry demand is originally D_1, industry output is Q_1 (100,000 units), and product price is P_1 ($50). This situation, from Figure 7.7, is one of long-run equilibrium. We saw that when demand increases

FIGURE 7.9
Long-run supply: constant-cost industry versus increasing-cost industry. (a) In a constant-cost industry, the entry of firms does not affect resource prices or, therefore, unit costs. So an increase in demand (D_1 to D_2) or a decrease in demand (D_1 to D_3) causes a change in industry output (Q_1 to Q_2 or Q_1 to Q_3) but no alteration in price ($50). This means that the long-run industry supply curve (S) is horizontal through points Z_3, Z_1, and Z_2. (b) In an increasing-cost industry, the entry of new firms in response to an increase in demand (D_3 to D_1 to D_2) will bid up resource prices and thereby increase unit costs. As a result, an increased industry output (Q_3 to Q_1 to Q_2) will be forthcoming only at higher prices ($45 to $50 to $55). The long-run industry supply curve (S) therefore slopes upward through points Y_3, Y_1, and Y_2.

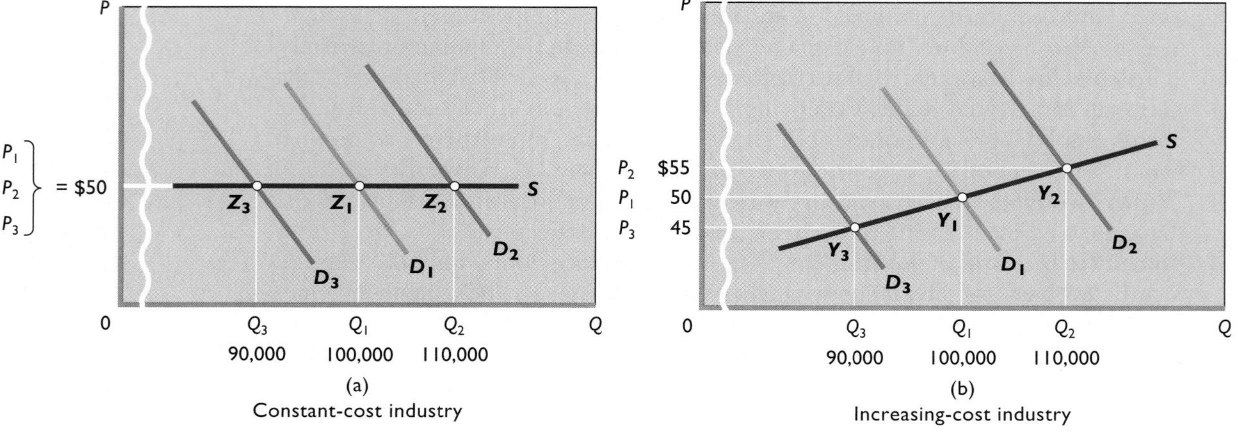

to D_2, upsetting this equilibrium, the resulting economic profits attract new firms. Because this is a constant-cost industry, entry continues and industry output expands until the price is driven back down to the level of the unchanged minimum ATC. This is at price P_2 (\$50) and output Q_2 (110,000).

From Figure 7.8, we saw that a decline in market demand from D_1 to D_3 causes an exit of firms and ultimately restores equilibrium at price P_3 (\$50) and output Q_3 (90,000 units). The points Z_1, Z_2, and Z_3 in Figure 7.9a represent these three price-quantity combinations. A line or curve connecting all such points shows the various price-quantity combinations that firms would produce if they had enough time to make all desired adjustments to changes in demand. This line or curve is the industry's long-run supply curve. In a constant-cost industry this curve (straight line) is horizontal, as in Figure 7.9a, thus representing perfectly elastic supply.

Long-Run Supply for an Increasing-Cost Industry

Constant-cost industries are a special case. Most industries are **increasing-cost industries,** in which firms' ATC curves shift upward as the industry expands and downward as the industry contracts. The construction industry and medical care industries are examples.

increasing-cost industry
An industry in which the entry of new firms raises the prices for resources and thus increases their production costs.

Usually, the entry of new firms will increase resource prices, particularly in industries using specialized resources whose supplies are not readily increased in response to an increase in resource demand. Higher resource prices result in higher long-run average total costs for all firms in the industry. These higher costs cause upward shifts in each firm's long-run ATC curve.

Thus, when an increase in product demand results in economic profits and attracts new firms to an increasing-cost industry, a two-way squeeze works to eliminate those profits. As before, the entry of new firms increases market supply and lowers the market price. But now the entire ATC curve shifts upward. The overall result is a higher-than-original equilibrium price. The industry produces a larger output at a higher product price because the industry expansion has increased resource prices and the minimum average total cost. We know that, in the long run, the product price must cover ATC.

Since greater output will be supplied at a higher price, the long-run industry supply curve is upsloping. Instead of supplying 90,000, 100,000, or 110,000 units at the same price of \$50, an increasing-cost industry might supply 90,000 units at \$45, 100,000 units at \$50, and 110,000 units at \$55. A higher price is required to induce more production, because costs per unit of output increase as production increases.

We show this in Figure 7.9b. Original market demand is D_1 and industry price and output are P_1 (\$50) and Q_1 (100,000 units), respectively, at equilibrium point Y_1. An increase in demand to D_2 upsets this equilibrium and leads to economic profits. New firms enter the industry, increasing both market supply and production costs of individual firms. A new price is established at point Y_2, where P_2 is \$55 and Q_2 is 110,000 units.

Conversely, a decline in demand from D_1 to D_3 makes production unprofitable and causes firms to leave the industry. The resulting decline in resource prices reduces the minimum average total cost of production for firms that stay. A new equilibrium price is established at some level below the original price, say, at point Y_3, where P_3 is \$45 and Q_3 is 90,000 units. Connecting these three equilibrium positions, we derive the upsloping long-run supply curve S in Figure 7.9b.

Long-Run Supply for a Decreasing-Cost Industry

decreasing-cost industry
An industry in which the entry of new firms lowers the prices of resources and thus decreases production costs.

In **decreasing-cost industries,** firms experience lower costs as the industry expands. The personal computer industry is an example. As demand for personal computers increased, new manufacturers of computers entered the industry and greatly increased the resource demand for the components used to build them (for example, memory chips, hard drives, monitors, and operating software). The expanded production of the components enabled the producers of those items to achieve substantial economies of scale. The decreased production costs of the components reduced their prices, which greatly lowered the computer manufacturers' average costs of production. The supply of personal computers increased by more than demand, and the price of personal computers declined. Although not shown in Figure 7.9, the long-run supply curve of a decreasing-cost industry is *downsloping*.

© Craig Aurness/CORBIS

Courtesy of Hewlett-Packard Company.

Photo Op Increasing-Cost versus Decreasing-Cost Industries

Mining is an example of an increasing-cost industry, whereas electronic goods is an example of a decreasing-cost industry.

Pure Competition and Efficiency

Our final goal in this chapter is to examine the efficiency aspects of pure competition. Whether a purely competitive industry is a constant-cost industry or an increasing-cost industry, the final long-run equilibrium positions of all firms have the same basic efficiency characteristics. As shown in Figure 7.10, price (and marginal revenue) will settle where it is equal to minimum average total cost: *P* (and MR) = minimum ATC. Moreover, since the marginal-cost curve intersects the average-total-cost curve at its minimum point, marginal cost and average total cost are equal: MC = minimum ATC. So in long-run equilibrium a multiple equality occurs: *P* (and MR) = MC = minimum ATC.

FIGURE 7.10
Long-run equilibrium of a competitive firm. The equality of price (*P*), marginal cost (MC), and minimum average total cost (ATC) indicates that the firm is achieving productive efficiency and allocative efficiency. It is using the most efficient technology, charging the lowest price, and producing the greatest output consistent with its costs. It is receiving only a normal profit, which is incorporated into the ATC curve. The equality of price and marginal cost indicates that society is allocating its scarce resources on the basis of consumer preferences.

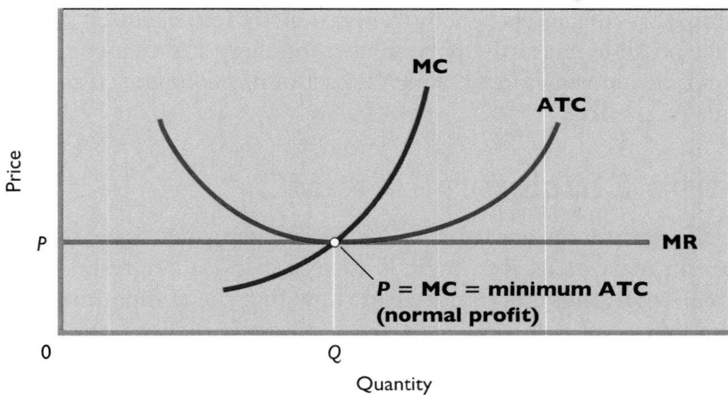

This triple equality tells us that although a competitive firm may realize economic profit or loss in the short run, it will earn only a normal profit by producing in accordance with the MR (=*P*) = MC rule in the long run. Also, this triple equality suggests certain conclusions of great social significance concerning the efficiency of a purely competitive economy.

Economists agree that, subject to Chapter 5's qualifications relating to public goods and externalities, an idealized purely competitive economy leads to an efficient use of society's scarce resources. A competitive market economy uses the limited amounts of resources available to society in a way that maximizes the satisfaction of consumers. As discussed in Chapter 5, efficient use of limited resources requires both productive efficiency and allocative efficiency.

Productive efficiency requires that goods be produced in the least costly way. Allocative efficiency requires that resources be apportioned among firms and industries so as to yield the mix of products and services that is most wanted by society (least-cost production assumed). Allocative efficiency has been realized when it is impossible to alter the combination of goods produced and achieve a net gain for society. Let's look at how productive and allocative efficiency would be achieved under purely competitive conditions.

Productive Efficiency: *P* = Minimum ATC

In the long run, pure competition forces firms to produce at the minimum average total cost of production and to charge a price that is just consistent with that cost. That is a highly favorable situation from the consumer's point of view. It means that unless firms use the best-available (least-cost) production methods and combinations of inputs, they will not survive. Stated differently, it means that the minimum amount of resources will be used to produce any particular output. Let's suppose that output in Figure 7.10 is cucumbers.

In the final equilibrium position shown in Figure 7.10, suppose each firm in the cucumber industry is producing 100 units (say, pickup truckloads) of output by using \$5000 (equal to average total cost of \$50 × 100 units) worth of resources. If one firm produced that same output at a total cost of, say, \$7000, its resources would be used inefficiently. Society would be faced with a net loss of \$2000 worth of alternative products. But this cannot happen in pure competition; this firm would incur a loss of \$2000, requiring it either to reduce its costs or go out of business.

Note, too, that consumers benefit from productive efficiency by paying the lowest product price possible under the prevailing technology and cost conditions. And the firm receives only a normal profit, which is part of its economic costs and thus incorporated in its ATC curve.

Allocative Efficiency: *P* = MC

Productive efficiency alone does not ensure the efficient allocation of resources. Least-cost production must be used to provide society with the "right goods"—the goods that consumers want most. Before we can show that the competitive market system does just that, we must discuss the social meaning of product prices. There are two critical elements here:

- The money price of any product is society's measure of the relative worth of an additional unit of that product—for example, cucumbers. So the price of a unit of cucumbers is the marginal benefit derived from that unit of the product.
- Similarly, recalling the idea of opportunity cost, we see that the marginal cost of an additional unit of a product measures the value, or relative worth, of the other goods sacrificed to obtain it. In producing cucumbers, resources are drawn away from producing other goods. The marginal cost of producing a unit of cucumbers measures society's sacrifice of those other products.

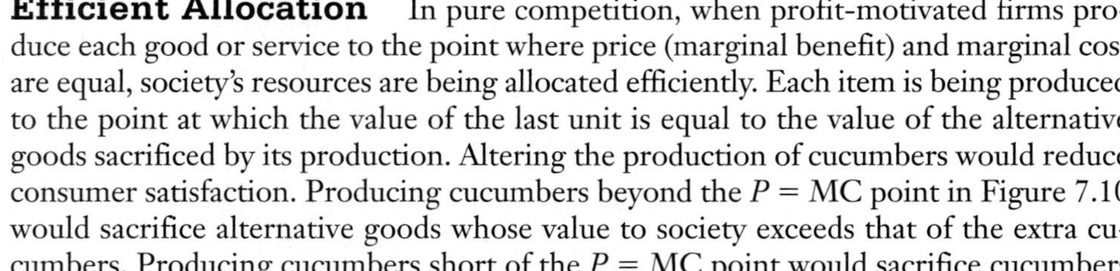

7.1 Allocative efficiency

Efficient Allocation In pure competition, when profit-motivated firms produce each good or service to the point where price (marginal benefit) and marginal cost are equal, society's resources are being allocated efficiently. Each item is being produced to the point at which the value of the last unit is equal to the value of the alternative goods sacrificed by its production. Altering the production of cucumbers would reduce consumer satisfaction. Producing cucumbers beyond the *P* = MC point in Figure 7.10 would sacrifice alternative goods whose value to society exceeds that of the extra cucumbers. Producing cucumbers short of the *P* = MC point would sacrifice cucumbers that society values more than the alternative goods its resources could produce.

Dynamic Adjustments A further attribute of purely competitive markets is their ability to restore efficiency when disrupted by changes in the economy. A change in consumer tastes, resource supplies, or technology will automatically set in motion the appropriate realignments of resources. For example, suppose that cucumbers and pickles become dramatically more popular. First, the price of cucumbers will increase, and so, at current output, the price of cucumbers will exceed their marginal cost. At this point efficiency will be lost, but the higher price will create economic profits in the cucumber industry and stimulate its expansion. The profitability of cucumbers will permit the industry to bid resources away from now less pressing uses, say, watermelons. Expansion of the industry will end only when the price of cucumbers and their marginal cost are equal—that is, when allocative efficiency has been restored.

Similarly, a change in the supply of a particular resource—for example, the field laborers who pick cucumbers—or in a production technique will upset an existing price–marginal-cost equality by either raising or lowering marginal cost. The resulting inequality will cause business managers, in either pursuing profit or avoiding loss, to reallocate resources until price once again equals marginal cost. In so doing, they will correct any inefficiency in the allocation of resources that the original change may have temporarily imposed on the economy.

"Invisible Hand" Revisited Finally, the highly efficient allocation of resources that a purely competitive economy promotes comes about because businesses and resource suppliers seek to further their self-interest. For private goods with no externalities (Chapter 5), the "invisible hand" (Chapter 2) is at work. The competitive system not only maximizes profits for individual producers but also, at the same time, creates a pattern of resource allocation that maximizes consumer satisfaction. The invisible hand thus organizes the private interests of producers in a way that is fully in sync with society's interest in using scarce resources efficiently. Striving for profit (and avoiding losses) produces highly desirable economic outcomes.

Summary

1. Economists group industries into four models based on their market structures: (a) pure competition, (b) monopolistic competition, (c) oligopoly, and (d) pure monopoly.
2. A purely competitive industry consists of a large number of independent firms producing a standardized product. Pure competition assumes that firms and resources are mobile among different industries.
3. In a competitive industry, no single firm can influence market price. This means that the firm's demand curve is perfectly elastic and price equals both marginal revenue and average revenue.
4. Provided price exceeds minimum average variable cost, a competitive firm maximizes profit or minimizes loss in the short run by producing the output at which price or marginal revenue equals marginal cost. If price is less than average variable cost, the firm minimizes its loss by shutting down. If price is greater than average variable cost but is less than average total cost, the firm minimizes its loss by producing the MR $(=P)$ = MC output. If price also exceeds average total cost, the firm maximizes its economic profit at the MR $(=P)$ = MC output.
5. Applying the MR $(=P)$ = MC rule at various possible market prices leads to the conclusion that the segment of the firm's short-run marginal-cost curve that lies above the firm's average-variable-cost curve is its short-run supply curve.
6. In the long run, the market price of a product will equal the minimum average total cost of production. At a higher price, economic profits would entice firms to enter the industry until those profits had been competed away. At a lower price, losses would force firms to exit the industry until the product price rose to equal average total cost.
7. The long-run supply curve is horizontal for a constant-cost industry, upsloping for an increasing-cost industry, and downsloping for a decreasing-cost industry.
8. The long-run equality of price and minimum average total cost means that competitive firms will use the most efficient known technology and charge the lowest price consistent with their production costs. It also means that the firm receives only a normal profit (which is one of its economic costs).

CHAPTER EIGHT

Pure Monopoly

In this chapter you will learn:

- The characteristics of pure monopoly.
- How a pure monopoly sets its profit-maximizing output and price.
- The economic effects of monopoly.
- Why a monopolist might prefer to charge different prices in different markets.
- The antitrust laws that are used to deal with monopoly.

We turn now from pure competition to pure monopoly (a single seller). You deal with monopolies—or near-monopolies—more often than you might think. This happens when you see the Microsoft Windows logo after you turn on your computer and when you swallow a prescription drug that is under patent. Depending on where you live, you may be patronizing a local or regional monopoly when you make a local telephone call, turn on your lights, or subscribe to cable TV.

What precisely do we mean by "pure monopoly," and what conditions enable it to arise and survive? How does a pure monopolist determine what price to charge? Does a pure monopolist achieve the efficiency associated with pure competition? If not, what should the government try to do about it? A model of pure monopoly will help us answer these questions.

An Introduction to Pure Monopoly

Pure monopoly exists when a single firm is the sole producer of a product for which there are no close substitutes. Here are the main characteristics of **pure monopoly:**

pure monopoly
An industry in which one firm is the sole producer or seller of a product or service for which there are no close substitutes.

- ***Single seller*** A pure, or absolute, monopoly is an industry in which a single firm is the sole producer of a specific good or the sole supplier of a service; the firm and the industry are synonymous.
- ***No close substitutes*** A pure monopoly's product is unique in that there are no close substitutes. The consumer who chooses not to buy the monopolized product must do without it.
- ***Price maker*** The pure monopolist controls the total quantity supplied and thus has considerable control over price; it is a *price maker.* (Unlike a pure competitor, which has no such control and therefore is a *price taker.*) The pure monopolist confronts the usual downward-sloping product demand curve. It can change its product price by changing the quantity of the product it supplies. The monopolist will use this power whenever it is advantageous to do so.
- ***Blocked entry*** A pure monopolist faces no immediate competition because certain barriers keep potential competitors from entering the industry. Those barriers may be economic, technological, legal, or of some other type. But entry is totally blocked in pure monopoly.

8.1
Monopoly

Examples of *pure* monopoly are relatively rare, but there are excellent examples of less pure forms. In many cities, government-owned or government-regulated public utilities—natural gas and electric companies, the water company, the cable TV company, and the local telephone company—are all monopolies or virtually so.

There are also many "near-monopolies" in which a single firm has the bulk of sales in a specific market. Intel, for example, provides 80 percent of the central microprocessors used in personal computers. First Data Corporation, via its Western Union subsidiary, accounts for 80 percent of the market for money order transfers. Brannock Device Company has an 80 percent market share of the shoe sizing devices found in shoe stores. Wham-O, through its Frisbee brand, sells 90 percent of plastic throwing disks. The De Beers diamond syndicate effectively controls 55 percent of the world's supply of rough-cut diamonds.

Professional sports teams are, in a sense, monopolies because they are the sole suppliers of specific services in large geographic areas. With a few exceptions, a single major-league team in each sport serves each large American city. If you want to see a live major-league baseball game in St. Louis or Seattle, you must patronize the Cardinals or the Mariners, respectively. Other geographic monopolies exist. For example, a small town may be served by only one airline or railroad. In a small, extremely isolated community, the local bank, movie theater, or grocery store may approximate a monopoly.

Of course, there is almost always some competition. Satellite television is a substitute for cable, and amateur softball is a substitute for professional baseball. The Linux operating system can substitute for Windows, and so on. But such substitutes are typically in some way less appealing.

Barriers to Entry

barriers to entry Any conditions that prevent the entry of firms into an industry.

The factors that prohibit firms from entering an industry are called **barriers to entry.** In pure monopoly, strong barriers to entry effectively block all potential competition. Somewhat weaker barriers may permit *oligopoly*, a market structure dominated by a few firms. Still weaker barriers may permit the entry of a fairly large number of competing firms, giving rise to *monopolistic competition*. And the absence of any effective entry barriers permits the entry of a very large number of firms, which provide the basis of pure competition. So barriers to entry are pertinent not only to the extreme case of pure monopoly but also to other market structures in which there is some degree of monopoly-like conditions and behavior.

Economies of Scale

Modern technology in some industries is such that economies of scale—declining average total cost with added firm size—are extensive. So a firm's long-run average-cost schedule will decline over a wide range of output. Given market demand, only a few large firms or, in the extreme, only a single large firm can achieve low average total costs.

If a pure monopoly exists in such an industry, economies of scale will serve as an entry barrier and will protect the monopolist from competition. New firms that try to enter the industry as small-scale producers cannot realize the cost economies of the monopolist and therefore cannot obtain the normal profits necessary for survival or growth. A new firm might try to start out big, that is, to enter the industry as a large-scale producer so as to achieve the necessary economies of scale. But the massive plant facilities required would necessitate huge amounts of financing, which a new and untried enterprise would find difficult to secure. In most cases the financial obstacles and risks to "starting big" are prohibitive. This explains why efforts to enter such industries as automobiles, computer operating software, commercial aircraft, and basic steel are so rare.

8.2 Minimum efficient scale

natural monopoly An industry in which economies of scale are so great that only a single firm can achieve minimum efficient scale.

In the extreme circumstance, in which the market demand curve cuts the long-run ATC curve where average total costs are still declining, the single firm is called a **natural monopoly.** It might seem that a natural monopolist's lower unit cost would enable it to charge a lower price than if the industry were more competitive. But that won't necessarily happen. A pure monopolist may, instead, set its price far above ATC and obtain substantial economic profit. In that event, the lowest-unit-cost advantage of a natural monopolist would accrue to the monopolist as profit and not as lower prices to consumers.

Legal Barriers to Entry: Patents and Licenses

Government also creates legal barriers to entry by awarding patents and licenses.

Patents A *patent* is the exclusive right of an inventor to use, or to allow another to use, her or his invention. Patents and patent laws aim to protect the inventor from rivals who would use the invention without having shared in the effort and expense of developing it. At the same time, patents provide the inventor with a monopoly position for the life of the patent. The world's nations have agreed on a uniform patent length of 20 years from the time of application. Patents have figured prominently in the growth of modern-day giants such as IBM, Merck, Kodak, Xerox, Polaroid, General Electric, and DuPont.

Research and development (R&D) is what leads to most patentable inventions and products. Firms that gain monopoly power through their own research or by purchasing the patents of others can use patents to strengthen their market position. The profit from one patent can finance the research required to develop new patentable products. In the pharmaceutical industry, patents on prescription drugs have produced large monopoly profits that have helped finance the discovery of new patentable medicines. So monopoly power achieved through patents may well be self-sustaining, even though patents eventually expire and generic drugs then compete with the original brand.

Licenses Government may also limit entry into an industry or occupation through *licensing*. At the national level, the Federal Communications Commission licenses only so many radio and television stations in each geographic area. In many large cities one of a limited number of municipal licenses is required to drive a taxicab. The consequent restriction of the supply of cabs creates economic profit for cab owners and drivers. New cabs cannot enter the industry to drive down prices and profits. In a few instances the government might "license" itself to provide some product and thereby create a public monopoly. For example, in some states only state-owned retail outlets can sell liquor. Similarly, many states have "licensed" themselves to run lotteries.

Ownership or Control of Essential Resources

A monopolist can use private property as an obstacle to potential rivals. For example, a firm that owns or controls a resource essential to the production process can prohibit the entry of rival firms. At one time the International Nickel Company of Canada (now called Inco) controlled a large percentage of the world's known nickel reserves. A local firm may own all the nearby deposits of sand and gravel. And it is very difficult for new sports leagues to be created because existing professional sports leagues have contracts with the best players and have long-term leases on the major stadiums and arenas.

Pricing and Other Strategic Barriers to Entry

Even if a firm is not protected from entry by, say, extensive economies of scale or ownership of essential resources, entry may effectively be blocked by the way the monopolist responds to attempts by rivals to enter the industry. Confronted with a new entrant, the monopolist may "create an entry barrier" by slashing its price, stepping up its advertising, or taking other strategic actions to make it difficult for the entrant to succeed.

Examples: In 1999 the U.S. Justice Department accused Dentsply, the dominant American maker of false teeth (75 percent market share) of unlawfully precluding independent distributors of false teeth from carrying competing brands. The lack of access to the distributors allegedly deterred potential foreign competitors from entering the U.S. market. In early 2005, this case was still pending in the courts. As another example, in 2001 a U.S. court of appeals upheld a lower court's finding that Microsoft used a series of illegal actions to maintain its monopoly in Intel-compatible PC operating systems (95 percent market share), partly by deterring potential entry from Netscape and Sun Microsystems. One such action was charging higher prices for its Windows operating system to computer manufacturers that featured Netscape's Navigator rather than Microsoft's Internet Explorer.

Column 4 in the table shows that marginal revenue is always less than the corresponding product price in column 2, except for the first unit of output. We show the relationship between the monopolist's demand curve and marginal-revenue curve in Figure 8.1b. For this figure, we extended the demand and marginal-revenue data of columns 1, 2, and 4 in the table, assuming that successive $10 price cuts each elicit 1 additional unit of sales. That is, the monopolist can sell 11 units at $62, 12 units at $52, and so on. Note that the monopolist's MR curve lies below the demand curve, indicating that marginal revenue is less than price at every output quantity except the very first unit.

The Monopolist Is a Price Maker

All imperfect competitors, whether they are pure monopolists, oligopolists, or monopolistic competitors, face downward-sloping demand curves. So firms in those industries can to one degree or another influence total supply through their own output decisions. In changing market supply, they can also influence product price. Firms with downsloping demand curves are *price makers.*

This is most evident in pure monopoly, where one firm controls total output. The monopolist faces a downsloping demand curve in which each output is associated with some unique price. Thus, in deciding on what volume of output to produce, the monopolist is also indirectly determining the price it will charge. Through control of output, it can "make the price." From columns 1 and 2 in the table in Figure 8.1 we find that the monopolist can charge a price of $72 if it produces and offers for sale 10 units, a price of $82 if it produces and offers for sale 9 units, and so forth.

Output and Price Determination

At what specific price-quantity combination will a profit-maximizing monopolist choose to operate? To answer this question, we must add production costs to our analysis.

Cost Data

On the cost side, we will assume that although the firm is a monopolist in the product market, it hires resources competitively and employs the same technology as Chapter 7's competitive firm does. This lets us use the cost data we developed in Chapter 6 and applied in Chapter 7, so we can compare the price-output decisions of a pure monopoly with those of a pure competitor. Columns 5 through 7 in the table in Figure 8.2 restate the pertinent cost data from the table in Figure 7.2.

MR = MC Rule

A monopolist seeking to maximize total profit will employ the same rationale as a profit-seeking firm in a competitive industry. If producing is preferable to shutting down, it will produce up to the output at which marginal revenue equals marginal cost (MR = MC).

A comparison of columns 4 and 7 in the table in Figure 8.2 indicates that the profit-maximizing output is 5 units, because the fifth unit is the last unit of output

FIGURE 8.2

Profit maximization by a pure monopolist. The pure monopolist maximizes profit by producing the MR = MC output, here $Q_m = 5$ units. Then, as seen from the demand curve, it will charge price $P_m = \$122$. Average total cost is $A = \$94$, so per-unit profit is $P_m - A$ and total profit is $5 \times (P_m - A)$. Total economic profit is thus $140, as shown by the gray rectangle.

Revenue Data				Cost Data			
(1) Quantity of Output	(2) Price (Average Revenue)	(3) Total Revenue, (1) × (2)	(4) Marginal Revenue	(5) Average Total Cost	(6) Total Cost, (1) × (5)	(7) Marginal Cost	(8) Profit (+) or Loss (−)
0	$172	$ 0			$ 100		$−100
1	162	162	$162	$190.00	190	$ 90	− 28
2	152	304	142	135.00	270	80	+ 34
3	142	426	122	113.33	340	70	+ 86
4	132	528	102	100.00	400	60	+128
5	***122***	***610***	***82***	***94.00***	***470***	***70***	***+140***
6	112	672	62	91.67	550	80	+122
7	102	714	42	91.43	640	90	+ 74
8	92	736	22	93.75	750	110	− 14
9	82	738	2	97.78	880	130	−142
10	72	720	−18	103.00	1030	150	−310

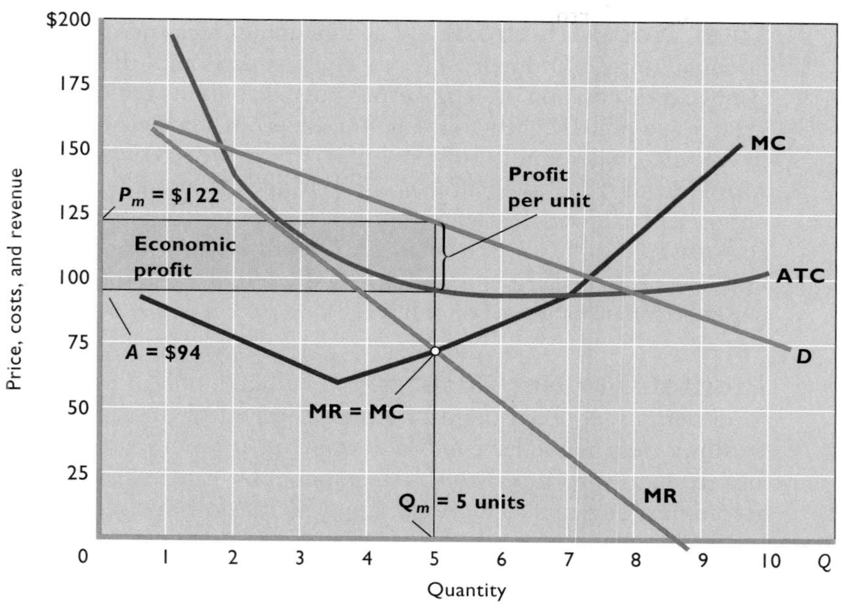

whose marginal revenue exceeds its marginal cost. What price will the monopolist charge? The demand schedule shown as columns 1 and 2 in the table indicates there is only one price at which 5 units can be sold: $122.

This analysis is shown in Figure 8.2, where we have graphed the demand, marginal-revenue, average-total-cost, and marginal-cost data from the table. The profit-maximizing output occurs at 5 units of output (Q_m), where the marginal-revenue (MR) and marginal-cost (MC) curves intersect. There, MR = MC.

To find the price the monopolist will charge, we extend a vertical line from Q_m up to the demand curve D. The unique price P_m at which Q_m units can be sold is $122. In this case, it is the profit-maximizing price. The monopolist sets the quantity at Q_m to charge its profit-maximizing price of $122.

8.1 Monopoly 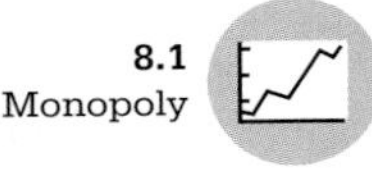

In columns 2 and 5 of the table we see that at 5 units of output, the product price ($122) exceeds the average total cost ($94). The monopolist thus earns an economic profit of $28 per unit, and the total economic profit is then $140 (=5 units × $28). In the graph in Figure 8.2, per-unit profit is $P_m - A$, where A is the average total cost of producing Q_m units. We find total economic profit of $140 (the gray rectangle) by multiplying this per-unit profit by the profit-maximizing output Q_m.

Misconceptions Concerning Monopoly Pricing

Our analysis exposes three fallacies concerning monopoly behavior.

Not Highest Price Because a monopolist can manipulate output and price, people often believe it "will charge the highest price possible." That is incorrect. There are many prices above P_m in Figure 8.2, but the monopolist shuns them because they yield a smaller-than-maximum total profit. The monopolist seeks maximum total profit, not maximum price. Some high prices that could be charged would reduce sales and total revenue too severely to offset any decrease in total cost.

Total, Not Unit, Profit The monopolist seeks maximum *total* profit, not maximum *unit* profit. In Figure 8.2 a careful comparison of the vertical distance between average total cost and price at various possible outputs indicates that per-unit profit is greater at a point slightly to the left of the profit-maximizing output Q_m. This is seen in the table, where unit profit at 4 units of output is $32 (=$132 − $100) compared with $28 (=$122 − $94) at the profit-maximizing output of 5 units. Here the monopolist accepts a lower-than-maximum per-unit profit because additional sales more than compensate for the lower unit profit. A profit-seeking monopolist would rather sell 5 units at a profit of $28 per unit (for a total profit of $140) than 4 units at a profit of $32 per unit (for a total profit of only $128).

Profitability Not Ensured The likelihood of economic profit is greater for a pure monopolist than for a pure competitor. In the long run the pure competitor is destined to have only a normal profit, whereas barriers to entry mean that any economic profit realized by the monopolist can persist. In pure monopoly there are no new entrants to increase supply, drive down price, and eliminate economic profit.

But pure monopoly does not guarantee profit. Despite dominance in its market (as, say, a seller of home sewing machines), a monopoly enterprise can suffer a loss because of weak demand and relatively high costs. If the demand and cost situation faced by the monopolist is far less favorable than that in Figure 8.2, the monopolist can incur losses. Like the pure competitor, the monopolist will not persist in operating at a loss in the long run. Faced with continuing losses, the firm's owners will move their resources to alternative industries that offer better profit opportunities. Thus we can expect monopolists to realize a normal profit or better in the long run.

Economic Effects of Monopoly

Let's now evaluate pure monopoly from the standpoint of society as a whole. Our reference for this evaluation will be the outcome of long-run efficiency in a purely competitive market, identified by the triple equality P = MC = minimum ATC.

Price, Output, and Efficiency

Figure 8.3 graphically contrasts the price, output, and efficiency outcomes of pure monopoly and a purely competitive *industry*. Figure 8.3a reminds us that the purely competitive industry's market supply curve S is the horizontal sum of the marginal-cost curves of all the firms in the industry. Let's suppose there are 1000 such firms. Comparing their combined supply curve S with market demand D, we get the purely competitive price and output of P_c and Q_c.

Recall that this price-output combination results in both productive efficiency and allocative efficiency. *Productive efficiency* is achieved because free entry and exit force firms to operate where their average total cost is at a minimum. The sum of the minimum-ATC outputs of the 1000 pure competitors is the industry output, here, Q_c. Product price is at the lowest level consistent with minimum average total cost. The *allocative efficiency* of pure competition results because production occurs up to that output at which price (the measure of a product's value or marginal benefit to society) equals marginal cost (the worth of the alternative products forgone by society in producing any given commodity). In short: P = MC = minimum ATC.

FIGURE 8.3

Inefficiency of pure monopoly relative to a purely competitive industry. (a) In a purely competitive industry, entry and exit of firms ensures that price (P_c) equals marginal cost (MC) and that the minimum average-total-cost output (Q_c) is produced. Both productive efficiency (P = minimum ATC) and allocative efficiency (P = MC) are obtained. (b) In pure monopoly, the MR curve lies below the demand curve. The monopolist maximizes profit at output Q_m, where MR = MC, and charges price P_m. So output is lower (Q_m rather than Q_c) and price is higher (P_m rather than P_c) than they would be in a purely competitive industry. Monopoly is inefficient, since output is less than that required for achieving minimum ATC (here, at Q_c) and because the monopolist's price exceeds MC.

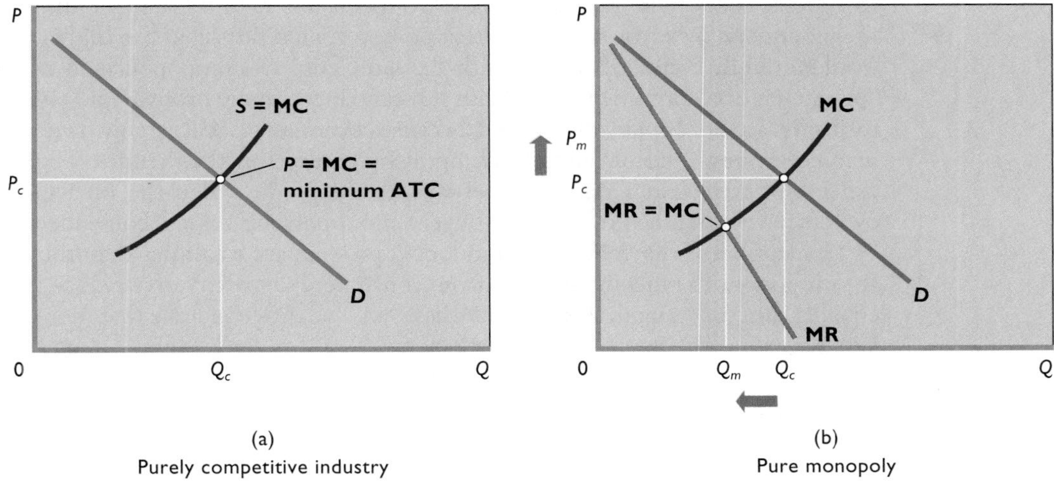

Now let's suppose that this industry becomes a pure monopoly (Figure 8.3b) as a result of one firm buying out all its competitors. We also assume that no changes in costs or market demand result from this dramatic change in the industry structure. What formerly were 1000 competing firms are now a single pure monopolist consisting of 1000 noncompeting branches.

The competitive market supply curve *S* has become the marginal-cost curve (MC) of the monopolist, the summation of the MC curves of its many branch plants. The important change, however, is on the demand side. From the viewpoint of each of the 1000 individual competitive firms, demand was perfectly elastic, and marginal revenue was therefore equal to price. Each firm equated MR (= price) and MC in maximizing profits. But market demand and individual demand are the same to the pure monopolist. The firm *is* the industry, and thus the monopolist sees the downsloping demand curve *D* shown in Figure 8.3b.

This means that marginal revenue is less than price, that graphically the MR curve lies below demand curve *D*. In using the MR = MC rule, the monopolist selects output Q_m and price P_m. A comparison of both graphs in Figure 8.3 reveals that the monopolist finds it profitable to sell a smaller output at a higher price than do the competitive producers. Monopoly yields neither productive nor allocative efficiency. The monopolist's output is less than Q_c, the output at which average total cost is lowest.

And price is higher than the competitive price P_c, which in long-run-equilibrium pure competition equals minimum average total cost. Thus the monopoly price *exceeds* minimum average total cost. Also, at the monopolist's Q_m output, product price is considerably higher than marginal cost, meaning that society values additional units of this monopolized product more highly than it values the alternative products the resources could otherwise produce.

So the monopolist's profit-maximizing output results in an underallocation of resources. The monopolist finds it profitable to restrict output and therefore employ fewer resources than is justified from society's standpoint. So the monopolist does not achieve allocative efficiency. In monopoly, then

- *P* exceeds MC.
- *P* exceeds minimum ATC.

Income Transfer

In general, monopoly transfers income from consumers to the stockholders who own the monopoly. By virtue of their market power, monopolists charge a higher price than would a purely competitive firm with the same costs. So monopolists in effect levy a "private tax" on consumers and obtain substantial economic profits. These monopolistic profits are not equally distributed, because corporate stock is largely owned by high-income groups. The owners of monopolistic enterprises thus tend to benefit at the expense of the consumers, who "overpay" for the product. Because, on average, these owners have more income than the buyers, monopoly increases income inequality.

Exception: If the buyers of a monopoly product are wealthier than the owners of the monopoly, the income transfer from consumers to owners may reduce income inequality. But, in general, this is not the case, and we thus conclude that monopoly contributes to income inequality.

Cost Complications

Our conclusion has been that, given identical costs, a purely monopolistic industry will charge a higher price, produce a smaller output, and allocate economic resources less efficiently than a purely competitive industry. These inferior results are rooted in the entry barriers present in monopoly.

Now we must recognize that costs may not be the same for purely competitive and monopolistic producers. The unit cost incurred by a monopolist may be either larger or smaller than that incurred by a purely competitive firm. There are four reasons why costs may differ: (1) economies of scale, (2) a factor called "X-inefficiency," (3) the need for monopoly-preserving expenditures, and (4) the "very long run" perspective, which allows for technological advance.

Economies of Scale Once Again Where there are extensive economies of scale, market demand may not be sufficient to support a large number of competing firms, each producing at minimum efficient scale (MES). In such cases, an industry of one or two firms would have a lower average total cost than would the same industry made up of numerous competitive firms. At the extreme, only a single firm—a natural monopoly—might be able to achieve the lowest long-run average total cost.

Some firms relating to new information technologies—for example, computer software, Internet service, and wireless communications—have displayed extensive economies of scale. As these firms have grown, their long-run average total costs have declined because of greater use of specialized inputs, the spreading of product development costs, and learning by doing. Also, *simultaneous consumption* and *network effects* have reduced costs.

A product's ability to satisfy a large number of consumers at the same time is called **simultaneous consumption.** Dell Computers needs to produce a personal computer for each customer, but Microsoft needs to produce its Windows program only once. Then, at very low marginal cost, Microsoft delivers its program by disk or Internet to millions of consumers. The same is true for Internet service providers, music producers, and wireless communication firms. Because marginal costs are so low, the average total cost of output typically declines as more customers are added.

simultaneous consumption
A product's ability to satisfy a large number of consumers at the same time.

Network effects are increases in the value of a product to each user, including existing users, as the total number of users rises. Good examples are computer software, cell phones, pagers, palm computers, and other products related to the Internet. When other people have Internet service and devices to access it, a person can conveniently send e-mail messages to them. And when they have similar software, then documents, spreadsheets, and photos can be attached to the e-mail messages. The greater the number of persons connected to the system, the greater are the benefits of the product to each person.

network effects
Increases in the value of a product to each user as the total number of users rises.

Such network effects may drive a market toward monopoly because consumers tend to choose standard products that everyone else is using. The focused demand for these products permits their producers to grow rapidly and thus achieve economies of scale. Smaller firms, which have higher-cost "right" products or the "wrong" products, get acquired or go out of business.

Economists generally agree that some new information firms have not yet exhausted their economies of scale. But most economists question whether such firms are truly natural monopolies. Most firms eventually achieve their minimum efficient scale at less than the full size of the market.

Even if natural monopoly develops, it's unlikely that the monopolist will pass cost reductions along to consumers as price reductions. So, with perhaps a handful of exceptions, economies of scale do not change the general conclusion that monopolies are inefficient relative to more competitive industries.

8.3 X-inefficiency 

X-inefficiency The production of output, whatever its level, at higher than the lowest average (and total) cost possible.

X-Inefficiency In constructing all the average-total-cost curves used in this book, we have assumed that the firm uses the most efficient existing technology. In other words, it uses the procedures and combinations of inputs that permit it to achieve the lowest average total cost of whatever level of output it decides to produce. In contrast, **X-inefficiency** occurs when a firm produces output, whatever its level, at higher than the lowest possible cost of producing it. For example, in Figure 8.2 the ATC and MC curves might be located above those shown, indicating higher costs at each level of output.

Why is X-inefficiency allowed to occur if it reduces profits? The answer harks back to our early discussion of the principal-agent problem. Managers may have goals, such as expanding power, having an easier work life, avoiding business risk, or giving jobs to incompetent relatives, that conflict with cost minimization. Or X-inefficiency may arise because a firm's workers are poorly motivated or ineffectively supervised. Or a firm may simply become lethargic and inert, relying on rules of thumb or intuition in decision making as opposed to relevant calculations of costs and revenues.

Presumably, monopolistic firms tend more toward X-inefficiency than competitive producers do. Firms in competitive industries are continually under pressure from rivals, forcing them to be internally efficient to survive. But monopolists are sheltered from such competitive forces by entry barriers, and that lack of pressure may lead to X-inefficiency.

There is no indisputable evidence regarding X-inefficiency, but what evidence we have suggests that it increases as competition decreases. A reasonable estimate is that X-inefficiency may be 10 percent or more of costs for monopolists but only 5 percent for an "average" oligopolistic industry in which the four largest firms produce 60 percent of total output.[1] In the words of one authority: "The evidence is fragmentary, but it points in the same direction. X-inefficiency exists, and it is more apt to be reduced when competitive pressures are strong than when firms enjoy insulated market positions."[2]

rent-seeking behavior Any action designed to gain special benefits from government at taxpayers' or someone else's expense.

Rent-Seeking Expenditures Economists define **rent-seeking behavior** as any activity designed to transfer income or wealth to a particular firm or resource supplier at someone else's, or even society's, expense. We have seen that a monopolist can obtain an economic profit even in the long run. Therefore, it is no surprise that a firm may go to great expense to acquire or maintain a monopoly granted by government through legislation or an exclusive license. Such rent-seeking expenditures add nothing to the firm's output, but they clearly increase its costs. They imply that monopoly involves higher costs and less efficiency than suggested in Figure 8.3b.

Technological Advance In the very long run, firms can reduce their costs through the discovery and implementation of new technology. If monopolists are more likely than competitive producers to develop more efficient production techniques over time, then the inefficiency of monopoly might be overstated. The general view of economists is that a pure monopolist will not be technologically progressive. Although its economic profit provides ample means to finance research and development, it has little incentive to implement new techniques (or products). The absence

---

[1] William G. Shepherd, *The Economics of Industrial Organization*, 4th ed. (Englewood Cliffs, N.J.: Prentice-Hall, 1997), p. 107.

[2] F. M. Scherer and David Ross, *Industrial Market Structure and Economic Performance*, 3d ed. (Chicago: Rand McNally College Publishing, 1990), p. 672.

of competitors means that there is no external pressure for technological advance in a monopolized market. Because of its sheltered market position, the pure monopolist can afford to be inefficient and lethargic; there is no major penalty for being so.

One caveat: Recall that entirely new products and new methods of production can suddenly supplant existing monopoly through the process of creative destruction (Chapter 2). Recognizing this threat, the monopolist may continue to engage in R&D and seek technological advance to avoid falling prey to future rivals. In this case technological advance is essential to the maintenance of monopoly. But forestalling creative destruction means that it is *potential competition*, not the monopoly market structure, which is driving the technological advance. By assumption, no such competition exists in the pure-monopoly model because entry is entirely blocked.

Applying the Analysis

Is De Beers' Diamond Monopoly Forever?

De Beers, a Swiss-based company controlled by a South African corporation, produces about 45 percent of the world's rough-cut diamonds and purchases for resale a sizable number of the rough-cut diamonds produced by other mines worldwide. As a result, De Beers markets about 55 percent of the world's diamonds to a select group of diamond cutters and dealers. But that percentage has declined from 80 percent in the mid-1980s. Therein lies the company's problem.

De Beers' past monopoly behavior and results are a classic example of the monopoly model illustrated in Figure 8.2. No matter how many diamonds it mined or purchased, it sold only the quantity of diamonds that would yield an "appropriate" (monopoly) price. That price was well above production costs, and De Beers and its partners earned monopoly profits.

When demand fell, De Beers reduced its sales to maintain price. The excess of production over sales was then reflected in growing diamond stockpiles held by De Beers. It also attempted to bolster demand through advertising ("Diamonds are forever"). When demand was strong, it increased sales by reducing its diamond inventories.

De Beers used several methods to control the production of many mines it did not own. First, it convinced a number of independent producers that "single-channel" or monopoly marketing through De Beers would maximize their profit. Second, mines that circumvented De Beers often found their market suddenly flooded with similar diamonds from De Beers' vast stockpiles. The resulting price decline and loss of profit often would encourage a "rogue" mine into the De Beers fold. Finally, De Beers simply purchased and stockpiled diamonds produced by independent mines to keep their added supplies from undercutting the market.

Several factors have come together to unravel the monopoly. New diamond discoveries resulted in a growing leakage of diamonds into world markets outside De Beers' control. For example, significant prospecting and trading in Angola occurred. Recent diamond discoveries in Canada's Northwest Territories posed another threat. Although De Beers is a participant in that region, a large uncontrolled supply of diamonds has begun to emerge. Similarly, although Russia's diamond monopoly Alrosa is part of the De Beers monopoly, it is allowed to sell one-half of its large diamond stock directly to diamond cutters.

Moreover, the international media began to focus heavily on the role that diamonds play in financing the bloody civil wars in Africa. Fearing a consumer boycott of diamonds, De Beers pledged that it would not buy these "conflict" diamonds or do business with any firms that did. These diamonds, however, continue to find their way into the marketplace, eluding De Beers' control.

In mid-2000 De Beers announced it was abandoning its attempt to control the supply of diamonds. Since then it has tried to transform itself from a diamond cartel to a modern international corporation selling "premium" diamonds under the De Beers label. It has gradually reduced its $4 billion stockpile of diamonds and turned its efforts to increasing the demand for its "branded" diamonds through advertising. De Beers' new strategy is to establish itself as "the diamond supplier of choice."

With its high market share and ability to control its own production levels, De Beers still wields considerable influence over the price of rough-cut diamonds. But it looks like the De Beers' diamond monopoly was not forever.

Question:
De Beers' advertising is trying to establish the tradition of giving diamond anniversary rings. What is the logic behind its efforts? Use Figure 8.2 to demonstrate this graphically.

Price Discrimination

8.4 Price discrimination

price discrimination The selling of a product to different buyers at different prices when the price differences are not justified by differences in costs.

We have thus far assumed that the monopolist charges a single price to all buyers. But under certain conditions the monopolist can increase its profit by charging different prices to different buyers. In so doing, the monopolist is engaging in **price discrimination,** the practice of selling a specific product at more than one price when the price differences are not justified by cost differences.

Price discrimination is a common business practice that rarely reduces competition and therefore is rarely challenged by government. The exception occurs when a firm engages in price discrimination as part of a strategy to block entry or drive out competitors.

Conditions

The opportunity to engage in price discrimination is not readily available to all sellers. Price discrimination is possible when the following conditions are realized:

- ***Monopoly power*** The seller must be a monopolist or, at least, must possess some degree of monopoly power, that is, some ability to control output and price.
- ***Market segregation*** At relatively low cost to itself, the seller must be able to segregate buyers into distinct classes, each of which has a different willingness or ability to pay for the product. This separation of buyers is usually based on different elasticities of demand, as the examples below will make clear.
- ***No resale*** The original purchaser cannot resell the product or service. If buyers in the low-price segment of the market could easily resell in the high-price segment, the monopolist's price-discrimination strategy would create competition in the high-price segment. This competition would reduce the price in the high-price segment and undermine the monopolist's price-discrimination policy. This condition suggests that service industries such as the transportation industry or legal and medical services, where resale is impossible, are candidates for price discrimination.

Examples

Price discrimination is widely practiced in the U.S. economy. For example, airlines charge high fares to business travelers, whose demand for travel is inelastic, and offer lower "Saturday night stayover rates" and "14-day advance purchase fares" to attract vacationers and others whose demands are more elastic.

Electric utilities frequently segment their markets by end uses, such as lighting and heating. The absence of reasonable lighting substitutes means that the demand for electricity for illumination is inelastic and that the price per kilowatt-hour for such use is high. But the availability of natural gas and petroleum for heating makes the demand for electricity for this purpose less inelastic and the price lower.

Movie theaters and golf courses vary their charges on the basis of time (for example, higher evening and weekend rates) and age (for example, lower rates for children, senior discounts). Railroads vary the rate charged per ton-mile of freight according to the market value of the product being shipped. The shipper of 10 tons of television sets or refrigerators is charged more than the shipper of 10 tons of gravel or coal.

The issuance of discount coupons, redeemable at purchase, is a form of price discrimination. It permits firms to give price discounts to their most price-sensitive customers who have elastic demand. Less price-sensitive consumers who have less elastic demand are not as likely to undertake the clipping and redeeming of coupons. The firm thus makes a larger profit than if it had used a single-price, no-coupon strategy.

Finally, price discrimination often occurs in international trade. A Russian aluminum producer, for example, might sell aluminum for less in the United States than in Russia. In the United States, this seller faces an elastic demand because several substitute suppliers are available. But in Russia, where the manufacturer dominates the market and trade barriers impede imports, consumers have fewer choices and thus demand is less elastic.

Graphical Analysis

Figure 8.4 demonstrates price discrimination graphically. The unusual back-to-back graphs are for a single pure monopolist selling its product, say, software, in two segregated parts of the market. For example, one segment might be small-business customers and the other students. Student versions of the software are identical to the versions sold to businesses but are available (1 per person) only to customers with a student ID. Presumably, students have lower ability to pay for the software and are charged a discounted price.

The demand curve D_b, located to the right of the vertical axis, represents the relatively inelastic demand for the product of business customers. The demand curve D_s, located to the left of the vertical axis, reflects the elastic demand of students. The marginal revenue curves (MR_b and MR_s) lie below their respective demand curves, reflecting the demand–marginal revenue relationship previously described. Quantity demanded is measured left to right from the origin for business customers and right to left from the origin for students. For visual clarity we have assumed that average total cost (ATC) is constant. Therefore marginal cost (MC) equals average total cost (ATC) at all quantities of output. These costs are the same for both versions of the software and therefore appear as the single straight line labeled "MC = ATC."

What price will the pure monopolist charge to each set of customers? Using the MR = MC rule for profit maximization, the firm will offer Q_b units of the software for sale to small businesses. It can sell that profit-maximizing output by charging price P_b. Again using the MR = MC rule, the monopolist will offer Q_s units of software to students. To sell those Q_s units, the firm will charge students the lower price P_s.

FIGURE 8.4
Price discrimination to different groups of buyers The price discriminating monopolist represented here maximizes its total profit by dividing the market into two segments based on differences in elasticity of demand. It then produces and sells the MR = MC output in each market segment. (For visual clarity, average total cost (ATC) is assumed to be constant. Therefore MC equals ATC at all output levels.) The firm charges a higher price (here, P_b) to customers who have a less elastic demand curve and a lower price (here, P_s) to customers with a more elastic demand. The price discriminator's total profit is larger than it would be with no discrimination and therefore a single price.

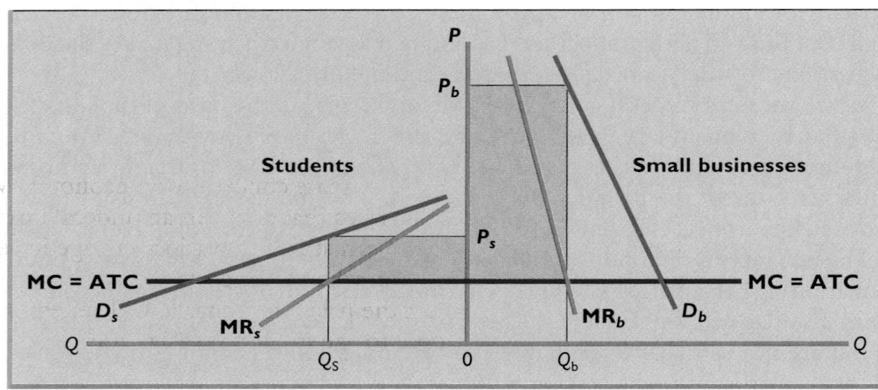

Firms engage in price discrimination because it enhances their profit. The numbers (not shown) behind the curves in Figure 8.4 would reveal that the sum of the two profit rectangles shown in gray exceeds the single profit rectangle the firm would obtain from a single monopoly price. How do consumers fare? In this case, students clearly benefit by paying a lower price than they would if the firm charged a single monopoly price; in contrast, the price discrimination results in a higher price for business customers. Therefore, compared to the single-price situation, students buy more of the software and small businesses buy less.

Price Discrimination at the Ballpark

Professional baseball teams earn substantial revenues through ticket sales. To maximize profit, they offer significantly lower ticket prices for children (whose demand is elastic) than those for adults (whose demand is inelastic). This discount may be as much as 50 percent.

If this type of price discrimination increases revenue and profit, why don't teams also price-discriminate at the concession stands? Why don't they offer half-price hot dogs, soft drinks, peanuts, and Cracker Jack to children? The answer involves the three requirements for successful price discrimination. All three requirements are met for game tickets: (1) The team has monopoly power; (2) it can segregate ticket buyers by age group, each group having a different elasticity of demand; and (3) children cannot resell their discounted tickets to adults.

It's a different situation at the concession stands. Specifically, the third condition is *not* met. If the team had dual prices, it could not prevent the exchange or "resale" of the concession goods from children to adults. Many adults would send children to buy food and soft drinks for them: "Here's some money, Billy. Go buy *10* hot dogs for all of us." In this case, price discrimination would reduce, not increase, team profit. Thus, children and adults are charged the same high prices at the concession stands.

Question:
Why are the prices for concessions at the games quite high compared to prices for the same or similar items at the local convenience store?

Monopoly and Antitrust Policy

For reasons we have discussed, monopoly is a legitimate concern to an economy. Monopolists can charge higher-than-competitive prices that result in an underallocation of resources to the monopolized product. They can stifle innovation, engage in rent-seeking behavior, and foster X-inefficiency. Even when their costs are low because of economies of scale, there is no guarantee that the price they charge will reflect those low costs. The cost savings may simply accrue to the monopoly as greater economic profit.

Not Widespread

Fortunately, however, monopoly is not widespread in the economy. Barriers to entry are seldom completely successful. Although research and technological advance may strengthen the market position of a monopoly, technology may also undermine monopoly power. Over time, the creation of new technologies may work to destroy monopoly positions (creative destruction). For example, the development of courier delivery, fax machines, and e-mail has eroded the monopoly power of the U.S. Postal Service. Cable television monopolies are now challenged by satellite TV and by new technologies that permit the transmission of audio and visual signals over the Internet.

Similarly, patents eventually expire; and even before they do, the development of new and distinct substitutable products often circumvents existing patent advantages. New sources of monopolized resources sometimes are found, and competition from foreign firms may emerge. (See Global Snapshot 8.1.) Finally, if a monopoly is sufficiently fearful of future competition from new products, it may keep its prices relatively low so as to discourage rivals from developing such products. If so, consumers may pay nearly competitive prices even though competition is currently lacking.

Antitrust Policy

But what should government do about monopoly when it arises and persists in the real world? Economists agree that government needs to look carefully at monopoly on a case-by-case basis. If the monopoly appears to be unsustainable over a long period of time, say, because of emerging new technology, society can simply choose to ignore it. In contrast, the government may want to file charges against a monopoly under the antitrust laws if the monopoly was achieved through anticompetitive actions, creates substantial economic inefficiency, and appears to be long-lasting. (Monopolies were once called "trusts.") The relevant antitrust law is the Sherman Act of 1890, which has two main provisions:

Competition from Foreign Multinational Corporations

Competition from foreign multinational corporations diminishes the market power of firms in the United States. Here are just a few of the hundreds of foreign multinational corporations that compete strongly with U.S. firms in certain American markets.

Company (Country)	Main Products
Bayer (Germany)	chemicals
BP Amoco (United Kingdom)	gasoline
Michelin (France)	tires
NEC (Japan)	computers
Nestlé (Switzerland)	food products
Nokia (Finland)	wireless phones
Royal Dutch/Shell (Netherlands)	gasoline
Royal Philips (Netherlands)	electronics
Sony (Japan)	electronics
Toyota (Japan)	automobiles
Unilever (Netherlands)	food products

Source: Compiled from the Forbes 2000 listing of the world's largest firms, www.forbes.com.

- ***Section 1*** "Every contract, combination in the form of a trust or otherwise, or conspiracy, in restraint of trade or commerce among the several States, or with foreign nations is declared to be illegal."
- ***Section 2*** "Every person who shall monopolize, or attempt to monopolize, or combine or conspire with any person or persons, to monopolize any part of the trade or commerce among the several States, or with foreign nations, shall be deemed guilty of a felony...." (as later amended from "misdemeanor").

In the 1911 Standard Oil case, the Supreme Court found Standard Oil guilty of monopolizing the petroleum industry through a series of abusive and anticompetitive actions. The Court's remedy was to divide Standard Oil into several competing firms. But the Standard Oil case left open an important question: Is every monopoly in violation of Section 2 of the Sherman Act or just those created or maintained by anticompetitive actions?

rule of reason The court ruling that only monopolies unreasonably attained or maintained are illegal.

In the 1920 U.S. Steel case, the courts established a **rule of reason** interpretation of Section 2, saying that it is not illegal to be a monopoly. Only monopolies that "unreasonably" restrain trade violate Section 2 of the Sherman Act and are subject to antitrust action. Size alone was not an offense. Although U.S. Steel clearly possessed monopoly power, it was innocent of "monopolizing" because it had not resorted to illegal acts against competitors in obtaining that power nor had it unreasonably used its monopoly power. Unlike Standard Oil, which was a "bad trust," U.S. Steel was a "good trust" and therefore not in violation of the law. The rule of reason was attacked and once reversed by the courts, but today it is the accepted legal interpretation of the Sherman Act's monopoly provisions.

Today, the U.S. Department of Justice, the Federal Trade Commission, injured private parties, or state attorney generals can file antitrust suits against alleged violators of the Sherman Act. The courts can issue injunctions to prohibit anticompetitive practices (a behavior remedy) or, if necessary, break up monopolists into competing firms (a structural remedy). Courts can also fine and imprison violators. Also, parties injured by monopolies can sue for *treble damages*—an award of three times the amount of the monetary injury done to them. In some cases, these damages have summed to millions or even billions of dollars.

The largest and most significant monopoly case of recent times is the Microsoft case, which is the subject of the application that follows.

Applying the Analysis

United States v. Microsoft

In May 1998 the U.S. Justice Department, 19 individual states, and the District of Columbia (hereafter, "the government") filed antitrust charges against Microsoft under the Sherman Antitrust Act. The government charged that Microsoft had violated Section 2 of the act through a series of unlawful actions designed to maintain its "Windows" monopoly. It also charged that some of that conduct violated Section 1 of the Sherman Act, which prohibits actions that restrain trade or commerce.

Microsoft denied the charges, arguing it had achieved its success through product innovation and lawful business practices. Microsoft contended it should not be penalized for its superior foresight, business acumen, and technological prowess. It also insisted that its monopoly was highly transitory because of rapid technological advance.

In June 2000 the district court ruled that the relevant market was software used to operate Intel-compatible personal computers (PCs). Microsoft's 95 percent share of that market clearly gave it monopoly power. The court pointed out, however, that being a monopoly is not illegal. The violation of the Sherman Act occurred because Microsoft used anticompetitive means to maintain its monopoly power.

According to the court, Microsoft feared that the success of Netscape's Navigator, which allowed people to browse the Internet, might allow Netscape to expand its software to include a competitive PC operating system—software that would threaten the Windows monopoly. It also feared that Sun's Internet applications of its Java programming language might eventually threaten Microsoft's Windows monopoly.

To counter these and similar threats, Microsoft illegally signed contracts with PC makers that required them to feature its Internet Explorer on the PC desktop and penalized companies that promoted software products that competed with Microsoft products. Moreover, it gave friendly companies coding that linked Windows to software applications and withheld such coding from companies featuring Netscape. Finally, under license from Sun, Microsoft developed Windows-related Java software that made Sun's own software incompatible with Windows.

The district court ordered Microsoft to split into two competing companies, one initially selling the Windows operating system and the other initially selling Microsoft applications (such as Word, Hotmail, MSN, PowerPoint, and Internet

Explorer). Both companies would be free to develop new products that compete with each other, and both could derive those products from the intellectual property embodied in the common products existing at the time of divestiture.

In late 2000 Microsoft appealed the district court decision to a U.S. court of appeals. In 2001 the higher court affirmed that Microsoft illegally maintained its monopoly, but tossed out the district court's decision to break up Microsoft. It agreed with Microsoft that the company was denied due process during the penalty phase of the trial and concluded that the district court judge had displayed an appearance of bias by holding extensive interviews with the press. The appeals court sent the remedial phase of the case to a new district court judge to determine appropriate remedies. The appeals court also raised issues relating to the wisdom of a structural remedy.

At the urging of the new district court judge, the Federal government and Microsoft negotiated a proposed settlement. With minor modification, the settlement became the final court order in 2002. The breakup was rescinded and replaced with a behavioral remedy. It (1) prevents Microsoft from retaliating against any firm that is developing, selling, or using software that competes with Microsoft Windows or Internet Explorer or is shipping a personal computer that includes both Windows and a non-Microsoft operating system; (2) requires Microsoft to establish uniform royalty and licensing terms for computer manufacturers wanting to include Windows on their PCs; (3) requires that manufacturers be allowed to remove Microsoft icons and replace them with other icons on the Windows desktop; and (4) calls for Microsoft to provide technical information to other companies so those firms can develop programs that work as well with Windows as Microsoft's own products.

Question:
Is the 2002 Microsoft settlement mainly a structural remedy for monopoly, or is it a behavioral remedy?

Source: *United States v. Microsoft* (District Court Conclusions of Law), April 2000; *United States v. Microsoft* (court of appeals), June 2001; *U.S.. v. Microsoft* (Final Judgment), November 2002; and Reuters and Associated Press news services.

Summary

1. A pure monopolist is the sole producer of a good or service for which there are no close substitutes.
2. The existence of pure monopoly is explained by barriers to entry in the form of (a) economies of scale, (b) patent ownership and research, (c) ownership or control of essential resources, and (d) pricing and other strategic behavior.
3. The pure monopolist's market situation differs from that of a competitive firm in that the monopolist's demand curve is downsloping, causing the marginal-revenue curve to lie below the demand curve. Like the competitive seller, the pure monopolist will maximize profit by equating marginal revenue and marginal cost. Barriers to entry may permit a monopolist to acquire economic profit even in the long run. However, (a) the monopolist does not charge "the highest price possible"; (b) the price that yields maximum total profit to the monopolist rarely coincides with the price that yields maximum unit profit; and (c) high costs and a weak demand may prevent the monopolist from realizing any profit at all.
4. With the same costs, the pure monopolist will find it profitable to restrict output and charge a higher price than would sellers in a purely

competitive industry. This restriction of output causes a misallocation of resources, as is evidenced by the fact that price exceeds marginal cost in monopolized markets.

5. In general, monopoly transfers income from consumers to the owners of the monopoly. Because, on average, consumers of monopolized products have less income than the corporate owners, monopoly increases income inequality.
6. The costs monopolists and competitive producers face may not be the same. On the one hand, economies of scale may make lower unit costs available to monopolists but not to competitors. Also, pure monopoly may be more likely than pure competition to reduce costs via technological advance because of the monopolist's ability to realize economic profit, which can be used to finance research. On the other hand, X-inefficiency—the failure to produce with the least costly combination of inputs—is more common among monopolists than among competitive firms. Also, monopolists may make costly expenditures to maintain monopoly privileges that are conferred by government. Finally, the blocked entry of rival firms weakens the monopolist's incentive to be technologically progressive.
7. A firm can increase its profit through price discrimination provided it (a) has monopoly pricing power, (b) can segregate buyers on the basis of elasticities of demand, and (c) can prevent its product or service from being readily transferred between the segregated markets.
8. The cornerstone of antimonopoly law is the Sherman Act of 1890, particularly Section 2. According to the rule of reason, possession of monopoly power is not illegal. But monopoly that is unreasonably gained or unreasonably maintained is a violation of the law.
9. If a company is found guilty of violating the Sherman Act, the government can either break up the monopoly into competing firms (a structural remedy) or prohibit it from engaging in specific anticompetitive business practices (a behavioral remedy).

Terms and Concepts

pure monopoly
barriers to entry
natural monopoly
simultaneous consumption
network effects
X-inefficiency
rent-seeking behavior
price discrimination
rule of reason

Study Questions

1. "No firm is completely sheltered from rivals; all firms compete for consumer dollars. If that is so, then pure monopoly does not exist." Do you agree? Explain.
2. Discuss the major barriers to entry into an industry. Explain how each barrier can foster either monopoly or oligopoly. Which barriers, if any, do you feel give rise to monopoly that is socially justifiable?
3. How does the demand curve faced by a purely monopolistic seller differ from that confronting a purely competitive firm? Why does it differ? Of what significance is the difference? Why is the pure monopolist's demand curve typically not perfectly inelastic?
4. Use the following demand schedule for a pure monopolist to calculate total revenue and marginal revenue at each quantity. Plot the monopolist's demand curve and marginal-revenue curve, and explain the relationships between them. Explain why the marginal revenue of the fourth unit of output is \$3.50, even though its price is \$5. What generalization can you make as to the relationship between the monopolist's demand and its marginal revenue? Suppose the marginal cost of successive units of output was zero. What output would the single-price monopolist produce, and what price would it charge?

Price (P)	Quantity Demanded (Q)	Price (P)	Quantity Demanded (Q)
\$7.00	0	\$4.50	5
6.50	1	4.00	6
6.00	2	3.50	7
5.50	3	3.00	8
5.00	4	2.50	9

5. Suppose a pure monopolist is faced with the demand schedule shown on the next page and the same cost data as the competitive producer discussed in question 3 at the end of Chapter 7. Calculate the missing total-revenue and marginal-revenue amounts, and determine the profit-maximizing price and profit-earning output for this monopolist. What is the monopolist's profit? Verify your answer graphically and by comparing total revenue and total cost.

CHAPTER NINE

Monopolistic Competition and Oligopoly

In this chapter you will learn:

- The characteristics of monopolistic competition.
- Why monopolistic competitors earn only a normal profit in the long run.
- The characteristics of oligopoly.
- How game theory relates to oligopoly.
- Why the demand curve of an oligopolist may be kinked.
- The incentives and obstacles to collusion among oligopolists.
- The positive and potential negative effects of advertising.

Most markets in the U.S. economy fall between the two poles of pure competition (Chapter 7) and pure monopoly (Chapter 8). Real-world industries usually have fewer than the hundreds of producers required for pure competition and more than the single producer that defines pure monopoly. Most firms have distinguishable rather than standardized products and have some discretion over the prices they charge. Competition often occurs on the basis of price, quality, location, service, and advertising. Entry to most real-world industries ranges from easy to very difficult but is rarely completely blocked.

This chapter examines two models that more closely approximate these widespread markets. You will discover that *monopolistic competition* mixes a small amount of monopoly power with a large amount of competition. *Oligopoly,* in contrast, blends a large amount of monopoly power, a small amount of competition through entry, and considerable rivalry among industry firms.

© Robert Landau/CORBIS

© Royalty-Free/CORBIS

Photo Op Monopolistic Competition versus Oligopoly

Furniture is produced in a monopolistically competitive industry, whereas refrigerators are produced in an oligopolistic industry.

Monopolistic Competition

Let's begin by examining **monopolistic competition,** which is characterized by (1) a relatively large number of sellers, (2) differentiated products (often promoted by heavy advertising), and (3) easy entry to, and exit from, the industry. The first and third characteristics provide the "competitive" aspect of monopolistic competition; the second characteristic provides the "monopolistic" aspect. In general, however, monopolistically competitive industries are much more competitive than they are monopolistic.

monopolistic competition
A market structure in which many firms sell a differentiated product and entry into and exit from the market are relatively easy.

Relatively Large Number of Sellers

9.1
Monopolistic competition

Monopolistic competition is characterized by a fairly large number of firms, say, 25, 35, 60, or 70, not by the hundreds or thousands of firms in pure competition. Consequently, monopolistic competition involves:

- ***Small market shares*** Each firm has a comparatively small percentage of the total market and consequently has limited control over market price.
- ***No collusion*** The presence of a relatively large number of firms ensures that collusion by a group of firms to restrict output and set prices is unlikely.
- ***Independent action*** With numerous firms in an industry, there is no feeling of interdependence among them; each firm can determine its own pricing policy without considering the possible reactions of rival firms. A single firm may realize

a modest increase in sales by cutting its price, but the effect of that action on competitors' sales will be nearly imperceptible and will probably trigger no response.

Differentiated Products

product differentiation A form of nonprice competition in which a firm tries to distinguish its product or service from all competing ones on the basis of attributes such as design and quality.

In contrast to pure competition, in which there is a standardized product, monopolistic competition is distinguished by **product differentiation.** Monopolistically competitive firms turn out variations of a particular product. They produce products with slightly different physical characteristics, offer varying degrees of customer service, provide varying amounts of locational convenience, or proclaim special qualities, real or imagined, for their products.

These aspects of product differentiation require more attention.

Product Attributes Product differentiation may entail physical or qualitative differences in the products themselves. Real differences in functional features, materials, design, and workmanship are vital aspects of product differentiation. Personal computers, for example, differ in terms of storage capacity, speed, graphic displays, and included software. There are dozens of competing principles of economics textbooks that differ in content, organization, presentation and readability, pedagogical aids, and graphics and design. Most cities have a variety of retail stores selling men's and women's clothes that differ greatly in styling, materials, and quality of work. Similarly, one furniture manufacturer may feature its solid oak furniture, while a competitor stresses its solid maple furniture.

Service Service and the conditions surrounding the sale of a product are forms of product differentiation too. One grocery store may stress the helpfulness of its clerks who bag your groceries and carry them to your car; a warehouse competitor may leave bagging and carrying to its customers but feature lower prices. Customers may prefer 1-day over 3-day dry cleaning of equal quality. The prestige appeal of a store, the courteousness and helpfulness of clerks, the firm's reputation for servicing or exchanging its products, and the credit it makes available are all service aspects of product differentiation.

Location Products may also be differentiated through the location and accessibility of the stores that sell them. Small convenience stores manage to compete with large supermarkets, even though these minimarts have a more limited range of products and charge higher prices. They compete mainly on the basis of location—being close to customers and situated on busy streets. A motel's proximity to an interstate highway gives it a locational advantage that may enable it to charge a higher room rate than nearby motels in less convenient locations.

Brand Names and Packaging Product differentiation may also be created through the use of brand names and trademarks, packaging, and celebrity connections. Most aspirin tablets are very much alike, but many headache sufferers believe that one brand—for example, Bayer, Anacin, or Bufferin—is superior and worth a higher price than a generic substitute. A celebrity's name associated with jeans, perfume, or athletic equipment may enhance the appeal of those products for some buyers. Many customers prefer one style of ballpoint pen to another. Packaging that touts "natural spring" bottled water may attract additional customers.

Some Control over Price Despite the relatively large number of firms, monopolistic competitors do have some control over their product prices because of product differentiation. If consumers prefer the products of specific sellers, then within limits they will pay more to satisfy their preferences. Sellers and buyers are not linked randomly, as in a purely competitive market. But the monopolistic competitor's control over price is quite limited, since there are numerous potential substitutes for its product.

Easy Entry and Exit

Entry into monopolistically competitive industries is relatively easy compared to oligopoly or pure monopoly. Because monopolistic competitors are typically small firms, both absolutely and relatively, economies of scale are few and capital requirements are low. On the other hand, compared with pure competition, financial barriers may result from the need to develop and advertise a product that differs from rivals' products. Some firms may have trade secrets relating to their products or hold trademarks on their brand names, making it difficult and costly for other firms to imitate them.

Exit from monopolistically competitive industries is relatively easy. Nothing prevents an unprofitable monopolistic competitor from holding a going-out-of-business sale and shutting down.

Advertising

The expense and effort involved in product differentiation would be wasted if consumers were not made aware of product differences. Thus, monopolistic competitors advertise their products, often heavily. The goal of product differentiation and advertising—so-called **nonprice competition**—is to make price less of a factor in consumer purchases and make product differences a greater factor. If successful, the demand for the firm's product will increase. The firm's demand may also become less elastic because of the greater loyalty to the firm's product.

nonprice competition
A selling strategy in which one firm tries to distinguish its product or service from all competing ones on the basis of attributes other than price.

Monopolistically Competitive Industries

Several manufacturing industries approximate monopolistic competition. Examples of manufactured goods produced in monopolistically competitive industries are jewelry, asphalt, wood pallets, commercial signs, leather goods, plastic pipes, textile bags, and kitchen cabinets. In addition, many retail establishments in metropolitan areas are monopolistically competitive, including grocery stores, gasoline stations, barbershops, dry cleaners, clothing stores, and restaurants. Also, many providers of professional services such as medical care, legal assistance, real estate sales, and basic bookkeeping are monopolistic competitors.

Price and Output in Monopolistic Competition

How does a monopolistically competitive firm decide what quantity to produce and what price to charge? Initially, we assume that each firm in the industry is producing a specific differentiated product and engaging in a particular amount of advertising. Later we'll see how changes in the product and in the amount of advertising modify our conclusions.

The Firm's Demand Curve

Our explanation is based on Figure 9.1. The basic feature of that diagram is the elasticity of demand, as shown by the individual firm's demand curve. The demand curve faced by a monopolistically competitive seller is highly, but not perfectly, elastic. It is precisely this feature that distinguishes monopolistic competition from pure monopoly and pure competition. The monopolistic competitor's demand is more elastic than the demand faced by a pure monopolist because the monopolistically competitive seller has many competitors producing closely substitutable goods. The pure monopolist has no rivals at all. Yet, for two reasons, the monopolistic competitor's demand is not perfectly elastic like that of the pure competitor. First, the monopolistic competitor has fewer rivals; second, its products are differentiated, so they are not perfect substitutes.

FIGURE 9.1

A monopolistically competitive firm: short run and long run. The monopolistic competitor maximizes profit or minimizes loss by producing the output at which MR = MC. The economic profit shown in (a) will induce new firms to enter, eventually eliminating economic profit. The loss shown in (b) will cause an exit of firms until normal profit is restored. After such entry and exit, the price will settle in (c) to where it just equals average total cost at the MR = MC output. At this price P_3 and output Q_3, the monopolistic competitor earns only a normal profit, and the industry is in long-run equilibrium.

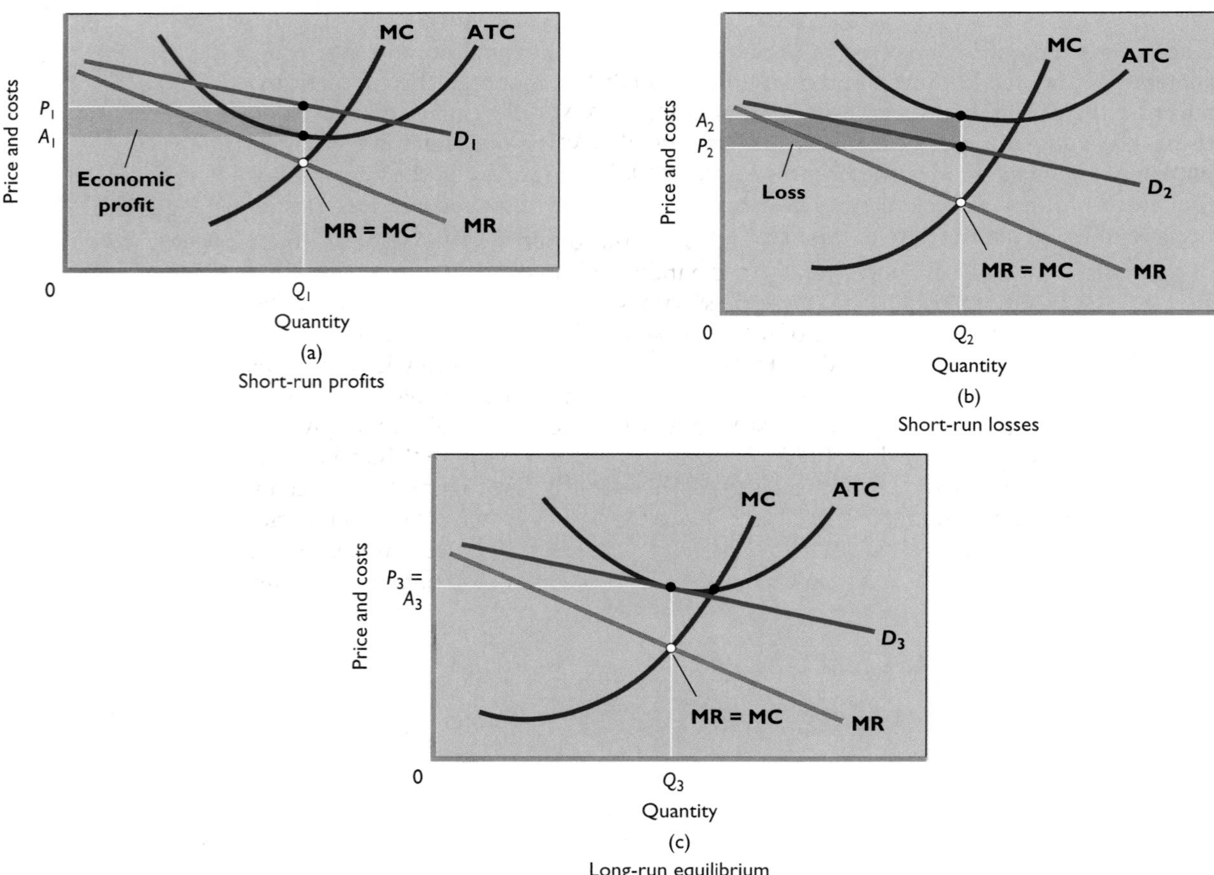

The price elasticity of demand faced by the monopolistically competitive firm depends on the number of rivals and the degree of product differentiation. The larger the number of rivals and the weaker the product differentiation, the greater the price elasticity of each seller's demand, that is, the closer monopolistic competition will be to pure competition.

The Short Run: Profit or Loss

The monopolistically competitive firm maximizes its profit or minimizes its loss in the short run just as do the other firms we have discussed: by producing the output at which marginal revenue equals marginal cost (MR = MC). In Figure 9.1a the firm produces output Q_1, where MR = MC. As shown by demand curve D_1, it then can charge price P_1. It realizes an economic profit, shown by the gray area [= $(P_1 - A_1) \times Q_1$].

But with less favorable demand or costs, the firm may incur a loss in the short run. We show this possibility in Figure 9.1b, where the firm's best strategy is to minimize its loss. It does so by producing output Q_2 (where MR = MC) and, as determined by demand curve D_2, by charging price P_2. Because price P_2 is less than average total cost A_2, the firm incurs a per-unit loss of $A_2 - P_2$ and a total loss represented as the red area [= $(A_2 - P_2) \times Q_2$].

The Long Run: Only a Normal Profit

In the long run, firms will enter a profitable monopolistically competitive industry and leave an unprofitable one. So a monopolistic competitor will earn only a normal profit in the long run or, in other words, will only break even. (Remember that the cost curves include both explicit and implicit costs, including a normal profit.)

Profits: Firms Enter In the case of short-run profit (Figure 9.1a), economic profits attract new rivals, because entry to the industry is relatively easy. As new firms enter, the demand curve faced by the typical firm shifts to the left (falls). Why? Because each firm has a smaller share of total demand and now faces a larger number of close-substitute products. This decline in the firm's demand reduces its economic profit. When entry of new firms has reduced demand to the extent that the demand curve is tangent to the average-total-cost curve at the profit-maximizing output, the firm is just making a normal profit. This situation is shown in Figure 9.1c, where demand is D_3 and the firm's long-run equilibrium output is Q_3. As Figure 9.1c indicates, any greater or lesser output will entail an average total cost that exceeds product price P_3, meaning a loss for the firm. At the tangency point between the demand curve and ATC, total revenue equals total costs. With the economic profit gone, there is no further incentive for additional firms to enter.

Losses: Firms Leave When the industry suffers short-run losses, as in Figure 9.1b, some firms will exit in the long run. Faced with fewer substitute products and blessed with an expanded share of total demand, the surviving firms will see their demand curves shift to the right (rise), as to D_3. Their losses will disappear and give way to normal profits (Figure 9.1c). (For simplicity we have assumed a constant-cost industry; shifts in the cost curves as firms enter or leave would complicate our discussion slightly but would not alter our conclusions.)

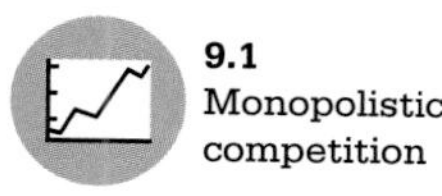

Monopolistic Competition and Efficiency

We know from Chapter 8 that economic efficiency requires the triple equality P = MC = minimum ATC. The equality of P and ATC yields *productive efficiency*. The good is being produced in the least costly way, and the price is just sufficient to cover average total cost, including a normal profit. The equality of P and MC yields *allocative efficiency*. The right amount of output is being produced, and thus the right amount of society's scarce resources is being devoted to this specific use.

How efficient is monopolistic competition, as measured against this triple equality?

Neither Productive nor Allocative Efficiency

In monopolistic competition, neither productive nor allocative efficiency occurs in long-run equilibrium. We show this in Figure 9.2, which enlarges part of Figure 9.1c and adds detail. First note that the profit-maximizing price P_3 slightly exceeds the lowest average total cost, A_4. Therefore, in producing the profit-maximizing output Q_3, the firm's average total cost is slightly higher than optimal from society's perspective—productive efficiency is not achieved. Also note that the profit-maximizing price P_3 exceeds marginal cost (here, M_3), meaning that monopolistic competition causes an

FIGURE 9.2
The inefficiency of monopolistic competition. In long-run equilibrium a monopolistic competitor achieves neither productive nor allocative efficiency. Productive efficiency is not realized because production occurs where the average total cost A_3 exceeds the minimum average total cost A_4. Allocative efficiency is not realized because the product price P_3 exceeds the marginal cost M_3. The result is an underallocation of resources and excess productive capacity of $Q_4 - Q_3$.

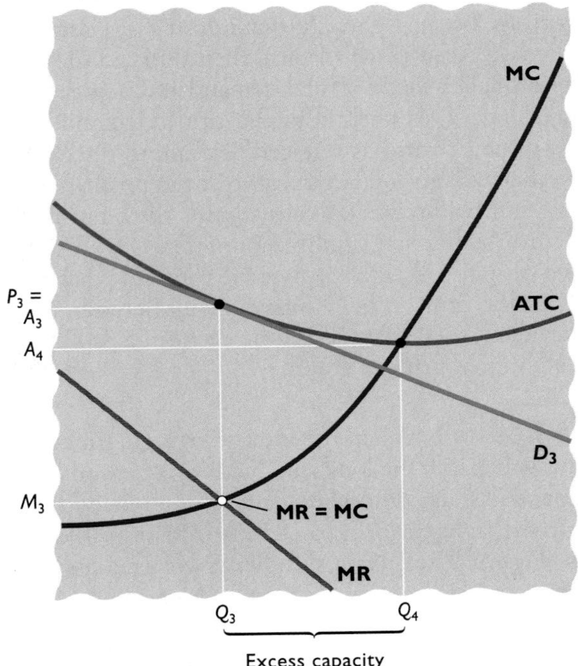

underallocation of resources. Society values each unit of output between Q_3 and Q_4 more highly than the goods it would have to forgo to produce those units. Thus, to a modest extent, monopolistic competition also fails the allocative-efficiency test. Consumers pay a higher-than-competitive price and obtain a less-than-optimal output. Indeed, monopolistic competitors must charge a higher-than-competitive price in the long run in order to achieve a normal profit.

Excess Capacity

In monopolistic competition, the gap between the minimum-ATC output and the profit-maximizing output identifies **excess capacity:** plant and equipment that are underused because firms are producing less than the minimum-ATC output. We show this gap as the distance between Q_4 and Q_3 in Figure 9.2. If each monopolistic competitor could profitably produce at the minimum-ATC output, fewer firms could produce the same total output, and the product could be sold at a lower price. Monopolistically competitive industries thus are overcrowded with firms, each operating below its optimal capacity. This situation is typified by many kinds of retail establishments. For example, in most cities there is an abundance of small motels and restaurants that operate well below half capacity.

excess capacity Plant or equipment that is underused because the firm is producing less than the minimum-ATC output.

Product Variety and Improvement

But monopolistic competition also has two notable virtues. It promotes product variety and product improvement. A monopolistic competitor is rarely satisfied with the situation portrayed in Figure 9.1c because it means only a normal profit. Instead, it may try to regain its economic profit through further product differentiation and better advertising. By developing or improving its product, it may be able to re-create, at least for a while, the profit outcome of Figure 9.1a.

The product variety and product improvement that accompany the drive to regain economic profit in monopolistic competition are benefits for society—ones that may offset the cost of the inefficiency associated with monopolistic competition. Consumers have a wide diversity of tastes: Some people like Italian salad dressing, others prefer French dressing; some people like contemporary furniture, others prefer traditional furniture. If a product is differentiated, then at any time the consumer will be offered a wide range of types, styles, brands, and quality gradations of that product. Compared with pure competition, this provides an advantage to the consumer. The range of choice is widened, and producers more fully meet the wide variation in consumer tastes.

The product improvement promoted by monopolistic competition further differentiates products and expands choices. And a successful product improvement by one firm obligates rivals to imitate or improve on that firm's temporary market advantage or else lose business. So society benefits from new and improved products.

Oligopoly

In terms of competitiveness, the spectrum of market structures reaches from pure competition, to monopolistic competition, to oligopoly, to pure monopoly. We now direct our attention to **oligopoly,** a market dominated by a few large producers of a homogeneous or differentiated product. Because of their "fewness," oligopolists have considerable control over their prices, but each must consider the possible reaction of rivals to its own pricing, output, and advertising decisions.

oligopoly A market structure dominated by a few large producers of homogeneous or differentiated products.

A Few Large Producers

The phrase "a few large producers" is necessarily vague because the market model of oligopoly covers much ground, ranging between pure monopoly, on the one hand, and monopolistic competition, on the other. Oligopoly encompasses the U.S. aluminum industry, in which three huge firms dominate an entire national market, and the situation in which four or five much smaller auto-parts stores enjoy roughly equal shares of the market in a medium-size town. Generally, however, when you hear a term such as "Big Three," "Big Four," or "Big Six," you can be sure it refers to an oligopolistic industry. Examples of U.S. industries that are oligopolies are tires, beer, cigarettes, copper, greeting cards, lightbulbs, aircraft, motor vehicles, gypsum products, and breakfast cereals. There are numerous others.

Either Homogeneous or Differentiated Products

homogeneous oligopoly
An oligopoly in which the firms produce a standardized product.

differentiated oligopoly
An oligopoly in which the firms produce a differentiated product.

An oligopoly may be either a **homogeneous oligopoly** or a **differentiated oligopoly,** depending on whether the firms in the oligopoly produce standardized or differentiated products. Many industrial products (steel, zinc, copper, aluminum, lead, cement, industrial alcohol) are virtually standardized products that are produced in oligopolies. Alternatively, many consumer goods industries (automobiles, tires, household appliances, electronic equipment, breakfast cereals, cigarettes, and many sporting goods) are differentiated oligopolies. These differentiated oligopolies typically engage in considerable nonprice competition supported by heavy advertising.

Control over Price, but Mutual Interdependence

strategic behavior
Self-interested behavior that takes into account the reactions of others.

mutual interdependence
A situation in which a change in strategy (usually price) by one firm will affect the sales and profits of other firms.

Because firms are few in oligopolistic industries, each firm is a "price maker"; like the monopolist, it can set its price and output levels to maximize its profit. But unlike the monopolist, which has no rivals, the oligopolist must consider how its rivals will react to any change in its price, output, product characteristics, or advertising. Oligopoly is thus characterized by *strategic behavior* and *mutual interdependence.* By **strategic behavior,** we simply mean self-interested behavior that takes into account the reactions of others. Firms develop and implement price, quality, location, service, and advertising strategies to "grow their business" and expand their profits. But because rivals are few, there is **mutual interdependence:** a situation in which each firm's profit depends not entirely on its own price and sales strategies but also on those of the other firms. So oligopolistic firms base their decisions on how they think rivals will react. Example: In deciding whether to increase the price of its baseball gloves, Rawlings will try to predict the response of the other major producers, such as Wilson. Second example: In deciding on its advertising strategy, Burger King will take into consideration how McDonald's might react.

Creative Strategic Behavior

The following story, offered with tongue in cheek, illustrates a localized market that exhibits some characteristics of oligopoly, including strategic behavior.

Tracy Martinez's Native American Arts and Crafts store is located in the center of a small tourist town that borders on a national park. In its early days, Tracy had a minimonopoly. Business was brisk, and prices and profits were high.

To Tracy's annoyance, two "copycat" shops opened adjacent to her store, one on either side of her shop. Worse yet, the competitors named their shops to take advantage of Tracy's advertising. One was "Native Arts and Crafts"; the other, "Indian Arts and Crafts." These new sellers drew business away from Tracy's store, forcing her to lower her prices. The three side-by-side stores in the small, isolated town constituted a localized oligopoly for Native American arts and crafts.

Tracy began to think strategically about ways to boost profit. She decided to distinguish her shop from those on either side by offering a greater mix of high-quality, expensive products and a lesser mix of inexpensive souvenir items. The tactic worked for a while, but the other stores eventually imitated her product mix.

Then, one of the competitors next door escalated the rivalry by hanging up a large sign proclaiming "We Sell for Less!" Shortly thereafter, the other shop put up a large sign stating "We Won't Be Undersold!"

Not to be outdone, Tracy painted a colorful sign of her own and hung it above her door. It read "Main Entrance."

Question:
How do you think the two rivals will react to Tracy's strategy?

Entry Barriers

The same barriers to entry that create pure monopoly also contribute to the creation of oligopoly. Economies of scale are important entry barriers in a number of oligopolistic industries, such as the aircraft, rubber, and copper industries. In those industries, three or four firms might each have sufficient sales to achieve economies of scale, but new firms would have such a small market share that they could not do so. They would then be high-cost producers, and as such they could not survive. A closely related barrier is the large expenditure for capital—the cost of obtaining necessary plant and equipment—required for entering certain industries. The jet engine, automobile, commercial aircraft, and petroleum-refining industries, for example, are all characterized by very high capital requirements.

The ownership and control of raw materials help explain why oligopoly exists in many mining industries, including gold, silver, and copper. In the electronics, chemicals, office equipment, and pharmaceutical industries, patents have served as entry barriers. Moreover, oligopolists can sometimes preclude the entry of new competitors through preemptive and retaliatory pricing and advertising strategies.

Mergers

Some oligopolies have emerged mainly through the growth of the dominant firms in a given industry (examples: breakfast cereals, chewing gum, candy bars). But for other industries the route to oligopoly has been through mergers (examples: steel, in its early history; and, more recently, airlines, banking, and entertainment). Section 7 of the Clayton Act (1914) outlaws mergers that *substantially* lessen competition. But the implied "rule of reason" leaves room for considerable interpretation. As a result, many mergers between firms in the same industry go unchallenged by government.

The combining of two or more firms in the same industry may significantly increase their market share, which may allow the new firm to achieve greater economies of scale. The merger may also increase the firm's monopoly power (pricing power) through greater control over market supply. Finally, because the new firm is a larger buyer of inputs, it may be able to obtain lower prices (costs) on its production inputs.

Oligopoly Behavior: A Game-Theory Overview

Oligopoly pricing behavior has the characteristics of certain games of strategy, such as poker, chess, and bridge. The best way to play such a game depends on the way one's opponent plays. Players (and oligopolists) must pattern their actions according to the actions and expected reactions of rivals. The study of how people or firms behave in strategic situations is called **game theory.** We will use a simple game-theory example to analyze the pricing behavior of oligopolists. We assume that a duopoly, or two-firm oligopoly, is producing athletic shoes. Each of the two firms—for example, RareAir and Uptown—has a choice of two pricing strategies: price high or price low. The profit each firm earns will depend on the strategy it chooses and the strategy its rival chooses.

game theory
The study of how people or firms behave in strategic situations.

9.2
Game theory

There are four possible combinations of strategies for the two firms, and a lettered cell in Figure 9.3 represents each combination. For example, cell C represents a low-price strategy for Uptown along with a high-price strategy for RareAir. Figure 9.3 is called a *payoff matrix*, because each cell shows the payoff (profit) to each firm that would result from each combination of strategies. Cell C shows that if Uptown adopts a low-price strategy and RareAir a high-price strategy, then Uptown will earn $15 million (gray portion) and RareAir will earn $6 million (lavender portion).

Mutual Interdependence Revisited

The data in Figure 9.3 are hypothetical, but their relationships are typical of real situations. Recall that oligopolistic firms can increase their profits, and influence their rivals' profits, by changing their pricing strategies. Each firm's profit depends on its own

FIGURE 9.3
Profit payoff (in millions) for a two-firm oligopoly. Each firm has two possible pricing strategies. RareAir's strategies are shown in the top margin, and Uptown's in the left margin. Each lettered cell of this four-cell payoff matrix represents one combination of a RareAir strategy and an Uptown strategy and shows the profit that combination would earn for each firm.

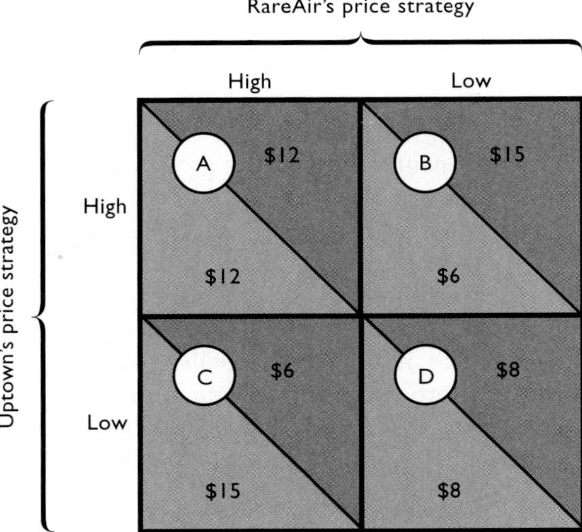

pricing strategy and that of its rivals. This mutual interdependence of oligopolists is the most obvious point demonstrated by Figure 9.3. If Uptown adopts a high-price strategy, its profit will be $12 million provided that RareAir also employs a high-price strategy (cell A). But if RareAir uses a low-price strategy against Uptown's high-price strategy (cell B), RareAir will increase its market share and boost its profit from $12 million to $15 million. RareAir's higher profit will come at the expense of Uptown, whose profit will fall from $12 million to $6 million. Uptown's high-price strategy is a good strategy only if RareAir also employs a high-price strategy.

Collusive Tendencies

Figure 9.3 also suggests that oligopolists often can benefit from **collusion**—that is, cooperation with rivals. Collusion occurs whenever firms in an industry reach an agreement to fix prices, divide up the market, or otherwise restrict competition among them. To see the benefits of collusion, first suppose that both firms in Figure 9.3 are acting independently and following high-price strategies. Each realizes a $12 million profit (cell A).

collusion A situation in which firms act together and in agreement to fix prices, divide markets, or otherwise restrict competition.

Note that either RareAir or Uptown could increase its profit by switching to a low-price strategy (cell B or C). The low-price firm would increase its profit to $15 million, and the profit of the high-price firm would fall to $6 million. The high-price firm would be better off if it, too, adopted a low-price policy because its profit would rise from $6 million to $8 million (cell D). The effect of all this independent strategy shifting would be the reduction of both firms' profits from $12 million (cell A) to $8 million (cell D).

In real situations, too, independent action by oligopolists may lead to mutually "competitive" low-price strategies: Independent oligopolists compete with respect to price, and this leads to lower prices and lower profits. This outcome is clearly beneficial to consumers but not to the oligopolists, whose profits decrease.

How could oligopolists avoid the low-profit outcome of cell D? The answer is that they could collude, rather than establish prices competitively or independently. In our example, the two firms could agree to establish and maintain a high-price policy. So each firm will increase its profit from $8 million (cell D) to $12 million (cell A).

Incentive to Cheat

The payoff matrix also explains why an oligopolist might be strongly tempted to cheat on a collusive agreement. Suppose Uptown and RareAir agree to maintain high-price policies, with each earning $12 million in profit (cell A). Both are tempted to cheat on this collusive pricing agreement, because either firm can increase its profit to $15 million by lowering its price. If Uptown secretly cheats on the agreement by charging low prices, the payoff moves from cell A to cell C. Uptown's profit rises to $15 million, and RareAir's falls to $6 million. If RareAir cheats, the payoff moves from cell A to cell B, and RareAir gets the $15 million.

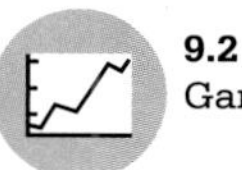

9.2 Game theory

Kinked-Demand Model

Our game-theory discussion is helpful in understanding more traditional, graphical oligopoly models. We begin by examining a model in which rivals do not overtly collude to fix a common price. Such collusion is, in fact, illegal in the United States. Specifically, Section 1 of the Sherman Act of 1890 outlaws conspiracies to restrain

per se violation
A collusive action, such as an attempt to fix prices or divide a market, that violates the antitrust laws, even if the action is unsuccessful.

trade. In antitrust law, these violations are known as **per se violations;** they are "in and of themselves" illegal, and therefore not subject to the rule of reason (Chapter 8). To gain a conviction, the government needs to show only that there was a conspiracy to fix prices, rig bids, or divide up markets, not that the conspiracy succeeded or caused serious damage to other parties.

Kinked-Demand Curve

Imagine an oligopolistic industry made up of three law-abiding firms (Arch, King, and Dave's), each having about one-third of the total market for a differentiated product. The question is, "What does each firm's demand curve look like?"

Let's focus on Arch, understanding that the analysis is applicable to each firm. Assume that the going price for the product is P_0 and Arch is currently selling output Q_0, as shown in Figure 9.4. Suppose Arch is considering a price increase. But if Arch raises its price above P_0 and its rivals ignore the price increase, Arch will lose sales significantly to its two rivals, who will be underpricing it. If that is the case, the demand and marginal-revenue curves faced by Arch will resemble the straight lines D_2 and MR_2 in Figure 9.4. Demand in this case is quite elastic: Arch's total revenue will fall. Because of product differentiation, however, Arch's sales and total revenue will not fall to zero when it raises its price; some of Arch's customers will pay the higher price because they have a strong preference for Arch's product.

And what about a price cut? It is reasonable to expect that King and Dave's will exactly match any price cut to prevent Arch from gaining an advantage over them. Arch's sales will increase only modestly. The small increase in sales that Arch (and its two rivals) will realize is at the expense of other industries; Arch will gain no sales from King

FIGURE 9.4
The kinked-demand curve. In all likelihood an oligopolist's rivals will ignore a price increase above the going price P_0 but follow a price cut below P_0. This causes the oligopolist's demand curve (D_2eD_1) to be kinked at *e* (price P_0) and the marginal-revenue curve to have a vertical break, or gap (*fg*). The firm will be highly reluctant to raise or lower its price. Moreover, any shift in marginal costs between MC_1 and MC_2 will cut the vertical (dashed) segment of the marginal-revenue curve and produce no change in price P_0 or output Q_0.

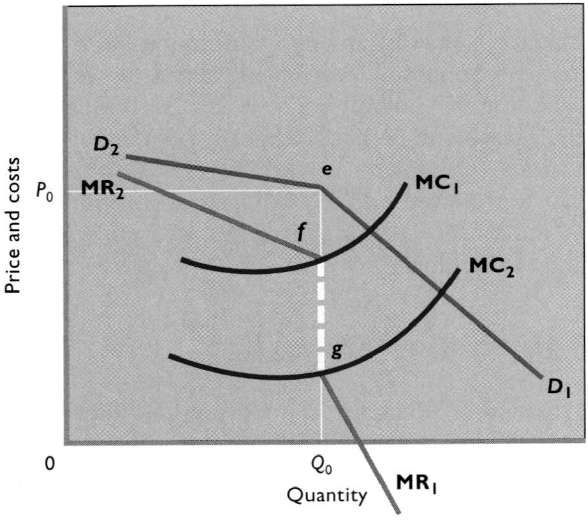

and Dave's. So Arch's demand and marginal-revenue curves below price P_0 will look like the straight lines labeled D_1 and MR_1 in Figure 9.4.

Graphically, the D_2e "rivals ignore" segment of Arch's demand curve seems relevant for price increases, and the D_1e "rivals match" segment of demand seems relevant for price cuts. It is logical, then, or at least a reasonable assumption, that the noncollusive oligopolist faces the **kinked-demand curve** D_2eD_1, as shown in Figure 9.4. Demand is highly elastic above the going price P_0 but much less elastic or even inelastic below that price.

kinked-demand curve
A demand curve based on the assumption that rivals will ignore a price increase and follow a price decrease.

Note also that if rivals ignore a price increase but match a price decrease, the marginal-revenue curve of the oligopolist will also have an odd shape. It, too, will be made up of two segments: the left-hand marginal-revenue curve MR_2f in Figure 9.4 and the right-hand marginal-revenue curve MR_1g. Because of the sharp difference in elasticity of demand above and below the going price, there is a gap, or what we can simply treat as a vertical segment, in the marginal-revenue curve. This gap is the dashed segment fg in the combined marginal-revenue curve MR_2fgMR_1.

Price Inflexibility

This analysis helps explain why prices are generally stable in noncollusive oligopolistic industries. There are both demand and cost reasons.

On the demand side, the kinked-demand curve gives each oligopolist reason to believe that any change in price will be for the worse. If it raises its price, many of its customers will desert it. If it lowers its price, its sales will increase very modestly, since rivals will match the lower price. Even if a price cut increases the oligopolist's total revenue somewhat, its costs may increase by a greater amount. And if its demand is inelastic to the right of Q_0, as it may well be, then the firm's profit will surely fall. Its total revenue will decline at the same time that the production of a larger output increases its total cost.

On the cost side, the broken marginal-revenue curve suggests that even if an oligopolist's costs change substantially, the firm may have no reason to change its price. In particular, all positions of the marginal-cost curve between MC_1 and MC_2 in Figure 9.4 will result in the firm's deciding on exactly the same price and output. For all those positions, MR equals MC at output Q_0; at that output, it will charge price P_0.

Price Leadership

The uncertainties of the reactions of rivals create a major problem for oligopolists. There are times when wages and other input prices rise beyond the marginal costs associated with MC_1 in Figure 9.4. If no oligopolist dare raise its price, profits for all rivals will be severely squeezed. In many industries a pattern of price leadership has emerged to handle these situations. **Price leadership** involves an implicit understanding by which oligopolists can coordinate prices without engaging in outright collusion based on formal agreements and secret meetings. Rather, a practice evolves whereby the "dominant firm"—usually the largest or most efficient in the industry—initiates price changes and all other firms more or less automatically follow the leader. Many industries, including farm machinery, cement, copper, newsprint, glass containers, steel, beer, fertilizer, cigarettes, and tin, are practicing, or have in the recent past practiced, price leadership.

price leadership
An implicit understanding that other firms will follow the lead when a certain firm in the industry initiates a price change.

An examination of price leadership in a variety of industries suggests that the price leader is likely to observe the following tactics.

- ***Infrequent price changes*** Because price changes always carry the risk that rivals will not follow the lead, price adjustments are made only infrequently. The price leader does not respond to minuscule day-to-day changes in costs and demand. Price is changed only when cost and demand conditions have been altered significantly and on an industry basis as the result of, for example, industry wage increases, an increase in excise taxes, or an increase in the price of some basic input such as energy. In the automobile industry, price adjustments traditionally have been made when new models are introduced each fall.
- ***Communications*** The price leader often communicates impending price adjustments to the industry through speeches by major executives, trade publication interviews, or press releases. By publicizing "the need to raise prices," the price leader seeks agreement among its competitors regarding the actual increase.
- ***Avoidance of price wars*** Price leaders try to prevent price wars that can damage industry profits. Such wars can lead to successive rounds of price cuts as rivals attempt to maintain their market shares.

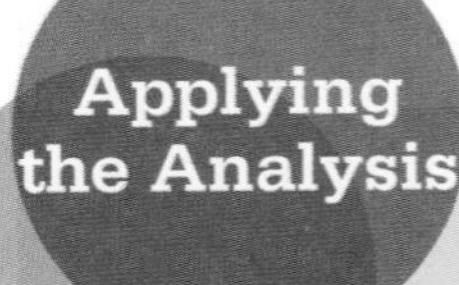

Challenges to Price Leadership

Despite attempts to maintain orderly price leadership, price wars occasionally break out in oligopolistic industries. Sometimes price wars result from attempts to establish new price leaders; other times, they result from attempts to "steal" business from rivals.

Consider the breakfast cereal industry, in which Kellogg traditionally had been the price leader. General Mills countered Kellogg's leadership in 1995 by reducing the prices of its cereals by 11 percent. In 1996, another rival, Post, responded to General Mills' action with a 20 percent price cut. Kellogg then followed with a 20 percent cut of its own. Not to be outdone, Post reduced its prices by another 11 percent. In short, a full-scale price war broke out between General Mills, Post, and Kellogg.

As another example, in late 2002 Burger King set off a price war by offering its bacon cheeseburger for 99¢. McDonald's retaliated by placing a price tag of $1 on its Big "N" Tasty burger, which competes directly against Burger King's popular and profitable Whopper. Burger King then countered with a "limited-time special" of 99¢ for Whoppers. The limited-time aspect of the offer signaled McDonald's that Burger King was willing to end the price war in the near future.

Most price wars eventually run their course. When all firms recognize that low prices are severely reducing their profits, they again yield price leadership to one of the industry's dominant firms. That firm then begins to raise prices back to their previous levels, and the other firms willingly follow. Orderly pricing is then restored.

Question:
How might a low-cost price leader "enforce" its leadership through implied threats to rivals?

Collusion

The disadvantages and uncertainties of kinked-demand oligopolies and price leadership make collusion tempting. By controlling price through collusion, oligopolists may be able to reduce uncertainty, increase profits, and perhaps even prohibit the entry of new rivals. Collusion may assume a variety of forms. The most comprehensive form is the **cartel**, a group of producers that typically creates a formal written agreement specifying how much each member will produce and charge. The cartel members must control output—divide up the market—in order to maintain the agreed-upon price. The collusion is *overt*, or open to view, and typically involves a group of foreign nations or foreign producers. More common forms of collusion are *covert*, or hidden from view. They include conspiracies to fix prices, rig bids, and divide up markets. Such conspiracies sometimes occur even though they are illegal.

cartel
A formal agreement among producers to set the price and the individual firm's output levels of a product.

Joint-Profit Maximization

To see the benefits of a cartel or other form of collusion, assume there are three hypothetical oligopolistic firms (Gypsum, Sheetrock, and GSR) producing, in this instance, gypsum drywall panels for finishing interior walls. Suppose all three firms produce a homogeneous product and have identical cost, demand, and marginal-revenue curves. Figure 9.5 represents the position of each of our three oligopolistic firms.

What price and output combination should, say, Gypsum select? If Gypsum were a pure monopolist, the answer would be clear: Establish output at Q_0, where marginal revenue equals marginal cost, charge the corresponding price P_0, and enjoy the maximum profit attainable. However, Gypsum does have two rivals selling identical products, and if Gypsum's assumption that its rivals will match its price of P_0 proves to be incorrect, the consequences could be disastrous for Gypsum. Specifically, if Sheetrock and GSR actually charge prices below P_0, then Gypsum's demand curve D will shift sharply to the left as its potential customers turn to its rivals, which are now selling the

FIGURE 9.5
Collusion and the tendency toward joint-profit maximization. If oligopolistic firms face identical or highly similar demand and cost conditions, they may collude to limit their joint output and to set a single, common price. Thus each firm acts as if it were a pure monopolist, setting output at Q_0 and charging price P_0. This price and output combination maximizes each firm's profit (gray area) and thus the joint profits of all.

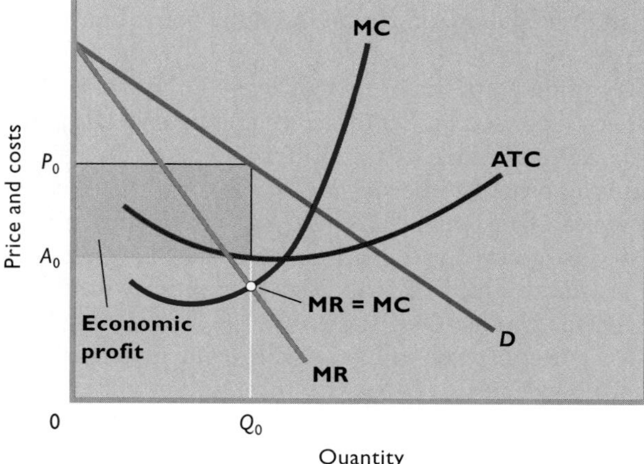

same product at a lower price. Of course, Gypsum can retaliate by cutting its price too, but this will move all three firms down their demand curves, lowering their profits. It may even drive them to a point where average total cost exceeds price and losses are incurred.

So the question becomes, "Will Sheetrock and GSR want to charge a price below P_0?" Under our assumptions, and recognizing that Gypsum has little choice except to match any price they may set below P_0, the answer is no. Faced with the same demand and cost circumstances, Sheetrock and GSR will find it in their interest to produce Q_0 and charge P_0. This is a curious situation; each firm finds it most profitable to charge the same price, P_0, but only if its rivals actually do so! How can the three firms ensure the price P_0 and quantity Q_0 solution in which each is keenly interested? How can they avoid the less profitable outcomes associated with either higher or lower prices?

The answer is evident: They can collude. They can get together, talk it over, and agree to charge the same price, P_0. In addition to reducing the possibility of price wars, this will give each firm the maximum profit. For society, the result will be the same as would occur if the industry were a pure monopoly composed of three identical plants.

Applying the Analysis

Cartels and Collusion

Undoubtedly the most significant international cartel is the Organization of Petroleum Exporting Countries (OPEC), comprising 11 oil-producing nations (Saudi Arabia, Iran, Venezuela, UAE, Nigeria, Kuwait, Libya, Indonesia, Algeria, Qatar, and Iraq). OPEC produces 40 percent of the world's oil and supplies 60 percent of all oil traded internationally. In the late 1990s it reacted vigorously to very low oil prices by greatly restricting supply. Some non-OPEC producers supported the cutback in production, and within a 15-month period the price of oil shot up from $11 a barrel to $34 a barrel. Fearing a global political and economic backlash from the major industrial nations, OPEC upped the production quotas for its members in mid-2000. The increases in oil supply that resulted reduced the price of oil to about $25, where it remained through 2002. It is clear that the OPEC cartel has sufficient market power to hold the price of oil substantially above its marginal cost of production. (In 2005, supply uncertainties associated with the Iraq war and rising demand for oil in China helped push the price up to over $60 a barrel!)

Because cartels among domestic firms are illegal in the United States, any collusion that exists is covert or secret. Yet there are numerous examples of collusion, as shown by evidence from antitrust (antimonopoly) cases. In 1993 Borden, Pet, and Dean Food, among others, either pleaded guilty to or were convicted of rigging bids on the prices of milk products sold to schools and military bases. By phone or at luncheons, company executives agreed in advance on which firm would submit the low bid for each school district or military base. In 1996 American agribusiness Archer Daniels Midland and three Japanese and South Korean firms were found to have conspired to fix the worldwide price and sales volume of a livestock feed additive. Executives for the firms secretly met in Hong Kong, Paris, Mexico City, Vancouver, and Zurich to discuss their plans.

There are many other relatively recent examples of price fixing: ConAgra and Hormel agreed to pay more than $21 million to settle their roles in a nationwide price-fixing case involving catfish. The U.S. Justice Department fined UCAR International $110 million for scheming with rivals to fix prices and divide the world market for graphite electrodes used in steel mills. The auction houses Sotheby's and Christy's were found guilty of conspiring over a 6-year period to set the same commission rates for sellers at auctions. Bayer AG pleaded guilty to, and was fined $66 million for, taking part in a conspiracy to divide up the market and set prices for chemicals used in rubber manufacturing.

Question:
In what way might mergers be an alternative to illegal collusion? In view of your answer, why is it important to enforce laws that outlaw mergers which substantially reduce competition?

Obstacles to Collusion

Normally, cartels and similar collusive arrangements are difficult to establish and maintain. Below are several barriers to collusion beyond the antitrust laws.

Demand and Cost Differences When oligopolists face different costs and demand curves, it is difficult for them to agree on a price. This is particularly the case in industries where products are differentiated and change frequently. Even with highly standardized products, firms usually have somewhat different market shares and operate with differing degrees of productive efficiency. Thus it is unlikely that even homogeneous oligopolists would have the same demand and cost curves.

In either case, differences in costs and demand mean that the profit-maximizing price will differ among firms; no single price will be readily acceptable to all, as we assumed was true in Figure 9.5. So price collusion depends on compromises and concessions that are not always easy to obtain and hence act as an obstacle to collusion.

Number of Firms Other things equal, the larger the number of firms, the more difficult it is to create a cartel or some other form of price collusion. Agreement on price by three or four producers that control an entire market may be relatively easy to accomplish. But such agreement is more difficult to achieve where there are, say, 10 firms, each with roughly 10 percent of the market, or where the Big Three have 70 percent of the market while a competitive fringe of 8 or 10 smaller firms battles for the remainder.

Cheating As the game-theory model makes clear, there is a temptation for collusive oligopolists to engage in secret price cutting to increase sales and profit. The difficulty with such cheating is that buyers who are paying a high price for a product may become aware of the lower-priced sales and demand similar treatment. Or buyers receiving a price concession from one producer may use the concession as a wedge to get even larger price concessions from a rival producer. Buyers' attempts to play producers against one another may precipitate price wars among the producers. Although secret price concessions are potentially profitable, they threaten collusive oligopolies over time. Collusion is more likely to succeed when cheating is easy to detect and punish. Then the conspirators are less likely to cheat on the price agreement.

Recession Long-lasting recession usually serves as an enemy of collusion because slumping markets increase average total cost. In technical terms, as the oligopolists' demand and marginal-revenue curves shift to the left in Figure 9.5 in response to a recession, each firm moves leftward and upward to a higher operating point on its average-total-cost curve. Firms find they have substantial excess production capacity, sales are down, unit costs are up, and profits are being squeezed. Under such conditions, businesses may feel they can avoid serious profit reductions (or even losses) by cutting price and thus gaining sales at the expense of rivals.

Potential Entry The greater prices and profits that result from collusion may attract new entrants, including foreign firms. Since that would increase market supply and reduce prices and profits, successful collusion requires that colluding oligopolists block the entry of new producers.

Oligopoly and Advertising

We have noted that oligopolists would rather not compete on the basis of price and may become involved in price collusion. Nonetheless, each firm's share of the total market is typically determined through product development and advertising, for two reasons:

- Product development and advertising campaigns are less easily duplicated than price cuts. Price cuts can be quickly and easily matched by a firm's rivals to cancel any potential gain in sales derived from that strategy. Product improvements and successful advertising, however, can produce more permanent gains in market share because they cannot be duplicated as quickly and completely as price reductions.
- Oligopolists have sufficient financial resources to engage in product development and advertising. For most oligopolists, the economic profits earned in the past can help finance current advertising and product development.

In 2004, firms spent an estimated $264 billion on advertising in the United States. *Advertising is prevalent in both monopolistic competition and oligopoly.* Table 9.1 lists the 10 leading U.S. advertisers in 2004.

TABLE 9.1
The Largest U.S. Advertisers, 2004

Company	Advertising Spending Millions of $
General Motors	$3997.4
Procter & Gamble	3919.7
Time Warner	3283.1
Pfizer	2957.3
SBC Communications	2686.8
DaimlerChrysler	2462.1
Ford Motor	2458.0
Walt Disney	2241.5
Verizon	2197.3
Johnson & Johnson	2175.7

Source: *Advertising Age*, www.adage.com/

Advertising may affect prices, competition, and efficiency either positively or negatively, depending on the circumstances. While our focus here is on advertising by oligopolists, the analysis is equally applicable to advertising by monopolistic competitors.

Positive Effects of Advertising

In order to make rational (efficient) decisions, consumers need information about product characteristics and prices. Media advertising may be a low-cost means for consumers to obtain that information. Suppose you are in the market for a high-quality camera and there is no advertising of such a product in newspapers or magazines. To make a rational choice, you may have to spend several days visiting stores to determine the availability, prices, and features of various brands. This search entails both direct costs (gasoline, parking fees) and indirect costs (the value of your time). By providing information about the available options, advertising reduces your search time and minimizes these direct and indirect costs.

By providing information about the various competing goods that are available, advertising diminishes monopoly power. In fact, advertising is frequently associated with the introduction of new products designed to compete with existing brands. Could Toyota and Honda have so strongly challenged U.S. auto producers without advertising? Could Federal Express have sliced market share away from UPS and the U.S. Postal Service without advertising?

Viewed this way, advertising is an efficiency-enhancing activity. It is a relatively inexpensive means of providing useful information to consumers and thus lowering their search costs. By enhancing competition, advertising results in greater economic efficiency. By facilitating the introduction of new products, advertising speeds up technological progress. By increasing output, advertising can reduce long-run average total cost by enabling firms to obtain economies of scale.

Potential Negative Effects of Advertising

Not all the effects of advertising are positive, of course. Much advertising is designed simply to manipulate or persuade consumers—that is, to alter their preferences in favor of the advertiser's product. A television commercial that indicates that a popular personality drinks a particular brand of soft drink—and therefore that you should too—conveys little or no information to consumers about price or quality. In addition, advertising is sometimes based on misleading and extravagant claims that confuse consumers rather than enlighten them. Indeed, in some cases advertising may well persuade consumers to pay high prices for much-acclaimed but inferior products, forgoing better but unadvertised products selling at lower prices. Example: *Consumer Reports* has found that heavily advertised premium motor oils and fancy additives provide no better engine performance and longevity than do cheaper brands.

Firms often establish substantial brand-name loyalty and thus achieve monopoly power via their advertising (see Global Snapshot 9.1 on the next page). As a consequence, they are able to increase their sales, expand their market shares, and enjoy greater profits. Larger profit permits still more advertising and further enlargement of the firm's market share and profit. In time, consumers may lose the advantages of competitive markets and face the disadvantages of monopolized markets. Moreover, new entrants to the industry need to incur large advertising costs in order to establish their products in the marketplace; thus, advertising costs may be a barrier to entry.

The World's Top 10 Brand Names

Here are the world's top 10 brands, based on four criteria: the brand's market share within its category, the brand's world appeal across age groups and nationalities, the loyalty of customers to the brand, and the ability of the brand to "stretch" to products beyond the original product.

World's Top 10 Brands

Coca-Cola
Microsoft
IBM
General Electric
Intel
Nokia
Disney
McDonald's
Toyota
Marlboro

Source: Interbrand, www.interbrand.com/. Data are for 2005.

Advertising can also be self-canceling. The advertising campaign of one fast-food hamburger chain may be offset by equally costly campaigns waged by rivals, so each firm's demand actually remains unchanged. Few, if any, extra burgers will be purchased, and each firm's market share will stay the same. But because of the advertising, the cost and hence the price of hamburgers will be higher.

When advertising either leads to increased monopoly power or is self-canceling, economic inefficiency results.

Oligopoly and Efficiency

Is oligopoly, then, an efficient market structure from society's standpoint? How do the price and output decisions of the oligopolist measure up to the triple equality $P = \text{MC} = \text{minimum ATC}$ that occurs in pure competition?

Inefficiency

Many economists believe that the outcome of some oligopolistic markets is approximately as shown in Figure 9.5. This view is bolstered by evidence that many oligopolists sustain sizable economic profits year after year. In that case, the oligopolist's production occurs where price exceeds marginal cost and average total cost. Moreover, production is below the output at which average total cost is minimized. In this view, neither productive efficiency ($P = \text{minimum ATC}$) nor allocative efficiency ($P = \text{MC}$) is likely to occur under oligopoly. A few observers assert that oligopoly is actually less desirable than pure monopoly, because government usually regulates pure monopoly in the United States to guard against abuses of monopoly power. Informal collusion among oligopolists may yield price and output results similar to those under pure monopoly yet give the outward appearance of competition involving independent firms.

Qualifications

We should note, however, three qualifications to this view:

- ***Increased foreign competition*** In recent decades foreign competition has increased rivalry in a number of oligopolistic industries—steel, automobiles, photographic film, electric shavers, outboard motors, and copy machines, for example. This has helped to break down such cozy arrangements as price leadership and to stimulate much more competitive pricing.
- ***Limit pricing*** Recall that some oligopolists may purposely keep prices below the short-run profit-maximizing level in order to bolster entry barriers. In essence, consumers and society may get some of the benefits of competition—prices closer to marginal cost and minimum average total cost—even without the competition that free entry would provide.
- ***Technological advance*** Over time, oligopolistic industries may foster more rapid product development and greater improvement of production techniques than would be possible if they were purely competitive. Oligopolists have large economic profits from which they can fund expensive research and development (R&D). Moreover, the existence of barriers to entry may give the oligopolist some assurance that it will reap the rewards of successful R&D. Oligopolists account for the bulk of the more than $200 billion that U.S. businesses spend on R&D each year. Thus, the short-run economic inefficiencies of oligopolists may be partly or wholly offset by the oligopolists' contributions to better products, lower prices, and lower costs over time.

Applying the Analysis

Oligopoly in the Beer Industry

The beer industry serves as a good case study for oligopoly. This industry was once populated by hundreds of firms and an even larger number of brands. But it now is an oligopoly dominated by a handful of producers. While the five largest brewers sold only 19 percent of the nation's beer in 1947, the Big Four brewers (Anheuser-Busch, SABMiller, Coors, and Pabst) currently sell 84 percent of the nation's beer. The Big Two—Anheuser-Busch (at 49 percent) and SABMiller (at 20 percent)—produce 69 percent. The industry is clearly an oligopoly.

Changes on the demand side of the market have contributed to the "shakeout" of small brewers from the industry. First, consumer tastes have generally shifted from the stronger-flavored beers of the small brewers to the light products of the larger brewers. Second, there has been a shift from the consumption of beer in taverns to consumption of it in the home. The beer consumed in taverns was mainly "draft" or "tap" beer from kegs, supplied by local and regional brewers that could deliver the kegs in a timely fashion at relatively low transportation cost. But the large increase in the demand for beer consumed at home opened the door for large brewers that sold their beer in bottles and aluminum cans. The large brewers could ship their beer by truck or rail over long distances and compete directly with the local brewers.

Developments on the supply side of the market have been even more profound. Technological advances speeded up the bottling and canning lines. Today, large brewers can fill and close 2000 cans per line per minute. Large plants are also able to reduce labor costs through the automating of brewing and warehousing. Furthermore, plant construction costs per barrel are about one-third less for a 4.5-million-barrel plant than for a 1.5-million-barrel plant. As a consequence of these and other factors, the minimum efficient scale in brewing is a plant size of about 4.5 million barrels, with multiple plants. Because the construction cost of a modern brewery of that size averages about $300 million, economies of scale may now constitute a significant barrier to entry.

"Blindfold" taste tests confirm that most mass-produced American beers taste alike. So brewers greatly emphasize advertising. And here Anheuser-Busch, SAB-Miller, and Coors, which sell national brands, enjoy major cost advantages over producers such as Pabst that have many regional brands (for example, Lonestar, Rainer, Schaefer, and Schmidts). The reason is that national television advertising is less costly *per viewer* than local spot TV advertising.

Although mergers have occurred in the brewing industry, they have not been a fundamental cause of the rising concentration. Rather, they largely have been the result of failing smaller breweries' (such as Heileman's) selling out. Dominant firms have expanded by heavily advertising their main brands and by creating new brands such as Lite, Bud Light, Genuine Draft, Keystone, and Icehouse rather than acquiring other brewers. This has sustained significant product differentiation, despite the declining number of major brewers.

The story of the last two decades has been Anheuser-Busch (A-B), which has greatly expanded its market share. A-B now makes the nation's top two brands: Bud Light and Budweiser account for nearly half the beer sold in the United States. Part of A-B's success owes to the demise of regional competitors. But part also is the result of A-B's strategic prowess. It has constructed state-of-the-art breweries, created effective advertising campaigns, and forged strong relationships with regional distributors. Meanwhile, Miller's market share has declined slightly in recent years. In 2002 Philip Morris sold Miller to South African Breweries (SAB). SABMiller, as the firm is now called, redesigned Miller's labeling to enhance its appeal and to expand its presence overseas.

Imported beers such as Beck, Corona, and Guinness constitute about 9 percent of the market, with individual brands seeming to wax and wane in popularity. Some local or regional microbreweries such as Samuel Adams and Pyramid, which brew "craft" or specialty beers and charge super-premium prices, have slightly whittled into the sales of the major brewers. A-B and Miller have taken notice, responding with specialty brands of their own (for example, Red Wolf, Red Dog, Killarney's, and Icehouse) and buying stakes in microbrewers Redhook Ale and Celis. But despite their local success, microbreweries account for only about 3 percent of the beer consumed in the United States and pose less of a threat to the majors than does "trendy" imported beer.

Source: Based on Kenneth G. Elzinga, "Beer," in Walter Adams and James Brock (eds.), *The Structure of American Industry,* 10th ed. (Upper Saddle River, N.J.: Prentice-Hall, 2001), pp. 85–113; and Douglas F. Greer, "Beer: Causes of Structural Change," in Larry Duetsch (ed.), *Industry Studies,* 2d ed. (New York: M. E. Sharpe, 1998), pp. 28–64. Updated data and information are mainly from *Beer Marketer's Insights,* www.beerinsights.com, and the Association of Brewers, www.beertown.com.

Summary

1. The distinguishing features of monopolistic competition are (a) there are enough firms in the industry to ensure that each firm has only limited control over price, mutual interdependence is absent, and collusion is nearly impossible; (b) products are characterized by real or perceived differences so that economic rivalry entails both price and nonprice competition; and (c) entry to the industry is relatively easy. Many aspects of retailing, and some manufacturing industries in which economies of scale are few, approximate monopolistic competition.
2. Monopolistically competitive firms may earn economic profits or incur losses in the short run. The easy entry and exit of firms result in only normal profits in the long run.
3. The long-run equilibrium position of the monopolistically competitive producer is less efficient than that of the pure competitor. Under monopolistic competition, price exceeds marginal cost, suggesting an underallocation of resources to the product, and price exceeds minimum average total cost, indicating that consumers do not get the product at the lowest price that cost conditions might allow.
4. Nonprice competition provides a way that monopolistically competitive firms can offset the long-run tendency for economic profit to fall to zero. Through product differentiation, product development, and advertising, a firm may strive to increase the demand for its product more than enough to cover the added cost of such nonprice competition. Consumers benefit from the wide diversity of product choice that monopolistic competition provides.
5. In practice, the monopolistic competitor seeks the specific combination of price, product, and advertising that will maximize profit.
6. Oligopolistic industries are characterized by the presence of few firms, each having a significant fraction of the market. Firms thus situated engage in strategic behavior and are mutually interdependent: The behavior of any one firm directly affects, and is affected by, the actions of rivals. Products may be either virtually uniform or significantly differentiated. Various barriers to entry, including economies of scale, underlie and maintain oligopoly.
7. Game theory (a) shows the interdependence of oligopolists' pricing policies, (b) reveals the tendency of oligopolists to collude, and (c) explains the temptation of oligopolists to cheat on collusive arrangements.
8. Noncollusive oligopolists may face a kinked-demand curve. This curve and the accompanying marginal-revenue curve help explain the price rigidity that often characterizes oligopolies; they do not, however, explain how the actual prices of products were first established.
9. Price leadership is an informal means of overcoming difficulties relating to kinked-demand curves whereby one firm, usually the largest or most efficient, initiates price changes and the other firms in the industry follow the leader.
10. Collusive oligopolists such as cartels maximize joint profits—that is, they behave like pure monopolists. Demand and cost differences, a "large" number of firms, cheating through secret price concessions, recessions, and the antitrust laws are all obstacles to collusive oligopoly.
11. Market shares in oligopolistic industries are usually determined on the basis of product development and advertising. Oligopolists emphasize nonprice competition because (a) advertising and product variations are less easy for rivals to match and (b) oligopolists frequently have ample resources to finance nonprice competition.
12. Advertising may affect prices, competition, and efficiency either positively or negatively. Positive: It can provide consumers with low-cost information about competing products, help introduce new competing products into concentrated industries, and generally reduce monopoly power and its attendant inefficiencies. Negative: It can promote monopoly power via persuasion and the creation of entry barriers. Moreover, it can be self-canceling when engaged in by rivals; then it boosts costs and creates inefficiency while accomplishing little else.
13. Neither productive nor allocative efficiency is realized in oligopolistic markets, but oligopoly may be superior to pure competition in promoting research and development and technological progress.

Terms and Concepts

monopolistic competition
product differentiation
nonprice competition
excess capacity
oligopoly
homogeneous oligopoly
differentiated oligopoly
strategic behavior
mutual interdependence

game theory

collusion

per se violation

kinked-demand curve

price leadership

cartel

Study Questions

1. How does monopolistic competition differ from pure competition in its basic characteristics? How does it differ from pure monopoly? Explain fully what product differentiation may involve. Explain how the entry of firms into its industry affects the demand curve facing a monopolistic competitor and how that, in turn, affects its economic profit.
2. Compare the elasticity of the monopolistic competitor's demand with that of a pure competitor and a pure monopolist. Assuming identical long-run costs, compare graphically the prices and outputs that would result in the long run under pure competition and under monopolistic competition. Contrast the two market structures in terms of productive and allocative efficiency. Explain: "Monopolistically competitive industries are characterized by too many firms, each of which produces too little."
3. "Monopolistic competition is monopolistic up to the point at which consumers become willing to buy close-substitute products and competitive beyond that point." Explain.
4. "Competition in quality and service may be just as effective as price competition in giving buyers more for their money." Do you agree? Why? Explain why monopolistically competitive firms frequently prefer nonprice competition to price competition.
5. Why do oligopolies exist? List five or six oligopolists whose products you own or regularly purchase. What distinguishes oligopoly from monopolistic competition?
6. Explain the general meaning of the following profit payoff matrix for oligopolists C and D. All profit figures are in thousands.

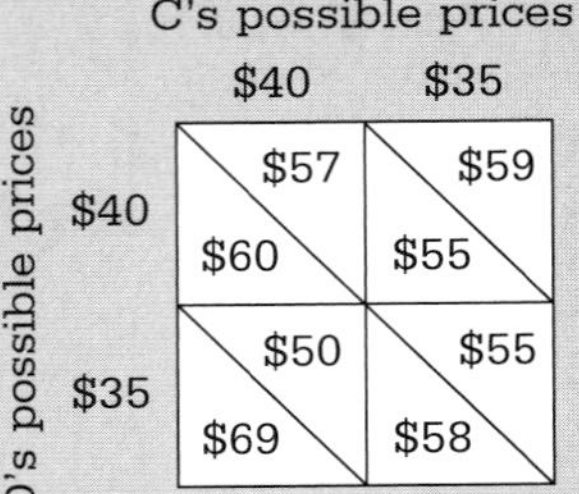

   a. Use the payoff matrix to explain the mutual interdependence that characterizes oligopolistic industries.
   b. Assuming no collusion between C and D, what is the likely pricing outcome?
   c. In view of your answer to 6b, explain why price collusion is mutually profitable. Why might there be a temptation to cheat on the collusive agreement?
7. What assumptions about a rival's response to price changes underlie the kinked-demand curve for oligopolists? Why is there a gap in the oligopolist's marginal-revenue curve? How does the kinked-demand curve explain price rigidity in oligopoly?
8. Why might price collusion occur in oligopolistic industries? Assess the economic desirability of collusive pricing. What are the main obstacles to collusion? Speculate as to why price leadership is legal in the United States, whereas price fixing is not.
9. Why is there so much advertising in monopolistic competition and oligopoly? How does such advertising help consumers and promote efficiency? Why might it be excessive at times?
10. Construct a game-theory matrix involving two firms and their decisions on high versus low advertising budgets and the effects of each on profits. Show a circumstance in which both firms select high advertising budgets even though both would be more profitable with low advertising budgets. Why won't they unilaterally cut their advertising budgets?
11. What firm dominates the beer industry? What demand and supply factors have contributed to "fewness" in this industry?

Website Questions

At the text's Website, www.brueonline.com, you will find three multiple-choice quizzes on this chapter's content. We encourage you to take the quizzes to see how you do. Also, you will find one or more Web-based questions that require information from the Internet to answer.

PART FOUR

Resource Markets

10 Wage Determination

11 Income Inequality and Poverty

CHAPTER TEN

Wage Determination

In this chapter you will learn:

- Why the firm's marginal revenue product curve is its labor demand curve.
- The factors that increase or decrease labor demand.
- The determinants of elasticity of labor demand.
- How wage rates are determined in competitive and monopsonistic labor markets.
- How unions increase wage rates.
- The major causes of wage differentials.

We now turn from the pricing and production of *goods and services* to the pricing and employment of *resources*. Although firms come in various sizes and operate under highly different market conditions, they each have a demand for productive resources. They obtain those resources from households—the direct or indirect owners of land, labor, capital, and entrepreneurial resources. So, referring to the circular flow diagram (Figure 2.2, page 39), we shift our attention from the bottom loop (where businesses supply products that households demand) to the top loop (where businesses demand resources that households supply).

A Focus on Labor

The basic principles we develop in this chapter apply to land, labor, and capital resources, but we will emphasize the pricing and employment of labor. About 72 percent of all income in the United States flows to households in the form of wages and salaries. More than 140 million of us go to work each day in the United States. We have an amazing variety of jobs with thousands of different employers and receive large differences in pay. What determines our hourly wage or annual salary? Why is the salary of, say, a topflight major-league baseball player $15 million or more a year, whereas the pay for a first-rate schoolteacher is $50,000? Why are starting salaries for college graduates who major in engineering and accounting so much higher than those for graduates majoring in journalism and sociology?

Demand and supply analysis helps us answer these questions. We begin by examining labor demand and labor supply in a **purely competitive labor market.** In such a market,

purely competitive labor market A labor market in which a large number of similarly qualified workers independently offer their labor services to a large number of employers, none of whom can set the wage rate.

- Numerous employers compete with one another in hiring a specific type of labor.
- Each of many workers with identical skills supplies that type of labor.
- Individual employers and individual workers are "wage takers" because neither can control the market wage rate.

Labor Demand

Labor demand is the starting point for any discussion of wages and salaries. The demand for labor is an inverse relationship between the price of labor (hourly wage) and the quantity of labor demanded. As with all resources, labor demand is a **derived demand:** It results from the products that labor helps produce. Labor resources usually do not directly satisfy customer wants but do so indirectly through their use in producing goods and services. No one wants to consume directly the labor services of a software engineer, but people do want to use the software that the engineer helps create.

derived demand The demand for a resource that results from the demand for the products it helps produce.

Marginal Revenue Product

The derived nature of labor demand means that the strength of the demand will depend on the productivity of the labor—its ability to produce goods and services—and the price of the good or service it helps produce. A resource that is highly productive in turning out a highly valued commodity will be in great demand. In contrast, a relatively unproductive resource that is capable of producing only a minimally valued commodity will be in little demand. And there will be no demand at all for a resource that is phenomenally efficient in producing something that no one wants to buy.

Consider the table in Figure 10.1, which shows the roles of marginal productivity and product price in determining labor demand.

Productivity Columns 1 and 2 give the number of units of labor employed and the resulting total product (output). Column 3 provides the marginal product (MP), or additional output, resulting from using each additional unit of labor. Columns 1 through 3 remind us that the law of diminishing returns applies here, causing the marginal product of labor to fall beyond some point. For simplicity, we assume that those diminishing marginal returns—those declines in marginal product—begin with the second worker hired.

FIGURE 10.1
The purely competitive seller's demand for labor. The MRP-of-labor curve is the labor demand curve; each of its points relates a particular wage rate (=MRP when profit is maximized) with a corresponding quantity of labor demanded. The downward slope of the D = MRP curve results from the law of diminishing marginal returns.

(1) Units of Labor	(2) Total Product (Output)	(3) Marginal Product (MP)	(4) Product Price	(5) Total Revenue, (2) × (4)	(6) Marginal Revenue Product (MRP)
0	0		$2	$ 0	
		7			$14
1	7		2	14	
		6			12
2	13		2	26	
		5			10
3	18		2	36	
		4			8
4	22		2	44	
		3			6
5	25		2	50	
		2			4
6	27		2	54	
		1			2
7	28		2	56	

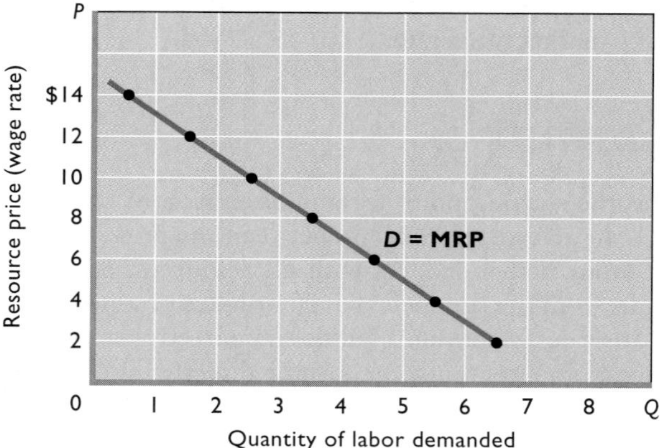

Product Price The derived demand for labor depends also on the market value (product price) of the good or service. Column 4 in the table in Figure 10.1 adds this price information to the mix. Because we are assuming a competitive product market, product price equals marginal revenue. The firm is a price taker and will sell units of output only at this market price. And this price will also be the firm's marginal revenue. In this case, both price and marginal revenue are a constant $2.

Multiplying column 2 by column 4 gives us the total-revenue data of column 5. These are the amounts of revenue the firm realizes from the various levels of employment. From these total-revenue data we can compute the **marginal revenue product (MRP)** of labor—the change in total revenue resulting from the use of each additional unit of labor. In equation form,

marginal revenue product (MRP) The change in a firm's total revenue when it employs 1 more unit of labor.

$$\text{Marginal revenue product} = \frac{\text{change in total revenue}}{\text{unit change in labor}}$$

The MRPs are listed in column 6 in the table.

Rule for Employing Labor: MRP = MRC

The MRP schedule, shown as columns 1 and 6, is the firm's demand schedule for labor. To explain why, we must first discuss the rule that guides a profit-seeking firm in hiring any resource: To maximize profit, a firm should hire additional units of labor as long as each successive unit adds more to the firm's total revenue than to its total cost.

Economists use special terms to designate what each additional unit of labor (or any other variable resource) adds to total revenue and what it adds to total cost. We have seen that MRP measures how much each successive unit of labor adds to total revenue. The amount that each additional unit of labor adds to the firm's total cost is called its **marginal resource cost (MRC).** In equation form,

$$\text{Marginal resource cost} = \frac{\text{change in total (labor) cost}}{\text{unit change in labor}}$$

marginal resource cost (MRC) The change in a firm's total cost when it employs 1 more unit of labor.

So we can restate our rule for hiring resources as follows: It will be profitable for a firm to hire additional units of labor up to the point at which labor's MRP is equal to its MRC. If the number of workers a firm is currently hiring is such that the MRP of the last worker exceeds his or her MRC, the firm can profit by hiring more workers. But if the number being hired is such that the MRC of the last worker exceeds his or her MRP, the firm is hiring workers who are not "paying their way" and it can increase its profit by discharging some workers. You may have recognized that this **MRP = MRC rule** is similar to the MR = MC profit-maximizing rule employed throughout our discussion of price and output determination. The rationale of the two rules is the same, but the point of reference is now *inputs* of a resource, not *outputs* of a product.

MRP = MRC rule The principle that to maximize profit a firm should expand employment until the marginal revenue product (MRP) of labor equals the marginal resource cost (MRC) of labor.

MRP as Labor Demand Schedule

In a competitive labor market, market supply and market demand establish the wage rate. Because each firm hires such a small fraction of the market supply of labor, an individual firm cannot influence the market wage rate; it is a wage taker, not a wage maker. This means that for each additional unit of labor hired, total labor cost increases by exactly the amount of the constant market wage rate. The MRC of labor exactly equals the market wage rate. Thus, resource "price" (the market wage rate) and resource "cost" (marginal resource cost) are equal for a firm that hires labor in a competitive labor market. Then the MRP = MRC rule tells us that a competitive firm will hire units of labor up to the point at which the market *wage rate* (its MRC) is equal to its MRP.

In terms of the data in columns 1 and 6 in Figure 10.1's table, if the market wage rate is, say, \$13.95, the firm will hire only one worker. This is the outcome because the first worker adds \$14 to total revenue and slightly less—\$13.95—to total cost. In other words, because MRP exceeds MRC for the first worker, it is profitable to hire that worker. For each successive worker, however, MRC (=\$13.95) exceeds MRP (=\$12 or less), indicating that it will not be profitable to hire any of those workers. If the wage rate is \$11.95, by the same reasoning we discover that it will pay the firm to hire both the first and second workers. Similarly, if the wage rate is \$9.95, three will be hired; if it is \$7.95, four; if it is \$5.95, five; and so forth. *The MRP schedule therefore constitutes the firm's demand for labor because each point on this schedule (or curve) indicates the quantity of labor units the firm would hire at each possible wage rate.* In the graph in Figure 10.1, we show the D = MRP curve based on the data in the table. The competitive firm's labor demand curve reflects an inverse relationship between the wage rate and the quantity of labor demanded. The curve slopes downward because of diminishing returns.[1]

Market Demand for Labor

We have now explained the individual firm's demand curve for labor. Recall that the total, or market, demand curve for a *product* is found by summing horizontally the demand curves of all individual buyers in the market. The market demand curve for a particular *resource* is derived in essentially the same way. Economists sum the individual labor demand curves of all firms hiring a particular kind of labor to obtain the market demand for that labor.

Changes in Labor Demand

What will alter the demand for labor (shift the labor demand curve)? The fact that labor demand is derived from *product demand* and depends on *resource productivity* suggests two "resource demand shifters." Also, our analysis of how changes in the prices of other products can shift a product's demand curve (Chapter 3) suggests another factor: changes in the prices of other *resources*.

Changes in Product Demand

Other things equal, an increase in the demand for a product will increase the demand for a resource used in its production, whereas a decrease in product demand will decrease the resource demand.

Let's see how this works. The first thing to recall is that a change in the demand for a product will normally change its price. In the table in Figure 10.1, let's assume that an increase in product demand boosts product price from $2 to $3. You should calculate the new labor demand schedule (columns 1 and 6) that would result, and plot it in the graph to verify that the new labor demand curve lies to the right of the old demand curve. Similarly, a decline in the product demand (and price) will shift the labor demand curve to the left. The fact that labor demand changes along with product demand demonstrates that labor demand is derived from product demand.

Example: With no offsetting change in supply, an increase in the demand for new houses will drive up house prices. Those higher prices will increase the MRP of construction workers, and therefore the demand for construction workers will rise. The labor demand curve will shift to the right.

Changes in Productivity

Other things equal, an increase in the productivity of a resource will increase the demand for the resource and a decrease in productivity will reduce the resource demand. If we doubled the MP data of column 3 in the table in Figure 10.1, the MRP data of column 6 would also double, indicating a rightward shift of the labor demand curve in the graph.

---

[1] Note that we plot the points in Figure 10.1 halfway between succeeding numbers of labor units. For example, we plot the MRP of the second unit ($12) not at 1 or 2 but at 1½. This "smoothing" enables us to sketch a continuously downsloping curve rather than one that moves downward in discrete steps as each new unit of labor is hired.

The productivity of any resource may be altered in several ways:

- ***Quantities of other resources*** The marginal productivity of any resource will vary with the quantities of the other resources used with it. The greater the amount of capital and land resources used with labor, the greater will be labor's marginal productivity and, thus, labor demand.
- ***Technological advance*** Technological improvements that increase the quality of other resources, such as capital, have the same effect. The better the *quality* of capital, the greater the productivity of labor used with it. Dockworkers employed with a specific amount of capital in the form of unloading cranes are more productive than dockworkers with the same amount of capital embodied in older conveyor-belt systems.
- ***Quality of labor*** Improvements in the quality of labor will increase its marginal productivity and therefore its demand. In effect, there will be a new demand curve for a different, more skilled, kind of labor.

Changes in the Prices of Other Resources

Changes in the prices of other resources may change the demand for labor.

Substitute Resources Suppose that labor and capital are substitutable in a certain production process. A firm can produce some specific amount of output using a relatively small amount of labor and a relatively large amount of capital, or vice versa. What happens if the price of machinery (capital) falls? The effect on the demand for labor will be the net result of two opposed effects: the substitution effect and the output effect.

- ***Substitution effect*** The decline in the price of machinery prompts the firm to substitute machinery for labor. This allows the firm to produce its output at lower cost. So at the fixed wage rate, smaller quantities of labor are now employed. This **substitution effect** decreases the demand for labor. More generally, the substitution effect indicates that a firm will purchase more of an input whose relative price has declined and, conversely, use less of an input whose relative price has increased.
- ***Output effect*** Because the price of machinery has declined, the costs of producing various outputs must also decline. With lower costs, the firm can profitably produce and sell a greater output. The greater output increases the demand for all resources, including labor. So this **output effect** increases the demand for labor. More generally, the output effect means that the firm will purchase more of one particular input when the price of the other input falls and less of that particular input when the price of the other input rises.
- ***Net effect*** The substitution and output effects are both present when the price of an input changes, but they work in opposite directions. For a decline in the price of capital, the substitution effect decreases the demand for labor and the output effect increases it. The net change in labor demand depends on the relative sizes of the two effects: If the substitution effect outweighs the output effect, a decrease in the price of capital decreases the demand for labor. If the output effect exceeds the substitution effect, a decrease in the price of capital increases the demand for labor.

substitution effect
The replacement of labor by capital when the price of capital falls.

output effect
An increase in the use of labor when the price of capital falls and the firm then increases its output because of the lower production costs.

Complementary Resources Resources may be complements rather than substitutes in the production process; an increase in the quantity of one of them also requires an increase in the amount of the other used, and vice versa. Suppose a small design firm does computer-assisted design (CAD) with relatively expensive personal computers as its basic piece of capital equipment. Each computer requires a single design engineer to operate it; the machine is not automated—it will not run itself—and a second engineer would have nothing to do.

Now assume that these computers substantially decline in price. There can be no substitution effect because labor and capital must be used in *fixed proportions:* one person for one machine. Capital cannot be substituted for labor. But there *is* an output effect. Other things equal, the reduction in the price of capital goods means lower production costs. It will therefore be profitable to produce a larger output. In doing so, the firm will use both more capital and more labor. When labor and capital are complementary, a decline in the price of capital increases the demand for labor through the output effect.

We have cast our analysis of substitute resources and complementary resources mainly in terms of a decline in the price of capital. Obviously, an *increase* in the price of capital causes the opposite effects on labor demand.

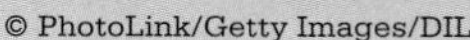

© PhotoLink/Getty Images/DIL

© Royalty-Free/CORBIS

Photo Op Substitute Resources versus Complementary Resources

Automatic teller machines (ATMs) and human tellers are substitute resources, whereas construction equipment and their operators are complementary resources.

Applying the Analysis

Occupational Employment Trends

Changes in labor demand are of considerable significance because they affect employment in specific occupations. Other things equal, increases in labor demand for certain occupational groups result in increases in their employment; decreases in labor demand result in decreases in their employment. For illustration, let's look at occupations that are growing and declining in demand.

TABLE 10.1

The 10 Fastest-Growing and Most Rapidly Declining U.S. Occupations, in Percentage Terms, 2002–2012

Occupation	Employment, Thousands of Jobs 2002	2012	Percentage Change*
Fastest Growing			
Medical assistants	365	579	59%
Data communication analysts	186	292	57
Physician assistants	63	94	49
Social and human service assistants	305	454	49
Home care aides	580	859	48
Medical record technicians	147	216	47
Physical therapist aides	37	54	46
Software engineers, applications	394	573	46
Software engineers, systems	281	409	45
Physical therapist assistants	50	73	45
Most Rapidly Declining			
Telephone operators	50	22	−56
Word processors and typists	241	148	−39
Textile machine operators	179	124	−31
Sewing machine operators	315	216	−31
Roof bolters, mining	4	3	−28
Fishers and fishing workers	36	27	−27
Shoe machine operators	7	5	−26
Fabric and apparel pattern makers	11	8	−25
Railroad brake, signal, and switch operators	15	12	−23
Farmers and ranchers	1158	920	−21

* Percentages may not correspond with employment numbers due to rounding of the employment data and the percentages.

Source: Bureau of Labor Statistics, "Employment Projections," www.bls.gov.

Table 10.1 lists the 10 fastest-growing and 10 most rapidly declining U.S. occupations (in percentage terms) for 2002 to 2012, as projected by the Bureau of Labor Statistics. Notice that service occupations dominate the fastest-growing list. In general, the demand for service workers is rapidly outpacing the demand for manufacturing, construction, and mining workers in the United States.

Of the 10 fastest-growing occupations in percentage terms, several are related to health care. The rising demands for these types of labor are derived from the growing demand for health services, caused by several factors. The aging of the U.S. population has brought with it more medical problems, the rising standard of income has led to greater expenditures on health care, and the growing presence of private and public insurance has allowed people to buy more health care than most could afford individually.

Three of the fastest-growing occupations are directly related to computers. The increase in the demand for computer software engineers and data communication analysts arises from the rapid rise in the demand for computers, computer services, and the Internet. It also results from the rising marginal revenue productivity of these particular workers, given the vastly improved quality of the computer and communications equipment they work with. Moreover, price declines on such equipment have had stronger output effects than substitution effects, increasing the demand for these kinds of labor.

Table 10.1 also lists the 10 U.S. occupations with the greatest projected job loss (in percentage terms) between 2002 and 2012.These occupations are more diverse than the fastest-growing occupations. Four of the ten are related to textiles, apparel, and shoes. The U.S. demand for these goods is increasingly being fulfilled through imports. Also, the decline in the demand for word processors and typists partially reflects increased outsourcing of that work to workers abroad. Declines in other occupations in the list (for example, telephone operators and railroad brake, signal, and switch operators) have resulted from technological advances that have enabled firms to replace workers with automated or computerized equipment. The decline in the employment of farmers and ranchers reflects an income-inelastic demand for food, enhanced physical productivity of farm equipment, and the consolidation of smaller farms into larger agribusinesses.

Question:
Name some occupation (other than those listed) that you think will grow in demand over the next decade. Name an occupation that you think will decline in demand. In each case, explain your reasoning.

Elasticity of Labor Demand

The employment changes we have just discussed have resulted from shifts in the locations of labor demand curves. Such changes in demand must be distinguished from changes in the quantity of labor demanded caused by a change in the wage rate. Such a change is caused not by a shift of the demand curve but, rather, by a movement from one point to another on a fixed labor demand curve. Example: In Figure 10.1 we note that an increase in the wage rate from $5 to $7 will reduce the quantity of labor demanded from 5 units to 4 units. This is a change in the *quantity of labor demanded* as distinct from a *change in labor demand*.

elasticity of labor demand
A measure of the responsiveness of employers to a change in the wage rate.

The sensitivity of employers to changes in wage rates is measured by the **elasticity of labor demand** (or *wage elasticity of demand*). In coefficient form,

$$E_w = \frac{\text{percentage change in labor quantity}}{\text{percentage change in wage rate}}$$

When E_w is greater than 1, labor demand is elastic; when E_w is less than 1, labor demand is inelastic; and when E_w equals 1, labor demand is unit-elastic. Several factors interact to determine the wage elasticity of demand.

10.1 Elasticity of resource demand

Ease of Resource Substitutability

The greater the substitutability of other resources for labor, the more elastic is the demand for labor. Example: Because automated voice-mail systems are highly substitutable for telephone receptionists, the demand for receptionists is quite elastic. In contrast, there are few good substitutes for physicians, so demand for them is less elastic or even inelastic.

Time can play a role in the input substitution process. For example, a firm's truck drivers may obtain a substantial wage increase with little or no immediate decline in employment. But over time, as the firm's trucks wear out and are replaced, that wage increase may motivate the company to purchase larger trucks and in that way deliver the same total output with fewer drivers.

Elasticity of Product Demand

The greater the elasticity of product demand, the greater is the elasticity of labor demand. The derived nature of resource demand leads us to expect this relationship. A small rise in the price of a product (caused by a wage increase) will sharply reduce output if product demand is elastic. So a relatively large decline in the amount of labor demanded will result. This means that the demand for labor is elastic.

Ratio of Labor Cost to Total Cost

The larger the proportion of total production costs accounted for by labor, the greater is the elasticity of demand for labor. In the extreme, if labor cost is the only production cost, then a 20 percent increase in wage rates will increase marginal cost and average total cost by 20 percent. If product demand is elastic, this substantial increase in costs will cause a relatively large decline in sales and a sharp decline in the amount of labor demanded. So labor demand is highly elastic. But if labor cost is only 50 percent of production cost, then a 20 percent increase in wage rates will increase costs by only 10 percent. With the same elasticity of product demand, this will cause a relatively small decline in sales and therefore in the amount of labor demanded. In this case the demand for labor is much less elastic.

Market Supply of Labor

Let's now turn to the supply side of a purely competitive labor market. The supply curve for each type of labor slopes upward, indicating that employers as a group must pay higher wage rates to obtain more workers. This is the case because employers must bid workers away from other industries, occupations, and localities. Within limits, workers have alternative job opportunities. For example, they may work in other industries in the same locality, or they may work in their present occupations in different cities or states, or they may work in other occupations.

Firms that want to hire these workers must pay higher wage rates to attract them away from the alternative job opportunities available to them. They must also pay higher wages to induce people who are not currently in the labor force—who are

FIGURE 10.2
A purely competitive labor market. In a purely competitive labor market (a) the equilibrium wage rate W_c and the number of workers Q_c are determined by labor supply *S* and labor demand *D*. Because this market wage rate is given to the individual firm (b) hiring in this market, its labor supply curve *s* = MRC is perfectly elastic. Its labor demand curve, *d*, is its MRP curve (here labeled *mrp*). The firm maximizes its profit by hiring workers up to the point where MRP = MRC.

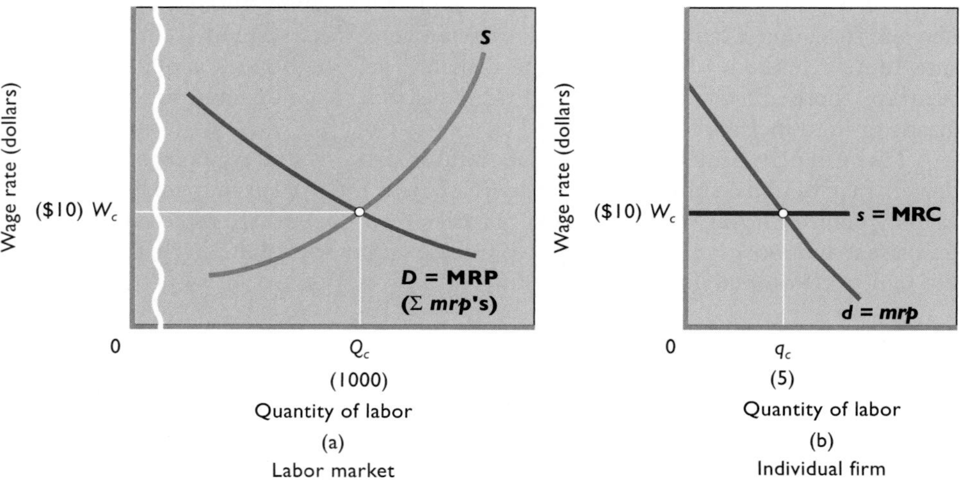

perhaps doing household activities or enjoying leisure—to seek employment. In short, assuming that wages are constant in other labor markets, higher wages in a particular labor market entice more workers to offer their labor services in that market. This fact results in a direct relationship between the wage rate and the quantity of labor supplied, as represented by the upward-sloping market supply-of-labor curve *S* in Figure 10.2a.

Wage and Employment Determination

What determines the market wage rate and how do firms respond to it? Suppose 200 firms demand a particular type of labor, say, carpenters. These firms need not be in the same industry; industries are defined according to the products they produce and not the resources they employ. Thus, firms producing wood-framed furniture, wood windows and doors, houses and apartment buildings, and wood cabinets will demand carpenters. To find the total, or market, labor demand curve for a particular labor service, we sum horizontally the labor demand curves (the marginal revenue product curves) of the individual firms, as indicated in Figure 10.2. The horizontal summing of the 200 labor demand curves like *d* in Figure 10.2b yields the market labor demand curve *D* in Figure 10.2a.

The intersection of the market labor demand curve *D* and the market supply curve *S* in Figure 10.2a determines the equilibrium wage rate and the level of employment in this labor market. Observe that the equilibrium wage rate is W_c ($10) and the number of workers hired is Q_c (1000).

To the individual firm (Figure 10.2b) the market wage rate W_c is given at $10. Each of the many firms employs such a small fraction of the total available supply of

TABLE 10.2

The Supply of Labor: Pure Competition in the Hire of Labor

(1) Units of Labor	(2) Wage Rate	(3) Total Labor Cost (Wage Bill)	(4) Marginal Resource (Labor) Cost
0	$10	$ 0	
			$10
1	10	10	
			10
2	10	20	
			10
3	10	30	
			10
4	10	40	
			10
5	10	50	
			10
6	10	60	

this type of labor that none of them can influence the wage rate. The supply of this labor is perfectly elastic to individual employers, as shown by horizontal line *s* in Figure 10.2b. This fact is clarified in Table 10.2, where we see that the marginal cost of labor MRC is constant at $10 and is equal to the wage rate. Each additional unit of labor employed adds precisely its own wage rate (here, $10) to the firm's total resource cost.

Each individual firm will apply the MRP = MRC rule to determine its profit-maximizing level of employment. So the competitive firm maximizes its profit by hiring units of labor to the point at which its wage rate (= MRC) equals MRP. In Figure 10.2b the employer will hire q_c (5) units of labor, paying each unit the market wage rate W_c ($10). The other 199 firms (not shown) in this labor market will do the same. The workers will receive pay based on their contribution to the firm's output and thus revenues.

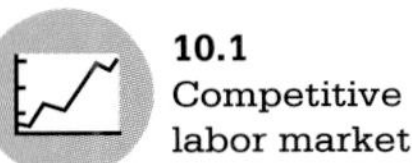
10.1 Competitive labor market

Monopsony

In the purely competitive labor market, each firm can hire as little or as much labor as it needs at the market wage rate, as reflected in its horizontal labor supply curve. The situation is strikingly different in **monopsony,** a market in which a single employer of labor has substantial buying (hiring) power. Labor market monopsony has the following characteristics:

monopsony A market structure in which there is only a single buyer of a good, service, or resource.

- There is only a single buyer of a particular type of labor.
- This type of labor is relatively immobile, either geographically or because workers would have to acquire new skills.
- The firm is a "wage maker," because the wage rate it must pay varies directly with the number of workers it employs.

As is true of monopoly power, there are various degrees of monopsony power. In *pure* monopsony such power is at its maximum, because there is only a single employer in the labor market. The best real-world examples are probably the labor markets in some towns that depend almost entirely on one major firm. For example, a silver-mining company may be almost the only source of employment in a remote Idaho or Colorado town. A Wisconsin paper mill or an Iowa food processor may provide most of the employment in its locale. In other cases three or four firms may each hire a large

10.2 Monopsony

portion of the supply of labor in a certain market and therefore have some monopsony power. Moreover, if they illegally act in concert in hiring labor, they greatly enhance their monopsony power.

Upward-Sloping Labor Supply to Firm

When a firm hires most of the available supply of a particular type of labor, its decision to employ more or fewer workers affects the wage rate it pays to those workers. Specifically, if a firm is large in relation to the size of the labor market, it will have to pay a higher wage rate to obtain more labor. Suppose there is only one employer of a particular type of labor in a certain geographic area. In that extreme case, the labor supply curve for that firm and the total supply curve for the labor market are identical. This supply curve is upward-sloping, indicating that the firm must pay a higher wage rate to attract more workers. The supply curve, *S* in Figure 10.3, is also the average-cost-of-labor curve for the firm; each point on it indicates the wage rate (cost) per worker that must be paid to attract the corresponding number of workers.

MRC Higher than the Wage Rate

When a monopsonist pays a higher wage to attract an additional worker, it must pay that higher wage to all the workers it is currently employing at a lower wage. If not, labor morale will deteriorate, and the employer will be plagued with labor unrest because of wage-rate differences existing for the same job. Paying a uniform wage to all workers means that the cost of an extra worker—the marginal resource (labor) cost (MRC) —is the sum of that worker's wage rate and the amount necessary to bring the wage rate of all current workers up to the new wage level.

Table 10.3 illustrates this point. One worker can be hired at a wage rate of \$6. But hiring a second worker forces the firm to pay a higher wage rate of \$7. The marginal resource cost of the second worker is \$8—the \$7 paid to the second worker plus a \$1 raise for the first worker. From another viewpoint, total labor cost is now \$14 (=2 × \$7), up from \$6. So the MRC of the second worker is \$8 (=\$14 − \$6), not just the \$7

FIGURE 10.3

Monopsony. In a monopsonistic labor market the employer's marginal resource (labor) cost curve (MRC) lies above the labor supply curve *S*. Equating MRC with MRP at point *b*, the monopsonist hires Q_m workers (compared with Q_c under competition). As indicated by point *c* on *S*, it pays only wage rate W_m (compared with the competitive wage W_c).

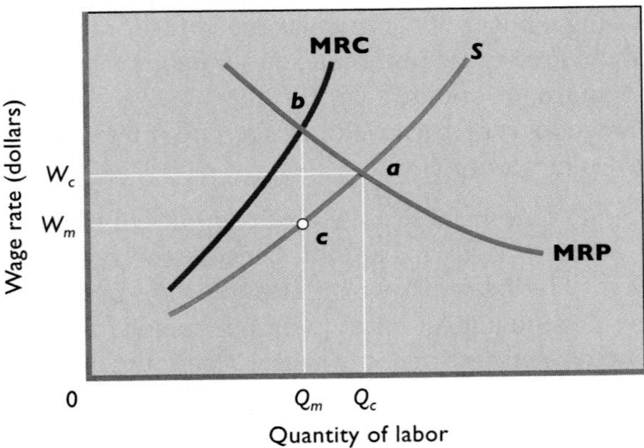

TABLE 10.3
The Supply of Labor: Monopsony in the Hire of Labor

(1) Units of Labor	(2) Wage Rate	(3) Total Labor Cost (Wage Bill)	(4) Marginal Resource (Labor) Cost
0	$ 5	$ 0	
			$ 6
1	6	6	
			8
2	7	14	
			10
3	8	24	
			12
4	9	36	
			14
5	10	50	
			16
6	11	66	

wage rate paid to that worker. Similarly, the marginal labor cost of the third worker is $10—the $8 that must be paid to attract this worker from alternative employment plus $1 raises, from $7 to $8, for the first two workers.

The important point is that to the monopsonist, marginal resource cost exceeds the wage rate. Graphically, the MRC curve lies above the average-cost-of-labor curve, or labor supply curve *S*, as is clearly shown in Figure 10.3.

Equilibrium Wage and Employment

How many units of labor will the monopsonist hire, and what wage rate will it pay? To maximize profit, the monopsonist will employ the quantity of labor Q_m in Figure 10.3, because at that quantity MRC and MRP are equal (point *b*). The monopsonist next determines how much it must pay to attract these Q_m workers. From the supply curve *S*, specifically point *c*, it sees that it must pay wage rate W_m. Clearly, it need not pay a wage equal to MRP; it can attract exactly the number of workers it wants (Q_m) with wage rate W_m. And that is what it will pay.

Contrast these results with those that would prevail in a competitive labor market. With competition in the hiring of labor, the level of employment would be greater (at Q_c) and the wage rate would be higher (at W_c). Other things equal, the monopsonist maximizes its profit by hiring a smaller number of workers and thereby paying a less-than-competitive wage rate. Society gets a smaller output, and workers get a wage rate that is less by *bc* than their marginal revenue product.

Monopsony Power

Monopsonistic labor markets are not common in the U.S. economy; typically, many potential employers compete for most workers, particularly for workers who are occupationally and geographically mobile. Also, where monopsony labor market outcomes might have otherwise occurred, unions have sprung up to counteract that power by forcing firms to negotiate wages. Nevertheless, economists have found evidence of monopsony power in such diverse labor markets as the markets for nurses, professional athletes, public school teachers, newspaper employees, and some building-trade workers.

In the case of nurses, the major employers in most locales are a relatively small number of hospitals. Further, the highly specialized skills of nurses are not readily transferable to other occupations. It has been found, in accordance with the monopsony model, that, other things equal, the smaller the number of hospitals in a town or city (that is, the greater the degree of monopsony), the lower the beginning salaries of nurses.

Professional sports leagues also provide a good example of monopsony, particularly as it relates to the pay of first-year players. The National Football League, the National Basketball Association, and Major League Baseball assign first-year players to teams through "player drafts." That device prohibits other teams from competing for a player's services, at least for several years, until the player becomes a "free agent." In this way the league exercises monopsony power, which results in lower salaries than would occur under competitive conditions.

Question:
The salaries of star players often increase substantially when they become free agents. How does that fact relate to monopsony power?

Union Models

We have assumed so far that workers compete with one another in selling their labor services. In some labor markets, however, workers sell their labor services collectively through labor unions. In the United States, about 12 percent of wage and salary workers belong to unions. (As shown in Global Snapshot 10.1, this percentage is low relative to some other nations.)

Union efforts to raise wage rates are mainly concentrated on the supply side of the labor market.

Global Snapshot 10.1

Union Membership

Compared with the percentages unionized in most other industrialized nations, union membership in the United States is small.

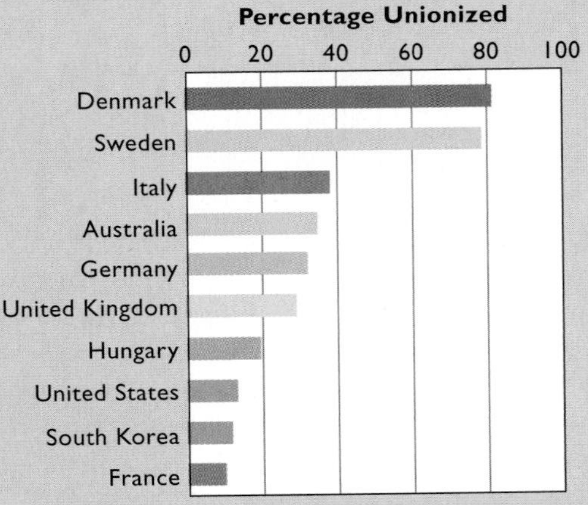

Source: Statistical agencies in individual countries. Latest data.

Exclusive or Craft Union Model

One way in which unions can boost wage rates is to reduce the supply of labor, and over the years organized labor has favored policies to do just that. For example, labor unions have supported legislation that has (1) restricted immigration, (2) reduced child labor, (3) encouraged compulsory retirement, and (4) enforced a shorter workweek.

Moreover, certain types of workers have adopted techniques designed to restrict the number of workers who can join their union. This is especially true of *craft unions*, whose members possess a particular skill, such as carpenters or brick masons or plumbers. Craft unions have frequently forced employers to agree to hire only union members, thereby gaining virtually complete control of the labor supply. Then, by following restrictive membership policies—for example, long apprenticeships, very high initiation fees, and limits on the number of new members admitted—they have artificially restricted labor supply. As indicated in Figure 10.4, such practices result in higher wage rates and constitute what is called **exclusive unionism.** By excluding workers from unions and therefore from the labor supply, craft unions succeed in elevating wage rates.

exclusive unionism The union practice of restricting the supply of skilled union labor to increase the wage rate received by union members.

This craft union model is also applicable to many professional organizations, such as the American Medical Association, the National Education Association, the American Bar Association, and hundreds of others. Such groups seek to limit competition for their services from less qualified labor suppliers. One way to accomplish that is through **occupational licensing.** Here, a group of workers in a given occupation pressure Federal, state, or municipal government to pass a law that says that some occupational group (for example, barbers, physicians, lawyers, plumbers, cosmetologists, egg graders, pest controllers) can practice their trade only if they meet certain requirements. Those requirements might include level of education, amount of work experience, and the passing of an examination. Members of the licensed occupation typically dominate the licensing board that administers such laws. The result is self-regulation, which can lead to policies that restrict entry to the occupation and reduce labor supply.

occupational licensing Government laws that require a worker to satisfy certain specified requirements and obtain a license from a licensing board before engaging in a particular occupation.

The purpose of licensing is supposedly to protect consumers from incompetent practitioners—surely a worthy goal. But such licensing, if abused, simply results in above-competitive wages and earnings for those in the licensed occupation (Figure 10.4). Moreover, licensing requirements often include a residency requirement, which inhibits the interstate movement of qualified workers. Some 600 occupations are now licensed in the United States.

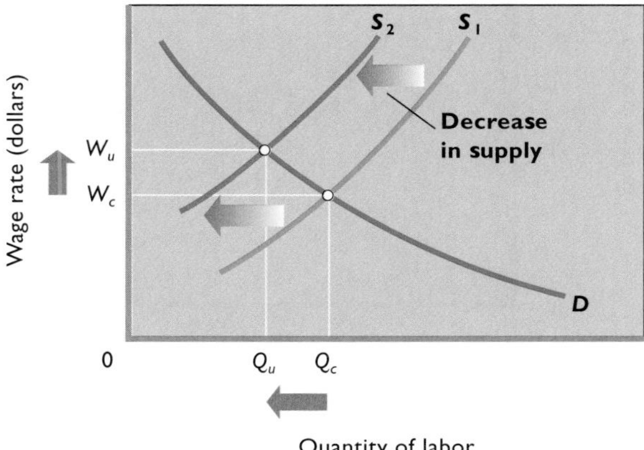

FIGURE 10.4 **Exclusive or craft unionism.** By reducing the supply of labor (say, from S_1 to S_2) through the use of restrictive membership policies, exclusive unions achieve higher wage rates (W_c to W_u). However, restriction of the labor supply also reduces the number of workers employed (Q_c to Q_u).

Inclusive or Industrial Union Model

Instead of trying to limit their membership, however, most unions seek to organize all available workers. This is especially true of the *industrial unions*, such as those of the automobile workers and steelworkers. Such unions seek as members all available unskilled, semiskilled, and skilled workers in an industry. A union can afford to be exclusive when its members are skilled craftspersons for whom there are few substitutes. But for a union composed of unskilled and semiskilled workers, a policy of limited membership would make available to the employers numerous nonunion workers who are highly substitutable for the union workers.

An industrial union that includes virtually all available workers in its membership can put firms under great pressure to agree to its wage demands. Because of its legal right to strike, such a union can threaten to deprive firms of their entire labor supply. And an actual strike can do just that.

inclusive unionism The union practice of including as members all workers employed in an industry.

We illustrate such **inclusive unionism** in Figure 10.5. Initially, the competitive equilibrium wage rate is W_c and the level of employment is Q_c. Now suppose an industrial union is formed that demands a higher, above-equilibrium wage rate of, say, W_u. That wage rate W_u would create a perfectly elastic labor supply over the range *ae* in Figure 10.5. If firms wanted to hire any workers in this range, they would have to pay the union-imposed wage rate. If they decide against meeting this wage demand, the union will supply no labor at all, and the firms will be faced with a strike. If firms decide it is better to pay the higher wage rate than to suffer a strike, they will cut back on employment from Q_c to Q_u.

By agreeing to the union's W_u wage demand, individual employers become wage takers. Because labor supply is perfectly elastic over range *ae*, the marginal resource (labor) cost is equal to the wage rate W_u over this range. The Q_u level of employment is the result of employers' equating this MRC (now equal to the wage rate) with MRP, according to our profit-maximizing rule.

Note from point *e* on labor supply curve *S* that Q_e workers desire employment at wage W_u. But as indicated by point *b* on labor demand curve *D*, only Q_u workers are employed. The result is a surplus of labor of $Q_e - Q_u$ (also shown by distance *eb*). In a

FIGURE 10.5

Inclusive or industrial unionism. By organizing virtually all available workers in order to control the supply of labor, inclusive industrial unions may impose a wage rate, such as W_u, which is above the competitive wage rate W_c. In effect, this changes the labor supply curve from *S* to *aeS*. At wage rate W_u, employers will cut employment from Q_c to Q_u.

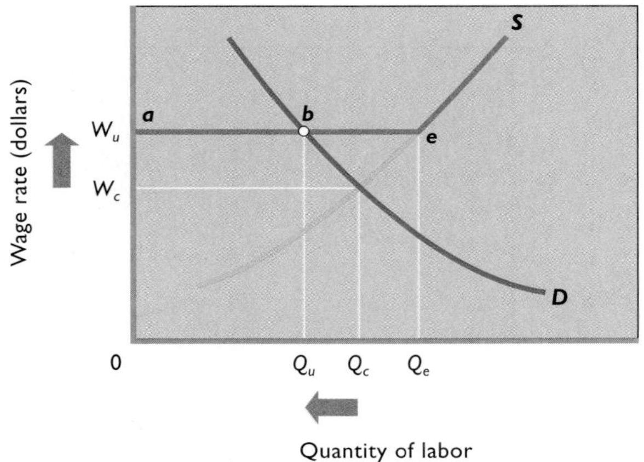

purely competitive labor market without the union, the effect of a surplus of unemployed workers would be lower wages. Specifically, the wage rate would fall to the equilibrium level W_c, where the quantity of labor supplied equals the quantity of labor demanded (each, Q_c). But this drop in wages does not happen, because workers are acting collectively through their union. Individual workers cannot offer to work for less than W_u; nor can employers pay less than that.

Wage Increases and Unemployment

Evidence suggests that union members on average achieve a 15-percent wage advantage over nonunion workers. Why not even more? As Figures 10.4 and 10.5 suggest, the effect of wage-raising actions achieved by both exclusive and inclusive unionism is reduced employment. A union's success in achieving above-equilibrium wage rates thus tends to be accompanied by a decline in the number of workers employed. That result acts as a restraining influence on union wage demands. A union cannot expect to maintain solidarity within its ranks if it seeks a wage rate so high that joblessness will result for, say, 20 percent or 30 percent of its members.

Wage Differentials

wage differentials The differences between the wage received by one worker or group of workers and that received by another worker or group of workers.

Hourly wage rates and annual salaries differ greatly among occupations. In Table 10.4 we list average annual salaries for a number of occupations to illustrate such **wage differentials.** For example, observe that aircraft pilots on average earn six times as much

TABLE 10.4 Average Annual Wages in Selected Occupations, 2003

Occupation	Average Annual Wages
Surgeons	$182,690
Aircraft pilots	129,230
Law professors	94,620
Financial managers	88,470
Petroleum engineers	88,050
Chemical engineers	78,410
Dental hygienists	58,730
Registered nurses	52,810
Police officers	45,560
Electricians	44,290
Travel agents	29,430
Barbers	23,300
Retail salespersons	22,540
Recreation workers	21,370
Teacher aides	20,100
Fast-food cooks	15,130

Source: Bureau of Labor Statistics, *Occupational Employment and Wages,* www.bls.gov/, 2005.

as retail salespersons. Not shown, there are also large wage differentials within some of the occupations listed. For example, some highly experienced pilots earn several times as much income as pilots just starting their careers. And, although average wages for retail salespersons are relatively low, some top salespersons selling on commission make several times the average wages listed for their occupation.

What explains wage differentials such as these? Once again, the forces of demand and supply are highly revealing. As we demonstrate in Figure 10.6, wage differentials can arise on either the supply or the demand side of labor markets. Panels (a) and (b) in Figure 10.6 represent labor markets for two occupational groups that have identical *labor supply curves*. Labor market (a) has a relatively high equilibrium wage (W_a) because labor demand is very strong. In labor market (b) the equilibrium wage is relatively low (W_b) because labor demand is weak. Clearly, the wage differential between occupations (a) and (b) results solely from differences in the magnitude of labor demand.

Contrast that situation with panels (c) and (d) in Figure 10.6, where the *labor demand curves* are identical. In labor market (c) the equilibrium wage is relatively high (W_c) because labor supply is highly restricted. In labor market (d) labor supply is highly abundant, so the equilibrium wage (W_d) is relatively low. The wage differential between (c) and (d) results solely from the differences in the magnitude of labor supply.

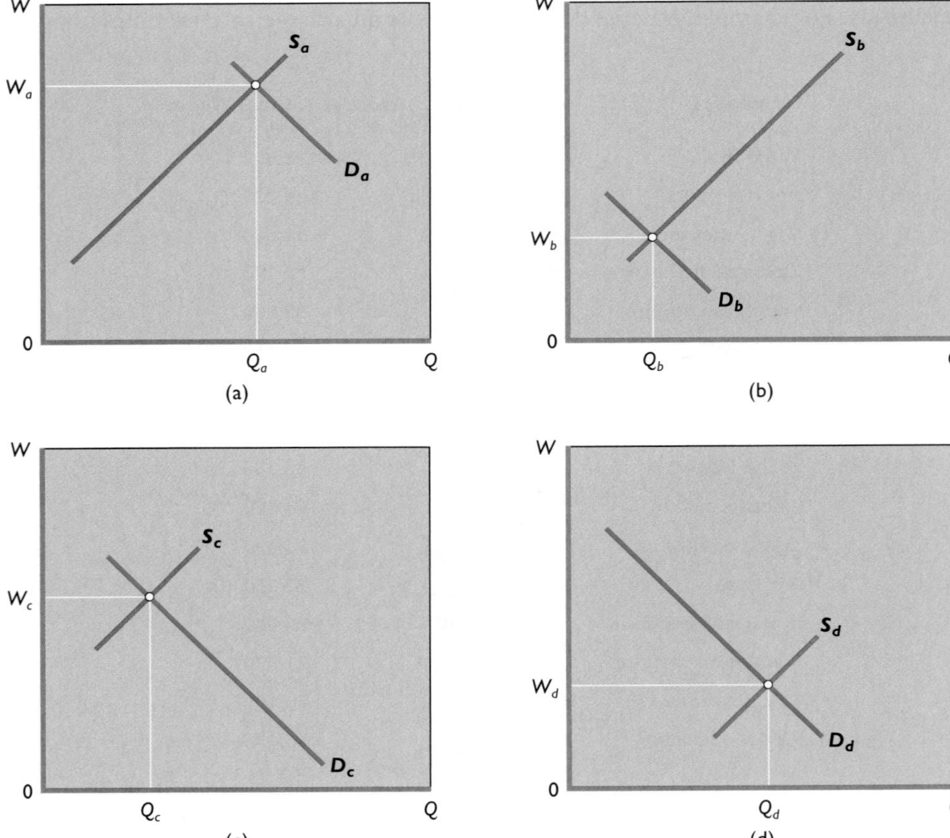

FIGURE 10.6 **Labor demand, labor supply, and wage differentials.** The wage differential between labor markets (a) and (b) results solely from differences in labor demand. In labor markets (c) and (d), differences in labor supply are the sole cause of the wage differential.

Although Figure 10.6 provides a good starting point for understanding wage differentials, we need to know *why* demand and supply conditions differ in various labor markets. There are several reasons.

Marginal Revenue Productivity

The strength of labor demand—how far rightward the labor demand curve is located—differs greatly among occupations due to differences in how much various occupational groups contribute to their employers' revenue. This revenue contribution, in turn, depends on the workers' productivity and the strength of the demand for the products they are helping to produce. Where labor is highly productive and product demand is strong, labor demand also is strong and, other things equal, pay is high. Top professional athletes, for example, are highly productive at producing sports entertainment, for which millions of people are willing to pay billions of dollars over the course of a season. So the marginal revenue productivity of these top players is exceptionally high, as are their salaries (as represented in Figure 10.6a). In contrast, in most occupations workers generate much more modest revenue for their employers, so their pay is lower (as in Figure 10.6b).

Noncompeting Groups

On the supply side of the labor market, workers are not homogeneous; they differ in their mental and physical capacities and in their education and training. At any given time the labor force is made up of many noncompeting groups of workers, each representing several occupations for which the members of that particular group qualify. In some groups qualified workers are relatively few, whereas in others they are highly abundant. And workers in one group do not qualify for the occupations of other groups.

Ability Only a few workers have the ability or physical attributes to be brain surgeons, concert violinists, top fashion models, research chemists, or professional athletes. Because the supply of these particular types of labor is very small in relation to labor demand, their wages are high (as in Figure 10.6c). The members of these and similar groups do not compete with one another or with other skilled or semiskilled workers. The violinist does not compete with the surgeon, nor does the surgeon compete with the violinist or the fashion model.

Education and Training Another source of wage differentials is differing amounts of **human capital,** which is the personal stock of knowledge, know-how, and skills that enables a person to be productive and thus to earn income. Such stocks result from investments in human capital. Like expenditures on machinery and equipment, productivity-enhancing expenditures on education or training are investments. In both cases, people incur *present costs* with the intention that those expenditures will lead to a greater flow of *future earnings.*

10.3
Human capital

human capital
The personal stock of knowledge, know-how, and skills that enables a person to be productive and thus to earn income.

Figure 10.7 indicates that workers who have made greater investments in education achieve higher incomes during their careers. The reason is twofold: (1) There are fewer such workers, so their supply is limited relative to less educated workers, and (2) more educated workers tend to be more productive and thus in greater demand. Figure 10.7 also indicates that the incomes of better-educated workers generally rise more rapidly than those of poorly educated workers. The primary reason is that employers

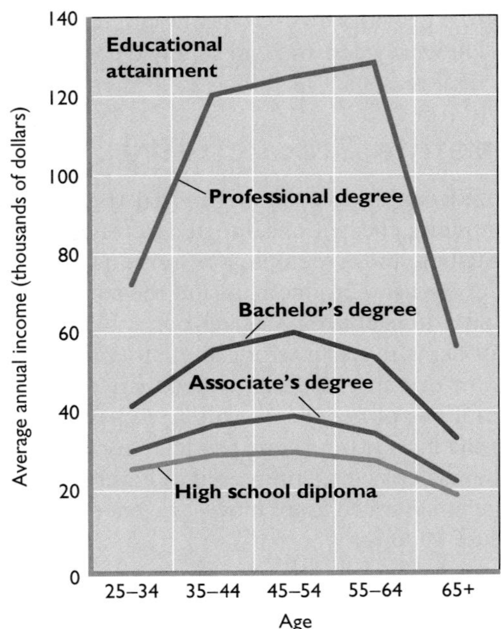

FIGURE 10.7
Education levels and average annual income. Annual income by age is higher for workers with more education than less. Investment in education yields a return in the form of earnings differences enjoyed over one's work life.

Source: U.S. Bureau of the Census, www.census.gov. Data are for 2003 and include both men and women.

provide more on-the-job training to the better-educated workers, boosting their marginal revenue productivity and therefore their earnings.

Although education yields higher incomes, it carries substantial costs. A college education involves not only direct costs (tuition, fees, books) but indirect or opportunity costs (forgone earnings) as well. Does the higher pay received by better-educated workers compensate for these costs? The answer is yes. Rates of return are estimated to be 10 to 13 percent for investments in secondary education and 8 to 12 percent for investments in college education. One generally accepted estimate is that each year of schooling raises a worker's wage by about 8 percent. Currently, college graduates on average earn about $1.70 for each $1 earned by high school graduates.

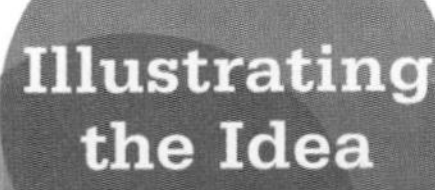

My Entire Life

For some people, high earnings have little to do with actual hours of work and much to do with their tremendous skill, which reflects their accumulated stock of human capital. The point is demonstrated in the following story: It is said that a tourist once spotted the famous Spanish artist Pablo Picasso (1881–1973) in a Paris café. The tourist asked Picasso if he would do a sketch of his wife for pay. Picasso sketched the wife in a matter of minutes and said, "That will be 10,000 francs [roughly $2000]." Hearing the high price, the tourist became irritated, saying, "But that took you only a few minutes."

"No," replied Picasso, "it took me my entire life!"

Question:

In general, how do the skill requirements of the highest-paying occupations in Table 10.4 compare with the skill requirements of the lowest-paying occupations?

Compensating Differences

If the workers in a particular noncompeting group are equally capable of performing several different jobs, you might expect the wage rates to be identical for all these jobs. Not so. A group of high school graduates may be equally capable of becoming salesclerks or general construction workers, but these jobs pay different wages. In virtually all locales, construction laborers receive much higher wages than salesclerks. These wage differentials are called **compensating differences,** because they must be paid to compensate for nonmonetary differences in various jobs.

compensating differences Wage differentials received by workers to compensate them for nonmonetary disparities in their jobs.

The construction job involves dirty hands, a sore back, the hazard of accidents, and irregular employment, both seasonally and cyclically. The retail sales job means clean clothing, pleasant air-conditioned surroundings, and little fear of injury or layoff. Other things equal, it is easy to see why workers would rather pick up a credit card than a shovel. So labor supply is more limited to construction firms (as in Figure 10.6c) than to retail shops (as in Figure 10.6d). Construction firms must pay higher wages than retailers to compensate for the unattractive nonmonetary aspects of construction jobs.

Compensating differences play an important role in allocating society's scarce labor resources. If very few workers want to be garbage collectors, then society must pay high wages to garbage collectors to get the garbage collected. If many more people want to be salesclerks, then society need not pay them as much as it pays garbage collectors to get those services performed.

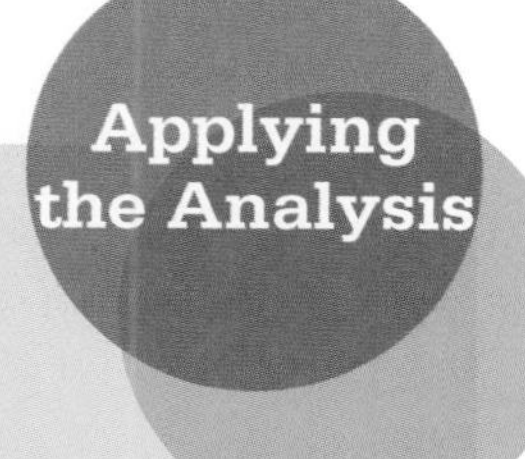

The Minimum Wage

Since the passage of the Fair Labor Standards Act in 1938, the United States has had a Federal minimum wage. That wage has ranged between 35 and 50 percent of the average wage paid to manufacturing workers and was $5.15 per hour in 2005. Several states, however, have minimum wages considerably above the Federal mandate. The purpose of minimum wages is to provide a "wage floor" that will help less skilled workers earn enough income to escape poverty.

Critics, reasoning in terms of Figure 10.5, contend that an above-equilibrium minimum wage (say, W_u) will simply push employers back up their labor demand curves, causing them to hire fewer workers. The higher labor costs may even force some firms out of business. In either case, some of the poor, low-wage workers whom the minimum wage was designed to help will find themselves out of work. Critics point out that a worker who is *unemployed* at a minimum wage of $5.15 per hour is clearly worse off than he or she would be if *employed* at a market wage rate of, say, $4.85 per hour.

A second criticism of the minimum wage is that it is "poorly targeted" to reduce household poverty. Critics point out that much of the benefit of the minimum wage accrues to workers, including many teenagers, who do not live in poverty households.

Advocates of the minimum wage say that critics analyze its impact in an unrealistic context, specifically a competitive labor market (Figure 10.2). But in a more real, low-pay labor market where there is some monopsony power (Figure 10.3), the minimum wage can increase wage rates without causing unemployment. Indeed, a higher minimum wage may even produce more jobs by eliminating the motive that monopsonistic firms have for restricting employment. For example, a minimum-wage floor of W_c in Figure 10.3 would change the firm's labor supply curve to $W_c aS$ and prompt the firm to increase its employment from Q_m workers to Q_c workers.

Moreover, a minimum wage may increase labor productivity, shifting the labor demand curve to the right and offsetting any reduced employment that the minimum wage might cause. For example, the higher wage rate might prompt firms to find more productive tasks for low-paid workers, thereby raising their productivity. Alternatively, the minimum wage may reduce *labor turnover* (the rate at which workers voluntarily quit). With fewer low-productive trainees, the *average* productivity of the firm's workers would rise. In either case, the higher labor productivity would justify paying the higher minimum wage. So the alleged negative employment effects of the minimum wage might not occur.

Which view is correct? Unfortunately, there is no clear answer. All economists agree there is some minimum wage so high that it would severely reduce employment. Consider $20 an hour, as an absurd example. Economists generally think a 10 percent increase in the minimum wage will reduce employment of unskilled workers by about 1 to 3 percent. But no current consensus exists on the employment effect of the *present level* of the minimum wage.

The overall effect of the minimum wage is thus uncertain. There seems to be a consensus emerging that, on the one hand, the employment and unemployment effects of the minimum wage are not as great as many critics fear. On the other hand, because a large part of its effect is dissipated on nonpoverty families, the minimum wage is not as strong an antipoverty tool as many supporters contend.

It is clear, however, that the minimum wage has strong political support. Perhaps this stems from two realities: (1) More workers are helped by the minimum wage than are hurt, and (2) the minimum wage gives society some assurance that employers are not "taking undue advantage" of vulnerable, low-skilled workers.

Question:
Have you ever worked for the minimum wage? If so, for how long? Would you favor increasing the minimum wage by $1? By $2? By $5? Explain your reasoning.

Summary

1. The demand for labor is derived from the product it helps produce. That means the demand for labor will depend on its productivity and on the market value (price) of the good it is producing.
2. Because the firm equates the wage rate and MRP in determining its profit-maximizing level of employment, the marginal revenue product curve is the firm's labor demand curve. Thus each point on the MRP curve indicates how many labor units the firm will hire at a specific wage rate.
3. The competitive firm's labor demand curve slopes downward because of the law of diminishing returns. Summing horizontally the demand curves of all the firms hiring that resource produces the market demand curve for labor.
4. The demand curve for labor will shift as the result of (a) a change in the demand for, and therefore the price of, the product the labor is producing; (b) changes in the productivity of labor; and (c) changes in the prices of substitutable and complementary resources.
5. The elasticity of demand for labor measures the responsiveness of employers to a change in the wage rate. The coefficient of the elasticity of labor demand is

$$E_w = \frac{\text{percentage change in labor quantity}}{\text{percentage change in wage rate}}$$

When E_w is greater than 1, labor demand is elastic; when E_w is less than 1, labor demand is inelastic; and when E_w equals 1, labor demand is unit-elastic.

6. The elasticity of labor demand will be greater (a) the greater the ease of substituting other resources for labor, (b) the greater the elasticity of demand for the product, and (c) the larger the proportion of total production costs attributable to labor.
7. Specific wage rates depend on the structure of the particular labor market. In a competitive labor market the equilibrium wage rate and level of employment are determined at the intersection of the labor supply curve and labor demand curve. For the individual firm, the market wage rate establishes a horizontal labor supply curve, meaning that the wage rate equals the firm's constant marginal resource cost. The firm hires workers to the point where its MRP equals its MRC.
8. Under monopsony the marginal resource cost curve lies above the resource supply curve because the monopsonist must bid up the wage rate to hire extra workers and must pay that higher wage rate to all workers. The monopsonist hires fewer workers than are hired under competitive conditions, pays less-than-competitive wage rates (has lower labor costs), and thus obtains greater profit.
9. A union may raise competitive wage rates by (a) restricting the supply of labor through exclusive unionism or (b) directly enforcing an above-equilibrium wage rate through inclusive unionism. On average, unionized workers realize wage rates 15 percent higher than those of comparable nonunion workers.
10. Wage differentials are largely explainable in terms of (a) marginal revenue productivity of various groups of workers; (b) noncompeting groups arising from differences in the capacities and education of different groups of workers; and (c) compensating wage differences, that is, wage differences that must be paid to offset nonmonetary differences in jobs.
11. Economists disagree about the desirability of the minimum wage. While it raises the income of some workers, it reduces the income of other workers whose skills are not sufficient to justify being paid the mandated wage.

Terms and Concepts

purely competitive labor market	substitution effect	occupational licensing
derived demand	output effect	inclusive unionism
marginal revenue product (MRP)	elasticity of labor demand	wage differentials
marginal resource cost (MRC)	monopsony	human capital
MRP = MRC rule	exclusive unionism	compensating differences

Study Questions

1. Explain the meaning and significance of the fact that the demand for labor is a derived demand. Why do labor demand curves slope downward?
2. At the bottom of the page, complete the labor demand table for a firm that is hiring labor competitively and selling its product in a purely competitive market.
   a. How many workers will the firm hire if the market wage rate is \$11.95? \$19.95? Explain why the firm will not hire a larger or smaller number of units of labor at each of these wage rates.
   b. Show in schedule form and graphically the labor demand curve of this firm.

Units of Labor	Total Product	Marginal Product	Product Price	Total Revenue	Marginal Revenue Product
0	0		\$2	\$____	
		____			\$____
1	17		2	____	
		____			____
2	31		2	____	
		____			____
3	43		2	____	
		____			____
4	53		2	____	
		____			____
5	60		2	____	
		____			____
6	65		2	____	

CHAPTER ELEVEN

Income Inequality and Poverty

In this chapter you will learn:

- How income inequality in the United States is measured and described.
- The extent and sources of income inequality.
- How income inequality has changed since 1970.
- The economic arguments for and against income inequality.
- How poverty is measured and its incidence by age, gender, ethnicity, and other characteristics.
- The major components of the income-maintenance program in the United States.

Evidence that suggests wide income disparity in the United States is easy to find. In 2004 talk-show host Oprah Winfrey earned an estimated $225 million, movie producer George Lucas earned $290 million, and golfer Tiger Woods earned $87 million. In contrast, the salary of the president of the United States is $400,000, and the typical schoolteacher earns $47,000. A full-time minimum-wage worker at a fast-food restaurant makes about $10,000. Cash welfare payments to a mother with two children average $5000.

In 2003 about 35.9 million Americans—or 12.5 percent of the population—lived in poverty. An estimated 500,000 people were homeless in that year. The richest fifth of American households received about 50 percent of total income, while the poorest fifth received less than 4 percent.

What are the sources of income inequality? Is income inequality rising or falling? Is the United States making progress against poverty? What are the major income-maintenance programs in the United States? Has welfare reform succeeded? These are some of the questions we will answer in this chapter.

Facts about Income Inequality

Average household income in the United States is among the highest in the world; in 2003, it was $59,067 per household (one or more persons occupying a housing unit). But that average tells us nothing about income inequality. To learn about that, we must examine how income is distributed around the average.

Distribution by Income Category

One way to measure **income inequality** is to look at the percentages of households in a series of income categories. Table 11.1 shows that about 17 percent of all households had annual before-tax incomes of less than $15,000 in 2003, while another 15 percent had annual incomes of $100,000 or more. The data in the table suggest considerable inequality of household income in the United States.

income inequality The unequal distribution of an economy's total income among households or families.

Distribution by Quintiles (Fifths)

A second way to measure income inequality is to divide the total number of individuals, households, or families (two or more persons related by birth) into five numerically equal groups, or *quintiles*, and examine the percentage of total personal (before-tax) income received by each quintile. We do this for households in the table in Figure 11.1, where we also provide the upper income limit for each quintile. Any amount of income greater than that listed in each row of column 3 would place a household into the next-higher quintile.

Lorenz curve A curve that shows an economy's distribution of income by measuring the cumulated percentage of income receivers along the horizontal axis and the cumulated percentage of income they receive along the vertical axis.

The Lorenz Curve and Gini Ratio

We can display the quintile distribution of personal income through a **Lorenz curve.** In Figure 11.1, we plot the cumulative percentage of households on the horizontal axis and the percentage of income they obtain on the vertical axis. The diagonal line $0e$ represents a *perfectly equal distribution of income* because each point along that line

TABLE 11.1

The Distribution of U.S. Income by Households, 2003

(1) Personal Income Category	(2) Percentage of All Households in This Category
Under $10,000	9.0
$10,000–$14,999	6.9
$15,000–$24,999	13.1
$25,000–$34,999	11.9
$35,000–$49,999	15.0
$50,000–$74,999	18.0
$75,000–$99,999	11.0
$100,000 and above	15.1
	100.0

Source: Bureau of the Census, www.census.gov/.

FIGURE 11.1

The Lorenz curve and Gini ratio. The Lorenz curve is a convenient way to show the degree of income inequality (here, household income by quintile). The area between the diagonal (the line of perfect equality) and the Lorenz curve represents the degree of inequality in the distribution of total income. This inequality is measured numerically by the Gini ratio—area A (shown in gold) divided by area $A + B$ (the gold + gray area). The Gini ratio for the distribution shown is 0.464.

(1) Quintile	(2) Percentage of Total Income*	(3) Upper Income Limit
Lowest 20%	3.4	$17,984
Second 20%	8.7	34,000
Third 20%	14.8	54,453
Fourth 20%	23.4	86,867
Highest 20%	49.8	No limit
Total	100.0	

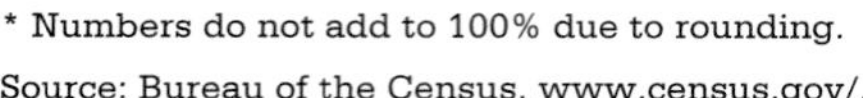

* Numbers do not add to 100% due to rounding.

Source: Bureau of the Census, www.census.gov/.

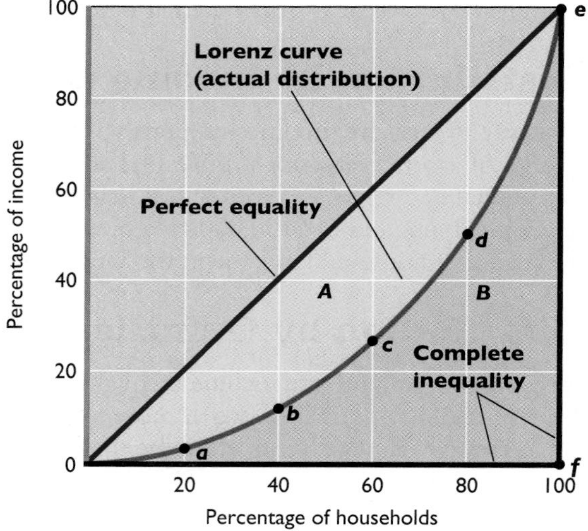

indicates that a particular percentage of households receive the same percentage of income. In other words, points representing 20 percent of all households receiving 20 percent of total income, 40 percent receiving 40 percent, 60 percent receiving 60 percent, and so on, all lie on the diagonal line.

By plotting the quintile data from the table in Figure 11.1, we obtain the Lorenz curve for 2003. Observe from point a that the bottom 20 percent of all households received 3.4 percent of the income; the bottom 40 percent received 12.1 percent (=3.4 + 8.7), as shown by point b; and so forth. The gold area between the diagonal line and the Lorenz curve is determined by the extent that the Lorenz curve sags away from the diagonal and indicates the degree of income inequality. If the actual income distribution were perfectly equal, the Lorenz curve and the diagonal would coincide and the gold area would disappear.

At the opposite extreme is complete inequality, where all households but one have zero income. In that case the Lorenz curve would coincide with the horizontal axis from 0 to point f (at 0 percent of income) and then would move immediately up from f to point e along the vertical axis (indicating that a single household has 100 percent of the total income). The entire area below the diagonal line (triangle $0ef$) would indicate this extreme degree of inequality. So the farther the Lorenz curve sags away from the diagonal, the greater is the degree of income inequality.

Gini ratio A numerical measure of the overall dispersion of income among an economy's income receivers.

We can easily transform the visual measurement of income inequality described by the Lorenz curve into the **Gini ratio**—a numerical measure of the overall dispersion of income:

$$\text{Gini ratio} = \frac{\text{area between Lorenz curve and diagonal}}{\text{total area below the diagonal}}$$

$$= \frac{A \text{ (gold area)}}{A + B \text{ (gold + gray area)}}$$

For the distribution of household income shown in Figure 11.1, the Gini ratio is 0.464. As the area between the Lorenz curve and the diagonal gets larger, the Gini ratio rises to reflect greater inequality. (Test your understanding of this idea by confirming that the Gini coefficient for complete income equality is zero and for complete inequality is 1.)

Because Gini ratios are numerical, they are easier to use than Lorenz curves for comparing the income distributions of different ethnic groups and countries. For example, in 2003 the Gini ratio of U.S. household income for African-Americans was 0.473; for Asians, 0.453; for Hispanics, 0.445; and for whites, 0.458.[1] Gini ratios for various nations range from 0.707 to 0.025. Just a few examples: Chile, 0.571; Mexico, 0.546; Russia, 0.456; France, 0.327; Japan, 0.249; and Denmark, 0.247.[2]

Income Mobility: The Time Dimension

The income data used so far have a major limitation: The income accounting period of 1 year is too short to be very meaningful. Because the Census Bureau data portray the distribution of income in only a single year, they may conceal a more equal distribution over a few years, a decade, or even a lifetime. If Brad earns $1000 in year 1 and $100,000 in year 2, while Jenny earns $100,000 in year 1 and only $1000 in year 2, do we have income inequality? The answer depends on the period of measurement. Annual data would reveal great income inequality, but there would be complete equality over the 2-year period.

This point is important because evidence suggests considerable "churning around" in the distribution of income over time. Such movement of individuals or households from one income quintile to another over time is called **income mobility.** For most income receivers, income starts at a relatively low level, reaches a peak during middle age, and then declines. It follows that if all people receive exactly the same stream of income over their lifetimes, considerable income inequality would still exist in any specific year because of age differences. In any single year, the young and the old would receive low incomes while the middle-aged receive high incomes.

income mobility
The extent to which income receivers move from one part of the income distribution to another over some period of time.

If we change from a "snapshot" view of income distribution in a single year to a "time exposure" portraying incomes over much longer periods, we find considerable movement of income receivers among income classes. For example, many relatively low-income students in professional programs in one year eventually graduate to become high-income doctors, lawyers, and accountants in subsequent years. Professional athletes and entertainers may have high incomes in one year and much lower incomes several years later. All this correctly suggests that income is more equally distributed over a 5-, 10-, or 20-year period than in a single year.

In short, there is significant individual and household income mobility over time; for many people, "low income" and "high income" are not permanent conditions.

Effect of Government Redistribution

The income data in the table in Figure 11.1 include wages, salaries, dividends, and interest. They also include all cash transfer payments such as Social Security, unemployment compensation benefits, and welfare assistance to needy households. The data are before-tax data and therefore do not take into account the effects of personal income

[1] U.S. Census Bureau, *Historical Income Tables*, www.census.gov.

[2] World Bank, *World Development Indicators, 2004*, pp. 60–62.

noncash transfers Government transfer payments in the form of goods and services (or vouchers to obtain them) rather than money.

and payroll (Social Security) taxes that are levied directly on income receivers. Nor do they include government-provided in-kind or **noncash transfers,** which make available specific goods or services rather than cash. Noncash transfers include such things as medical care, housing subsidies, subsidized school lunches, and food stamps. Such transfers are much like income because they enable recipients to "purchase" goods and services.

One economic function of government is to redistribute income, if society so desires. Figure 11.2 and its table reveal that government significantly redistributes income from higher- to lower-income households through taxes and transfers. Note that the U.S. distribution of household income before taxes and transfers are taken into account (dark green Lorenz curve) is substantially less equal than the distribution after taxes and transfers (light green Lorenz curve). Without government redistribution, the lowest 20 percent of households in 2003 would have received only 0.8 percent of total income. *With* redistribution, they received 4.5 percent, or five times as much.[3]

Which contributes more to redistribution, government taxes or government transfers? The answer is transfers. Because the U.S. tax system is only modestly progressive, after-tax data would reveal only about 20 percent less inequality. Roughly 80 percent of the reduction in income inequality is attributable to transfer payments, which account for more than 75 percent of the income of the lowest quintile. Together with growth of job opportunities, transfer payments have been the most important means of alleviating poverty in the United States.

[3] The "before" data in this table differ from the data in Figure 11.1 because the latter include cash transfers. Also, the data in Figure 11.2 are based on a broader concept of income than are the data in Figure 11.1.

FIGURE 11.2

The impact of taxes and transfers on U.S. income inequality. The distribution of income is significantly more equal after taxes and transfers are taken into account than before. Transfers account for most of the lessening of inequality and provide most of the income received by the lowest quintile of households.

Quintile	Percentage of Total Income Received, 2003* (1) Before Taxes and Transfers	(2) After Taxes and Transfers
Lowest 20 percent	0.8	4.5
Second 20 percent	7.2	10.7
Third 20 percent	14.8	16.4
Fourth 20 percent	24.0	24.0
Highest 20 percent	53.1	44.4

* The data include all money income from private sources, including realized capital gains and employer-provided health insurance. The "after taxes and transfers" data include the value of noncash transfers as well as cash transfers. Numbers may not add to 100% due to rounding.

Source: Bureau of the Census, www.census.gov/.

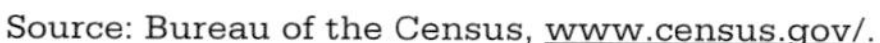

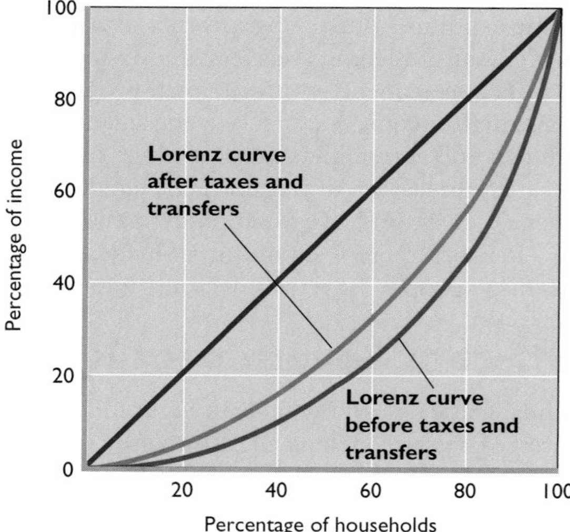

Causes of Income Inequality

There are several causes of income inequality in the United States. In general, the market system is an impersonal mechanism that embodies no conscience concerning what is an "equitable" or "just" distribution of income. It is permissive of a high degree of income inequality because it rewards individuals on the basis of the contribution their resources make in producing society's output.

More specifically, the factors that contribute to income inequality are the following.

Ability

People have different mental, physical, and aesthetic talents. Some have inherited the exceptional mental qualities that are essential to such high-paying occupations as medicine, corporate finance, and law. Others are blessed with the physical capacity and coordination to become highly paid professional athletes. A few have the talent to become great artists or musicians or have the beauty to become top fashion models. Others have very weak mental endowments and may work in low-paying occupations or may be incapable of earning any income at all. The intelligence and skills of most people fall somewhere in between.

Education and Training

Native ability alone rarely produces high income; people must develop and refine their capabilities through education and training. Individuals differ significantly in the amount of education and training they obtain and thus in their capacity to earn income. Such differences may be a matter of choice: Chin enters the labor force after graduating from high school, while Rodriguez takes a job only after earning a college degree. Other differences may be involuntary: Chin and her parents may simply be unable to finance a college education.

People also receive varying degrees of on-the-job training, which also contributes to income inequality. Some workers learn valuable new skills each year on the job and therefore experience significant income growth over time; others receive little or no on-the-job training and earn no more at age 50 than they did at age 30. Moreover, firms tend to select for advanced on-the-job training the workers who have the most formal education. That added training magnifies the education-based income differences between less educated and better-educated individuals.

Discrimination

Discrimination in education, hiring, training, and promotion undoubtedly contributes to income inequality in the United States, although the degree is uncertain. If discrimination restricts racial and ethnic minorities (or women) to low-paying occupations, the supply of labor will be great relative to demand in those occupations. So wages and incomes will be low. Conversely, discrimination reduces the competition that whites (or men) face in the occupations in which they are predominant. Thus, labor supply is artificially limited relative to demand in those occupations, with the result that wages and incomes are high.

Preferences and Risks

Incomes also differ because of differences in preferences for market work relative to leisure, market work relative to work in the household, and types of market work. People who choose to stay home with children, work part-time, or retire early usually have less income than those who make the opposite choices. Those who are willing to take arduous, unpleasant jobs (for example, underground mining or heavy construction), to work long hours with great intensity, or to "moonlight" will tend to earn more.

Individuals also differ in their willingness to assume risk. We refer here not only to the race driver or the professional boxer but also to the entrepreneur. Although many entrepreneurs fail, many of those who develop successful new products or services realize very substantial incomes. That contributes to income inequality.

Unequal Distribution of Wealth

Income is a *flow;* it represents a stream of wage and salary earnings, along with rent, interest, and profits, as depicted in Chapter 2's circular flow diagram. In contrast, wealth is a *stock*, reflecting at a particular moment the financial and real assets an individual has accumulated over time. A retired person may have very little income and yet own a home, mutual fund shares, and a pension plan that add up to considerable wealth. A new college graduate may be earning a substantial income as an accountant, middle manager, or engineer but have yet to accumulate significant wealth.

The ownership of wealth in the United States is more unequal than the distribution of income. According to the most recent (2001) Federal Reserve wealth data, the wealthiest 10 percent of families owned 70 percent of the total wealth and the top 1 percent owned 33 percent. The bottom 90 percent held only 30 percent of the total wealth. This wealth inequality leads to inequality in rent, interest, and dividends, which in turn contributes to income inequality. Those who own more machinery, real estate, farmland, stocks and bonds, and savings accounts obviously receive greater income from that ownership than people with less or no such wealth.

Market Power

The ability to "rig the market" on one's own behalf also contributes to income inequality. For example, in *resource* markets certain unions and professional groups have adopted policies that limit the supply of their services, thereby boosting the incomes of those "on the inside." Also, legislation that requires occupational licensing for, say, doctors, dentists, and lawyers can bestow market power that favors the licensed groups. In *product* markets, "rigging the market" means gaining or enhancing monopoly power, which results in greater profit and thus greater income to the firms' owners.

Luck, Connections, and Misfortune

Other forces also play a role in producing income inequality. Luck and "being in the right place at the right time" have helped individuals stumble into fortunes. Discovering oil on a ranch, owning land along a major freeway interchange, and hiring the right press agent have accounted for some high incomes. Personal contacts and political connections are other potential routes to attaining high income.

In contrast, economic misfortunes such as prolonged illness, serious accident, death of the family breadwinner, or unemployment may plunge a family into the low range of income. The burden of such misfortune is borne very unevenly by the population and thus contributes to income inequality.

Income inequality of the magnitude we have described is not exclusively an American phenomenon. Global Snapshot 11.1 compares income inequality in the United States (here by individuals, not by households) with that in several other nations. Income inequality tends to be greatest in South American nations, where land and capital resources are highly concentrated in the hands of very wealthy families.

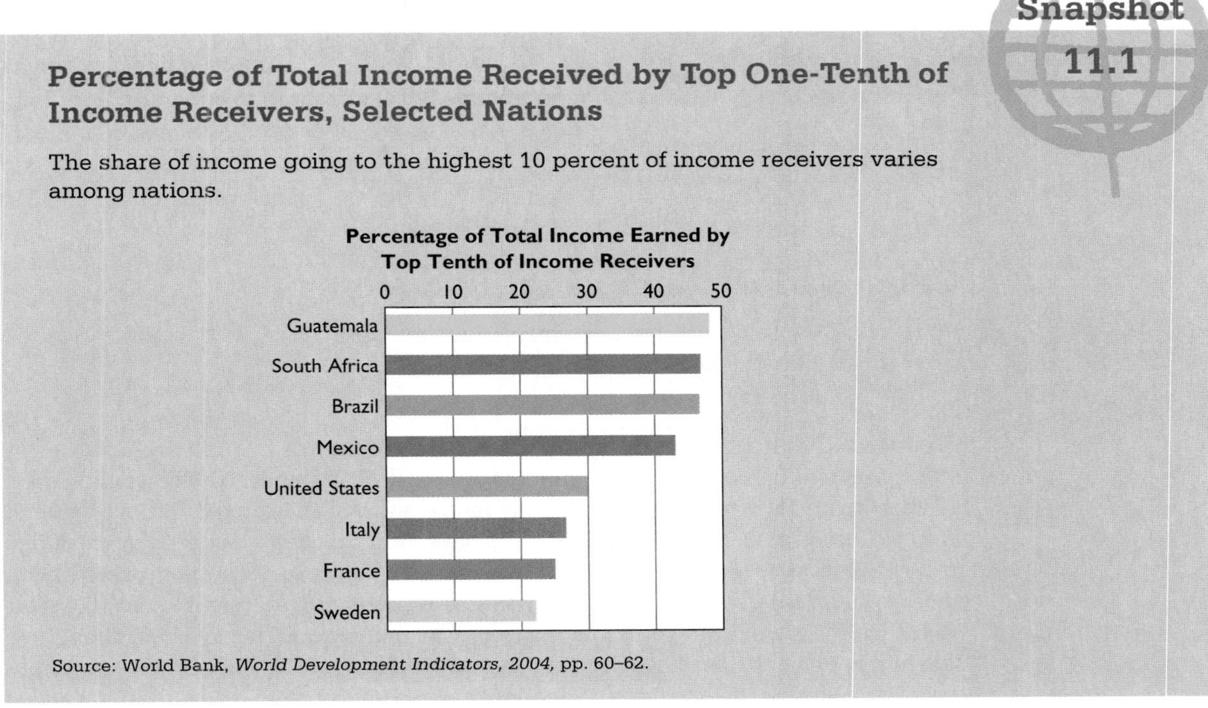

Source: World Bank, *World Development Indicators, 2004*, pp. 60–62.

Income Inequality over Time

Over a period of years economic growth has raised incomes in the United States: In *absolute* dollar amounts, the entire distribution of income has been moving upward. But incomes may move up in *absolute* terms while leaving the *relative* distribution of income less equal, more equal, or unchanged. Table 11.2 shows how the distribution of household income has changed since 1970. This income is "before tax" and includes cash transfers but not noncash transfers.

Rising Income Inequality since 1970

It is clear from Table 11.2 that the distribution of income by quintiles has become more unequal since 1970. In 2003 the lowest 20 percent of households received 3.4 percent of total before-tax income, compared with 4.1 in 1970. Meanwhile, the income share received by the highest 20 percent rose from 43.3 in 1970 to 49.8 percent in 2003. Also, the percentage of income received by the top 5 percent of households rose significantly over the 1970–2003 period.

TABLE 11.2
Percentage of Total Before-Tax Income Received by Each One-Fifth, and by the Top 5%, of Households, Selected Years*

Quintile	1970	1975	1980	1985	1990	1995	2003
Lowest 20%	4.1	4.4	4.3	4.0	3.9	3.7	3.4
Second 20%	10.8	10.5	10.3	9.7	9.6	9.1	8.7
Third 20%	17.4	17.1	16.9	16.3	15.9	15.2	14.8
Fourth 20%	24.5	24.8	24.9	24.6	24.0	23.3	23.4
Highest 20%	43.3	43.2	43.7	45.3	46.6	48.7	49.8
Total	100.0	100.0	100.0	100.0	100.0	100.0	100.0
Top 5%	16.6	15.9	15.8	17.0	18.6	21.0	21.4

* Numbers may not add to 100% due to rounding.

Source: Bureau of the Census, www.census.gov/.

Causes of Growing Inequality

Economists suggest several major explanations for the growing U.S. income inequality of the past several decades.

Greater Demand for Highly Skilled Workers Perhaps the most significant contributor to the growing income inequality has been an increasing demand by many firms for workers who are highly skilled and well educated. Moreover, several industries requiring highly skilled workers have either recently emerged or expanded greatly, such as the computer software, business consulting, biotechnology, health care, and Internet industries. Because highly skilled workers remain relatively scarce, their wages have been bid up. Consequently, the wage differences between them and less skilled workers have increased. In fact, between 1980 and 2003 the wage difference between college graduates and high school graduates rose from 36 to 69 percent for women and from 34 to 75 percent for men.

The rising demand for skill has also shown up in rapidly rising pay for chief executive officers (CEOs), sizable increases in income from stock options, substantial increases in income for professional athletes and entertainers, and huge fortunes for successful entrepreneurs. This growth of "superstar" pay has also contributed to rising income inequality.

Demographic Changes The entrance of large numbers of less experienced and less skilled "baby boomers" into the labor force during the 1970s and 1980s may have contributed to greater income inequality in those two decades. Because younger workers tend to earn less income than older workers, their growing numbers contributed to income inequality. There has also been a growing tendency for men and women with high earnings potential to marry each other, thus increasing family income among the highest income quintiles. Finally, the number of households headed by single or divorced women has increased greatly. That trend has increased income inequality because such households lack a second major wage earner and also because the poverty rate for female-headed households is very high.

International Trade, Immigration, and Decline in Unionism

Other factors are probably at work as well. Stronger international competition from imports has reduced the demand for and employment of less skilled (but highly paid) workers in such industries as the automobile and steel industries. The decline in such jobs has reduced the average wage for less skilled workers. It also has swelled the ranks of workers in already low-paying industries, placing further downward pressure on wages there.

Similarly, the transfer of jobs to lower-wage workers in developing countries has exerted downward wage pressure on less skilled workers in the United States. Also, an upsurge in immigration of unskilled workers has increased the number of low-income households in the United States. Finally, the decline in unionism in the United States has undoubtedly contributed to wage inequality, since unions tend to equalize pay within firms and industries.

Two cautions: First, when we note growing income inequality, we are not saying that the "rich are getting richer and the poor are getting poorer" in terms of absolute income. Both the rich and the poor are experiencing rises in real income. Rather, what has happened is that, while incomes have risen in all quintiles, income growth has been fastest in the top quintile. Second, increased income inequality is not solely a U.S. phenomenon. The recent rise of inequality has also occurred in several other industrially advanced nations.

The Lorenz curve can be used to contrast the distribution of income at different points in time. If we plotted Table 11.2's data as Lorenz curves, we would find that the curve shifted away from the diagonal between 1970 and 2003. The Gini ratio rose from 0.391 in 1970 to 0.464 in 2003.

Photo Op The Rich and the Poor in America

Wide disparities of income and wealth exist in the United States.

Equality versus Efficiency

The main policy issue concerning income inequality is how much is necessary and justified. While there is no general agreement on the justifiable amount, we can gain insight by exploring the economic cases for and against greater equality.

The Case for Equality: Maximizing Total Utility

The basic economic argument for an equal distribution of income is that income equality maximizes the total consumer satisfaction (utility) from any particular level of output and income. The rationale for this argument is shown in Figure 11.3, in which we assume that the money incomes of two individuals, Anderson and Brooks, are subject to the **law of diminishing marginal utility.** In any time period, income receivers spend the first dollars received on the products they value most—products whose marginal utility (extra satisfaction) is high. As a consumer's most pressing wants become satisfied, he or she then spends additional dollars of income on less important, lower-marginal-utility goods. So marginal-utility-from-income curves slope downward, as in Figure 11.3. The identical diminishing curves (MU_A and MU_B) reflect the assumption that Anderson and Brooks have the same capacity to derive utility from income. Each point on one of the curves measures the marginal utility of the last dollar of a particular level of income.

law of diminishing marginal utility The principle that the amount of extra satisfaction (marginal utility) from consuming a product declines as more of it is consumed.

FIGURE 11.3
The utility-maximizing distribution of income. With identical marginal-utility-of-income curves MU_A and MU_B, Anderson and Brooks will maximize their combined utility when any amount of income (say, $10,000) is equally distributed. If income is unequally distributed (say, $2500 to Anderson and $7500 to Brooks), the marginal utility derived from the last dollar will be greater for Anderson than for Brooks, and a redistribution toward equality will result in a net increase in total utility. The utility gained by equalizing income at $5000 each, shown by the blue area below curve MU_A in panel (a), exceeds the utility lost, indicated by the red area below curve MU_B in (b).

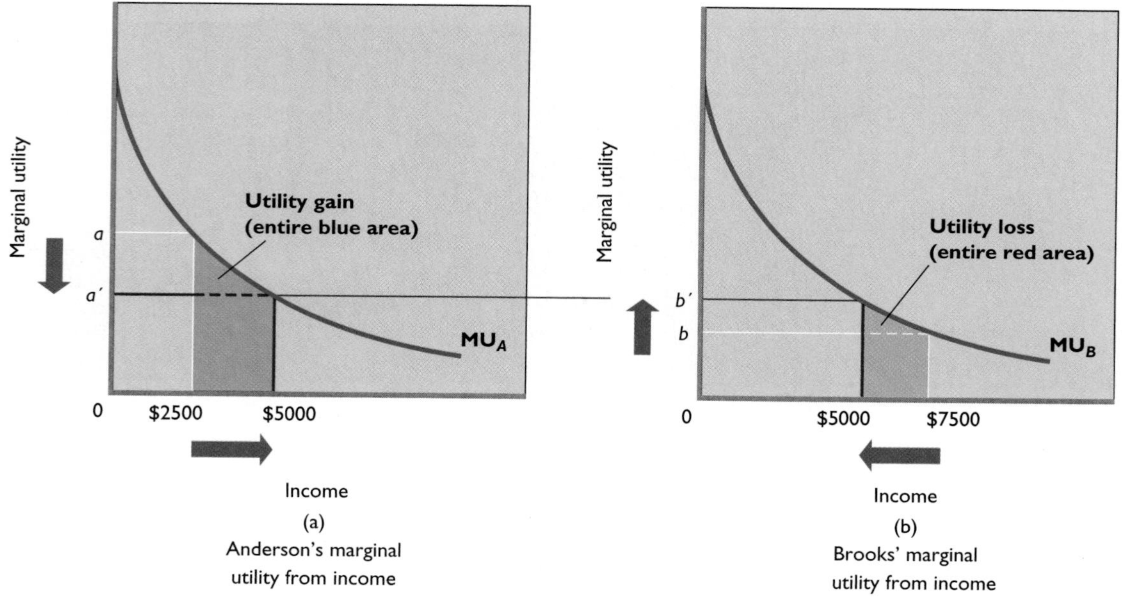

Now suppose that there is $10,000 worth of income (output) to be distributed between Anderson and Brooks. According to proponents of income equality, the optimal distribution is an equal distribution, which causes the marginal utility of the last dollar spent to be the same for both persons. We can confirm this by demonstrating that if the income distribution is initially unequal, then distributing income more equally can increase the combined utility of the two individuals.

Suppose that the $10,000 of income initially is distributed such that Anderson gets $2500 and Brooks $7500. The marginal utility, *a*, from the last dollar received by Anderson is high, and the marginal utility, *b*, from Brooks' last dollar of income is low. If a single dollar of income is shifted from Brooks to Anderson—that is, toward greater equality—then Anderson's utility increases by *a* and Brooks' utility decreases by *b*. The combined utility then increases by *a* minus *b* (Anderson's large gain minus Brooks' small loss). The transfer of another dollar from Brooks to Anderson again increases their combined utility, this time by a slightly smaller amount. Continued transfer of dollars from Brooks to Anderson increases their combined utility until the income is evenly distributed and both receive $5000. At that time their marginal utilities from the last dollar of income are equal (at a' and b'), and any further income redistribution beyond the $2500 already transferred would begin to create inequality and decrease their combined utility.

The area under the MU curve and to the left of the individual's particular level of income represents the total utility (the sum of the marginal utilities) of that income. Therefore, as a result of the transfer of the $2500, Anderson has gained utility represented by the blue area below curve MU_A, and Brooks has lost utility represented by the red area below curve MU_B. The blue area exceeds the red area, so income equality yields greater combined total utility than does the initial income inequality.

The Case for Inequality: Incentives and Efficiency

Although the logic of the argument for equality is sound, critics attack its fundamental assumption that there is some fixed amount of output produced and therefore income to be distributed. Critics of income equality argue that the way in which income is distributed is an important determinant of the amount of output or income that is produced and is available for distribution.

Suppose once again in Figure 11.3 that Anderson earns $2500 and Brooks earns $7500. In moving toward equality, society (the government) must tax away some of Brooks' income and transfer it to Anderson. This tax and transfer process diminishes the income rewards of high-income Brooks and raises the income rewards of low-income Anderson; in so doing, it reduces the incentives of both to earn high incomes. Why should high-income Brooks work hard, save and invest, or undertake entrepreneurial risks when the rewards from such activities will be reduced by taxation? And why should low-income Anderson be motivated to increase his income through market activities when the government stands ready to transfer income to him? Taxes are a reduction in the rewards from increased productive effort; redistribution through transfers is a reward for diminished effort.

In the extreme, imagine a situation in which the government levies a 100 percent tax on income and distributes the tax revenue equally to its citizenry. Why would anyone work hard? Why would anyone work at all? Why would anyone assume business risk? Or why would anyone save (forgo current consumption) in order to invest? The economic incentives to "get ahead" will have been removed, greatly reducing society's total production and income. That is, the way income is distributed affects the size of that income. The basic argument for income inequality is that inequality is essential to maintain incentives to produce output and income—to get the output produced and income generated year after year.

The Equality-Efficiency Tradeoff

equality-efficiency tradeoff The decrease in economic efficiency that may accompany an increase in income equality.

At the essence of the income equality-inequality debate is a fundamental tradeoff between equality and efficiency. In this **equality-efficiency tradeoff,** greater income equality (achieved through redistribution of income) comes at the opportunity cost of reduced production and income. And greater production and income (through reduced redistribution) comes at the expense of less equality of income. The tradeoff obligates society to choose how much redistribution it wants, in view of the costs. If society decides it wants to redistribute income, it needs to determine methods that minimize the adverse effects on economic efficiency.

Slicing the Pizza

The equality-efficiency tradeoff might better be understood through an analogy. Assume that society's income is a huge pizza, baked year after year, *with the sizes of the pieces going to people on the basis of their contribution to making it*. Now suppose that for fairness reasons, society decides some people are getting pieces that are too large and others are getting pieces too small. But when society redistributes the pizza to make the sizes more equal, they discover the result is a smaller pizza than before. Why participate in making the pizza if you get a decent-size piece without contributing?

The shrinkage of the pizza represents the efficiency loss—the loss of output and income—caused by the harmful effects of the redistribution on incentives to work, to save and invest, and to accept entrepreneurial risk. The shrinkage also reflects the resources that society must divert to the bureaucracies that administer the redistribution system.

How much pizza shrinkage will society accept while continuing to agree to the redistribution? If redistributing pizza to make it less unequal reduces the size of the pizza, what amount of pizza loss will society tolerate? Is a loss of 10 percent acceptable? 25 percent? 75 percent? This is the basic question in any debate over the ideal size of a nation's income redistribution program.

Question:
Why might "equality of opportunity" be a more realistic and efficient goal than "equality of income outcome"?

The Economics of Poverty

We now turn from the larger issue of income distribution to the more specific issue of very low income, or "poverty." A society with a high degree of income inequality can have a high, moderate, or low amount of poverty. In fact, it could have no poverty at all. We need to learn about the extent of poverty in the United States, the characteristics of the poor, and the programs designed to reduce poverty.

Definition of Poverty

Poverty is a condition in which a person or family does not have the means to satisfy basic needs for food, clothing, shelter, and transportation. The means include currently earned income, transfer payments, past savings, and property owned. The basic needs have many determinants, including family size and the health and age of its members.

The Federal government has established minimum income thresholds below which a person or a family is "in poverty." In 2003 an unattached individual receiving less than $9393 per year was said to be living in poverty. For a family of four, the poverty line was $18,810; for a family of six, it was $25,122. Using these thresholds, we find for 2003 that about 35.9 million Americans lived in poverty. In 2003 the **poverty rate**—the percentage of the population living in poverty—was 12.5 percent.

poverty rate The percentage of the population with incomes below the official poverty income levels established by the Federal government.

Incidence of Poverty

The poor are heterogeneous: They can be found in all parts of the nation; they are whites and nonwhites, rural and urban, young and old. But as Figure 11.4 indicates, poverty is far from randomly distributed. For example, the poverty rate for African-Americans is above the national average, as is the rate for Hispanics, while the rate for whites and Asians is below the average. In 2003, the poverty rates for African-Americans and Hispanics were 24.4 and 22.5 percent, respectively; the rate for whites and Asians, 10.5 and 11.8 percent.

Figure 11.4 shows that female-headed households, foreign-born noncitizens, and children under 18 years of age have very high incidences of poverty. Marriage and full-time, year-round work are associated with low poverty rates, and, because of the Social Security system, the incidence of poverty among the elderly is less than that for the population as a whole.

The high poverty rate for children is especially disturbing because poverty tends to breed poverty. Poor children are at greater risk for a range of long-term problems,

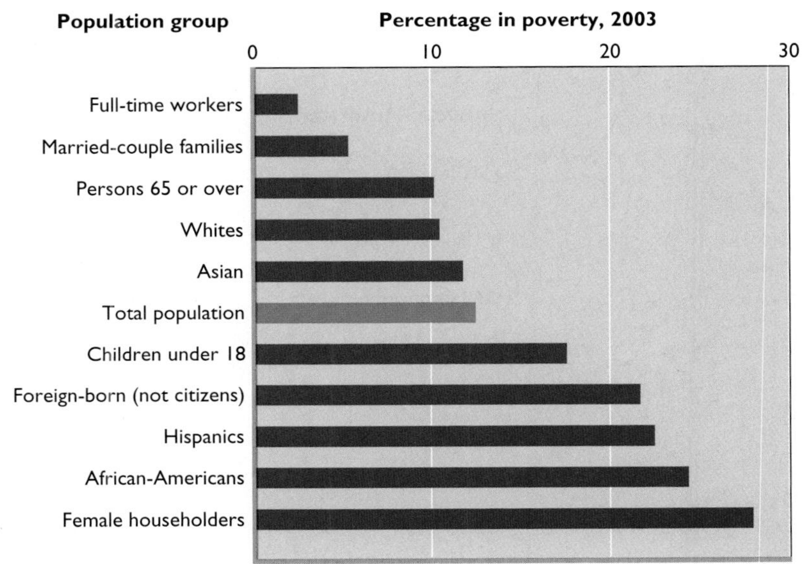

FIGURE 11.4
Poverty rates among selected population groups, 2003. Poverty is disproportionately borne by African-Americans, Hispanics, children, foreign-born residents who are not citizens, and families headed by women. People who are employed full-time or are married tend to have low poverty rates.

Source: Bureau of the Census, www.census.gov/.

including poor health and inadequate education, crime, drug use, and teenage pregnancy. Many of today's impoverished children will reach adulthood unhealthy and illiterate and unable to earn above-poverty incomes.

As many as half of people in poverty are poor for only 1 or 2 years before climbing out of poverty. But poverty is much more long-lasting among some groups than among others. In particular, African-American and Hispanic families, families headed by women, persons with little education and few labor market skills, and people who are dysfunctional because of drug use, alcoholism, or mental illness are more likely than others to remain in poverty. Also, long-lasting poverty is heavily present in depressed areas of cities, parts of the Deep South, and some Indian reservations.

Poverty Trends

As Figure 11.5 shows, the total poverty rate fell significantly between 1959 and 1969, stabilized at 11 to 13 percent over the next decade, and then rose in the early 1980s. In 1993 the rate was 15.1 percent, the highest since 1983. Between 1993 and 2000 the rate turned downward, falling to 11.3 percent in 2000. Because of recession and slow recovery, the rate rose to 11.7 percent in 2001, 12.1 percent in 2002, and 12.5 percent in 2003. During the second half of the 1990s, poverty rates plunged for African-Americans, Hispanics, and Asians.

FIGURE 11.5

Poverty-rate trends, 1959–2003. Although the national poverty rate declined sharply between 1959 and 1969, it stabilized in the 1970s only to increase significantly in the early 1980s. Between 1993 and 2000 it substantially declined, before rising slightly again in the immediate years following the 2001 recession. Although poverty rates for African-Americans and Hispanics are much higher than the average, they significantly declined during the 1990s.

Source: Bureau of the Census, www.census.gov/.

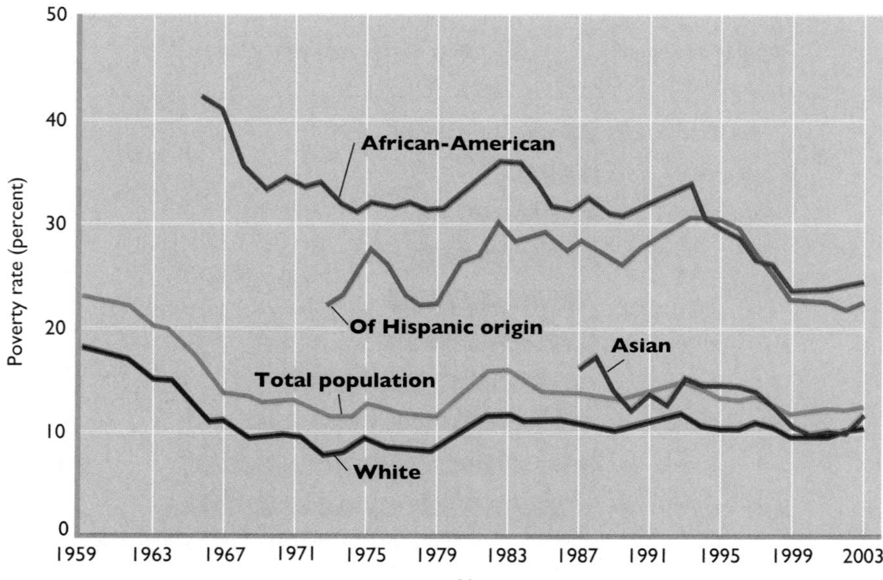

Measurement Issues

The poverty rates and trends in Figures 11.4 and 11.5 need to be interpreted cautiously. The official income thresholds for defining poverty are necessarily arbitrary and therefore may inadequately measure the true extent of poverty in the United States.

Some observers say that the high cost of living in major metropolitan areas means that the official poverty thresholds exclude millions of families whose income is slightly above the poverty level but clearly inadequate to meet basic needs for food, housing, and medical care. These observers use city-by-city studies on "minimal income needs" to show there is much more poverty in the United States than is officially measured and reported.

In contrast, some economists point out that using income to measure poverty understates the standard of living of many of the people who are officially poor. When individual, household, or family *consumption* is considered rather than family *income*, some of the poverty in the United States disappears. Some low-income families maintain their consumption by drawing down past savings, borrowing against future income, or selling homes. Moreover, many poverty families receive substantial noncash benefits such as food stamps and rent subsidies that boost their living standards. Such "in-kind" benefits are not included in determining a family's official poverty status.

The U.S. Income-Maintenance System

Regardless of how poverty is measured, economists agree that considerable poverty is present in the United States. Helping those who have very low income is a widely accepted goal of public policy. A wide array of antipoverty programs, including education and training programs, subsidized employment, minimum-wage laws, and antidiscrimination policies are designed to increase the earnings of the poor. In addition, there are a number of income-maintenance programs devised to reduce poverty, the most important of which are listed in Table 11.3. These programs involve large expenditures and numerous beneficiaries.

The U.S. income-maintenance system consists of two kinds of programs: (1) social insurance and (2) public assistance or "welfare." Both are known as **entitlement programs,** because all eligible persons are assured (entitled to) the benefits set forth in the programs.

entitlement programs Government programs that guarantee particular levels of transfer payments or noncash benefits to all who fit the programs' criteria.

Social Insurance Programs

Social insurance programs partially replace earnings that have been lost due to retirement, disability, or temporary unemployment; they also provide health insurance for the elderly. The main social insurance programs are Social Security, unemployment compensation, and Medicare. Benefits are viewed as earned rights and do not carry the stigma of public charity. These programs are financed primarily out of Federal payroll taxes. In these programs the entire population shares the risk of an individual's losing income because of retirement, unemployment, disability, or illness. Workers (and employers) pay a part of wages into a government fund while they are working. The workers are then entitled to benefits when they retire or when a specified misfortune occurs.

Social Security A Federal pension program (financed by payroll taxes on employers and employees) that replaces part of the earnings lost when workers retire, become disabled, or die.

Social Security and Medicare The major social insurance program known as **Social Security** replaces earnings lost when workers retire, become disabled, or die. This gigantic program ($449 billion in 2004) is financed by compulsory payroll taxes

TABLE 11.3

Characteristics of Major Income-Maintenance Programs

Program	Basis of Eligibility	Source of Funds	Form of Aid	Expenditures,* Billions	Beneficiaries, Millions
Social Insurance Programs					
Social Security	Age, disability, or death of parent or spouse; individual earnings	Federal payroll tax on employers and employees	Cash	$449	48
Medicare	Age or disability	Federal payroll tax on employers and employees	Subsidized health insurance	237	42
Unemployment compensation	Unemployment	State and Federal payroll taxes on employers	Cash	41	10
Public Assistance Programs					
Supplemental Security Income (SSI)	Age or disability; income	Federal revenues	Cash	38	7
Temporary Assistance for Needy Families (TANF)	Certain families with children; income	Federal-state-local revenues	Cash and services	11	5
Food stamps	Income	Federal revenues	Vouchers	22	22
Medicaid	Persons eligible for TANF or SSI and medically indigent	Federal-state-local revenues	Subsidized medical services	228	43
Earned-income tax credit (EITC)	Low-wage working families	Federal revenues	Refundable tax credit, cash	36	21

* Expenditures by Federal, state, and local governments; excludes administrative expenses.

Source: *Statistical Abstract of the United States, 2004–2005,* www.census.gov/; other government sources, latest data.

levied on both employers and employees. Workers currently may retire at age 65 and receive full retirement benefits or retire early at age 62 with reduced benefits. When a worker dies, benefits accrue to his or her family survivors. Special provisions provide benefits for disabled workers.

Social Security covers over 90 percent of the workforce; some 48 million people receive Social Security benefits averaging about $872 per month. In 2005, those benefits were financed with a combined Social Security and Medicare payroll tax of 15.3 percent, with both the worker and the employer paying 7.65 percent on their first $90,000 of earnings. The 7.65 percent tax comprises 6.2 percent for Social Security and 1.45 percent for Medicare. Self-employed workers pay a tax of 15.3 percent.

Medicare
A Federal insurance program (financed by payroll taxes on employers and employees) that provides health insurance benefits to those 65 or older.

Medicare provides hospital insurance for the elderly and disabled and is financed out of the payroll tax. This overall 2.9 percent tax is paid on all work income, not just on the first $90,000. Medicare also makes available a supplementary low-cost insurance program that helps pay doctor fees.

As we will detail in Chapter 14, the number of retirees drawing Social Security and Medicare benefits is rapidly rising relative to the number of workers paying payroll taxes. As a result, Social Security and Medicare face serious long-term funding problems. These fiscal imbalances have spawned calls to reform the programs.

Unemployment Compensation All 50 states sponsor unemployment insurance programs called **unemployment compensation.** This insurance is financed by a relatively small payroll tax, paid by employers, which varies by state and by the size of the firm's payroll. Any insured worker who becomes unemployed can, after a short waiting period, become eligible for benefit payments. The program covers almost all wage and salary workers. The size of payments and the number of weeks they are made available vary considerably from state to state. Generally, benefits approximate 33 percent of a worker's wages up to a certain maximum payment. In 2003 benefits averaged about $262 weekly. The number of beneficiaries and the level of total disbursements vary with economic conditions.

unemployment compensation
A Federal-State social insurance program (financed by payroll taxes on employers) that makes income available to workers who are unemployed.

Public Assistance Programs

Public assistance programs (welfare) provide benefits for those who are unable to earn income because of permanent handicaps or have no or very low income and also have dependent children. These programs are financed out of general tax revenues and are regarded as public charity. They include "means tests" which require that individuals and families demonstrate low incomes in order to qualify for aid. The Federal government finances about two-thirds of the welfare program expenditures, and the rest is paid for by the states.

Many needy persons who do not qualify for social insurance programs are assisted through the Federal government's **Supplemental Security Income (SSI)** program. The purpose of SSI is to establish a uniform, nationwide minimum income for the aged, blind, and disabled who are unable to work and who do not qualify for Social Security aid. Over half the states provide additional income supplements to the aged, blind, and disabled.

The **Temporary Assistance for Needy Families (TANF)** program is state-administered but is partly financed with Federal grants. The program provides cash assistance to families with children and also seeks to reduce welfare dependency by promoting job preparation and work. TANF's predecessor was the Aid to Families with Dependent Children (AFDC) program. But unlike that program, TANF has work requirements and limits on the length of time a family can receive welfare payments. In 2004 about 5 million people (including children) received TANF assistance.

The **food-stamp program** is designed to provide all low-income Americans with a "nutritionally adequate diet." Under the program, eligible households receive monthly allotments of coupons that are redeemable for food. The amount of food stamps received varies inversely with a family's earned income.

Medicaid helps finance the medical expenses of individuals participating in the SSI and the TANF programs.

The **earned-income tax credit (EITC)** is a tax credit for low-income working families, with or without children. The credit reduces the Federal income taxes that such families owe or provides them with cash payments if the credit exceeds their tax liabilities. The purpose of the credit is to offset Social Security taxes paid by low-wage earners and thus keep the Federal government from "taxing families into poverty." In essence, EITC is a wage subsidy from the Federal government that works out to be as much as $2 per hour for the lowest-paid workers with families. Under the program many people owe no income tax and receive direct checks from the Federal

Supplemental Security Income (SSI)
A Federal program (financed by general tax revenues) that provides a uniform nationwide minimum income for the aged, blind, and disabled who do not qualify for benefits under the Social Security program in the United States.

Temporary Assistance for Needy Families (TANF)
The basic welfare program (financed through general tax revenues) for low-income families in the United States.

food-stamp program
A Federal program (financed through general tax revenues) that permits eligible low-income persons to obtain vouchers that are usable to buy food.

Medicaid
A Federal program (financed by general tax revenues) that provides medical benefits to people covered by the Supplemental Security Income (SSI) and Temporary Assistance for Needy Families (TANF) programs.

earned-income tax credit (EITC)
A refundable Federal tax credit provided to low-income wage earners to supplement their families' incomes and encourage work.

government once a year. According to the Internal Revenue Service, 21 million taxpayers received $36 billion in payments from the EITC in 2003.

There are also several welfare programs that are not listed in Table 11.3. Most provide help in the form of noncash transfers. Head Start provides education, nutrition, and social services to economically disadvantaged 3- and 4-year-olds. Housing assistance in the form of rent subsidies and funds for construction is available to low-income families. Pell grants provide assistance to college students from low-income families.

Welfare Reform

In 1996 the public assistance or welfare part of the U.S. income-maintenance program underwent major reform. The reform grew out of the reality that welfare spending was not ending poverty. While the number of people receiving welfare benefits under the Aid to Families with Dependent Children (AFDC) program rose substantially in the 1980s and early 1990s, the number of people in poverty went up, instead of down. There was concern that the AFDC program was creating dependency on the government and thus robbing individuals and family members of motivation and dignity.

The Personal Responsibility Act of 1996 replaced AFDC with the *Temporary Assistance for Needy Families (TANF)* program, which ended the Federal government's six-decade-old welfare program based on cash assistance for poor families. Under the new law, the Federal government instead pays each state a lump sum of Federal money each year to operate its own welfare and work programs. These lump-sum payments are called TANF funds. But the TANF reform did much more. It:

- Set a lifetime limit of 5 years on receiving TANF benefits and required able-bodied adults to work after receiving assistance for 2 years.
- Ended food-stamp eligibility for able-bodied persons age 18 to 50 (with no dependents) who are not working or engaged in job training programs.
- Tightened the definition of "disabled children" as it applies to eligibility of low-income families for Supplemental Security Income (SSI) assistance.
- Established a 5-year waiting period on public assistance for new legal immigrants who have not become citizens.

Supporters of TANF believe that it already has played a key role in helping to end a "culture of welfare" in which dropping out of school, having a child, and going on welfare were allegedly becoming a normal way of life for part of the welfare population. They cite large declines in the welfare rolls as evidence of the law's effectiveness. In 1996 there were 12.6 million welfare recipients, including children, or 4.8 percent of the U.S. population. By the end of 2002 those totals had declined to 5.2 million and 2 percent of the population. Economists attribute about half the decline in "welfare caseloads" to welfare reform and the other half to the strong demand for labor and the low unemployment accompanying the economic expansion in the last half of the 1990s.

The recession of 2001 and the slack labor market in 2002 slowed the decline of welfare recipients but did not reverse the downward trend. Economists judge the positive results of the 1996 welfare reform as strong confirmation of two economic principles: Economic growth and high levels of employment are powerful antipoverty forces, and welfare program incentives (and disincentives) clearly matter.

Question:
Why are "declining welfare caseloads" and "declining poverty" not necessarily synonymous?

Summary

1. The distribution of income in the United States reflects considerable inequality. The richest 20 percent of families receive 49.8 percent of total income, while the poorest 20 percent receive 3.4 percent.
2. The Lorenz curve shows the percentage of total income received by each percentage of families. The extent of the gap between the Lorenz curve and a line of total equality illustrates the degree of income inequality.
3. The Gini ratio measures the overall dispersion of the income distribution and is found by dividing the area between the diagonal and the Lorenz curve by the entire area below the diagonal. Higher Gini ratios signify greater degrees of income inequality.
4. Recognizing that the positions of individual families in the distribution of income change over time and incorporating the effects of noncash transfers and taxes would reveal less income inequality than do standard census data. Government transfers (cash and noncash) greatly lessen the degree of income inequality; taxes also reduce inequality, but not by nearly as much as transfers.
5. Causes of income inequality include differences in abilities, in education and training, and in job tastes, along with discrimination, inequality in the distribution of wealth, and an unequal distribution of market power.
6. Census data show that income inequality has increased significantly since 1970. The major cause of recent increases in income inequality is a rising demand for highly skilled workers, which has boosted their earnings significantly.
7. The basic argument for income equality is that it maximizes consumer satisfaction (total utility) from a particular level of total income. The main argument for income inequality is that it provides the incentives to work, invest, and assume risk and is necessary for the production of output, which, in turn, creates income that is then available for distribution.
8. Current statistics reveal that 12.5 percent of the U.S. population lived in poverty in 2003. Poverty rates are particularly high for female-headed families, young children, African-Americans, and Hispanics.
9. The present income-maintenance program in the United States consists of social insurance programs (Social Security, Medicare, and unemployment compensation) and public assistance programs (SSI, TANF, food stamps, Medicaid, and earned-income tax credit).
10. In 1996 Congress established the Temporary Assistance for Needy Families (TANF) program, which shifted responsibility for welfare from the Federal government to the states. Among its provisions are work requirements for adults receiving welfare and a 5-year lifelong limit on welfare benefits.
11. A generally strong economy and TANF have reduced the U.S. welfare rolls by more than one-half since 1996.

CHAPTER TWELVE

Introduction to GDP, Growth, and Instability

In this chapter you will learn:

- How gross domestic product (GDP) is defined and measured.
- How economists distinguish between nominal GDP and real GDP.
- About the long-term trend of U.S. economic growth and the primary phases of the business cycle.
- How unemployment and inflation are measured.
- About the types of unemployment and inflation and their various economic impacts.

"Investment Stagnates." "GDP up 4 Percent." "Robust Expansion Continues." "Unemployment Rate Rises," "Inflation Remains Mild."

These macroeconomic headlines, typical of those in *The Wall Street Journal,* give knowledgeable readers valuable information on the state of the economy. This chapter will help you interpret such headlines and understand the stories reported under them. Specifically, it will explain how economists measure the economy's total output and will introduce you to key topics in macroeconomics: growth, business cycles, unemployment, and inflation.

Gross Domestic Product

The Bureau of Economic Analysis (BEA), an agency of the Commerce Department, compiles the **national income and product accounts (NIPA)** for the U.S. economy. The BEA derives the NIPA data from Census Bureau surveys and information available from government agencies.

national income and product accounts (NIPA)
The national accounts that measure the overall production and income of the economy for the nation as a whole.

The primary measure of the economy's performance is its annual total output of goods and services. This output is called **gross domestic product (GDP):** the total market value of all final goods and services produced within a nation's boundaries in a certain year. GDP includes all goods and services produced by either citizen-supplied or foreign-supplied resources employed within the country. If a final good or service is produced in the United States, it is part of U.S. GDP.

gross domestic product (GDP)
The total market value of all final goods and services produced annually within the boundaries of the United States, whether by U.S. or foreign-supplied resources.

A Monetary Measure

If the economy produces three sofas and two computers in year 1 and two sofas and three computers in year 2, in which year is output greater? We can't answer that question until we attach a price tag to each of the two products to indicate how society evaluates their relative worth.

That's what GDP does. It is a *monetary measure.* Without such a measure we would have no way of comparing the relative values of the vast number of goods and services produced in different years. In Table 12.1 the price of sofas is $500 and the price of computers is $2000. GDP would gauge the output of year 2 ($7000) as greater than the output of year 1 ($5500), because society places a higher monetary value on the output of year 2. Society is willing to pay $1500 more for the combination of goods produced in year 2 than for the combination of goods produced in year 1.

Avoiding Multiple Counting

To measure aggregate output accurately, all goods and services produced in a particular year must be counted once and only once. Because most products go through a series of production stages before they reach the market, some of their components are bought and sold many times. To avoid counting those components each time, GDP includes only the market value of *final goods* and ignores *intermediate goods* altogether.

Intermediate goods are goods and services that are purchased for resale or for further processing or manufacturing. **Final goods** are goods and services that are purchased for final use, not for resale or for further processing or manufacturing.

intermediate goods
Products that are purchased for resale or further processing or manufacturing.

final goods
Products that have been purchased for final use and not for resale or further processing or manufacturing.

Including the value of intermediate goods in calculating GDP would amount to *multiple counting,* and that would distort the value of GDP. For example, suppose that among other inputs an automobile manufacturer uses $4000 of steel, $2000 of glass, and $1000 of tires in producing a new automobile that sells for $20,000. The $20,000 final good already includes the $7000 of steel, glass, and tires. We would be greatly overstating GDP if we added the $7000 of components to the $20,000 price of the auto and obtained $27,000 of output.

TABLE 12.1
Comparing Heterogeneous Output by Using Money Prices

Year	Annual Output	Market Value
1	3 sofas and 2 computers	3 at $500 + 2 at $2000 = $5500
2	2 sofas and 3 computers	2 at $500 + 3 at $2000 = $7000

© Brand X Pictures/Punchstock/DIL

© Royalty-Free/CORBIS/DIL

Photo Op Intermediate versus Final Goods

Lumber is an intermediate good, and a new townhouse is a final good.

Excluding Secondhand Sales

Secondhand sales do not contribute to current production and therefore are excluded from GDP. If you sell your 1965 Ford Mustang to a friend, that transaction would be ignored in determining this year's GDP because it generates no current production. The same would be true if you sold a brand-new Mustang to a neighbor a week after you purchased it. It has already been counted in GDP.

© PhotoLink/Getty Images/DIL

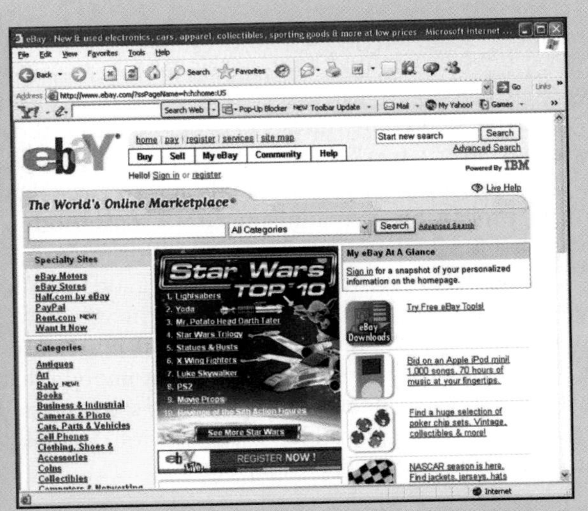

These materials have been reproduced with the permission of eBay Inc.

Photo Op New Goods versus Secondhand Goods

The goods offered for sale at a shopping mall are new goods and therefore included in current GDP. In contrast, the goods sold through eBay are usually secondhand items and thus not part of current GDP.

Measuring GDP

The simplest way to measure GDP is to add up all that was spent to buy total output in a certain year. Economists use precise terms for the four categories of spending.

Personal Consumption Expenditures (C)

The symbol C designates the **personal consumption expenditures** component of GDP. That term covers all expenditures by households on *durable consumer goods* (automobiles, refrigerators, cameras) that have lives of more than 3 years, *nondurable consumer goods* (bread, milk, toothpaste), and *consumer expenditures for services* (of lawyers, doctors, mechanics).

personal consumption expenditures (C) Expenditures by households for durable goods, nondurable goods, and services.

Gross Private Domestic Investment (I_g)

Under the heading **gross private domestic investment** are included (1) all final purchases of machinery, equipment, and tools by business enterprises; (2) all construction; and (3) changes in inventories.

gross private domestic investment (I_g) Expenditures for newly produced capital goods (such as plant and equipment) and for additions to inventories.

Notice that this list, except for the first item, includes more than we have meant by "economic investment" so far. The second item includes residential construction as well as the construction of new factories, warehouses, and stores. Why is residential construction investment rather than consumption? Because apartment buildings and houses, like factories and stores, earn income when they are rented or leased. Owner-occupied houses are treated as investment goods because they *could be* rented to bring in an income return. So all residential construction is treated as investment. Finally, an increase in inventories (unsold goods) is investment because it is "unconsumed output." For economists, all new output either is consumed or is capital. An increase in inventories is an addition (although temporary) to the stock of capital goods, and such additions are precisely how we define investment.

Positive and Negative Changes in Inventories We need to look at changes in inventories more closely. Inventories can either increase or decrease over some period. Suppose inventories rose by $10 billion between December 31, 2003, and December 31, 2004. That means the economy produced $10 billion more output than was purchased in 2004. We need to count all output produced in 2004 as part of that year's GDP, even though some of it remained unsold at the end of the year. This is accomplished by including the $10 billion increase in inventories as investment in 2004. That way the expenditures in 2004 will correctly measure the output produced that year.

Alternatively, suppose inventories fell by $10 billion in 2004. This "drawing down of inventories" means that the economy sold $10 billion more of output in 2004 than it produced that year. It did this by selling goods produced in prior years—goods already counted as GDP in those years. Unless corrected, expenditures in 2004 will overstate GDP for 2004. So in 2004 we consider the $10 billion decline in inventories as "negative investment" and subtract it from total investment that year. Thus, expenditures in 2004 will correctly measure the output produced in 2004.

Noninvestment Transactions So much for what investment is. You also need to know what it isn't. Investment does *not* include the transfer of paper assets (stocks, bonds) or the resale of tangible assets (houses, factories). Such transactions merely transfer the ownership of existing assets. Investment has to do with the creation of *new* capital assets—assets that create jobs and income. The mere transfer (sale) of claims to existing capital goods does not create new capital.

Gross Investment As we have seen, the category "gross private domestic investment" includes (1) all final purchases of machinery, equipment, and tools; (2) all construction; and (3) changes in inventories. The words "private" and "domestic" mean that we are speaking of spending by private businesses, not by government (public) agencies, and that the investment is taking place inside the country, not abroad.

The word "gross" means that we are referring to *all* investment goods—both those that replace machinery, equipment, and buildings that were used up (worn out or made obsolete) in producing the current year's output and any net additions to the economy's stock of capital. Gross investment includes investment in replacement capital *and* in added capital. [As opposed to net investment, for which replacement capital (depreciation) is subtracted from gross investment.]

The symbol I represents private domestic investment spending, along with the subscript g to signify gross investment.

Government Purchases (G)

government purchases (G) Government expenditures on final goods, services, and social capital.

The third category of expenditures in the national income accounts is **government purchases,** officially labeled "government consumption expenditures and gross investment." These expenditures have two components: (1) expenditures for goods and services that government consumes in providing public services and (2) expenditures for *social capital* such as schools and highways, which have long lifetimes. Government purchases (Federal, state, and local) include all government expenditures on final goods and all direct purchases of resources, including labor. It does *not* include government transfer payments such as Social Security payments, unemployment compensation, and veterans' benefits, because they merely transfer government receipts to certain households and generate no *current* production. The symbol G signifies government purchases.

Net Exports (X_n)

International trade transactions are a significant item in determining GDP. We know that GDP records all spending on goods and services produced in the United States, including spending on U.S. output by people abroad. So we must include the value of exports when we are adding up expenditures to determine GDP.

At the same time, we know that Americans spend a great deal of money on imports—goods and services produced abroad. That spending shows up in other nations' GDP. We must subtract the value of imports from U.S. spending to avoid overstating total production in the United States.

net exports (X_n) Exports minus imports.

Rather than add exports and then subtract imports, is it convenient to use "exports less imports," or **net exports.** We designate exports as X, imports as M, and net exports as X_n:

$$\text{Net exports } (X_n) = \text{exports } (X) - \text{imports } (M)$$

In 2004 Americans spent \$607 billion more on imports than foreigners spent on U.S. exports. That is, net exports in 2004 were a *minus* \$607 billion.

Adding It Up: GDP $= C + I_g + G + X_n$

Taken together, these four categories of expenditures provide a measure of the market value of a given year's total output—its GDP. For the United States in 2004,

$$\text{GDP} = \$8229 + 1927 + 2184 - 607 = \$11{,}734 \text{ billion (or } \$11.734 \text{ trillion)}$$

Global Snapshot 12.1 compares GDP in the United States to GDP in several other countries for 2004.

Global Snapshot 12.1

Comparative GDPs in Trillions of U.S. Dollars, Selected Nations, 2004

The United States, Japan, and Germany have the world's highest GDPs. The GDP data charted below have been converted to dollars via international exchange rates.

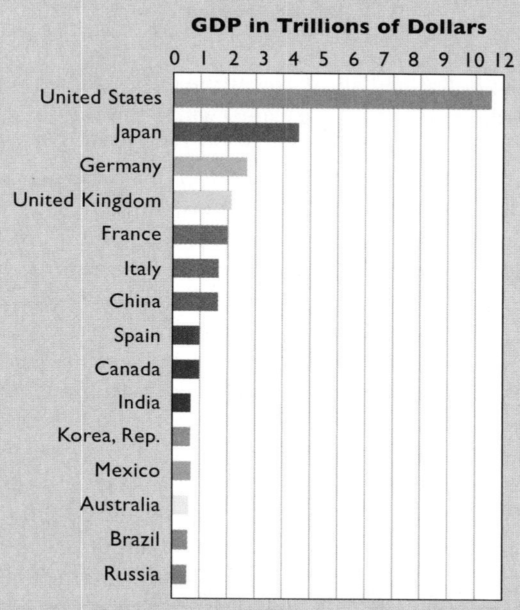

Source: World Bank, www.worldbank.org.

Nominal GDP versus Real GDP

Recall that GDP is a measure of the market or money value of all final goods and services produced by the economy in a given year. We use money or nominal values as a common denominator in order to sum that heterogeneous output into a meaningful total. But that creates a problem: How can we compare the market values of GDP from year to year if the value of money itself changes in response to inflation or deflation? After all, we determine the value of GDP by multiplying total output by market prices.

Whether there is a 5 percent increase in output with no change in prices or a 5 percent increase in prices with no change in output, the change in the monetary value of GDP will be the same. And yet it is the *quantity* of goods that get produced and distributed to households that affects our standard of living, not the price of the goods. The deluxe hamburger that sold for $4 in 2004 yields the same satisfaction as an identical hamburger that sold for 50 cents in 1970.

The way around this problem is to *deflate* GDP when prices rise and to *inflate* GDP when prices fall. These adjustments give us a measure of GDP for various years

TABLE 12.2
Calculating Real GDP (Base Year = Year 1)

Year	(1) Units of Output	(2) Price of Pizza per Unit	(3) Unadjusted, or Nominal, GDP, (1) × (2)	(4) Adjusted, or Real, GDP
1	5	$10	$ 50	$50
2	7	20	140	70
3	8	25	200	80
4	10	30	___	___
5	11	28	___	___

as if the value of the dollar had always been the same as it was in some reference year. A GDP based on the prices that prevailed when the output was produced is called *unadjusted GDP*, or **nominal GDP.** A GDP that has been deflated or inflated to reflect changes in the price level is called *adjusted GDP*, or **real GDP.**

nominal GDP Gross domestic product measured in terms of the price level at the time of measurement (i.e., GDP that is unadjusted for inflation).

real GDP Gross domestic product measured in terms of the price level in a base period (i.e., GDP that is adjusted for inflation).

Let's see how real GDP can be found. For simplicity, suppose the economy produces only one good, pizza, in the amounts indicated in Table 12.2 for years 1, 2, 3, 4, and 5. Also assume that we gather output and price data directly from the pizza business in various years. That is, we collect separate data on physical outputs (as in column 1) and their prices (as in column 2).

We can then determine the unadjusted, or nominal, GDP in each year by multiplying the number of units of output by the price per unit. Nominal GDP—here, the market value of pizza—is shown for each year in column 3.

We can also determine adjusted, or real, GDP from the data in Table 12.2. We want to know the market value of outputs in successive years *if the base-year price ($10) had prevailed.* In year 2, the 7 units of pizza would have a value of $70 (=7 units × $10) at the year-1 price. As column 4 shows, that $70 worth of output is year 2's real GDP. Similarly, we can determine the real GDP for year 3 by multiplying the 8 units of output that year by the $10 price in the base year. You should check your understanding of nominal versus real GDP by completing columns 3 and 4, where we purposely left the last rows blank.

Let's return to the real economy. As previously determined, nominal GDP in the United States was $11,734 billion in 2004. What was real GDP that year? Because prices rose between the 2000 base year and 2004, real GDP in 2004 turned out to be $10,842 billion. Or, in the language of economics, "GDP in 2004 was $10,842 billion in 2000 (base-year) prices."

The Underground Economy

Real GDP is a reasonably accurate and highly useful measure of how well or how poorly the economy is performing. But some production never shows up in GDP, which measures only the *market value* of output. Embedded in the U.S. economy is a flourishing, productive underground sector. Some of the people who conduct business there are gamblers, smugglers, prostitutes, "fences" of stolen goods, drug producers, and drug dealers. They have good reason to conceal their economic activities. When they do, their "contributions" to output do not show up in GDP.

Most participants in the underground economy, however, engage in perfectly legal activities but choose not to report their full incomes to the Internal Revenue Service (IRS). A bell captain at a hotel may report just a portion of the tips received from customers. Storekeepers may report only a portion of their sales receipts. Workers who want to hold on to their unemployment compensation benefits may take an "off-the-books" or "cash-only" job. A brick mason may agree to rebuild a neighbor's fireplace in exchange for the neighbor's repairing his boat engine. The value of none of these transactions shows up in GDP.

The value of underground transactions is estimated to be about 8 percent of the recorded GDP in the United States. That would mean that GDP in 2004 was understated by about $939 billion. Global Snapshot 12.2 shows estimates of the relative sizes of underground economies in selected nations.

Question:
How would decriminalization of drugs instantly increase a nation's real GDP? What might be the downside of decriminalization of drugs for growth of real GDP over time?

Global Snapshot 12.2

The Underground Economy as a Percentage of GDP, Selected Nations

Underground economies vary in size worldwide. Three factors that help explain the variation are (1) the extent and complexity of regulation, (2) the type and degree of taxation, and (3) the effectiveness of law enforcement.

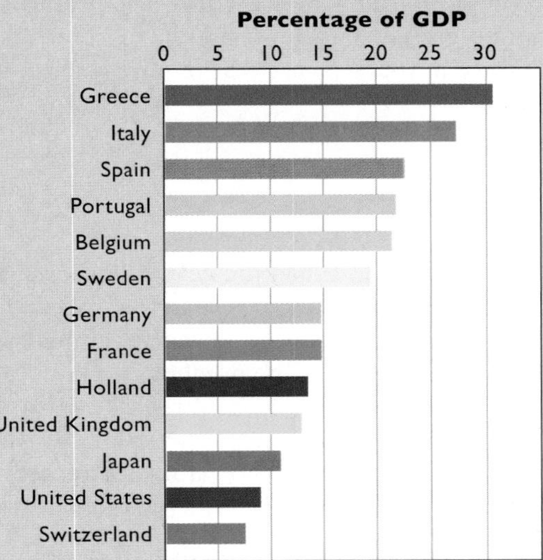

Source: Friedrich Schneider and Dominik H. Enste, "Shadow Economies: Size, Causes, and Consequences," *Journal of Economic Literature,* March 2000, p. 104.

Growth and the Business Cycle

economic growth The expansion of real GDP (or real GDP per capita) over time.

real GDP per capita Real output divided by population.

The NIPA data enable economists to calculate and analyze economic growth rates. Economists define and measure **economic growth** as either an *increase in real GDP* occurring over time or an *increase in real GDP per capita* occurring over time. **Real GDP per capita** (or output per person) is found by dividing real GDP by the size of the population. With either definition, economic growth is calculated as a percentage rate of growth per quarter (3-month period) or per year.

For measuring expansion of military potential or political preeminence, the growth of real GDP is more useful. Unless specified otherwise, growth rates reported in the news and by international agencies use this definition of economic growth. For comparing living standards, however, the second definition is superior. While China's GDP in 2003 was \$1410 billion compared with Denmark's \$212 billion, Denmark's real GDP per capita was \$33,750 compared with China's \$1110.

Growth as a Goal

Economic growth is a widely held economic goal. The expansion of total output relative to population results in rising real wages and incomes and thus higher standards of living. An economy that is experiencing economic growth is better able to meet people's wants and resolve socioeconomic problems. Rising real wages and income provide richer opportunities to individuals and families—a vacation trip, a personal computer, a higher education—without sacrificing other opportunities and pleasures. A growing economy can undertake new programs to alleviate poverty and protect the environment without impairing existing levels of consumption, investment, and public goods production.

In short, *growth lessens the burden of scarcity.* A growing economy, unlike a static economy, can consume more today while increasing its capacity to produce more in the future. By easing the burden of scarcity—by relaxing society's constraints on production—economic growth enables a nation to attain its economic goals more readily and to undertake new endeavors that require the use of goods and services to be accomplished.

Arithmetic of Growth

The mathematical approximation called the *rule of 70* shows the effect of compounding of economic growth rates over time. It tells us that we can find the number of years it will take for some measure to double, given its annual percentage increase, by dividing that percentage increase into the number 70. So

$$\text{Approximate number of years required to double real GDP} = \frac{70}{\text{annual percentage rate of growth}}$$

Examples: A 3 percent annual rate of growth will double real GDP in about 23 (=70/3) years. Growth of 8 percent per year will double it in about 9 (=70/8) years.

Illustrating the Idea

Growth Rates Matter!

Small absolute differences in rates of economic growth add up to substantial differences in real GDP and standards of living. Consider three hypothetical countries—Alpha, Bravo, and Charlie. Suppose that in 2004 these countries have identical levels of real GDP ($6 trillion), population (200 million), and real GDP per capita ($30,000). Also, assume that annual real GDP growth is 2 percent in Alpha, 3 percent in Bravo, and 4 percent in Charlie.

How will these alternative growth rates affect real GDP and real GDP per capita over a long period, say, the 70-year average life span of an American? By 2074 the 2, 3, and 4 percent growth rates would boost real GDP from $6 trillion to $24 trillion in Alpha, $47 trillion in Bravo, and $93 trillion in Charlie.

For illustration, let's assume that each country experienced an average annual population growth of 1 percent over the 70 years. Then, in 2074 real GDP per capita would be about $60,000 in Alpha, $118,000 in Bravo, and $233,000 in Charlie.

No wonder economists pay so much attention to small changes in the rate of economic growth. For the United States, with a current real GDP of about $12 trillion, the difference between a 3 percent and a 4 percent rate of growth is about $120 billion of output each year. For a poor country, a difference of one-half of a percentage point in the rate of growth may mean the difference between starvation and mere hunger. Economic growth rates matter!

Question:
Why would gaps in GDP per capita for Alpha and Charlie be even more dramatic if population growth was faster in Alpha than in Charlie?

Main Sources of Economic Growth

We analyze the sources of economic growth (so-called *growth accounting*) in Chapter 17. For now, you simply need to know that there are two fundamental ways society can increase its real output and income: (1) by increasing its inputs of resources and (2) by increasing the productivity of those inputs. Other things equal, increases in land, labor, capital, and entrepreneurial resources yield additional output. But economic growth also occurs through increases in *productivity*—measured broadly as real output per unit of input. Productivity rises when the health, training, education, and motivation of workers are improved; when workers have more and better machinery and natural resources with which to work; when production is better organized and managed; and when labor is reallocated from less efficient industries to more efficient industries. About one-third of U.S. growth comes from more inputs. The remaining two-thirds results from improved productivity.

Growth in the United States

Table 12.3 gives an overview of economic growth in the United States over past periods. Column 2 reveals strong growth as measured by increases in real GDP. Note that real GDP increased more than sixfold between 1950 and 2004. But the U.S. population also increased over these years. Nevertheless, in column 4 we find that real GDP per capita rose more than threefold.

TABLE 12.3
Real GDP and Per Capita Real GDP, Selected Years, 1950–2004

(1) Year	(2) Real GDP, Billions of 2000 $	(3) Population, Millions	(4) Real Per Capita GDP, 2000 $ (2) ÷ (3)
1950	1777	152	11,691
1960	2502	181	13,823
1970	3772	205	18,400
1980	5162	228	22,640
1990	7113	250	28,452
1995	8032	267	30,082
2000	9817	282	34,812
2004	10,842	293	37,003

Source: Bureau of Economic Analysis, www.bea.doc.gov, and U.S. Census Bureau, www.census.gov.

What has been the *rate* of U.S. growth? Real GDP grew at an annual rate of about 3.4 percent between 1950 and 2004. Real GDP per capita increased about 2.1 percent per year over that time.

Viewed from the perspective of the last half-century, economic growth in the United States lagged behind that in Japan, Germany, Italy, Canada, and France. Japan's annual growth rate, in fact, averaged twice that of the United States. But economic growth since 1994 is quite another matter. As shown in Global Snapshot 12.3, the U.S. growth rate generally topped the rates of growth in Japan and other major industrial nations.

Global Snapshot 12.3

Average Annual Growth Rates, 1996–2004, Selected Nations

Between 1996 and 2004, economic growth in the United States exceeded that of several other major countries. U.S. economic growth greatly slowed in 2001 and 2002 before rising again in 2003 and 2004.

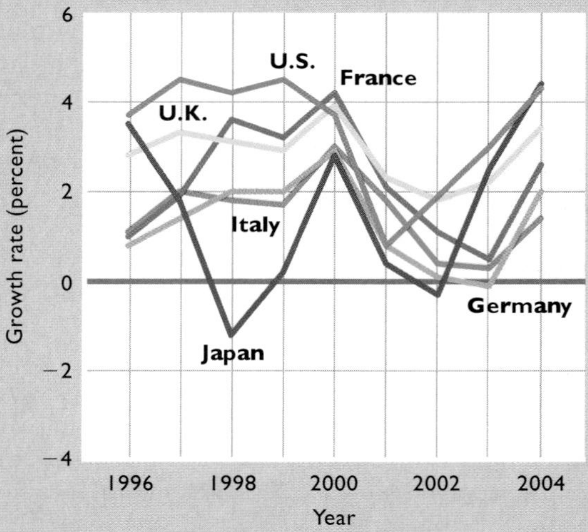

Source: *Economic Report of the President, 2005.*

Business Cycles

12.1 Business cycles

We have seen that the long-run growth trend of the U.S. economy is one of expansion. But growth has been interrupted by periods of economic instability usually associated with *business cycles*. The term **business cycles** refers to alternating rises and declines in the level of economic activity, sometimes over several years. Individual cycles (one "up" followed by one "down") vary substantially in duration and intensity.

business cycles Recurring increases and decreases in the level of economic activity over periods of time.

As shown in Figure 12.1, the two primary phases of business cycles are recessions and expansions ("peaks" and "troughs" are merely turning points). A **recession** is a period of decline in total output, income, and employment. This downturn, which lasts 6 months or more, is marked by the widespread contraction of business activity in many sectors of the economy—that is, by declines in real GDP and significant increases in unemployment. Table 12.4 documents the 10 recessions in the United States since 1950.

recession A period of declining real GDP, accompanied by lower income and higher unemployment.

A recession is usually followed by a recovery and **expansion,** a period in which real GDP, income, and employment rise. At some point, full employment is again achieved. If spending then expands more rapidly than does production capacity, prices of nearly all goods and services will rise. In other words, inflation will occur.

expansion A generalized increase in output, income, and business activity.

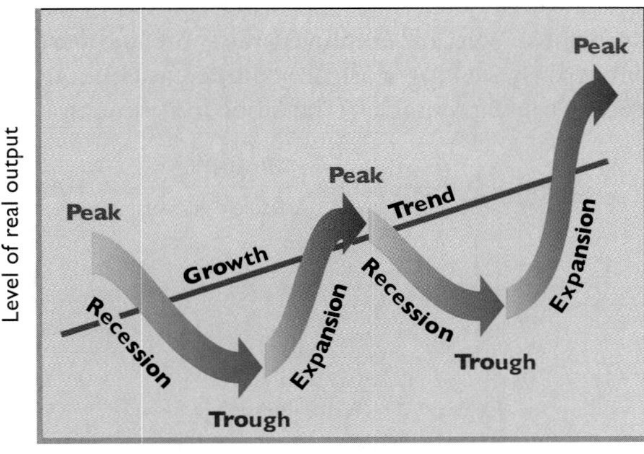

FIGURE 12.1
The business cycle. Economists distinguish two primary phases of the business cycle (recession and expansion); the duration and strength of each phase may vary.

TABLE 12.4
U.S. Recessions since 1950

Period	Duration, Months	Depth (Decline in Real Output)
1953–54	10	−3.7%
1957–58	8	−3.9
1960–61	10	−1.6
1969–70	11	−1.0
1973–75	16	−4.9
1980	6	−2.3
1981–82	16	−3.3
1990–91	8	−1.8
2001	8	−0.5

Source: *Economic Report of the President, 1993,* updated.

Unemployment

The twin problems that arise from business cycles are unemployment and inflation. Let's look at unemployment first.

Measurement of Unemployment

The U.S. Bureau of Labor Statistics (BLS) conducts a nationwide random survey of some 60,000 households each month to determine who is employed and who is not employed. In a series of questions it asks which members of the household are working, unemployed and looking for work, not looking for work, and so on. From the answers it determines an unemployment rate for the entire nation.

Figure 12.2 helps explain the mathematics. It divides the total U.S. population into three groups. One group is made up of people less than 16 years of age and people who are institutionalized, for example, in mental hospitals or correctional institutions. Such people are not considered potential members of the labor force. A second group, labeled "Not in labor force," is composed of adults who are potential workers but are not employed and are not seeking work. For example, they are homemakers, full-time students, or retirees. The third group is the **labor force,** which constituted about 50 percent of the total population in 2004. The labor force consists of people who are able and willing to work. Both those who are employed full-time and part-time and those who are unemployed but actively seeking work are counted as being in the labor force. The **unemployment rate** is the percentage of the labor force unemployed:

labor force Persons 16 years and older who are not in institutions and who are either employed or unemployed and seeking work.

unemployment rate The percentage of the labor force unemployed.

$$\text{Unemployment rate} = \frac{\text{unemployed}}{\text{labor force}} \times 100$$

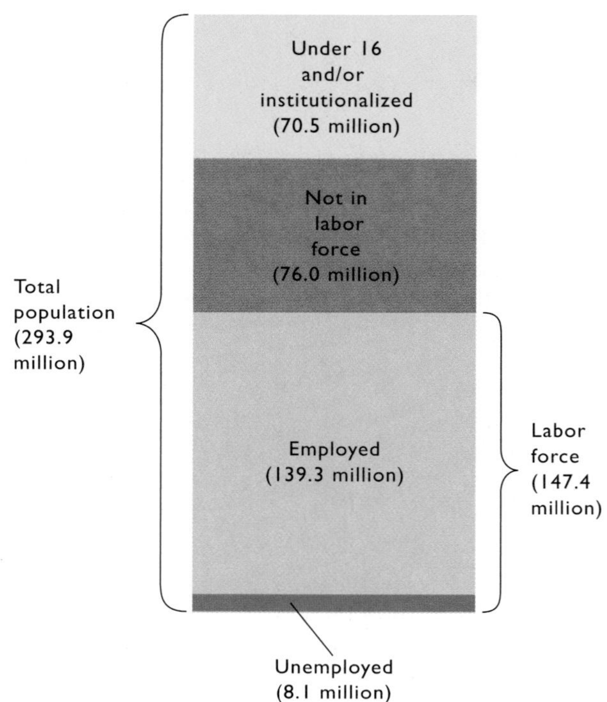

FIGURE 12.2 **The labor force, employment, and unemployment, 2004.** The labor force consists of persons 16 years of age or older who are not in institutions and who are (1) employed or (2) unemployed but seeking employment.

Source: Bureau of Labor Statistics, www.bls.gov (civilian labor force data, which excludes military employment).

The statistics included in Figure 12.2 show that in 2004 the unemployment rate averaged

$$\frac{8{,}149{,}000}{147{,}400{,}000} \times 100 = 5.5\%$$

Types of Unemployment

There are three *types* of unemployment: frictional, structural, and cyclical.

Frictional Unemployment At any moment some workers are "between jobs." Some of them will be moving voluntarily from one job to another. Others will have been fired and will be seeking reemployment. Still others will have been laid off temporarily because of seasonal demand. In addition to those between jobs, many young workers will be searching for their first jobs.

As these unemployed people find jobs or are called back from temporary layoffs, other job seekers and laid-off workers will replace them in the "unemployment pool." So even though the workers who are unemployed for such reasons change from month to month, this type of unemployment persists.

Economists use the term **frictional unemployment**—consisting of *search unemployment* and *wait unemployment*—for workers who are either searching for jobs or waiting to take jobs in the near future. The word "frictional" implies that the labor market does not operate perfectly and instantaneously (without friction) in matching workers and jobs.

frictional unemployment Unemployment that is associated with people searching for jobs or waiting to take jobs in the near future.

Frictional unemployment is inevitable and, at least in part, desirable. Many people who are frictionally unemployed are moving into the labor force or from low-paying, low-productivity jobs to higher-paying, higher-productivity positions. That means greater income for the workers, a better allocation of labor resources, and a larger real GDP for the economy.

Structural Unemployment Frictional unemployment blurs into a category called **structural unemployment.** Here, economists use "structural" in the sense of "compositional." Changes over time in consumer demand and in technology alter the "structure" of the total demand for labor, both occupationally and geographically.

structural unemployment Unemployment that is associated with a mismatch between available jobs and the skills or locations of those unemployed.

Occupationally, the demand for certain skills (for example, sewing clothes or working on farms) may decline or even vanish. The demand for other skills (for example, designing software or maintaining computer systems) will intensify. Unemployment results because the composition of the labor force does not respond immediately or completely to the new structure of job opportunities. Workers who find that their skills and experience have become obsolete or unneeded thus find that they have no marketable talents. They are structurally unemployed until they adapt or develop skills that employers want.

Geographically, the demand for labor also changes over time. An example: migration of industry and thus of employment opportunities from the Snow Belt to the Sun Belt over the past few decades. Another example is the movement of jobs from inner-city factories to suburban industrial parks. As job opportunities shift from one place to another, some workers become structurally unemployed.

cyclical unemployment Unemployment that is associated with the recessionary phase of a business cycle.

Cyclical Unemployment Unemployment caused by a decline in total spending is called **cyclical unemployment** and typically begins in the recession phase of the business cycle. As the demand for goods and services decreases, employment falls and unemployment rises. The 25 percent unemployment rate in the depth of the Great Depression in 1933 reflected mainly cyclical unemployment, as did significant parts of the 9.7 percent unemployment rate in 1982, the 7.5 percent rate in 1992, and the 5.8 percent rate in 2002.

Cyclical unemployment is a very serious problem when it occurs. To understand its costs, we need to define "full employment."

Definition of Full Employment

Because frictional and structural unemployment is largely unavoidable in a dynamic economy, *full employment* is something less than 100 percent employment of the labor force. Economists say that the economy is "fully employed" when it is experiencing only frictional and structural unemployment. That is, full employment occurs when there is no cyclical unemployment. Today, most economists believe that the economy is fully employed when the unemployment rate is less than 5 percent. The level of real GDP that would occur precisely at "full employment" is called **potential output** (or *potential GDP*).

potential output The level of real GDP that would occur if there was full employment.

Economic Cost of Unemployment

The basic economic cost of unemployment is forgone output. When the economy fails to create enough jobs for all who have the necessary skills and are willing to work, potential production of goods and services is irretrievably lost. In terms of Chapter 1's analysis, cyclical unemployment means that society is operating at some point inside its production possibilities curve. Economists call this sacrifice of output a **GDP gap**—the difference between actual and potential GDP. That is:

GDP gap The negative or positive difference between actual GDP and potential GDP.

$$\text{GDP gap} = \text{actual GDP} - \text{potential GDP}$$

The GDP gap can be either a negative number (actual GDP is less than potential GDP) or a positive number (actual GDP exceeds potential GDP). There is a close correlation between the actual unemployment rate and the GDP gap. The higher the unemployment rate, the greater is the negative GDP gap.

Society's cost of unemployment—its forgone output—translates to forgone income for individuals. This loss of income is borne unequally. Some groups have higher unemployment rates than others and bear the brunt of rising rates during recessions. For instance, workers in lower-skilled occupations (for example, laborers) have higher unemployment rates than workers in higher-skilled occupations (for example, professionals). Lower-skilled workers have more and longer spells of structural unemployment than higher-skilled workers. They also are less likely to be self-employed than are higher-skilled workers. Moreover, lower-skilled workers usually bear the brunt of recessions. Businesses generally retain most of their higher-skilled workers, in whom they have invested the expense of training.

Also, teenagers have much higher unemployment rates than adults. Teenagers have lower skill levels, quit their jobs more frequently, are more frequently "fired," and have less geographic mobility than adults. Many unemployed teenagers are new in the labor market, searching for their first jobs. Male African-American teenagers, in particular, have very high unemployment rates.

Finally, the overall unemployment rate for African-Americans and Hispanics is higher than that for whites and Asians. The causes of the higher rates include lower rates of educational attainment, greater concentration in lower-skilled occupations, and discrimination in the labor market. In general, the unemployment rate for African-Americans is twice that of whites.

International Comparisons

Unemployment rates differ greatly among nations at any given time. One reason is that nations have different unemployment rates when their economies are fully employed. Another is that nations may be in recessions or expansions. Global Snapshot 12.4 shows unemployment rates for five industrialized nations in recent years. Between 1994 and 2004, the U.S. unemployment rate was considerably lower than the rates in Italy, France, and Germany.

Global Snapshot 12.4

Unemployment Rates in Five Industrial Nations, 1994–2004

Compared with Italy, France, and Germany, the United States had a relatively low unemployment rate in recent years.

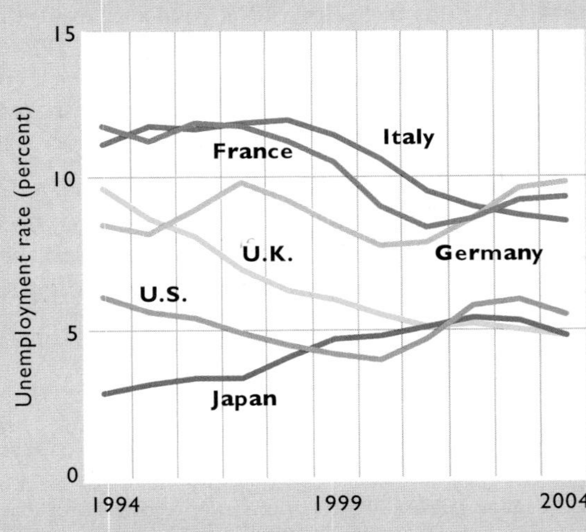

Source: *Economic Report of the President, 2005.*

Inflation

We now turn to inflation, another aspect of macroeconomic instability. The problems inflation poses are subtler than those posed by unemployment.

Meaning of Inflation

Inflation is a rise in the *general level of prices*. When inflation occurs, each dollar of income will buy fewer goods and services than before. Inflation reduces the "purchasing power" of money. But inflation does not mean that *all* prices are rising. Even during periods of rapid inflation, some prices may be relatively constant while others are falling. For example, although the United States experienced high rates of inflation in the 1970s and early 1980s, the prices of video recorders, digital watches, and personal computers declined.

inflation
A rise in the general level of prices in an economy.

Measurement of Inflation

Consumer Price Index (CPI)
An index that compares the price of a market basket of consumer goods and services in one period with the price of the same (or highly similar) market basket in a base period.

The main measure of inflation in the United States is the **Consumer Price Index (CPI),** compiled by the Bureau of Labor Statistics (BLS). The government uses this index to report inflation rates each month and each year. It also uses the CPI to adjust Social Security benefits and income tax brackets for inflation. The CPI reports the price of a "market basket" of some 300 consumer goods and services that presumably are purchased by a typical urban consumer.

The composition of the market basket for the CPI is based on spending patterns of urban consumers in a specific period, presently 2002–2003. The BLS updates the composition of the market basket every 2 years so that it reflects the most recent patterns of consumer purchases and captures the inflation that consumers are currently experiencing. The BLS arbitrarily sets the CPI equal to 100 for 1982–1984. So the CPI for any particular year is found as follows:

$$\text{CPI} = \frac{\text{price of the most recent market basket in the particular year}}{\text{price of the same market basket in 1982–1984}}$$

The rate of inflation for a certain year is found by comparing, in percentage terms, that year's index with the index in the previous year. For example, the CPI rose from 184.0 in 2003 to 188.9 in 2004. So the rate of inflation for 2004 was 2.7 percent.

$$\text{Rate of inflation} = \frac{188.9 - 184.0}{184.0} \times 100 = 2.7\%$$

Recall that the mathematical approximation called the *rule of 70* tells us that we can find the number of years it will take for some measure to double, given its annual percentage increase, by dividing that percentage increase into the number 70. For example, annual rates of inflation of 3 percent will double the price level in about 23 (=70/3) years.

FIGURE 12.3
Annual inflation rates in the United States, 1960–2004. The major periods of inflation in the United States in the past 40 years were in the 1970s and 1980s.

Source: Bureau of Labor Statistics, www.bls.gov (December-to-December data).

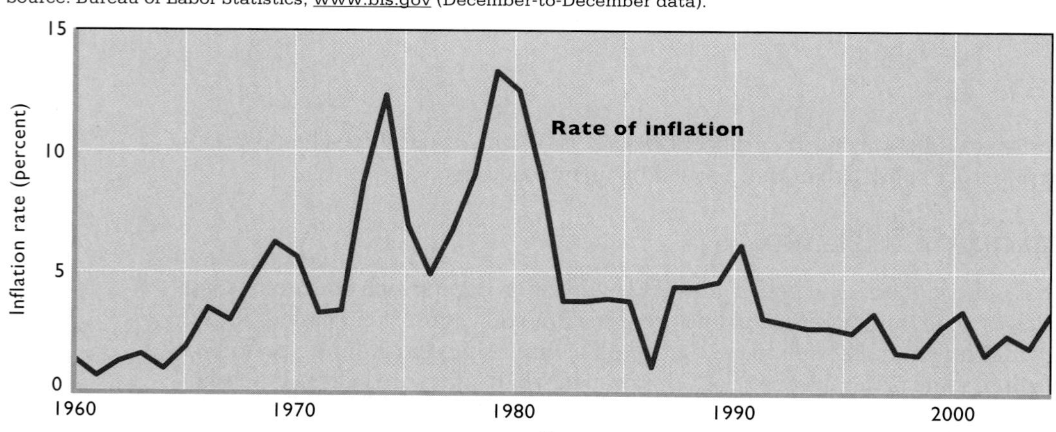

Facts of Inflation

Figure 12.3 shows the annual rates of inflation in the United States between 1960 and 2004. Observe that inflation reached double-digit rates in the 1970s and early 1980s but has since declined and has been relatively mild recently.

In recent years U.S. inflation has been neither unusually high nor unusually low relative to inflation in several other industrial countries (see Global Snapshot 12.5). Some nations (not shown) have had double-digit or even higher annual rates of inflation in recent years. In 2004, for example, the annual inflation rate in Venezuela was 24 percent, in the Dominican Republic, 55 percent; in Angola, 56 percent; and in Zimbabwe, 350 percent.

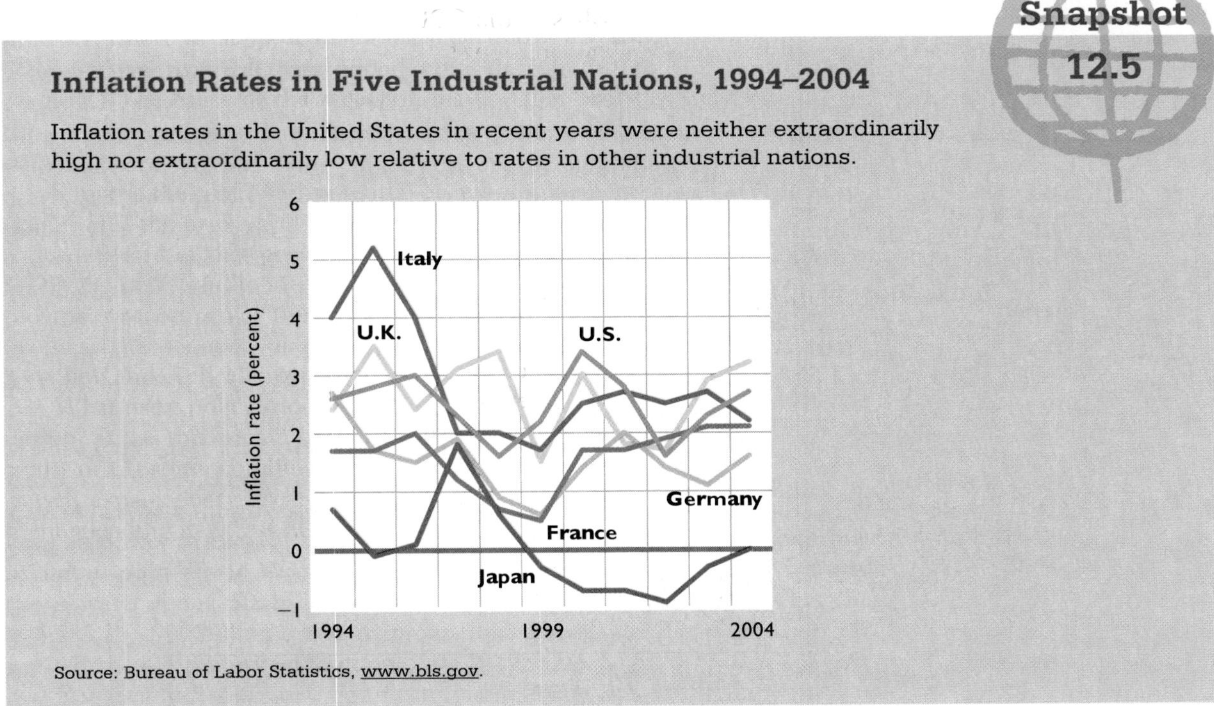

Inflation Rates in Five Industrial Nations, 1994–2004

Inflation rates in the United States in recent years were neither extraordinarily high nor extraordinarily low relative to rates in other industrial nations.

Source: Bureau of Labor Statistics, www.bls.gov.

Types of Inflation

Economists distinguish between two types of inflation: *demand-pull inflation* and *cost-push inflation.*

Demand-Pull Inflation Usually, changes in the price level are caused by an excess of total spending beyond the economy's capacity to produce. Where inflation is rapid and sustained, the cause invariably is an overissuance of money by the central bank (the Federal Reserve in the United States). When resources are already fully employed, the business sector cannot respond to excess demand by expanding output. So the excess demand bids up the prices of the limited output, producing **demand-pull inflation.** The essence of this type of inflation is "too much spending chasing too few goods."

demand-pull inflation
Increases in the price level (inflation) caused by excessive spending.

Illustrating the Idea

Clipping Coins

Some interesting early episodes of demand-pull inflation occurred in Europe during the ninth to the fifteenth centuries under feudalism. In that economic system *lords* (or *princes*) ruled individual fiefdoms, and their *vassals* (or *peasants*) worked the fields. The peasants initially paid parts of their harvest as taxes to the princes. Later, when the princes began issuing "coins of the realm," peasants began paying their taxes with gold coins.

Some princes soon discovered a way to transfer purchasing power from their vassals to themselves without explicitly increasing taxes. As coins came into the treasury, princes clipped off parts of the gold coins, making them slightly smaller. From the clippings they minted new coins and used them to buy more goods for themselves.

This practice of clipping coins was a subtle form of taxation. The quantity of goods being produced in the fiefdom remained the same, but the number of gold coins increased. With "too much money chasing too few goods," inflation occurred. Each gold coin earned by the peasants therefore had less purchasing power than previously because prices were higher. The increase of the money supply shifted purchasing power away from the peasants and toward the princes just as surely as if the princes had increased taxation of the peasants.

In more recent eras some dictators have simply printed money to buy more goods for themselves, their relatives, and their key loyalists. These dictators, too, have levied hidden taxes on their population by creating inflation.

The moral of the story is quite simple: A society that values price-level stability should not entrust the control of its money supply to people who benefit from inflation.

Question:
Why might a government with a huge foreign debt be tempted to increase its domestic money supply and cause inflation?

Cost-Push Inflation Inflation may also arise on the supply, or cost, side of the economy. During some periods in U.S. economic history, including the mid-1970s, the price level increased even though total spending was not excessive. These were periods when output and employment were both *declining* (evidence that total spending was not excessive) while the general price level was *rising*.

cost-push inflation Increases in the price level (inflation) caused by sharp rises in the cost of key resources.

The theory of **cost-push inflation** explains rising prices in terms of factors that raise the average cost of a particular level of output. Rising average production costs squeeze profits and reduce the economy's supply of goods and services. In this scenario, costs are *pushing* the price level upward, whereas in demand-pull inflation demand is *pulling* it upward.

The major source of cost-push inflation has been so-called *supply shocks*. Specifically, abrupt increases in the costs of raw materials or energy inputs have on occasion driven up per-unit production costs and thus product prices. The rocketing prices of imported oil in 1973–1974 and again in 1979–1980 are good illustrations. As energy prices surged upward during these periods, the costs of producing and transporting virtually every product in the economy rose. Rapid cost-push inflation ensued.

Redistribution Effects of Inflation

Inflation hurts some people, leaves others unaffected, and actually helps still others. That is, inflation redistributes real income from some people to others. Who gets hurt? Who benefits? Before we can answer, we need some terminology. There is a difference between money (or nominal) income and real income. **Nominal income** is the number of dollars received as wages, rent, interest, or profits. **Real income** is a measure of the amount of goods and services nominal income can buy; it is the purchasing power of nominal income, or income adjusted for inflation. That is,

nominal income
The number of dollars received as wages, rent, interest, and profit.

$$\text{Real income} = \frac{\text{nominal income}}{\text{price index (in hundredths)}}$$

real income
The purchasing power of nominal income; the amount of goods and services that nominal income can buy.

Inflation need not alter an economy's overall real income—its total purchasing power. It is evident from the above equation that real income will remain the same when nominal income and the price index rise at the same percentage rate.

But when inflation occurs, not everyone's nominal income rises at the same pace as the price level. Therein lies the potential for redistribution of real income from some to others. If the change in the price level differs from the change in a person's nominal income, his or her real income will be affected.

The redistribution effects of inflation depend on whether or not it is expected. With fully expected or *anticipated inflation*, an income receiver may be able to avoid or lessen the adverse effects of inflation on real income. The generalizations that follow assume *unanticipated inflation*—inflation whose full extent was not expected.

Who Is Hurt by Inflation?

Unanticipated inflation hurts fixed-income recipients, savers, and creditors. It redistributes real income away from them and toward others.

Fixed-Income Receivers People whose incomes are fixed see their real incomes fall when inflation occurs. The classic case is the elderly couple living on a private pension or annuity that provides a fixed amount of nominal income each month. They may have retired on what appeared to be an adequate pension. However, years later they discover that inflation has severely cut the purchasing power of that pension—their real income.

Similarly, landlords who receive lease payments of fixed dollar amounts will be hurt by inflation as they receive dollars of declining value over time. Likewise, public sector workers whose incomes are dictated by fixed pay schedules may suffer from inflation. The fixed "steps" (the upward yearly increases) in their pay schedules may not keep up with inflation. Minimum-wage workers and families living on fixed welfare incomes will also be hurt by inflation.

Savers Unanticipated inflation hurts savers. As prices rise, the real value, or purchasing power, of an accumulation of savings deteriorates. Paper assets such as savings accounts, insurance policies, and annuities, which once were adequate to meet rainy-day contingencies or provide for a comfortable retirement, decline in real value during periods of inflation.

Creditors Unanticipated inflation harms creditors (lenders). Suppose Chase Bank lends Bob $1000, to be repaid in 2 years. If in that time the price level doubles, the $1000 that Bob repays will have only half the purchasing power of the $1000 he borrowed. True, if we ignore interest charges, the same number of dollars will be repaid as was borrowed. But because of inflation, each of those dollars will buy only half as much as it did when the loan was negotiated. As prices go up, the value of the dollar goes down. So the borrower pays back less valuable dollars than those received from the lender. The owners of Chase Bank suffer a loss of real income.

Who Is Unaffected or Helped by Inflation?

Some people are unaffected by inflation, and others are actually helped by it. For the second group, inflation redistributes real income toward them and away from others.

Flexible-Income Receivers People who have flexible incomes may escape inflation's harm or even benefit from it. For example, individuals who derive their incomes solely from Social Security are largely unaffected by inflation because Social Security payments are *indexed* to the CPI. Benefits automatically increase when the CPI increases, preventing erosion of benefits from inflation. Some union workers also get automatic *cost-of-living adjustments (COLAs)* in their pay when the CPI rises, although such increases rarely equal the full percentage rise in inflation.

Some flexible-income receivers are helped by unanticipated inflation. The strong product demand and labor shortages implied by rapid demand-pull inflation may cause some nominal incomes to spurt ahead of the price level, thereby enhancing real incomes. As an example, property owners faced with an inflation-induced real estate boom may be able to boost flexible rents more rapidly than the rate of inflation. Also, some business owners may benefit from inflation. If their product prices rise faster than their resource prices, business revenues will increase more rapidly than costs. In those cases, the growth rate of profit incomes will outpace the rate of inflation.

Debtors Unanticipated inflation benefits debtors (borrowers). In our earlier example, Chase Bank's loss of real income from inflation is Bob's gain of real income. Debtor Bob borrows "dear" dollars but, because of inflation, pays back the principal and interest with "cheap" dollars whose purchasing power has been eroded by inflation. Real income is redistributed away from the owners of Chase Bank toward borrowers such as Bob.

Anticipated Inflation

The redistribution effects of inflation are less severe or are eliminated altogether if people anticipate inflation and can adjust their nominal incomes to reflect the expected price-level rises. The prolonged inflation that began in the late 1960s prompted many workers in the 1970s to insist on high wage and salary increases that would protect them from expected inflation.

Similarly, if inflation is anticipated, the redistribution of income from lender to borrower may be altered. Suppose a lender (perhaps a bank) and a borrower (a household) both agree that 5 percent is a fair rate of interest on a 1-year loan provided the price level is stable. But assume that inflation has been occurring and is expected to be 6 percent over the next year. The lender will neutralize inflation by charging an *inflation premium* of 6 percent, the amount of the anticipated inflation.

FIGURE 12.4
The inflation premium and nominal and real interest rates. The inflation premium—the expected rate of inflation—gets built into the nominal interest rate. Here, the nominal interest rate of 11 percent comprises the real interest rate of 5 percent plus the inflation premium of 6 percent.

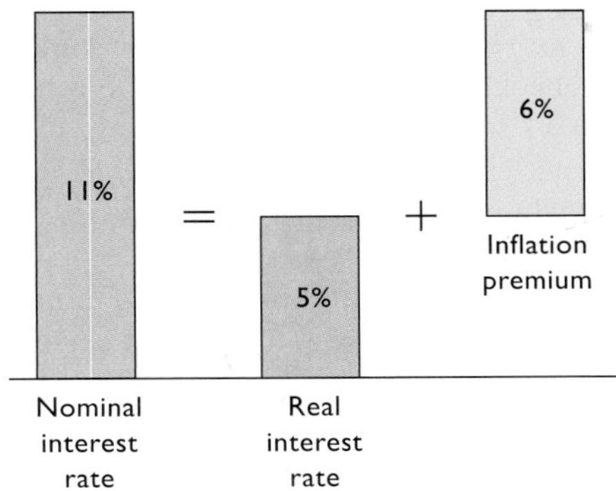

Our example reveals the difference between the real rate of interest and the nominal rate of interest. The **real interest rate** is the percentage increase in *purchasing power* that the borrower pays the lender. In our example the real interest rate is 5 percent. The **nominal interest rate** is the percentage increase in *money* that the borrower pays the lender, including that resulting from the built-in expectation of inflation, if any. In equation form:

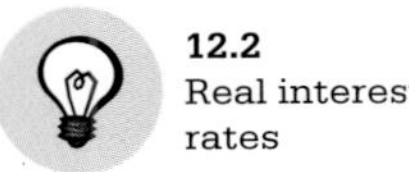

real interest rate
The percentage increase in purchasing power that a borrower pays a lender; the nominal interest rate less the expected rate of inflation.

nominal interest rate
The percentage increase in money that a borrower pays a lender.

$$\text{Nominal interest rate} = \text{real interest rate} + \text{inflation premium (the expected rate of inflation)}$$

As illustrated in Figure 12.4, the nominal interest rate in our example is 11 percent.

Does Inflation Affect Output?

Thus far, our discussion has focused on how inflation redistributes a given level of total real income. But inflation may also affect an economy's level of real output (and thus its level of real income). The direction and significance of this effect on output depends on the type of inflation and its severity.

Cost-Push Inflation and Real Output

Recall that abrupt and unexpected rises in key resource prices such as oil can sufficiently drive up overall production costs to cause cost-push inflation. As prices rise, the quantity of goods and services demanded falls. So firms respond by producing less output, and unemployment goes up. In short, cost-push inflation reduces real output. It redistributes a decreased level of real income.

Demand-Pull Inflation and Real Output

Economists do not fully agree on the effects of mild inflation (less than 3 percent) on real output. One perspective is that even low levels of inflation reduce real output, because inflation diverts time and effort toward activities designed to hedge against inflation. For example, businesses must incur the cost of changing thousands of prices on their shelves and in their computers simply to reflect inflation. Also, households and businesses must spend considerable time and effort obtaining the information they need to distinguish between real and nominal values such as prices, wages, and interest rates. Further, to limit the loss of purchasing power from inflation, people try to limit the amount of money they hold in their billfolds and checking accounts at any one time and instead put more money into interest-bearing accounts and stock and bond funds. But cash and checking deposits are needed in even greater amounts to buy the higher-priced goods and services. Therefore, people must make more frequent trips, phone calls, or Internet visits to financial institutions to transfer funds to checking accounts and billfolds, when needed. Bottom line: From this perspective even mild inflation reduces total output.

In contrast, other economists point out that full employment and economic growth depend on strong levels of total spending. Such spending creates high profits, strong demand for labor, and a powerful incentive for firms to expand their plants and equipment. In this view, the mild inflation that is a by-product of strong spending is a small price to pay for full employment and continued economic growth. Defenders of mild inflation say that it is much better for an economy to err on the side of strong spending, full employment, economic growth, and mild inflation than on the side of weak spending, unemployment, recession, and **deflation**—a decline in the general level of prices in the economy.

deflation
A decline in the general level of prices in the economy.

Hyperinflation

All economists agree that *hyperinflation*, which is extraordinarily rapid inflation, can have a devastating impact on real output and employment.

As prices shoot up sharply and unevenly during hyperinflation, normal economic relationships are disrupted. Business owners do not know what to charge for their products. Consumers do not know what to pay. Resource suppliers want to be paid with actual output, rather than with rapidly depreciating money. Creditors avoid debtors to keep them from repaying their debts with cheap money. Money eventually becomes almost worthless and ceases to do its job as a medium of exchange. The economy may be thrown into a state of barter, and production and exchange drop dramatically. The net result is economic, social, and possibly political chaos.

Examples of hyperinflation are Germany after the First World War and Japan after the Second World War. In Germany, "prices increased so rapidly that waiters changed the prices on the menu several times during the course of a lunch. Sometimes customers had to pay double the price listed on the menu when they ordered."* In postwar Japan, in 1947 "fishermen and farmers...used scales to weigh currency and change, rather than bothering to count it."†

There are also more recent examples: Between June 1986 and March 1991 the cumulative inflation in Nicaragua was 11,895,866,143 percent. From November 1993 to December 1994 the cumulative inflation rate in the

Democratic Republic of Congo was 69,502 percent. From February 1993 to January 1994 the cumulative inflation rate in Serbia was 156,312,790 percent.[‡]

Such dramatic hyperinflations are almost invariably the consequence of highly imprudent expansions of the money supply by government. The rocketing money supply produces frenzied total spending and severe demand-pull inflation.

Question:

How would you alter your present spending plans if you were quite certain that the prices of everything were going to double in the coming week?

* Theodore Morgan, *Income and Employment,* 2d ed. (Englewood Cliffs, N.J.: Prentice-Hall, 1952), p. 361.

† Raburn M. Williams, *Inflation! Money, Jobs, and Politicians* (Arlington Heights, Ill.: AHM Publishing, 1980), p. 2.

‡ Stanley Fischer, Ratna Sahay, and Carlos Végh, "Modern Hyper- and High Inflations," *Journal of Economic Literature,* September 2002, p. 840.

Summary

1. Gross domestic product (GDP) is the market value of all final goods and services produced within the borders of a nation in a year. Intermediate goods and secondhand sales are purposely excluded in calculating GDP.
2. GDP can be calculated by adding consumer purchases of goods and services, gross investment spending by businesses, government purchases, and net exports: GDP = $C + I_g + G + X_n$.
3. Nominal (current-dollar) GDP measures each year's output valued in terms of the prices prevailing in that year. Real (constant-dollar) GDP measures each year's output in terms of the prices that prevailed in a selected base year. Because real GDP is adjusted for price-level changes, differences in real GDP are due only to differences in output.
4. Economic growth is either (a) an increase of real GDP over time or (b) an increase in real GDP per capita over time. Growth lessens the burden of scarcity and provides increases in real GDP that can be used to resolve socioeconomic problems.
5. Business cycles are recurring ups and downs in economic activity. Their two primary phases are expansions and recessions.
6. Economists distinguish between frictional, structural, and cyclical unemployment. The rate of unemployment at full employment consists of frictional and structural unemployment and currently is about 5 percent.
7. The economic cost of unemployment, as measured by the negative GDP gap, consists of the goods and services forgone by society when its resources are involuntarily idle.
8. Inflation is a rise in the general price level and is measured in the United States by the Consumer Price Index (CPI). When inflation occurs, each dollar of income will buy fewer goods and services than before. That is, inflation reduces the purchasing power of money.
9. Economists discern both demand-pull and cost-push (supply-side) inflation. Demand-pull inflation results from an excess of total spending relative to the economy's capacity to produce. The main source of cost-push inflation is abrupt and rapid increases in the prices of key resources. These supply shocks push up per-unit production costs and ultimately the prices of consumer goods.
10. Unanticipated inflation arbitrarily redistributes real income at the expense of fixed-income receivers, creditors, and savers. If inflation is anticipated, individuals and businesses may be able to take steps to lessen or eliminate adverse redistribution effects.
11. Cost-push inflation reduces real output and employment. Proponents of zero inflation argue that even mild demand-pull inflation (1 to 3 percent) reduces the economy's real output. Other economists say that mild inflation may be a necessary by-product of the high and growing spending that produces high levels of output, full employment, and economic growth.

CHAPTER THIRTEEN

Aggregate Demand and Aggregate Supply

In this chapter you will learn:

- About aggregate demand (AD) and the factors that cause it to change.
- About aggregate supply (AS) and the factors that cause it to change.
- How AD and AS determine an economy's equilibrium price level and level of real GDP.
- How the AD-AS model explains periods of demand-pull inflation, cost-push inflation, and recession.

In early 2000, Alan Greenspan, chair of the Federal Reserve, made the following statement:

> Through the so-called wealth effect, the [recent stock market gains] have tended to foster increases in aggregate demand beyond the increases in supply. It is this imbalance . . . that contains the potential seeds of rising inflationary . . . pressures that could undermine the current expansion. Our goal [at the Federal Reserve] is to extend the expansion by containing its imbalances and avoiding the very recession that would complete the business cycle.[1]

Although the Federal Reserve held inflation in check, it did not accomplish its goal of extending the decade-long economic expansion. In March 2001 the U.S. economy experienced its ninth recession since 1950. The economy has since recovered and returned to the expansion phase of the business cycle.

We will say more about the recession and expansion soon, but our immediate focus is the terminology in the Greenspan quotation. This is precisely the language of the **aggregate demand–aggregate supply model (AD-AS model).** The AD-AS model—the subject of this chapter—enables us to analyze changes in real GDP and the price level simultaneously. The AD-AS model therefore provides keen insights on inflation, recession, unemployment, and economic growth. In later chapters, we will also use it to show the logic of macroeconomic stabilization policies, such as those implied by Greenspan.

[1] Alan Greenspan, speech to the New York Economics Club, Jan. 13, 2000.

Aggregate Demand

aggregate demand–aggregate supply (AD-AS) model The macroeconomic model that uses aggregate demand and aggregate supply to determine and explain the price level and level of real domestic output.

Aggregate demand is a schedule or curve that shows the quantities of real domestic output (real GDP) that buyers collectively want to purchase at each possible price level. The relationship between the price level (as measured by the GDP price index) and the amount of real output demanded is inverse or negative: When the price level rises, the quantity of real GDP demanded falls; when the price level falls, the quantity of real GDP demanded rises.

Figure 13.1 shows the inverse relationship between the price level and real GDP. The downward slope of the AD curve reflects the fact that higher U.S. price levels discourage domestic buyers (households and businesses) and foreign buyers from purchasing U.S. real GDP. Lower price levels encourage them to buy more U.S. real output.

aggregate demand A schedule or curve that shows the total quantity of goods and services demanded (purchased) at different price levels.

Changes in Aggregate Demand

Other things equal, a change in the price level will change the amount of total spending and therefore change the amount of real GDP demanded by the economy. Movements along a fixed aggregate demand curve represent these changes in real GDP. However, if one or more of those "other things" change, the entire aggregate demand curve will shift. We call these other things **determinants of aggregate demand.** When they change, they shift the AD curve. These AD shifters are listed in the table in Figure 13.2. In that figure, the rightward shift of the curve from AD_1 to AD_2 shows an increase in aggregate demand. The leftward shift from AD_1 to AD_3 shows a decrease in aggregate demand. Notice that the categories of spending are the same as those in the national income and product accounts (Chapter 12). To provide a clear understanding of these AD shifters, we need to elaborate on them.

determinants of aggregate demand Factors that shift the aggregate demand curve when they change.

Consumer Spending

If consumers decide to buy more output at each price level, the aggregate demand curve will shift to the right, as from AD_1 to AD_2 in Figure 13.2. If they decide to buy less output, the aggregate demand curve will shift to the left, as from AD_1 to AD_3.

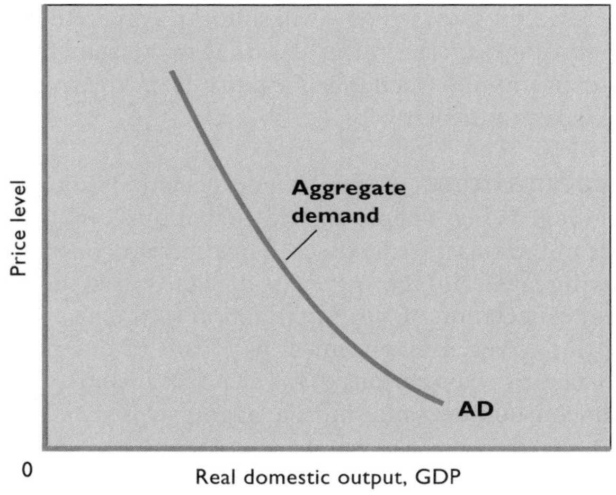

FIGURE 13.1
The aggregate demand curve.
The downsloping aggregate demand curve AD indicates an inverse (or negative) relationship between the price level and the amount of real output purchased.

FIGURE 13.2

Changes in aggregate demand. A change in one or more of the listed determinants of aggregate demand will shift the aggregate demand curve. The rightward shift from AD_1 to AD_2 represents an increase in aggregate demand; the leftward shift from AD_1 to AD_3 shows a decrease in aggregate demand.

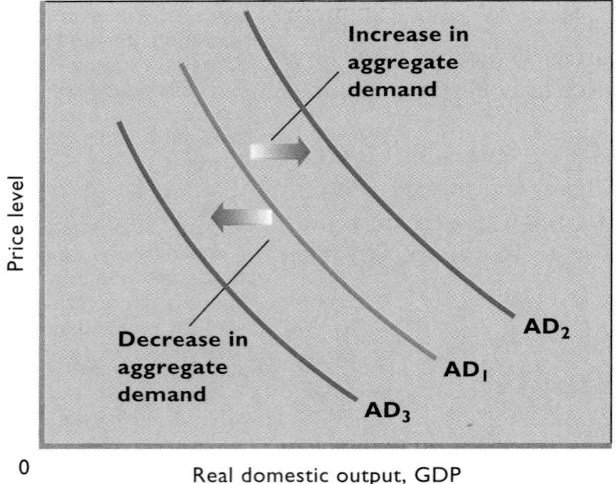

Determinants of Aggregate Demand: Factors That Shift the Aggregate Demand Curve

1. Change in consumer spending
   a. Consumer wealth
   b. Consumer expectations
   c. Household indebtedness
   d. Personal taxes
2. Change in investment spending
   a. Interest rates
   b. Expected returns
      - Expected future business conditions
      - Technology
      - Degree of excess capacity
      - Business taxes
3. Change in government spending
4. Change in net export spending
   a. National income abroad
   b. Exchange rates

Several factors can change consumer spending and therefore shift the aggregate demand curve. As the table in Figure 13.2 shows, those factors are real consumer wealth, consumer expectations, household indebtedness, and personal taxes.

Consumer Wealth Consumer wealth includes both financial assets such as stocks and bonds and physical assets such as houses and land. A sharp increase in the real value of consumer wealth (for example, because of a rise in stock market values) prompts people to save less and buy more products. The resulting increase in consumer spending—called the *wealth effect*—will shift the aggregate demand curve to the right. In contrast, a major decrease in the real value of consumer wealth at each price level will reduce consumption spending *(negative wealth effect)* and thus shift the aggregate demand curve to the left.

Consumer Expectations Changes in expectations about the future may alter consumer spending. When people expect their future real incomes to rise, they tend to spend more of their current incomes. Thus current consumption spending increases (current saving falls), and the aggregate demand curve shifts to the right. Similarly, a widely held expectation of surging inflation in the near future may increase aggregate demand today because consumers will want to buy products before their prices escalate. Conversely, expectations of lower future income or lower future prices may reduce current consumption and shift the aggregate demand curve to the left.

Household Indebtedness Households finance some of their spending by borrowing. If household indebtedness from past spending rises beyond normal levels, consumers may be forced to cut current spending in order to pay the interest and principal on their debt. Consumption spending will then decline, and the aggregate demand curve will shift to the left. Alternatively, when household indebtedness is unusually low, consumers have considerable leeway to borrow and spend today. Then the aggregate demand curve may shift to the right.

Personal Taxes A reduction in personal income tax rates raises take-home income and increases consumer purchases at each possible price level. Tax cuts shift the aggregate demand curve to the right. Tax increases reduce consumption spending and shift the curve to the left.

What Wealth Effect?

The consumption component of aggregate demand is usually relatively stable even during rather extraordinary times. Between March 2000 and July 2002, the U.S. stock market lost a staggering $3.7 trillion of value (yes, trillion). Yet consumption spending was greater at the end of that period than at the beginning. How can that be? Why didn't a negative wealth effect reduce consumption?

There are a number of reasons. Of greatest importance, the amount of consumption spending in the economy depends mainly on the *flow* of income, not the *stock* of wealth. Disposable income (after-tax income) in the United States is nearly $9 trillion annually, and consumers spend a large portion of it. Even though there was a mild recession in 2001, disposable income and consumption spending were both greater in July 2002 than in March 2000. Second, the Federal government cut personal income tax rates during this period, and that bolstered consumption spending. Third, household wealth did not fall by the full amount of the $3.7 trillion stock market loss because the value of houses increased dramatically over this period. Finally, lower interest rates during this period enabled many households to refinance their mortgages, reduce monthly loan payments, and increase their current consumption.

For all these offsetting reasons, the consumption component of aggregate demand held up in the face of the extraordinary loss of stock market value.

Question:
Which do you think will increase consumption more: a 10 percent increase in after-tax income or a 10 percent increase in stock market values? Explain.

Investment Spending

Investment spending (the purchase of capital goods) is a second major determinant of aggregate demand. Increases in investment spending at each price level boost aggregate demand, and decreases in investment spending reduce it.

The investment decision is a marginal-benefit–marginal-cost decision. The marginal benefit of the investment is a stream of higher profits that is expected to result from the investment. In percentage terms, economists call these higher profits (net of new operation expenses) the *expected return on the investment, r*. For example, suppose the owner of a small cabinetmaking shop is considering whether to invest in a new sanding machine that costs $1000, expands output, and has a useful life of only 1 year.

(Extending the life of the machine beyond 1 year complicates the economic calculation but does not change the fundamental analysis.) Suppose the net expected revenue from the machine (that is, after such operating costs as power, lumber, labor, and certain taxes have been subtracted) is \$1100. Then the expected net revenue is sufficient to cover the initial \$1000 cost of the machine and leave a profit of \$100. Comparing this \$100 to the \$1000 initial cost of the machine, we find that the expected rate of return, r, on the investment is 10 percent (=\$100/\$1000).

It is important to note that the return just discussed is an *expected* rate of return, not a *guaranteed* rate of return. Investment involves risk, so the investment may or may not pay off as anticipated. Moreover, investment faces diminishing returns. As more of it occurs, the best investment projects are completed and the subsequent projects produce lower expected rates of return. So, the expected return, r, tends to fall as firms undertake more and more investment.

The marginal cost of the investment to a firm is reflected in either the explicit costs of borrowing money from others or the implicit cost of using its own retained earnings to make the investment. In percentage terms, and adjusted for expected inflation, this cost is the real interest rate, i.

13.1 Interest-rate–investment relationship

The business firm compares the real interest rate (marginal cost) with the expected return on investment (marginal benefit). If the expected rate of return (for example, 6 percent) exceeds the interest rate (say, 5 percent), the investment is undertaken. The firm expects the investment to be profitable. But if the interest rate (for example, 7 percent) exceeds the expected rate of return (6 percent), the investment will not be undertaken. The firm expects the investment to be unprofitable. The profit-maximizing firm will undertake all investment that it thinks will be profitable. That means it will invest up to the point where $r = i$ in order to exhaust all investment possibilities for which r exceeds i.

So real interest rates and expected returns are the two main determinants of investment spending.

Real Interest Rates We will discover that a nation's central bank—the Federal Reserve in the United States—can take monetary actions to increase and decrease interest rates. When it takes those actions, it shifts the nation's aggregate demand curve. Other things equal, increases in real interest rates will lower investment spending and reduce aggregate demand. Declines in interest rates will have the opposite effects.

Expected Returns Higher expected returns on investment projects will increase the demand for capital goods and shift the aggregate demand curve to the right. Alternatively, declines in expected returns will decrease investment and shift the curve to the left. Expected returns are influenced by several factors:

- ***Future business conditions*** If firms are generally optimistic about future business conditions, they are more likely to forecast high rates of return on current investment and therefore may invest more today. In contrast, if they think the economy will deteriorate in the future, they will forecast low rates of return and perhaps will invest less today.
- ***Technology*** New and improved technologies enhance expected returns on investment and thus increase aggregate demand. For example, recent advances in microbiology have motivated pharmaceutical companies to establish new labs and production facilities.

- ***Degree of excess capacity*** A rise in excess capacity—unused capital—will reduce the expected return on new investment and hence decrease aggregate demand. Other things equal, firms operating factories at well below capacity have little incentive to build new factories. But when firms realize that their excess capacity is dwindling or has completely disappeared, their expected returns on new investment in factories and capital equipment rise. Thus, they increase their investment spending, and the aggregate demand curve shifts to the right.
- ***Business taxes*** An increase in business taxes will reduce after-tax profits from capital investment and lower expected returns. So investment and aggregate demand will decline. A decrease in business taxes will have the opposite effects.

The variability of interest rates and investment expectations makes investment quite volatile. In contrast to consumption, investment spending rises and falls quite often, independent of changes in total income. Investment, in fact, is the least stable component of aggregate demand.

Global Snapshot 13.1 compares investment spending relative to GDP for several nations in a recent year.

Global Snapshot 13.1

Gross Investment Expenditures as a Percentage of GDP, Selected Nations

As a percentage of GDP, investment varies widely by nation. These differences, of course, can change from year to year.

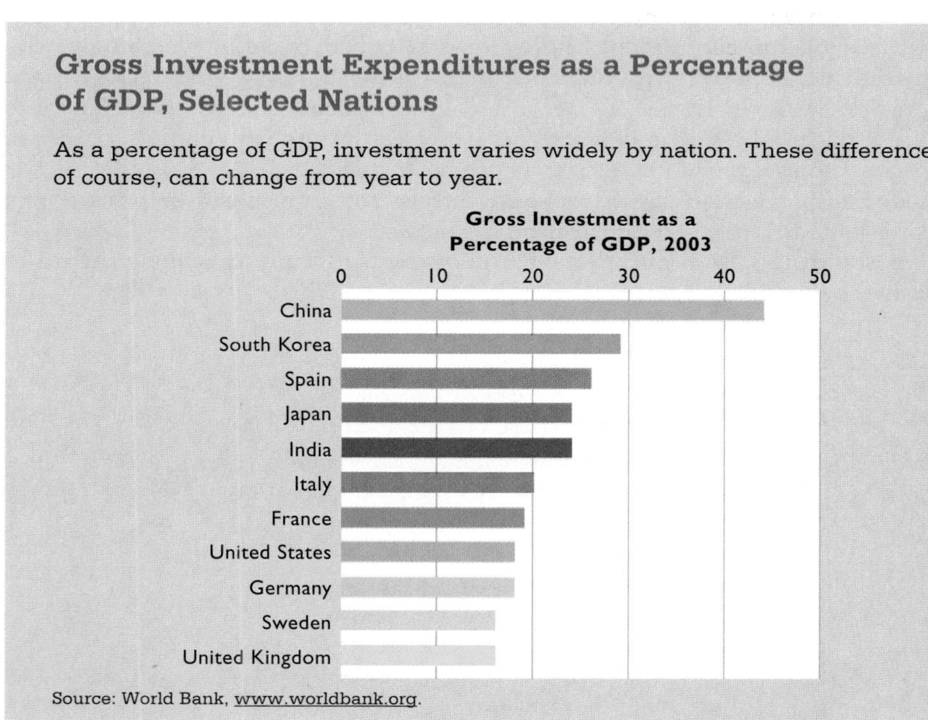

Source: World Bank, www.worldbank.org.

Government Spending

Government purchases are the third determinant of aggregate demand. An increase in government purchases (for example, more military equipment) will shift the aggregate demand curve to the right, as long as tax collections and interest rates do not change as a result. In contrast, a reduction in government spending (for example, fewer transportation projects) will shift the curve to the left.

Net Export Spending

The final determinant of aggregate demand is net export spending. Other things equal, higher U.S. *exports* mean an increased foreign demand for U.S. goods. So a rise in net exports (higher exports relative to imports) shifts the aggregate demand curve to the right. In contrast, a decrease in U.S. net exports shifts the aggregate demand curve leftward.

What might cause net exports to change, other than the price level? Two possibilities are changes in national income abroad and changes in exchange rates.

National Income Abroad Rising national income abroad encourages foreigners to buy more products, some of which are made in the United States. So U.S. net exports rise, and the U.S. aggregate demand curve shifts to the right. Declines in national income abroad do the opposite: They reduce U.S. net exports and shift the U.S. aggregate demand curve to the left.

exchange rates
The prices of foreign currencies in terms of one's own currency.

Exchange Rates Changes in **exchange rates**—the prices of foreign currencies in terms of one's own currency—may affect U.S. net exports and therefore aggregate demand. When the dollar *depreciates* (declines in value) against foreign currencies, it takes more dollars to buy foreign goods. So foreign goods become more expensive in dollar terms, and Americans reduce their imports. On the opposite side, the depreciation of the dollar means that other currencies *appreciate* (rise in value) relative to the dollar. U.S. exports rise because those foreign currencies can buy more American goods. Conclusion: Dollar depreciation increases net exports (imports go down; exports go up) and therefore increases aggregate demand.

Dollar appreciation has the opposite effects: Net exports fall (imports go up; exports go down) and aggregate demand declines.

As shown in Global Snapshot 13.2, net exports vary greatly among the major industrial nations.

Global Snapshot 13.2

Net Exports of Goods, Selected Nations, 2003

Some nations, such as Germany and Japan, have positive net exports; other countries, such as the United States and the United Kingdom, have negative net exports.

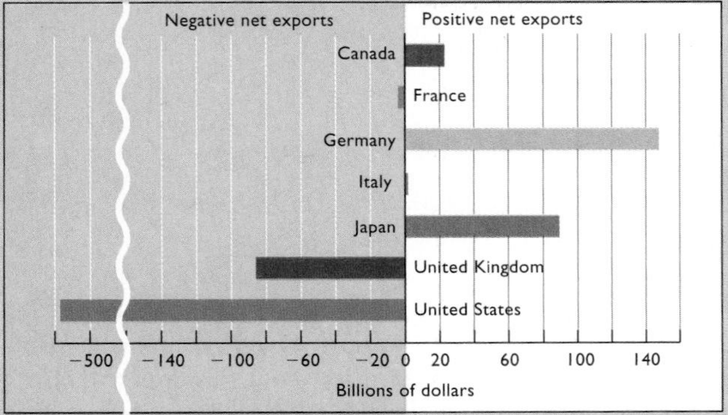

Source: World Trade Organization, www.wto.org.

Aggregate Supply

Aggregate supply is a schedule or curve showing the level of real domestic output that firms will produce at each price level. The production responses of firms to changes in the price level differ in the *long run*, which in macroeconomics is a period in which nominal wages (and other resource prices) match changes in the price level, and the *short run*, a period in which nominal wages (and other resource prices) do not respond to price-level changes. So the long and short runs vary by degree of wage adjustment, not by a set length of time such as 1 month, 1 year, or 3 years.

aggregate supply A schedule or curve that shows the total quantity of goods and services supplied (produced) at different price levels.

Aggregate Supply in the Long Run

In the long run, the aggregate supply curve is vertical at the economy's full-employment output (or its potential output), as represented by AS_{LR} in Figure 13.3. When changes in wages respond completely to changes in the price level, those price-level changes do not alter the amount of real GDP produced and offered for sale.

Consider a one-firm economy in which the firm's owners must receive a real profit of $20 in order to produce the full-employment output of 100 units. The real reward the owner receives, not the level of prices, is what really counts. Assume the owner's only input (aside from entrepreneurial talent) is 10 units of hired labor at $8 per worker, for a total wage cost of $80. Also assume that the 100 units of output sell for $1 per unit, so total revenue is $100. The firm's nominal profit is $20 (=$100 − $80), and using the $1 price to designate the base-price index of 100, its real profit is also $20 (=$20/1.00). Well and good—the full-employment output is produced.

Next, suppose the price level doubles. Would the owner earn more than the $20 of real profit and therefore boost production beyond the 100-unit full-employment output? The answer is no, given the assumption that nominal wages and the price level rise by the same amount, as is true in the long run. Once the product price has doubled to $2, total revenue will be $200 (=100 × $2). But the cost of 10 units of labor will double from $80 to $160 because the wage rate rises from $8 to $16. Nominal profit thus increases to $40 (=$200 − $160). What about real profit? By

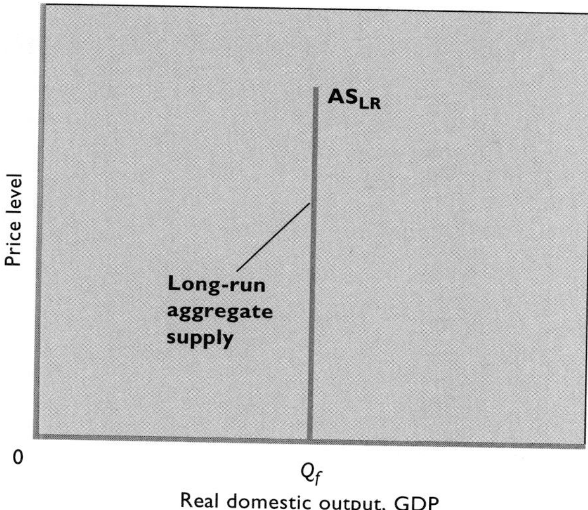

FIGURE 13.3 **Aggregate supply in the long run.** The long-run aggregate supply curve AS_{LR} is vertical at the full-employment level of real GDP (Q_f) because in the long run wages and other input prices rise and fall to match changes in the price level. So price-level changes do not affect firms' profits, and thus they create no incentive for firms to alter their output.

dividing the nominal profit of $40 by the new price index of 200 (expressed as a decimal), we obtain real profit of $20 (=$40/2.00). Because real profit does not change, the firm will not alter its production. Real GDP will remain at its full-employment level.

In the long run, wages and other input prices rise or fall to match changes in the price level. Changes in the price level therefore do not change real profit, and there is no change in real output. As shown in Figure 13.3, the **long-run aggregate supply curve** is vertical at the economy's potential output (or full-employment output). We will say more about long-run aggregate supply in Chapter 17 on economic growth.

long-run aggregate supply curve
The aggregate supply curve associated with a period of time in which wages and other input prices fully respond to changes in the price level.

Aggregate Supply in the Short Run

In reality, nominal wages adjust only slowly to changes in the price level, and perfect adjustment may take several months or even a number of years. Reconsider our previous one-firm economy. If the $8 nominal wage for each of the 10 workers is unresponsive to the price-level change, the doubling of the price level will boost total revenue from $100 to $200 but leave total cost unchanged at $80. Nominal profit will rise from $20 (=$100 − $80) to $120 (=$200 − $80). Dividing that $120 profit by the new price index of 200 (=2.0 in hundredths), we find that the real profit is now $60. The rise in the real reward from $20 to $60 prompts firms to produce more output. Conversely, price-level declines reduce real profits and cause firms collectively to reduce their output. So, in the short run, there is a direct or positive relationship between the price level and real output.

short-run aggregate supply curve
An aggregate supply curve relevant to a time period in which wages and other input prices do not change in response to changes in the price level.

The **short-run aggregate supply curve** is upsloping, as shown in Figure 13.4. A rise in the price level increases real output; a fall in the price level reduces it. Per-unit production costs underlie the aggregate supply curve. In equation form,

FIGURE 13.4
The aggregate supply curve (short run). The upsloping aggregate supply curve AS indicates a direct (or positive) relationship between the price level and the amount of real output that firms will offer for sale. The AS curve is relatively flat below the full-employment output because unemployed resources and unused capacity allow firms to respond to price-level rises with large increases in real output. It is relatively steep beyond the full-employment output because resource shortages and capacity limitations make it difficult to expand real output as the price level rises.

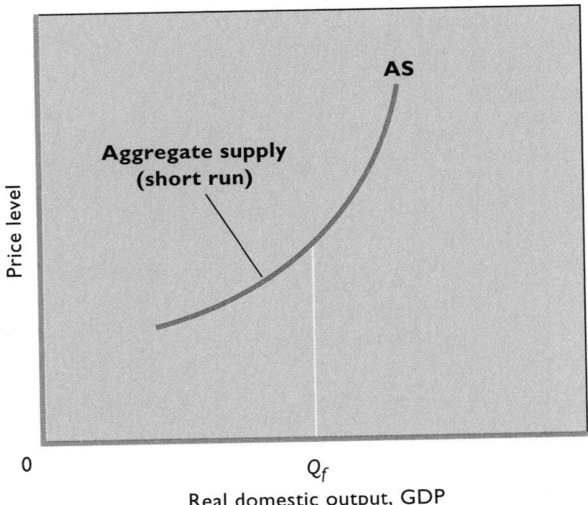

$$\text{Per-unit production cost} = \frac{\text{total input cost}}{\text{units of output}}$$

The per-unit production cost of any specific level of output establishes that output's price level because the price level must cover all the costs of production, including profit "costs."

As the economy expands in the short run, per-unit production costs generally rise because of reduced efficiency and rising input prices. But the extent of that rise depends on where the economy is operating relative to its capacity. The aggregate supply curve in Figure 13.4 is relatively flat at outputs below the full-employment output Q_f and relatively steep at outputs above it. Why the difference?

When the economy is operating below its full-employment output, it has large amounts of unused machinery and equipment and unemployed workers. Firms can put these idle human and property resources back to work with little upward pressure on per-unit production costs. Workers unemployed for 2 or 3 months will hardly expect a wage increase when recalled to their jobs. And as output expands, few if any shortages of inputs or production bottlenecks will arise to raise per-unit production costs.

When the economy is operating beyond its full-employment output, the vast majority of its available resources are already employed. Adding more workers to a relatively fixed number of highly used capital resources such as plant and equipment creates congestion in the workplace and reduces the efficiency (on average) of workers. Adding more capital, given the limited number of available workers, leaves equipment idle and reduces the efficiency of capital. Adding more land resources when capital and labor are highly constrained reduces the efficiency of land resources. Under these circumstances, total output rises less rapidly than total input cost. So per-unit production costs increase.

Moreover, individual firms may try to expand their own production by bidding resources away from other firms. But the resources and additional production that one firm gains will be largely lost by the other firms. The bidding will raise input prices, but real output will rise very little, if at all. That is a prescription for higher per-unit production costs.

Unless stated otherwise, all our references to "aggregate supply" will be to aggregate supply in the short run. When we bring long-run aggregate supply into the picture, we will add the adjective "long-run."

Changes in Aggregate Supply

An existing aggregate supply curve identifies the relationship between the price level and real output, other things equal. But when other things change, the curve itself shifts. The rightward shift of the curve from AS_1 to AS_2 in Figure 13.5 represents an increase in aggregate supply, indicating that firms are willing to produce and sell more real output at each price level. A decrease in aggregate supply is shown by the leftward shift of the curve from AS_1 to AS_3. At each price level, firms produce less output than before.

The table in Figure 13.5 lists the factors that collectively position the aggregate supply curve. They are called the **determinants of aggregate supply,** and shift the curve when they change. Changes in these determinants raise or lower per-unit production costs *at each price level (or each level of output)*. These changes in per-unit

determinants of aggregate supply
Factors that shift the aggregate supply curve when they change.

FIGURE 13.5

Changes in aggregate supply. A change in one or more of the listed determinants of aggregate supply will shift the aggregate supply curve. The rightward shift of the aggregate supply curve from AS_1 to AS_2 represents an increase in aggregate supply; the leftward shift of the curve from AS_1 to AS_3 shows a decrease in aggregate supply.

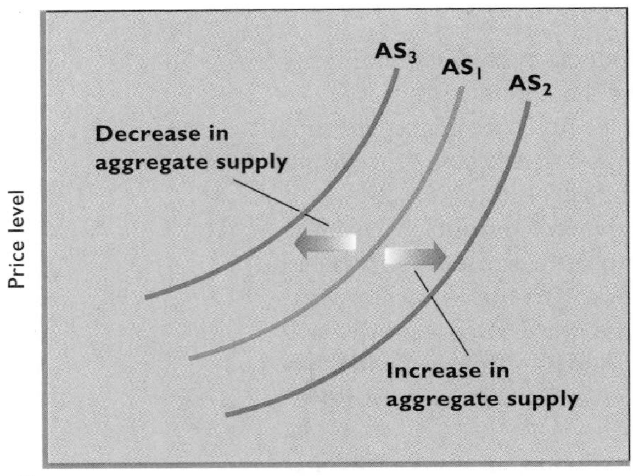

Determinants of Aggregate Supply: Factors That Shift the Aggregate Supply Curve

1. Change in input prices
   a. Domestic resource prices
   b. Prices of imported resources
   c. Market power
2. Change in productivity
3. Change in legal-institutional environment
   a. Business taxes
   b. Government regulations

production costs affect profits, thereby leading firms to alter the amount of output they are willing to produce *at each price level.* For example, firms may collectively offer \$7 trillion of real output at a price level of 1.0 (=100 in index-value terms), rather than \$6.8 trillion. Or they may offer \$6.5 trillion rather than \$7 trillion. The point is that when one of the determinants listed in Figure 13.5 changes, the aggregate supply curve shifts to the right or left. Changes that reduce per-unit production costs shift the aggregate supply curve to the right, as from AS_1 to AS_2; changes that increase per-unit production costs shift it to the left, as from AS_1 to AS_3. *When per-unit production costs change for reasons other than changes in real output, the aggregate supply curve shifts.*

The aggregate supply determinants listed in Figure 13.5 are very important and therefore require more discussion.

Input Prices

Input or resource prices—to be distinguished from the output prices that make up the price level—are a major ingredient of per-unit production costs and therefore a key determinant of aggregate supply. These resources can be either domestic or imported.

Domestic Resource Prices Wages and salaries make up about 75 percent of all business costs. Other things equal, decreases in wages reduce per-unit production costs. So the aggregate supply curve shifts to the right. Increases in wages shift the curve to the left. Examples:

- Labor supply increases because of substantial immigration. Wages and per-unit production costs fall, shifting the AS curve to the right.

- Labor supply decreases because of a rapid rise in pension income and early retirements. Wage rates and per-unit production costs rise, shifting the AS curve to the left.

Similarly, the aggregate supply curve shifts when the prices of land and capital inputs change. Examples:

- The price of machinery and equipment falls because of declines in the prices of steel and electronic components. Per-unit production costs decline, and the AS curve shifts to the right.
- Land resources expand through discoveries of mineral deposits, irrigation of land, or technical innovations that transform "nonresources" (say, vast desert lands) into valuable resources (productive lands). The price of land declines, per-unit production costs fall, and the AS curve shifts to the right.

Prices of Imported Resources Just as foreign demand for U.S. goods contributes to U.S. aggregate demand, resources imported from abroad (such as oil, tin, and copper) add to U.S. aggregate supply. Added supplies of resources—whether domestic or imported—typically reduce per-unit production costs. A decrease in the price of imported resources increases U.S. aggregate supply, while an increase in their price reduces U.S. aggregate supply.

Exchange-rate fluctuations are one factor that may alter the price of imported resources. Suppose that the dollar appreciates, enabling U.S. firms to obtain more foreign currency with each dollar. This means that domestic producers face a lower *dollar* price of imported resources. U.S. firms will respond by increasing their imports of foreign resources, thereby lowering their per-unit production costs at each level of output. Falling per-unit production costs will shift the U.S. aggregate supply curve to the right.

A depreciation of the dollar will have the opposite set of effects.

Market Power A change in the degree of market power—the ability to set prices above competitive levels—held by sellers of major inputs also can affect input prices and aggregate supply. An example is the fluctuating market power held by the Organization of Petroleum Exporting Countries (OPEC) over the past several decades. The 10-fold increase in the price of oil that OPEC achieved during the 1970s drove up per-unit production costs and jolted the U.S. aggregate supply curve leftward. Then a steep reduction in OPEC's market power during the mid-1980s resulted in a sharp decline in oil prices and a rightward shift of the U.S. aggregate supply curve. In 1999 OPEC temporarily reasserted its market power, raising oil prices and therefore per-unit production costs for some U.S. producers (for example, airlines and truckers).

Productivity

The second major determinant of aggregate supply is **productivity**, which is a measure of the relationship between a nation's level of real output and the amount of resources used to produce that output. Thus productivity is a measure of average real output, or of real output per unit of input:

productivity A measure of real output per unit of input.

$$\text{Productivity} = \frac{\text{total output}}{\text{total inputs}}$$

With no change in resource prices, increases in productivity reduce the per-unit production cost of output. Recall that this cost is determined by dividing the total cost of production by the dollar amount of output. For example, if the total cost of production is \$20 billion and total output is \$40 billion, per-unit production cost is \$.50. If productivity rises such that output increases from \$40 billion to \$60 billion, the per-unit production cost will fall from \$.50 (=\$20/\$40) to \$.33 (=\$20/\$60).

The generalization is this: By reducing per-unit production costs, increases in productivity shift the aggregate supply curve to the right. The main source of productivity advance is improved production technology, often embodied within new plant and equipment that replaces old plant and equipment. Other sources of productivity increases are a better-educated and -trained workforce, improved forms of business enterprises, and the reallocation of labor resources from lower- to higher-productivity uses.

Much rarer, decreases in productivity increase per-unit production costs and therefore reduce aggregate supply (shift the AS curve to the left).

Legal-Institutional Environment

Changes in the legal-institutional setting in which businesses operate are the final determinant of aggregate supply. Such changes may alter the per-unit costs of output and, if so, shift the aggregate supply curve. Two changes of this type are (1) changes in business taxes and (2) changes in the extent of regulation.

Business Taxes Higher business taxes, such as sales, excise, and payroll taxes, increase per-unit costs and reduce short-run aggregate supply in much the same way as a wage increase does. An increase in such taxes paid by businesses will increase per-unit production costs and shift aggregate supply to the left.

Government Regulation It is usually costly for businesses to comply with government regulations. More regulation therefore tends to increase per-unit production costs and shift the aggregate supply curve to the left. "Supply-side" proponents of deregulation of the economy have argued forcefully that, by increasing efficiency and reducing the paperwork associated with complex regulations, deregulation will reduce per-unit costs and shift the aggregate supply curve to the right. Other economists are less certain. Deregulation that results in accounting manipulations, monopolization, and business failures is likely to shift the AS curve to the left rather than to the right.

equilibrium price level
The price level at which the aggregate demand curve and the aggregate supply curve intersect.

equilibrium real output
The level of real GDP at which the aggregate demand curve and aggregate supply curve intersect.

Equilibrium Price Level and Real GDP

Of all the possible combinations of price levels and levels of real GDP, which combination will the economy gravitate toward, at least in the short run? Figure 13.6 and its accompanying table provide the answer. Equilibrium occurs at the price level that equalizes the amounts of real output demanded and supplied. The intersection of the aggregate demand curve AD and the aggregate supply curve AS establishes the economy's **equilibrium price level** and **equilibrium real output.** So aggregate demand and aggregate supply jointly establish the price level and level of real GDP.

FIGURE 13.6

The equilibrium price level and equilibrium real GDP. The intersection of the aggregate demand curve and the aggregate supply curve determines the economy's equilibrium price level. At the equilibrium price level of 100 (in index-value terms) the $510 billion of real output demanded matches the $510 billion of real output supplied. So equilibrium real GDP is $510 billion.

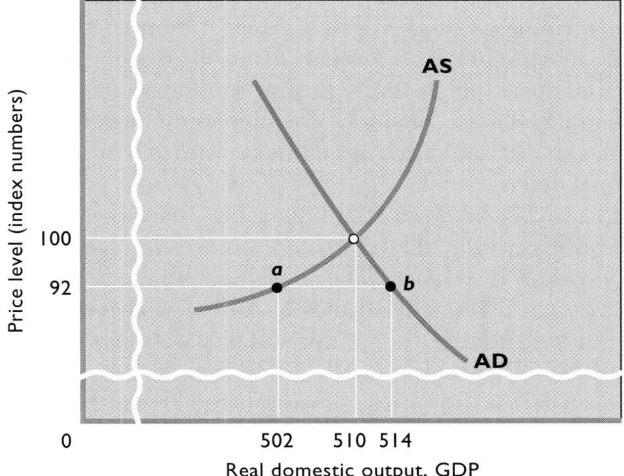

Real Output Demanded (Billions)	Price Level (Index Number)	Real Output Supplied (Billions)
$506	108	$513
508	104	512
510	***100***	***510***
512	96	507
514	92	502

In Figure 13.6 the equilibrium price level and level of real output are 100 and $510 billion, respectively. To illustrate why, suppose the price level is 92 rather than 100. We see from the table that the lower price level will encourage businesses to produce real output of $502 billion. This is shown by point *a* on the AS curve in the graph. But, as revealed by the table and point *b* on the aggregate demand curve, buyers will want to purchase $514 billion of real output at price level 92. Competition among buyers to purchase the lesser available real output of $502 billion will eliminate the $12 billion (=$514 billion − $502 billion) shortage and pull up the price level to 100.

As the table and graph show, the rise in the price level from 92 to 100 encourages producers to increase their real output from $502 billion to $510 billion and causes buyers to scale back their purchases from $514 billion to $510 billion. When equality occurs between the amounts of real output produced and purchased, as it does at price level 100, the economy has achieved equilibrium (here, at $510 billion of real GDP).

13.1 Aggregate demand–aggregate supply

Changes in the Price Level and Real GDP

Aggregate demand and aggregate supply typically change from one period to the next. If aggregate demand and aggregate supply increase proportionately over time, real GDP will expand and neither demand-pull inflation nor cyclical unemployment will occur. But we know from our discussion of the business cycle that macroeconomic stability is not always certain. A number of less desirable situations can confront the economy. Let's apply the model to several such situations. For simplicity we will use P and Q symbols, rather than actual numbers. Remember that these symbols represent price index values and amounts of real GDP.

Demand-Pull Inflation

Suppose the economy is operating at its full-employment output and businesses and government increase their spending—actions that shift the aggregate demand curve to the right. Our list of determinants of aggregate demand (Figure 13.2) provides several reasons why this shift might occur. Perhaps firms boost their investment spending because they anticipate higher future profits from investments in new capital. Those profits are predicated on having new equipment and facilities that incorporate a number of new technologies. And perhaps government increases spending to expand national defense.

As shown by the rise in the price level from P_1 to P_2 in Figure 13.7, the increase in aggregate demand beyond the full-employment level of output moves the economy from *a* to *b* and causes inflation. This is *demand-pull inflation*, because the price level is being pulled up by the increase in aggregate demand. Also, observe that the increase in demand expands real output from Q_f to Q_1. The distance between Q_1 and Q_f is a positive *GDP gap:* Actual GDP exceeds potential GDP.*

A classic American example of demand-pull inflation occurred in the late 1960s. The escalation of the war in Vietnam resulted in a 40 percent increase in defense spending between 1965 and 1967 and another 15 percent increase in 1968. The rise in government spending, imposed on an already growing economy, shifted the economy's aggregate demand curve to the right, producing the worst inflation in two decades. Actual GDP exceeded potential GDP, and inflation jumped from 1.6 percent in 1965 to 5.7 percent by 1970.

A more recent example of demand-pull inflation occurred in the late 1980s. As aggregate demand expanded beyond its full-employment level between 1986 and 1990, the price level rose at an increasing rate. Specifically, the annual rate of inflation increased from 1.9 percent in 1986 to 3.6 percent in 1987 to 4.1 percent in 1988 to 4.8 percent in 1989. In terms of Figure 13.7, the aggregate demand

* This positive GDP gap cannot last forever because eventually the price of labor and other inputs will increase and therefore shift the short-run AS curve leftward. The economy will eventually return to its full-employment output, Q_f, along its vertical long-run aggregate supply curve (not shown) that is located there.

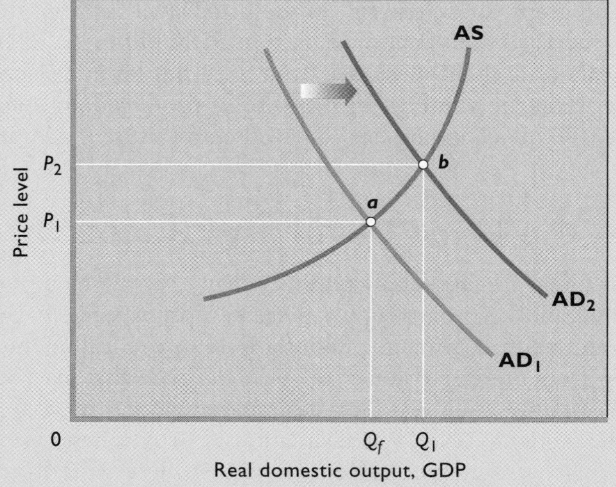

FIGURE 13.7 **Demand-pull inflation.** The increase of aggregate demand from AD_1 to AD_2 moves the economy from *a* to *b*, causing demand-pull inflation of P_1 to P_2. It also causes a positive GDP gap of Q_1 minus Q_f.

curve moved rightward from year to year, raising the price level and the size of the positive GDP gap. The gap closed and the rate of inflation fell as the expansion gave way to the recession of 1990–1991.

Question:
How is the upward slope of the aggregate supply curve important in explaining demand-pull inflation?

Applying the Analysis

Cost-Push Inflation

Inflation can also arise on the aggregate supply side of the economy. Suppose that warfare in the Middle East severely disrupts world oil supplies and drives up oil prices by some huge amount, say, 300 percent. Higher energy prices would spread through the economy, driving up production and distribution costs on a wide variety of goods. The U.S. aggregate supply curve would spring to the left, say, from AS_1 to AS_2 in Figure 13.8. The resulting increase in the price level would be *cost-push inflation.*

The effects of a leftward shift in aggregate supply are doubly bad. When aggregate supply shifts from AS_1 to AS_2, the economy moves from *a* to *b*. The price level rises from P_1 to P_2 and real output declines from Q_f to Q_1. Along with the cost-push inflation, a recession (and negative GDP gap) occurs. That is exactly what happened in the United States in the mid-1970s when the price of oil rocketed upward.

Today, the effect of oil prices on the U.S. economy has weakened relative to earlier periods. In the mid-1970s, oil expenditures were about 10 percent of U.S. GDP, compared to only 3 percent today. So the U.S. economy is now less vulnerable to cost-push inflation arising from oil-related "aggregate supply shocks."

Question:
Which is costlier to an economy in terms of lost real output, an equal degree of demand-pull inflation or cost-push inflation?

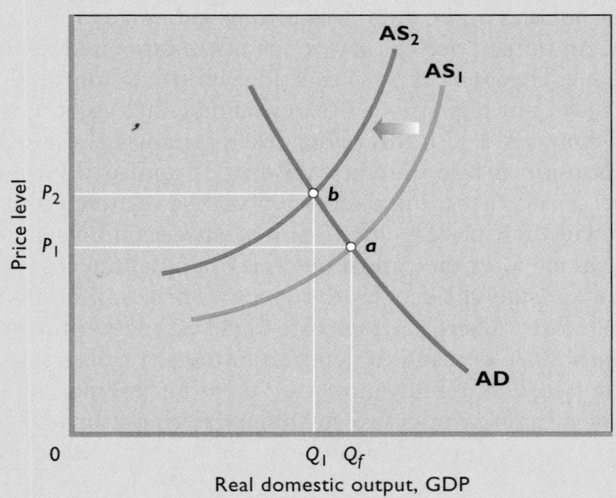

FIGURE 13.8 Cost-push inflation. A leftward shift of aggregate supply from AS_1 to AS_2 moves the economy from *a* to *b*, raises the price level from P_1 to P_2, and produces cost-push inflation. Real output declines and a negative GDP gap (of Q_1 minus Q_f) occurs.

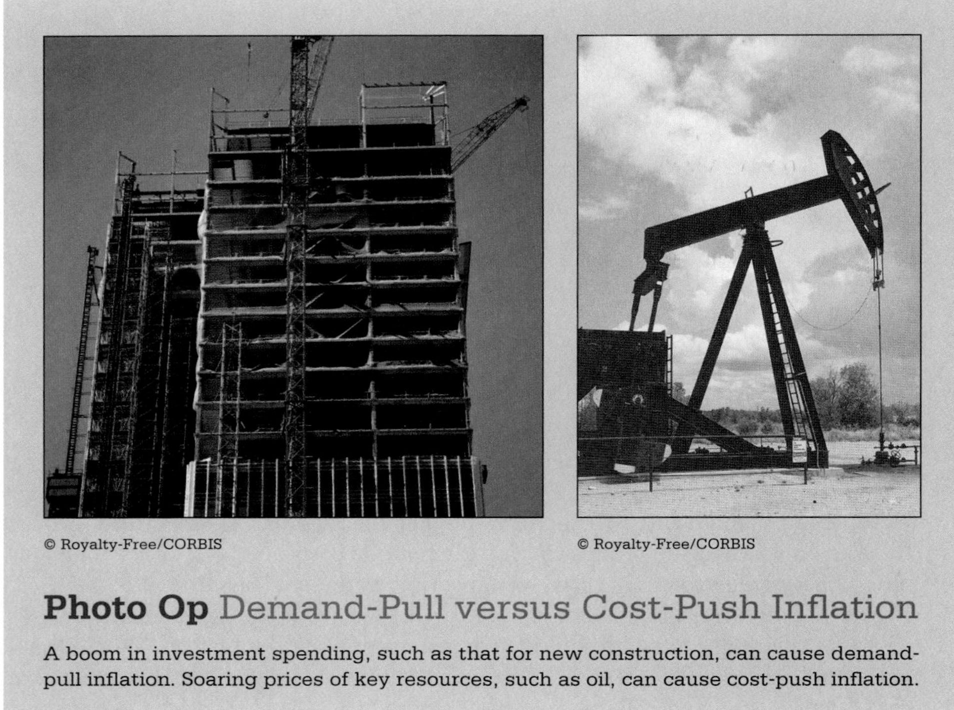

© Royalty-Free/CORBIS © Royalty-Free/CORBIS

Photo Op Demand-Pull versus Cost-Push Inflation

A boom in investment spending, such as that for new construction, can cause demand-pull inflation. Soaring prices of key resources, such as oil, can cause cost-push inflation.

Downward Price-Level Inflexibility

We have just seen that the price level is readily flexible upward. But in the U.S. economy, deflation (a decline in the price level) rarely occurs even though the rate of inflation rises and falls. Why is the price level "sticky" or inflexible on the downside? Economists have offered several possible reasons for this:

- ***Fear of price wars*** Some oligopolists may be concerned that if they reduce their prices, rivals not only will match their price cuts but may retaliate by making even deeper cuts. An initial price cut may touch off an unwanted *price war:* successively deeper and deeper rounds of price cuts. In such a situation, all the firms end up with far less profit or higher losses than would be the case if they had simply maintained their prices. For this reason, each firm may resist making the initial price cut, choosing instead to reduce production and lay off workers.
- ***Menu costs*** Firms that think a recession will be relatively short-lived may be reluctant to cut their prices. One reason is what economists metaphorically call *menu costs*, named after their most obvious example: the cost of printing new menus when a restaurant decides to reduce its prices. But lowering prices also creates other costs. There are the costs of (1) estimating the magnitude and duration of the shift in demand to determine whether prices should be lowered, (2) repricing items held in inventory, (3) printing and mailing new catalogs, and (4) communicating new prices to customers, perhaps through advertising. When menu costs are present, firms may choose to avoid them by retaining current prices. That is, they may wait to see if the decline in aggregate demand is permanent.

- ***Wage contracts*** It usually is not profitable for firms to cut their product prices if they cannot also cut their wage rates. Wages are usually inflexible downward because large parts of the labor force work under contracts prohibiting wage cuts for the duration of the contract. (It is not uncommon for collective bargaining agreements in major industries to run for 3 years.) Similarly, the wages and salaries of nonunion workers are usually adjusted once a year, rather than quarterly or monthly.
- ***Morale, effort, and productivity*** Wage inflexibility downward is reinforced by the reluctance of many employers to reduce wage rates. If worker productivity (output per hour of work) remains constant, lower wages *do* reduce labor costs per unit of output. But lower wages might impair worker morale and work effort, thereby reducing productivity. Considered alone, lower productivity raises labor costs per unit of output because less output is produced. If the higher labor costs resulting from reduced productivity exceed the cost savings from the lower wage, then wage cuts will increase rather than reduce labor costs per unit of output. In such situations, firms will resist lowering wages when they are faced with a decline in aggregate demand.
- ***Minimum wage*** The minimum wage imposes a legal floor under the wages of the least skilled workers. Firms paying those wages cannot reduce that wage rate when aggregate demand declines.

Conclusion: In the United States, the price level readily rises but only reluctantly falls.

The Ratchet Effect

A *ratchet analogy* is a good way to think about the asymmetry of price-level changes. A ratchet is a tool or mechanism such as a winch, car jack, or socket wrench that cranks a wheel forward but does not allow it to go backward. Properly set, each allows the operator to move an object (boat, car, or nut) in one direction while preventing it from moving in the opposite direction.

The price level, wage rates, and per-unit production costs readily rise when aggregate demand increases along the aggregate supply curve. In the United States, the price level has increased in every year but one since 1950.

But the price level, wage rates, and per-unit production costs are inflexible downward when aggregate demand declines. The U.S. price level has fallen in only a single year (1955) since 1950, even though aggregate demand and real output have declined in a number of years.

In terms of our analogy, increases in aggregate demand ratchet the U.S. price level upward. Once in place, the higher price level remains until it is ratcheted up again. The higher price level tends to remain even with declines in aggregate demand. Inflation rates *do* rise and fall in the United States, but the price level mainly rises.

Question:
Does the ratchet analogy also apply to changes in real GDP? Why or why not?

Recession and Cyclical Unemployment

Decreases in aggregate demand, combined with downward price-level inflexibility, can create recessions. For example, suppose that for some reason investment spending sharply declines. In Figure 13.9 we show the resulting decline in aggregate demand as a leftward shift from AD_1 to AD_2.

With the price level inflexible downward at P_1, the decline in aggregate demand moves the economy from *a* to *b* and reduces real output from Q_f to Q_1. The distance between Q_1 and Q_f measures the negative GDP gap—the amount by which actual output falls short of potential output. Because fewer workers are needed to produce the lower output, *cyclical unemployment* arises.

All recent demand-caused recessions in the United States have mimicked the "GDP gap but no deflation" scenario shown in Figure 13.9. Consider the recession of 2001, which resulted from a significant decline in investment spending. Because of the resulting decline of aggregate demand, GDP fell short of potential output by an average of $67 billion for each of the last three quarters of the year. Between February 2001 and December 2001, unemployment increased by 1.8 million workers, and the nation's unemployment rate rose from 4.2 percent to 5.8 percent. Although the rate of inflation fell (an outcome called *disinflation*), the price level did not decline. That is, deflation did not occur.

Question:
How can an increase in the real interest rate, combined with a decline in expected investment returns, jointly contribute to a recession?

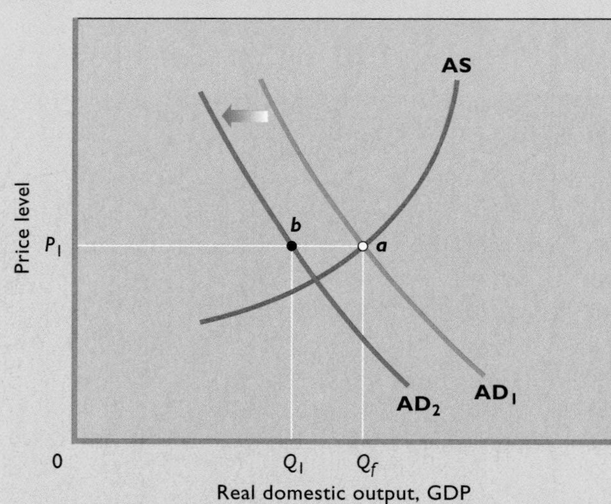

FIGURE 13.9
A recession. If the price level is downwardly inflexible, a decline of aggregate demand from AD_1 to AD_2 will move the economy from *a* to *b* and reduce real GDP from Q_f to Q_1. Idle production capacity, cyclical unemployment, and a negative GDP gap (of Q_1 minus Q_f) will result.

An Important Caution

There is some evidence that the price level and average level of wages are becoming more flexible downward in the United States. Intense international competition and declining power of unions in the United States seem to be undermining the ability of firms and workers to resist price and wage cuts when faced with falling aggregate demand. This increased flexibility of some prices and wages may be one reason the recession of 2001 was relatively mild. The U.S. auto manufacturers, for example, maintained output in the face of falling demand by offering zero-interest loans on auto purchases. This, in effect, was a disguised price cut.

In theory, fully flexible downward prices and wages would automatically "self-correct" a recession. Reduced aggregate demand, with its accompanying negative GDP gap and greater unemployment, would reduce the price level and level of (nominal) wages. In Figure 13.9, the lower wages would reduce per-unit production costs and shift the AS curve rightward. Eventually the economy would return to its full-employment output, but at a considerably lower price level than before. That is, the economy would move back to its long-run aggregate supply curve (not shown), which is a vertical line running upward at the economy's full-employment level of output.

In reality, the government and monetary authorities have been reluctant to wait for these slow and uncertain "corrections." Instead, they focus on trying to move the aggregate demand curve to its prerecession location. For example, throughout 2001 the Federal Reserve lowered interest rates to try to halt the recession and promote recovery. Those Fed actions, along with large Federal tax cuts, increased military spending, and strong demand for new housing, helped increase aggregate demand and spur recovery. Real GDP grew by 1.9 percent in 2002, 3.0 percent in 2003, and 4.4 percent in 2004. The unemployment rate remained stubbornly high during this period. It rose from 4.7 percent in 2001 to 6.0 percent in 2003, before declining to 5.5 percent in 2004. We will examine stabilization policies, such as those undertaken by the Federal government and the Federal Reserve, in the following chapter.

Summary

1. The aggregate demand–aggregate supply model (AD-AS model) enables analysis of simultaneous changes of real GDP and the price level.
2. The aggregate demand curve shows the level of real output that the economy will purchase at each price level. It slopes downward because higher price levels dissuade U.S. businesses and households, along with foreign buyers, from purchasing as much output as before.
3. The determinants of aggregate demand consist of spending by domestic consumers, businesses, and government and by foreign buyers. Changes in the factors listed in Figure 13.2 alter the spending by these groups and shift the aggregate demand curve.
4. The aggregate supply curve shows the levels of real output that businesses will produce at various possible price levels. The long-run aggregate supply curve assumes that nominal wages and other input prices fully match any change in the price level. The curve is vertical at the full-employment output.
5. The short-run aggregate supply curve (or simply "aggregate supply curve") assumes nominal wages and other input prices do not respond to price-level changes. The aggregate supply curve is generally upsloping because per-unit production costs, and hence the prices that firms must receive, rise as real output expands. The aggregate supply curve is relatively steep to the right of the full-employment output and relatively flat to the left of it.
6. Figure 13.5 lists the determinants of aggregate supply: input prices, productivity, and the legal-institutional environment. A change in any one of these factors will change per-unit production costs at each level of output and therefore will shift the aggregate supply curve.
7. The intersection of the aggregate demand and aggregate supply curves determines an economy's equilibrium price level and real GDP. At the intersection, the quantity of real GDP demanded equals the quantity of real GDP supplied.
8. Increases in aggregate demand beyond the full-employment output cause inflation and positive

GDP gaps (actual GDP exceeds potential GDP). Such gaps eventually evaporate as wages and other input prices rise to match the increase in the price level.

9. Leftward shifts of the aggregate supply curve reflect increases in per-unit production costs at each level of output and cause cost-push inflation, with accompanying negative GDP gaps.
10. Shifts of the aggregate demand curve to the left of the full-employment output cause recession, negative GDP gaps, and cyclical unemployment. The price level typically does not fall during U.S. recessions because of downwardly inflexible prices and wages. This inflexibility results from fear of price wars, menu costs, wage contracts, morale concerns, and minimum wages.
11. In theory, price and wage flexibility would allow the economy automatically to self-correct from a recession. In reality, downward price and wage flexibility make the process slow and uncertain. Recessions usually prompt the Federal government and the Federal Reserve to take actions to try to increase aggregate demand.
12. Following the recession of 2001, the U.S. economy entered the expansion phase of the business cycle. Real GDP expanded by 1.9 percent in 2002, 3.0 percent in 2003, and 4.4 percent in 2004.

Terms and Concepts

aggregate demand–aggregate supply (AD-AS) model

aggregate demand

determinants of aggregate demand

exchange rates

aggregate supply

long-run aggregate supply curve

short-run aggregate supply curve

determinants of aggregate supply

productivity

equilibrium price level

equilibrium real output

Study Questions

1. What is the general relationship between a country's price level and the quantity of its domestic output (real GDP) demanded? Who are the buyers of U.S. real GDP?
2. Why is the long-run aggregate supply curve vertical? Explain the shape of the short-run aggregate supply curve. Why is the short-run curve relatively flat to the left of the full-employment output and relatively steep to the right?
3. Suppose that the aggregate demand and supply schedules for a hypothetical economy are as shown below:

Amount of Real GDP Demanded, Billions	Price Level (Price Index)	Amount of Real GDP Supplied, Billions
$100	300	$450
200	250	400
300	200	300
400	150	200
500	100	100

   a. Use these sets of data to graph the aggregate demand and aggregate supply curves. What are the equilibrium price level and the equilibrium level of real output in this hypothetical economy? Is the equilibrium real output also necessarily the full-employment real output? Explain.
   b. Why will a price level of 150 not be an equilibrium price level in this economy? Why not 250?
   c. Suppose that buyers desire to purchase $200 billion of extra real output at each price level. Sketch in the new aggregate demand curve as AD_1. What factors might cause this change in aggregate demand? What are the new equilibrium price level and level of real output?
4. Suppose that a hypothetical economy has the following relationship between its real output and the input quantities necessary for producing that output:

Input Quantity	Real GDP
150.0	$400
112.5	300
75.0	200

a. What is productivity in this economy?
b. What is the per-unit cost of production if the price of each input unit is $2?
c. Assume that the input price increases from $2 to $3 with no accompanying change in productivity. What is the new per-unit cost of production? In what direction would the $1 increase in input price push the economy's aggregate supply curve? What effect would this shift of aggregate supply have on the price level and the level of real output?
d. Suppose that the increase in input price does not occur but, instead, that productivity increases by 100 percent. What would be the new per-unit cost of production? What effect would this change in per-unit production cost have on the economy's aggregate supply curve? What effect would this shift of aggregate supply have on the price level and the level of real output?

5. Other things equal, what effects would each of the following have on aggregate demand or aggregate supply? In each case use a diagram to show the expected effects on the equilibrium price level and the level of real output.
a. A reduction in the economy's real interest rate.
b. A major increase in Federal spending for health care (with no increase in taxes).
c. The complete disintegration of OPEC, causing oil prices to fall by one-half.
d. A 10 percent reduction in personal income tax rates (with no change in government spending).
e. A sizable increase in labor productivity (with no change in nominal wages).
f. A 12 percent increase in nominal wages (with no change in productivity).
g. A sizable depreciation in the international value of the dollar.

6. Other things equal, what effect will each of the following have on the equilibrium price level and level of real output?
a. An increase in aggregate demand in the steep portion of the aggregate supply curve.
b. An increase in aggregate supply, with no change in aggregate demand (assume that prices and wages are flexible upward and downward).
c. Equal increases in aggregate demand and aggregate supply.
d. A reduction in aggregate demand in the relatively flat portion of the aggregate supply curve.
e. An increase in aggregate demand and a decrease in aggregate supply.

7. Why does a reduction in aggregate demand tend to reduce real output, rather than the price level?

8. Explain: "Unemployment can be caused by a decrease of aggregate demand or a decrease of aggregate supply." In each case, specify the price-level outcomes.

9. In early 2001 investment spending sharply declined in the United States. In the 2 months following the September 11, 2001, attacks on the United States, consumption also declined. Use AD-AS analysis to show the two impacts on real GDP.

Website Questions

At the text's Website, www.brueonline.com, you will find three multiple-choice quizzes on this chapter's content. We encourage you to take the quizzes to see how you do. Also, you will find one or more Web-based questions that require information from the Internet to answer.

CHAPTER FOURTEEN

Fiscal Policy, Deficits, and Debt

In this chapter you will learn:

- The purposes, tools, and limitations of fiscal policy.
- The role of built-in stabilizers in dampening business cycles.
- How the standardized budget reveals the status of U.S. fiscal policy.
- About the size, composition, and consequences of the U.S. public debt.
- Why there is a long-run fiscal imbalance in the Social Security system.

In the previous chapter we saw that an excessive increase in aggregate demand can cause demand-pull inflation and that a significant decline in aggregate demand can cause recession and cyclical unemployment. For those reasons, central governments sometimes use budgetary actions to try to "stimulate the economy" or "rein in inflation." Such countercyclical **fiscal policy** consists of deliberate changes in government spending and tax collections designed to achieve full employment, control inflation, and encourage economic growth. (The adjective "fiscal" simply means "financial.")

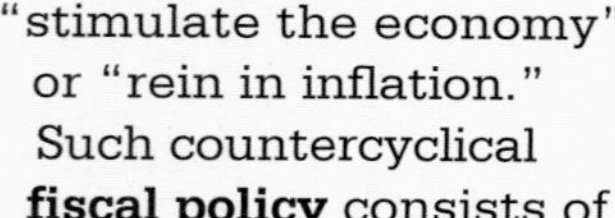

We begin this chapter by examining the logic behind fiscal policy, its current status, and its limitations. Then we examine two related topics: the U.S. public debt and the Social Security funding problem.

Fiscal Policy and the AD-AS Model

The fiscal policy that we have been describing is *discretionary* (or "active"). It is often initiated on the advice of the president's **Council of Economic Advisers (CEA),** a group of three economists appointed by the president to provide expertise and assistance on economic matters. Such changes in government spending and taxes are *at the option* of the Federal government. They do not occur automatically, independent of congressional action. The latter changes are *nondiscretionary* (or "passive" or "automatic"), and we will examine them later in this chapter.

fiscal policy
Deliberate changes in government spending or taxation to promote full employment, price-level stability, and economic growth.

Council of Economic Advisers (CEA)
A group of three economists appointed by the U.S. president to provide advice and assistance on economic matters.

Expansionary Fiscal Policy

When recession occurs, an **expansionary fiscal policy** may be in order. Consider Figure 14.1, where we suppose that a sharp decline in investment spending has shifted the economy's aggregate demand curve to the left from AD_1 to AD_2. (Disregard the arrow for now.) The cause of the recession may be that profit expectations on investment projects have dimmed, curtailing investment spending and reducing aggregate demand.

Suppose the economy's potential or full-employment output is $510 billion in Figure 14.1. If the price level is inflexible downward at P_1, the aggregate demand curve slides leftward at that price level and reduces real GDP to $490 billion. A negative GDP gap of $20 billion (=$490 billion − $510 billion) arises. An increase in unemployment accompanies this negative GDP gap because fewer workers are needed to produce the reduced output. In short, the economy depicted is suffering both recession and cyclical unemployment.

What fiscal policy should the Federal government adopt to try to remedy the situation? It has three main options: (1) government-spending increases, (2) tax reductions, or (3) some combination of the two. If the Federal budget is balanced at the outset, expansionary fiscal policy will create a government **budget deficit** (government spending in excess of tax revenues).

expansionary fiscal policy
An increase in government spending, a decrease in taxes, or some combination of the two for the purpose of increasing aggregate demand and real output.

budget deficit
The amount by which expenditures of the Federal government exceed its revenues in any year.

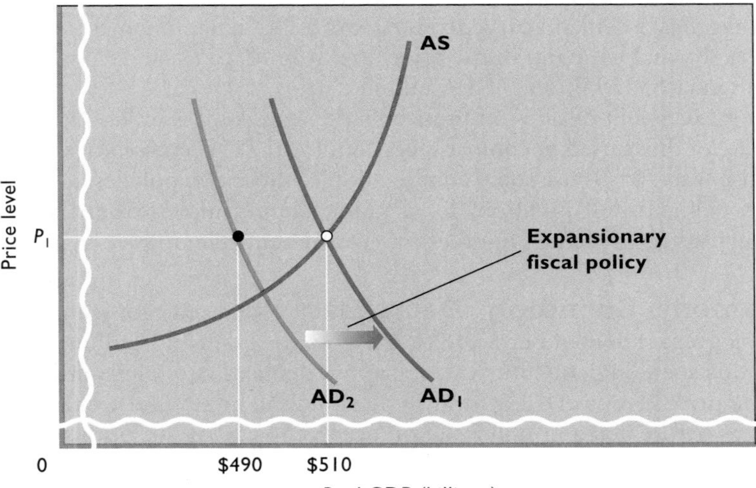

FIGURE 14.1
Expansionary fiscal policy. Expansionary fiscal policy uses increases in government spending, tax cuts, or a combination of both to increase aggregate demand and push the economy out of recession. Here, this policy increases aggregate demand from AD_2 to AD_1, increases real GDP from $490 billion to $510 billion, and restores full employment.

Government Spending Increases To increase aggregate demand, the Federal government can increase its spending. For example, it might boost spending on highways, education, and health care. Other things equal, a sufficient increase in government spending will shift an economy's aggregate demand curve to the right, as from AD_2 to AD_1 in Figure 14.1. Observe that real output rises to \$510 billion, up \$20 billion from its recessionary level of \$490 billion. Firms increase their employment to the full-employment level, output increases, and the negative GDP gap disappears.

Tax Reductions Alternatively, the government could reduce taxes to shift the aggregate demand curve rightward, as from AD_2 to AD_1. Suppose the government cuts personal income taxes, which increases disposable income. Households will spend a large part of that income and save the rest. The part spent—the new consumption spending—will increase aggregate demand. In Figure 14.1, this increase in aggregate demand from AD_2 to AD_1 expands real GDP by \$20 billion, eliminating the negative GDP gap. Employment increases accordingly, and the unemployment rate falls.

A tax cut must be larger than an increase in government spending to achieve the same rightward shift of the aggregate demand curve. This is because households save part of the higher after-tax income provided by the tax cut. Only the part of the tax cut that increases consumption spending shifts the aggregate demand curve to the right.

Combined Government Spending Increases and Tax Reductions The government may combine spending increases and tax cuts to produce the desired initial increase in spending and the eventual increase in aggregate demand and real GDP. In the economy depicted in Figure 14.1, there is some combination of greater government spending and lower taxes (increased consumption spending) that will shift the aggregate demand curve from AD_2 to AD_1 and remove the negative GDP gap.

Contractionary Fiscal Policy

contractionary fiscal policy
A decrease in government spending, an increase in taxes, or some combination of the two for the purpose of decreasing aggregate demand and halting inflation.

When demand-pull inflation occurs, a restrictive or **contractionary fiscal policy** may help control it. Take a look at Figure 14.2, where the full-employment level of real GDP is \$510 billion. Suppose a sharp increase in investment and net export spending shifts the aggregate demand curve from AD_3 to AD_4. The outcomes are demand-pull inflation, as shown by the rise of the price level from P_1 to P_2, and a positive GDP gap of \$12 billion (=\$522 billion − \$510 billion).

If the government decides on fiscal policy to control this inflation, its options are the opposite of those used to combat recession. It can (1) decrease government spending, (2) raise taxes, or (3) use some combination of those two policies. When the economy faces demand-pull inflation, fiscal policy should move toward a government **budget surplus** (tax revenues in excess of government spending).

budget surplus
The amount by which revenues of the Federal government exceed its expenditures in any year.

Government Spending Decreases Reduced government spending shifts the aggregate demand curve leftward to control demand-pull inflation. In Figure 14.2, this spending cut shifts the aggregate demand curve leftward from AD_4 to AD_3. If the price level were downwardly flexible, the price level would return to P_1, where it was before demand-pull inflation occurred. That is, deflation would occur.

Unfortunately, the actual economy is not as simple and tidy as Figure 14.2 suggests. Increases in aggregate demand tend to ratchet the price level upward, but

FIGURE 14.2

Contractionary fiscal policy. Contractionary fiscal policy uses decreases in government spending, increases in taxes, or a combination of both to reduce aggregate demand and slow or eliminate demand-pull inflation. Here, this policy shifts the aggregate demand curve from AD_4 to AD_3, removes the upward pressure on the price level, and halts the demand-pull inflation.

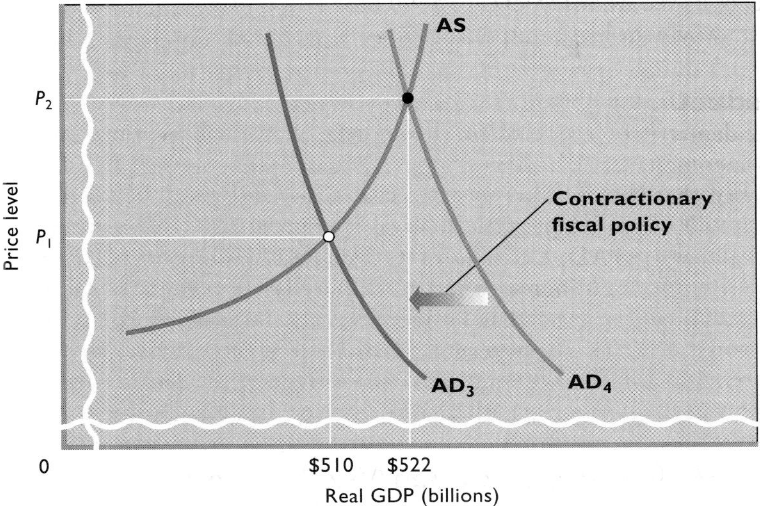

declines in aggregate demand do not seem to push the price level downward. So stopping inflation is a matter of halting the rise of the price level, not trying to lower it to the previous level. Demand-pull inflation usually is experienced as a continual rightward shifting of the aggregate demand curve. Contractionary fiscal policy is designed to stop a further shift, not to restore a lower price level. Successful fiscal policy eliminates a continuing positive (and thus inflationary) GDP gap and prevents the price level from continuing its inflationary rise. Nevertheless, Figure 14.2 displays the basic principle: Reductions in government expenditures can be used as a fiscal policy action to tame demand-pull inflation.

Tax Increases Just as government can use tax cuts to increase consumption spending, it can use tax increases to reduce consumption spending. In the economy in Figure 14.2, the government must raise taxes sufficiently to reduce consumption such that the aggregate demand curve will shift leftward from AD_4 to AD_3. That way, the demand-pull inflation will have been controlled.

Because part of any tax increase reduces saving rather than consumption, a tax increase must exceed a decrease in government spending to cause the same leftward shift of the aggregate demand curve. Only the part of the tax increase that lowers consumption spending reduces aggregate demand.

Combined Government Spending Decreases and Tax Increases

The government may choose to combine spending decreases and tax increases in order to reduce aggregate demand and check inflation. Some combination of lower government spending and higher taxes will shift the aggregate demand curve from AD_4 to AD_3.

Built-In Stability

To some degree, government tax revenues change automatically over the course of the business cycle and in ways that stabilize the economy. This automatic response, or built-in stability, constitutes nondiscretionary (or "passive" or "automatic") budgetary policy and results from the makeup of most tax systems. We did not include this built-in stability in our discussion of fiscal policy because we implicitly assumed that the same amount of tax revenue was being collected at each level of GDP. But the actual U.S. tax system is such that *net tax revenues* vary directly with GDP. (*Net taxes* are tax revenues less transfers and subsidies. From here on, we will use the simpler "taxes" to mean "net taxes.")

Virtually any tax will yield more tax revenue as GDP (and therefore total income) rises. In particular, personal income taxes have progressive rates and thus generate more-than-proportionate increases in tax revenues as GDP expands. Furthermore, as GDP rises and more goods and services are purchased, revenues from corporate income taxes and from sales taxes and excise taxes also increase. And, similarly, revenues from payroll taxes rise as economic expansion creates more jobs and income. Conversely, when GDP declines, tax receipts from all these sources also decline.

Transfer payments (or "negative taxes") behave in the opposite way from tax revenues. For example, welfare and unemployment compensation payments decline during an economic expansion and increase during an economic contraction.

Automatic or Built-In Stabilizers

built-in stabilizer Anything that increases the government's budget deficit (or reduces its budget surplus) during a recession and increases its budget surplus (or reduces its budget deficit) during expansion without requiring explicit action by policymakers.

A **built-in stabilizer** is anything that increases the government's budget deficit (or reduces its budget surplus) during a recession and increases its budget surplus (or reduces its budget deficit) during inflation without requiring explicit action by policymakers. As Figure 14.3 reveals, this is precisely what the U.S. tax system does. Government expenditures *G* are fixed and assumed to be independent of the level of GDP. Congress decides on a particular level of spending, but it does not determine the magnitude of tax revenues. Instead, it establishes tax rates, and the tax revenues then vary directly with the level of GDP that the economy achieves. Line *T* represents that direct relationship between tax revenues and GDP.

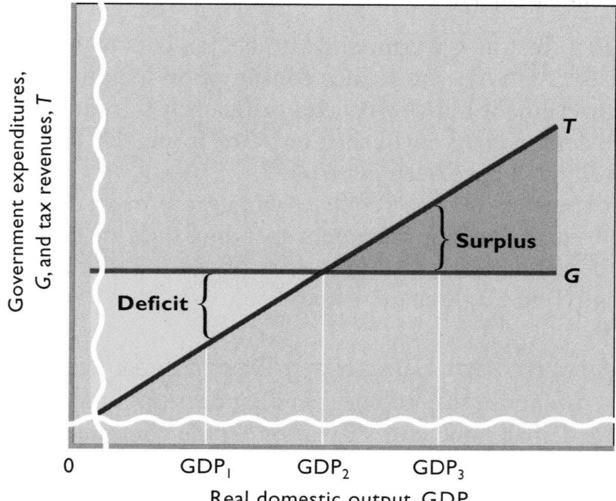

FIGURE 14.3
Built-in stability. Tax revenues *T* vary directly with GDP, and government spending *G* is assumed to be independent of GDP. As GDP falls in a recession, deficits occur automatically and help alleviate the recession. As GDP rises during expansion, surpluses occur automatically and help offset possible inflation.

Economic Importance

The economic importance of the direct relationship between tax receipts and GDP becomes apparent when we consider that:

- Taxes reduce spending and aggregate demand.
- Reductions in spending are desirable when the economy is moving toward inflation, whereas increases in spending are desirable when the economy is slumping.

As shown in Figure 14.3, tax revenues automatically increase as GDP rises during prosperity, and since taxes reduce household and business spending, they restrain the economic expansion. That is, as the economy moves toward a higher GDP, tax revenues automatically rise and move the budget from deficit toward surplus. In Figure 14.3, observe that the high and perhaps inflationary income level GDP_3 automatically generates a contractionary budget surplus.

Conversely, as output and income fall during recession, tax revenues automatically decline, increasing spending and cushioning the economic contraction. With a falling GDP, tax receipts decline and move the government's budget from surplus toward deficit. In Figure 14.3, the low level of income GDP_1 will automatically yield an expansionary budget deficit.

Built-in stability has reduced the severity of U.S. business fluctuations, perhaps by as much as 8 percent of the change in GDP that otherwise would have occurred.[1] For example, as the economy expanded vigorously in the late 1990s, the Federal budget swung from deficit to surplus. That swing helped dampen private spending and forestall demand-pull inflation. When the recession of 2001 hit, tax revenues automatically dropped off, slowing the decline in aggregate demand. But built-in stabilizers can only diminish, not eliminate, swings in real GDP. Discretionary fiscal policy (changes in tax rates and expenditures) or monetary policy (central bank-caused changes in interest rates) may be needed to correct recession or inflation of any appreciable magnitude.

Evaluating Fiscal Policy

How can we determine whether discretionary fiscal policy is expansionary, neutral, or contractionary in a particular period? We cannot simply examine changes in the actual budget deficits or surpluses, because those changes may reflect automatic changes in tax revenues that accompany changes in GDP, not changes in discretionary fiscal policy. Moreover, the strength of any deliberate change in government spending or taxes depends on how large it is relative to the size of the economy. So, in evaluating the status of fiscal policy, we must adjust deficits and surpluses to eliminate automatic changes in tax revenues and compare the sizes of the adjusted budget deficits (or surpluses) to the levels of potential GDP.

Economists use the **standardized budget** (or *full-employment budget*) to adjust the actual Federal budget deficits and surpluses to eliminate the automatic changes in tax revenues. The standardized budget measures what the Federal budget deficit or surplus would be with existing tax rates and government spending programs if the economy had achieved its full-employment level of GDP (its potential output) in each year. The idea is to compare *actual* government expenditures for each year with the tax

standardized budget
A measure of what the Federal budget deficit or surplus would be with existing tax rates and government spending programs if the economy had achieved its full-employment GDP in the year.

[1] Alan J. Auerbach and Daniel Feenberg, "The Significance of Federal Taxes as Automatic Stabilizers," *Journal of Economic Perspectives*, Summer 2000, p. 54.

revenues *that would have occurred* in that year if the economy had achieved full-employment GDP. That procedure removes budget deficits or surpluses that arise simply because of changes in GDP and thus tell us nothing about changes in discretionary fiscal policy.

Consider Figure 14.4, where line *G* represents government expenditures and line *T* represents tax revenues. In full-employment year 1, government expenditures of $500 billion equal tax revenues of $500 billion, as indicated by the intersection of lines *G* and *T* at point *a*. The actual budget deficit and the standardized budget deficit in year 1 are zero—government expenditures equal tax revenues, and government spending equals the tax revenues forthcoming at the full-employment output GDP_1. Obviously, the standardized budget deficit *as a percentage of potential GDP* is also zero.

Now suppose that a recession occurs and GDP falls from GDP_1 to GDP_2, as shown in Figure 14.4. Let's also assume that the government takes no discretionary action, so lines *G* and *T* remain as shown in the figure. Tax revenues automatically fall to $450 billion (point *c*) at GDP_2, while government spending (we assume) remains unaltered at $500 billion (point *b*). A $50 billion actual budget deficit (represented by distance *bc*) arises. But this **cyclical deficit** is simply a by-product of the economy's slide into recession, not the result of discretionary fiscal actions by the government. We would be wrong to conclude from this deficit that the government is engaging in an expansionary fiscal policy.

cyclical deficit A Federal budget deficit that is caused by a recession and the consequent decline in tax revenues.

That fact is highlighted when we consider the standardized budget deficit for year 2 in Figure 14.4. The $500 billion of government expenditures in year 2 is shown by *b* on line *G*. And, as shown by *a* on line *T*, $500 billion of tax revenues

FIGURE 14.4
Standardized budget deficits. The standardized budget deficit is zero at the full-employment output GDP_1. But it is also zero at the recessionary output GDP_2, because the $500 billion of government expenditures at GDP_2 equals the $500 billion of tax revenues that would be forthcoming at the full-employment GDP_1. Here, fiscal policy did not change as the economy slid into recession. The deficit that arose is simply a cyclical deficit.

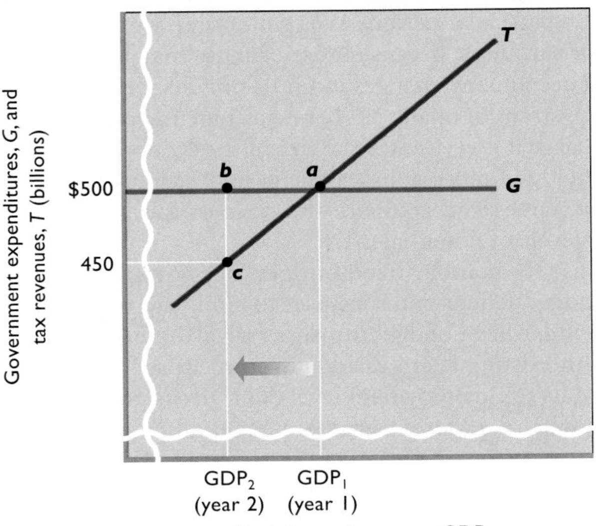

would have occurred if the economy had achieved its full-employment GDP. Because both *b* and *a* represent $500 billion, the standardized budget deficit in year 2 is zero, as is this deficit as a percentage of potential GDP. Since the full-employment deficits are zero in both years, we know that government did not change its discretionary fiscal policy, even though a recession occurred and an actual deficit of $50 billion resulted.

In contrast, if we observed a standardized deficit of zero in a specific year, followed by a standardized budget deficit in the next, we could conclude that fiscal policy is expansionary. Because the standardized budget adjusts for automatic changes in tax revenues, the increase in the standardized budget deficit reveals that government either increased its spending (G) or decreased tax rates such that tax revenues (T) decreased. In Figure 14.4, the government either shifted the line G upward or the line T downward. These changes in G and T are precisely the discretionary actions that we have identified as elements of an *expansionary* fiscal policy. Similarly, if we observed a standardized deficit of zero in one year, followed by a standardized budget surplus in the next, we could conclude that fiscal policy is contractionary. Government either decreased its spending (G) or increased tax rates such that tax revenues (T) increased. We know that these changes in G and T are elements of a *contractionary* fiscal policy.

Global Snapshot 14.1 shows the extent of the standardized budget deficits or surpluses of a number of countries in a recent year.

Global Snapshot 14.1

Standardized Budget Deficits or Surpluses as a Percentage of Potential GDP, Selected Nations

In 2005 some nations had standardized budget surpluses, while others had standardized budget deficits. These surpluses and deficits varied as a percentage of each nation's potential GDP. Generally, the surpluses represented contractionary fiscal policy and the deficits expansionary fiscal policy.

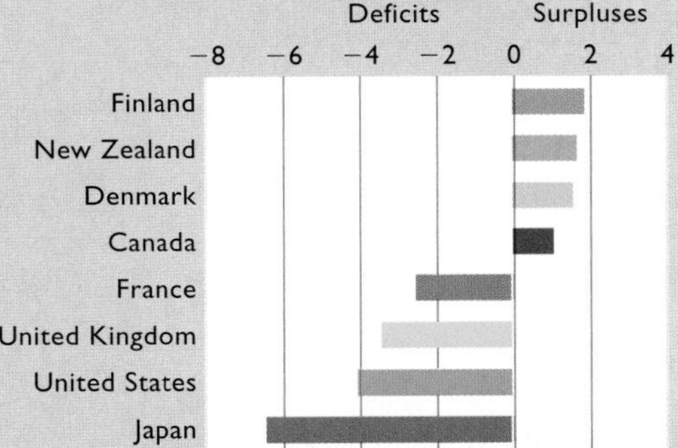

Source: Organization for Economic Cooperation and Development, www.oecd.org. Data are 2005 estimates.

Recent U.S. Fiscal Policy

Table 14.1 lists the actual U.S. budget deficits and surpluses (column 2) and the standardized deficits and surpluses (column 3), as percentages of actual and potential GDP, respectively, for recent years. Observe that the standardized deficits are generally smaller than the actual deficits. This is because the actual deficits include cyclical deficits, whereas the standardized deficits do not. The latter deficits provide the information needed to assess discretionary fiscal policy.

Column 3 shows that fiscal policy was expansionary in the early 1990s. Consider 1992, for example. From the table we see that the actual budget deficit was 4.5 percent of GDP and the standardized budget deficit was 2.9 percent of potential GDP. The economy was recovering from the 1990–1991 recession, so tax revenues were relatively low. But even if the economy were at full employment in 1992, with the greater tax revenues that would imply, the Federal budget would have been in deficit by 2.9 percent. And that percentage was greater than the deficits in the prior 2 years. So the standardized budget deficit in 1992 clearly reflected expansionary fiscal policy.

TABLE 14.1
Federal Deficits (−) and Surpluses (+) as Percentages of GDP, 1990–2004

(1) Year	(2) Actual Deficit or Surplus	(3) Standardized Deficit or Surplus*
1990	−3.9%	−2.2%
1991	−4.4	−2.5
1992	−4.5	−2.9
1993	−3.8	−2.9
1994	−2.9	−2.1
1995	−2.2	−2.0
1996	−1.4	−1.2
1997	−0.3	−1.0
1998	+0.8	−0.4
1999	+1.4	+0.1
2000	+2.5	+1.2
2001	+1.3	+1.1
2002	−1.5	−1.1
2003	−3.4	−2.7
2004	−3.5	−2.4

* As a percentage of potential GDP.

Source: Congressional Budget Office. www.cbo.gov.

But the large standardized budget deficits were projected to continue even when the economy fully recovered from the 1990–1991 recession. The concern was that the large actual and full-employment deficits would cause high interest rates, low levels of investment, and slow economic growth. In 1993 the Clinton administration and Congress increased personal income and corporate income tax rates to prevent these potential outcomes. Observe from column 3 of Table 14.1 that the standardized budget deficits shrunk each year and eventually gave way to surpluses in 1999, 2000, and 2001.

On the basis of projections that actual budget surpluses would accumulate to as much as $5 trillion between 2000 and 2010, the Bush administration and Congress passed a major tax reduction package in 2001. The tax cuts went into effect over a number of years. For example, the cuts reduced tax liabilities by an estimated $44 billion in 2001 and $52 billion in 2002. In terms of fiscal policy, the timing was good since the economy entered a recession in March 2001 and absorbed a second economic blow from the terrorist attacks on September 11, 2001. The government greatly increased its spending on war abroad and homeland security. Also, in March 2002 Congress passed a "recession-relief" bill that extended unemployment compensation benefits and offered business tax relief. That legislation was specifically designed to interject $51 billion into the economy in 2002 and another $71 billion over the following 2 years.

As seen in Table 14.1, the standardized budget moved from a *surplus* of 1.1 percent of potential GDP in 2000 to a *deficit* of 1.1 percent in 2002. Clearly, fiscal policy had turned expansionary. Nevertheless, the economy remained very sluggish in 2003. In June of that year, Congress again cut taxes, this time by an enormous $350 billion over several years. Specifically, the tax legislation accelerated the reduction of marginal tax rates already scheduled for future years and slashed tax rates on income from dividends and capital gains. It also increased tax breaks for families and small businesses. This tax package, along with expanded government spending, increased the standardized budget deficit greatly. As a percentage of potential GDP, it rose to −2.7 percent in 2003 and to −2.4 percent in 2004. The purpose of this expansionary fiscal policy was to prevent another recession, reduce unemployment, and increase economic growth.

Figure 14.5 shows the actual and projected budget deficits and surpluses (both nonstandardized) from 1992 to 2012. Clearly, the United States has been experiencing large budget deficits recently and these are expected to continue for several years. But projected deficits and surpluses change periodically as government alters fiscal policy and the growth of GDP rises or slows. So we suggest that you update this figure by going to the Congressional Budget Office Website, www.cbo.gov, and selecting "Current Budget Projections" and then "CBO's Baseline Budget Projections." The relevant numbers are in the row "Surplus or Deficit (−)."

Question:

Use Figure 14.4 to demonstrate how each of the following contributed to increased actual budget deficits in recent years: (a) the recession of 2001; (b) the war on terrorism in the United States and abroad; and (c) the Bush administration tax cuts.

FIGURE 14.5
Federal budget deficits and surpluses, actual and projected, fiscal years 1992–2012 (in billions of nominal dollars). The annual budget deficits of 1992 through 1997 gave way to budget surpluses from 1998 through 2001. Deficits reappeared in 2002 and are projected to continue through 2011.

Source: Congressional Budget Office, www.cbo.gov.

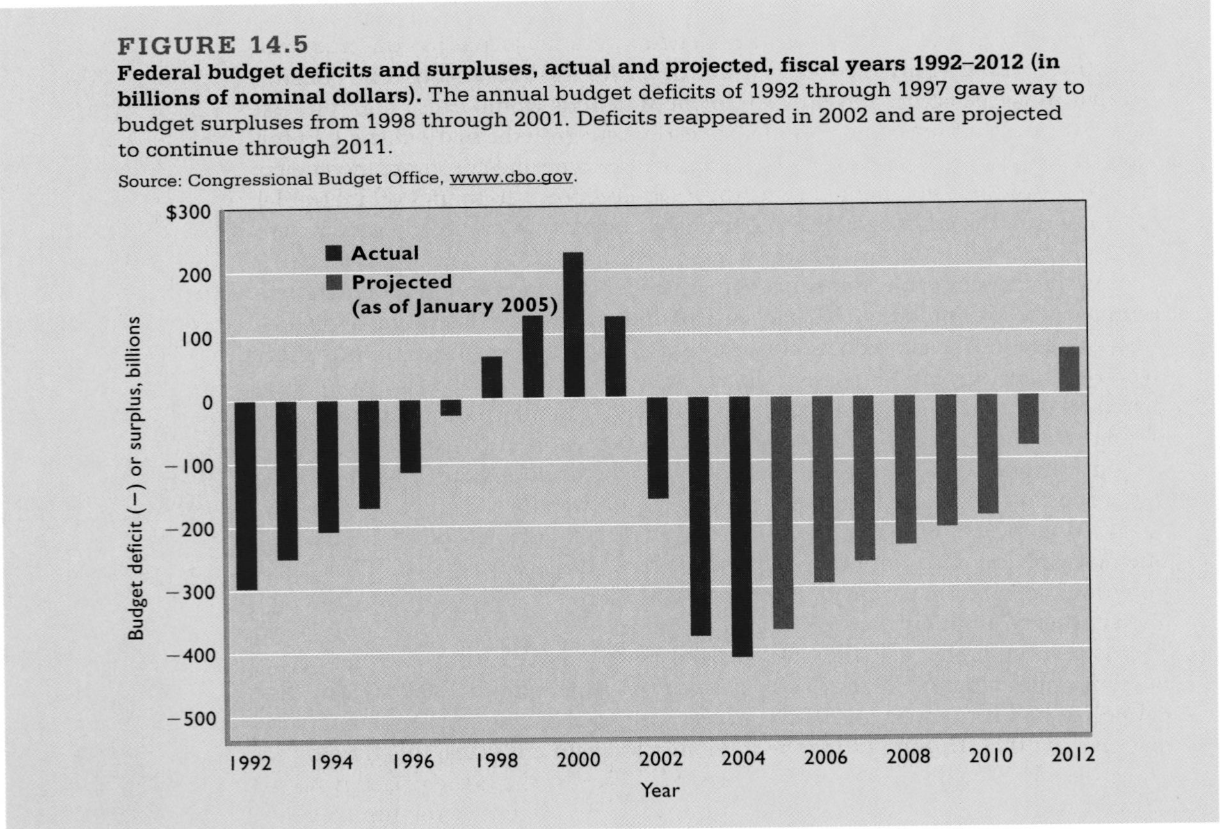

Problems, Criticisms, and Complications

Economists recognize that governments may encounter a number of significant problems in enacting and applying fiscal policy.

Problems of Timing

Several problems of timing may arise in connection with fiscal policy:

- ***Recognition lag*** The recognition lag is the time between the beginning of recession or inflation and the certain awareness that it is actually happening. This lag arises because of the difficulty in predicting the future course of economic activity. Although macroeconomic forecasting models provide clues to the direction of the economy, the economy may be 4 or 6 months into a recession or inflation before that fact appears in relevant statistics and is acknowledged. Meanwhile, the economic downslide or the inflation may become more serious than it would have if the situation had been identified and acted on sooner.
- ***Administrative lag*** The wheels of democratic government turn slowly. There will typically be a significant lag between the time the need for fiscal action is

recognized and the time action is taken. Following the terrorist attacks of September 11, 2001, the U.S. Congress was stalemated for 5 months before passing a compromise economic stimulus law in March 2002. (In contrast, the Federal Reserve began lowering interest rates the week after the attacks.)

- ***Operational lag*** A lag also occurs between the time fiscal action is taken and the time that action affects output, employment, or the price level. Although changes in tax rates can be put into effect relatively quickly, government spending on public works—new dams, interstate highways, and so on—requires long planning periods and even longer periods of construction. Such spending is of questionable use in offsetting short (for example, 6- to 12-month) periods of recession. Consequently, discretionary fiscal policy has increasingly relied on tax changes rather than on changes in spending as its main tool.

Political Considerations

Fiscal policy is conducted in a political arena. That reality not only may slow the enactment of fiscal policy but also may create the potential for political considerations swamping economic considerations in its formulation. It is a human trait to rationalize actions and policies that are in one's self-interest. Politicians are very human—they want to get reelected. A strong economy at election time will certainly help them. So they may favor large tax cuts under the guise of expansionary fiscal policy even though that policy is economically inappropriate. Similarly, they may rationalize increased government spending on popular items such as farm subsidies, health care, education, and homeland security.

At the extreme, elected officials and political parties might collectively "hijack" fiscal policy for political purposes, cause inappropriate changes in aggregate demand, and thereby cause (rather than avert) economic fluctuations. They may stimulate the economy using expansionary fiscal policy before elections and use contractionary fiscal policy to dampen excessive aggregate demand after the election. Such **political business cycles** are difficult to document and prove, but there is little doubt that political considerations weigh heavily in the formulation of fiscal policy. The question is how often, if ever, those political considerations run counter to "sound economics."

political business cycle
The alleged tendency of presidential administrations and Congress to create macroeconomic instability by reducing taxes and increasing government spending before elections and to raise taxes and reduce expenditures after elections.

Future Policy Reversals

Fiscal policy may fail to achieve its intended objectives if households expect future reversals of policy. Consider a tax cut, for example. If taxpayers believe the tax reduction is temporary, they may save a large portion of their tax saving, reasoning that rates will return to their previous level in the future. At that time, they can draw on this extra saving to maintain their consumption then. So a tax reduction thought to be temporary may not increase present consumption spending and aggregate demand by as much as our simple model (Figure 14.1) suggests.

The opposite may be true for a tax increase. If taxpayers think it is temporary, they may reduce their saving to pay the tax while maintaining their present consumption. They may reason that they can restore their saving when the tax rate again falls. So the tax increase may not reduce current consumption and aggregate demand by as much as the policymakers desired.

To the extent that this so-called *consumption smoothing* occurs over time, fiscal policy will lose some of its strength. The lesson is that tax-rate changes that households view as permanent are more likely to alter consumption and aggregate demand than tax changes they view as temporary.

Offsetting State and Local Finance

The fiscal policies of state and local governments are frequently *pro-cyclical*, meaning that they worsen rather than correct recession or inflation. Unlike the Federal government, most state and local governments face constitutional or other legal requirements to balance their budgets. Like households and private businesses, state and local governments increase their expenditures during prosperity and cut them during recession. During the Great Depression of the 1930s, most of the increase in Federal spending was offset by decreases in state and local spending. During and immediately following the recession of 2001, many state and local governments had to increase tax rates, impose new taxes, and reduce spending to offset lower tax revenues resulting from the reduced personal income and spending of their citizens.

Crowding-Out Effect

crowding-out effect A decrease in private investment caused by higher interest rates that result from the Federal government's increased borrowing to finance deficits (or debt).

14.1 Crowding out

14.2 Crowding out

Another potential flaw of fiscal policy is the so-called **crowding-out effect:** An expansionary fiscal policy (deficit spending) may increase the interest rate and reduce private spending, thereby weakening or canceling the stimulus of the expansionary policy. In this view, fiscal policy may be largely or totally ineffective!

Suppose the economy is in recession and government enacts a discretionary fiscal policy in the form of increased government spending. Also suppose that the monetary authorities hold the supply of money constant. To finance its budget deficit, the government borrows funds in the money market. The resulting increase in the demand for money raises the price paid for borrowing money: the interest rate. Because investment spending varies inversely with the interest rate, some investment will be choked off or crowded out. (Some interest-sensitive consumption spending such as purchases of automobiles on credit may also be crowded out.)

Nearly all economists agree that a budget deficit is inappropriate when the economy has achieved full employment. Such a deficit will surely crowd out some private investment. But there is disagreement on whether crowding out exists under all circumstances. Many economists believe that little crowding out will occur when fiscal policy is used to move the economy from recession. The added amount of government financing resulting from typical budget deficits is small compared to the total amount of private and public financing occurring in the money market. Therefore, interest rates are not likely to be greatly affected. Moreover, both increased government spending and increased consumption spending resulting from tax cuts may improve the profit expectations of businesses. The greater expected returns on private investment may encourage more of it. Thus, private investment need not fall, even though interest rates do rise. (We will soon see that the financing of the entire public debt, as opposed to the financing of new debt from annual deficits, is more likely to raise interest rates.)

Current Thinking on Fiscal Policy

Where do these complications leave us as to the advisability and effectiveness of discretionary fiscal policy? In view of the complications and uncertain outcomes of fiscal policy, some economists argue that it is better not to engage in it at all. Those holding that view point to the superiority of monetary policy (changes in interest rates engineered by the Federal Reserve) as a stabilizing device or believe that most economic fluctuations tend to be mild and self-correcting.

But most economists believe that fiscal policy remains an important, useful policy lever in the government's macroeconomic toolkit. The current popular view is that fiscal policy can help "push the economy" in a particular direction but cannot "fine-tune it" to a precise macroeconomic outcome. Mainstream economists generally agree that monetary policy is the best month-to-month stabilization tool for the U.S. economy. If monetary policy is doing its job, the government should maintain a relatively neutral fiscal policy, with a standardized budget deficit or surplus of no more than 2 percent of potential GDP. It should hold major discretionary fiscal policy in reserve to help counter situations where recession threatens to be deep and long-lasting or where inflation threatens to escalate rapidly despite the efforts of the Federal Reserve to stabilize the economy.

Finally, there is general agreement that proposed fiscal policy should be evaluated for its potential positive and negative impacts on long-run productivity growth. The short-run policy tools used for conducting active fiscal policy often have long-run impacts. Countercyclical fiscal policy should be shaped to strengthen, or at least not impede, the growth of long-run aggregate supply (shown as a rightward shift of the long-run aggregate supply curve in Figure 13.3). For example, a tax cut might be structured to enhance work effort, strengthen investment, and encourage innovation. Or an increase in government spending might center on preplanned projects for "public capital" (highways, mass transit, ports, airports) that are complementary to private investment and thus conducive to long-term economic growth.

The Public Debt

The national or **public debt** is essentially the total accumulation of the deficits (minus the surpluses) the Federal government has incurred through time. These deficits have emerged mainly because of war financing, recessions, and fiscal policy. Lack of political will by Congress has also contributed to the size of the debt. In 2004 the total public debt was $7.4 trillion—$4.3 trillion held by the public and $3.1 trillion held by agencies of the Federal government.

public debt
The total amount of money owed by the Federal government to the owners of government securities; equal to the sum of past government budget deficits less government budget surpluses.

Ownership

The total public debt represents the total amount of money owed by the Federal government to the holders of **U.S. securities:** Treasury bills, Treasury notes, Treasury bonds, and U.S. savings bonds. Figure 14.6 shows that the public held 58 percent of the public debt in 2004 and that Federal government agencies and the Federal Reserve (the U.S. central bank) held the other 42 percent. In this case the "public" consists of individuals here and abroad, state and local governments, and U.S. financial institutions. People and institutions abroad held about 26 percent of the total debt. So most of the debt is internally held, not externally held. Americans owe roughly three-fourths of the debt to Americans.

U.S. securities
Treasury bills, Treasury notes, Treasury bonds, and U.S. savings bonds issued by the Federal government to finance expenditures that exceed tax revenues.

Debt and GDP

A simple statement of the absolute size of the debt ignores the fact that the wealth and productive ability of the U.S. economy is also vast. A wealthy, highly productive nation can incur and carry a large public debt more easily than a poor nation can. It is more meaningful to measure the public debt in relation to an economy's GDP. Figure 14.7

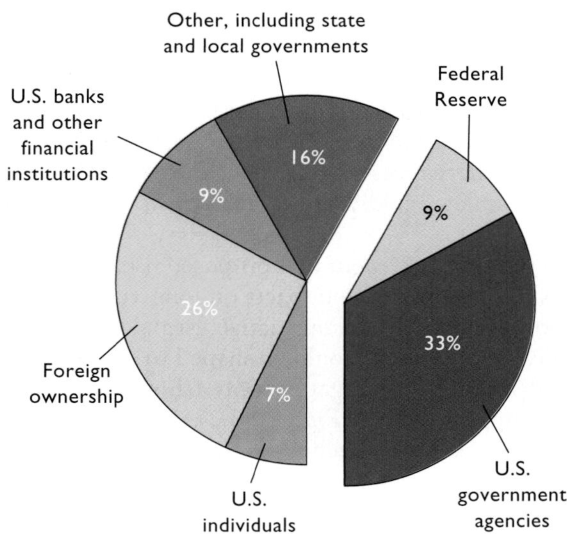

FIGURE 14.6 Ownership of the total public debt, 2004. The total public debt can be divided into the proportion held by the public (58 percent) and the proportion held by Federal agencies and the Federal Reserve System (42 percent). Of the total debt, 26 percent is foreign-owned.

Source: U.S. Treasury, www.fms.treas.gov/.

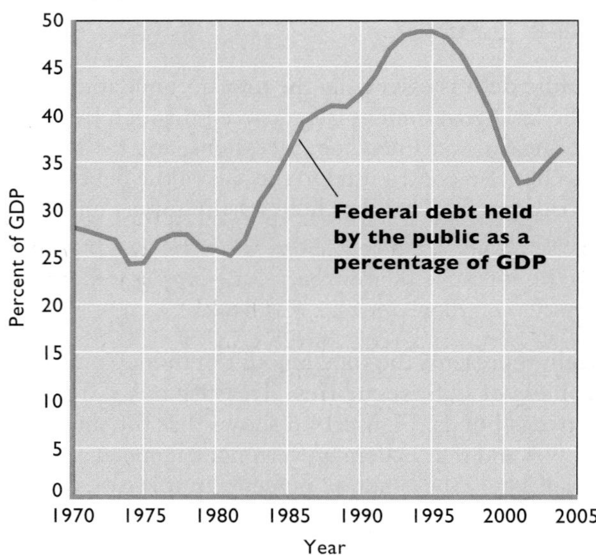

FIGURE 14.7 Federal debt held by the public as a percentage of GDP, 1970–2004. As a percentage of GDP, the Federal debt held by the public (held outside the Federal Reserve and government agencies) increased sharply over the 1980–1995 period and declined significantly between 1995 and 2001. Since 2001, the percentage has gone up again, but remains lower than it was in the 1990s.

shows the relative size of the Federal debt held by the public (as opposed to the Federal Reserve and Federal agencies) over time. Notice this percentage has increased since 2001, but remains below the percentages in the 1990s.

International Comparisons

It is not uncommon for countries to have public debts. Global Snapshot 14.2 lists publicly held government debts as percentages of GDP for several countries.

Global Snapshot 14.2

Publicly Held Debt: International Comparisons

Although the United States has the world's largest public debt, a number of other nations have larger publicly held debts as a percentage of their GDPs.

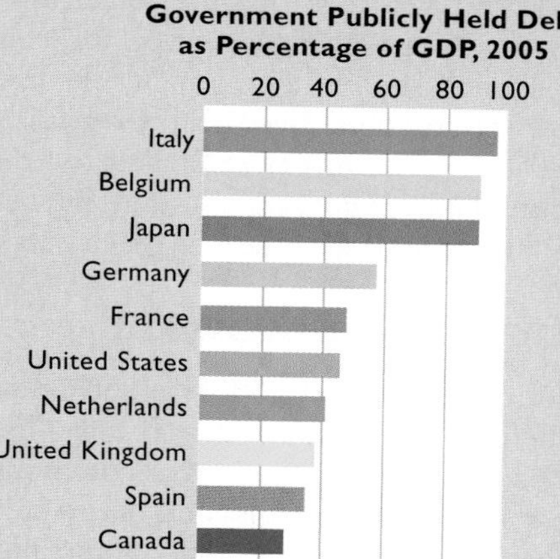

Source: Organization for Economic Cooperation and Development, www.oecd.org/. Data are 2005 estimates.

Interest Charges

Many economists conclude that the primary burden of the debt is the annual interest charge accruing on the bonds sold to finance the debt. In 2004 interest on the total public debt was $160 billion and is now the fourth-largest item in the Federal budget (behind income security, national defense, and health).

Interest payments were 1.4 percent of GDP in 2004. That percentage reflects the level of taxation (the average tax rate) required to pay the interest on the public debt. That is, in 2004 the Federal government had to collect taxes equal to 1.4 percent of GDP to service the total public debt.

False Concerns

You may wonder if the large public debt might bankrupt the United States or at least place a tremendous burden on your children and grandchildren. Fortunately, these are false concerns.

Bankruptcy

The large U.S. public debt does not threaten to bankrupt the Federal government, leaving it unable to meet its financial obligations. There are two main reasons: refinancing and taxation.

Refinancing The public debt is easily refinanced. As portions of the debt come due on maturing Treasury bills, notes, and bonds each month, the government does not cut expenditures or raise taxes to provide the funds required. Rather, it refinances the debt by selling new bonds and using the proceeds to pay off holders of the maturing bonds. The new bonds are in strong demand, because lenders can obtain a relatively good interest return with no risk of default by the Federal government.

Taxation The Federal government has the constitutional authority to levy and collect taxes. A tax increase is a government option for gaining sufficient revenue to pay interest and principal on the public debt. Financially distressed private households and corporations cannot extract themselves from their financial difficulties by taxing the public. If their incomes or sales revenues fall short of their expenses, they can indeed go bankrupt. But the Federal government does have the option to impose new taxes or increase existing tax rates if necessary to finance its debt.

Burdening Future Generations

In 2004 public debt per capita was $25,200. Was each child born in 2004 handed a $25,200 bill from the Federal government? Not really. The public debt does not impose as much of a burden on future generations as commonly thought.

The United States owes a substantial portion of the public debt to itself. U.S. citizens and institutions (banks, businesses, insurance companies, governmental agencies, and trust funds) own about 74 percent of the U.S. government securities. While that part of the public debt is a liability to Americans (as taxpayers), it is simultaneously an asset to Americans (as holders of Treasury bills, Treasury notes, Treasury bonds, and U.S. savings bonds).

To eliminate the American-owned part of the public debt would require a gigantic transfer payment from Americans to Americans. Taxpayers would pay higher taxes, and holders of the debt would receive an equal amount for their U.S. securities. Purchasing power in the United States would not change. Only the repayment of the 26 percent of the public debt owned by foreigners would negatively impact U.S. purchasing power.

The public debt increased sharply during the Second World War. But the decision to finance military purchases through the sale of government bonds did not shift the economic burden of the war to future generations. The economic cost of the Second World War consisted of the civilian goods society had to forgo in shifting scarce resources to war goods production (recall production possibilities analysis). Regardless of whether society financed this reallocation through higher taxes or through borrowing, the real economic burden of the war would have been the same. That burden was borne almost entirely by those who lived during the war. They were the ones who did without a multitude of consumer goods to enable the United States to arm itself and its allies. The next generation inherited the debt from the war but also an equal amount of government bonds. It also inherited the enormous benefits from the victory—namely, preserved political and economic systems at home and the "export" of those systems to Germany, Italy, and Japan. Those outcomes enhanced postwar U.S. economic growth and helped raise the standard of living of future generations of Americans.

Substantive Issues

Although the above issues are of false concern, there are a number of substantive issues relating to the public debt. Economists, however, attach varying degrees of importance to them.

Income Distribution

The distribution of ownership of government securities is highly uneven. Some people own much more than the $25,200-per-person portion of government securities; other people own less or none at all. In general, the ownership of the public debt is concentrated among wealthier groups who own a large percentage of all stocks and bonds. Because the overall Federal tax system is only mildly progressive, payment of interest on the public debt probably increases income inequality. Income is transferred from people who, on average, have lower incomes to the higher-income bondholders. If greater income equality is one of society's goals, then this redistribution is undesirable.

Incentives

The current public debt necessitates annual interest payments of $160 billion. With no increase in the size of the debt, that interest charge must be paid out of tax revenues. Higher taxes may dampen incentives to bear risk, to innovate, to invest, and to work. So, in this indirect way, a large public debt may impair economic growth.

Foreign-Owned Public Debt

The 26 percent of the U.S. debt held by citizens and institutions of foreign countries *is* an economic burden to Americans. Because we do not owe that portion of the debt "to ourselves," the payment of interest and principal on this **external public debt** enables foreigners to buy some of our output. In return for the benefits derived from the borrowed funds, the United States transfers goods and services to foreign lenders. Of course, Americans also own debt issued by foreign governments, so payment of principal and interest by those governments transfers some of their goods and services to Americans.

external public debt
The part of the public debt owed to foreign citizens, firms, and institutions.

Crowding Out Revisited

There is a potentially more serious problem. The financing (and continual refinancing) of the large public debt can transfer a real economic burden to future generations by passing a smaller stock of capital goods on to them. This possibility involves the previously discussed crowding-out effect: the idea that public borrowing drives up real interest rates, which reduces private investment spending. If the amount of current investment crowded out is extensive, future generations will inherit an economy with a smaller production capacity and, other things equal, a lower standard of living.

A Graphical Look at Crowding Out We know from Chapter 13 there is an inverse relationship between the real interest rate and the amount of investment spending. When graphed, that relationship is shown as a downward-sloping **investment demand curve,** such as either ID_1 or ID_2 in Figure 14.8. Let's first consider curve ID_1. (Ignore curve ID_2 for now.) Suppose that government borrowing increases the real interest rate from 6 to 10 percent. Then, investment spending will fall from $25 billion to $15 billion, as shown by the economy's move from *a* to *b*. That is, the financing of the debt will compete with the financing of private investment projects and crowd out $10 billion of private investment. So the stock of private capital handed down to future generations will be $10 billion less than it would have been without the need to finance the public debt.

investment demand curve
A curve that shows the amount of investment forthcoming in an economy at each real interest rate in a series of such rates.

FIGURE 14.8
The investment demand curve and the crowding-out effect. If the investment demand curve (ID_1) is fixed, the increase in the interest rate from 6 to 10 percent caused by financing a large public debt will move the economy from *a* to *b* and crowd out $10 billion of private investment and decrease the size of the capital stock inherited by future generations. However, if the public goods enabled by the debt improve the investment prospects of businesses, the private investment demand curve will shift rightward, as from ID_1 to ID_2. That shift may offset the crowding-out effect wholly or in part. In this case, it moves the economy from *a* to *c*.

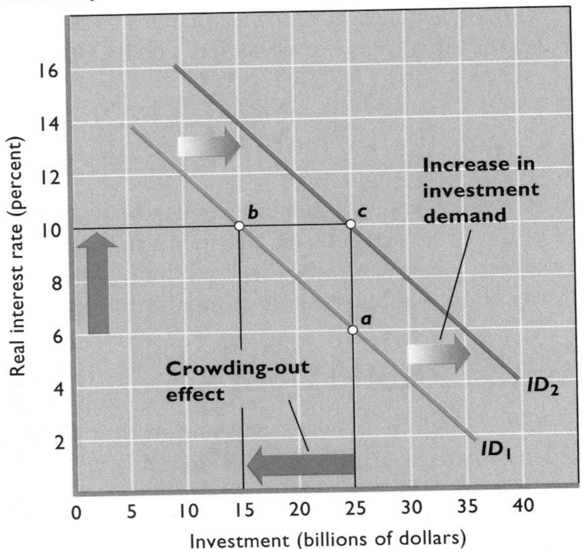

Public Investments and Public-Private Complementarities

But even with crowding out, there are two factors that could partly or fully offset the net economic burden shifted to future generations. First, just as private goods may involve either consumption or investment, so it is with public goods. Part of the government spending enabled by the public debt is for public investment outlays (for example, highways, mass-transit systems, and electric power facilities) and "human capital" (for example, investments in education, job training, and health). Like private expenditures on machinery and equipment, those **public investments** increase the economy's future production capacity. Because of the financing through debt, the stock of public capital passed on to future generations may be higher than otherwise. That greater stock of public capital may offset the diminished stock of private capital resulting from the crowding-out effect, leaving overall production capacity unimpaired.

public investments Government expenditures on public capital (such as highways, bridges, mass-transit systems, and electric power facilities) and on human capital (such as education, training, and health).

So-called public-private complementarities are a second factor that could reduce the crowding-out effect. Some public and private investments are complementary. Thus, the public investment financed through the debt could spur some private sector investment by increasing its expected rate of return. For example, a Federal building in a city may encourage private investment in the form of nearby office buildings, shops, and restaurants. Through its complementary effect, the spending on public capital may shift the private investment demand curve to the right, as from ID_1 to ID_2 in Figure 14.8. Even though the government borrowing boosts the interest rate from 6 to 10 percent, total private investment need not fall. In the case shown as the move from *a* to *c* in Figure 14.8, it remains at $25 billion. Of course, the increase in investment demand might be smaller than that shown. If it were smaller, the crowding-out effect would not be fully offset. But the point is that an increase in private investment demand may counter the decline in investment that would otherwise result from the higher interest rate.

The Long-Run Fiscal Imbalance: Social Security

The most significant fiscal issue in the United States is not the budget deficit or the public debt but, rather, the long-term funding imbalance in the Social Security and Medicare programs. The total unfunded liabilities of the two programs exceeded $10 trillion in 2004. We will focus our attention on Social Security.

The Future Funding Shortfall

The Social Security program (excluding Medicare) has grown from less than one-half of 1 percent of U.S. GDP in 1950 to 4.4 percent of GDP today. That percentage is projected to grow to 6.5 percent of GDP in 2035 and even higher thereafter. There is a severe long-run shortfall in Social Security funding because of growing payments to retiring baby boomers.

The Social Security program is largely a "pay-as-you-go" plan, meaning that most of the current revenues from the 12.4 percent Social Security tax (the rate when the 2.9 percent Medicare tax is excluded) are paid out to current Social Security retirees. In anticipation of the large benefits owed to the baby boomers when they retire, however, the Social Security Administration has been placing an excess of current revenues over current payouts into the **Social Security trust fund,** consisting of U.S. Treasury securities. But the accumulation of money in the trust fund will be greatly inadequate for paying the retirement benefits promised to all future retirees.

Social Security trust fund
A Federal fund that saves excessive Social Security tax revenues received in one year to meet Social Security benefit obligations that exceed Social Security tax revenues in some subsequent year.

In 2017 Social Security retirement revenues will fall below Social Security retirement benefits, and the system will begin dipping into the trust fund to make up the difference. The trust fund will be exhausted in 2041, after which the promised retirement benefits will immediately exceed the Social Security tax revenues by an estimated 37 percent annually, rising to 56 percent annually in 2075. The Federal government faces a several-trillion-dollar shortfall of long-run revenues for funding Social Security.

As shown in Figure 14.9, the problem is one of demographics. The percentage of the American population age 62 or older will rise substantially over the next several decades, with the greatest increases for people who are age 75 and older. High fertility rates during the "baby boom" (1946–1964), declining birthrates thereafter, and rising life expectancies have combined to produce an aging population. In the future, more people will be receiving Social Security benefits for longer periods, and fewer workers will pay for each person's benefits. The number of workers per Social Security beneficiary was 5:1 in 1960. Today it is 3:1, and by 2040 it will be only 2:1.

There is no easy way to restore long-run balance to Social Security funding. Either benefits must be reduced or revenues must be increased. The Social Security Administration concludes that bringing projected Social Security revenues and payments

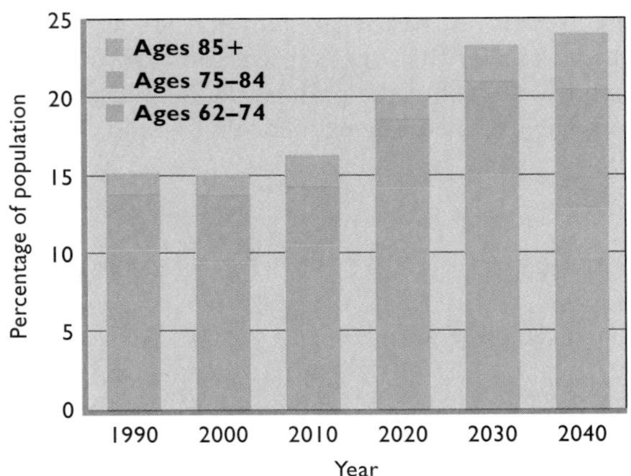

FIGURE 14.9
The aging U.S. population. The percentage of the U.S. population that is age 62 or older is rapidly rising. Depending on policy responses, this could result in a severe funding shortfall for Social Security in the decades ahead.

into balance over the next 75 years would require a 13 percent permanent reduction in Social Security benefits, a 15 percent permanent increase in tax revenues, or some combination of the two.[2]

© Ryan McVay/Getty Images/DIL

© Jack Hollingsworth/Getty Images/DIL

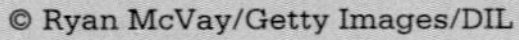

Photo Op Will Social Security Be There for You?

Social Security is largely a "pay-as-you-go" plan, in which current retirement benefits are paid out of current payroll taxes. But the number of retirees in the United States is growing faster than the number of workers, foretelling a future funding shortfall.

Policy Options

Several suggestions have been offered to help make Social Security financially sound. One idea is to boost the trust fund by investing all or part of it in corporate stocks and bonds. The Federal government would own the stock investments, and an appointed panel would oversee the direction of those investments. The presumed higher returns

[2] Social Security Board of Trustees, "Status of the Social Security and Medicare Programs: A Summary of the 2002 Annual Reports," www.ssa.gov.

on the investments relative to the lower returns on U.S. securities would stretch out the life of the trust fund. Nevertheless, a substantial increase in the payroll tax would still be needed to cover the shortfalls after the trust fund is exhausted.

Another option is to increase the payroll tax immediately—perhaps by as much as 1.5 percentage points—and allocate the new revenues to individual accounts. Government would own the accumulations in the accounts, but individuals could direct their investments to a restricted list of broad stock or bond funds. When they retire, recipients could convert these individual account balances to annuities—securities paying monthly payments for life. That annuity income would supplement reduced monthly benefits from the pay-as-you-go system when the trust fund is exhausted.

A different route is to place half the payroll tax into accounts that individuals, not the government, would own, maintain, and bequeath. Individuals could invest these funds in bank certificates of deposit or in approved stock and bond funds and draw upon the accounts when they reach retirement age. A flat monthly benefit would supplement the accumulations in the private accounts. The personal security accounts would be phased in over time, so people now receiving or about to receive Social Security benefits would continue to receive benefits.

These general ideas do not exhaust the possible reforms, since the variations on each plan are nearly endless. Reaching consensus on Social Security reform will be difficult because every citizen has a direct economic stake in the outcome. Nevertheless, society will eventually need to confront the problem of trillions of dollars of unfunded Social Security liabilities.

Summary

1. Fiscal policy consists of deliberate changes in government spending, taxes, or some combination of both to promote full employment, price-level stability, and economic growth. Fiscal policy requires increases in government spending, decreases in taxes, or both—a budget deficit—to increase aggregate demand and push an economy from a recession. Decreases in government spending, increases in taxes, or both—a budget surplus—are appropriate fiscal policy for dealing with demand-pull inflation.
2. Built-in stability arises from net tax revenues, which vary directly with the level of GDP. During recession, the Federal budget automatically moves toward a stabilizing deficit; during expansion, the budget automatically moves toward an anti-inflationary surplus. Built-in stability lessens, but does not fully correct, undesired changes in real GDP.
3. The standardized budget measures the Federal budget deficit or surplus that would occur if the economy operated at full employment throughout the year. Cyclical deficits or surpluses are those that result from changes in GDP. Changes in the standardized deficit or surplus provide meaningful information as to whether the government's fiscal policy is expansionary, neutral, or contractionary. Changes in the actual budget deficit or surplus do not, since such deficits or surpluses can include cyclical deficits or surpluses.
4. Certain problems complicate the enactment and implementation of fiscal policy. They include (a) timing problems associated with recognition, administrative, and operational lags; (b) the potential for misuse of fiscal policy for political rather than economic purposes; (c) the fact that state and local finances tend to be pro-cyclical; (d) potential ineffectiveness if households expect future policy reversals; and (e) the possibility of fiscal policy crowding out private investment.
5. Most economists believe that fiscal policy can help move the economy in a desired direction but cannot reliably be used to fine-tune the economy to a position of price stability and full employment. Nevertheless, fiscal policy is a valuable backup tool for aiding monetary policy in fighting significant recession or inflation.
6. The large Federal budget deficits of the 1980s and early 1990s prompted Congress in 1993 to increase tax rates and limit government spending.

As a result of these policies, along with a very rapid and prolonged economic expansion, the deficits dwindled to $22 billion in 1997. Large budget surpluses occurred in 1999, 2000, and 2001. In 2001 the Congressional Budget Office projected that $5 trillion of annual budget surpluses would accumulate between 2000 and 2010.

7. In 2001 the Bush administration and Congress chose to reduce marginal tax rates and phase out the Federal estate tax. A recession occurred in 2001, the stock market crashed, and Federal spending for the war on terrorism rocketed. The Federal budget swung from a surplus of $127 billion in 2001 to a deficit of $158 billion in 2002. In 2003 the Bush administration and Congress accelerated the tax reductions scheduled under the 2001 tax law and cut tax rates on capital gains and dividends. The purposes were to stimulate a sluggish economy. In 2004 the budget deficit reached $412 billion, and deficits were projected to continue through 2011 before surpluses again reemerge.
8. The public debt is the total accumulation of the government's deficits (minus surpluses) over time and consists of Treasury bills, Treasury notes, Treasury bonds, and U.S. savings bonds. In 2004 the U.S. public debt was $7.4 trillion, or $25,200 per person. The public (here including banks and state and local governments) holds 58 percent of that debt, while the Federal Reserve and Federal agencies hold the other 42 percent. Foreigners hold 26 percent of the U.S. public debit. Interest payments as a percentage of GDP were about 1.4 percent in 2004.
9. The concern that a large public debt may bankrupt the government is a false worry because (a) the debt need only be refinanced rather than refunded and (b) the Federal government has the power to increase taxes to make interest payments on the debt.
10. In general, the public debt is not a vehicle for shifting economic burdens to future generations. Americans inherit not only most of the public debt (a liability) but also most of the U.S. securities (an asset) that finance the debt.
11. More substantive problems associated with public debt include the following: (a) Payment of interest on the debt may increase income inequality. (b) Interest payments on the debt require higher taxes, which may impair incentives. (c) Paying interest or principal on the portion of the debt held by foreigners means a transfer of real output to abroad. (d) Government borrowing to refinance or pay interest on the debt may increase interest rates and crowd out private investment spending, leaving future generations with a smaller stock of capital than they would have otherwise.
12. The increase in investment in public capital that may result from debt financing may partly or wholly offset the crowding-out effect of the public debt on private investment. Also, the added public investment may stimulate private investment, where the two are complements.
13. The Social Security system has a significant long-run funding problem. The number of Social Security beneficiaries is projected to significantly rise in future years, and those retirees, on average, are expected to live longer than current retirees. Meanwhile, the number of workers paying Social Security taxes will increase relatively slowly. So a large gap between Social Security revenues and payments will eventually arise. This problem has created calls for various kinds of Social Security reform.

Terms and Concepts

fiscal policy
Council of Economic Advisers (CEA)
expansionary fiscal policy
budget deficit
contractionary fiscal policy
budget surplus
built-in stabilizer
standardized budget
cyclical deficit
political business cycle
crowding-out effect
public debt
U.S. securities
external public debt
investment demand curve
public investments
Social Security trust fund

Study Questions

1. The Federal government establishes its budget to decide what programs to provide and how to pay for them. How does fiscal policy differ from this ordinary fiscal activity of budgeting?
2. What are government's fiscal policy options for moving the economy out of a recession? Use the aggregate demand–aggregate supply model to show the impact of these policies on real GDP.

Checkable Deposits The safety and convenience of checks has made checkable deposits a large component of the $M1$ money supply. You would not think of stuffing $4896 in bills in an envelope and dropping it in a mailbox to pay a debt. But writing and mailing a check for a large sum is commonplace. The person cashing a check must endorse it (sign it on the reverse side); the writer of the check subsequently receives a record of the cashed check as a receipt attesting to the fulfillment of the obligation. Similarly, because the writing of a check requires a signature, the theft or loss of your checkbook is not nearly as calamitous as losing an identical amount of currency. Finally, it is more convenient to write a check than to transport and count out a large sum of currency. For all these reasons, **checkable deposits** (checkbook money) are a large component of the stock of money in the United States. About 49 percent of $M1$ is in the form of checkable deposits, on which checks can be drawn.

checkable deposits Deposits in banks or thrifts against which checks may be written.

It might seem strange that checking account balances are regarded as part of the money supply. But the reason is clear: Checks are nothing more than a way to transfer the ownership of deposits in banks and other financial institutions and are generally acceptable as a medium of exchange. Although checks are less generally accepted than currency for small purchases, for major purchases most sellers willingly accept checks as payment. Moreover, people can convert checkable deposits into paper money and coins on demand; checks drawn on those deposits are thus the equivalent of currency.

To summarize:

$$\text{Money, } M1 = \text{currency} + \text{checkable deposits}$$

Institutions That Offer Checkable Deposits In the United States, a variety of financial institutions allow customers to write checks in any amount on the funds they have deposited. **Commercial banks** are the primary depository institutions. They accept the deposits of households and businesses, keep the money safe until it is demanded via checks, and in the meantime use it to make available a wide variety of loans. Commercial bank loans provide short-term financial capital to businesses, and they finance consumer purchases of automobiles and other durable goods.

commercial banks Firms that engage in the business of banking (accepting deposits, offering checking accounts, and making loans).

Savings and loan associations (S&Ls), mutual savings banks, and credit unions supplement the commercial banks and are known collectively as savings or **thrift institutions,** or simply "thrifts." *Savings and loan associations* and *mutual savings banks* accept the deposits of households and businesses and then use the funds to finance housing mortgages and to provide other loans. *Credit unions* accept deposits from and lend to "members," who usually are a group of people who work for the same company.

thrift institutions Savings and loan associations, mutual savings banks, or credit unions that offer savings and checking accounts.

The checkable deposits of banks and thrifts are known variously as demand deposits, NOW (negotiable order of withdrawal) accounts, ATS (automatic transfer service) accounts, and share draft accounts. Their commonality is that depositors can write checks on them whenever, and in whatever amount, they choose.

A Qualification We must qualify our discussion in an important way. Currency held by commercial banks or other financial institutions is *excluded* from $M1$ and other measures of the money supply.

A paper dollar in the hands of, say, Emma Buck obviously constitutes just $1 of the money supply. But if we counted currency held by banks as part of the money supply, the same $1 would count for $2 when it was deposited in a bank. It would count for a $1 checkable deposit owned by Buck and also for $1 of currency resting in the bank's till or vault. By excluding currency resting in banks in determining the total money supply, we avoid this problem of double counting.

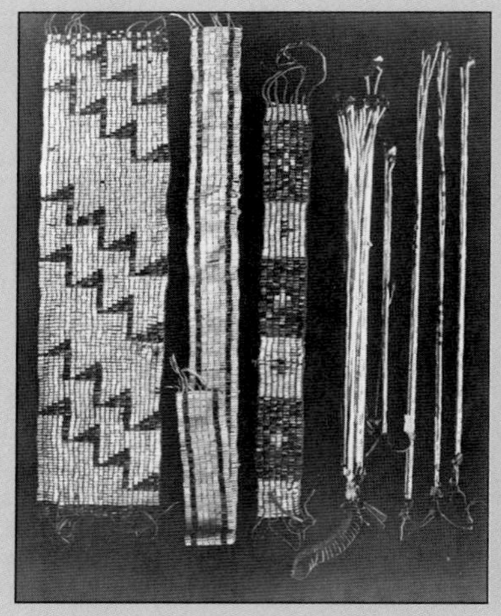
© CORBIS

© PhotoLink/Getty Images/DIL

© Getty Images/DIL

Photo Op Money: Then and Now

Items such as wampum belts were once used as money. Today, bills and coins, along with checkable deposits, constitute the *M*1 money supply.

Money Definition: *M*2

near-monies
Financial assets that do not directly serve as a medium of exchange but readily can be converted into narrowly defined money (currency + checkable deposits).

***M*2**
A more broadly defined money supply, equal to *M*1 plus noncheckable savings accounts (including money market deposit accounts), time deposits of less than $100,000, and individual money market mutual fund balances.

savings account
An interest-earning account (at a bank or thrift) from which funds normally can be withdrawn at any time.

A second and broader definition of money includes *M*1 plus several near-monies. **Near-monies** are certain highly liquid financial assets that do not function directly or fully as a medium of exchange but can be readily converted into currency or checkable deposits. There are three categories of near-monies included in the ***M*2** definition of money:

- ***Savings deposits, including money market deposit accounts*** A depositor can withdraw funds from an interest-earning **savings account** at a bank or thrift or simply request that the funds be transferred to a checkable account. A person can also withdraw funds from a **money market deposit account (MMDA),** which is an interest-earning account containing interest-earning short-term securities. MMDAs, however, have a minimum-balance requirement and a limit on how often a person can withdraw funds.
- ***Small (less than $100,000) time deposits*** Funds from **time deposits** become available at their maturity. For example, a person can convert a 6-month time deposit ("certificate of deposit" or simply "CD") to currency without penalty 6 months or more after it has been deposited. In return for this withdrawal limitation, the financial institution pays a higher interest rate on such deposits than it does on its MMDAs. Also, a person can "cash in" a CD before its maturity but must pay a severe penalty.
- ***Money market mutual funds*** By making a telephone call, using the Internet, or writing a check for $500 or more, a depositor can redeem shares in a **money market mutual fund (MMMF)** offered by a mutual fund company. Such companies combine the funds of individual shareholders to buy interest-bearing short-term credit instruments such as certificates of deposit and U.S. government securities. Then they can offer interest on the MMMF accounts of the shareholders (depositors) who jointly own those financial assets.

All three categories of near-monies imply substantial liquidity. In summary, *M*2 includes the immediate medium-of-exchange items (currency and checkable deposits) that constitute *M*1 plus certain near-monies that can be easily converted into currency and checkable deposits. In Figure 15.1 we see that the addition of all these items yields an *M*2 money supply that is about five times larger than the narrower *M*1 money supply. Thus, to summarize in equation form,

Money, *M*2 = *M*1 + savings deposits, including MMDAs + small (less than $100,000) time deposits + MMMFs

money market deposit account (MMDA) An interest-earning account (at a bank or thrift) consisting of short-term securities and on which a limited number of checks can be written each year.

time deposits Interest-earning deposits (at a bank or thrift) such as certificates of deposit (CDs) that depositors can withdraw without penalty after the end of a specified period.

money market mutual fund (MMMF) An interest-earning account at an investment company, which pools the funds of depositors to purchase short-term securities.

Actually, there is an entire spectrum of assets that vary slightly in terms of their liquidity or "moneyness" that are not included in *M*1 or *M*2. Because the simple *M*1 definition includes only items directly and immediately usable as a medium of exchange, it is often cited in discussions of the money supply. But, for some purposes economists prefer the broader *M*2 definition. For example, *M*2 is used as one of the 10 trend variables in the index of leading indicators (an economic forecasting tool). Still broader definitions of money are so inclusive that they have limited usefulness.

We will use the narrow *M*1 definition of the money supply in our discussion and analysis, unless stated otherwise. The important principles we will develop relating to *M*1 also apply to *M*2 because *M*1 is included in *M*2.

What "Backs" the Money Supply?

The money supply in the United States essentially is "backed" (guaranteed) by government's ability to keep the value of money relatively stable. Nothing more! Paper currency and checkable deposits have no intrinsic value. A $5 bill is just an inscribed piece of paper. A checkable deposit is merely a bookkeeping entry. And coins, we know, have less intrinsic value than their face value. Nor will government redeem the paper money you hold for anything tangible, such as gold. In effect, the government has chosen to "manage" the nation's money supply. Its monetary authorities attempt to provide the amount of money needed for the particular volume of business activity that will promote full employment, price-level stability, and economic growth.

Nearly all today's economists agree that managing the money supply is more sensible than linking it to gold or to some other commodity whose supply might change arbitrarily and capriciously. A large increase in the nation's gold stock as the result of a new gold discovery might increase the money supply too rapidly and thereby trigger rapid inflation. Or a long-lasting decline in gold production might reduce the money supply to the point where recession and unemployment resulted.

In short, people cannot convert paper money into a fixed amount of gold or any other precious commodity. Money is exchangeable only for paper money. If you ask the government to redeem $5 of your paper money, it will swap one paper $5 bill for another bearing a different serial number. That is all you can get. Similarly, checkable deposits can be redeemed not for gold but only for paper money, which, as we have just seen, the government will not redeem for anything tangible.

Value of Money

So why are currency and checkable deposits money, whereas, say, Monopoly (the game) money is not? What gives a $20 bill or a $100 checking account entry its value? The answer to these questions has three parts.

Acceptability Currency and checkable deposits are money because people accept them as money. By virtue of long-standing business practice, currency and checkable deposits perform the basic function of money: They are acceptable as a medium of exchange. We accept paper money in exchange because we are confident it will be exchangeable for real goods, services, and resources when we spend it.

legal tender
A legal designation of a nation's official currency (bills and coins).

Legal Tender Our confidence in the acceptability of paper money undoubtedly is strengthened because government has designated currency as **legal tender.** Specifically, each bill contains the statement "This note is legal tender for all debts, public and private." That means paper money is a valid and legal means of payment of debt. (But private firms and government are not mandated to accept cash. It is not illegal for them to specify payment in noncash forms such as checks, cashier's checks, money orders, or credit cards.)

The general acceptance of paper currency as money is more important than the government's decree that money is legal tender, however. The government has never decreed checks to be legal tender, and yet they serve as such in many of the economy's exchanges of goods, services, and resources. But it is true that government agencies—the Federal Deposit Insurance Corporation (FDIC) and the National Credit Union Administration (NCUA)—insure individual deposits of up to $100,000 at commercial banks and thrifts. That fact enhances our willingness to store money in checkable accounts and write checks on those accounts to buy goods, services, and resources.

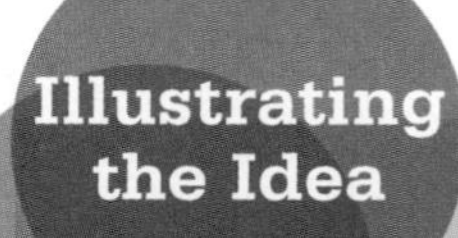

Are Credit Cards Money?

You may wonder why we have ignored credit cards such as Visa and MasterCard in our discussion of the money supply. After all, credit cards are a convenient way to buy things and account for about 25 percent of the dollar value of all transactions in the United States. The answer is that a credit card is not money. Rather, it is a convenient means of obtaining a short-term loan from the financial institution that issued the card.

What happens when you purchase an item with a credit card? The bank that issued the card will reimburse the store, charging it a transaction fee, and later you will reimburse the bank. Rather than reduce your cash or checking account with each purchase, you bunch your payments once a month. You may have to pay an annual fee for the services provided, and if you pay the bank in installments, you will pay a sizable interest charge on the loan. Credit cards are merely a means of deferring or postponing payment for a short period. Your checking account balance used to pay your monthly credit card bill *is* money; the credit card is *not* money.*

Although credit cards are not money, they allow individuals and businesses to "economize" in the use of money. Credit cards enable people to hold less currency in their billfolds and have smaller checkable deposit balances (prior to the due date for paying the credit card bill) in their bank accounts. Credit cards also help people coordinate the timing of their expenditures with their receipt of income.

Question:
If credit cards are not money, why are they so popular?

*A bank debit card, however, is very similar to a blank check in your checkbook. Unlike a purchase with a credit card, a purchase with a debit card creates a direct "debit" (a subtraction) from your checking account balance. That checking account balance *is* money—it is part of *M*1.

Relative Scarcity The value of money, like the economic value of anything else, depends on its supply and demand. Money derives its value from its scarcity relative to its utility (its want-satisfying power). The utility of money lies in its capacity to be exchanged for goods and services, now or in the future. The economy's demand for money thus depends on the total dollar volume of transactions in any period plus the amount of money individuals and businesses want to hold for future transactions. With a reasonably constant demand for money, the supply of money will determine the value or "purchasing power" of the monetary unit (dollar, yen, peso, or whatever).

Money and Prices

The purchasing power of money is the amount of goods and services a unit of money will buy. When money rapidly loses its purchasing power, it loses its role as money.

The Purchasing Power of the Dollar The amount a dollar will buy varies inversely with the price level, meaning a reciprocal relationship exists between the general price level and the purchasing power of the dollar. When the Consumer Price Index or "cost-of-living" index goes up, the purchasing power of the dollar goes down, and vice versa. Higher prices lower the purchasing power of the dollar, because more dollars are needed to buy a particular amount of goods, services, or resources. For example, if the price level doubles, the purchasing power of the dollar declines by one-half, or 50 percent.

Conversely, lower prices increase the purchasing power of the dollar, because fewer dollars are needed to obtain a specific quantity of goods and services. If the price level falls by, say, one-half, or 50 percent, the purchasing power of the dollar doubles.

Inflation and Acceptability In Chapter 12 we noted situations in which a nation's currency became worthless and unacceptable in exchange. They were circumstances in which the government issued so many pieces of paper currency that the purchasing power of each of those units of money was almost totally undermined. The infamous post-World War I inflation in Germany is an example. In December 1919 there were about 50 billion marks in circulation. Four years later there were 496,585,345,900 billion marks in circulation! The result? The German mark in 1923 was worth an infinitesimal fraction of its 1919 value.[3]

Runaway inflation may significantly depreciate the purchasing power of money between the time it is received and the time it is spent. Rapid declines in the purchasing power of a currency may cause it to cease being used as a medium of exchange. Businesses and households may refuse to accept paper money in exchange because they do not want to bear the loss in its value that will occur while it is in their possession. (All this despite the fact that the government says that paper currency is legal tender!) Without an acceptable domestic medium of exchange, the economy may simply revert to barter. Alternatively, more internally stable currencies such as the U.S. dollar may come into widespread use.

Similarly, people will use money as a store of value only as long as there is no sizable deterioration in the value of that money because of inflation. And an economy can effectively employ money as a unit of account only when its purchasing power is

---

[3] Frank G. Graham, *Exchange, Prices and Production in Hyperinflation Germany, 1920–1923* (Princeton, N.J.: Princeton University Press, 1930), p. 13.

relatively stable. A monetary yardstick that no longer measures a yard (in terms of purchasing power) does not permit buyers and sellers to establish the terms of trade clearly. When the value of the dollar is declining rapidly, sellers will not know what to charge, and buyers will not know what to pay, for goods and services.

The Federal Reserve and the Banking System

Federal Reserve System
A central component of the U.S. banking system, consisting of the Board of Governors of the Federal Reserve and 12 regional Federal Reserve Banks.

A key element of the U.S. banking system is the **Federal Reserve System** (the "Fed"). As shown in Figure 15.2, a Board of Governors directs the activities of 12 Federal Reserve Banks, which in turn control the lending activity of the nation's banks and thrift institutions.

Board of Governors

Board of Governors
The seven-member group that supervises and controls the money and banking system of the United States; the Board of Governors of the Federal Reserve System; the Federal Reserve Board.

The central authority of the U.S. money and banking system is the **Board of Governors** of the Federal Reserve System. The U.S. president, with the confirmation of the Senate, appoints the seven Board members. Terms are 14 years and staggered so that one member is replaced every 2 years. In addition, new members are appointed when resignations occur. The president selects the chairperson and vice-chairperson of the Board from among the members. Those officers serve 4-year terms and can be reappointed to new 4-year terms by the president. The long-term appointments provide the Board with continuity, experienced membership, and independence from political pressures that could result in inflation.

The 12 Federal Reserve Banks

The 12 **Federal Reserve Banks,** which blend private and public control, collectively serve as the nation's "central bank." These banks also serve as bankers' banks.

FIGURE 15.2
The framework of the Federal Reserve System and its relationship to the nonbank public.
With the aid of the Federal Open Market Committee, the Board of Governors makes the basic policy decisions that provide monetary control of the U.S. money and banking system. The 12 Federal Reserve Banks implement these decisions.

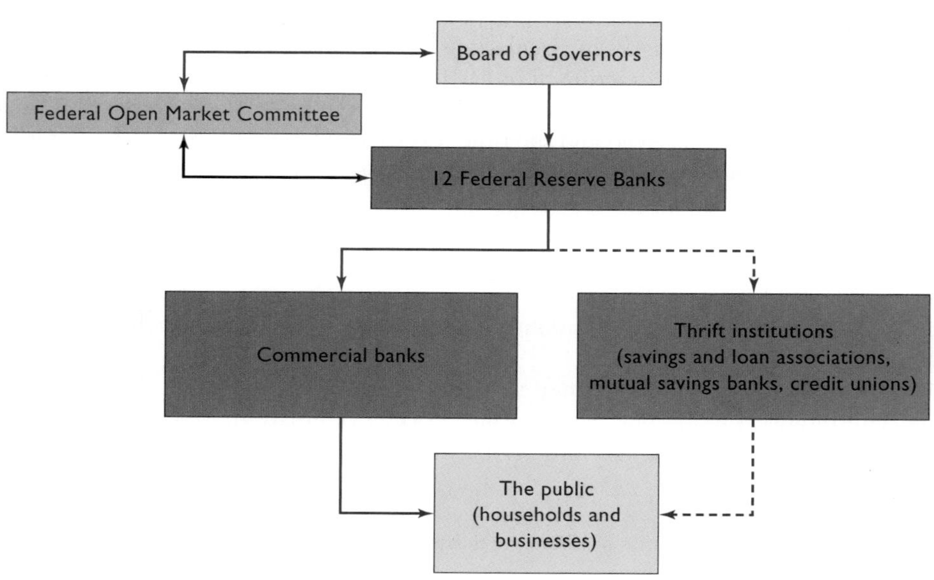

Central Banks Most nations have a single central bank—for example, Britain's Bank of England or Japan's Bank of Japan. The United States' central bank consists of 12 banks whose policies are coordinated by the Fed's Board of Governors. The 12 Federal Reserve Banks accommodate the geographic size and economic diversity of the United States and the nation's large number of commercial banks and thrifts.

Federal Reserve Banks
The 12 banks chartered by the U.S. government to control the money supply and perform other functions.

Figure 15.3 locates the 12 Federal Reserve Banks and indicates the district that each serves. These banks implement the basic policy of the Board of Governors.

Quasi-Public Banks The 12 Federal Reserve Banks are quasi-public banks, which blend private ownership and public control. Each Federal Reserve Bank is owned by the private commercial banks in its district. (Federally chartered commercial banks are required to purchase shares of stock in the Federal Reserve Bank in their district.) But the Board of Governors is an independent, quasi-government body that sets the basic policies that the Federal Reserve Banks pursue.

Despite their private ownership, the Federal Reserve Banks are in practice public institutions. Unlike private firms, they are not motivated by profit. The policies they follow are designed by the Board of Governors to promote the well-being of the economy as a whole. Also, the Federal Reserve Banks do not compete with commercial banks. In general, they do not deal with the public; rather, they interact with the government and commercial banks and thrifts.

Bankers' Banks The Federal Reserve Banks are "bankers' banks." They perform essentially the same functions for banks and thrifts as those institutions perform for the public. Just as banks and thrifts accept the deposits of and make loans to the public, so the central banks accept the deposits of and make loans to banks and thrifts. Normally, these loans average only about $150 million a day. But in emergency circumstances the Federal Reserve Banks become the "lender of last resort" to the banking system and can lend out as much as needed to ensure that banks and thrifts can meet their cash obligations. On the day after terrorists attacked the United States on September 11, 2001, the Fed lent $45 *billion* to U.S. banks and thrifts to make sure that the destruction and disruption did not precipitate a nationwide banking crisis.

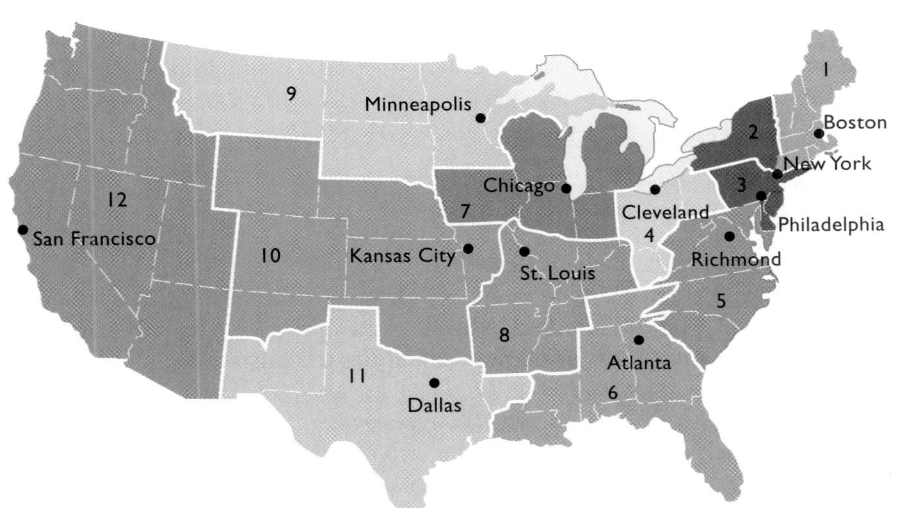

FIGURE 15.3
The 12 Federal Reserve Districts. The Federal Reserve System divides the United States into 12 districts, each having one central bank and in some instances one or more branches of the central bank. Hawaii and Alaska are included in the twelfth district.

Source: Federal Reserve System, www.federalreserve.gov.

But the Federal Reserve Banks have a third function, which banks and thrifts do not perform: They issue currency. Congress has authorized the Federal Reserve Banks to put into circulation Federal Reserve Notes, which constitute the economy's paper money supply.

FOMC

Federal Open Market Committee (FOMC)
The 12-member Federal Reserve group that determines the purchase and sale policies of the Federal Reserve Banks in the market for U.S. government securities.

The **Federal Open Market Committee (FOMC)** aids the Board of Governors in conducting monetary policy. The FOMC is made up of 12 individuals:

- The seven members of the Board of Governors.
- The president of the New York Federal Reserve Bank.
- Four of the remaining presidents of Federal Reserve Banks on a 1-year rotating basis.

The FOMC meets regularly to direct the purchase and sale of government securities (bills, notes, bonds) in the open market in which such securities are bought and sold on a daily basis. We will find in Chapter 16 that the purpose of these aptly named *open-market operations* is to control the nation's money supply and influence interest rates. The Federal Reserve Bank in New York City conducts most of the Fed's open-market operations.

Commercial Banks and Thrifts

There are about 7600 commercial banks. Roughly three-fourths are *state banks*, which are chartered (authorized) by individual states to operate within those states. The other one-fourth of all banks are *national banks*, chartered by the Federal government to operate nationally. Some of the U.S. national banks are very large, ranking among the world's largest financial institutions (see Global Snapshot 15.1). The 11,400 thrift institutions—the vast majority of which are credit unions—are regulated by agencies separate and apart from the Board of Governors and the Federal Reserve Banks. For example, the operations of savings and loan associations are regulated and monitored by the Treasury Department's Office of Thrift Supervision. But the thrifts *are* subject to monetary control by the Federal Reserve System. In particular, like the banks, thrifts are required to keep a certain percentage of their checkable deposits as reserves. In Figure 15.2 we use dashed arrows to indicate that the thrift institutions are partially subject to the control of the Board of Governors and the central banks. Decisions concerning monetary policy affect the thrifts along with the commercial banks.

Fed Functions and Responsibilities

The Fed performs several functions, some of which we have already mentioned. They and other functions are worth summarizing:

- ***Issuing currency*** The Federal Reserve Banks issue Federal Reserve Notes, the paper currency used in the U.S. monetary system. (The Federal Reserve Bank that issued a particular bill is identified in black in the upper left of the front of the newly designed bills. "A1," for example, identifies the Boston bank, "B2" the New York bank, and so on.)
- ***Setting reserve requirements and holding reserves*** The Fed sets legal reserve ratios, which are the fractions of checking account balances that banks must maintain as currency reserves. The central banks accept as deposits from the banks and thrifts any portion of their mandated reserves not held as vault cash.

Global Snapshot 15.1

The World's 12 Largest Financial Institutions

The world's 12 largest private sector financial institutions are headquartered in Europe, Japan, and the United States (2003 data).

	Assets (millions of U.S. dollars)
Mizuho Financial (Japan)	$1,282,589
Citigroup (U.S.)	1,264,032
Allianz (Germany)	1,178,643
UBS (Switzerland)	1,118,553
J.P Morgan Chase (U.S.)	1,097,475
HSBC Holdings (U.K.)	1,034,216
Deutsche Bank (Germany)	1,011,991
Fannie Mae (U.S.)	1,009,569
Mitsubishi Toyota (Japan)	992,695
Credit Agricole (France)	989,863
BNP Paribas (France)	986,128
ING Group (Netherlands)	980,706

Source: *Wall Street Journal*, Sept. 27, 2004, p. R12.

- ***Lending money to banks and thrifts*** From time to time the Fed lends money to banks and thrifts and charges them an interest rate called the *discount rate.* In times of financial emergencies, the Fed serves as a lender of last resort to the U.S. banking industry.
- ***Providing for check collection*** The Fed provides the banking system with a means for collecting checks. If Sue writes a check on her Miami bank or thrift to Joe, who deposits it in his Dallas bank or thrift, how does the Dallas bank collect the money represented by the check drawn against the Miami bank? Answer: The Fed handles it in 2 or 3 days by adjusting the reserves (deposits) of the two banks.
- ***Acting as fiscal agent*** The Fed acts as the fiscal agent (provider of financial services) for the Federal government. The government collects huge sums through taxation, spends equally large amounts, and sells and redeems bonds. To carry out these activities, the government uses the Fed's facilities as its bank.
- ***Supervising banks*** The Fed supervises the operations of banks. It makes periodic examinations to assess bank profitability, to ascertain that banks perform in accordance with the many regulations to which they are subject, and to uncover questionable practices or fraud.[4]

[4] The Fed is not alone in this task of supervision. The individual states supervise all banks that they charter. The Comptroller of the Currency supervises all national banks, and the Office of Thrift Supervision supervises all thrifts. Also, the Federal Deposit Insurance Corporation supervises all banks and thrifts whose deposits it insures.

- ***Controlling the money supply*** Finally, the major task of the Fed is to manage the nation's money supply, and thus indirectly set interest rates, according to the needs of the economy. This involves making an amount of money available that is consistent with high and rising levels of output and employment and a relatively constant price level. While all the other functions of the Fed are routine activities or have a service nature, managing the nation's money supply requires making basic, but unique, policy decisions. (We discuss those decisions in detail in Chapter 16.)

Federal Reserve Independence

Congress purposely established the Fed as an independent agency of government. The objective was to protect the Fed from political pressures so that it could effectively control the money supply and interest rates in order to maintain price-level stability. Political pressures on Congress and the executive branch may at times result in inflationary fiscal policies, including tax cuts and special-interest spending. If Congress and the executive branch also controlled the nation's monetary policy, citizens and lobbying groups undoubtedly would pressure elected officials to keep interest rates low even though at times high interest rates are necessary to reduce aggregate demand and thus control inflation. An independent monetary authority (the Fed) can take actions to increase interest rates when higher rates are needed to stem inflation. Studies show that countries that have independent central banks like the Fed have lower rates of inflation, on average, than countries that have little or no central bank independence.

The Fractional Reserve System

fractional reserve banking system A banking system in which banks and thrifts are required to hold less than 100 percent of their checkable-deposit liabilities as cash reserves.

We have seen that the *M*1 money supply consists of currency (coins and Federal Reserve Notes) and checkable deposits. The U.S. Mint creates the coins and the U.S. Bureau of Engraving creates the Federal Reserve Notes. So who creates the checkable deposits that make up about half the nation's *M*1 money supply? Surprisingly, it is loan officers at banks and thrifts!

The United States, like most other countries today, has a **fractional reserve banking system** in which only a portion (fraction) of the total money supply is held in reserve as currency. Our goal is to explain how commercial banks and thrifts can create checkable deposits by issuing loans. Our examples will involve commercial banks, but remember that thrift institutions also provide checkable deposits. So the analysis applies to banks and thrifts alike.

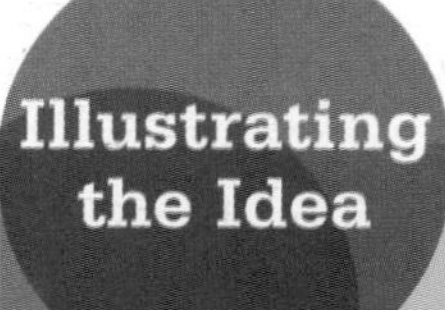

The Goldsmiths

Here is the history behind the idea of the fractional reserve system.

When early traders began to use gold in making transactions, they soon realized that it was both unsafe and inconvenient to carry gold and to have it weighed and assayed (judged for purity) every time they negotiated a transaction. So by the sixteenth century they had begun to deposit their gold with goldsmiths, who would store it in vaults for a fee. On receiving a gold deposit, the goldsmith would issue a receipt to the depositor. Soon people were paying for goods with goldsmiths' receipts, which served as the first kind of paper money.

At this point the goldsmiths—embryonic bankers—used a 100 percent reserve system; they backed their circulating paper money receipts fully with the gold that they held "in reserve" in their vaults. But because of the public's acceptance of the goldsmiths' receipts as paper money, the goldsmiths soon realized that owners rarely redeemed the gold they had in storage. In fact, the goldsmiths observed that the amount of gold being deposited with them in any week or month was likely to exceed the amount that was being withdrawn.

Then some clever goldsmith hit on the idea that paper "receipts" could be issued in excess of the amount of gold held. Goldsmiths would put these receipts, which were redeemable in gold, into circulation by making interest-earning loans to merchants, producers, and consumers. Borrowers were willing to accept loans in the form of gold receipts because the receipts were accepted as a medium of exchange in the marketplace.

This was the beginning of the fractional reserve system of banking, in which reserves in bank vaults are a fraction of the total money supply. If, for example, the goldsmith issued $1 million in receipts for actual gold in storage and another $1 million in receipts as loans, then the total value of paper money in circulation would be $2 million—twice the value of the gold. Gold reserves would be a fraction (one-half) of outstanding paper money.

Question:
Explain how the gold receipts issued by goldsmiths performed the three major functions of money.

The goldsmith story highlights two significant characteristics of fractional reserve banking. First, banks can create money through lending. In fact, goldsmiths created money when they made loans by giving borrowers paper money that was not fully backed by gold reserves. The quantity of such money goldsmiths could create depended on the amount of reserves they deemed prudent to have available. The smaller the amount of reserves thought necessary, the larger the amount of paper money the goldsmiths could create. Today, gold is no longer used as bank reserves. Instead, the creation of checkable-deposit money by banks (via their lending) is limited by the amount of *currency reserves* that the banks feel obligated, or are required by law, to keep.

A second reality is that banks operating on the basis of fractional reserves are vulnerable to "panics" or "runs." A goldsmith who issued paper money equal to twice the value of his gold reserves would be unable to convert all that paper money into gold in the event that all the holders of that money appeared at his door at the same time demanding their gold. In fact, many European and U.S. banks were once ruined by this unfortunate circumstance. However, a bank panic is highly unlikely if the banker's reserve and lending policies are prudent. Indeed, one reason why banking systems are highly regulated industries is to prevent runs on banks. This is also the reason why the United States has a system of deposit insurance.

A Single Commercial Bank

To illustrate the workings of the modern fractional reserve banking system, we need to examine a commercial bank's balance sheet.

The **balance sheet** of a commercial bank (or thrift) is a statement of assets and claims on assets that summarizes the financial position of the bank at a certain time.

balance sheet
A statement of the assets, liabilities, and net worth of a firm, individual, or institution at some time.

Every balance sheet must balance; this means that the value of *assets* must equal the amount of claims against those assets. The claims shown on a balance sheet are divided into two groups: the claims of nonowners against the firm's assets, called *liabilities*, and the claims of the owners of the firm against the firm's assets, called *net worth*. A balance sheet is balanced because

Assets = liabilities + net worth.

For every $1 change in assets, there must be an offsetting $1 change in liabilities + net worth. For every $1 change in liabilities + net worth, there must be an offsetting $1 change in assets.

Now let's work through a series of bank transactions involving balance sheets to establish how individual banks can create money.

Transaction 1: Creating a Bank

Suppose some farsighted citizens of the town of Somewhere decide their town needs a new commercial bank to provide banking services for that growing community. Once they have secured a state or national charter for their bank, they turn to the task of selling, say, $250,000 worth of stock certificates (equity shares) to buyers, both in and out of the community. Their efforts meet with success and the Bank of Somewhere comes into existence—at least on paper. What does its balance sheet look like at this stage?

The founders of the bank have sold $250,000 worth of shares of stock in the bank—some to themselves, some to other people. As a result, the bank now has $250,000 in cash on hand and $250,000 worth of stock certificates outstanding. The cash is an asset to the bank. Cash held by a bank is sometimes called *vault cash* or *till money*. The shares of stock outstanding constitute an equal amount of claims that the owners have against the bank's assets. Those shares of stock constitute the net worth of the bank. The bank's balance sheet reads:

Creating a Bank

Balance Sheet 1: Somewhere Bank

Assets		Liabilities and net worth	
Cash	$250,000	Stock shares	$250,000

Each item listed in a balance sheet such as this is called an *account*.

Transaction 2: Acquiring Property and Equipment

The board of directors (who represent the bank's owners) must now get the new bank off the drawing board and make it a reality. First, property and equipment must be acquired. Suppose the directors, confident of the success of their venture, purchase a building for $220,000 and pay $20,000 for office equipment. This simple transaction changes the composition of the bank's assets. The bank now has $240,000 less in cash and $240,000 of new property assets. Using blue to denote accounts affected by each transaction, we show that the bank's balance sheet at the end of transaction 2 appears as follows:

Acquiring Property and Equipment Balance Sheet 2: Somewhere Bank			
Assets		**Liabilities and net worth**	
Cash	$ 10,000	Stock shares	$250,000
Property	240,000		

Note that the balance sheet still balances, as it must.

Transaction 3: Accepting Deposits

Commercial banks have two basic functions: to accept deposits of money and to make loans. Now that the bank is operating, suppose that the citizens and businesses of Somewhere decide to deposit $100,000 in the Somewhere bank. What happens to the bank's balance sheet?

The bank receives cash, which is an asset to the bank. Suppose this money is deposited in the bank as checkable deposits (checking account entries), rather than as savings accounts or time deposits. These newly created *checkable deposits* constitute claims that the depositors have against the assets of the Somewhere bank and thus are a new liability account. The bank's balance sheet now looks like this:

Accepting Deposits Balance Sheet 3: Somewhere Bank			
Assets		**Liabilities and net worth**	
Cash	$110,000	Checkable deposits	$100,000
Property	240,000	Stock shares	250,000

There has been no change in the economy's total supply of money as a result of transaction 3, but a change has occurred in the composition of the money supply. Bank money, or checkable deposits, has increased by $100,000, and currency held by the public has decreased by $100,000. Currency held by a bank, you will recall, is not part of the economy's money supply.

A withdrawal of cash will reduce the bank's checkable-deposit liabilities and its holdings of cash by the amount of the withdrawal. This, too, changes the composition, but not the total supply, of money in the economy.

Transaction 4: Depositing Reserves in a Federal Reserve Bank

required reserves The funds that banks and thrifts must deposit with the Federal Reserve Bank (or hold as vault cash) to meet the Fed's reserve requirement.

reserve ratio The legally required percentage of reserves for every $1 of a bank or thrift's checkable deposits.

All commercial banks and thrift institutions that provide checkable deposits must by law keep **required reserves.** Required reserves are an amount of funds equal to a specified percentage of the bank's own deposit liabilities. A bank must keep these reserves on deposit with the Federal Reserve Bank in its district or as cash in the bank's vault. To simplify, we suppose the Bank of Somewhere keeps its required reserves entirely as deposits in the Federal Reserve Bank of its district. But remember that vault cash is counted as reserves and real-world banks keep a significant portion of their own reserves in their vaults.

The "specified percentage" of checkable-deposit liabilities that a commercial bank must keep as reserves is known as the **reserve ratio**—the ratio of the required reserves the commercial bank must keep to the bank's own outstanding checkable-deposit liabilities:

$$\text{Reserve ratio} = \frac{\text{commercial bank's required reserves}}{\text{commercial bank's checkable-deposit liabilities}}$$

If the reserve ratio is $\frac{1}{10}$, or 10 percent, the Somewhere bank, having accepted \$100,000 in deposits from the public, would have to keep \$10,000 as reserves. If the ratio is $\frac{1}{5}$, or 20 percent, \$20,000 of reserves would be required. If $\frac{1}{2}$, or 50 percent, \$50,000 would be required.

The Fed has the authority to establish and vary the reserve ratio within limits legislated by Congress. A 10 percent reserve is required on checkable deposits over \$45.4 million, although the Fed can vary that percentage between 8 and 14 percent. Also, after consultation with appropriate congressional committees, the Fed for 180 days may impose reserve requirements outside the 8–14 percent range.

In order to simplify, we will suppose that the reserve ratio for checkable deposits in commercial banks is $\frac{1}{5}$, or 20 percent. Although 20 percent obviously is higher than the requirement really is, the figure is convenient for calculations. The main point is that reserve requirements are fractional, meaning that they are less than 100 percent.

By depositing \$20,000 in the Federal Reserve Bank, the Somewhere bank will just be meeting the required 20 percent ratio between its reserves and its own deposit liabilities. We will use "reserves" to mean the funds commercial banks deposit in the Federal Reserve Banks, to distinguish those funds from the public's deposits in commercial banks.

But suppose the Somewhere bank anticipates that its holdings of checkable deposits will grow in the future. Then, instead of sending just the minimum amount, \$20,000, it sends an extra \$90,000, for a total of \$110,000. In so doing, the bank will avoid the inconvenience of sending additional reserves to the Federal Reserve Bank each time its own checkable-deposit liabilities increase. And, as you will see, it is these extra reserves that enable banks to lend money and earn interest income.

Actually, the bank would not deposit *all* its cash in the Federal Reserve Bank. However, because (1) banks as a rule hold vault cash only in the amount of $1\frac{1}{2}$ or 2.0 percent of their total assets and (2) vault cash can be counted as reserves, we can assume that all the bank's cash is deposited in the Federal Reserve Bank and therefore constitutes the commercial bank's actual reserves. Then we do not need to bother adding two assets—"cash" and "deposits in the Federal Reserve Bank"—to determine reserves.

After the Somewhere bank deposits \$110,000 of reserves at the Fed, its balance sheet becomes:

Depositing Reserves at the Fed
Balance Sheet 4: Somewhere Bank

Assets		Liabilities and net worth	
Cash	\$ 0	Checkable deposits	\$100,000
Reserves	110,000	Stock shares	250,000
Property	240,000		

excess reserves Actual bank or thrift reserves minus legally required reserves.

actual reserves The funds that a bank or thrift has on deposit at a Federal Reserve Bank or is holding as vault cash.

There are three things to note about this latest transaction.

Excess Reserves A bank's **excess reserves** are found by subtracting its *required reserves* (or legally required reserves) from its **actual reserves:**

Excess reserves = actual reserves − required reserves

In this case,

Actual reserves	\$110,000
Required reserves	−20,000
Excess reserves	\$ 90,000

The only reliable way of computing excess reserves is to multiply the bank's checkable-deposit liabilities by the reserve ratio to obtain required reserves (\$100,000 × 20 percent = \$20,000) and then to subtract the required reserves from the actual reserves listed on the asset side of the bank's balance sheet.

To test your understanding, compute the bank's excess reserves from balance sheet 4, assuming that the reserve ratio is (1) 10 percent, (2) $33\frac{1}{3}$ percent, and (3) 50 percent.

We will soon demonstrate that the ability of a commercial bank to make loans depends on the existence of excess reserves. Understanding this concept is crucial in seeing how the banking system creates money.

Control You might think the basic purpose of reserves is to enhance the liquidity of a bank and protect commercial bank depositors from losses. Reserves would constitute a ready source of funds from which commercial banks could meet large, unexpected cash withdrawals by depositors.

But this reasoning breaks down under scrutiny. Although historically reserves have been seen as a source of liquidity and therefore as protection for depositors, a bank's required reserves are not great enough to meet sudden, massive cash withdrawals. If the banker's nightmare should materialize—everyone with checkable deposits appearing at once to demand those deposits in cash—the legal reserves held as vault cash or at the Federal Reserve Bank would be insufficient. The banker simply could not meet this "bank panic." Because reserves are fractional, checkable deposits are usually much greater than a bank's required reserves.

So commercial bank deposits must be protected by other means. Periodic bank examinations are one way of promoting prudent commercial banking practices. Furthermore, as we have mentioned, government-sponsored deposit insurance funds insure individual deposits in banks and thrifts up to \$100,000.

If it is not the purpose of reserves to provide for commercial bank liquidity, then what is their function? *Control* is the answer. Required reserves help the Fed control the lending ability of commercial banks. The Fed can take certain actions that either increase or decrease commercial bank reserves and affect the ability of banks to grant credit. The objective is to prevent banks from overextending or underextending bank credit. To the degree that these policies successfully influence the volume of commercial bank credit, the Fed can help the economy avoid business fluctuations. Another function of reserves is to facilitate the collection or "clearing" of checks.

Transaction 5: Clearing a Check Drawn against the Bank

Assume that Fred Bradshaw, a Somewhere farmer, deposited a substantial portion of the \$100,000 in checkable deposits that the Somewhere bank received in transaction 3. Now suppose that Fred buys \$50,000 of farm machinery from the Ajax Farm

Implement Company of Elsewhere. Bradshaw pays for this machinery by writing a $50,000 check against his deposit in the Somewhere bank. He gives the check to the Ajax Company. What are the results?

Ajax deposits the check in its account with the Elsewhere bank. The Elsewhere bank increases Ajax's checkable deposits by $50,000 when Ajax deposits the check. Ajax is now paid in full. Bradshaw is pleased with his new machinery.

Now the Elsewhere bank has Bradshaw's check. This check is simply a claim against the assets of the Somewhere bank. The Elsewhere bank will collect this claim by sending the check (along with checks drawn on other banks) to the regional Federal Reserve Bank. Here a clerk will clear, or collect, the check for the Elsewhere bank by increasing Elsewhere's reserve in the Federal Reserve Bank by $50,000 and decreasing the Somewhere bank's reserve by that same amount. The check is "collected" merely by making bookkeeping notations to the effect that Somewhere's claim against the Federal Reserve Bank is reduced by $50,000 and Elsewhere's claim is increased by $50,000.

Finally, the Federal Reserve Bank sends the cleared check back to the Somewhere bank, and for the first time the Somewhere bank discovers that one of its depositors has drawn a check for $50,000 against his checkable deposit. Accordingly, the Somewhere bank reduces Bradshaw's checkable deposit by $50,000 and notes that the collection of this check has caused a $50,000 decline in its reserves at the Federal Reserve Bank. All the balance sheets balance: The Somewhere bank has reduced both its assets and its liabilities by $50,000. The Elsewhere bank has $50,000 more in assets (reserves) and in checkable deposits. Ownership of reserves at the Federal Reserve Bank has changed—with Somewhere owning $50,000 less and Elsewhere owning $50,000 more—but total reserves stay the same.

Whenever a check is drawn against one bank and deposited in another bank, collection of that check will reduce both the reserves and the checkable deposits of the bank on which the check is drawn. Conversely, if a bank receives a check drawn on another bank, the bank receiving the check will, in the process of collecting it, have its reserves and deposits increased by the amount of the check. In our example, the Somewhere bank loses $50,000 in both reserves and deposits to the Elsewhere bank. But there is no loss of reserves or deposits for the banking system as a whole. What one bank loses, another bank gains.

If we bring all the other assets and liabilities back into the picture, the Somewhere bank's balance sheet looks like this at the end of transaction 5:

Clearing a Check

Balance Sheet 5: Somewhere Bank

Assets		Liabilities and net worth	
Reserves	$ 60,000	Checkable deposits	$ 50,000
Property	240,000	Stock shares	250,000

Verify that with a 20 percent reserve requirement, the bank's excess reserves now stand at $50,000.

Transaction 6: Granting a Loan (Creating Money)

In addition to accepting deposits, commercial banks grant loans to borrowers. What effect does lending by a commercial bank have on its balance sheet?

Suppose the Gristly Meat Packing Company of Somewhere decides it is time to expand its facilities. Suppose, too, that the company needs exactly $50,000—which just happens to be equal to the Somewhere bank's excess reserves—to finance this project.

Gristly goes to the Somewhere bank and requests a loan for this amount. The Somewhere bank knows the Gristly Company's fine reputation and financial soundness and is convinced of its ability to repay the loan. So the loan is granted. In return, the president of Gristly hands a promissory note—a fancy IOU—to the Somewhere bank. Gristly wants the convenience and safety of paying its obligations by check. So, instead of receiving a bushel basket full of currency from the bank, Gristly gets a $50,000 increase in its checkable-deposit account in the Somewhere bank.

The Somewhere bank has acquired an interest-earning asset (the promissory note, which it files under "Loans") and has created checkable deposits (a liability) to "pay" for this asset. Gristly has swapped an IOU for the right to draw an additional $50,000 worth of checks against its checkable deposit in the Somewhere bank. Both parties are pleased.

At the moment the loan is completed, the Somewhere bank's position is shown by balance sheet 6a:

When a Loan Is Negotiated
Balance Sheet 6a: Somewhere Bank

Assets		Liabilities and net worth	
Reserves	$ 60,000	Checkable	
Loans	50,000	deposits	$100,000
Property	240,000	Stock shares	250,000

All this looks simple enough. But a close examination of the Somewhere bank's balance statement reveals a startling fact: *When a bank makes loans, it creates money.* The president of Gristly went to the bank with something that is *not* money—her IOU—and walked out with something that *is* money—a checkable deposit.

Contrast transaction 6a with transaction 3, in which checkable deposits were created but only as a result of currency having been taken out of circulation. There was a change in the *composition* of the money supply in that situation but no change in the *total supply* of money. But when banks lend, they create checkable deposits that *are* money. By extending credit, the Somewhere bank has "monetized" an IOU. Gristly and the Somewhere bank have created and then swapped claims. The claim created by Gristly and given to the bank is not money; an individual's IOU is not acceptable as a medium of exchange. But the claim created by the bank and given to Gristly *is* money; checks drawn against a checkable deposit are acceptable as a medium of exchange.

Much of the money we use in our economy is created through the extension of credit by commercial banks. This checkable-deposit money may be thought of as "debts" of commercial banks and thrift institutions. Checkable deposits are bank debts in the sense that they are claims that banks and thrifts promise to pay "on demand."

But there are factors limiting the ability of a commercial bank to create checkable deposits ("bank money") by lending. The Somewhere bank can expect the newly created checkable deposit of $50,000 to be a very active account. Gristly would not borrow $50,000 at, say, 7, 10, or 12 percent interest for the sheer joy of knowing that funds were available if needed.

Assume that Gristly awards a $50,000 building contract to the Quickbuck Construction Company. Quickbuck, true to its name, completes the expansion promptly and is paid with a check for $50,000 drawn by Gristly against its checkable deposit in the Somewhere bank. Quickbuck does not deposit this check in the Somewhere bank but instead deposits it in the Elsewhere bank. Elsewhere now has a $50,000 claim against the Somewhere bank. The check is collected in the manner described in transaction 5. As a result, the Somewhere bank loses both reserves and deposits equal to the amount of the check; Elsewhere acquires $50,000 of reserves and deposits.

In summary, assuming a check is drawn by the borrower for the entire amount of the loan ($50,000) and is given to a firm that deposits it in some other bank, the Somewhere bank's balance sheet will read as follows *after the check has been cleared against it:*

After a Check Is Drawn on the Loan
Balance Sheet 6b: Somewhere Bank

Assets		Liabilities and net worth	
Reserves	$ 10,000	Checkable deposits	$ 50,000
Loans	50,000		
Property	240,000	Stock shares	250,000

After the check has been collected, the Somewhere bank just meets the required reserve ratio of 20 percent (=$10,000/$50,000). The bank has *no* excess reserves. This poses a question: Could the Somewhere bank have lent more than $50,000—an amount greater than its excess reserves—and still have met the 20 percent reserve requirement when a check for the full amount of the loan was cleared against it? The answer is no; the bank is "fully loaned up."

Here is why: Suppose the Somewhere bank had lent $55,000 to the Gristly company. Collection of the check against the Somewhere bank would have lowered its reserves to $5000 (=$60,000 − $55,000), and checkable deposits would once again stand at $50,000 (=$105,000 − $55,000). The ratio of actual reserves to checkable deposits would then be $5000/$50,000, or only 10 percent. The Somewhere bank could thus not have lent $55,000.

By experimenting with other amounts over $50,000, you will find that the maximum amount the Somewhere bank could lend at the outset of transaction 6 is $50,000. This amount is identical to the amount of excess reserves the bank had available when the loan was negotiated. *A single commercial bank in a multibank banking system can lend only an amount equal to its initial preloan excess reserves.* When it lends, the lending bank faces the possibility that checks for the entire amount of the loan will be drawn and cleared against it. If that happens, the lending bank will lose (to other banks) reserves equal to the amount it lends. So, to be safe, it limits its lending to the amount of its excess reserves.

The Banking System: Multiple-Deposit Expansion

Thus far we have seen that a single bank in a banking system can lend one dollar for each dollar of its excess reserves. The situation is different for all commercial banks as a group. We will find that the commercial banking system can lend—that is, can create money—by a multiple of its excess reserves. This multiple lending is accomplished even though each bank in the system can lend only "dollar for dollar" with its excess reserves.

How do these seemingly paradoxical results come about? To answer this question, we must keep our analysis uncluttered and rely on three simplifying assumptions:

- The reserve ratio for all commercial banks is 20 percent.
- Initially all banks are meeting this 20 percent reserve requirement exactly. No excess reserves exist; or, in the parlance of banking, they are "loaned up" (or "loaned out") fully in terms of the reserve requirement.
- If any bank can increase its loans as a result of acquiring excess reserves, an amount equal to those excess reserves will be lent to one borrower, who will write a check for the entire amount of the loan and give it to someone else, who will deposit the check in another bank. This third assumption means that the worst thing possible happens to every lending bank—a check for the entire amount of the loan is drawn and cleared against it in favor of another bank.

The Banking System's Lending Potential

Suppose a junkyard owner finds a $100 bill while dismantling a car that has been on the lot for years. He deposits the $100 in bank A, which adds the $100 to its reserves. We will record only changes in the balance sheets of the various commercial banks. The deposit changes bank A's balance sheet as shown by entries (a_1):

Multiple-Deposit Expansion Process
Balance Sheet: Commercial Bank A

Assets		Liabilities and net worth	
Reserves	\$+100 (a_1) − 80 (a_3)	Checkable deposits	\$+100 (a_1) + 80 (a_2) − 80 (a_3)
Loans	+ 80 (a_2)		

Recall from transaction 3 that this \$100 deposit of currency does not alter the money supply. While \$100 of checkable-deposit money comes into being, it is offset by the \$100 of currency no longer in the hands of the nonbank public (the junkyard owner). But bank A *has* acquired excess reserves of \$80. Of the newly acquired \$100 in currency, 20 percent, or \$20, must be earmarked for the required reserves on the new \$100 checkable deposit, and the remaining \$80 goes to excess reserves. Remembering that a single commercial bank can lend only an amount equal to its excess reserves, we conclude that bank A can lend a maximum of \$80. When a loan for this amount is made, bank A's loans increase by \$80 and the borrower gets an \$80 checkable deposit. We add these figures—entries (a_2)—to bank A's balance sheet.

But now we employ our third assumption: The borrower draws a check (\$80) for the entire amount of the loan and gives it to someone who deposits it in bank B, a different bank. As we saw in transaction 6, bank A loses both reserves and deposits equal to the amount of the loan, as indicated in entries (a_3). The net result of these transactions is that bank A's reserves now stand at +\$20 (=\$100 − \$80), loans at +\$80, and checkable deposits at +\$100 (=\$100 + \$80 − \$80). When the dust has settled, bank A is just meeting the 20 percent reserve ratio.

Recalling our previous discussion, we know that bank B acquires both the reserves and the deposits that bank A has lost. Bank B's balance sheet is changed as in entries (b_1) at the top of the next page.

Multiple-Deposit Expansion Process
Balance Sheet: Commercial Bank B

Assets		Liabilities and net worth	
Reserves	\$+80 (b_1) −64 (b_3)	Checkable deposits	\$+80 (b_1) +64 (b_2) −64 (b_3)
Loans	+64 (b_2)		

When the borrower's check is drawn and cleared, bank A loses \$80 in reserves and deposits and bank B gains \$80 in reserves and deposits. But 20 percent, or \$16, of bank B's new reserves must be kept as required reserves against the new \$80 in checkable deposits. This means that bank B has \$64 (=\$80 − \$16) in excess reserves. It can therefore lend \$64 [entries (b_2)]. When the new borrower draws a check for the entire amount and deposits it in bank C, the reserves and deposits of bank B both fall by \$64 [entries (b_3)]. As a result of these transactions, bank B's reserves now stand at +\$16 (=\$80 − \$64), loans at +\$64, and checkable deposits at +\$80 (=\$80 + \$64 − \$64). After all this, bank B is just meeting the 20 percent reserve requirement.

We could go ahead with this procedure by bringing banks C, D, E, . . . , N into the picture. But that might be annoying! Instead, we summarize the entire analysis in Table 15.1. Our conclusion is startling: On the basis of only \$80 in excess reserves (acquired by the banking system when someone deposited \$100 of currency in bank A), the entire commercial banking system is able to lend \$400, the sum of the amounts in

TABLE 15.1

Expansion of the Money Supply by the Commercial Banking System

Bank	(1) Acquired Reserves and Deposits	(2) Required Reserves (Reserve Ratio = .2)	(3) Excess Reserves, (1) − (2)	(4) Amount Bank Can Lend; New Money Created = (3)
Bank A	\$100.00 (a_1)	\$20.00	**\$80.00**	\$ 80.00 (a_2)
Bank B	80.00 (a_3, b_1)	16.00	64.00	64.00 (b_2)
Bank C	64.00	12.80	51.20	51.20
Bank D	51.20	10.24	40.96	40.96
Bank E	40.96	8.19	32.77	32.77
Bank F	32.77	6.55	26.21	26.21
Bank G	26.21	5.24	20.97	20.97
Bank H	20.97	4.20	16.78	16.78
Bank I	16.78	3.36	13.42	13.42
Bank J	13.42	2.68	10.74	10.74
Bank K	10.74	2.15	8.59	8.59
Bank L	8.59	1.72	6.87	6.87
Bank M	6.87	1.37	5.50	5.50
Bank N	5.50	1.10	4.40	4.40
Other banks	21.99	4.40	17.59	17.59
Total amount of money created (sum of the amounts in column 4)				**\$400.00**

column 4. The banking system can lend excess reserves by a multiple of 5 when the reserve ratio is 20 percent. Yet each single bank in the banking system is lending only an amount equal to its own excess reserves. How do we explain this? How can the banking system lend by a multiple of its excess reserves, when each individual bank can lend only dollar for dollar with its excess reserves?

The answer is that reserves lost by a single bank are not lost to the banking system as a whole. The reserves lost by bank A are acquired by bank B. Those lost by B are gained by C. C loses to D, D to E, E to F, and so forth. Although reserves can be, and are, lost by individual banks in the banking system, there is no loss of reserves for the banking system as a whole.

An individual bank can safely lend only an amount equal to its excess reserves, but the commercial banking system can lend by a multiple of its excess reserves. Commercial banks as a group can create money by lending in a manner very different from that of the individual banks in the group.

The Monetary Multiplier

The banking system magnifies any original excess reserves into a larger amount of newly created checkable-deposit money. The *checkable-deposit multiplier*, or **monetary multiplier,** exists because the reserves and deposits lost by one bank become reserves of another bank. It magnifies excess reserves into a larger creation of checkable-deposit money. The monetary multiplier m is the reciprocal of the required reserve ratio R (the leakage into required reserves that occurs at each step in the lending process). In short,

monetary multiplier
The multiple of its excess reserves by which the banking system can expand checkable deposits and thus the money supply by making new loans.

$$\text{Monetary multiplier} = \frac{1}{\text{required reserve ratio}}$$

or, in symbols,

$$m = \frac{1}{R}$$

In this formula, m represents the maximum amount of new checkable-deposit money that can be created by a single dollar of excess reserves, given the value of R. By multiplying the excess reserves E by m, we can find the maximum amount of new checkable-deposit money, D, that can be created by the banking system. That is,

$$\text{Maximum checkable-deposit creation} = \text{excess reserves} \times \text{monetary multiplier}$$

or, more simply,

$$D = E \times m$$

In our example in Table 15.1, R is .20, so m is 5 (=1/.20). Then

$$D = \$80 \times 5 = \$400$$

Reversibility: The Multiple Destruction of Money

The process we have described is reversible. Just as money is created when banks make loans, money is destroyed when loans are paid off. Loan repayment, in effect, sets off a process of multiple destruction of money akin to the multiple creation process. Because loans are both made and paid off in any period, the direction of the money supply in a given period will depend on the net effect of the two processes. If the dollar amount of loans made in some period exceeds the dollar amount of loans paid off, checkable deposits will expand and the money supply will increase. In contrast, if the dollar amount of loans made in some period is less than the dollar amount of loans paid off, checkable deposits will contract and the money supply will decline.

The Bank Panics of 1930 to 1933

In the early months of the Great Depression, before there was deposit insurance, several financially weak banks went out of business. As word spread that customers of those banks had lost their deposits, a general concern arose that something similar could happen at other banks. Depositors became frightened that their banks did not, in fact, still have all the money they had deposited. And, of course, that is a reality in a fractional reserve banking system. Acting on their fears, people en masse tried to "cash out" their bank accounts by withdrawing their money before it was all gone. This "run on the banks" caused many previously financially sound banks to declare bankruptcy. More than 9000 banks failed within 3 years.

The massive conversion of checkable deposits to currency during 1930 to 1933 reduced the nation's money supply. This might seem strange, since a check written for "cash" reduces checkable-deposit money and increases currency in the hands of the public by the same amount. So how does the money supply decline? Our discussion of the money-creation process provides the answer, but now the story becomes one of money destruction.

Suppose that people collectively cash out $10 billion from their checking accounts. As an immediate result, checkable-deposit money declines by $10 billion, while currency held by the public increases by $10 billion. But here is the catch: Assuming a reserve ratio of 20 percent, the $10 billion of currency in the banks had been supporting $50 billion of deposit money, the $10 billion of deposits plus $40 billion created through loans. The $10 billion withdrawal of currency forces banks to reduce loans (and thus checkable-deposit money) by $40 billion to continue to meet their reserve requirement. In short, a $40 billion destruction of deposit money occurs. This is the scenario that occurred in the early years of the 1930s.

Accompanying this multiple contraction of checkable deposits was the banks' "scramble for liquidity" to try to meet further withdrawals of currency. To obtain more currency, they sold many of their holdings of government securities to the public. A bank's sale of government securities to the public, like a reduction in loans, reduces the money supply. People write checks for the securities, reducing their checkable deposits, and the bank uses the currency it obtains to meet the ongoing bank run. In short, the loss of reserves from the banking system, in conjunction with the scramble for security, reduced the amount of checkable-deposit money by far more than the increase in currency in the hands of the public. Thus, the money supply collapsed.

In 1933, President Franklin Roosevelt ended the bank panics by declaring a "national bank holiday," which closed all national banks for 1 week and resulted in the federally insured deposit program. Meanwhile, the nation's money supply had plummeted by about 23 percent, the largest such drop in U.S. history. This decline in the money supply contributed to the nation's deepest and longest depression.

Today, a multiple contraction of the money supply of the 1930–1933 magnitude is unthinkable. FDIC deposit insurance has kept individual bank failures from becoming general panics. Also, while the Fed stood idly by during the bank panics of 1930 to 1933, today it would take immediate and dramatic actions to maintain the banking system's reserves and the nation's money supply. Those actions are the subject of Chapter 16.

Question:
Why do fractional reserve banking and deposit insurance closely accompany one another in modern banking systems?

Summary

1. Conceptually, money is any item that society accepts as (a) a medium of exchange, (b) a unit of monetary account, and (c) a store of value.
2. In the United States, two "official" definitions of money are *M*1, consisting of currency (outside banks) and checkable deposits, and *M*2, consisting of *M*1 plus savings deposits, including money market deposit accounts, small (less than $100,000) time deposits, and money market mutual fund balances.
3. Money has value because of the goods, services, and resources it will command in the market. Maintaining the purchasing power of money depends largely on the government's effectiveness in managing the money supply to prevent inflation.
4. The U.S. banking system consists of (a) the Board of Governors of the Federal Reserve System, (b) the 12 Federal Reserve Banks, and (c) some 7600 commercial banks and 11,400 thrift institutions (mainly credit unions). The Board of Governors is the basic policymaking body for the entire banking system. The directives of the Board and the Federal Open Market Committee (FOMC) are made effective through the 12 Federal Reserve Banks, which are simultaneously (a) central banks, (b) quasi-public banks, and (c) bankers' banks.
5. The major functions of the Fed are to (a) issue Federal Reserve Notes, (b) set reserve requirements and hold reserves deposited by banks and thrifts, (c) lend money to banks and thrifts, (d) provide for the rapid collection of checks, (e) act as the fiscal agent for the Federal government, (f) supervise the operations of the banks, and (g) control the supply of money in the best interests of the economy.
6. The Fed is essentially an independent institution, controlled neither by the president of the United States nor by Congress. This independence shields the Fed from political pressure and allows it to raise and lower interest rates (via changes in the money supply) as needed to promote full employment, price stability, and economic growth.
7. Modern banking systems are fractional reserve systems: Only a fraction of checkable deposits is backed by currency. Commercial banks keep required reserves on deposit in a Federal Reserve Bank or as vault cash. These required reserves are equal to a specified percentage of the commercial bank's checkable-deposit liabilities. Excess reserves are equal to actual reserves minus required reserves.
8. Commercial banks create money—checkable deposits, or checkable-deposit money—when they make loans. The ability of a single commercial bank to create money by lending depends on the size of its excess reserves. Generally, a commercial bank can lend only an amount equal to its excess reserves. Money creation is thus limited because, in all likelihood, checks drawn by borrowers will be deposited in other banks, causing a loss of reserves and deposits to the lending bank equal to the amount of money lent.
9. The commercial banking system as a whole can lend by a multiple of its excess reserves because the system as a whole cannot lose reserves. Individual banks, however, can lose reserves to other banks in the system. The multiple by which the banking system can lend on the basis of each dollar of excess reserves is the reciprocal of the reserve ratio.
10. The bank panics of 1930–1933 resulted in a significant contraction of the U.S. money supply, contributed to the Great Depression, and gave rise to Federal deposit insurance.

Short-Term Nominal Interest Rates, Selected Nations

These data show the short-term nominal interest rates (percentage rates on 3-month loans) in various countries in 2004. Because these are nominal rates, much of the variation reflects differences in rates of inflation. But differences in central bank monetary policies and in risk of default also explain the variations.

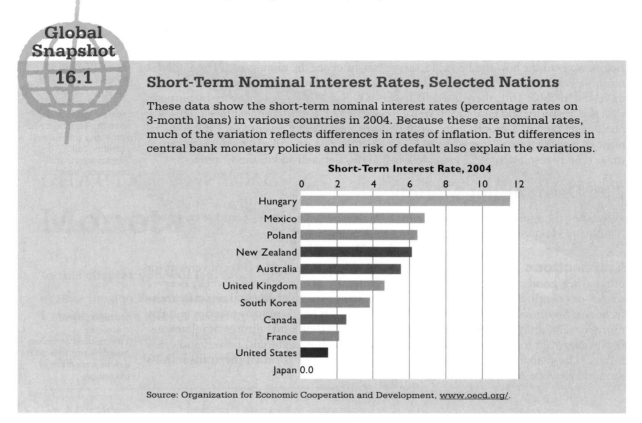

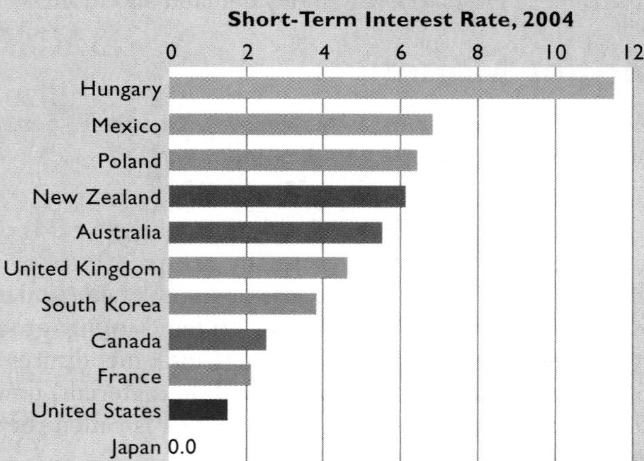

Source: Organization for Economic Cooperation and Development, www.oecd.org/.

The level of nominal GDP is the main determinant of the amount of money demanded for transactions. The larger the total money value of all goods and services exchanged in the economy, the larger the amount of money needed to negotiate those transactions. The transactions demand for money varies directly with nominal GDP. We specify *nominal* GDP because households and firms will want more money for transactions if prices rise or if real output increases. In both instances there will be a need for a larger dollar volume to accomplish the desired transactions.

In Figure 16.1a we graph the quantity of money demanded for transactions against the interest rate. For simplicity, let's assume that the amount demanded depends exclusively on the level of nominal GDP and is independent of the real interest rate. (In reality, higher interest rates are associated with slightly lower volumes of money demanded for transactions.) Our simplifying assumption allows us to graph the transactions demand, D_t, as a vertical line. This demand curve is positioned at $100 billion, on the assumption that each dollar held for transactions purposes is spent an average of three times per year and that nominal GDP is $300 billion. Thus the public needs $100 billion (=$300 billion/3) to purchase that GDP.

Asset Demand, D_a The second reason for holding money derives from money's function as a store of value. People may hold their financial assets in many forms, including corporate stocks, corporate or government bonds, or money. To the extent they want to hold money as an asset, there is an **asset demand** for money.

asset demand
The amount of money people want to hold as a store of value.

FIGURE 16.1

The demand for money, supply of money, and equilibrium interest rate. The total demand for money D_m is determined by horizontally adding the asset demand for money D_a to the transactions demand D_t. The transactions demand is vertical because it is assumed to depend solely on nominal GDP rather than on the interest rate. The asset demand varies inversely with the interest rate because of the opportunity cost involved in holding currency and checkable deposits that pay no interest or very low interest. Combining the money supply S_m with the total money demand D_m portrays the money market and determines the equilibrium interest rate i_e.

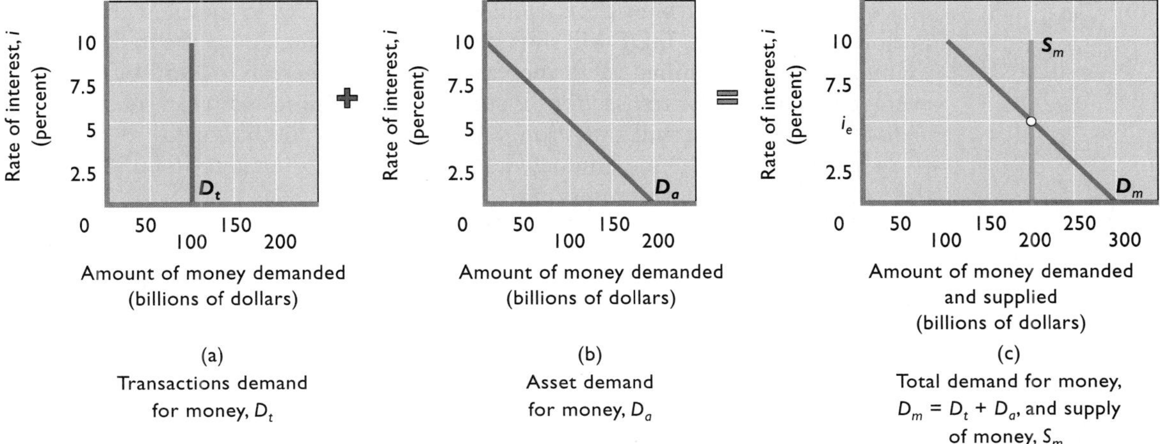

16.1 Liquidity preference

People like to hold some of their financial assets as money (apart from using it to buy goods and services) because money is the most liquid of all financial assets; it is immediately usable for purchasing other assets when opportunities arise. Money is also an attractive asset to hold when the prices of other assets such as bonds are expected to decline. For example, when the price of a bond falls, the bondholder who sells the bond prior to the payback date of the full principal will suffer a loss (called a *capital loss*). That loss will partially or fully offset the interest received on the bond. There is no such risk of capital loss in holding money.

The disadvantage of holding money as an asset is that it earns no or very little interest. Checkable deposits pay either no interest or lower interest rates than bonds. Idle currency, of course, earns no interest at all.

Knowing these advantages and disadvantages, the public must decide how much of its financial assets to hold as money, rather than other assets such as bonds. The answer depends primarily on the rate of interest. A household or a business incurs an opportunity cost when it holds money; in both cases, interest income is forgone or sacrificed. If a bond pays 6 percent interest, for example, it costs $6 per year of forgone income to hold $100 as cash or in a noninterest checkable account.

The amount of money demanded as an asset therefore varies inversely with the rate of interest (the opportunity cost of holding money as an asset). When the interest rate rises, it becomes more costly to be liquid and to avoid capital losses. The public reacts by reducing its holdings of money as an asset. When the interest rate falls, the cost of being liquid and avoiding capital losses also declines. The public therefore increases the amount of financial assets that it wants to hold as money. This inverse relationship just described is shown by D_a in Figure 16.1b.

total demand for money The sum of the transaction demand and asset demand for money.

Total Money Demand, D_m As shown in Figure 16.1, we find the **total demand for money,** D_m, by horizontally adding the asset demand to the transactions demand. The resulting downward-sloping line in Figure 16.1c represents the total amount of money the public wants to hold, both for transactions and as an asset, at each possible interest rate.

Recall that the transactions demand for money depends on the nominal GDP. A change in the nominal GDP—working through the transactions demand for money—will shift the total money demand curve. Specifically, an increase in nominal GDP means that the public wants to hold a larger amount of money for transactions, and that extra demand will shift the total money demand curve to the right. In contrast, a decline in the nominal GDP will shift the total money demand curve to the left. As an example, suppose nominal GDP increases from $300 billion to $450 billion and the average dollar held for transactions is still spent three times per year. Then the transactions demand curve will shift from $100 billion (=$300 billion/3) to $150 billion (=$450 billion/3). The total money demand curve will then lay $50 billion farther to the right at each possible interest rate.

The Equilibrium Interest Rate

16.1 Equilibrium interest rate 

money market The market in which the demand for and the supply of money determine the interest rate (or series of interest rates) in the economy.

We can combine the demand for money with the supply of money to determine the equilibrium rate of interest. In Figure 16.1c the vertical line, S_m, represents the money supply. It is a vertical line because the monetary authorities and financial institutions have provided the economy with some particular stock of money. Here it is $200 billion.

Just as in a product market or a resource market, the intersection of demand and supply in the **money market** determines equilibrium price. Here, the equilibrium "price" is the *real* interest rate (i_e)—the inflation-adjusted price that is paid for the use of money over some time period.

That Is Interest

Interest is needed to entice individuals to give up liquidity or sacrifice their present consumption, that is, to let someone else use their money for a period of time. The following story told by economist Irving Fisher (1867–1947) helps illustrate the idea of the "time value of money." The irony is that it was Fisher who had earlier formalized this exact idea in his theory of interest.

> In the process of a massage, a masseur informed Fisher that he was a socialist who believed that "interest is the basis of capitalism and is robbery." Following the massage, Fisher asked, "How much do l owe you?"
>
> The masseur replied, "Thirty dollars."
>
> "Very well," said Fisher, "I will give you a note payable a hundred years hence. I suppose you have no objections to taking this note without any interest. At the end of that time, you, or perhaps your grandchildren, can redeem it."
>
> "But I cannot afford to wait that long," said the masseur.
>
> "I thought you said that interest was robbery. If interest is robbery, you ought to be willing to wait indefinitely for the money. If you are willing to wait ten years, how much would you require?"
>
> "Well, I would have to get more than thirty dollars."
>
> His point now made, Fisher replied, "That is interest."*

Question:
Who benefits most from lending at interest: the lender or the borrower?

* Irving Fisher, as quoted in Irving Norton Fisher, *My Father Irving Fisher* (New York: Comet, 1956), p. 77.

Tools of Monetary Policy

We can now explore how the Federal Reserve (the "Fed") can change the supply of money in the economy and therefore alter the interest rate. The Fed has three tools of monetary control it can use to alter the money supply: open-market operations, the reserve ratio, and the discount rate.

16.2 Tools of monetary policy

Open-Market Operations

Bond markets are "open" to all buyers and sellers of corporate and government bonds (securities). The Federal Reserve is the largest single holder of U.S. government securities. The U.S. government, not the Fed, issued these Treasury bills (short-term securities), Treasury notes (mid-term securities), and Treasury bonds (long-term securities) to finance past budget deficits. Over the decades, the Fed has purchased these securities from major financial institutions that buy and sell government and corporate securities for themselves or their customers.

The Fed's **open-market operations** consist of the buying of government bonds from, or the selling of government bonds to, commercial banks and the general public. (The Fed actually buys and sells the government bonds to commercial banks and the public through two-dozen or so large financial firms called *primary dealers*.) Open-market operations are the Fed's most important instrument for influencing the money supply.

open-market operations
The buying and selling of U.S. government securities by the Fed for purposes of carrying out monetary policy.

Buying Securities Suppose the Federal Open Market Committee (FOMC) directs the Federal Reserve Bank of New York to buy $100 million of government bonds. The Federal Reserve Bank indirectly purchases these bonds from commercial banks (or thrifts) or the public. In both cases the reserves of the commercial banks will increase.

When a Federal Reserve Bank buys government bonds from *commercial banks*, those banks send some of their holdings of securities to the Federal Reserve Bank. In paying for the securities, the Federal Reserve Bank in essence writes checks for $100 million to the commercial banks. The banks deposit the $100 million of checks in their own accounts. When the checks clear against the Federal Reserve Bank, $100 million of reserves flow to the commercial banks. Because there are no new checkable deposits, the entire $100 million of new reserves in the banking system are excess reserves.

We know from Chapter 15 that excess reserves allow the banking system to make loans (expand the money supply) by a multiple of excess reserves. Suppose the reserve requirement is 20 percent, so the monetary multiplier is 5. Then commercial banks can expand the $100 million of excess reserves to $500 million of new checkable deposit money.

The effect on commercial bank reserves is much the same when a Federal Reserve Bank purchases securities from the *general public* rather than directly from banks. The Federal Reserve Bank buys the $100 million of securities by issuing checks to the sellers, who deposit the checks in their checkable-deposit accounts at their commercial banks. When the checks clear, \$100 million of new reserves flow from the Federal Reserve Bank to the commercial banks. Because the banks need only 20 percent of the new reserves for the \$100 million of new checkable deposits, the commercial banks have excess reserves of \$80 million (=\$100 million of actual reserves − \$20 million of required reserves). They lend out the excess reserves, expanding checkable deposits by \$400 million (=5 × \$80 million). When added to the original checkable deposits of \$100 million, the \$400 million of loan-created checkable deposits result in a total of \$500 million of new money in the economy.

Selling Securities As you may suspect, when a Federal Reserve Bank sells government bonds, the reserves of commercial banks are reduced. Let's see why, this time dispensing with the math because it is the exact reverse of the prior examples.

When a Federal Reserve Bank sells securities in the open market to commercial banks, the Federal Reserve Bank gives up securities that the commercial banks acquire. To pay for those securities, the commercial banks in essence write checks payable to the Federal Reserve Bank. When the checks clear, reserves flow from the commercial banks to the Federal Reserve Bank. If all excess reserves are already lent out, this decline in commercial bank reserves produces a multiple decline in money created through lending. That is, the nation's money supply declines. This multiple decline in money will equal the decline in reserves times the monetary multiplier.

The outcome is the same when a Federal Reserve Bank sells securities to the public rather than directly to banks. The public pays for the securities with checks drawn on individuals' banks. When the checks clear, the commercial banks send reserves to the Federal Reserve Bank and reduce accordingly the checkable deposits of customers who wrote the checks. The lower reserves mean a multiple contraction of the money supply.

The Reserve Ratio

The Fed can also manipulate the reserve ratio in order to influence the ability of commercial banks to lend. Suppose a commercial bank's balance sheet shows that reserves are \$5000 and checkable deposits are \$20,000. If the reserve ratio is 20 percent (row 2, Table 16.2), the bank's required reserves are \$4000. Since actual reserves are \$5000, the excess reserves of this bank are \$1000. On the basis of \$1000 of excess reserves, this one bank can lend \$1000; however, the banking system as a whole can create a maximum of \$5000 of new checkable-deposit money by lending (column 7).

TABLE 16.2

The Effects of Changes in the Reserve Ratio on the Lending Ability of Commercial Banks

(1) Reserve Ratio, %	(2) Checkable Deposits	(3) Actual Reserves	(4) Required Reserves	(5) Excess Reserves, (3) − (4)	(6) Money-Creating Potential of Single Bank, = (5)	(7) Money-Creating Potential of Banking System
(1) 10	\$20,000	\$5000	\$2000	\$ 3000	\$ 3000	\$30,000
(2) 20	20,000	5000	4000	1000	1000	5,000
(3) 25	20,000	5000	5000	0	0	0
(4) 30	20,000	5000	6000	−1000	−1000	−3,333

Raising the Reserve Ratio Now, what if the Fed raised the reserve ratio from 20 to 25 percent? (See row 3.) Required reserves would jump from \$4000 to \$5000, shrinking excess reserves from \$1000 to zero. Raising the reserve ratio increases the amount of required reserves banks must keep. As a consequence, either the banks lose excess reserves, diminishing their ability to create money by lending, or they find their reserves deficient and are forced to contract checkable deposits and therefore the money supply. In the example in Table 16.2, excess reserves are transformed into required reserves, and the money-creating potential of our single bank is reduced from \$1000 to zero (column 6). Moreover, the banking system's money-creating capacity declines from \$5000 to zero (column 7).

What if the Fed increases the reserve requirement to 30 percent? (See row 4.) The commercial bank, to protect itself against the prospect of failing to meet this requirement, would be forced to lower its checkable deposits and at the same time increase its reserves. To reduce its checkable deposits, the bank could let outstanding loans mature and be repaid without extending new credit. This action would reduce the supply of money.

Lowering the Reserve Ratio What would happen if the Fed lowered the reserve ratio from the original 20 percent to 10 percent? (See row 1.) In this case, required reserves would decline from \$4000 to \$2000, and excess reserves would jump from \$1000 to \$3000. The single bank's lending (money-creating) ability would increase from \$1000 to \$3000 (column 6), and the banking system's money-creating potential would expand from \$5000 to \$30,000 (column 7). Lowering the reserve ratio transforms required reserves into excess reserves and enhances the ability of banks to create new money by lending.

The examples in Table 16.2 show that a change in the reserve ratio affects the money-creating ability of the *banking system* in two ways:

- It changes the amount of excess reserves.
- It changes the size of the monetary multiplier.

For example, when the legal reserve ratio is raised from 10 to 20 percent, excess reserves are reduced from \$3000 to \$1000 and the monetary multiplier is reduced from 10 to 5. The money-creating potential of the banking system declines from \$30,000 (=\$3000 × 10) to \$5000 (=\$1000 × 5). Raising the reserve ratio forces banks to reduce the amount of checkable deposits they create through lending.

Although changing the reserve ratio is a powerful technique of monetary control, it is infrequently used. The last such change was in 1992, when the Fed lowered the reserve ratio from 12 percent to 10 percent.

The Discount Rate

One of the functions of a central bank is to be a "lender of last resort." Occasionally, commercial banks have unexpected and immediate needs for additional funds. In such cases, each Federal Reserve Bank will make short-term loans to commercial banks in its district.

When a commercial bank borrows, it gives the Federal Reserve Bank a promissory note (IOU) drawn against itself and secured by acceptable collateral—typically U.S. government securities. Just as commercial banks charge interest on their loans, so too Federal Reserve Banks charge interest on loans they grant to commercial banks. The interest rate they charge is called the **discount rate.**

discount rate
The interest rate the Federal Reserve Banks charge on the loans they make to commercial banks and thrifts.

In providing the loan, the Federal Reserve Bank increases the reserves of the borrowing commercial bank. Since no required reserves need be kept against loans from Federal Reserve Banks, all new reserves acquired by borrowing from Federal Reserve Banks are excess reserves. In short, borrowing from the Federal Reserve Banks by commercial banks increases the reserves of the commercial banks and enhances their ability to extend credit.

The Fed has the power to set the discount rate at which commercial banks borrow from Federal Reserve Banks. From the commercial banks' point of view, the discount rate is a cost of acquiring reserves. A lowering of the discount rate entices commercial banks to obtain additional reserves, if needed, by borrowing from Federal Reserve Banks. When the commercial banks lend new reserves to bank customers, the money supply increases.

An increase in the discount rate discourages commercial banks from obtaining additional reserves through borrowing from the Federal Reserve Banks. So the Fed may raise the discount rate when it wants to restrict the money supply.

Easy Money and Tight Money

Suppose the economy faces recession and unemployment. The Fed decides that an increase in the supply of money is needed to increase aggregate demand so as to employ idle resources. To increase the supply of money, the Fed must increase the excess reserves of commercial banks. How can it do that?

- ***Buy securities*** By purchasing securities in the open market, the Fed can increase commercial bank reserves. When the Fed's checks for the securities are cleared against it, the commercial banks discover that they have more reserves.
- ***Lower the reserve ratio*** By lowering the reserve ratio, the Fed changes required reserves into excess reserves and increases the size of the monetary multiplier.
- ***Lower the discount rate*** By lowering the discount rate, the Fed may entice commercial banks to borrow more reserves from the Fed.

easy money policy Fed actions designed to increase the money supply, lower interest rates, and expand real GDP.

These actions are called an **easy money policy** (or *expansionary monetary policy*). Its purpose is to make bank loans less expensive and more available and thereby increase aggregate demand, output, and employment.

Suppose, on the other hand, excessive spending is pushing the economy into an inflationary spiral. Then the Fed should try to reduce aggregate demand by limiting or contracting the supply of money. That means reducing the reserves of commercial banks. How is that done?

- ***Sell securities*** By selling government bonds in the open market, the Federal Reserve Banks can reduce commercial bank reserves.
- ***Increase the reserve ratio*** An increase in the reserve ratio will automatically strip commercial banks of their excess reserves and decrease the size of the monetary multiplier.
- ***Raise the discount rate*** A boost in the discount rate will discourage commercial banks from borrowing from Federal Reserve Banks in order to build up their reserves.

tight money policy Fed actions to reduce (or restrict) the growth of the nation's money supply, increase interest rates, and restrain inflation.

These actions are called a **tight money policy** (or *restrictive monetary policy*). The objective is to tighten the supply of money in order to reduce spending and control inflation.

Relative Importance

Of the three instruments of monetary control, buying and selling securities in the open market is clearly the most important. This technique has the advantage of flexibility—government securities can be purchased or sold in large or small amounts—and the impact on bank reserves is prompt. And, compared with reserve-requirement changes, open-market operations work subtly and less directly. Furthermore, there is virtually no question about the ability of the Federal Reserve Banks to affect commercial bank reserves through the purchase and sale of bonds. The Federal Reserve Banks have very large holdings of government securities ($720 billion in 2005, for example). The sale of those securities could theoretically reduce commercial bank reserves to zero.

Changing the reserve requirement is a less important instrument of monetary control, and the Fed has used this technique only sparingly. Normally, it can accomplish its monetary goals easier through open-market operations. The limited use of changes in the reserve ratio undoubtedly relates to the fact that reserves earn no interest. Consequently, raising or lowering reserve requirements has a substantial effect on bank profits.

The discount rate has become a passive, not active, tool of monetary policy. The Fed now sets the discount rate at 1 percentage point above the Fed's targeted rate of interest on the overnight loans that commercial banks make to other commercial banks that need the funds to meet the required reserve ratio. When the interest rate on overnight loans rises or falls, the discount rate automatically rises or falls along with it. We will say more about the very important interest rate on overnight loans later in the chapter.

Monetary Policy, Real GDP, and the Price Level

16.2 Monetary policy

So far we have explained only how the Fed can change the money supply. Now we need to link up the money supply, the interest rate, investment spending, and aggregate demand to see how monetary policy affects the economy. How does monetary policy work?

Cause-Effect Chain

The three diagrams in Figure 16.2 will help you understand how monetary policy works toward achieving its goals.

Market for Money Figure 16.2a represents the market for money, in which the demand curve for money and the supply curve of money are brought together. Recall that the total demand for money is made up of the transactions and asset demands. The transactions demand is directly related to the nominal GDP. The asset demand is inversely related to the interest rate. The interest rate is the opportunity cost of holding money as an asset; the higher that cost, the smaller the amount of money the public wants to hold. The total demand for money D_m is thus inversely related to the interest rate, as is indicated in Figure 16.2a. Also, recall that an increase in nominal GDP will shift D_m to the right and a decline in nominal GDP will shift D_m to the left.

FIGURE 16.2

Monetary policy and equilibrium GDP. An easy money policy that shifts the money supply curve rightward from S_{m1} to S_{m2} lowers the interest rate from 10 to 8 percent. As a result, investment spending increases from \$15 billion to \$20 billion, shifting the aggregate demand curve rightward from AD_1 to AD_2, and real output rises from the recessionary level Q_1 to the full-employment level Q_f. A tight money policy that shifts the money supply curve leftward from S_{m3} to S_{m2} increases the interest rate from 6 to 8 percent. Investment spending thus falls from \$25 billion to \$20 billion, and the aggregate demand curve shifts leftward from AD_3 to AD_2, curtailing inflation.

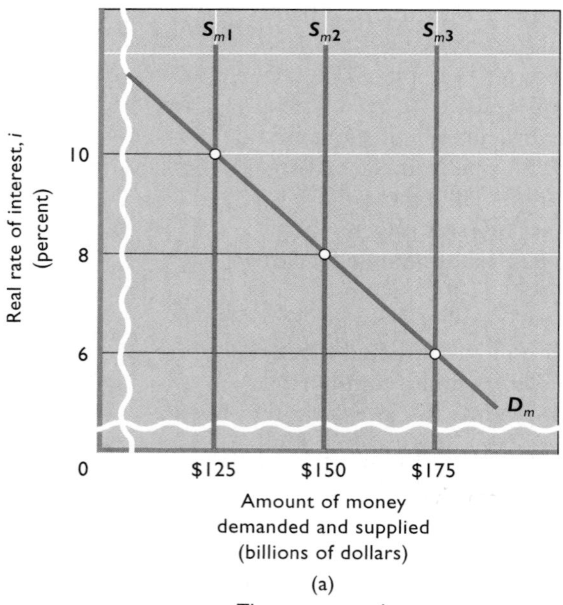

(a)
The money market

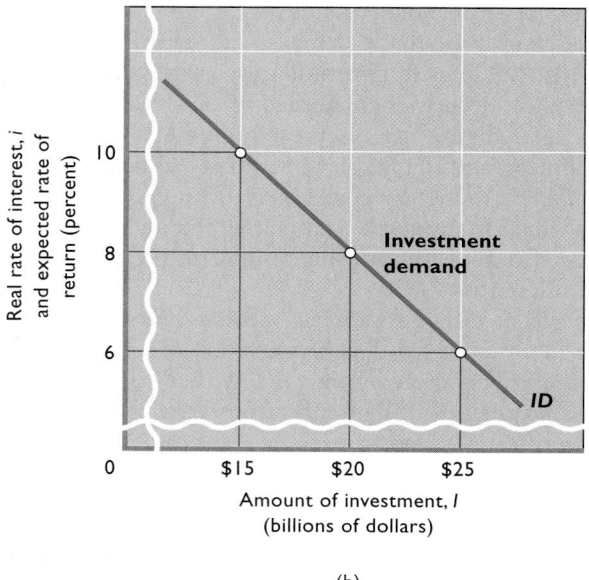

(b)
Investment demand

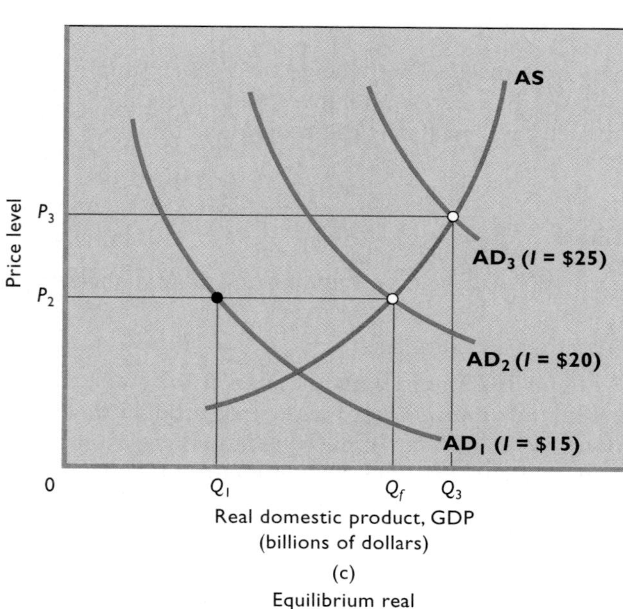

(c)
Equilibrium real GDP and the price level

This figure also shows three potential money supply curves, S_{m1}, S_{m2}, and S_{m3}. In each case the money supply is shown as a vertical line representing some fixed amount of money determined by the Fed. While monetary policy (specifically, the supply of money) helps determine the interest rate, the interest rate does not determine the location of the money supply curve.

The equilibrium interest rate is the rate at which the amount of money demanded and the amount supplied are equal. With money demand D_m in Figure 16.2a, if the supply of money is \$125 billion (S_{m1}), the equilibrium interest rate is 10 percent. With a money supply of \$150 billion (S_{m2}), the equilibrium interest rate is 8 percent; with a money supply of \$175 billion (S_{m3}), it is 6 percent.

Investment These 10, 8, and 6 percent real interest rates are carried rightward to the investment demand curve in Figure 16.2b. This curve shows the inverse relationship between the interest rate—the cost of borrowing to invest—and the amount of investment spending. At the 10 percent interest rate it will be profitable for the nation's businesses to invest \$15 billion; at 8 percent, \$20 billion; at 6 percent, \$25 billion.

Changes in the interest rate mainly affect the investment component of total spending, although they also affect spending on durable consumer goods (such as autos) that are purchased on credit. The impact of changing interest rates on investment spending is great because of the large cost and long-term nature of capital purchases. Manufacturing equipment, factory buildings, and warehouses are tremendously expensive. In absolute terms, interest charges on funds borrowed for these purchases are considerable.

Similarly, the interest cost on a house purchased on a long-term contract is very large: A percentage-point change in the interest rate would amount to thousands of dollars in the total cost of a typical home.

Also, changes in the interest rate may affect investment spending by changing the relative attractiveness of purchases of capital equipment versus purchases of bonds. In purchasing capital goods, the interest rate is the cost of borrowing the funds to make the investment. In purchasing bonds, the interest rate is the return on the financial investment. If the interest rate increases, the cost of buying capital goods increases while the return on bonds increases. Businesses are then more inclined to use business savings to buy securities than to buy equipment. Conversely, a drop in the interest rate makes purchases of capital goods relatively more attractive than bond ownership.

In brief, the impact of changing interest rates is mainly on investment (and, through that, on aggregate demand, output, employment, and the price level). Moreover, as Figure 16.2b shows, investment spending varies inversely with the interest rate.

Equilibrium GDP Figure 16.2c shows the impact of our three interest rates and corresponding levels of investment spending on aggregate demand. As noted, aggregate demand curve AD_1 is associated with the \$15 billion level of investment, AD_2 with investment of \$20 billion, and AD_3 with investment of \$25 billion. That is, investment spending is one of the determinants of aggregate demand. Other things equal, the greater the investment spending, the farther to the right lies the aggregate demand curve.

Suppose the money supply in Figure 16.2a is \$150 billion (S_{m2}), producing an equilibrium interest rate of 8 percent. In Figure 16.2b we see that this 8 percent interest rate will bring forth $20 billion of investment spending. This $20 billion of investment spending joins with consumption spending, net exports, and government spending to yield aggregate demand curve AD_2 in Figure 16.2c. The equilibrium levels of real output and prices are Q_f and P_2, as determined by the intersection of AD_2 and the aggregate supply curve AS.

To test your understanding of these relationships, explain why each of the other two levels of money supply in Figure 16.2a results in a different interest rate, level of investment, aggregate demand curve, and equilibrium real output.

Effects of an Easy Money Policy

Next, suppose that the money supply is $125 billion ($S_{m1}$) in Figure 16.2a. Because the resulting real output Q_1 in Figure 16.2c is far below the full-employment output, Q_f, the economy must be experiencing recession and substantial unemployment. The Fed therefore should institute an easy money policy.

To increase the money supply, the Federal Reserve Banks will take some combination of the following actions: (1) Buy government securities from banks and the public in the open market, (2) lower the legal reserve ratio, and (3) lower the discount rate. The intended outcome will be an increase in excess reserves in the commercial banking system. Because excess reserves are the basis on which commercial banks and thrifts can earn profit by lending and thus creating checkable-deposit money, the nation's money supply probably will rise. An increase in the money supply will lower the interest rate, increasing investment, aggregate demand, and equilibrium GDP.

For example, an increase in the money supply from $125 billion to $150 billion ($S_{m1}$ to S_{m2}) will reduce the interest rate from 10 to 8 percent, as indicated in Figure 16.2a, and will boost investment from $15 billion to $20 billion, as shown in Figure 16.2b. This $5 billion increase in investment will shift the aggregate demand curve rightward, as shown by the shift from AD_1 to AD_2 in Figure 16.2c. This rightward shift in the aggregate demand curve will eliminate the negative GDP gap by increasing GDP from Q_1 to the full-employment GDP of Q_f.[1]

Column 1 in Table 16.3 summarizes the chain of events associated with an easy money policy.

Effects of a Tight Money Policy

Now let's assume that the money supply is $175 billion ($S_{m3}$) in Figure 16.2a. This results in an interest rate of 6 percent, investment spending of $25 billion, and aggregate demand AD_3. As you can see in Figure 16.2c, we have depicted a positive GDP gap of $Q_3 - Q_f$ and demand-pull inflation. Aggregate demand AD_3 is excessive relative to the economy's full-employment level of real output Q_f. To rein in spending, the Fed will institute a tight money policy.

The Federal Reserve Board will direct Federal Reserve Banks to undertake some combination of the following actions: (1) Sell government securities to banks and the public in the open market, (2) increase the legal reserve ratio, and (3) increase the dis-

---

[1] For simplicity we assume that the increase in real GDP does not increase the demand for money. In reality, the transactions demand for money would rise, slightly dampening the decline in the interest rate shown in Figure 16.2a. We also assume that the price level was inflexible downward at P_3 when the economy entered the recession. So the easy money policy expands real GDP from Q_1 to Q_f without causing inflation.

TABLE 16.3
Monetary Policies for Recession and Inflation

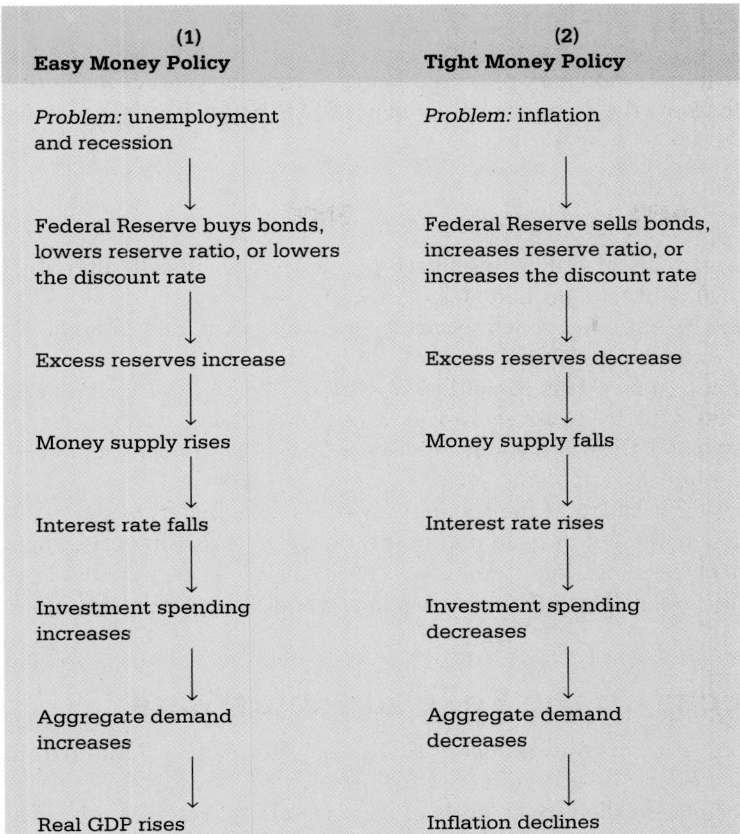

(1) Easy Money Policy	(2) Tight Money Policy
Problem: unemployment and recession	*Problem:* inflation
↓	↓
Federal Reserve buys bonds, lowers reserve ratio, or lowers the discount rate	Federal Reserve sells bonds, increases reserve ratio, or increases the discount rate
↓	↓
Excess reserves increase	Excess reserves decrease
↓	↓
Money supply rises	Money supply falls
↓	↓
Interest rate falls	Interest rate rises
↓	↓
Investment spending increases	Investment spending decreases
↓	↓
Aggregate demand increases	Aggregate demand decreases
↓	↓
Real GDP rises	Inflation declines

count rate. Banks then will discover that their reserves are below those required. So they will need to reduce their checkable deposits by refraining from issuing new loans as old loans are paid back. This will shrink the money supply and increase the interest rate. The higher interest rate will discourage investment, lowering aggregate demand and restraining demand-pull inflation.

If the Fed reduces the money supply from $175 billion to $150 billion ($S_{m3}$ to S_{m2} in Figure 16.2a), the interest rate will rise from 6 to 8 percent and investment will decline from $25 billion to $20 billion (Figure 16.2b). This $5 billion decrease in investment will shift the aggregate demand curve leftward from AD_3 to AD_2 (Figure 16.2c). This leftward shift of the aggregate demand curve will eliminate the excessive spending and halt the demand-pull inflation. In the real world, of course, the goal will be to stop inflation—that is, to halt further increases in the price level—rather than to actually drive down the price level, which tends to be inflexible downward.[2]

Column 2 in Table 16.3 summarizes the cause-effect chain of a tight money policy.

[2] Again, we assume for simplicity that the decrease in nominal GDP does not feed back to reduce the demand for money and thus the interest rate. In reality, this would occur, slightly dampening the increase in the interest rate shown in Figure 16.2a.

Monetary Policy in Action

We now turn from monetary policy in theory to monetary policy in action. Monetary policy has become the dominant component of U.S. national stabilization policy. It has two key advantages over fiscal policy:

- Speed and flexibility.
- Isolation from political pressure.

Compared with fiscal policy, monetary policy can be quickly altered. Recall that congressional deliberations may delay the application of fiscal policy for months. In contrast, the Fed can buy or sell securities from day to day and thus affect the money supply and interest rates almost immediately.

Also, because members of the Fed's Board of Governors are appointed and serve 14-year terms, they are relatively isolated from lobbying and need not worry about retaining their popularity with voters. Thus, the Board, more readily than Congress, can engage in politically unpopular policies (higher interest rates) that may be necessary for the long-term health of the economy. Moreover, monetary policy is a subtler and more politically neutral measure than fiscal policy. Changes in government spending directly affect the allocation of resources, and changes in taxes can have extensive political ramifications. Because monetary policy works more subtly, it is more politically palatable.

The Focus on the Federal Funds Rate

Federal funds rate
The interest rate banks and thrifts charge one another on overnight loans made out of their excess reserves.

The Fed currently focuses monetary policy on altering the **Federal funds rate** as needed to stabilize the economy. Normal day-to-day flows of funds to banks rarely leave all banks with their exact levels of legally required reserves. Also, funds held at the Federal Reserve Banks are highly liquid, but they do not draw interest. Banks therefore lend these excess reserves to other banks on an overnight basis to earn interest without sacrificing long-term liquidity. Banks that borrow in this Federal funds market—the market for immediately available reserve balances at the Federal Reserve—do so because they are temporarily short of required reserves. The interest rate paid on these overnight loans is called the *Federal funds rate.*

Because the Federal Reserve can control the supply of Federal funds—the supply of reserves in the banking system—it can control the Federal Funds interest rate. The Fed is a monopoly supplier of reserves. When it wants to increase the Federal funds rate, it sells securities in the open market to reduce (or withdraw) bank reserves. This is a "tighter" or "more restrictive" monetary policy. When it wants to reduce the Federal funds rate, it buys securities in the open market to increase (or inject) reserves. This is an "easier" or "more accommodating" monetary policy.

The Fed can target the Federal funds rate because it knows that interest rates in general typically rise and fall with that rate. For example, in Figure 16.3 observe that the **prime interest rate** generally parallels the Federal funds rate. The prime interest rate is the benchmark rate that banks use as a reference point for a wide range of interest rates on loans to businesses and individuals. By changing the Federal funds rate, the Fed in effect alters the economy's prime interest rate along with a wide array of other short-term interest rates.

prime interest rate
The benchmark interest rate that banks and thrifts use as a reference point for a wide range of loans to businesses and individuals.

Why the lockstep pattern between the Federal funds rate and the prime interest rate? Sales of securities by the Fed in the open market reduce excess reserves in the banking system, lessening the supply of excess reserves available for overnight loans in

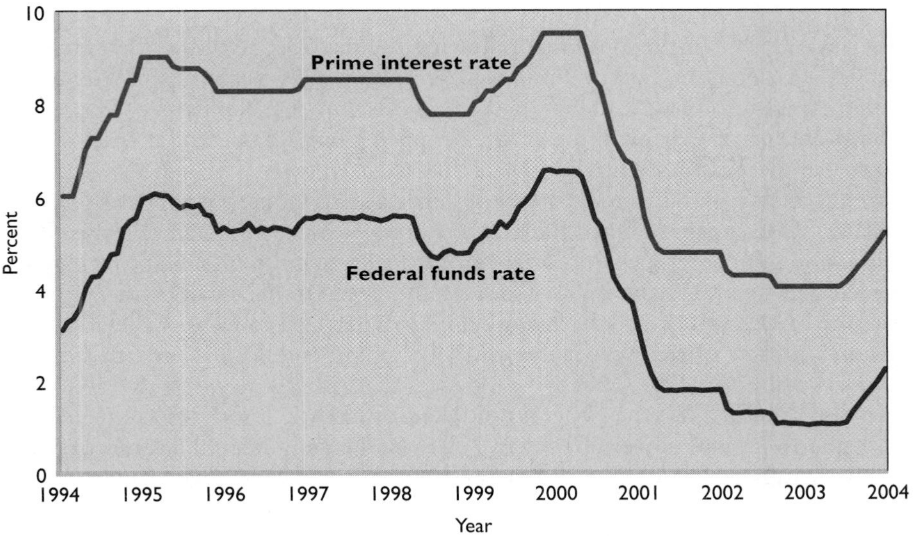

FIGURE 16.3
The prime interest rate and the Federal funds rate in the United States, 1994–2004. The prime interest rate rises and falls with changes in the Federal funds rate.

Source: Federal Reserve data, www.federalreserve.gov/.

the Federal funds market. The decreased supply of excess reserves in that market increases the Federal funds rate. In addition, reduced excess reserves decrease the amount of bank lending and hence the amount of checkable-deposit money. Declines in the supply of money produce higher interest rates in general, including the prime interest rate.

Purchases of securities by the Fed in the open market increase the supply of reserves in the Federal funds market, reducing the Federal funds rate. The money supply rises because the increased supply of excess reserves leads to more lending and thus greater creation of checkable-deposit money. As a result, interest rates in general fall, including the prime interest rate.

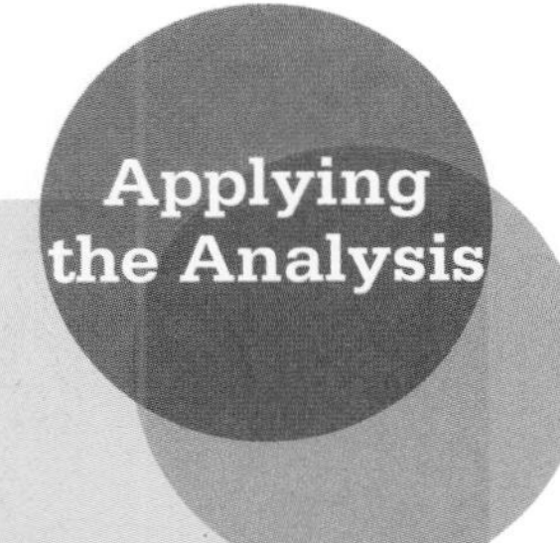

Recent U.S. Monetary Policy

In the early 1990s, the Fed's easy money policy helped the economy recover from the 1990–1991 recession. The expansion of GDP that began in 1992 continued through the rest of the decade. By 2000 the U.S. unemployment rate had declined to 4 percent—the lowest rate in 30 years. To counter potential inflation during that strong expansion, in 1994 and 1995, and then again in early 1997, the Fed reduced reserves in the banking system to raise the interest rate. In 1998 the Fed temporarily reversed its course and moved to an easier monetary policy to make sure that the U.S. banking system had plenty of liquidity in the face of a severe financial crisis in southeast Asia. The economy continued to expand briskly, and in 1999 and 2000 the Fed, in a series of steps, boosted interest rates to make sure that inflation remained under control.

Significant inflation did not occur in the late 1990s. But in the last quarter of 2000 the economy abruptly slowed. The Fed responded by cutting interest rates by a full percentage point in two increments in January 2001. Despite these rate cuts, the economy entered a recession in March 2001. Between March 20, 2001, and August 21, 2001, the Fed cut the Federal funds rate from 5 percent to 3.5 percent in a series of steps. In the 3 months following the terrorist attacks of September 11, 2001, it lowered the Federal funds rate from 3.5 to 1.75 percent, and it left the rate there until it lowered it to 1.25 percent in November 2002. Partly because of the Fed's actions, the prime interest rate dropped from 9.5 percent at the end of 2000 to 4.25 percent in December 2002.

Economists generally credit the Fed's adroit use of monetary policy as one of a number of factors that helped the U.S. economy achieve and maintain the rare combination of full employment, price stability, and strong economic growth that occurred between 1996 and 2000. The Fed also deserves high marks for helping to keep the recession of 2001 relatively mild, particularly in view of the adverse economic impacts of the terrorist attacks of September 11, 2001, and the steep stock market drop in 2001–2002.

In 2003 the Fed left the Federal funds rate at historic lows. But as the economy began to expand more robustly in 2004, the Fed engineered a series of five separate quarter-percentage-point hikes in the Federal funds rate. It continued to raise the rate in the first-half of 2005. The purpose was to boost the prime interest rate (6.5 percent in August 2005) to make sure that aggregate demand continued to grow at a noninflationary pace.

Question:
What is the current monetary policy stance of the Fed? Has it been increasing interest rates, decreasing them, or leaving them unchanged in recent months? (Answer this question by going to the Federal Reserve's Website, www.federalreserve.gov.)

Problems and Complications

Despite its recent successes in the United States, monetary policy has certain limitations and faces real-world complications.

Lags Recall that three elapses of time (lags)—a recognition lag, an administrative lag, and an operational lag—hinder the timing of fiscal policy. Monetary policy faces a similar recognition lag and operational lag, but avoids the administrative lag. Because of monthly variations in economic activity and changes in the price level, it may take the Fed a while to recognize that the economy is receding or the rate of inflation is rising (recognition lag). And once the Fed acts, it may take 3 to 6 months or more for interest-rate changes to have their full impacts on investment, aggregate demand, real GDP, and the price level (operational lag). These two lags thus complicate the timing of monetary policy.

cyclical asymmetry The potential problem of monetary policy successfully controlling inflation during the expansionary phase of the business cycle but failing to expand spending and real GDP during the recessionary phase of the cycle.

Cyclical Asymmetry Monetary policy may be highly effective in slowing expansions and controlling inflation but less reliable in pushing the economy from a severe recession. Economists say that monetary policy may suffer from **cyclical asymmetry.**

If pursued vigorously, a tight money policy could deplete commercial banking reserves to the point where banks would be forced to reduce the volume of loans. That would mean a contraction of the money supply, higher interest rates, and reduced aggregate demand. The Fed can turn down the monetary spigot and eventually achieve its goal.

But it cannot be certain of achieving its goal when it turns up the monetary spigot. An easy money policy suffers from a "You can lead a horse to water, but you cannot make it drink" problem. The Fed can create excess reserves, but it cannot guarantee that the banks will actually make the added loans and thus increase the supply of money. If commercial banks seek liquidity and are unwilling to lend, the efforts of the Fed will be of little avail. Similarly, businesses can frustrate the intentions of the Fed by not borrowing excess reserves. And the public may use money paid to them through Fed sales of U.S. securities to pay off existing bank loans.

Furthermore, a severe recession may so undermine business confidence that the investment demand curve shifts to the left and frustrates an easy money policy. That is what happened in Japan in the 1990s and early 2000s. Although its central bank drove the real interest rate to 0 percent, investment spending remained low and the Japanese economy stayed mired in recession. In fact, deflation—a fall in the price level—occurred. The Japanese experience reminds us that monetary policy is not an assured cure for the business cycle.

In March 2003 some members of the Fed's Open Market Committee expressed concern about potential deflation in the United States if the economy remained weak. But the economy began to expand, and deflation did not occur.

Pushing on a String

In the late 1990s and early 2000s, the central bank of Japan used an easy money policy to reduce real interest rates to zero. Even with "interest-free" loans available, most consumers and businesses did not borrow and spend more. Japan's economy continued to sputter in and out of recession.

The Japanese circumstance illustrates the possible *asymmetry* of monetary policy, which economists have likened to "pulling versus pushing on a string." A string may be effective at pulling something back to a desirable spot, but it is ineffective at pushing it toward a desired location. So it is with monetary policy, say some economists. Monetary policy can readily *pull* the aggregate demand curve to the left, reducing demand-pull inflation. There is no limit on how much a central bank can restrict a nation's money supply and hike interest rates. Eventually, a sufficiently tight money policy will reduce aggregate demand and inflation.

But during severe recession, participants in the economy may be highly pessimistic about the future. If so, an easy money policy may not be able to *push* the aggregate demand curve to the right, increasing real GDP. The central bank can produce excess reserves in the banking system by reducing the reserve ratio, lowering the discount rate, and purchasing government securities. But commercial banks may not be able to find willing borrowers for those excess reserves, no matter how low interest rates fall. Instead of borrowing and spending, consumers and businesses may be more intent on reducing debt and increasing saving in preparation for expected worse times ahead. If so, monetary policy will be ineffective. Using it under those circumstances will be much like pushing on a string.

Question:
What levers does government have to push the economy from recession, if monetary policy fails?

"Artful Management" or "Inflation Targeting"?

Under the leadership of Alan Greenspan, the Fed and FOMC have artfully managed the money supply to avoid escalating inflation, on the one hand, and deep recession and deflation, on the other. The emphasis has been on achieving a multiple set of objectives: primarily to maintain price stability but also to smooth the business cycle, maintain high levels of employment, and promote strong economic growth. Greenspan and the FOMC have used their best judgment (and, some suggest, "Greenspan's personal intuition") to determine appropriate changes in monetary policy.

Some economists are concerned that this "artful management" may be unique to Greenspan and that someone less insightful may not be as successful. These economists say it would be beneficial to replace or combine the artful management of monetary policy with so-called **inflation targeting**—the annual statement of a target range of inflation, say, 1 to 2 percent, for the economy over some period such as 2 years. The Fed would then undertake monetary policy to achieve that goal, explaining to the public how each monetary action fits within its overall strategy. If the Fed missed its target, it would need to explain what went wrong. So inflation targeting would increase the "transparency" (openness) of monetary policy and increase Fed accountability. Several countries, including Canada, New Zealand, Sweden, and the United Kingdom, have adopted inflation targeting.

inflation targeting The annual statement of a target range of inflation for future years, coupled with monetary policy designed to achieve the goal.

Proponents of inflation targeting say that, along with increasing transparency and accountability, it would focus the Fed on what should be its main mission: controlling inflation. They say that an explicit commitment to price-level stability will create more certainty for households and firms about future product and input prices and create greater output stability. In the advocates' view, setting and meeting an inflation target is the single best way for the Fed to achieve its important subsidiary goals of full employment and strong economic growth.

But many economists are unconvinced by the arguments for inflation targeting. They say that the overall success of the countries that have adopted the policy has come at a time in which inflationary pressures, in general, have been weak. The truer test will occur under more severe economic conditions. Critics of inflation targeting say that it assigns too narrow a role for the Fed. They do not want to limit the Fed's discretion to adjust the money supply and interest rates to smooth the business cycle, independent of meeting a specific inflation target. Those who oppose inflation targeting say the recent U.S. monetary policy owes its success to adherence to sound principles of monetary policy, not simply to Greenspan's intuition. In view of the overall success of the Fed's monetary policies since 1990, ask critics, why saddle it with an explicit inflation target?

Summary

1. There are a set of interest rates that vary by loan purpose, size, risk, maturity, and taxability. Nevertheless, economists often speak of a single interest rate in order to simplify their analysis.
2. The total demand for money consists of the transactions demand and asset demand for money. The amount of money demanded for transactions varies directly with the nominal GDP; the amount of money demanded as an asset varies inversely with the interest rate. The money market combines the total demand for money with the money supply to determine equilibrium interest rates.

3. The goal of monetary policy is to help the economy achieve price stability, full employment, and economic growth.
4. The three instruments of monetary policy are (a) open-market operations, (b) the reserve ratio, and (c) the discount rate.
5. The Fed's most often used monetary policy tool is its open-market operations. The Fed injects reserves into the banking system (and reduces interest rates) by buying securities from commercial banks and the general public. The Fed withdraws reserves from the banking system (and increases interest rates) by selling securities to commercial banks and the general public.
6. Monetary policy affects the economy through a complex cause-effect chain: (a) Policy decisions affect commercial bank reserves; (b) changes in reserves affect the money supply; (c) changes in the money supply alter the interest rate; (d) changes in the interest rate affect investment; (e) changes in investment affect aggregate demand; (f) changes in aggregate demand affect the equilibrium real GDP and the price level. Table 16.3 draws together all the basic ideas relevant to the use of monetary policy.
7. The advantages of monetary policy include its flexibility and political acceptability. Recently, the Fed has targeted changes in the Federal funds rate as the immediate focus of its monetary policy. When it deems it necessary, the Fed uses open-market operations to change that rate, which is the interest rate banks charge one another on overnight loans of excess reserves. Interest rates in general, including the prime interest rate, rise and fall with the Federal funds rate. The prime interest rate is the benchmark rate that banks use as a reference rate for a wide range of interest rates on short-term loans to businesses and individuals.
8. In the recent past, the Fed has adroitly used monetary policy to hold inflation in check as the economy boomed, to limit the depth of the recession of 2001, and to promote economic recovery. Today, nearly all economists view monetary policy as a significant stabilization tool.
9. Monetary policy has two major limitations and potential problems: (a) Recognition and operation lags complicate the timing of monetary policy. (b) In a severe recession, the reluctance of firms to borrow and spend on capital goods may limit the effectiveness of an expansionary monetary policy.
10. Some economists recommend that the United States follow the lead of several other nations, including Canada and the United Kingdom, in replacing or combining the "artful management" of monetary policy with inflation targeting. Opponents of this idea believe it may unduly reduce the Fed's flexibility in smoothing business cycles.

Terms and Concepts

monetary policy
transactions demand
asset demand
total demand for money
money market
open-market operations
discount rate
easy money policy
tight money policy
Federal funds rate
prime interest rate
cyclical asymmetry
inflation targeting

Study Questions

1. What is the basic determinant of (a) the strength of the transactions demand for money (the location of the transactions demand for money curve) and (b) the amount of money demanded for assets, given a particular asset demand for money curve? How is the equilibrium interest rate in the market for money determined? Use a graph to show the impact of an increase in the total demand for money on the equilibrium interest rate (no change in money supply). Use your general knowledge of equilibrium prices to explain why the previous interest rate is no longer sustainable.
2. Assume that the following data characterize a hypothetical economy: money supply = \$200 billion; quantity of money demanded for transactions = \$150 billion; quantity of money demanded as an asset = \$10 billion at 12 percent interest, increasing by \$10 billion for each 2-percentage-point fall in the interest rate.
   a. What is the equilibrium interest rate? Explain.
   b. At the equilibrium interest rate, what are the quantity of money supplied, the total quantity of money demanded, the amount of money demanded for transactions, and the amount of money demanded as an asset?

Production Possibilities Analysis

To put the six factors underlying economic growth in proper perspective, let's first use the production possibilities analysis introduced in Chapter 1.

Growth and Production Possibilities

Recall that a curve like *AB* in Figure 17.1 is a production possibilities curve. It indicates the various *maximum* combinations of products an economy can produce with its fixed quantity and quality of natural, human, and capital resources and its stock of technological knowledge. An improvement in any of the supply factors will push the production possibilities curve outward, as from *AB* to *CD*.

But the demand factor reminds us that an increase in total spending is needed to move the economy from point *a* to a point on *CD*. And the efficiency factor reminds us that we need least-cost production and an optimal location on *CD* for the resources to make their maximum possible dollar contribution to total output. You will recall from Chapter 1 that this "best allocation" is determined by expanding production of each good until its marginal cost equals its marginal benefit. Here, we assume that this optimal combination of capital and consumer goods occurs at point *b*.

Example: The net increase in the size of the labor force in the United States in recent years has been 1.5 million to 2 million workers per year. That increment raises the economy's production capacity. But obtaining the extra output that these added workers could produce depends on their success in finding jobs. It also depends on whether or not the jobs are in firms and industries where the workers' talents are fully and optimally used. Society does not want new labor-force entrants to be unemployed. Nor does it want pediatricians working as plumbers or pediatricians producing services for which marginal costs exceed marginal benefits.

Normally, increases in total spending match increases in production capacity, and the economy moves from a point on the previous production possibilities curve to a point on the expanded curve. Moreover, the competitive market system tends to drive

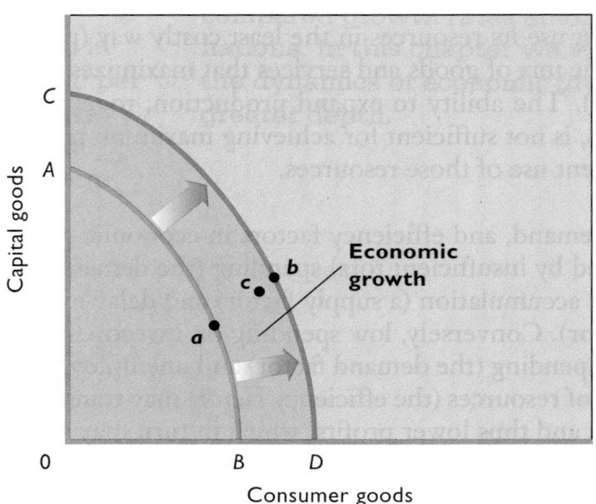

FIGURE 17.1
Economic growth and the production possibilities curve. Economic growth is made possible by the four supply factors that shift the production possibilities curve outward, as from *AB* to *CD*. Economic growth is realized when the demand factor and the efficiency factor move the economy from point *a* to *b*.

the economy toward productive and allocative efficiency. Occasionally, however, the curve may shift outward but leave the economy behind at some level of operation such as *c* in Figure 17.1. Because *c* is inside the new production possibilities curve *CD*, the economy has not realized its potential for economic growth.

Production Possibilities and Aggregate Supply

Economic growth can also be thought of as an expansion of an economy's long-run aggregate supply. Recall from Chapter 13 that the long-run aggregate supply curve shows the amount of real output forthcoming at various price levels, assuming an economy's wage and other input prices have responded fully to changes in the price level. The long-run aggregate supply curve graphs as a vertical line, located at the economy's potential (full-employment) level of output.

The supply factors that shift the economy's production possibilities curve outward also shift its long-run aggregate supply curve rightward. As shown in Figure 17.2, the outward shift of the production possibilities curve from *AB* to *CD* in graph (a) is equivalent to the rightward shift of the economy's long-run aggregate supply curve from AS_{LR1} to AS_{LR2} in graph (b). The two long-run aggregate supply curves are vertical because an economy's potential output—its full-employment output—is determined by the supply and efficiency factors, not by its price level. Whatever the price level, the economy's potential output remains the same. Moreover, just as price-level changes do not shift an economy's production possibilities curve, they do not shift an economy's long-run aggregate supply curve.

17.1 Growth theory

FIGURE 17.2

Production possibilities and long-run aggregate supply. (a) Supply factors shift an economy's production possibilities curve outward, as from *AB* to *CD*. (b) The same factors (along with the efficiency factor) shift the economy's long-run aggregate supply curve to the right, as from AS_{LR1} to AS_{LR2}.

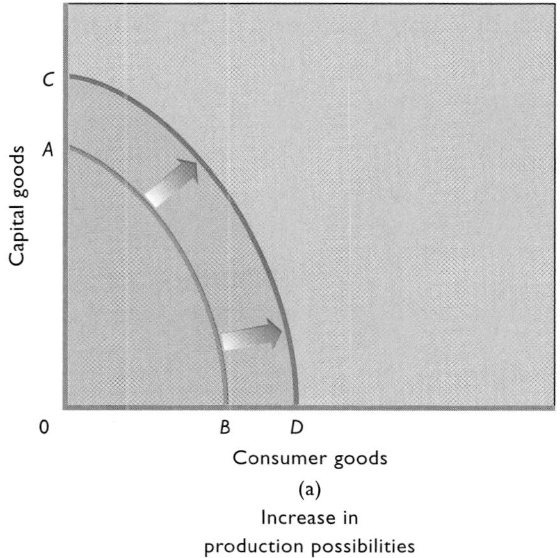

(a) Increase in production possibilities

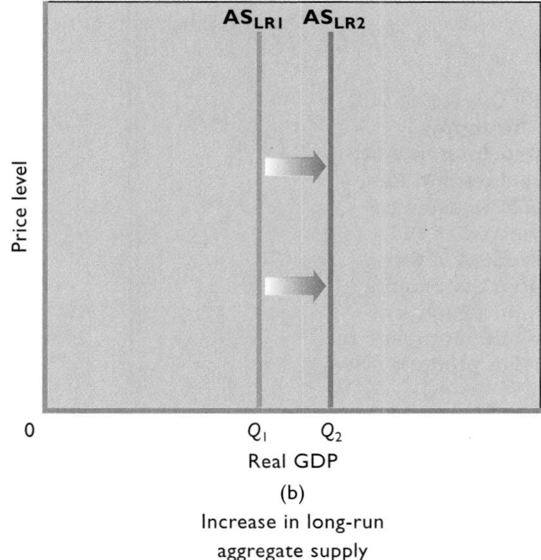

(b) Increase in long-run aggregate supply

Inputs and Productivity

Society can increase long-run aggregate supply, and thus expand its output and income, in two fundamental ways: (1) by increasing its inputs of resources, and (2) by raising the productivity of those inputs. Figure 17.3 concentrates on the input of *labor* and provides a useful framework for discussing the role of supply factors in growth. A nation's real GDP in any year depends on the input of labor (measured in hours of work) multiplied by **labor productivity** (measured as real output per hour of work).

labor productivity Real output per hour of work.

So, thought of this way, a nation's economic growth from one year to the next depends on its *increase* in labor inputs (if any) and its *increase* in labor productivity (if any).

Illustration: Assume that the cool economy of Rapland has 10 workers in year 1, each working 2000 hours per year (50 weeks at 40 hours per week). The total input of labor therefore is 20,000 hours. If productivity (average real output per hour of work) is $10, then real GDP in Rapland will be $200,000 (=20,000 × $10). If work hours rise to 20,200 and labor productivity rises to $10.40, Rapland's real GDP will increase to $210,080 in year 2. Rapland's rate of economic growth will be about 5 percent [=($210,080 − $200,000)/$200,000] for the year.

Hours of Work What determines the number of hours worked each year? As shown in Figure 17.3, the hours of labor input depend on the size of the employed labor force and the length of the average workweek. Labor-force size depends on the size of the working-age population and the **labor-force participation rate**—the percentage of the working-age population actually in the labor force. The length of the average workweek is governed by legal and institutional considerations and by collective bargaining.

labor-force participation rate The percentage of the working-age population actually in the labor force.

Labor Productivity Figure 17.3 tells us that labor productivity is determined by technological progress, the quantity of capital goods available to workers, the quality of the labor itself, and the efficiency with which inputs are allocated, combined, and managed. Productivity rises when the health, training, education, and motivation of workers improve, when workers have more and better machinery and natural resources with which to work, when production is better organized and managed, and when labor is reallocated from less efficient industries to more efficient industries.

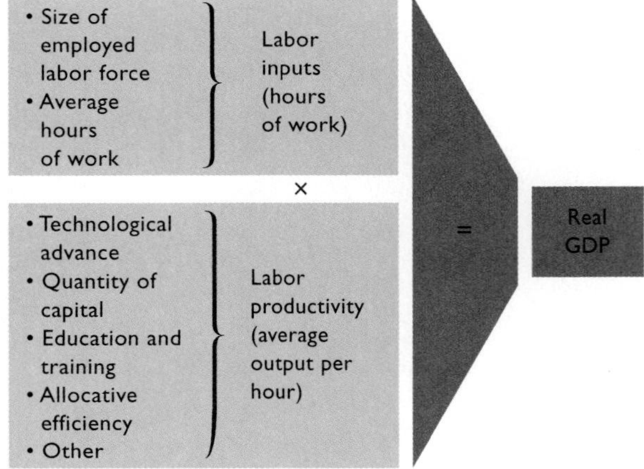

FIGURE 17.3 The supply determinants of real output. Real GDP is usefully viewed as the product of the quantity of labor inputs (hours of work) multiplied by labor productivity.

Applying the Analysis

U.S. Economic Growth Rates

More resources and greater productivity have fueled the growth of real GDP in the United States. Moreover, this output growth has far outstripped the population growth, resulting in a rise in real GDP per capita (=real GDP/population). Figure 17.4 shows the average annual growth rates of real GDP and real per capita GDP in the United States from 1950 through 2004. Over all these years, real GDP grew by 3.5 percent annually, whereas real GDP per capita grew by 2.3 percent a year. Economic growth was particularly strong in the 1960s but declined during the 1970s and 1980s. Although the average annual growth rate for the 1990s only slightly exceeded that of the 1980s, real GDP surged between 1996 and 1999. Specifically, it grew by 3.7 percent in 1996, 4.5 percent in 1997, 4.2 percent in 1998, and 4.5 percent in 1999. These growth rates were higher than previous rates in the 1990s and also higher than those in most other advanced industrial nations during that period.

Economic growth continued strong in 2000 in the United States, but it collapsed during the recessionary year 2001. Specifically, the rate was 3.7 percent in 2000 and 0.8 percent in 2001. Growth rates rebounded to 1.9 percent in 2002, 3.0 percent in 2003, and 4.4 percent in 2004.

Question:
Briefly explain why real GDP per capita traditionally has grown less rapidly than real GDP in the United States.

FIGURE 17.4

U.S. economic growth, annual averages for five decades. Growth of real GDP has averaged about 3.5 percent annually since 1950, and annual growth of real GDP per capita has averaged about 2.3 percent. Growth rates in the 1970s and 1980s were less than those in the 1960s, but the rates rebounded over the 1995–2004 period (not shown).

Source: Bureau of Economic Analysis, www.bea.gov/.

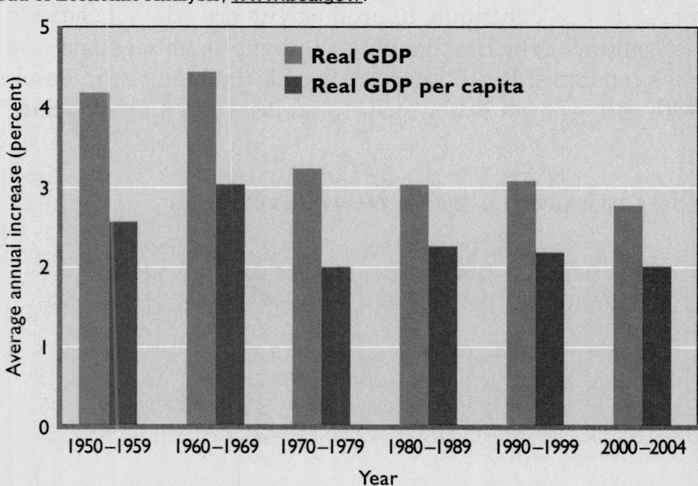

Accounting for Growth

growth accounting The bookkeeping of the supply-side elements that contribute to changes in real GDP.

The Council of Economic Advisers uses **growth accounting**—the bookkeeping of the supply-side elements that contribute to changes in real GDP—to assess the factors underlying economic growth. Ultimately, that accounting leads to the two main categories that we have just discussed:

- Increases in hours of work.
- Increases in labor productivity.

Labor Inputs versus Labor Productivity

Table 17.1 provides the relevant data for four periods. The symbol "Q" in the table stands for "quarter" of the year. The beginning points for the first three periods are business-cycle peaks, and the last period includes future projections by the Council of Economic Advisers. It is clear from the table that both increases in the quantity of labor and rises in labor productivity are important sources of economic growth. Between 1953 and 2004, the labor force increased from 63 million to 148 million workers. Over that period the average length of the workweek remained relatively stable. Falling birthrates slowed the growth of the native population, but increased immigration partly offset that slowdown. Of particular significance was a surge of women's participation in the labor force, from 34 percent in 1953 to 59 percent in 2004. Partly as a result, U.S. labor-force growth averaged 1.7 million workers per year over the past 51 years.

The growth of labor productivity has also been important to economic growth. In fact, productivity growth has usually been the more significant factor, with the exception of 1973–1995 when productivity growth greatly slowed. For example, between 2001 and 2004, productivity growth was responsible for 1.8 percentage points, or 64 percent, of the 2.8 percent average annual economic growth. Between 2004 and 2010, productivity growth is projected to account for 70 percent of the growth of real GDP.

Technological Advance

The importance of productivity growth to economic growth calls for a fuller explanation of the factors that contribute to productivity growth. The largest contributor is technological advance, which is thought to account for about 40 percent of productivity growth. As economist Paul Romer has stated, "Human history teaches us that economic growth springs from better recipes, not just from more cooking."

TABLE 17.1

Accounting for Growth of Real GDP, 1953–2010 (Average Annual Percentage Changes)*

Item	1953 Q2 to 1973 Q4	1973 Q4 to 1995 Q2	1995 Q2 to 2001 Q1	2001 Q1 to 2004 Q3	2004 Q3 to 2010 Q4
Increase in real GDP	3.6	2.8	3.8	2.8	3.3
Increase in quantity of labor	1.2	1.5	1.7	1.0	1.0
Increase in labor productivity	2.4	1.3	2.1	1.8	2.3

* Rates beyond 2004 are projected rates.

Source: Derived from *Economic Report of the President, 2005*, p. 45.

Technological advance includes not only innovative production techniques but new managerial methods and new forms of business organization that improve the process of production. Generally, technological advance is generated by the discovery of new knowledge, which allows resources to be combined in improved ways that increase output. Once discovered and implemented, new knowledge soon becomes available to entrepreneurs and firms at relatively low cost. Technological advance therefore eventually spreads through the entire economy, boosting productivity and economic growth.

Technological advance and capital formation (investment) are closely related because technological advance usually promotes investment in new machinery and equipment. In fact, technological advance is often *embodied* within new capital. For example, the purchase of new computers brings into industry speedier, more powerful computers that incorporate new technology.

Technological advance has been both rapid and profound. Gas and diesel engines, conveyor belts, and assembly lines are significant developments of the past. So, too, are fuel-efficient commercial aircraft, integrated microcircuits, personal computers, xerography, and containerized shipping. More recently, technological advance has exploded, particularly in the areas of computers, wireless communications, and the Internet. Other fertile areas of recent innovation are medicine and biotechnology.

Quantity of Capital

A second major contributor to productivity growth is increased capital, which explains roughly 30 percent of productivity growth. More and better plant and equipment make workers more productive. And a nation acquires more capital by saving some of its income and using that saving to invest in plant and equipment.

Although some capital substitutes for labor, most capital is complementary to labor—it makes labor more productive. A key determinant of labor productivity is the amount of capital goods available *per worker*. If both the aggregate stock of capital goods and the size of the labor force increase over a given period, the individual worker is not necessarily better equipped and productivity will not necessarily rise. But the quantity of capital equipment available per U.S. worker has increased greatly over time. (In 2003 it was about $83,466 per worker.)

Public investment in the U.S. **infrastructure** (highways and bridges, public transit systems, water and sewage systems, airports, industrial parks, educational facilities, and so on) has also grown over the years. This public capital (infrastructure) complements private capital. Investments in new highways promote private investment in new factories and retail stores along their routes. Industrial parks developed by local governments attract manufacturing and distribution firms.

infrastructure
Public and private capital goods that buttress an economy's production capacity (for example, highways, bridges, airports, public transit systems, wastewater treatment facilities, educational facilities, and telecommunications systems that complement private capital).

Private investment in infrastructure also plays a large role in economic growth. One example is the tremendous growth of private capital relating to communications systems over the years.

Education and Training

Ben Franklin once said, "He that hath a trade hath an estate," meaning that education and training contribute to a worker's stock of **human capital**—the knowledge and skills that make a worker productive. Investment in human capital includes not only formal education but also on-the-job training. Like investment in physical capital, investment in human capital is an important means of increasing labor productivity and earnings. An estimated 15 percent of productivity growth owes to such investment in people's education and skills.

human capital
The knowledge and skills that make a worker productive.

© Royalty-Free/CORBIS

© Royalty-Free/CORBIS

Photo Op Public and Private Investment in Infrastructure

Both public infrastructure investments (such as highways and bridges) and private infrastructure investments (such as wireless communications systems) have increased the nation's stock of private and public capital and help expand real GDP.

One measure of a nation's quality of labor is its level of educational attainment. Figure 17.5 shows large gains in educational attainment over the past several decades. In 1960 only 41 percent of the U.S. population age 25 or older had at least a high school education; and only 8 percent had a college education or more. By 2004, those numbers had increased to 85 and 28 percent, respectively. Clearly, education has become accessible to more people in the United States during the recent past.

But all is not upbeat with education in the United States. Many observers think that the quality of education in the United States has declined. For example, U.S. students in science and mathematics perform poorly on tests on those subjects relative to students in many other nations. The United States has been producing fewer native-born engineers and scientists, a problem that may trace back to inadequate training in math and science in elementary and high schools. And it is argued that on-the-job training programs (apprenticeship programs) in several European nations are superior to those in the United States. For these reasons, much recent public policy discussion and legislation has been directed toward improving the quality of the U.S. education and training system.

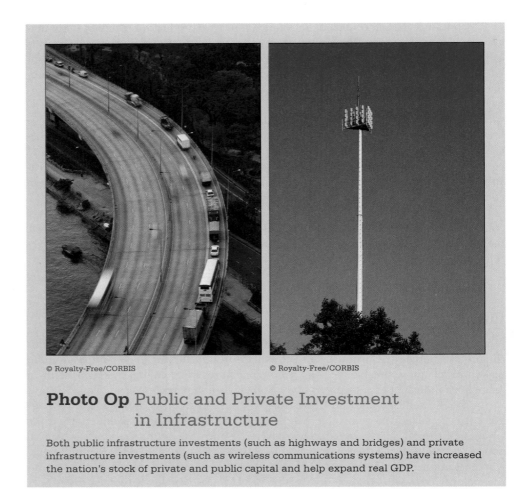

FIGURE 17.5
Changes in the educational attainment of the U.S. adult population. The percentage of the U.S. adult population, age 25 or more, completing high school and college has been rising over recent decades.

Source: U.S. Census Bureau, www.census.gov.

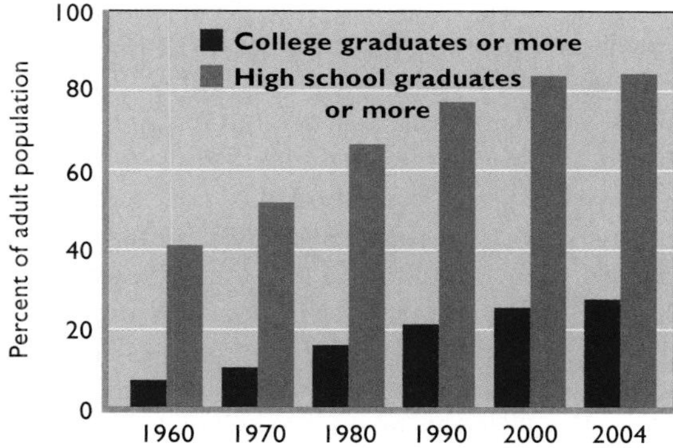

Economies of Scale and Resource Allocation

Economies of scale and improved resource allocation are a third and fourth source of productivity growth, and together they explain about 15 percent of productivity growth.

Economies of Scale Reductions in per-unit cost that result from increases in the size of markets and firms are called **economies of scale.** Markets have increased in size over time, allowing firms to achieve production advantages associated with greater size. As firms expand their size and output, they are able to use larger, more productive equipment and employ methods of manufacturing and delivery that increase productivity. They also are better able to recoup substantial investments in developing new products and production methods. Examples: A large manufacturer of autos can use elaborate assembly lines with computerization and robotics, while smaller producers must settle for less advanced technologies using more labor inputs. Large pharmaceutical firms greatly reduce the average amount of labor (researchers, production workers) needed to produce each pill as they increase the number of pills produced. Accordingly, economies of scale result in greater real GDP and thus contribute to economic growth.

economies of scale Reductions in per-unit cost that result from increases in the size of markets and firms.

Improved Resource Allocation Improved resource allocation means that workers over time have moved from low-productivity employment to high-productivity employment. Historically, much labor has shifted from agriculture, where labor productivity is low, to manufacturing, where it is quite high. More recently, labor has shifted away from some manufacturing industries to even higher productivity industries such as computer software, business consulting, and pharmaceuticals. As a result of such shifts, the average productivity of U.S. workers has increased.

Also, we will discover in Chapter 18 that tariffs, import quotas, and other barriers to international trade tend to relegate resources to relatively unproductive pursuits. The long-run movement toward liberalized international trade through international agreements has improved the allocation of resources, increased labor productivity, and expanded real output, both here and abroad.

Finally, discrimination in education and the labor market has historically deterred some women and minorities from entering high-productivity jobs. With the decline of such discrimination over time many members of those groups have shifted from low-productivity jobs to higher-productivity jobs. The result has been higher overall labor productivity and real GDP.

Other Factors

Several difficult-to-measure factors influence a nation's rate of economic growth. The overall social-cultural-political environment of the United States, for example, has fostered economic growth. The capitalistic system that has prevailed in the United States has fostered many income and profit incentives that promote growth. The United States has also had a stable political system characterized by democratic principles, internal order, the right of property ownership, the legal status of enterprise, and the enforcement of contracts. Economic freedom and political freedom have been "growth-friendly."

Unlike some nations, there are virtually no social or moral taboos on production and material progress in the United States. The nation's social philosophy has embraced material advance as an attainable and desirable economic goal. The inventor, the innovator, and the businessperson are accorded high degrees of prestige and respect in American society.

Moreover, Americans have had positive attitudes toward work and risk taking, resulting in an ample supply of willing workers and innovative entrepreneurs. A flow of energetic immigrants has greatly augmented that supply.

The Productivity Acceleration: A New Economy?

Figure 17.6 shows the growth of labor productivity (as measured by changes in the index of labor productivity for the full business sector) in the United States from 1973 to 2004, along with separate trend lines for 1973–1995 and 1995–2004. Labor productivity grew by an average of only 1.4 percent yearly over the 1973–1995 period. But productivity growth averaged 2.9 percent between 1995 and 2004. Many economists believe that this higher productivity growth resulted from a significant new wave of technological advance, coupled with global competition. A few economists say that the United States has achieved a **New Economy**—one with a higher projected trend rate of productivity growth and therefore greater potential economic growth than in the 1973–1995 period.

New Economy The post-1995 economy, characterized by accelerated productivity growth, rapid technological advance, and enhanced global competition.

This increase in productivity growth is important because real output, real income, and real wages are linked to labor productivity. To see why, suppose you are alone on an uninhabited island. The number of fish you can catch or coconuts you can pick per hour—your productivity—is your real wage (or real income) per hour. By *increasing* your productivity, you can improve your standard of living because greater output per hour means there are more fish and coconuts (goods) available to consume.

So it is for the economy as a whole: Over long periods, the economy's labor productivity determines its average real hourly wage. The economy's income per hour is equal to its output per hour. Productivity growth therefore is its main route for increasing its standard of living. It allows firms to pay higher wages without lowering their business profits. Even a seemingly small percentage change in productivity growth, if sustained over several years, can make a substantial difference as to how fast a nation's standard of living rises. We know from the *rule of 70* (Chapter 12) that if a nation's productivity grows by 2.9 percent annually rather than 1.4, its standard of living will double in 24 years rather than 50 years. That is a big deal!

FIGURE 17.6

Growth of labor productivity in the United States, 1973–2004. U.S. labor productivity (here, for the business sector) increased at an average annual rate of only 1.4 percent from 1973 to 1995. But between 1995 and 2004 it accelerated to an annual rate of 2.9 percent.

Source: U.S. Bureau of Labor Statistics, www.bls.gov/.

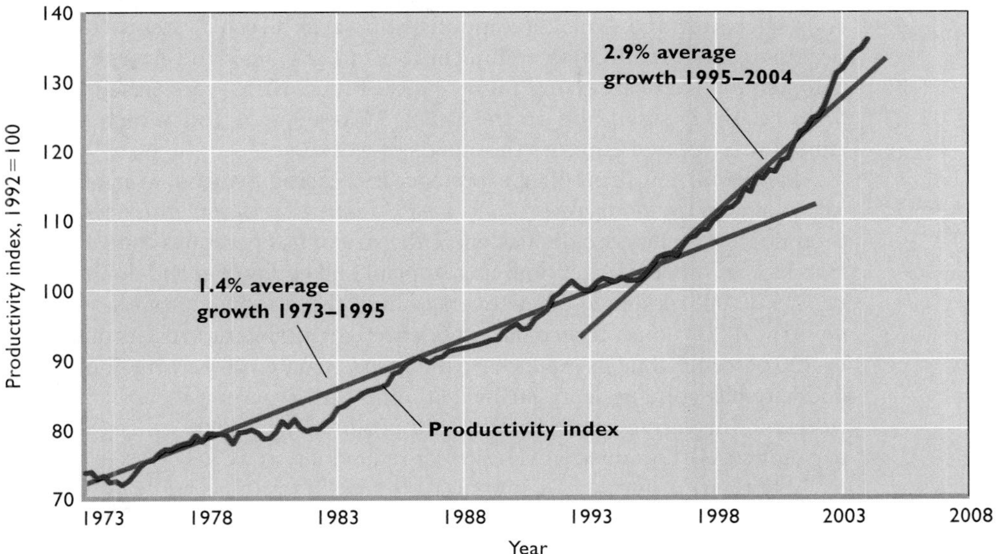

Reasons for the Productivity Acceleration

Why has productivity growth increased relative to earlier periods? What is "new" about the New Economy?

The Microchip and Information Technology The core element of the productivity speedup is an explosion of entrepreneurship and innovation based on the microprocessor, or *microchip*, which bundles transistors on a piece of silicon. Many observers liken the invention of the microchip to that of electricity, the automobile, air travel, the telephone, and television in importance and scope.

The microchip has found its way into thousands of applications. It has helped create a wide array of new products and services and new ways of doing business. Its immediate results were the pocket calculator, the bar-code scanner, the personal computer, the laptop computer, and more powerful business computers. But the miniaturization of electronic circuits also advanced the development of many other products such as cell phones and pagers, computer-guided lasers, deciphered genetic codes, global positioning equipment, energy conservation systems, Doppler radar, and digital cameras.

Perhaps of greatest significance, the widespread availability of personal and laptop computers stimulated the desire to tie them together. That desire promoted rapid development of the Internet and all its many manifestations, such as business-to-household and business-to-business electronic commerce *(e-commerce)*. The combination of the computer, fiber optic cable, wireless technology, and the Internet constitutes a spectacular advance in **information technology,** which has been used to connect all parts of the world.

information technology
New and more efficient methods of delivering and receiving information through use of computers, fax machines, wireless phones, and the Internet.

start-up firms New firms focused on creating and introducing particular new products or employing specific new production or distribution methods.

New Firms and Increasing Returns Hundreds of new **start-up firms** advanced various aspects of the new information technology. Many of these firms created more "hype" than goods and services and quickly fell by the wayside. But a number of firms flourished, eventually to take their places among the nation's largest firms. Examples of those firms include Intel (microchips); Apple and Dell (personal computers); Microsoft and Oracle (computer software); Cisco Systems (Internet switching systems); Yahoo and Google (Internet search engines); and Amazon.com (electronic commerce). There are scores more! Most of these firms were either "not on the radar" or "a relatively small blip on the radar" 30 years ago. Today each of them has large annual revenue and employs thousands of workers.

increasing returns An increase in a firm's output by a larger percentage than the increase in its inputs.

Successful new firms often experience **increasing returns,** which occur *when a firm's output increases by a larger percentage than the increase in its inputs (resources).* For example, suppose that Techco decides to double the size of its operations to meet the growing demand for its services. After doubling its plant and equipment and doubling its workforce, say, from 100 workers to 200 workers, it finds that its total output has tripled from 8000 units to 24,000 units. Techco has experienced increasing returns; its output has increased by 200 percent, while its inputs have increased by only 100 percent. That is, its labor productivity has gone up from 80 (=8000 units/100 workers) to 120 (=24,000 units/200 workers). Increasing returns boost labor productivity, which, other things equal, lowers per-unit costs of production. These cost reductions, as we know, are *economies of scale.*

There are a number of sources of increasing returns and economies of scale for emerging firms:

- ***More specialized inputs*** Firms can use more specialized and thus more productive capital and workers as they expand their operations. A growing new e-commerce business, for example, can purchase highly specialized inventory management systems and hire specialized personnel such as accountants, marketing managers, and system maintenance experts.
- ***Spreading of development costs*** Firms can spread high product development costs over greater output. For example, suppose that a new software product costs $100,000 to develop and only $2 per unit to manufacture and sell. If the firm sells 1000 units of the software, its cost per unit will be $102 [=($100,000 + $2000)/1000], but if it sells 500,000 units, that cost will drop to only $2.20 [=($100,000 + $1 million)/500,000].
- ***Simultaneous consumption*** Many of the products and services of the New Economy can satisfy many customers at the same time. Unlike a gallon of gas that needs to be produced for each buyer, a software program needs to be produced only once. It then becomes available at very low expense to thousands or even millions of buyers. The same is true of entertainment delivered on CDs, movies distributed on DVDs, and information disseminated through the Internet.
- ***Network effects*** Software and Internet service become more beneficial to a buyer the greater the number of households and businesses that also buy them. When others have Internet service, you can send e-mail messages to them. And when they also have software that allows display of documents and photos, you can attach those items to your e-mail messages. These system advantages are called **network effects,** which are increases in the value of the product to each user, including existing users, as the total number of users rises. The domestic and global expansion of the Internet in particular has produced network effects, as have cell phones, pagers, palm computers, and other aspects of wireless communication. Network effects magnify the value of output well beyond the costs of inputs.

network effects Increases in the value of a product to each user, including existing users, as the total number of users rises.

- ***Learning by doing*** Finally, firms that produce new products or pioneer new ways of doing business experience increasing returns through **learning by doing.** Tasks that initially may have taken firms hours may take them only minutes once the methods are perfected.

learning by doing Achieving greater productivity and lower average total costs through gains in knowledge and skill that accompany repetition of a task.

Whatever the particular source of increasing returns, the result is higher productivity, which tends to reduce the per-unit cost of producing and delivering products.

Global Competition The recent economy is characterized not only by information technology and increasing returns but also by heightened global competition. The collapse of the socialist economies in the late 1980s and early 1990s, together with the success of market systems, has led to a reawakening of capitalism throughout the world. The new information technologies have "shrunk the globe" and made it imperative for all firms to lower their costs and prices and to innovate in order to remain competitive. Free-trade zones such as those created by the North American Free Trade Agreement (NAFTA) and the European Union (EU) have also heightened competition internationally by removing trade protection from domestic firms. So, too, has trade liberalization through the World Trade Organization (WTO). The larger geographic markets and lower tariffs, in turn, have enabled emerging and old-line firms to expand beyond their national borders.

Implication: More-Rapid Economic Growth

Other things equal, stronger productivity growth and heightened global competition allow the economy to achieve a higher rate of economic growth. A glance back at Figure 17.2 will help make this point. If the shifts of the curves reflect annual changes in the old economy, then the New Economy would be depicted by an outward shift of the production possibilities curve beyond *CD* in Figure 17.2a, and a shift of the long-run aggregate supply curve farther to the right than AS_{LR2} in Figure 17.2b. When coupled with economic efficiency and increased total spending, the economy's real GDP would rise by more than that shown. That is, the economy would achieve a higher rate of economic growth.

If the productivity acceleration is permanent, the economy has a higher "safe speed limit" than previously because production capacity rises more rapidly. The New Economy can grow by, say, 3.5 or 4 percent, rather than 2 or 3 percent, each year without igniting demand-pull inflation. Increases in aggregate demand that in the past would have caused inflation do not cause inflation because they are buffered by faster productivity growth. Even when wage increases rise to match the productivity increases, as is desirable and as they usually do, per-unit production costs and therefore prices can remain stable.

Global competition in the New Economy also contributes to price stability by reducing the pricing power (or market power) of U.S. firms.

A caution: Those who champion the idea of a New Economy emphasize that it does not mean that the business cycle is dead. Indeed, the economy slowed in the first two months of 2001 and receded over the following eight months of that year. The New Economy is simply one for which the *trend lines* of productivity growth and economic growth are steeper than they were in the preceding two decades. Real output may periodically deviate below and above the steeper trend lines.

© Royalty-Free/CORBIS/DIL

Courtesy of Google Inc.

© age footstock/SuperStock

Photo Op Key Elements of the U.S. Productivity Acceleration

A combination of information technology, emerging new firms, and globalization helps explain the speedup in U.S. productivity growth since 1995.

Skepticism about Permanence

Although most macroeconomists have revised their forecasts for long-term productivity growth upward, at least slightly, others are still skeptical and urge a "wait-and-see" approach. Skeptics acknowledge that the economy has experienced a rapid advance of new technology, some new firms have experienced increasing returns, and global competition has increased. But they wonder if these factors are sufficiently profound to produce a 15- to 20-year period of substantially higher rates of productivity growth and real GDP growth.

Skeptics point out that productivity surged between 1975 and 1978 and between 1983 and 1986 but in each case soon reverted to its lower long-run trend. The higher trend line of productivity inferred from the short-run spurt of productivity could prove to be an illusion. Only by looking backward over long periods can economists distinguish the start of a new long-run secular trend from a shorter-term boost in productivity related to the business cycle and temporary factors.

What Can We Conclude?

Given the different views on the New Economy, what should we conclude? Perhaps the safest conclusions are these:

- The prospects for a more rapid long-run trend of productivity growth are good (see Global Snapshot 17.1). Studies indicate that productivity advance related to information technology has spread to a wide range of industries, including services. Even in the recession year 2001 and in 2002, when the economy was sluggish, productivity growth remained strong. Specifically, it averaged about 3.4 percent in the business sector over those two years. It rose by 4.5 percent in 2003 and 4.0 percent in 2004 as the economy vigorously expanded.
- Time will tell. It will be several more years before economists can declare the recent productivity acceleration a long-term reality.

Global Snapshot 17.1

Growth Competitiveness Index

The World Economic Forum annually compiles a growth competitiveness index, which uses various factors (such as innovativeness, effective transfer of technology among sectors, efficiency of the financial system, rates of investment, and degree of integration with the rest of the world) to measure the ability of a country to achieve economic growth over time. Here is its latest top 10 list:

Country	Growth Competitiveness Ranking, 2004
Finland	1
United States	2
Sweden	3
Taiwan	4
Denmark	5
Norway	6
Singapore	7
Switzerland	8
Japan	9
Iceland	10

Source: World Economic Forum, www.weforum.org/.

Is Growth Desirable and Sustainable?

Economists typically see economic growth as desirable and sustainable. But not all social observers agree.

The Antigrowth View

Critics of growth say industrialization and growth result in pollution, global warming, ozone depletion, and other environmental problems. These adverse spillover costs occur because inputs in the production process reenter the environment as some form of waste. The more rapid our growth and the higher our standard of living, the more waste the environment must absorb—or attempt to absorb. In an already wealthy society, further growth usually means satisfying increasingly trivial wants at the cost of mounting threats to the ecological system.

Critics of growth also argue that there is little compelling evidence that economic growth has solved sociological problems such as poverty, homelessness, and discrimination. Consider poverty: In the antigrowth view, American poverty (and, for that matter, world poverty) is a problem of distribution, not production. The requisite for solving the problem is commitment and political courage to redistribute wealth and income, not further increases in output.

Antigrowth sentiment also says that while growth may permit us to "make a better living," it does not give us "the good life." We may be producing more and enjoying it less. Growth means frantic paces on jobs, worker burnout, and alienated employees who have little or no control over decisions affecting their lives. The changing technology at the core of growth poses new anxieties and new sources of insecurity for workers. Both high-level and low-level workers face the prospect of having their hard-earned skills and experience rendered obsolete by an onrushing technology. High-growth economies are high-stress economies, which may impair our physical and mental health.

Finally, critics of high rates of growth doubt that they are sustainable. The planet Earth has finite amounts of natural resources available, and they are being consumed at alarming rates. Higher rates of economic growth simply speed up the degradation and exhaustion of the earth's resources. In this view, slower economic growth that is sustainable is preferable to faster growth.

In Defense of Economic Growth

The primary defense of growth is that it is the path to the greater material abundance and higher living standards desired by the vast majority of people. Rising output and incomes allow people to buy

> more education, recreation, and travel, more medical care, closer communications, more skilled personal and professional services, and better-designed as well as more numerous products. It also means more art, music, and poetry, theater, and drama. It can even mean more time and resources devoted to spiritual growth and human development.[1]

Growth also enables society to improve the nation's infrastructure, enhance the care of the sick and elderly, provide greater access for the disabled, and provide more police and fire protection. Economic growth may be the only realistic way to reduce poverty, since there is little political support for greater redistribution of income. The way to improve the economic position of the poor is to increase household incomes through higher productivity and economic growth. Also, a no-growth policy among industrial nations might severely limit growth in poor nations. Foreign investment and development assistance in those nations would fall, keeping the world's poor in poverty longer.

Economic growth has not made labor more unpleasant or hazardous, as critics suggest. New machinery is usually less taxing and less dangerous than the machinery it replaces. Air-conditioned workplaces are more pleasant than steamy workshops. Furthermore, why would an end to economic growth reduce materialism or alienation? The loudest protests against materialism are heard in those nations and groups that now enjoy the highest levels of material abundance! The high standard of living that growth provides has increased our leisure and given us more time for reflection and self-fulfillment.

Does growth threaten the environment? The connection between growth and environment is tenuous, say growth proponents. Increases in economic growth need not mean increases in pollution. Pollution is not so much a by-product of growth as it is a "problem of the commons." Much of the environment—streams, lakes, oceans, and the air—is treated as "common property," with no or insufficient restrictions on its

[1] Alice M. Rivlin, *Reviving the American Dream* (Washington, D.C.: Brookings Institution, 1992), p. 36.

use. The commons have become our dumping grounds; we have overused and debased them. Environmental pollution is a case of spillover or external costs, and correcting this problem involves regulatory legislation, specific taxes ("effluent charges"), or market-based incentives to remedy misuse of the environment.

Those who support growth admit there are serious environmental problems but say that limiting growth is the wrong solution. Growth has allowed economies to reduce pollution, be more sensitive to environmental considerations, set aside wilderness, create national parks and monuments, and clean up hazardous waste, while still enabling rising household incomes.

Is growth sustainable? Yes, say the proponents of growth. If we were depleting natural resources faster than their discovery, we would see the prices of those resources rise. That has not been the case for most natural resources; in fact, the prices of most of them have declined. And if one natural resource becomes too expensive, another resource will be substituted for it. Moreover, say economists, economic growth has to do with the expansion and application of human knowledge and information, not of extractable natural resources. In this view, economic growth—and solving any problems it may create—is limited only by human imagination.

Applying the Analysis

Growth in the Low-Income Nations

It is difficult for most of us in the United States, where per capita GDP in 2004 was nearly $37,000, to grasp the fact that about 2.8 billion people, or nearly half the world population, live on $2 or less a day. Hunger, squalor, and disease are the norm in many nations of the world. For those nations, economic growth—and the higher standard of living that usually accompanies it—is a critical, life-sustaining priority.

These poor nations include numerous Sub-Saharan African countries such as Angola, Chad, Ethiopia, Mauritania, Mozambique, Niger, and Sudan. They also include nations such as Afghanistan Bangladesh, Nepal, and Pakistan in South Asia; Nicaragua in Latin American; and Indonesia in East Asia. All have relatively low levels of industrialization. In general, literacy rates are low, unemployment is high, and population growth is rapid. Capital equipment is minimal, production technologies are simple, and labor productivity is very low.

The world's poorest nations face daunting tasks. There simply are no magic methods for achieving quick economic development. But economists suggest that poor nations can pursue several policies to foster their economic growth.

First, they need to establish and implement the rule of law. Clearly defined and regularly enforced property rights bolster economic growth by ensuring that individuals receive and retain the fruits of their labor. Since legal protections reduce investment risk, the rule of law encourages direct investments by firms from the high-income nations. Government itself must live by the law. The presence of corruption in the government sanctions criminality throughout the economic system. Such criminality undermines the growth of output by diverting scarce resources toward activities that "transfer" income away from activities that produce goods and services.

Another route to growth of GDP per capita is controlling population growth. Slower population growth converts increases in real output and income to increases in real per capita output and income. Families with fewer children consume less and save more; they also free up time for women to improve their education and participate in the labor market.

Programs that encourage literacy, education, and labor market skills also enhance economic growth. In particular, policies that close the education gap between women and men spur economic growth in developing countries. Higher-education loans and grants should contain strong incentives for recipients to remain in the home country (or to return to the home country) after receiving their degrees.

Low-income economies can speed development by opening their doors to international trade and investment. Other things equal, open economies grow faster than closed economies. Low-income countries that welcome direct foreign investment enjoy greater growth rates than countries that view such investment suspiciously and put severe obstacles in its way.

There are other policies that can aid development, such as establishing independent central banks and realistic exchange-rate policies. High rates of inflation are not conducive to economic investment and growth. Poor nations can help keep inflation in check by establishing independent central banks to maintain proper control over their money supplies. Studies indicate that low-income countries that control inflation enjoy higher growth rates than those that do not. Exchange rates that are fixed at unrealistic levels invite balance-of-payments problems and speculative trading in currencies. Often, such trading forces a nation into an abrupt reevaluation of its currency, sending shock waves throughout its economy. More flexible exchange rates may enable more gradual adjustments and thus less susceptibility to major currency shocks and the domestic disruption they cause.

Also, many economists say that poor nations would benefit by converting some state enterprises into private firms. State enterprises often are inefficient, more concerned with providing employment than with introducing modern technology and delivering goods and services at minimum per-unit cost. Moreover, state enterprises are poor "incubators" for the development of profit-focused, entrepreneurial persons who leave the firm to set up their own businesses.

Finally, low-income countries can enhance economic growth by making peace with neighbors. Countries at war or in fear of war with neighboring nations divert scarce resources to armaments, rather than to private capital or public infrastructure. Sustained peace among neighboring nations eventually leads to economic cooperation and integration, broadened markets, and stronger growth.

What can the advanced industrial countries such as the United States, Germany, and Japan do to improve living conditions and promote growth in the developing nations? Here there is more disagreement among the experts. Economists offer a variety of suggestions.

Some experts say that the wealthy nations should direct more of their foreign aid to the poorest developing nations. Much of the foreign aid is strongly influenced by political and military considerations rather than allocated on the basis of economic need or degree of destitution. Only a fraction of foreign aid goes to the countries in which most of the world's poorest people live.

Advanced industrial nations can also help the poorest developing nations by reducing tariffs, import quotas, and farm subsidies. Trade barriers in the wealthy nations are often highest for labor-intensive manufactured goods such as textiles, clothing, footwear, and processed agricultural products. These are precisely the sorts of products for which some of the poorest nations have a comparative advantage. Moreover, large agricultural subsidies in the high-income nations encourage excessive production of food and fiber in the high-income nations. The overproduction flows into world markets, where it depresses agricultural prices. Low-income nations, which typically do not subsidize farmers, therefore face artificially low prices for any farm exports they can muster. The high-income nations could greatly help the low-income nations by reducing farm subsidies along with tariffs.

There is little doubt that the high-income nations could greatly help the lowest of the low-income nations by providing debt forgiveness. The current debt of the poorest nations is so large that it serves as a severe roadblock to their growth. And, in fact, the process of debt forgiveness has begun. A group of high-income nations have agreed to provide debt relief for highly indebted poor nations. The World Bank has also agreed to additional debt relief.

Question:
Because real capital is supposed to earn a higher return where it is scarce, how do you explain the fact that most international investment flows from high-income nations to other high-income nations (where capital is relatively abundant) rather than to the low-income nations (where capital is very scarce)?

Summary

1. Economic growth—measured as either an increase in real output or an increase in real output per capita—increases material abundance and raises a nation's standard of living.
2. The supply factors in economic growth are (a) the quantity and quality of a nation's natural resources, (b) the quantity and quality of its human resources, (c) its stock of capital facilities, and (d) its technology. Two other factors—a sufficient level of aggregate demand and economic efficiency—are necessary for the economy to realize its growth potential.
3. The growth of production capacity is shown graphically as an outward shift of a nation's production possibilities curve or as a rightward shift of its long-run aggregate supply curve. Growth is realized when total spending rises sufficiently to match the growth of production capacity.
4. Between 1950 and 2004 the annual growth rate of real GDP for the United States averaged about 3.5 percent; the annual growth rate of real GDP per capita was about 2.3 percent.
5. U.S. real GDP has grown partly because of increased inputs of labor and primarily because of increases in the productivity of labor. The increases in productivity have resulted mainly from technological progress, increases in the quantity of capital per worker, improvements in the quality of labor, economies of scale, and an improved allocation of labor.
6. Over long time periods, the growth of labor productivity underlies an economy's growth of real wages and its standard of living.
7. Productivity rose by 2.9 percent annually between 1995 and 2004, compared to 1.4 percent annually between 1973 and 1995. Some economists think this productivity acceleration will be long-lasting and is reflective of a New Economy—one of faster productivity growth and greater noninflationary economic growth.
8. The productivity speedup is based on (a) rapid technological change in the form of the microchip and information technology, (b) increasing returns and lower per-unit costs, and (c) heightened global competition that holds down prices.

- Exports of goods and services make up about 10 percent of total U.S. output. That percentage is much lower than the percentage in many other nations, including Canada, Italy, France, and the United Kingdom (see Global Snapshot 18.2).
- China has become a major international trader, with an estimated $583 billion of exports in 2004. Other Asian economies—including South Korea, Taiwan, and Singapore—are also active in international trade. Their combined exports exceed those of France, Britain, or Italy.
- International trade and finance are often at the center of economic policy.

With this information in mind, let's look more closely at the economics of international trade.

Global Snapshot 18.2

Exports of Goods and Services as a Percentage of GDP, Selected Countries

Although the United States is the world's second-largest exporter, it ranks relatively low among trading nations in terms of exports as a percentage of GDP.

Exports as a Percentage of GDP

0 10 20 30 40 50 60

Netherlands
Canada
Germany
New Zealand
Spain
France
Italy
United Kingdom
Japan
United States

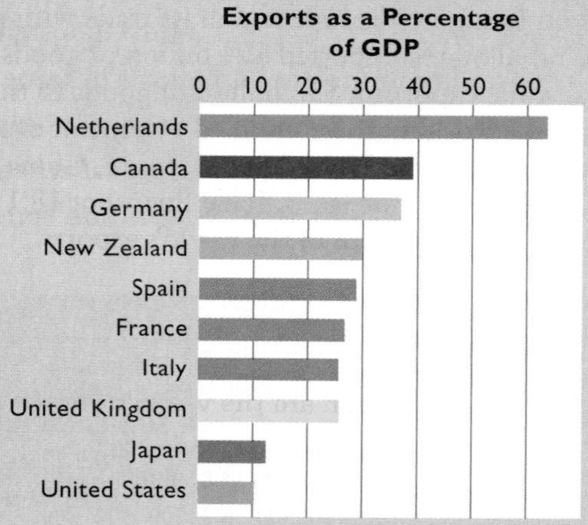

Source: Derived from data in IMF, *International Financial Statistics*, March 2005.

Comparative Advantage and Specialization

Given the presence of an *open economy*—one that includes the international sector—the United States produces more of certain goods (exports) and fewer of other goods (imports) than it would otherwise. Thus U.S. labor and other resources are shifted toward export industries and away from import industries. For example, the United States uses more resources to make computers and to grow wheat and less to make sporting goods and clothing. So we ask: "Do shifts of resources like these make economic sense? Do they enhance U.S. total output and thus the U.S. standard of living?"

The answers are affirmative. Specialization and international trade increase the productivity of a nation's resources and allow for greater total output than would otherwise be possible. This idea is not new. Adam Smith had this to say in 1776:

> It is the maxim of every prudent master of a family, never to attempt to make at home what it will cost him more to make than to buy. The taylor does not attempt to make his own shoes, but buys them of the shoemaker. The shoemaker does not attempt to make his own clothes, but employs a taylor. The farmer attempts to make neither the one nor the other, but employs those different artificers. . . .
>
> What is prudence in the conduct of every private family, can scarce be folly in that of a great kingdom. If a foreign country can supply us with a commodity cheaper than we can make it, better buy it of them with some part of the produce of our own industry, employed in a way in which we have some advantage.[1]

Nations specialize and trade for the same reasons that individuals do: Specialization and exchange result in greater overall output and income. In the early 1800s British economist David Ricardo expanded on Smith's idea by observing that it pays for a person or a country to specialize and trade even if a nation is more productive than a potential trading partner in *all* economic activities. We demonstrate Ricardo's principle in the examples that follow.

A CPA and a House Painter

Consider the certified public accountant (CPA) who is also a skilled house painter. Suppose the CPA is a swifter painter than the professional painter she is thinking of hiring. Also suppose that she can earn \$50 per hour as an accountant but would have to pay the painter \$15 per hour. And say it would take the accountant 30 hours to paint her house but the painter would take 40 hours.

Should the CPA take time from her accounting to paint her own house, or should she hire the painter? The CPA's opportunity cost of painting her house is \$1500 (=30 hours of sacrificed CPA time × \$50 per CPA hour). The cost of hiring the painter is only \$600 (=40 hours of painting × \$15 per hour of painting). Although the CPA is better at both accounting and painting, she will get her house painted at lower cost by specializing in accounting and using some of her earnings from accounting to hire a house painter.

Similarly, the house painter can reduce his cost of obtaining accounting services by specializing in painting and using some of his income to hire the CPA to prepare his income tax forms. Suppose it would take the painter 10 hours to prepare his tax return, while the CPA could handle the task in 2 hours. The house painter would sacrifice \$150 of income (=10 hours of painting time × \$15 per hour) to do something he could hire the CPA to do for \$100 (=2 hours of CPA time × \$50 per CPA hour). By using the CPA to prepare his tax return, the painter lowers the cost of getting his tax return prepared.

What is true for our CPA and house painter is also true for nations. Specializing enables nations to reduce the cost of obtaining the goods and services they desire.

Question:
How might the specialization described above change once the CPA retires? What generalization about the permanency of a particular pattern of specialization can you draw from your answer?

---

[1] Adam Smith, *The Wealth of Nations* (New York: Modern Library, 1937), p. 424. (Originally published in 1776.)

Comparative Advantage: Production Possibilities Analysis

Our simple example shows that the reason specialization is economically desirable is that it results in more efficient production. Now let's put specialization into the context of trading nations and use the familiar concept of the production possibilities table for our analysis.

Assumptions and Comparative Costs Suppose the production possibilities for one product in Mexico and for one product in the United States are as shown in Tables 18.1 and 18.2. Both tables reflect constant costs. Each country must give up a constant amount of one product to secure a certain increment of the other product. (This assumption simplifies our discussion without impairing the validity of our conclusions. Later we will allow for increasing costs.)

Also for simplicity, suppose that the labor forces in the United States and Mexico are of equal size. The data then tell us that the United States has an *absolute advantage* in producing both products. If the United States and Mexico use their entire (equal-size) labor forces to produce avocados, the United States can produce 90 tons compared with Mexico's 60 tons. Similarly, the United States can produce 30 tons of soybeans compared to Mexico's 15 tons. There are greater production possibilities in the United States, using the same number of workers as in Mexico. So labor productivity (output per worker) in the United States exceeds that in Mexico in producing both products.

Although the United States has an absolute advantage in producing both goods, gains from specialization and trade are possible. Specialization and trade are mutually beneficial or "profitable" to the two nations if the *comparative* costs of producing the two products within the two nations differ. What are the comparative costs of avocados and soybeans in Mexico? By comparing production alternatives A and B in Table 18.1, we see that Mexico must sacrifice 5 tons of soybeans (=15 − 10) to produce 20 tons of avocados (=20 − 0). Or, more simply, in Mexico it costs 1 ton of soybeans (S) to produce 4 tons of avocados (A); that is, 1S ≡ 4A. (The "≡" sign simply means "equivalent to.") Because we assumed constant costs, this domestic opportunity cost will not change as Mexico expands the output of either product. This is evident from

TABLE 18.1
Mexico's Production Possibilities Table (in Tons)

	Production Alternatives				
Product	**A**	**B**	**C**	**D**	**E**
Avocados	0	20	24	40	60
Soybeans	15	10	9	5	0

TABLE 18.2
U.S. Production Possibilities Table (in Tons)

	Production Alternatives				
Product	**R**	**S**	**T**	**U**	**V**
Avocados	0	30	33	60	90
Soybeans	30	20	19	10	0

production possibilities B and C, where we see that 4 more tons of avocados (=24 − 20) cost 1 unit of soybeans (=10 − 9).

Similarly, in Table 18.2, comparing U.S. production alternatives R and S reveals that in the United States it costs 10 tons of soybeans (=30 − 20) to obtain 30 tons of avocados (=30 − 0). That is, the domestic (internal) comparative-cost ratio for the two products in the United States is 1S ≡ 3A. Comparing production alternatives S and T reinforces this conclusion: an extra 3 tons of avocados (=33 − 30) comes at the sacrifice of 1 ton of soybeans (=20 − 19).

The comparative costs of the two products within the two nations are obviously different. Economists say that the United States has a **comparative advantage** over Mexico in soybeans. The United States must forgo only 3 tons of avocados to get 1 ton of soybeans, but Mexico must forgo 4 tons of avocados to get 1 ton of soybeans. In terms of opportunity costs, soybeans are relatively cheaper in the United States. *A nation has a comparative advantage in some product when it can produce that product at a lower opportunity cost than can a potential trading partner.* Mexico, in contrast, has a comparative advantage in avocados. While 1 ton of avocados costs $\frac{1}{3}$ ton of soybeans in the United States, it costs only $\frac{1}{4}$ ton of soybeans in Mexico. Comparatively speaking, avocados are cheaper in Mexico. We summarize the situation in Table 18.3. Be sure to give it a close look.

comparative advantage A lower relative or comparative opportunity cost than that of another person, producer, or country.

Because of these differences in comparative costs, Mexico should produce avocados and the United States should produce soybeans. If both nations specialize according to their comparative advantages, each can achieve a larger total output with the same total input of resources. Together they will be using their scarce resources more efficiently.

18.1 Absolute and comparative advantage

Terms of Trade

The United States can shift production between soybeans and avocados at the rate of 1S for 3A. Thus, the United States would specialize in soybeans only if it could obtain *more than* 3 tons of avocados for 1 ton of soybeans by trading with Mexico. Similarly, Mexico can shift production at the rate of 4A for 1S. So it would be advantageous to Mexico to specialize in avocados if it could get 1 ton of soybeans for *less than* 4 tons of avocados.

Suppose that through negotiation the two nations agree on an exchange rate of 1 ton of soybeans for $3\frac{1}{2}$ tons of avocados. These **terms of trade** are mutually beneficial to both countries, since each can "do better" through such trade than through domestic production alone. The United States can get $3\frac{1}{2}$ tons of avocados by sending 1 ton of soybeans to Mexico, while it can get only 3 tons of avocados by shifting its own resources domestically from soybeans to avocados. Mexico can obtain 1 ton of soybeans

terms of trade The rate at which units of one product can be exchanged for units of another product.

TABLE 18.3
Comparative-Advantage Example: A Summary

Soybeans	Avocados
Mexico: Must give up 4 tons of avocados to get 1 ton of soybeans	**Mexico:** Must give up $\frac{1}{4}$ ton of soybeans to get 1 ton of avocados
United States: Must give up 3 tons of avocados to get 1 ton of soybeans	**United States:** Must give up $\frac{1}{3}$ ton of soybeans to get 1 ton of avocados
Comparative advantage: United States	**Comparative advantage:** Mexico

at a lower cost of $3\frac{1}{2}$ tons of avocados through trade with the United States, compared to the cost of 4 tons if Mexico produced the 1 ton of soybeans itself.

Gains from Specialization and Trade Let's pinpoint the gains in total output from specialization and trade. Suppose that, before specialization and trade, production alternative C in Table 18.1 and alternative T in Table 18.2 were the optimal product mixes for the two countries. That is, Mexico preferred 24 tons of avocados and 9 tons of soybeans (Table 18.1) and the United States preferred 33 tons of avocados and 19 tons of soybeans (Table 18.2) to all other available domestic alternatives. These outputs are shown in column 1 in Table 18.4.

Now assume that both nations specialize according to their comparative advantages, with Mexico producing 60 tons of avocados and no soybeans (alternative E) and the United States producing no avocados and 30 tons of soybeans (alternative R). These outputs are shown in column 2 in Table 18.4. Using our $1S \equiv 3\frac{1}{2}A$ terms of trade, assume that Mexico exchanges 35 tons of avocados for 10 tons of U.S. soybeans. Column 3 in Table 18.4 shows the quantities exchanged in this trade, with a minus sign indicating exports and a plus sign indicating imports. As shown in column 4, after the trade Mexico has 25 tons of avocados and 10 tons of soybeans, while the United States has 35 tons of avocados and 20 tons of soybeans. Compared with their optimal product mixes before specialization and trade (column 1), *both* nations now enjoy more avocados and more soybeans! Specifically, Mexico has gained 1 ton of avocados and 1 ton of soybeans. The United States has gained 2 tons of avocados and 1 ton of soybeans. These gains are shown in column 5.

Specialization based on comparative advantage improves global resource allocation. The same total inputs of world resources and technology result in a larger global output. If Mexico and the United States allocate all their resources to avocados and soybeans, respectively, the same total inputs of resources can produce more output between them, indicating that resources are being allocated more efficiently.

Through specialization and international trade a nation can overcome the production constraints imposed by its domestic production possibilities table and curve. Our discussion of Tables 18.1, 18.2, and 18.4 has shown just how this is done. The domestic production possibilities data (Tables 18.1 and 18.2) of the two countries have not changed, meaning that neither nation's production possibilities curve has shifted. But specialization and trade mean that citizens of both countries can enjoy increased consumption (column 5 of Table 18.4).

TABLE 18.4

Specialization According to Comparative Advantage and the Gains from Trade (in Tons)

Country	(1) Outputs before Specialization	(2) Outputs after Specialization	(3) Amounts Traded	(4) Outputs Available after Trade	(5) Gains from Specialization and Trade (4) − (1)
Mexico	24 avocados	60 avocados	−35 avocados	25 avocados	1 avocados
	9 soybeans	0 soybeans	+10 soybeans	10 soybeans	1 soybeans
United States	33 avocados	0 avocados	+35 avocados	35 avocados	2 avocados
	19 soybeans	30 soybeans	−10 soybeans	20 soybeans	1 soybeans

Trade with Increasing Costs

To explain the basic principles underlying international trade, we simplified our analysis in several ways. For example, we limited discussion to two products and two nations. But multiproduct and multinational analysis yields the same conclusions. We also assumed constant opportunity costs, which is a more substantive simplification. Let's consider the effect of allowing increasing opportunity costs to enter the picture.

As before, suppose that comparative advantage indicates that the United States should specialize in soybeans and Mexico in avocados. But now, as the United States begins to expand soybean production, its cost of soybeans will rise. It will eventually have to sacrifice more than 3 tons of avocados to get 1 additional ton of soybeans. Resources are no longer perfectly substitutable between alternative uses, as our constant-cost assumption implied. Resources less and less suitable to soybean production must be allocated to the U.S. soybean industry in expanding soybean output, and that means increasing costs—the sacrifice of larger and larger amounts of avocados for each additional ton of soybeans.

Photo Op The Fruits of Free Trade*

Because of specialization and exchange, fruits from all over the world appear in our grocery stores. For example, apples may be from New Zealand; bananas, from Ecuador; coconuts, from the Philippines; pineapples, from Costa Rica; raspberries, from Mexico; plums, from Chile; and grapes, from Peru.

* This example is from "The Fruits of Free Trade," Federal Reserve Bank of Dallas, Annual Report 2002, p. 3.

Similarly, Mexico will find that its cost of producing an additional ton of avocados will rise beyond 4 tons of soybeans as it produces more avocados. Resources transferred from soybean to avocado production will eventually be less suitable to avocado production.

At some point the differing domestic cost ratios that underlie comparative advantage will disappear, and further specialization will become uneconomical. And, most importantly, this point of equal cost ratios may be reached while the United States is still producing some avocados along with its soybeans and Mexico is producing some soybeans along with its avocados. The primary effect of increasing opportunity costs is less-than-complete specialization. For this reason we often find domestically produced products competing directly against identical or similar imported products within a particular economy.

The Foreign Exchange Market

foreign exchange market
A market in which foreign currencies are exchanged and relative currency prices are established.

exchange rates
The rates at which national currencies trade for one another.

Buyers and sellers (whether individuals, firms, or nations) use money to buy products or to pay for the use of resources. Within the domestic economy, prices are stated in terms of the domestic currency and buyers use that currency to purchase domestic products. In Mexico, for example, buyers have pesos, and that is what sellers want.

International markets are different. Sellers set their prices in terms of their domestic currencies, but buyers often possess entirely different currencies. How many dollars does it take to buy a truckload of Mexican avocados selling for 3000 pesos, a German automobile selling for 50,000 euros, or a Japanese motorcycle priced at 300,000 yen? Producers in Mexico, Germany, and Japan want payment in pesos, euros, and yen, respectively, so that they can pay their wages, rent, interest, dividends, and taxes.

A **foreign exchange market,** a market in which various national currencies are exchanged for one another, serves this need. The equilibrium prices in such currency markets are called **exchange rates.** An exchange rate is the rate at which the currency of one nation can be exchanged for the currency of another nation. (See Global Snapshot 18.3.)

Exchange Rates: Foreign Currency per U.S. Dollar

The amount of foreign currency that a dollar will buy varies greatly from nation to nation and fluctuates in response to supply and demand changes in the foreign exchange market. The amounts shown here are for April 2005.

$1 Will Buy
43.65 Indian rupees
.53 British pounds
1.22 Canadian dollars
11.17 Mexican pesos
1.20 Swiss francs
.77 European euros
108 Japanese yen
1012 South Korean won
7.10 Swedish kronors
2146 Venezuelan bolivars

© PhotoLink/Getty Images/DIL

Photo Op Foreign Currencies

The world is awash with hundreds of national currencies. Currency markets determine the rates of exchange between them.

The market price or exchange rate of a nation's currency is an unusual price; it links all domestic prices with all foreign prices. Exchange rates enable consumers in one country to translate prices of foreign goods into units of their own currency: They need only multiply the foreign product price by the exchange rate. If the U.S. dollar–yen exchange rate is \$.01 (1 cent) per yen, a Sony television set priced at ¥20,000 will cost \$200 (=20,000 × \$.01) in the United States. If the exchange rate rises to \$.02 (2 cents) per yen, the television will cost \$400 (=20,000 × \$.02) in the United States. Similarly, all other Japanese products would double in price to U.S. buyers in response to the altered exchange rate.

Exchange Rates

18.1 Exchange rates

Let's examine the rate, or price, at which U.S. dollars might be exchanged for British pounds. In Figure 18.1 we show the dollar price of 1 pound on the vertical axis and the quantity of pounds on the horizontal axis. The demand for pounds is D_1 and the supply of pounds is S_1 in this market for British pounds.

The *demand-for-pounds curve* is downward-sloping because all British goods and services will be cheaper to the United States if pounds become less expensive to the United States. That is, at lower dollar prices for pounds, the United States can obtain more pounds for each dollar and therefore buy more British goods and services per

FIGURE 18.1

The market for foreign currency (pounds). The intersection of the demand-for-pounds curve D_1 and the supply-of-pounds curve S_1 determines the equilibrium dollar price of pounds, here, \$2. That means that the exchange rate is \$2 = £1. The upward blue arrow is a reminder that a higher dollar price of pounds (say, \$3 = £1, caused by a shift in either the demand or the supply curve) means that the dollar has depreciated (the pound has appreciated). The downward blue arrow tells us that a lower dollar price of pounds (say, \$1 = £1, again caused by a shift in either the demand or the supply curve) means that the dollar has appreciated (the pound has depreciated).

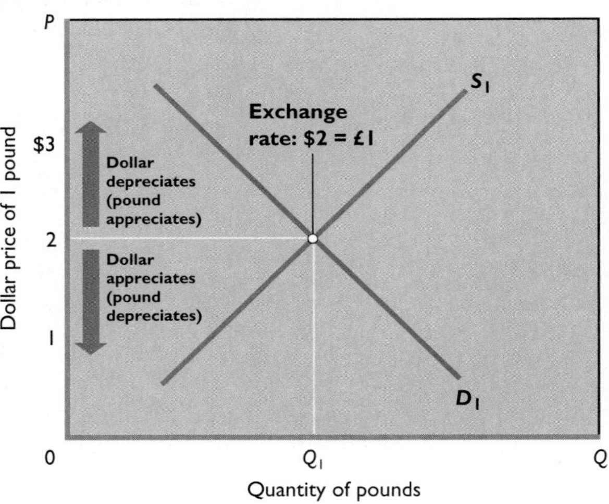

dollar. To buy those cheaper British goods, U.S. consumers will increase the quantity of pounds they demand.

The *supply-of-pounds curve* slopes upward because the British will purchase more U.S. goods when the dollar price of pounds rises (that is, as the pound price of dollars falls). When the British buy more U.S. goods, they supply a greater quantity of pounds to the foreign exchange market. In other words, they must exchange pounds for dollars to purchase U.S. goods. So, when the dollar price of pounds rises, the quantity of pounds supplied goes up.

The intersection of the supply curve and the demand curve will determine the dollar price of pounds. In Figure 18.1, that price (exchange rate) is \$2 for £1.

Depreciation and Appreciation

depreciation (of a currency)
A decrease in the value of a currency relative to another currency.

appreciation (of a currency)
An increase in the value of a currency relative to another currency.

An exchange rate determined by market forces can, and often does, change daily like stock and bond prices. These price changes result from changes in the supply of, or demand for, a particular currency. When the dollar price of pounds *rises*, for example, from \$2 = £1 to \$3 = £1, the dollar has *depreciated* relative to the pound (and the pound has appreciated relative to the dollar). A **depreciation** of a currency means that more units of it (dollars) are needed to buy a single unit of some other currency (a pound).

When the dollar price of pounds *falls*, for example, from \$2 = £1 to \$1 = £1, the dollar has *appreciated* relative to the pound. An **appreciation** of a currency means that it takes fewer units of it (dollars) to buy a single unit of some other currency (a pound). For example, the dollar price of pounds might decline from \$2 to \$1. Each British product becomes less expensive in terms of dollars, so people in the United States purchase more British goods. In general, U.S. imports from the United Kingdom rise. Meanwhile, because it takes more pounds to get a dollar, U.S. exports to the United Kingdom fall.

In our U.S.-Britain illustrations, depreciation of the dollar means an appreciation of the pound, and vice versa. When the dollar price of a pound jumps from \$2 = £1 to \$3 = £1, the pound has appreciated relative to the dollar because it takes fewer pounds to buy \$1. At \$2 = £1, it took £1/2 to buy \$1; at \$3 = £1, it takes only £1/3 to buy \$1. Conversely, when the dollar appreciates relative to the pound, the pound depreciates relative to the dollar. More pounds are needed to buy a U.S. dollar.

Determinants of Exchange Rates

What factors would cause a nation's currency to appreciate or depreciate in the market for foreign exchange? Here are three generalizations (other things equal):

- If the demand for a nation's currency increases, that currency will appreciate; if the demand declines, that currency will depreciate.
- If the supply of a nation's currency increases, that currency will depreciate; if the supply decreases, that currency will appreciate.
- If a nation's currency appreciates, some foreign currency depreciates relative to it.

With these generalizations in mind, let's examine the determinants of exchange rates—the factors that shift the demand or supply curve for a certain currency.

Tastes Any change in consumer tastes or preferences for the products of a foreign country may alter the demand for that nation's currency and change its exchange rate. If technological advances in U.S. MP3 players make them more attractive to British consumers and businesses, then the British will supply more pounds in the exchange market in order to purchase more U.S. MP3 players. The supply-of-pounds curve will shift to the right, causing the pound to depreciate and the dollar to appreciate.

In contrast, the U.S. demand-for-pounds curve will shift to the right if British woolen apparel becomes more fashionable in the United States. So the pound will appreciate and the dollar will depreciate.

Relative Income A nation's currency is likely to depreciate if its growth of national income is more rapid than that of other countries. Here's why: A country's imports vary directly with its income level. As total income rises in the United States, people there buy both more domestic goods and more foreign goods. If the U.S. economy is expanding rapidly and the British economy is stagnant, U.S. imports of British goods, and therefore U.S. demands for pounds, will increase. The dollar price of pounds will rise, so the dollar will depreciate.

Relative Price Levels Changes in the relative price levels of two nations may change the demand for and supply of currencies and alter the exchange rate between the two nations' currencies. If, for example, the domestic price level rises rapidly in the United States and remains constant in Great Britain, U.S. consumers will seek out low-priced British goods, increasing the demand for pounds. The British will purchase fewer U.S. goods, reducing the supply of pounds. This combination of demand and supply changes will cause the pound to appreciate and the dollar to depreciate.

Relative Interest Rates Changes in relative interest rates between two countries may alter their exchange rate. Suppose that real interest rates rise in the United States but stay constant in Great Britain. British citizens will then find the United States an attractive place in which to make financial investments. To undertake these investments, they will have to supply pounds in the foreign exchange market to obtain dollars. The increase in the supply of pounds results in depreciation of the pound and appreciation of the dollar.

Speculation Currency speculators are people who buy and sell currencies with an eye toward reselling or repurchasing them at a profit. Suppose that, as a group, speculators anticipate that the pound will appreciate and the dollar will depreciate. Speculators holding dollars will therefore try to convert them into pounds. This effort will increase the demand for pounds and cause the dollar price of pounds to rise (that is, cause the dollar to depreciate). A self-fulfilling prophecy occurs: The pound appreciates and the dollar depreciates because speculators act on the belief that these changes will in fact take place. In this way, speculation can cause changes in exchange rates.

tariffs
Taxes imposed by a nation on imported goods.

import quotas
Limits imposed by nations on the quantities (or total values) of goods that may be imported during some period of time.

nontariff barriers (NTBs)
All impediments other than protective tariffs that nations establish to impede imports, including licensing requirements, unreasonable product-quality standards, unnecessary bureaucratic detail in customs procedures, and so on.

voluntary export restriction (VER)
An agreement by countries or foreign firms to limit their exports to a certain foreign nation to avoid enactment of formal trade barriers by that nation.

Government and Trade

If people and nations benefit from specialization and international exchange, why do governments sometimes try to restrict the free flow of imports or encourage exports? What kinds of world trade barriers can governments erect, and why would they do so?

Trade Protections and Subsidies

Trade interventions by government take several forms. Excise taxes on imported goods are called **tariffs.** A *protective tariff* is designed to shield domestic producers from foreign competition. Such tariffs impede free trade by causing a rise in the prices of imported goods, thereby shifting demand toward domestic products. An excise tax on imported shoes, for example, would make domestically produced shoes more attractive to consumers. Although protective tariffs are usually not high enough to stop the importation of foreign goods, they put foreign producers at a competitive disadvantage in selling in domestic markets.

Import quotas are limits on the quantities or total value of specific items that may be imported. Once a quota is "filled," further imports of that product are choked off. Import quotas are more effective than tariffs in retarding international commerce. With a tariff, a product can go on being imported in large quantities; with an import quota, however, all imports are prohibited once the quota is filled.

Nontariff barriers (NTBs) include onerous licensing requirements, unreasonable standards pertaining to product quality, or excessive bureaucratic paperwork in customs procedures. Some nations require that importers of foreign goods obtain licenses. By restricting the issuance of licenses, imports can be restricted. Although many nations carefully inspect imported agricultural products to prevent the introduction of potentially harmful insects, some countries use lengthy inspections to impede imports.

A **voluntary export restriction (VER)** is a trade barrier by which foreign firms "voluntarily" limit the amount of their exports to a particular country. Exporters agree to a VER, which has the effect of an import quota, to avoid more stringent trade barriers. In the late 1990s, for example, Canadian producers of softwood lumber (fir, spruce, cedar, pine) agreed to a VER on exports to the United States under the threat of a permanently higher U.S. tariff.

Export subsidies consist of government payments to domestic producers of export goods. By reducing production costs, the subsidies enable producers to charge lower prices and thus to sell more exports in world markets. Example: The United States and other nations have subsidized domestic farmers to boost the domestic food supply. Such subsidies have lowered the market price of agricultural commodities and have artificially lowered their export prices.

export subsidies Government payments to domestic producers to enable them to reduce the price of a product to foreign buyers.

Economic Impact of Tariffs

18.2 Mercantilism

Tariffs, quotas, and other trade restrictions have a series of economic effects predicted by supply and demand analysis and observed in reality. These effects vary somewhat by type of trade protection. So to keep things simple, we will focus on the effects of tariffs.

Direct Effects Because tariffs raise the price of goods imported to the United States, U.S. consumption of those goods declines. Higher prices reduce quantity demanded, as indicated by the law of demand. A tariff prompts consumers to buy fewer of the imported goods, and reallocate a portion of their expenditures to less desired substitute products. U.S. consumers are clearly injured by the tariff.

U.S. producers—who are not subject to the tariff—receive the higher price (pre-tariff foreign price + tariff) on the imported product. Because this new price is higher than before, the domestic producers respond by producing more. Higher prices increase quantity supplied, as indicated by the law of supply. So domestic producers increase their output. They therefore enjoy both a higher price and expanded sales; this explains why domestic producers lobby for protective tariffs. But from a social point of view, the greater domestic production means the tariff allows domestic producers to bid resources away from other, more efficient, U.S. industries.

Foreign producers are hurt by tariffs. Although the sales price of an imported good is higher, that higher amount accrues to the U.S. government as tariff revenue, not to foreign producers. The after-tariff price, or the per-unit revenue to foreign producers, remains as before, but the volume of U.S. imports (foreign exports) falls.

Government gains revenue from tariffs. This revenue is a transfer of income from consumers to government and does not represent any net change in the nation's economic well-being. The result is that government gains a portion of what consumers lose by paying more for imported goods.

Indirect Effects Tariffs have a subtle effect beyond those just mentioned. They also hurt domestic firms that use the protected goods as inputs in their production process. For example, a tariff on imported steel boosts the price of steel girders, thus hurting firms that build bridges and office towers. Also, tariffs reduce competition in the protected industries. With less competition from foreign producers, domestic firms may be slow to design and implement cost-saving production methods and introduce new products.

Because foreigners sell fewer imported goods in the United States, they earn fewer dollars and so must buy fewer U.S. exports. U.S. export industries must then cut production and release resources. These are highly efficient industries, as we know from their comparative advantage and their ability to sell goods in world markets.

Tariffs directly promote the expansion of inefficient industries that do not have a comparative advantage; they also indirectly cause the contraction of relatively efficient industries that do have a comparative advantage. Put bluntly, tariffs cause resources to be shifted in the wrong direction—and that is not surprising. We know that specialization and world trade lead to more efficient use of world resources and greater world output. But protective tariffs reduce world trade. Therefore, tariffs also reduce efficiency and the world's real output.

Net Costs of Tariffs

Tariffs impose costs on domestic consumers but provide gains to domestic producers and revenue to the Federal government. The consumer costs of trade restrictions are calculated by determining the effect the restrictions have on consumer prices. Protection raises the price of a product in three ways: (1) The price of the imported product goes up; (2) the higher price of imports causes some consumers to shift their purchases to higher-priced domestically produced goods; and (3) the prices of domestically produced goods rise because import competition has declined.

Study after study finds that the costs to consumers substantially exceed the gains to producers and government. A sizable net cost or efficiency loss to society arises from trade protection. Furthermore, industries employ large amounts of economic resources to influence Congress to pass and retain protectionist laws. Because these efforts divert resources away from more socially desirable purposes, trade restrictions also impose that cost on society.

Conclusion: The gains that U.S. trade barriers produce for protected industries and their workers come at the expense of much greater losses for the entire economy. The result is economic inefficiency.

So Why Government Trade Protections?

In view of the benefits of free trade, what accounts for the impulse to impede imports and boost exports through government policy? There are several reasons—some legitimate, most not.

Misunderstanding the Gains from Trade It is a commonly accepted myth that the greatest benefit to be derived from international trade is greater domestic sales and employment in the export sector. This suggests that exports are "good" because they increase domestic sales and employment, whereas imports are "bad" because they reduce domestic sales and deprive people of jobs at home. Actually, the true benefit created by international trade is the extra output obtained from abroad—the imports obtained for less cost than the cost if they were produced at home.

Political Considerations While a nation as a whole gains from trade, trade may harm particular domestic industries and particular groups of resource suppliers. In our earlier comparative-advantage example, specialization and trade adversely affected the U.S. avocado industry and the Mexican soybean industry. Understandably, those industries might seek to preserve their economic positions by persuading their respective governments to protect them from imports—perhaps through tariffs.

Those who directly benefit from import protection are relatively few in number but have much at stake. Thus, they have a strong incentive to pursue political activity to achieve their aims. Moreover, because the costs of import protection are buried in the price of goods and spread out over millions of citizens, the cost born by each individual citizen is quite small. However, the full cost of tariffs and quotas typically greatly exceeds the benefits. It is not uncommon to find that it costs the public $250,000 or more a year to protect a domestic job that pays less than one-fourth that amount.

In the political arena, the voice of the relatively few producers and unions demanding *protectionism* is loud and constant, whereas the voice of those footing the bill is soft or nonexistent. When political deal making is added in—"You back tariffs for the apparel industry in my state, and I'll back tariffs for the steel industry in your state"—the outcome can be a network of protective tariffs.

Buy American?

Will "buying American" make Americans better off? No, says Dallas Federal Reserve economist W. Michael Cox:

> A common myth is that it is better for Americans to spend their money at home than abroad. The best way to expose the fallacy of this argument is to take it to its logical extreme. If it is better for me to spend my money here than abroad, then it is even better yet to buy in Texas than in New York, better yet to buy in Dallas than in Houston . . . in my own neighborhood . . . within my own family . . . to consume only what I can produce. Alone and poor.*

* "The Fruits of Free Trade," Federal Reserve Bank of Dallas, Annual Report 2002, p. 16.

Three Arguments for Protection

Arguments for trade protection are many and diverse. Some—such as tariffs to protect "infant industries" or to create "military self-sufficiency"—have some legitimacy. But other arguments break down under close scrutiny. Three protectionist arguments, in particular, have persisted decade after decade in the United States.

Increased Domestic Employment Argument

Arguing for a tariff to "save U.S. jobs" becomes fashionable when the economy encounters a recession or experiences slow job growth during a recovery (as in the early 2000s in the United States). In an economy that engages in international trade, exports involve spending on domestic output and imports reflect spending to obtain part of another nation's output. So, in this argument, reducing imports will divert spending on another nation's output to spending on domestic output. Thus domestic output and employment will rise. But this argument has several shortcomings.

While imports may eliminate some U.S. jobs, they create others. Imports may have eliminated the jobs of some U.S. steel and textile workers in recent years, but other workers have gained jobs unloading ships, flying imported aircraft, and selling imported electronic equipment. Import restrictions alter the composition of employment, but they may have little or no effect on the volume of employment.

The *fallacy of composition*—the false idea that what is true for the part is necessarily true for the whole—is also present in this rationale for tariffs. All nations cannot simultaneously succeed in restricting imports while maintaining their exports; what is true for one nation is not true for all nations. The exports of one nation must be the imports of another nation. To the extent that one country is able to expand its economy through an excess of exports over imports, the resulting excess of imports over exports worsens another economy's unemployment problem. It is no wonder that tariffs and import quotas meant to achieve domestic full employment are called "beggar my neighbor" policies: They achieve short-run domestic goals by making trading partners poorer.

Moreover, nations adversely affected by tariffs and quotas are likely to retaliate, causing a "trade-barrier war" that will choke off trade and make all nations worse off. The **Smoot-Hawley Tariff Act** of 1930 is a classic example. Although that act was meant to reduce imports and stimulate U.S. production, the high tariffs it authorized prompted adversely affected nations to retaliate with tariffs equally high. International trade fell, lowering the output and income of all nations. Economic historians generally agree that the Smoot-Hawley Tariff Act was a contributing cause of the Great Depression.

Smoot-Hawley Tariff Act
Legislation passed in 1930 that established very high U.S. tariffs designed to reduce imports and stimulate the domestic economy. Instead, the law resulted only in retaliatory tariffs by other nations and a decline in trade worldwide.

Finally, forcing an excess of exports over imports cannot succeed in raising domestic employment over the long run. It is through U.S. imports that foreign nations earn dollars for buying U.S. exports. In the long run a nation must import in order to export. The long-run impact of tariffs is not an increase in domestic employment but, at best, a reallocation of workers away from export industries and to protected domestic industries. This shift implies a less efficient allocation of resources.

Cheap Foreign Labor Argument

The cheap foreign labor argument says that government must shield domestic firms and workers from the ruinous competition of countries where wages are low. If protection is not provided, cheap imports will flood U.S. markets and the prices of U.S. goods—along with the wages of U.S. workers—will be pulled down. That is, the domestic living standard in the United States will be reduced.

This argument can be rebutted at several levels. The logic of the argument suggests that it is not mutually beneficial for rich and poor persons to trade with one another. However, that is not the case. A relatively low-income mechanic may fix the Mercedes owned by a wealthy lawyer, and both may benefit from the transaction. And both U.S. consumers and Chinese workers gain when they "trade" a pair of athletic shoes priced at $30 as opposed to a similar shoe made in the U.S. for $60.

Also, recall that gains from trade are based on comparative advantage, not on absolute advantage. Again, think back to our U.S.-Mexico (soybean-avocado) example in which the United States had greater labor productivity than Mexico in producing both soybeans and avocados. Because of that greater productivity, wages and living standards will be higher for U.S. labor. Mexico's less productive labor will receive lower wages.

The cheap foreign labor argument suggests that, to maintain American living standards, the United States should not trade with low-wage Mexico. Suppose it forgoes trade with Mexico. Will wages and living standards rise in the United States as a result? Absolutely not! To obtain avocados, the United States will have to reallocate a portion of its labor from its relatively efficient soybean industry to its relatively inefficient avocado industry. As a result, the average productivity of U.S. labor will fall, as will real wages and living standards for American workers. The labor forces of both countries will have diminished standards of living because without specialization and trade they will have less output available to them. Compare column 4 with column 1 in Table 18.4 to confirm this point.

Protection-against-Dumping Argument

This argument contends that tariffs are needed to protect domestic firms from "dumping" by foreign producers. **Dumping** is the selling of excess goods in a foreign market at a price below average cost or below the price charged in the home market. Economists cite two plausible reasons for this behavior. First, firms may use dumping abroad to drive out domestic competitors there, thus obtaining monopoly power and monopoly prices and profits for the importing firm. The long-term economic profits resulting from this strategy may more than offset the earlier losses that accompany the below-cost sales.

dumping
The sale of products in a foreign country at prices either below costs or below the prices charged at home.

Second, dumping may be a form of price discrimination, which we know from Chapter 8 is charging different prices to different customers even though costs are the same. The foreign seller may find it can maximize its profit by charging a high price in its monopolized domestic market while unloading its surplus output at a lower price in the United States. The surplus output may be needed so that the firm can obtain the overall per-unit cost saving associated with large-scale production. The higher profit in the home market more than makes up for the losses incurred on sales abroad.

Because dumping is an "unfair trade practice," most nations prohibit it. For example, where dumping is shown to injure U.S. firms, the Federal government imposes tariffs called *antidumping duties* on the specific goods. But there are relatively few documented cases of dumping each year, and specific instances of unfair trade do not justify widespread, permanent tariffs. Moreover, antidumping duties can be abused. Often, what appears to be dumping is simply comparative advantage at work.

Trade Adjustment Assistance

A nation's comparative advantage in the production of a certain product is not forever fixed. As national economies evolve, the size and quality of their labor forces may change, the volume and composition of their capital stocks may shift, new technologies may develop, and even the quality of land and the quantity of natural resources may be altered. As these changes take place, the relative efficiency with which a nation can produce specific goods will also change. Also, new trade agreements can suddenly leave formerly protected industries highly vulnerable to major disruption or even collapse.

Shifts in patterns of comparative advantage and removal of trade protection can hurt specific groups of workers. For example, the erosion of the United States' once strong comparative advantage in steel has caused production plant shutdowns and layoffs in the U.S. steel industry. The textile and apparel industries in the United States face similar difficulties. Clearly, not everyone wins from free trade (or freer trade). Some workers lose.

The **Trade Adjustment Assistance Act** of 2002 has introduced some new, novel elements to help those hurt by shifts in international trade patterns. The law provides cash assistance (beyond unemployment insurance) for up to 78 weeks for workers displaced by imports or plant relocations abroad. To obtain the assistance, workers must participate in job searches, training programs, or remedial education. There also are relocation allowances to help displaced workers move geographically to new jobs within the United States. Refundable tax credits for health insurance serve as payments to help workers maintain their insurance coverage during the retraining and job search period. Also, workers who are 50 years of age or older are eligible for "wage insurance," which replaces some of the difference in pay (if any) between their old and new jobs.

Trade Adjustment Assistance Act
A U.S. law passed in 2002 that provides cash assistance, education and training benefits, health care subsidies, and wage subsidies (for persons age 50 or more) to workers displaced by imports or plant relocations abroad.

Trade adjustment assistance not only helps workers hurt by international trade but also helps create the political support necessary to reduce trade barriers and export subsidies. For both reasons, many economists support it.

But not all observers are fans of trade adjustment assistance. Loss of jobs from imports or plant relocations abroad is only a small fraction (about 3 percent in recent years) of total job loss in the economy each year. Many workers also lose their jobs because of changing patterns of demand, changing technology, bad management, and other dynamic aspects of a market economy. Some critics ask, "What makes losing one's job to international trade worthy of such special treatment, compared to losing one's job to, say, technological change?" There is no totally satisfying answer.

Applying the Analysis

Is Offshoring Bad?

offshoring The practice of shifting work previously done by American workers to workers located in other nations.

In recent years U.S. firms have found it increasingly profitable to outsource work abroad. Economists call this business activity **offshoring:** shifting work previously done by American workers to workers located in other nations. Offshoring is not a new practice but traditionally has involved components for U.S. manufacturing goods. For example, Boeing has long offshored the production of major airplane parts for its "American" aircraft.

Recent advances in computer and communications technologies have enabled U.S. firms to offshore service jobs such as data entry, book composition, software coding, call-center operations, medical transcription, and claims processing to countries such as India. Where offshoring occurs, some of the value added in the production process occurs in foreign countries rather than the United States. So part of the income generated from the production of U.S. goods is paid to foreigners, not to American workers.

Offshoring is obviously costly to Americans who lose their jobs, but it is not generally bad for the economy. Offshoring simply reflects a growing international trade in services. That trade has been made possible by recent trade agreements and new information and communication technologies. Like trade in goods, trade in services reflects comparative advantage and is beneficial to both trading parties. Moreover, the United States has a sizable trade surplus with other nations in services. The U.S. gains by specializing in high-valued services such as transportation services, accounting services, legal services, and advertising services, where it still has a comparative advantage. It then "trades" to obtain lower-valued services such as call-center and data entry work, for which comparative advantage has gone abroad.

Offshoring also increases the demand for complementary jobs in the United States. Jobs that are close substitutes for existing U.S. jobs are lost, but complementary jobs in the United States are expanded. For example, the lower price of offshore maintenance of aircraft and reservation centers reduces the price of airline tickets. That means more domestic and international flights by American carriers, which in turn means more jobs for U.S.-based pilots, flight attendants, baggage handlers, and check-in personnel. Moreover, offshoring encourages domestic investment and expansion of firms in the United States by reducing their production costs and keeping them competitive worldwide. Some observers equate "offshoring jobs" to "importing competitiveness."

Question:
What has enabled white-collar labor services to become the world's newest export and import commodity even though such labor itself remains in place?

Multilateral Trade Agreements and Free-Trade Zones

Being aware of the overall benefits of free trade, nations have worked to lower tariffs worldwide. Their pursuit of free trade has been aided by the growing power of free-trade interest groups: Exporters of goods and services, importers of foreign components used in "domestic" products, and domestic sellers of imported products all strongly support lower tariffs. And, in fact, tariffs have generally declined during the past half-century.

General Agreement on Tariffs and Trade (GATT)
An international accord reached in 1947 in which 23 nations agreed to give equal and nondiscriminatory treatment to one another, to reduce tariffs through multilateral negotiations, and to eliminate import quotas.

General Agreement on Tariffs and Trade

Following the Second World War, the major nations of the world set upon a general course of liberalizing trade. In 1947 some 23 nations, including the United States, signed the **General Agreement on Tariffs and Trade (GATT).** GATT was based on the principles of equal, nondiscriminatory trade treatment for all member nations and the reduction of tariffs and quotas by multilateral negotiation. Basically, GATT provided a continuing forum for the negotiation of reduced trade barriers on a multilateral basis among nations.

Since 1947, member nations have completed eight "rounds" of GATT negotiations to reduce trade barriers. The *Uruguay Round* agreement of 1993 phased in trade liberalizations between 1995 and 2005.

World Trade Organization (WTO)
An organization of 148 nations (as of 2005) that oversees the provisions of the current world trade agreement, resolves disputes stemming from it, and holds forums for further rounds of trade negotiations.

World Trade Organization

The Uruguay Round of 1993 established the **World Trade Organization (WTO)** as GATT's successor. In 2005, 148 nations belonged to the WTO, which oversees trade agreements and rules on disputes relating to them. It also provides forums for further rounds of trade negotiations. The ninth and latest round of negotiations—the **Doha Round**—was launched in Doha, Qatar, in late 2001. (The trade rounds occur over several years in several geographic venues but are named after the city or country of origination.) The negotiations are aimed at further reducing tariffs and quotas, as well as agricultural subsidies that distort trade. One of this chapter's questions asks you to update the progress of the Doha Round via an Internet search.

Doha Round
The latest, uncompleted (as of 2005) sequence of trade negotiations by members of the World Trade Organization; named after Doha, Qatar, where the set of negotiations began.

GATT and the WTO have been positive forces in the trend toward liberalized world trade. The trade rules agreed upon by the member nations provide a strong and necessary bulwark against the protectionism called for by the special-interest groups in the various nations. For that reason and others, the WTO is controversial.

Applying the Analysis

The WTO Protests

The general public came to know the WTO in November 1999, when tens of thousands of people took part in sometimes-violent demonstrations in Seattle. Since then, international WTO meetings have drawn large numbers of angry demonstrators. The groups involved include some labor unions (which fear loss of jobs and labor protections), environmental groups (which oppose environmental degradation), socialists (who dislike capitalism and multinational corporations), and a few anarchists (who detest government authority of any kind). Dispersed within the crowds are other, smaller groups such as European farmers who fear the WTO will threaten their livelihoods by reducing agricultural tariffs and farm subsidies.

The most substantive WTO issues involve labor protections and environmental standards. Labor unions in industrially advanced countries (hereafter, "advanced countries") would like the international trade rules to include such labor standards as collective bargaining rights, minimum wages, and workplace safety standards. Such rules are fully consistent with the long-standing values and objectives of unions.

But there is a hitch. Imposing labor standards on low-income developing countries (hereafter, "developing countries") would raise labor and production costs in those nations. The higher costs in the developing countries would raise the relative price of their goods, making them less competitive with goods produced in the advanced countries (which already meet the labor standards). So the trade rules would increase the demands for products and workers in the advanced countries and reduce them in the developing countries. Union workers in the advanced countries would benefit; consumers in the advanced countries and workers in the developing countries would be harmed. The trade standards would contribute to poverty in the world's poorest nations.

Not surprisingly, the developing countries say "thanks, but no thanks" to the protesters' pleas for labor standards. Instead, they want the advanced countries to reduce or eliminate tariffs on goods imported from the developing countries. That would expand the demand for products and workers in the developing countries, boosting their wages. As living standards in the developing countries rise, those countries then can afford to devote more of their annual productivity advances to improved working conditions.

Environmental standards are the second substantive WTO issue. Critics are concerned that trade liberalization will encourage more activities that degrade sensitive forests, fisheries, and mining lands and contribute to air, water, and solid-waste pollution. Critics would like the WTO to establish trade rules that set minimum environmental standards for the member nations. The WTO nations respond that environmental standards are outside the mandate of the WTO and must be established by the individual nations via their own political processes.

Moreover, imposing such standards on low-income developing countries may simply provide competitive cost advantages to firms in the advanced countries. As with labor standards, environmental standards will simply slow economic growth and prolong poverty in the developing countries. Studies show that economic growth and rising living standards are strongly associated with greater environmental protections. In the early phases of their development, low-income developing nations typically choose to trade off some environmental damage to achieve higher real wages. But studies show that the tradeoff is usually reversed once standards of living rise beyond threshold levels.

Question:

Do you think the WTO protests will build in momentum over the next decade or largely subside? Briefly explain your reasoning.

European Union

Countries have also sought to reduce tariffs by creating regional *free-trade zones*—also called *trade blocs*. The most dramatic example is the **European Union (EU).** In 2005 the EU was composed of 25 European nations.[2]

The EU has abolished tariffs and import quotas on nearly all products traded among the participating nations and established a common system of tariffs applicable to all goods received from nations outside the EU. It has also liberalized the movement of capital and labor within the EU and has created common policies in other economic matters of joint concern, such as agriculture, transportation, and business practices. The EU is now a strong **trade bloc:** a group of countries having common identity, economic interests, and trade rules. Of the 25 EU countries, 12 use the **euro** as a common currency.

EU integration has achieved for Europe what the U.S. constitutional prohibition on tariffs by individual states has achieved for the United States: increased regional specialization, greater productivity, greater output, and faster economic growth. The free flow of goods and services has created large markets for EU industries. The resulting economies of large-scale production have enabled those industries to achieve much lower costs than they could have achieved in their small, single-nation markets.

European Union (EU)
An association of 25 European nations that has eliminated tariffs and quotas among them, established common tariffs for imported goods from outside the member nations, reduced barriers to the free movement of capital, and created other common economic policies.

trade bloc
A group of nations that lower or abolish trade barriers among themselves.

euro
The common currency unit used by 12 (as of 2005) European nations in the European Union.

North American Free Trade Agreement

In 1993 Canada, Mexico, and the United States formed a major trade bloc. The **North American Free Trade Agreement (NAFTA)** established a free-trade zone that has about the same combined output as the EU but encompasses a much larger geographic area. NAFTA has greatly reduced tariffs and other trade barriers between Canada, Mexico, and the United States and will eliminate them entirely by 2008.

Critics of NAFTA feared that it would cause a massive loss of U.S. jobs as firms moved to Mexico to take advantage of lower wages and weaker regulations on pollution and workplace safety. Also, there was concern that Japan and South Korea would build plants in Mexico and transport goods tariff-free to the United States, further hurting U.S. firms and workers.

In retrospect, critics were much too pessimistic. In the 11-year period (1993–2004) following passage of NAFTA, employment in the United States rose by more than 19 million workers and the unemployment rate fell from 6.9 percent to 5.4 percent. Increased trade among Canada, Mexico, and the United States has enhanced the standard of living in all three countries.

Not all aspects of trade blocs are positive. By giving preferences to countries within their free-trade zones, trade blocs such as the EU and NAFTA tend to reduce their members' trade with non-bloc members. Thus, the world loses some of the benefits of a completely open global trading system. Eliminating that disadvantage has been one of the motivations for liberalizing global trade through the World Trade Organization. Its liberalizations apply equally to all 148 nations that belong to the WTO.

North American Free Trade Agreement (NAFTA)
A 1993 agreement establishing, over a 15-year period, a free-trade zone composed of Canada, Mexico, and the United States.

---

[2] France, Germany, United Kingdom, Italy, Belgium, the Netherlands, Luxembourg, Denmark, Ireland, Greece, Spain, Portugal, Austria, Finland, Sweden, Poland, Hungary, Czech Republic, Slovakia, Lithuania, Latvia, Estonia, Slovenia, Malta, and Cyprus.

U.S. Trade Deficits

As indicated in Figure 18.2, the United States has experienced large and persistent trade deficits over the past several years. These deficits climbed steeply between 1994 and 2000, fell slightly in the recessionary year 2001, and rose again between 2002 and 2004. In 2004 the trade deficit on goods was $665 billion and the trade deficit on goods and services was $617 billion. Large trade deficits are expected to continue for many years.

Causes of the Trade Deficits

There are several reasons for these large trade deficits. First, over recent years the U.S. economy has grown more rapidly than the economies of several of its major trading partners. The strong growth of U.S. income that accompanies economic growth has enabled Americans to buy more imported goods. In contrast, Japan and some European nations have either suffered recession or experienced slow income growth. So their purchases of U.S. exports have not kept pace with the growing U.S. imports. Large trade deficits with Japan and Germany have been particularly noteworthy in this regard.

Second, large trade deficits with China have emerged, reaching $162 billion in 2004. This is even greater than the U.S. trade imbalance with Japan ($77 billion in 2004) or Germany ($47 billion in 2004). The United States is China's largest export market, and although China has increased its imports from the United States, its standard of living has not yet increased enough for its citizens to afford large quantities of U.S. goods and services.

Finally, a declining U.S. saving rate (=saving/total income) undoubtedly has also contributed to U.S. trade deficits. Over the last 10 years, the saving rate has diminished while the investment rate (=investment/total income) has remained stable or

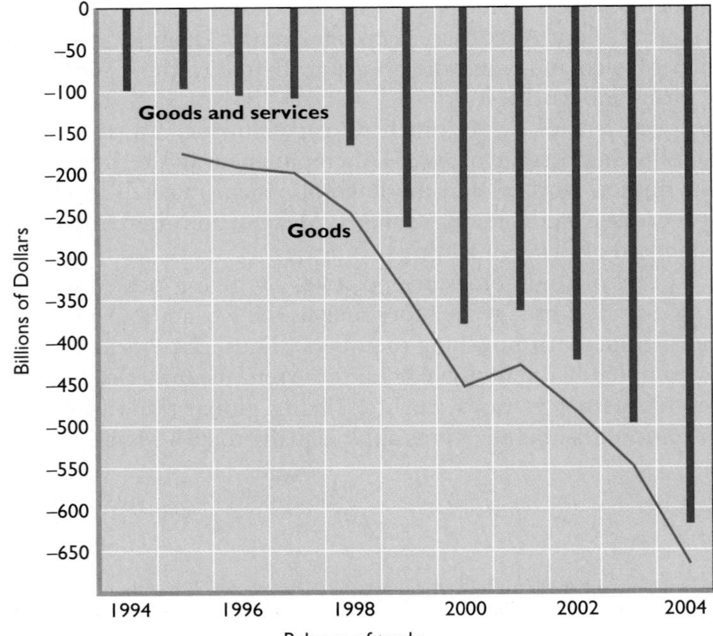

FIGURE 18.2
U.S. trade deficits, 1994–2004. The United States experienced large deficits in goods and in goods and services between 1994 and 2004. These deficits were particularly large in 2003 and 2004 and are expected to continue at least throughout the current decade.

Source: U.S. Census Bureau, Foreign Trade Division, www.census.gov/foreign-trade/statistics.

increased. The gap between saving and investment has been met through foreign purchases of U.S. real and financial assets. Because foreign savers are willingly financing a larger part of U.S. investment, Americans are able to save less than otherwise and consume more. Part of that added consumption spending is on imported goods. That is, the inflow of funds from abroad may be one cause of the trade deficits, not just a result of those deficits.

The U.S. recession of 2001 temporarily lowered income and reduced U.S. imports and trade deficits. But the general trend toward higher trade deficits quickly reemerged in 2002 and ballooned in 2003 and 2004.

Implications of U.S. Trade Deficits

There is disagreement on whether the large trade deficits should be of major policy concern for the United States. Most economists see both benefits and costs to trade deficits but are increasingly anxious about the size of these deficits.

Increased Current Consumption At the time a trade deficit is occurring, American consumers benefit. A trade deficit means that the United States is receiving more goods and services as imports from abroad than it is sending out as exports. Taken alone, a trade deficit augments the domestic standard of living. But there is a catch: The gain in present consumption may come at the expense of reduced future consumption.

Increased U.S. Indebtedness A trade deficit is considered "unfavorable" because it must be financed by borrowing from the rest of the world, selling off assets, or dipping into foreign currency reserves. Trade deficits are financed primarily by net inpayments of foreign currencies to the United States. When U.S. exports are insufficient to finance U.S. imports, the United States increases both its debt to people abroad and the value of foreign claims against assets in the United States. Financing of the U.S. trade deficit has resulted in a larger foreign accumulation of claims against U.S. financial and real assets than the U.S. claim against foreign assets. Today, the United States is the world's largest debtor nation. In 2003 foreigners owned $2.4 billion more of U.S. assets (corporations, land, stocks, bonds, loan notes) than U.S. citizens and institutions owned of foreign assets.

If the United States wants to regain ownership of these domestic assets, at some future time it will have to export more than it imports. At that time, domestic consumption will be lower because the United States will need to send more of its output abroad than it receives as imports. Therefore, the current consumption gains delivered by U.S. trade deficits may mean permanent debt, permanent foreign ownership, or large sacrifices of future consumption.

We say "may mean" above because the foreign lending to U.S. firms and foreign investment in the United States increase the stock of American capital. U.S. production capacity might increase more rapidly than otherwise because of a large inflow of funds to offset the trade deficits. We know that faster increases in production capacity and real GDP enhance the economy's ability to service foreign debt and buy back real capital, if that is desired.

Downward Pressure on the Dollar Finally, the large U.S. trade deficits place downward pressure on the exchange value of the U.S. dollar. The surge of

Appendix

Graphs and Their Meaning

If you glance quickly through this text, you will find many graphs. These graphs are included to help you visualize and understand economic relationships. Most of our principles or models explain relationships between just two sets of economic data, which can be conveniently represented with two-dimensional graphs.

Construction of a Graph

A graph is a visual representation of the relationship between two variables. The table in Figure A.1 is a hypothetical illustration showing the relationship between income and consumption for the economy as a whole. Because people tend to buy more goods and services when their incomes go up, it is not surprising to find in the table that total consumption in the economy increases as total income increases.

The information in the table is also expressed graphically in Figure A.1. Here is how it is done: We want to show visually or graphically how consumption changes as income changes. Since income is the determining factor, we follow mathematical custom and represent it on the horizontal axis of the graph. And because consumption depends on income, it is represented on the vertical axis of the graph.

The vertical and horizontal scales of the graph reflect the ranges of values of consumption and income, marked in convenient increments. As you can see, the values on the scales cover all the values in the table.

FIGURE A.1

Graphing the direct relationship between consumption and income. Two sets of data that are positively or directly related, such as consumption and income, graph as an upsloping line.

Income per Week	Consumption per Week	Point
$ 0	$ 50	*a*
100	100	*b*
200	150	*c*
300	200	*d*
400	250	*e*

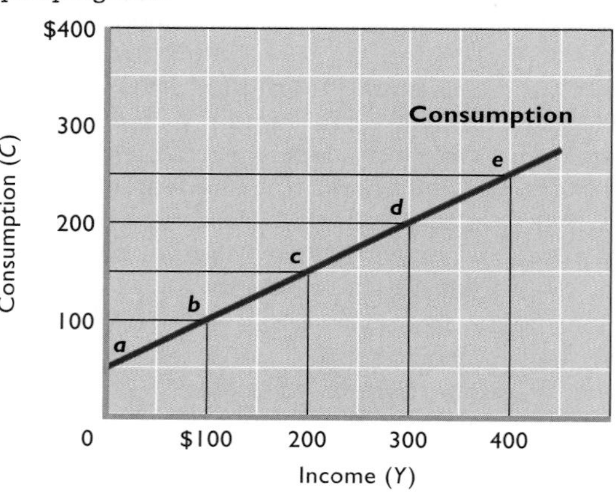

Because the graph has two dimensions, each point within it represents an income value and its associated consumption value. To find a point that represents one of the five income-consumption combinations in the table, we draw lines from the appropriate values on the vertical and horizontal axes. For example, to plot point *c* (the \$200 income–\$150 consumption point), lines are drawn up from the horizontal (income) axis at \$200 and across from the vertical (consumption) axis at \$150. These lines intersect at point *c*, which represents this particular income-consumption combination. You should verify that the other income-consumption combinations shown in the table in Figure A.1 are properly located in the graph that is there.

Finally, by assuming that the same general relationship between income and consumption prevails for all other incomes, we draw a line or smooth curve to connect these points. That line or curve represents the income-consumption relationship.

If the graph is a straight line, as in Figure A.1, the relationship is said to be *linear*.

Direct and Inverse Relationships

The line in Figure A.1 slopes upward to the right, so it depicts a **direct relationship** between income and consumption. A direct relationship, or positive relationship, means that two variables (here, consumption and income) change in the same direction. An increase in consumption is associated with an increase in income; a decrease in consumption accompanies a decrease in income. When two sets of data are positively or directly related, they always graph as an upsloping line, as in Figure A.1.

direct relationship The (positive) relationship between two variables that change in the same direction.

In contrast, two sets of data may be inversely related. Consider the table in Figure A.2, which shows the relationship between the price of basketball tickets and game attendance for Big Time University (BTU). Here there is an **inverse relationship,** or negative relationship, because the two variables change in opposite

inverse relationship The (negative) relationship between two variables that change in opposite directions.

FIGURE A.2

Graphing the inverse relationship between ticket prices and game attendance. Two sets of data that are negatively or inversely related, such as ticket price and the attendance at basketball games, graph as a downsloping line.

Ticket Price	Attendance, Thousands	Point
\$50	0	*a*
40	4	*b*
30	8	*c*
20	12	*d*
10	16	*e*
0	20	*f*

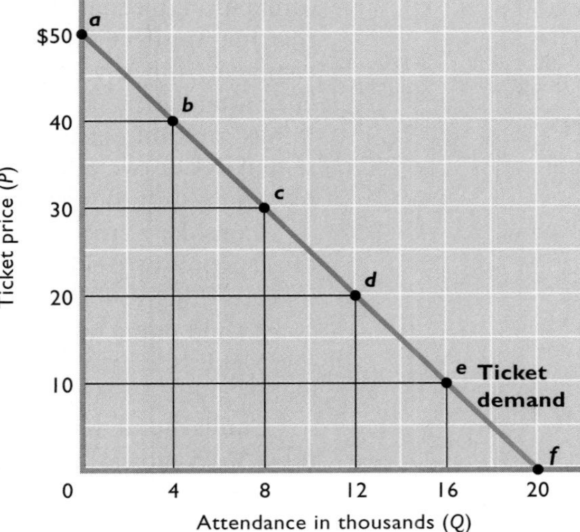

directions. When ticket prices for the games decrease, attendance increases. When ticket prices increase, attendance decreases. The six data points in the table are plotted in the graph in Figure A.2. This inverse relationship graphs as a downsloping line.

Dependent and Independent Variables

independent variable
The variable causing a change in some other (dependent) variable; the "causal variable."

dependent variable
The variable that changes as result of a change in some other (independent) variable; the "outcome variable."

Economists seek to determine which variable is the "cause" and which the "effect." Or, more formally, they seek the independent variable and the dependent variable. The **independent variable** is the cause or source; it is the variable that changes first. The **dependent variable** is the effect or outcome; it is the variable that changes because of the change in the independent variable. As noted in our income-consumption example, income generally is the independent variable and consumption the dependent variable. Income causes consumption to be what it is rather than the other way around. Similarly, ticket prices (set in advance of the season) determine attendance at BTU basketball games; attendance at games does not determine the printed ticket prices for those games. Ticket price is the independent variable, and the quantity of tickets purchased is the dependent variable.

Mathematicians always put the independent variable (cause) on the horizontal axis and the dependent variable (effect) on the vertical axis. Economists are less tidy; their graphing of independent and dependent variables is more arbitrary. Their conventional graphing of the income-consumption relationship is consistent with mathematical presentation, but economists historically put price and cost data on the vertical axis of their graphs. Contemporary economists have followed the tradition. So economists' graphing of BTU's ticket price–attendance data conflicts with normal mathematical procedure.

Other Things Equal

Our simple two-variable graphs purposely ignore many other factors that might affect the amount of consumption occurring at each income level or the number of people who attend BTU basketball games at each possible ticket price. When economists plot the relationship between any two variables, they employ the *ceteris paribus* (other-things-equal) assumption. Thus, in Figure A.1 all factors other than income that might affect the amount of consumption are presumed to be constant or unchanged. Similarly, in Figure A.2 all factors other than ticket price that might influence attendance at BTU basketball games are assumed constant. In reality, "other things" are not equal; they often change, and when they do, the relationship represented in our two tables and graphs will change. Specifically, the lines we have plotted would shift to new locations.

Consider a stock market "crash." The dramatic drop in the value of stocks might cause people to feel less wealthy and therefore less willing to consume at each level of income. The result might be a downward shift of the consumption line. To see this, you should plot a new consumption line in Figure A.1, assuming that consumption is, say, $20 less at each income level. Note that the relationship remains direct; the line merely shifts downward to reflect less consumption spending at each income level.

Similarly, factors other than ticket prices might affect BTU game attendance. If BTU loses most of its games, attendance at BTU games might be less at each ticket price. To see this, redraw Figure A.2, assuming that 2000 fewer fans attend BTU games at each ticket price.

Slope of a Line

Lines can be described in terms of their slopes. The **slope of a straight line** is the ratio of the vertical change (the rise or drop) to the horizontal change (the run) between any two points of the line.

slope (of a straight line)
The ratio of the vertical change (the rise or fall) to the horizontal change (the run) between any two points on a line.

Positive Slope Between point *b* and point *c* in the graph in Figure A.1 the rise or vertical change (the change in consumption) is +\$50 and the run or horizontal change (the change in income) is +\$100. Therefore:

$$\text{Slope} = \frac{\text{vertical change}}{\text{horizontal change}} = \frac{+50}{+100} = \frac{1}{2} = .5$$

Note that our slope of $\frac{1}{2}$ or .5 is positive because consumption and income change in the same direction; that is, consumption and income are directly or positively related.

Negative Slope Between any two of the identified points in the graph of Figure A.2, say, point *c* and point *d*, the vertical change is −10 (the drop) and the horizontal change is +4 (the run). Therefore:

$$\text{Slope} = \frac{\text{vertical change}}{\text{horizontal change}} = \frac{-10}{+4} = -2\frac{1}{2} = -2.5$$

This slope is negative because ticket price and attendance have an inverse relationship.

Slopes and Marginal Analysis Economists are largely concerned with changes in values. The concept of slope is important in economics because it reflects marginal changes—those involving 1 more (or 1 less) unit. For example, in Figure A.1 the .5 slope shows that \$.50 of extra or marginal consumption is associated with each \$1 change in income. In this example, people collectively will consume \$.50 of any \$1 increase in their incomes and reduce their consumption by \$.50 for each \$1 decline in income. Careful inspection of Figure A.2 reveals that every \$1 increase in ticket price for BTU games will decrease game attendance by 400 people and every \$1 decrease in ticket price will increase game attendance by 400 people.

Infinite and Zero Slopes Many variables are unrelated or independent of one another. For example, the quantity of wristwatches purchased is not related to the price of bananas. In Figure A.3a the price of bananas is measured on the vertical axis and the quantity of watches demanded on the horizontal axis. The graph of their relationship is the line parallel to the vertical axis, indicating that the same quantity of watches is purchased no matter what the price of bananas. The slope of such a line is infinite.

Similarly, aggregate consumption is completely unrelated to the nation's divorce rate. In Figure A.3b we put consumption on the vertical axis and the divorce rate on the horizontal axis. The line parallel to the horizontal axis represents this lack of relatedness. This line has a slope of zero.

Slope of a Nonlinear Curve We now move from the simple world of linear relationships (straight lines) to the somewhat more complex world of nonlinear

FIGURE A.3
Infinite and zero slopes. (a) A line parallel to the vertical axis has an infinite slope. Here, purchases of watches remain the same no matter what happens to the price of bananas. (b) A line parallel to the horizontal axis has a slope of zero. Here, total consumption remains the same no matter what happens to the divorce rate. In both (a) and (b), the two variables are totally unrelated to one another.

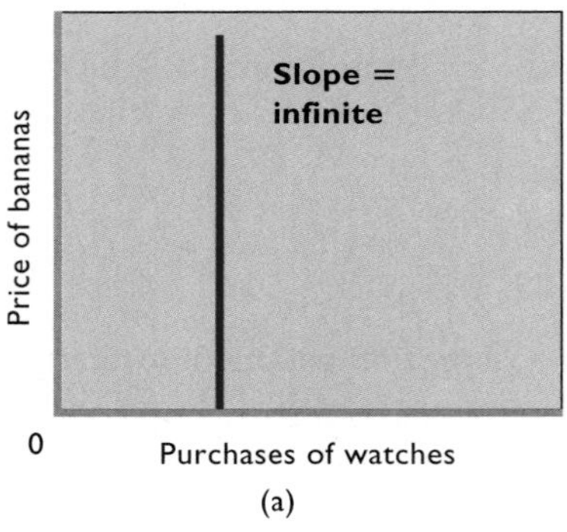

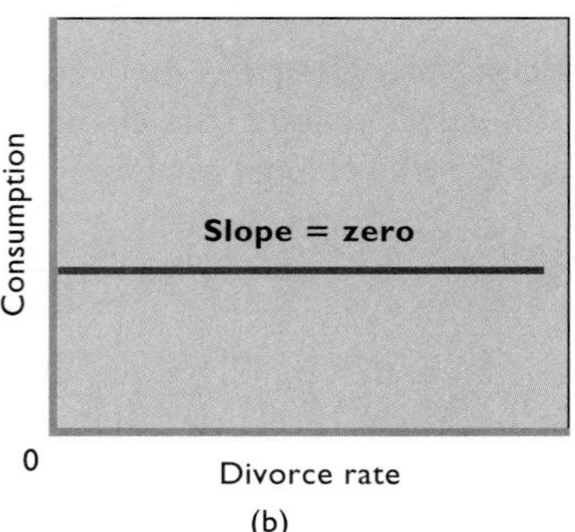

relationships. The slope of a straight line is the same at all its points. The slope of a line representing a nonlinear relationship changes from one point to another. Such lines are referred to as *curves*. (It is also permissible and customary to refer to a straight line as a "curve.")

Consider the downsloping curve in Figure A.4. Its slope is negative throughout, but the curve flattens as we move down along it. Thus, its slope constantly changes; the curve has a different slope at each point.

To measure the slope at a specific point, we draw a straight line tangent to the curve at that point. A line is tangent at a point if it touches, but does not intersect, the curve at that point. So line *aa* is tangent to the curve in Figure A.4 at point *A*. The slope of the curve at that point is equal to the slope of the tangent line. Specifically, the total vertical change (drop) in the tangent line *aa* is -20 and the total horizontal change (run) is $+5$. Because the slope of the tangent line *aa* is $-20/+5$, or -4, the slope of the curve at point *A* is also -4.

FIGURE A.4
Determining the slopes of curves. The slope of a nonlinear curve changes from point to point on the curve. The slope at any point (say, *B*) can be determined by drawing a straight line that is tangent to that point (line *bb*) and calculating the slope of that line.

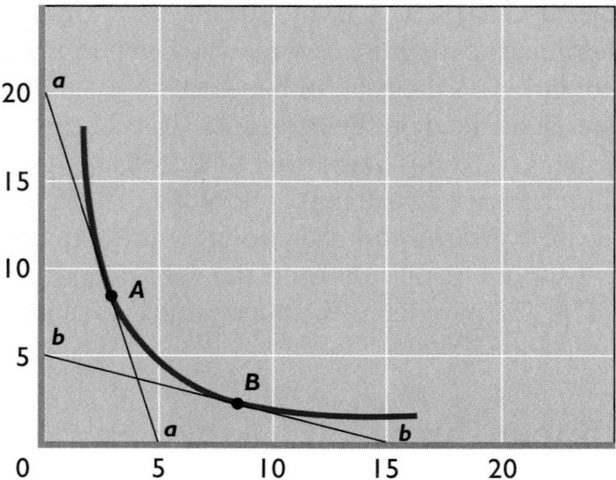

Line *bb* in Figure A.4 is tangent to the curve at point *B*. Using the same procedure, we find the slope at *B* to be $-5/+15$, or $-\frac{1}{3}$. Thus, in this flatter part of the curve, the slope is less negative.

Several of the Appendix questions are of a "workbook" variety, and we urge you to go through them carefully to check your understanding of graphs and slopes.

APPENDIX SUMMARY

1. Graphs are a convenient and revealing way to represent economic relationships.
2. Two variables are positively or directly related when their values change in the same direction. The line (curve) representing two directly related variables slopes upward.
3. Two variables are negatively or inversely related when their values change in opposite directions. The curve representing two inversely related variables slopes downward.
4. The value of the dependent variable (the "effect") is determined by the value of the independent variable (the "cause").
5. When the "other factors" that might affect a two-variable relationship are allowed to change, the graph of the relationship will likely shift to a new location.
6. The slope of a straight line is the ratio of the vertical change to the horizontal change between any two points. The slope of an upsloping line is positive; the slope of a downsloping line is negative.
7. The slope of a line or curve is especially relevant for economics because it measures marginal changes.
8. The slope of a horizontal line is zero; the slope of a vertical line is infinite.
9. The slope of a curve at any point is determined by calculating the slope of a straight line tangent to the curve at that point.

APPENDIX TERMS AND CONCEPTS

direct relationship

inverse relationship

independent variable

dependent variable

slope of a straight line

APPENDIX STUDY QUESTIONS

1. Briefly explain the use of graphs as a way to represent economic relationships. What is an inverse relationship? How does it graph? What is a direct relationship? How does it graph? Graph and explain the relationships (other things equal) you would expect to find between (a) the number of inches of rainfall per month and the sale of umbrellas, (b) the price of bottled water and the number of bottles sold per year, and (c) the popularity of an entertainer and the price of her concert tickets.

   In each case cite and explain how variables other than those specifically mentioned might upset the expected relationship. Is your graph in part *b*, above, consistent with the fact that, historically, the quantity and price of bottled water have both increased? If not, explain any difference.
2. Indicate how each of the following might affect the data shown in the table and graph in Figure A.2 of this Appendix:
   a. BTU's athletic director hires away the coach from a perennial champion.
   b. An NBA team locates in the city where BTU plays.
   c. BTU contracts to have all its home games televised.
3. The following table contains data on the relationship between saving and income. Rearrange these data into a meaningful order and graph them on the accompanying grid. What is the slope of the line? Interpret the meaning of the slope. What would you predict saving to be at the $12,500 level of income?

Income per Year	Saving per Year
$15,000	$1,000
0	−500
10,000	500
5,000	0
20,000	1,500

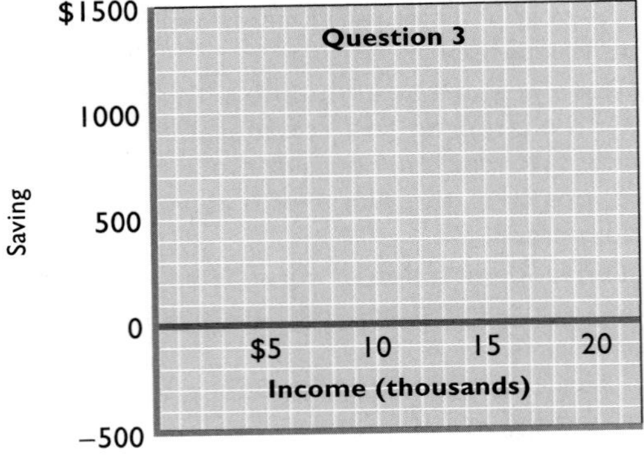

4. Construct a table from the data shown on the graph below. Which is the dependent variable and which the independent variable?

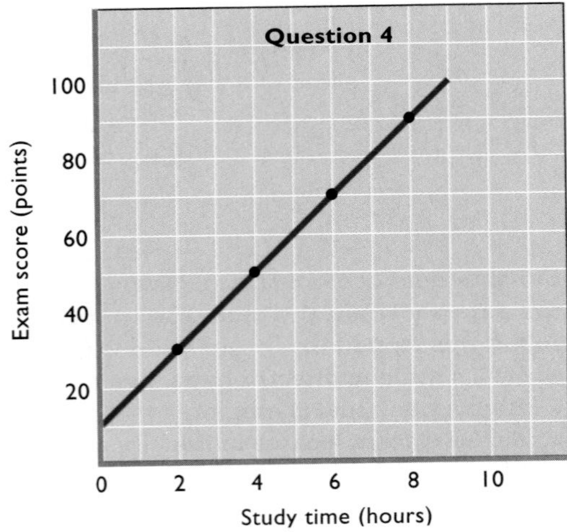

5. Suppose that when the price of gold is $100 an ounce, gold producers find it unprofitable to sell gold. However, when the price is $200 an ounce, 5000 ounces of output (production) is profitable. At $300, a total of 10,000 ounces of output is profitable. Similarly, total production increases by 5000 ounces for each successive $100 increase in the price of gold. Describe the relevant relationship between the price of gold and the production of gold in words, in a table, and on a graph. Put the price of gold on the vertical axis and the output of gold on the horizontal axis. Comment on the advantages and disadvantages of the verbal, tabular, and graphical forms of description.

6. The accompanying graph shows curve XX' and tangents to the curve at points A, B, and C. Calculate the slope of the curve at each of these three points.

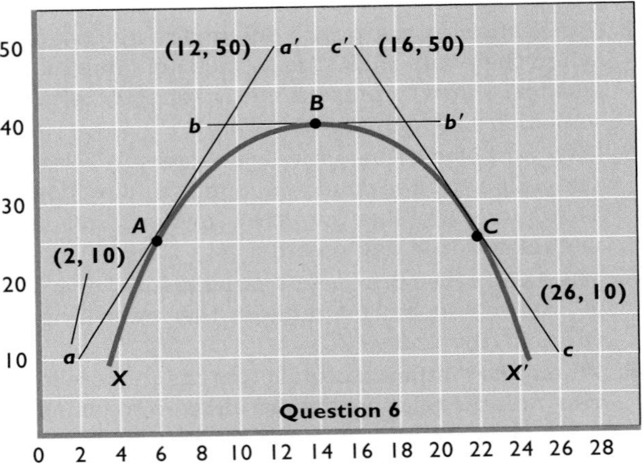

7. In the accompanying graph, is the slope of curve AA' positive or negative? Does the slope increase or decrease as we move along the curve from A to A'? Answer the same two questions for curve BB'.

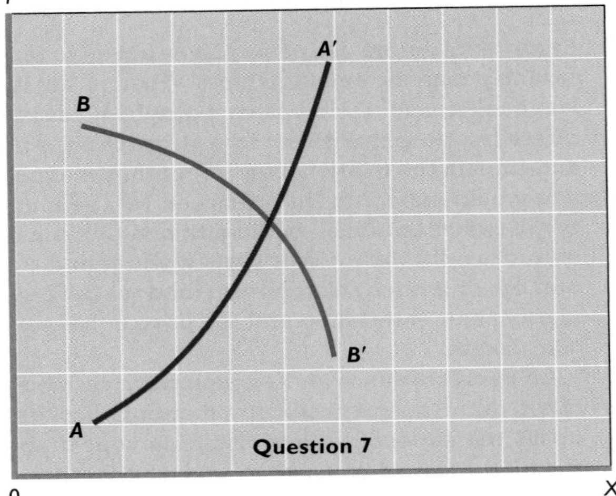

Glossary

A

ability-to-pay principle The idea that those who have greater income (or wealth) should pay a greater proportion of it as taxes than those who have less income (or wealth).

actual reserves The funds that a bank has on deposit at the Federal Reserve Bank of its district (plus its vault cash).

advertising A seller's activities in communicating its message about its product to potential buyers.

aggregate A collection of specific economic units treated as if they were one. For example, all prices of individual goods and services are combined into a price level, or all the units of output are aggregated into gross domestic product.

aggregate demand A schedule or curve that shows the total quantity of goods and services demanded (purchased) at different price levels.

aggregate demand–aggregate supply model The macroeconomic model that uses aggregate demand and aggregate supply to determine and explain the price level and the real domestic output.

aggregate supply A schedule or curve showing the total quantity of goods and services supplied (produced) at different price levels.

aggregate supply shocks Sudden, large changes in resource costs that shift an economy's aggregate supply curve.

allocative efficiency The apportionment of resources among firms and industries to obtain the production of the products most wanted by society (consumers); the output of each product at which its marginal cost and price or marginal benefit are equal.

anticipated inflation Increases in the price level (inflation) that occur at the expected rate.

antitrust laws Legislation (including the Sherman Act) that prohibits anticompetitive business activities such as price fixing, bid rigging, monopolization, and tying contracts.

appreciation (of the dollar) An increase in the value of the dollar relative to the currency of another nation, so a dollar buys a larger amount of the foreign currency and thus of foreign goods.

asset Anything of monetary value owned by a firm or individual.

asset demand for money The amount of money people want to hold as a store of value; this amount varies inversely with the interest rate.

average fixed cost A firm's total fixed cost divided by output (the quantity of product produced).

average product The total output produced per unit of a resource employed (total product divided by the quantity of that employed resource).

average revenue Total revenue from the sale of a product divided by the quantity of the product sold (demanded); equal to the price at which the product is sold when all units of the product are sold at the same price.

average tax rate Total tax paid divided by total (taxable) income, as a percentage.

average total cost A firm's total cost divided by output (the quantity of product produced); equal to average fixed cost plus average variable cost.

average variable cost A firm's total variable cost divided by output (the quantity of product produced).

B

balance sheet A statement of the assets, liabilities, and net worth of a firm or individual at some given time.

bank deposits The deposits that individuals or firms have at banks (or thrifts) or that banks have at the Federal Reserve Banks.

bankers' bank A bank that accepts the deposits of and makes loans to depository institutions; in the United States, a Federal Reserve Bank.

bank reserves The deposits of commercial banks and thrifts at Federal Reserve Banks plus bank and thrift vault cash.

barrier to entry Anything that artificially prevents the entry of firms into an industry.

barter The exchange of one good or service for another good or service.

base year The year with which other years are compared when an index is constructed; for example, the base year for a price index.

benefits-received principle The idea that those who receive the benefits of goods and services provided by government should pay the taxes required to finance them.

Board of Governors The seven-member group that supervises and controls the money and banking system of the United States;, also called the *Board of Governors of the Federal Reserve System* and the *Federal Reserve Board.*

bond A financial device through which a borrower (a firm or government) is obligated to pay the principal and interest on a loan at a specific date in the future.

budget constraint The limit that the size of a consumer's income (and the prices that must be paid for goods and services) imposes on the ability of that consumer to obtain goods and services.

budget deficit The amount by which the expenditures of the Federal government exceed its revenues in any year.

budget line A line that shows the different combinations of two products a consumer can purchase with a specific money income, given the products' prices.

budget surplus The amount by which the revenues of the Federal government exceed its expenditures in any year.

built-in stabilizer A mechanism that increases government's budget deficit (or reduces its surplus) during a recession and increases government's budget surplus (or reduces its deficit) during expansion without any action by policymakers. The tax system is one such mechanism.

Bureau of Economic Analysis (BEA) An agency of the U.S. Department of Commerce that compiles the national income and product accounts.

business cycles Recurring increases and decreases in the level of economic activity over periods of years; a cycle consists of peak, recession, trough, and expansion phases.

business firm (See **firm.**)

C

capital Human-made resources (buildings, machinery, and equipment) used to produce goods and services; goods that do not directly satisfy human wants; also called *capital goods* and *investment goods.*

capital gain The gain realized when securities or properties are sold for a price greater than the price paid for them.

capital goods (See **capital.**)

capitalism An economic system in which property resources are privately owned and markets and prices are used to direct and coordinate economic activities.

capital stock The total available capital in a nation.

cartel A formal agreement among firms (or countries) in an industry to set the price of a product and establish the outputs of the individual firms (or countries) or to divide the market for the product geographically.

ceiling price (See **price ceiling.**)

central bank A bank whose chief function is the control of the nation's money supply; in the United States, the Federal Reserve System.

central economic planning Government determination of the objectives of the economy and how resources will be directed to attain those goals.

***ceteris paribus* assumption** (See **other-things-equal assumption.**)

change in demand A change in the quantity demanded of a good or service at every price; a shift of the demand curve to the left or right.

change in supply A change in the quantity supplied of a good or service at every price; a shift of the supply curve to the left or right.

checkable deposit Any deposit in a commercial bank or thrift institution against which a check may be written.

check clearing The process by which funds are transferred from the checking accounts of the writers of checks to the checking accounts of the recipients of the checks.

checking account A checkable deposit in a commercial bank or thrift institution.

circular flow diagram The flow of resources from households to firms and of products from firms to households. These flows are accompanied by reverse flows of money from firms to households and from households to firms.

Coase theorem The idea, first stated by economist Ronald Coase, that externality problems may be resolved through private negotiations of the affected parties.

coincidence of wants A situation in which the good or service that one trader desires to obtain is the same as that which another trader desires to give up and an item that the second trader wishes to acquire is the same as that which the first trader desires to surrender.

collusion A situation in which firms act together and in agreement (collude) to fix prices, divide a market, or otherwise restrict competition.

command system A method of organizing an economy in which property resources are publicly owned and government uses central economic planning to direct and coordinate economic activities; command economy; communism.

commercial bank A firm that engages in the business of banking (accepts deposits, offers checking accounts, and makes loans).

commercial banking system All commercial banks and thrift institutions as a group.

communism (See **command system.**)

comparative advantage A lower relative domesic opportunity cost than that of another producer or country.

compensating differences Differences in the wages received by workers in different jobs to compensate for nonmonetary differences in the jobs.

compensation to employees Wages and salaries plus wage and salary supplements paid by employers to workers.

competition The presence in a market of independent buyers and sellers competing with one another along with the freedom of buyers and sellers to enter and leave the market.

competitive industry's short-run supply curve The horizontal summation of the short-run supply curves of the firms in a purely competitive industry (see **pure competition**); a curve that shows the total quantities offered for sale at various prices by the firms in an industry in the short run.

competitive labor market (See **purely competitive labor market.**)

complementary goods Products and services that are used together. When the price of one falls, the demand for the other increases (and conversely).

constant-cost industry An industry in which expansion by the entry of new firms has no effect on the prices firms in the industry must pay for resources and thus no effect on production costs.

constant opportunity cost An opportunity cost that remains the same for each additional unit as a consumer (or society) shifts purchases (production) from one product to another along a straight-line budget line (production possibilities curve).

consumer goods Products and services that satisfy human wants directly.

Consumer Price Index (CPI) An index that measures the prices of a fixed "market basket" of some 300 goods and services bought by a "typical" consumer.

consumer sovereignty Determination by consumers of the types and quantities of goods and services that will be produced with the scarce resources of the economy; consumers' direction of production through their dollar votes.

contractionary fiscal policy A decrease in government purchases for goods and services, an increase in net taxes, or some combination of the two, for the purpose of decreasing aggregate demand and thus controlling inflation.

corporate income tax A tax levied on the net income (accounting profit) of corporations.

corporation A legal entity ("person") chartered by a state or the Federal government that is distinct and separate from the individuals who own it.

cost-benefit analysis A comparison of the marginal costs of a government project or program with the marginal benefits to decide whether or not to employ resources in that project or program and to what extent.

cost-of-living adjustment (COLA) An automatic increase in the incomes (wages) of workers when inflation occurs; guaranteed by a collective bargaining contract between firms and workers.

cost-push inflation Increases in the price level (inflation) resulting from an increase in resource costs (for example, raw-material prices) and hence in per-unit production costs; inflation caused by reductions in aggregate supply.

Council of Economic Advisers (CEA) A group of three persons that advises and assists the president of the United States on economic matters (including the preparation of the annual *Economic Report of the President*).

craft union A labor union that limits its membership to workers with a particular skill (craft).

creative destruction The hypothesis that the creation of new products and production methods simultaneously destroys the market power of existing monopolies.

credit union An association of persons who have a common tie (such as being employees of the same firm or members of the same labor union) that sells shares to (accepts deposits from) its members and makes loans to them.

crowding-out effect A rise in interest rates and a resulting decrease in investment caused by the Federal government's increased borrowing to finance budget deficits or debt.

currency Coins and paper money.

cyclical deficit A Federal budget deficit that is caused by a recession and the consequent decline in tax revenues.

cyclical unemployment A type of unemployment caused by insufficient total spending (or by insufficient aggregate demand).

D

decreasing-cost industry An industry in which expansion through the entry of firms lowers the prices that firms in the industry must pay for resources and therefore decreases their production costs.

deflating Finding the real gross domestic product by decreasing the dollar value of the GDP for a year in which prices were higher than in the base year.

deflation A decline in the economy's price level.

demand A schedule showing the amounts of a good or service that buyers (or a buyer) wish to purchase at various prices during some time period.

demand curve A curve illustrating demand.

demand-pull inflation Increases in the price level (inflation) resulting from an excess of demand over output at the existing price level, caused by an increase in aggregate demand.

dependent variable A variable that changes as a consequence of a change in some other (independent) variable; the "effect" or outcome.

depository institutions Firms that accept deposits of money from the public (businesses and persons); commercial banks, savings and loan associations, mutual savings banks, and credit unions.

depreciation (of the dollar) A decrease in the value of the dollar relative to another currency, so a dollar buys a smaller amount of the foreign currency and therefore of foreign goods.

derived demand The demand for a resource that depends on the demand for the products it helps to produce.

determinants of aggregate demand Factors such as consumption spending, investment, government spending, and net exports that, if they change, shift the aggregate demand curve.

determinants of aggregate supply Factors such as input prices, productivity, and the legal-institutional environment that, if they change, shift the aggregate supply curve.

determinants of demand Factors other than price that determine the quantities demanded of a good or service.

determinants of supply Factors other than price that determine the quantities supplied of a good or service.

developing countries Many countries of Africa, Asia, and Latin America that are characterized by lack of capital goods, use of nonadvanced technologies, low literacy rates, high unemployment, rapid population growth, and labor forces heavily committed to agriculture.

differentiated oligopoly An oligopoly in which the firms produce a differentiated product.

differentiated product A product that differs physically or in some other way from the similar products produced by other firms; a product such that buyers are not indifferent to the seller when the price charged by all sellers is the same.

diminishing marginal returns (See **law of diminishing returns.**)

direct relationship The relationship between two variables that change in the same direction, for example, product price and quantity supplied.

discount rate The interest rate that the Federal Reserve Banks charge on the loans they make to commercial banks and thrift institutions.

discretionary fiscal policy Deliberate changes in taxes (tax rates) and government spending by Congress to promote full employment, price stability, and economic growth.

discrimination The practice of according individuals or groups inferior treatment in hiring, occupational access, education and training, promotion, wage rates, or working conditions even though they have the same abilities, education, skills, and work experience as other workers.

diseconomies of scale Increases in the average total cost of producing a product as the firm expands the size of its plant (its output) in the long run.

dividends Payments by a corporation of all or part of its profit to its stockholders (the corporate owners).

division of labor The separation of the work required to produce a product into a number of different tasks that are performed by different workers; specialization of workers.

Doha Round The latest, uncompleted (as of 2005) sequence of trade negotiations by members of the World Trade Organization; named after Doha, Qatar, where the set of negotiations began.

dollar votes The "votes" that consumers and entrepreneurs cast for the production of consumer and capital goods, respectively, when they purchase those goods in product and resource markets.

dumping The sale of products in a foreign country at prices either below costs or below the prices charged at home.

durable good A consumer good with an expected life (use) of 3 or more years.

E

earned-income tax credit A refundable Federal tax credit for low-income working people designed to reduce poverty and encourage labor-force participation.

earnings The money income received by a worker; equal to the wage (rate) multiplied by the amount of time worked.

easy money policy Federal Reserve System actions to increase the money supply to lower interest rates and expand real GDP.

economic cost A payment that must be made to obtain and retain the services of a resource; the income a firm must provide to a resource supplier to attract the resource away from an alternative use; equal to the quantity of other products that cannot be produced when resources are instead used to make a particular product.

economic efficiency The use of the minimum necessary resources to obtain the socially optimal amounts of goods and services; entails both productive efficiency and allocative efficiency.

economic growth (1) An outward shift in the production possibilities curve that results from an increase in resource supplies or quality or an improvement in technology; (2) an increase of real output (gross domestic product) or real output per capita.

economic law An economic principle that has been tested and retested and has stood the test of time.

economic model A simplified picture of economic reality; an abstract generalization.

economic perspective A viewpoint that envisions individuals and institutions making rational decisions by comparing the marginal benefits and marginal costs associated with their actions.

economic policy A course of action intended to correct or avoid a problem.

economic principle A widely accepted generalization about the economic behavior of individuals or institutions.

economic problem The choices necessitated because society's economic wants for goods and services are unlimited but the resources available to satisfy these wants are limited (scarce).

economic profit The total revenue of a firm less its economic costs (which include both explicit costs and implicit costs); also called *pure profit* and *above-normal profit.*

economic resources The land, labor, capital, and entrepreneurial ability that are used in the production of goods and services; productive agents; factors of production.

economics The study of how people, institutions, and society make economic choices under conditions of scarcity.

economic system A particular set of institutional arrangements and a coordinating mechanism for solving the economizing problem; a method of organizing an economy, of which the market system and the command system are the two general types.

economic theory A statement of a cause-effect relationship; when accepted by nearly all economists, an economic principle.

economies of scale Reductions in the average total cost of producing a product as the firm expands the size of plant (its output) in the long run; the economies of mass production.

efficient allocation of resources That allocation of an economy's resources among the production of different products that leads to the maximum satisfaction of consumers' wants, thus producing the socially optimal mix of output with society's scarce resources.

elastic demand Product or resource demand whose price elasticity is greater than 1. This means the resulting change in quantity demanded is greater than the percentage change in price.

elasticity coefficient The number obtained when the percentage change in quantity demanded (or supplied) is divided by the percentage change in the price of the commodity.

elasticity formula (See **price elasticity of demand.**)

elasticity of labor demand A measure of the responsiveness of employers to a change in the wage rate; the percentage change in labor quantity divided by the percentage change in the wage rate.

elastic supply Product or resource supply whose price elasticity is greater than 1. This means the resulting change in quantity supplied is greater than the percentage change in price.

entitlement programs Government programs such as social insurance, food stamps, Medicare, and Medicaid that guarantee particular levels of transfer payments or noncash benefits to all who fit the programs' criteria.

entrepreneurial ability The human resource that combines the other resources to produce a product, makes nonroutine decisions, innovates, and bears risks.

equality-efficiency tradeoff The decrease in economic efficiency that may accompany a decrease in income inequality; the presumption that some income inequality is required to achieve economic efficiency.

equilibrium price The price in a competitive market at which the quantity demanded and the quantity supplied are equal, there is neither a shortage nor a surplus, and there is no tendency for price to rise or fall.

equilibrium price level The price level at which the aggregate demand curve intersects the aggregate supply curve.

equilibrium quantity (1) The quantity demanded and supplied at the equilibrium price in a competitive market; (2) the profit-maximizing output of a firm.

equilibrium real output The gross domestic product at which the total quantity of final goods and services purchased (aggregate expenditures) is equal to the total quantity of final goods and services produced (the real domestic output); the real domestic output at which the aggregate demand curve intersects the aggregate supply curve.

euro The common currency unit used by 12 European nations (Austria, Belgium, Finland, France, Germany, Greece, Ireland, Italy, Luxembourg, the Netherlands, Portugal, and Spain).

European Union (EU) An association of 25 European nations that has eliminated tariffs and quotas among them, established common tariffs for imported goods from outside the member nations, eliminated barriers to the free movement of capital, and created other common economic policies.

excess capacity Plant resources that are underused when imperfectly competitive firms produce less output than that associated with achieving minimum average total cost.

excess reserves The amount by which a bank's or thrift's actual reserves exceed its required reserves; actual reserves minus required reserves.

exchange rate The rate of exchange of one nation's currency for another nation's currency.

exchange-rate appreciation An increase in the value of a nation's currency in foreign exchange markets; an increase in the rate of exchange for foreign currencies.

exchange-rate depreciation A decrease in the value of a nation's currency in foreign exchange markets; a decrease in the rate of exchange for foreign currencies.

excise tax A tax levied on the production of a specific product or on the quantity of the product purchased.

exclusive unionism The practice of a labor union of restricting the supply of skilled union labor to increase the wages received by union members; the policies typically employed by a craft union.

expansion The phase of the business cycle in which output, income, and business activity rise.

expansionary fiscal policy An increase in government purchases of goods and services, a decrease in net taxes, or some combination of the two, for the purpose of increasing aggregate demand and expanding real output.

expectations The anticipations of consumers, firms, and others about future economic conditions.

expected rate of return The increase in profit a firm anticipates it will obtain by purchasing capital (or engaging in research and development); expressed as a percentage of the total cost of the investment (or R&D) activity.

explicit cost The monetary payment a firm must make to an outsider to obtain a resource.

exports Goods and services produced in a nation and sold to buyers in other nations.

export subsidies Government payments to domestic producers to enable them to reduce the price of a good or service to foreign buyers.

external benefit A benefit obtained without compensation by third parties from the production or consumption of sellers or buyers. Example: A beekeeper benefits when a neighboring farmer plants clover.

external cost A cost imposed without compensation on third parties by the production or consumption of sellers or buyers. Example: A manufacturer dumps toxic chemicals into a river, killing the fish sought by sport fishers.

externality A benefit or cost from production or consumption, accruing without compensation to nonbuyers and nonsellers of the product (see **external benefit** and **external cost**).

external public debt Public debt owed to foreign citizens, firms, and institutions.

F

factors of production Economic resources: land, capital, labor, and entrepreneurial ability.

fallacy of composition The false idea that what is true for the individual (or part) is necessarily true for the group (or whole).

Federal Deposit Insurance Corporation (FDIC) The federally chartered corporation that insures deposit liabilities (up to $100,000 per account) of commercial banks and thrift institutions (excluding credit unions, whose deposits are insured by the National Credit Union Administration).

Federal funds rate The interest rate banks and other depository institutions charge one another on overnight loans made out of their excess reserves.

Federal government The government of the United States, as distinct from the state and local governments.

Federal Open Market Committee (FOMC) The 12-member group that determines the purchase and sale policies of the Federal Reserve Banks in the market for U.S. government securities.

Federal Reserve Banks The 12 banks chartered by the U.S. government to control the money supply and perform other functions. (See **central bank, quasi-public bank,** and **bankers' bank.**)

Federal Reserve Note Paper money issued by the Federal Reserve Banks.

Federal Reserve System A central component of the U.S. banking system, consisting of the Board of Governors of the Federal Reserve and 12 regional Federal Reserve Banks.

final goods and services Goods and services that have been purchased for final use and not for resale or further processing or manufacturing.

financial capital Money available to purchase capital; simply money, as defined by economists.

firm An organization that employs resources to produce a good or service for profit and owns and operates one or more plants.

fiscal policy Changes in government spending and tax collections designed to achieve a full-employment and noninflationary domestic output; also called *discretionary fiscal policy.*

fixed cost Any cost that in total does not change when the firm changes its output; the cost of fixed resources.

fixed resource Any resource whose quantity cannot be changed by a firm in the short run.

food-stamp program A program permitting low-income persons to purchase for less than their retail value, or to obtain without cost, coupons that can be exchanged for food items at retail stores.

foreign exchange market A market in which the money (currency) of one nation can be used to purchase (can be exchanged for) the money of another nation.

foreign exchange rate (See **exchange rate.**)

fractional reserve A reserve requirement that is less than 100 percent of the checkable-deposit liabilities of a commercial bank or thrift institution.

freedom of choice The freedom of owners of property resources to employ or dispose of them as they see fit, of workers to enter any line of work for which they are qualified, and of consumers to spend their incomes in a manner that they think is appropriate.

freedom of enterprise The freedom of firms to obtain economic resources, to use those resources to produce products of the firm's own choosing, and to sell their products in markets of their choice.

free-rider problem The inability of potential providers of an economically desirable good or service to obtain payment from those who benefit, because of nonexcludability.

free trade The absence of artificial (government-imposed) barriers to trade among individuals and firms in different nations.

frictional unemployment A type of unemployment caused by workers voluntarily changing jobs and by temporary layoffs; unemployed workers between jobs.

full employment (1) The use of all available resources to produce want-satisfying goods and services; (2) the situation in which the unemployment rate is equal to the full-employment unemployment rate and there is frictional and structural but no cyclical unemployment (and the real GDP of the economy equals potential output).

full-employment unemployment rate The unemployment rate at which there is no cyclical unemployment of the labor force; equal to between 4 and 5 percent in the United States because some frictional and structural unemployment is unavoidable.

G

gains from trade The extra output that trading partners obtain through specialization of production and exchange of goods and services.

game theory A means of analyzing the pricing behavior of oligopolists that uses the theory of strategy associated with games such as chess and bridge.

GDP (See **gross domestic product.**)

GDP gap Actual gross domestic product minus potential output; may be either a positive amount (a positive GDP gap) or a negative amount (a negative GDP gap).

General Agreement on Tariffs and Trade (GATT) The international agreement reached in 1947 in which 23 nations agreed to give equal and nondiscriminatory treatment to one another, to reduce tariff rates by multinational negotiations, and to eliminate import quotas. It now includes most nations and has become the World Trade Organization.

Gini ratio A numerical measure of the overall dispersion of income among households, families, or individuals; found graphically by dividing the area between the diagonal line and the Lorenz curve by the entire area below the diagonal line.

government purchases Expenditures by government for goods and services that government consumes in providing public goods and for public (or social) capital that has a long lifetime; the expenditures of all governments in the economy for those final goods and services.

government transfer payment The disbursement of money (or goods and services) by government for which government receives no currently produced good or service in return.

gross domestic product (GDP) The total market value of all final goods and services produced annually within the boundaries of the United States, whether by U.S.- or foreign-supplied resources.

gross private domestic investment Expenditures for newly produced capital goods (such as machinery, equipment, tools, and buildings) and for additions to inventories.

growth accounting The bookkeeping of the supply-side elements that contribute to changes in real GDP over some specific time period.

H

homogeneous oligopoly An oligopoly in which the firms produce a standardized product.

household An economic unit (of one or more persons) that provides the economy with resources and uses the income received to purchase goods and services that satisfy economic wants.

human capital The accumulation of knowledge and skills that make a worker productive.

human capital investment Any expenditure undertaken to improve the education, skills, health, or mobility of workers, with an expectation of greater productivity and thus a positive return on the investment.

hyperinflation A very rapid rise in the price level; an extremely high rate of inflation.

hypothesis A tentative explanation of cause and effect that requires testing.

I

immobility The inability or unwillingness of a worker to move from one geographic area or occupation to another or from a lower-paying job to a higher-paying job.

imperfect competition Any market structure except pure competition; includes monopoly, monopolistic competition, and oligopoly.

implicit cost The monetary income a firm sacrifices when it uses a resource it owns rather than supplying the resource in the market; equal to what the resource could have earned in the best-paying alternative employment; includes a normal profit.

import quota A limit imposed by a nation on the quantity (or total value) of a good that may be imported during some period of time.

imports Spending by individuals, firms, and governments for goods and services produced in foreign nations.

inclusive unionism The practice of a labor union of including as members all workers employed in an industry.

income A flow of dollars (or purchasing power) per unit of time derived from the use of human or property resources.

income elasticity of demand The ratio of the percentage change in the quantity demanded of a good to a percentage change in consumer income; measures the responsiveness of consumer purchases to income changes.

income inequality The unequal distribution of an economy's total income among households or families.

income-maintenance system A group of government programs designed to eliminate poverty and reduce inequality in the distribution of income.

income mobility The extent to which income receivers move from one part of the income distribution to another over some period of time.

increase in demand An increase in the quantity demanded of a good or service at every price; a shift of the demand curve to the right.

increasing-cost industry An industry in which expansion through the entry of new firms raises the prices firms in the industry must pay for resources and therefore increases their production costs.

increasing marginal returns An increase in the marginal product of a resource as successive units of the resource are employed.

increasing returns An increase in a firm's output by a larger percentage than the percentage increase in its inputs.

increase in supply An increase in the quantity supplied of a good or service at every price; a shift of the supply curve to the right.

independent goods Products or services for which there is little or no relationship between the price of one and the demand for the other. When the price of one rises or falls, the demand for the other tends to remain constant.

independent variable The variable causing a change in some other (dependent) variable.

industrial union A labor union that accepts as members all workers employed in a particular industry (or by a particular firm).

industry A group of (one or more) firms that produce identical or similar products.

inelastic demand Product or resource demand for which the elasticity coefficient for price is less than 1. This means the resulting percentage change in quantity demanded is less than the percentage change in price.

inelastic supply Product or resource supply for which the price elasticity coefficient is less than 1. The percentage change in quantity supplied is less than the percentage change in price.

inferior good A good or service whose consumption declines as income rises (and conversely), price remaining constant.

inflation A rise in the general level of prices in an economy.

inflationary expectations The belief of workers, firms, and consumers that substantial inflation will occur in the future.

inflation premium The component of the nominal interest rate that reflects anticipated inflation.

inflation targeting The annual statement of a goal for a specific range of inflation in future years, coupled with monetary policy designed to achieve the goal.

information technology New and more efficient methods of delivering and receiving information through use of computers, fax machines, wireless phones, and the Internet.

infrastructure The capital goods usually provided by the public sector for the use of its citizens and firms (for example, highways, bridges, transit systems, wastewater treatment facilities, municipal water systems, and airports).

in-kind transfer The distribution by government of goods and services to individuals for which the government receives no currently produced good or service in return; a government transfer payment made in goods or services rather than in money; also called *noncash transfer.*

interest The payment made for the use of money (of borrowed funds).

interest rate The annual rate at which interest is paid; a percentage of the borrowed amount.

intermediate goods Products that are purchased for resale or further processing or manufacturing.

internally held public debt Public debt owed to citizens, firms, and institutions of the same nation that issued the debt.

inventories Goods that have been produced but remain unsold.

inverse relationship The relationship between two variables that change in opposite directions, for example, product price and quantity demanded.

investment Spending for the production and accumulation of capital and additions to inventories.

investment demand curve A curve that shows the amounts of investment demanded by an economy at a series of real interest rates.

investment goods (See **capital.**)

investment in human capital (See **human capital investment.**)

"invisible hand" The tendency of firms and resource suppliers that seek to further their own self-interests in competitive markets to also promote the interest of society.

K

kinked-demand curve The demand curve for a noncollusive oligopolist, which is based on the assumption that rivals will match a price decrease and will ignore a price increase.

L

labor People's physical and mental talents and efforts that are used to help produce goods and services.

labor force Persons 16 years of age and older who are not in institutions and who are employed or are unemployed and seeking work.

labor-force participation rate The percentage of the working-age population that is actually in the labor force.

labor productivity Total output divided by the quantity of labor employed to produce it; the average product of labor or output per hour of work.

labor union A group of workers organized to advance the interests of the group (to increase wages, shorten the hours worked, improve working conditions, and so on).

land Natural resources ("free gifts of nature") used to produce goods and services.

law of demand The principle that, other things equal, an increase in a product's price will reduce the quantity of it demanded, and conversely for a decrease in price.

law of diminishing marginal utility The principle that as a consumer increases the consumption of a good or service, the marginal utility obtained from each additional unit of the good or service decreases.

law of diminishing returns The principle that as successive increments of a variable resource are added to a fixed resource, the marginal product of the variable resource will eventually decrease.

law of increasing opportunity costs The principle that as the production of a good increases, the opportunity cost of producing an additional unit rises.

law of supply The principle that, other things equal, an increase in the price of a product will increase the quantity of it supplied, and conversely for a price decrease.

learning by doing Achieving greater productivity and lower average total cost through gains in knowledge and skill that accompany repetition of a task; a source of economies of scale.

legal tender A legal designation of a nation's official currency (bills and coins). Payment of debts must be accepted in this monetary unit, but creditors can specify the form of payment, for example, "cash only" or "check or credit card only."

liability A debt with a monetary value; an amount owed by a firm or an individual.

limited liability Restriction of the maximum loss to a predetermined amount for the owners (stockholders) of a corporation. The maximum loss is the amount they paid for their shares of stock.

liquidity The ease with which an asset can be converted quickly into cash with little or no loss of purchasing power. Money is said to be perfectly liquid, whereas other assets have a lesser degree of liquidity.

long run (1) In microeconomics, a period of time long enough to enable producers of a product to change the quantities of all the resources they employ; period in which all resources and costs are variable and no resources or costs are fixed. (2) In macroeconomics, a period sufficiently long for nominal wages and other input prices to change in response to a change in the nation's price level.

long-run aggregate supply curve The aggregate supply curve associated with a time period in which input prices (especially nominal wages) are fully responsive to changes in the price level.

long-run competitive equilibrium The price at which firms in pure competition neither obtain economic profit nor suffer losses in the long run and the total quantity demanded and supplied are equal; a price equal to the minimum long-run average total cost of producing the product.

long-run supply A schedule or curve showing the prices at which a purely competitive industry will make various quantities of the product available in the long run.

long-run supply curve A curve showing the prices at which a purely competitive industry will make various quantities of the product available in the long run.

Lorenz curve A curve showing the distribution of income in an economy. The cumulated percentage of families (income receivers) is measured along the horizontal axis, and cumulated percentage of income is measured along the vertical axis.

M

***M*1** The most narrowly defined money supply, equal to currency in the hands of the public and the checkable deposits of commercial banks and thrift institutions.

***M*2** A more broadly defined money supply, equal to *M*1 plus noncheckable savings accounts (including money market deposit accounts), small time deposits (deposits of less than $100,000), and individual money market mutual fund balances.

macroeconomics The part of economics concerned with the economy as a whole; with such major aggregates as the household, business, and government sectors; and with measures of the total economy.

marginal analysis The comparison of marginal ("extra" or "additional") benefits and marginal costs, usually for decision making.

marginal benefit The extra (additional) benefit of consuming 1 more unit of some good or service; the change in total benefit when 1 more unit is consumed.

marginal cost The extra (additional) cost of producing 1 more unit of output; equal to the change in total cost divided by the change in output (and, in the short run, to the change in total variable cost divided by the change in output).

marginal product The additional output produced when 1 additional unit of a resource is employed (the quantity of all other resources employed remaining constant); equal to the change in total product divided by the change in the quantity of a resource employed.

marginal resource cost The amount the total cost of employing a resource increases when a firm employs 1 additional unit of the resource (the quantity of all other resources employed remaining constant); equal to the change in the total cost of the resource divided by the change in the quantity of the resource employed.

marginal revenue The change in total revenue that results from the sale of 1 additional unit of a firm's product; equal to the change in total revenue divided by the change in the quantity of the product sold.

marginal revenue product The change in a firm's total revenue when it employs 1 additional unit of a resource (the quantity of all other resources employed remaining constant); equal to the change in total revenue divided by the change in the quantity of the resource employed.

marginal tax rate The tax rate paid on each additional dollar of income.

marginal utility The extra utility a consumer obtains from the consumption of 1 additional unit of a good or service; equal to the change in total utility divided by the change in the quantity consumed.

market Any institution or mechanism that brings together buyers (demanders) and sellers (suppliers) of a particular good or service.

market economy An economy in which only the private decisions of consumers, resource suppliers, and firms determine how resources are allocated; the market system.

market failure The inability of a market to bring about the allocation of resources that best satisfies the wants of society; in particular, the overallocation or underallocation of resources to the production of a particular good or service because of spillovers or informational problems or because markets do not provide desired public goods.

market for externality rights A market in which firms can buy rights to discharge pollutants. The price of such rights is determined by the demand for the right to discharge pollutants and a perfectly inelastic supply of such rights (the latter determined by the quantity of discharges that the environment can assimilate).

market period A period in which producers of a product are unable to change the quantity produced in response to a change in its price and in which there is a perfectly inelastic supply.

market system All the product and resource markets of a market economy and the relationships among them; a method that allows the prices determined in those markets to allocate the economy's scarce resources and to communicate and coordinate the decisions made by consumers, firms, and resource suppliers.

Medicaid A Federal program that helps finance the medical expenses of individuals covered by the Supplemental Security Income (SSI) and Temporary Assistance for Needy Families (TANF) programs.

Medicare A Federal program that is financed by payroll taxes and provides for (1) compulsory hospital insurance for senior citizens and (2) low-cost voluntary insurance to help older Americans pay physicians' fees.

medium of exchange Any item sellers generally accept and buyers generally use to pay for a good or service; money; a convenient means of exchanging goods and services without engaging in barter.

microeconomics The part of economics concerned with such individual units as a household, a firm, or an industry and with individual markets, specific goods and services, and product and resource prices.

minimum efficient scale The lowest level of output at which a firm can minimize long-run average total cost.

minimum wage The lowest wage employers may legally pay for an hour of work.

monetary multiplier The multiple of its excess reserves by which the banking system can expand checkable deposits and thus the money supply by making new loans (or buying securities); equal to 1 divided by the reserve requirement.

monetary policy A central bank's changing of the money supply to influence interest rates and assist the economy in achieving price stability, full employment, and economic growth.

money Any item that is generally acceptable to sellers in exchange for goods and services.

money income (See **nominal income.**)

money market The market in which the demand for and the supply of money determine the interest rate (or the level of interest rates) in the economy.

money market deposit account (MMDA) An interest-earning account (at a bank or thrift) consisting of short-term securities and on which a limited number of checks may be written each year.

money market mutual funds (MMMFs) Interest-bearing accounts offered by investment companies, which pool depositors' funds for the purchase of short-term securities. Depositors may write checks in minimum amounts or more against their accounts.

money supply Narrowly defined, *M*1; more broadly defined, *M*2. (See ***M*1, *M*2.**)

monopolistic competition A market structure in which many firms sell a differentiated product, into which entry is relatively easy, in which the firm has some control over its product price, and in which there is considerable nonprice competition.

monopoly A market structure in which the number of sellers is so small that each seller is able to influence the total supply and the price of the good or service. (Also see **pure monopoly.**)

monopsony A market structure in which there is only a single buyer of a good, service, or resource.

MR = MC rule The principle that a firm will maximize its profit (or minimize its losses) by producing the output at which marginal revenue and marginal cost are equal, provided product price is equal to or greater than average variable cost.

MRP = MRC rule The principle that to maximize profit (or minimize losses), a firm should employ the quantity of a resource at which its marginal revenue product (MRP) is equal to its marginal resource cost (MRC), the latter being the wage rate in pure competition.

multiple counting Wrongly including the value of intermediate goods in the gross domestic product; counting the same good or service more than once.

mutual interdependence A situation in which a change in price strategy (or in some other strategy) by one firm will affect the sales and profits of another firm (or other firms). Any firm that makes such a change can expect the other rivals to react to the change.

N

national bank A commercial bank authorized to operate by the U.S. government.

National Credit Union Administration (NCUA) The federally chartered agency that insures deposit liabilities (up to $100,000 per account) in credit unions.

national income Total income earned by resource suppliers for their contributions to gross domestic product; the sum of wages and salaries, rent, interest, profit, and proprietor's income.

national income accounting The techniques used to measure the overall production of the economy and other related variables for the nation as a whole.

national income and product accounts The national accounts that measure overall production and income of the economy and other related aggregates for the nation as a whole.

natural monopoly An industry in which economies of scale are so great that a single firm can produce the product at a lower average total cost than would be possible if more than one firm produced the product.

natural rate of unemployment The full-employment unemployment rate; the unemployment rate occurring when there is no cyclical unemployment and the economy is achieving its potential output; the unemployment rate at which actual inflation equals expected inflation.

near-money Financial assets, the most important of which are noncheckable savings accounts, time deposits, and U.S. short-term securities and savings bonds, which are not a medium of exchange but can be readily converted into money.

negative GDP gap A situation in which actual gross domestic product is less than potential output.

negative relationship (See **inverse relationship.**)

net exports Exports minus imports.

net taxes The taxes collected by government less government transfer payments.

network effects Increases in the value of a product to each user, including existing users, as the total number of users rises.

net worth The total assets less the total liabilities of a firm or an individual; for a firm, the claims of the owners against the firm's total assets; for an individual, his or her wealth.

New Economy The label attached by some economists and the popular press to the U.S. economy since 1995. The main characteristics are accelerated productivity growth and economic growth, caused by rapid technological advance and the emergence of the global economy.

nominal GDP Gross domestic product measured in terms of the price level at the time of the measurement; GDP that is unadjusted for inflation.

nominal income The number of dollars received by an individual or group for supplying resources during some period of time; income that is not adjusted for inflation.

nominal interest rate The interest rate expressed in terms of annual amounts currently charged for interest and not adjusted for inflation.

nominal wage The amount of money received by a worker per unit of time (hour, day, etc.); money wage that is not adjusted for inflation.

noncash transfer A government transfer payment in the form of goods and services rather than money, for example, food stamps, housing assistance, and job training; also called *in-kind transfer*.

noncollusive oligopoly An oligopoly in which the firms do not act together and in agreement to determine the price of the product and the output that each firm will produce.

noncompeting groups Collections of workers in the economy who do not compete with each other for employment because the skill and training of the workers in one group are substantially different from those of the workers in other groups.

nondiscretionary fiscal policy (See **built-in stabilizer.**)

nondurable good A consumer good with an expected life (use) of less than 3 years.

nonexcludability The inability to keep nonpayers (free riders) from obtaining benefits from a certain good; a public goods characteristic.

nonmarket transactions The production of goods and services excluded in the measurement of the gross domestic product because they are not bought and sold.

nonprice competition Competition based on distinguishing one's product by means of product differentiation and then advertising the distinguished product to consumers.

nonproduction transaction The purchase and sale of any item that is not a currently produced good or service.

nonrivalry The idea that one person's benefit from a certain good does not reduce the benefit available to others; a public goods characteristic.

nontariff barriers All barriers other than protective tariffs that nations erect to impede international trade, including import quotas, licensing requirements, unreasonable product-quality standards, unnecessary bureaucratic detail in customs procedures, and so on.

normal good A good or service whose consumption increases when income increases and falls when income decreases, price remaining constant.

normal profit The payment made by a firm to obtain and retain entrepreneurial ability; the minimum income entrepreneurial ability must receive to induce it to perform entrepreneurial functions for a firm.

North American Free Trade Agreement (NAFTA) A 1993 agreement establishing, over a 15-year period, a free-trade zone composed of Canada, Mexico, and the United States.

O

occupational licensing State and local laws that require a worker to satisfy certain specific requirements and obtain a license from a licensing board before engaging in a particular occupation.

offshoring The practice of shifting work previously done by American workers to workers located abroad.

oligopoly A market structure in which a few firms sell either a standardized or a differentiated product, into which entry is difficult, in which the firm has limited control over product price because of mutual interdependence (except when there is collusion among firms), and in which there is typically nonprice competition.

OPEC (See **Organization of Petroleum Exporting Countries.**)

open-market operations The buying and selling of U.S. government securities by the Federal Reserve Banks for purposes of carrying out monetary policy.

opportunity cost The value of the good, service, or time forgone to obtain something else.

Organization of Petroleum Exporting Countries (OPEC) A cartel of 11 oil-producing countries (Algeria, Indonesia, Iran, Iraq, Kuwait, Libya, Nigeria, Qatar, Saudi Arabia, Venezuela, and the UAE) that controls the quantity and price of crude oil exported by its members and that accounts for 60 percent of the world's export of oil.

other-things-equal assumption The assumption that factors other than those being considered are held constant; *ceteris paribus* assumption.

output effect The situation in which an increase in the price of one input will increase a firm's production costs and reduce its level of output, thus reducing the demand for other inputs; conversely for a decrease in the price of the input.

P

partnership An unincorporated firm owned and operated by two or more persons.

patent An exclusive right given to inventors to produce and sell a new product or machine for 20 years from the time of patent application.

payroll tax A tax levied on employers of labor equal to a percentage of all or part of the wages and salaries paid by them and on employees equal to a percentage of all or part of the wages and salaries received by them.

***P* = MC rule** The principle that a purely competitive firm will maximize its profit or minimize its loss by producing that output at which the price of the product is equal to marginal cost, provided that price is equal to or greater than average variable cost in the short run and equal to or greater than average total cost in the long run.

per capita GDP Gross domestic product (GDP) per person; the average GDP of a population.

per capita income A nation's total income per person; the average income of a population.

perfectly elastic demand Product or resource demand in which quantity demanded can be of any amount at a particular product price; graphs as a horizontal demand curve.

perfectly elastic supply Product or resource supply in which quantity supplied can be of any amount at a particular product or resource price; graphs as a horizontal supply curve.

perfectly inelastic demand Product or resource demand in which price can be of any amount at a particular quantity of the product or resource demanded; quantity demanded does not respond to a change in price; graphs as a vertical demand curve.

perfectly inelastic supply Product or resource supply in which price can be of any amount at a particular quantity of the product or resource demanded; quantity supplied does not respond to a change in price; graphs as a vertical supply curve.

per se violations Collusive actions, such as attempts to fix prices or divide markets, that are violations of the antitrust laws, even if the actions are unsuccessful.

personal consumption expenditures The expenditures of households for durable and nondurable consumer goods and services.

personal income tax A tax levied on the taxable income of individuals, households, and unincorporated firms.

per-unit production cost The average production cost of a particular level of output; total input cost divided by units of output.

political business cycle The alleged tendency of Congress to destabilize the economy by reducing taxes and increasing government expenditures before elections and to raise taxes and lower expenditures after elections.

positive GDP gap A situation in which actual gross domestic product exceeds potential output.

positive relationship A direct relationship between two variables.

potential output The real output (GDP) an economy can produce when it fully employs its available resources.

poverty A situation in which the basic needs of an individual or family exceed the means to satisfy them.

poverty rate The percentage of the population with incomes below the official poverty income levels that are established by the Federal government.

price The amount of money needed to buy a particular good, service, or resource.

price ceiling A legally established maximum price for a good or service.

price discrimination The selling of a product to different buyers at different prices when the price differences are not justified by differences in cost.

price elasticity of demand The ratio of the percentage change in quantity demanded of a product or resource to the percentage change in its price; a measure of the responsiveness of buyers to a change in the price of a product or resource.

price elasticity of supply The ratio of the percentage change in quantity supplied of a product or resource to the percentage change in its price; a measure of the responsiveness of producers to a change in the price of a product or resource.

price fixing The conspiring by two or more firms to set the price of their products; an illegal practice under the Sherman Act.

price floor A legally determined price above the equilibrium price.

price index An index number that shows how the weighted-average price of a "market basket" of goods changes over time.

price leadership An informal method that firms in an oligopoly may employ to set the price of their product: One firm (the leader) is the first to announce a change in price, and the other firms (the followers) soon announce identical or similar changes.

price level The weighted average of the prices of all the final goods and services produced in an economy.

price-level stability A steadiness of the price level from one period to the next; zero or low annual inflation; also called *price stability.*

price maker A seller (or buyer) of a product or resource that is able to affect the product or resource price by changing the amount it sells (or buys).

price support A minimum price that government allows sellers to receive for a good or service; a legally established or maintained minimum price.

price taker A seller (or buyer) of a product or resource that is unable to affect the price at which a product or resource sells by changing the amount it sells (or buys).

price war Successive and continued decreases in the prices charged by firms in an oligopolistic industry. Each firm lowers its price below rivals' prices, hoping to increase its sales and revenues at its rivals' expense.

prime interest rate The benchmark interest rate that banks use as a reference point for a wide range of loans to businesses and individuals.

principal-agent problem A conflict of interest that occurs when agents (workers or managers) pursue their own objectives to the detriment of the principals' (stockholders') goals.

private good A good or service that is individually consumed and that can be profitably provided by privately owned firms because they can exclude nonpayers from receiving the benefits.

private property The right of private persons and firms to obtain, own, control, employ, dispose of, and bequeath land, capital, and other property.

private sector The households and business firms of the economy.

product differentiation A strategy in which one firm's product is distinguished from competing products by means of its design, related services, quality, location, or other attributes (except price).

production possibilities curve A curve showing the different combinations of two goods or services that can be produced in a full-employment, full-production economy where the available supplies of resources and technology are fixed.

productive efficiency The production of a good in the least costly way; occurs when production takes place at the output at which average total cost is a minimum and marginal product per dollar's worth of input is the same for all inputs.

productivity A measure of average output or real output per unit of input. For example, the productivity of labor is determined by dividing real output by hours of work.

productivity growth The percentage increase in productivity from one period to another.

product market A market in which products are sold by firms and bought by households.

profit The return to the resource entrepreneurial ability (see **normal profit**); total revenue minus total cost (see **economic profit**).

progressive tax A tax whose average tax rate increases as the taxpayer's income increases and decreases as the taxpayer's income decreases.

property tax A tax on the value of property (capital, land, stocks and bonds, and other assets) owned by firms and households.

proportional tax A tax whose average tax rate remains constant as the taxpayer's income increases or decreases.

proprietor's income The net income of the owners of unincorporated firms (proprietorships and partnerships).

protective tariff A tariff designed to shield domestic producers of a good or service from the competition of foreign producers.

public assistance programs Government programs that pay benefits to those who are unable to earn income (because of permanent disabilities or because they have very low income and dependent children); financed by general tax revenues and viewed as public charity (rather than earned rights).

public debt The total amount owed by the Federal government to the owners of government securities; equal to the sum of past government budget deficits less government budget surpluses.

public good A good or service that is characterized by nonrivalry and nonexcludability; a good or service with these characteristics provided by government.

public investments Government expenditures on public capital (such as roads, highways, bridges, mass-transit systems, and electric power facilities) and on human capital (such as education, training, and health).

public sector The part of the economy that contains all government entities; government.

purchasing power The amount of goods and services that a monetary unit of income can buy.

pure competition A market structure in which a very large number of firms sell a standardized product, into which entry is very easy, in which the individual seller has no control over the product price, and in which there is no nonprice competition; a market characterized by a very large number of buyers and sellers.

purely competitive labor market A labor market in which a large number of similarly qualified workers independently offer their labor services to a large number of employers, none of whom can set the wage rate.

pure monopoly A market structure in which one firm sells a unique product, into which entry is blocked, in which the single firm has considerable control over product price, and in which nonprice competition may or may not be found.

Q

quantity demanded The amount of a good or service that buyers (or a buyer) desire to purchase at a particular price during some period.

quantity supplied The amount of a good or service that producers (or a producer) offer to sell at a particular price during some period.

quasi-public bank A bank that is privately owned but governmentally (publicly) controlled; each of the U.S. Federal Reserve Banks.

quasi-public good A good or service to which excludability could apply but that has such a large spillover benefit that government sponsors its production to prevent an underallocation of resources.

R

rate of return The gain in net revenue divided by the cost of an investment or an R&D expenditure; expressed as a percentage.

rational behavior Human behavior based on comparison of marginal costs and marginal benefits; behavior designed to maximize total utility.

real capital (See **capital.**)

real GDP (See **real gross domestic product.**)

real GDP per capita Real output (GDP) divided by population.

real gross domestic product (GDP) Gross domestic product adjusted for inflation; gross domestic product in a year divided by the GDP price index for that year, the index expressed as a decimal.

real income The amount of goods and services that can be purchased with nominal income during some period of time; nominal income adjusted for inflation.

real interest rate The interest rate expressed in dollars of constant value (adjusted for inflation) and equal to the nominal interest rate less the expected rate of inflation.

recession A period of declining real GDP, accompanied by lower real income and higher unemployment.

refinancing the public debt Paying owners of maturing government securities with money obtained by selling new securities or with new securities.

regressive tax A tax whose average tax rate decreases as the taxpayer's income increases and increases as the taxpayer's income decreases.

rent-seeking behavior The actions by persons, firms, or unions to gain special benefits from government at the taxpayers' or someone else's expense.

required reserves The funds that banks and thrifts must deposit with the Federal Reserve Bank (or hold as vault cash) to meet the legal reserve requirement; a fixed percentage of the bank's or thrift's checkable deposits.

reserve ratio The specified minimum percentage of its checkable deposits that a bank or thrift must keep on deposit at the Federal Reserve Bank in its district or hold as vault cash.

resource A natural, human, or manufactured item that helps produce goods and services; a productive agent or factor of production.

resource market A market in which households sell and firms buy resources or the services of resources.

rule of reason The rule stated and applied in the U.S. Steel case that only combinations and contracts unreasonably restraining trade are subject to actions under the antitrust laws and that size and possession of monopoly power are not illegal.

rule of 70 A method for determining the number of years it will take for some measure to double, given its annual percentage increase. Example: To determine the number of years it will take for the price level to double, divide 70 by the annual rate of inflation.

S

sales tax A tax levied on the cost (at retail) of a broad group of products.

saving Disposable income not spent for consumer goods; equal to disposable income minus personal consumption expenditures.

savings account A deposit that is interest-bearing and that the depositor can normally withdraw at any time.

savings institution (See **thrift institution.**)

scarce resources The limited quantities of land, capital, labor, and entrepreneurial ability that are never sufficient to satisfy people's virtually unlimited economic wants.

scientific method The procedure for the systematic pursuit of knowledge involving the observation of facts and the formulation and testing of hypotheses to obtain theories, principles, and laws.

secular trend A long-term tendency; a change in some variable over a very long period of years.

self-interest The most-advantageous outcome as viewed by each firm, property owner, worker, or consumer.

service An (intangible) act or use for which a consumer, firm, or government is willing to pay.

Sherman Act The Federal antitrust act of 1890 that makes monopoly and conspiracies to restrain trade criminal offenses.

shortage The amount by which the quantity demanded of a product exceeds the quantity supplied at a particular (below-equilibrium) price.

short run (1) In microeconomics, a period of time in which producers are able to change the quantities of some but not all of the resources they employ; a period in which some resources (usually plant) are fixed and some are variable. (2) In macroeconomics, a period in which nominal wages and other input prices do not change in response to a change in the price level.

short-run aggregate supply curve An aggregate supply curve relevant to a time period in which input prices (particularly nominal wages) do not change in response to changes in the price level.

short-run competitive equilibrium The price at which the total quantity of a product supplied in the short run in a purely competitive industry equals the total quantity of the product demanded and that is equal to or greater than average variable cost.

short-run supply curve A supply curve that shows the quantity of a product a firm in a purely competitive industry will offer to sell at various prices in the short run; the portion of the firm's short-run marginal cost curve that lies above its average-variable-cost curve.

shutdown case The circumstance in which a firm would experience a loss greater than its total fixed cost if it were to produce any output greater than zero; alternatively, a situation in which a firm would cease to operate when the price at which it can sell its product is less than its average variable cost.

simultaneous consumption A product's ability to satisfy a large number of consumers at the same time.

slope of a line The ratio of the vertical change (the rise or fall) to the horizontal change (the run) between any two points on a line. The slope of an upward-sloping line is positive, reflecting a direct relationship between two variables; the slope of a downward-sloping line is negative, reflecting an inverse relationship between two variables.

Smoot-Hawley Tariff Act Legislation passed in 1930 that established very high tariffs. Its objective was to reduce imports and stimulate the domestic economy, but it resulted only in retaliatory tariffs by other nations.

social insurance programs Programs that replace a portion of the earnings lost when people retire or are temporarily unemployed, that are financed by payroll taxes, and that are viewed as earned rights (rather than charity).

Social Security The Federal program, financed by compulsory payroll taxes, that partially replaces earnings lost when workers retire, become disabled, or die.

Social Security trust fund A Federal fund that saves excessive Social Security tax revenues received in one year to meet Social Security benefit obligations that exceed Social Security tax revenues in some subsequent year.

sole proprietorship An unincorporated firm owned and operated by one person.

special-interest effect Any result of government promotion of the interests (goals) of a small group at the expense of a much larger group.

specialization The use of the resources of an individual, a firm, a region, or a nation to concentrate production on one or a small number of goods and services.

speculation The activity of buying or selling with the motive of later reselling or rebuying for profit.

SSI (See **Supplemental Security Income.**)

standardized budget A measure of what the Federal budget deficit or budget surplus would be with the existing tax and government spending programs if the economy had achieved full-employment GDP in the year.

standardized product A product whose buyers are indifferent to the seller from whom they purchase it as long as the price charged by all sellers is the same; a product all units of which are identical and thus are perfect substitutes for each other.

Standard Oil case A 1911 antitrust case in which Standard Oil was found guilty of violating the Sherman Act by illegally monopolizing the petroleum industry. As a remedy the company was divided into several competing firms.

start-up (firm) A new firm focused on creating and introducing a particular new product or employing a specific new production or distribution method.

stock (corporate) An ownership share in a corporation.

store of value An asset set aside for future use; one of the three functions of money.

strategic behavior Self-interested economic actions that take into account the expected reactions of others.

strike The withholding of labor services by an organized group of workers (a labor union).

structural unemployment Unemployment of workers whose skills are not demanded by employers, who lack sufficient skill to obtain employment, or who cannot easily move to locations where jobs are available.

subsidy A payment of funds (or goods and services) by a government, firm, or household for which it receives no good or service in return. When made by a government, it is a government transfer payment.

substitute goods Products or services that can be used in place of each other. When the price of one falls, the demand for the other product falls; conversely, when the price of one product rises, the demand for the other product rises.

substitution effect The effect of a change in the price of a resource on the quantity of the resource employed by a firm, assuming no change in its output.

sunk cost A cost that has been incurred and cannot be recovered.

Supplemental Security Income (SSI) A federally financed and administered program that provides a uniform nationwide minimum income for the aged, blind, and disabled who do not qualify for benefits under Social Security in the United States.

supply A schedule showing the amounts of a good or service that sellers (or a seller) will offer at various prices during some period.

supply curve A curve illustrating supply.

surplus The amount by which the quantity supplied of a product exceeds the quantity demanded at a specific (above-equilibrium) price.

T

tacit collusion Any method used by an oligopolist to set prices and outputs that does not involve outright (or overt) collusion. Price leadership is a frequent example.

Index

Ability
income inequality and, 247
wage differentials and, 235
Ability-to-pay principle, 107
Absolute advantage, 414
Accounting
for economic growth, 273, 394–398
profit in, 119
Accounts, on balance sheet, 352
Actual reserves, 354–355, 372–373
Adams, Walter, 212n
AD-AS model. *See* Aggregate demand-aggregate supply (AD-AS) model
Administrative lag, 322–323
Advertising
differentiated oligopoly and, 198
oligopoly and, 208–210
positive effects of, 209
potential negative effects of, 209–210
product differentiation and, 193
African Americans
poverty of, 255, 256
unemployment and, 278–279
Aggregate, defined, 8
Aggregate demand, 291–296
changes in, 291–296
defined, 291
determinants of, 291–296
equilibrium price level and, 302–309
Aggregate demand-aggregate supply (AD-AS) model, 290
aggregate demand in, 291–296, 302–309
aggregate supply in, 297–309
equilibrium price level in, 302–309
fiscal policy in, 313–315
Aggregate supply, 297–302
changes in, 299–302
defined, 297
equilibrium price level and, 302–309
in the long run, 297–298
production possibilities model and, 391
in the short run, 298–299
Agriculture
exit of farmers from U.S., 157
fluctuating farm income and, 79–80
law of diminishing returns and, 122
price floors and, 65–66
Aid to Families with Dependent Children (AFDC), 259, 260
Alcoa, 138
Allianz, 349
Allocative efficiency
defined, 92
monopolistic competition and, 196–197
in pure competition, 162–163
pure monopoly and, 175–176
Amazon, 45
American Bar Association, 231
American Medical Association, 231
Anheuser-Busch, 211–212
Anticipated inflation, 283, 284–285
Antidumping duties, 427
Antiques Road Show, price elasticity of supply and, 85
Antitrust policy, 183–186, 199, 201–202
Appreciation of currency, 296, 420–421
Archer Daniels Midland, 206
Arthur Andersen, 117
Asians, poverty of, 255
Asset demand for money, 368–369
Assets, 352
Auerbach, Alan J., 317n
Australia
GDP in, 269
interest rates in, 368
union membership in, 230
Average cost (AC), 126, 127–128
Average fixed cost (AFC), 128
Average product (AP)
defined, 121
law of diminishing returns and, 123–125
Average revenue (AR)
defined, 143
in pure competition, 143–144
Averages, price elasticity of demand and, 71–72
Average tax rates, 107–108
Average total cost (ATC), 128
firm size and, 130–132
price discrimination and, 181–182
relation of marginal cost and average variable cost, 129–130
Average variable cost (AVC), 128
relation to marginal cost and average total cost, 129–130
Ayres, Ian, 102–103

Balance sheet
commercial bank, 351–352
defined, 351
Bank debit cards, 344n
Bankers' banks, Federal Reserve Banks as, 347
Bankruptcy, as false concern for public debt, 327–328
Barriers to entry, 168–169
antitrust policy and, 183
defined, 168
economies of scale, 168, 177
licenses, 169
oligopoly and, 199
ownership or control of essential resources, 169
patents, 168–169
pricing, 169
research and development (R&D), 169, 211
Barter
defined, 33
as medium of exchange, 33
Bayer AG, 184, 207
Belgium
exports of, 411
public debt of, 327
underground economy in, 271
Benefits-received principle, 106–107
Blocked entry, in pure monopoly, 167
BNP Paribas, 349
Board of Governors, Federal Reserve, 346
Boeing, 120–121, 136, 240
Bonds, defined, 115–116
Borden, 206
BP, 41
BP Amoco, 184
Brand names. *See also* Advertising
in product differentiation, 192
world's top ten, 210
Brannock Device Company, 167
Brazil
average income and, 9
GDP in, 269
income inequality and, 249
Index of Economic Freedom and, 29
Brock, James, 212n
Budget deficit
cyclical, 318
defined, 313
in full-employment economy, 324
as percentage of potential GDP, 318–319
Budget line
defined, 11
in microeconomics, 11–12
Budget surplus, defined, 314
Built-in stabilizers, 316–317
Burger King, 204

Bush, George W., 321
Business cycles
cyclical unemployment and, 277–278, 308
defined, 275
economic growth and, 272–274
political, 323
Businesses. *See also* Corporations
facts about U.S., 40–41
firm size and long-run production costs, 130–132
levels of, 115
population of, 115–117
taxes on, 108, 109, 295, 302, 333
Buyers, change in demand and, 52

Canada
exports of, 411–412
GDP in, 269
inflation targeting in, 384
interest rates in, 368
net exports and, 296
North American Free Trade Agreement (NAFTA) and, 401, 431
public debt of, 327
standardized budget surplus in, 319
Capital
defined, 13
economic growth and, 395
as economic resource, 13
efficient, 134
Capital accumulation, market system and, 36
Capital goods
defined, 14
in market system, 31
Capitalism, 27–28. *See also* Market system
Capital loss, 369
Carlin, George, 89
Cartels
collusion and, 205–207
defined, 205
Cause-effect chain, 375–378
Central banks, 347
Chaloupka, Frank, 81
Change in demand, 61–63
change in quantity demanded versus, 54
defined, 52, 54
determinants of, 52–53
illustration of, 51
Change in quantity demanded, 54
Change in quantity supplied, 57–58
Change in supply, 56–57, 61, 62–63
change in quantity supplied versus, 57–58
defined, 57
determinants of, 56–57
Cheating, oligopoly and, 201, 207
Checkable deposits, 353, 355
defined, 341
multiple-deposit expansion, 358–363
Checkable reserves, clearing checks and, 355–356
ChevronTexaco, 41
Chicago Board of Trade, 48
Children, poverty of, 255–256
China
average income and, 9
command system in, 27, 38
exports of, 411–412
GDP in, 269
gross investment expenditures in, 295
Index of Economic Freedom and, 29
Choice. *See also* Opportunity cost
in economic perspective, 4
in macroeconomics, 21–22
in microeconomics, 12
Christy's, 207
Circular flow model, 39–40, 248
Citigroup, 349
Clayton Act (1914), 199
Clean Air Act (1990), 105
Clean Water Act (1977), 105
Clinton, Bill, 321
Coase, Ronald, 98–99
Coase theorem, 98–99
Coca-Cola, 7, 115, 127, 210
Coins
clipping gold, 282
in currency, 340
College tuition, price elasticity of demand and, 81–82
Collusion, 205–208
defined, 201
lack of, in monopolistic competition, 191
obstacles to, 207–208
oligopoly and, 201, 205–208
Command system
defined, 27
demise of, 37–38
examples of, 27
Commercial banks
bank panics and, 362–363
checkable deposits and, 341, 353, 355, 358–363
defined, 341
Federal Reserve lending to, 349
fractional reserve banking system and, 350–358
money supply and, 358–363, 371–372
open-market operations and, 371–372
sample transactions of, 351–358
types of, 348
Comparative advantage, 414–416
assumptions of, 414–415
defined, 415
gains from specialization and trade, 416
terms of trade and, 415–416
Comparative economics. *See* International economics
Compensating differences, 237
Competition. *See also* Monopolistic competition; Oligopoly; Pure competition; Pure monopoly
defined, 30
from foreign corporations, 184
global, and New Economy, 401, 403
in market system, 30, 50–51
Complementary goods, 52–53
defined, 52
price changes in, 221–222
public-private complementarities and, 330–331
Composition, fallacy of, 425–426
Comptroller of the Currency, 349n
ConAgra, 207
Conflict of interest, in principal-agent problem, 116–117
Conglomerates, 115
Congo, inflation in, 287
Constant-cost industry
defined, 158
profit maximization in the long run and, 154, 158–159
Constant opportunity cost, 12
Constant returns to scale, 135
Consumer durables, 43
Consumer goods, defined, 14
Consumer nondurables, 43
Consumer Price Index (CPI), 280, 284, 345
Consumer sovereignty, 34–35
Consumer spending. *See* Personal consumption expenditures
Consumption smoothing, 323
Continuing economic loss, 34
Continuing economic profit, 34
Contractionary fiscal policy, 314–315
Coordination problem, in command system, 37–38
Coors, 211–212
Corporate income tax, U.S., as proportional, 109
Corporations
advantages of, 115–116
in business population, 115
competition from foreign, 184
defined, 40–41
facts about U.S., 40–41
largest U.S. advertisers, 208
principal-agent problem and, 116–117
world's ten largest, 41
world's twelve largest financial institutions, 349

currency in, 340
M2, components of, 340, 342–343
Macroeconomics, 12–22. *See also* Fiscal policy; Gross domestic product (GDP); Monetary policy; Recession; Unemployment
aggregate demand in, 291–296
aggregate supply in, 297–302
defined, 8
economic growth and. *See* Economic growth
opportunity cost in, 16–18, 21–22
production possibilities model in, 14–18, 21–22
resource categories and, 13–14
scarce resources and, 12–13
unemployment and, 19
Managerial specialization, 133–134
Marginal analysis
application of, 6
defined, 5
price discrimination and, 181–182
in production possibilities model, 17–18
for public goods, 95–96
Marginal benefits (MB), 17–18
Marginal cost (MC), 17–18, 126, 129–130
calculations for, 129
defined, 129, 130
graphical portrayal of, 129
MR = MC rule and, 145, 151–157, 172–174, 176
price discrimination and, 181–182
in pure competition, 145, 151–152
relation of average variable cost and average total cost to, 129–130
short-run supply and, 151–154
determinants of, 50–51
illustration of, 51
individual demand versus, 50–51, 91
for labor. *See* Labor demand
Market equilibrium, 58–60
application of, 50
price in, 59
quantity in, 59
Market failure, defined, 90, 91
Market period
defined, 83
price elasticity of supply and, 83–84
Market power
described, 301
income inequality and, 248
Markets, defined, 30–31
Market segregation, price discrimination and, 180
Market share, in monopolistic competition, 191
Market supply
determinants of, 55–56
of labor, 225–227, 228
supply curve, 56
Market system, 27–43
capitalism in, 27–28
characteristics of, 28–34
circular flow model and, 39–40, 248
competition in, 30, 50–51. *See also* Pure competition
defined, 27
fundamental questions of, 34–36
negative externalities and, 103–105
progress in, 36
MasterCard, 344
McDonald's, 35, 127, 204, 210
Medicaid, 258, 259
Microsoft, 4, 169, 177, 185–186, 210
Minimum efficient scale (MES), 135–136, 177
Minimum wage
downward price-level inflexibility and, 307
establishment of, 237
inflation and, 283
pros and cons of, 237–238
Mitsubishi Toyota, 349
Mizuho Financial, 349
Monetary multiplier, 361
Monetary policy, 366–385. *See also* Federal Reserve System; Money supply
"artful management" versus "inflation targeting" in, 384
cause-effect chain and, 375–378
easy money policy and, 374, 376, 378, 379
Federal funds rate and, 380–382
interest rates and, 367–370
problems and complications of, 382–383
recent U.S., 381–382
tight money policy and, 374, 376, 378–379
tools of, 371–375
Money. *See also* Currency; Exchange rates; Foreign exchange market
defined, 33
demand for, 367–370
market for, 375–377
in market system, 32–33
as medium of exchange, 33, 339
prices and, 345–346
as store of value, 339, 345–346
as unit of account, 339

International economics. *See also* International trade
average annual growth rates, 274
average income and, 9
comparative GDPs, 269
diamonds in, 167, 179–180
economic growth and, 401, 403, 405–407
gross investment as percentage of GDP, 295
income inequality and, 249
Index of Economic Freedom, 29
inflation in, 281, 286–287, 345
interest rates and, 368
multinational corporations in, 41, 184
net exports and, 296
productivity acceleration and, 401
public debt and, 326–327
standardized budget deficits and surpluses, 319
underground economy in, 271
unemployment and, 279
union membership and, 230
world's ten largest corporations, 41
world's top ten brand names, 210
world's twelve largest financial institutions, 349
International Monetary Fund (IMF), 412
International Nickel Company of Canada (Inco), 169
International trade, 410–435. *See also* International economics
arguments for protection of, 425–427
comparative advantage and, 414–416
comparative exports in, 411–412
facts concerning, 411–412

"Invisible hand" (Smith), 36–37, 163
Iran, Index of Economic Freedom and, 29
Italy
economic growth in, 274
exports of, 411–412
GDP in, 269
gross investment expenditures in, 295
income inequality and, 249
inflation in, 281
net exports and, 296
public debt of, 327
underground economy in, 271
unemployment in, 279
union membership in, 230

Japan
average income and, 9
central bank of, 347
economic growth in, 274
exports of, 411–412
GDP in, 269
gross investment expenditures in, 295
growth competitiveness index and, 403
inflation in, 281, 286
interest rates in, 368
net exports and, 296
public debt of, 327
recession in, 383
standardized budget deficit in, 319
underground economy in, 271
Johnson & Johnson, 208
Joint-profit maximization, 205–207
J.P. Morgan Chase, 349

Kellogg, 204

Labor demand, 217–220
changes in, 220–224
elasticity of, 224–225
marginal revenue product (MRP) and, 219–220
market, 220
MRP = MRC rule and, 219, 227, 229
occupational employment trends and, 222–224
ratio of labor cost to total cost, 225
Labor demand curves, 234–235
Labor force. *See also* Unemployment
defined, 276
Labor-force participation rate, 392
Labor supply curves, 234
Laissez-faire capitalism, 28
Land
defined, 13
as economic resource, 13
Law of demand, 49–50, 71
Law of diminishing marginal utility, 252–253
Law of diminishing returns, 121–125
applications of, 122, 125
defined, 121
relevancy for firms, 121–123
tabular and graphical representations of, 123–125
Law of increasing opportunity cost, 16–17
Law of supply, 55
Learning by doing
economies of scale and, 134, 401
start-up firms and, 401
Legal tender, 344

Money market, defined, 370
Money market deposit accounts (MMDAs), 342, 343
Money market mutual funds (MMMF), 342, 343
Money supply, 339–346. *See also* Federal Reserve System
backing for, 343–346
expansion of, by commercial banks, 358–361, 371–372
*M*1 and, 339–341
*M*2 and, 340, 342–343
prices and, 345–346
reduction of, by commercial banks, 361–362, 372
value of money and, 343–345
Monopolistic competition, 191–197
characteristics of, 191–193
defined, 141, 191
efficiency and, 196–197
price and output in, 193–195
virtues of, 197
Monopoly. *See* Pure monopoly
Monopoly power, price discrimination and, 180
Monopsony, 227–230
application of, 229–230
characteristics of, 227–230
defined, 227
Morale, downward price-level inflexibility and, 307
Morgan, Theodore, 287n
MR = MC rule
defined, 145
features of, 145
in the long run, 155–157
in pure competition, 152–157
in pure monopoly, 172–174, 176
in the short run, 152–154
MRP = MRC rule, 219, 227, 229
Multilateral trade agreements, 429–431
Multiplant firms, 115
Mutual interdependence
game theory and, 200–201
oligopoly and, 198–199, 200–201
Mutual savings banks, defined, 341

National banks, 348
National Credit Union Administration (NCUA), 344
National Educational Association, 231
National income abroad, 296
National income and product accounts (NIPA), 265
Natural monopoly, 168
Near-monies, 342–343
Near-monopolies, 167
NEC, 184

Necessities
defined, 10
price elasticity of demand and, 78–79
Negative externalities
correcting for, 100
defined, 97
government intervention and, 100–101
market-based approach to, 103–105
Nestlé, 184
Net costs, of tariffs, 424
Net effect, 221
Net exports
aggregate demand and, 296
comparative, 411–412
in GDP, 268
Netherlands
exports of, 411–412
public debt of, 327
underground economy in, 271
Netscape, 169, 185
Net tax revenues, 316
Network effects, 177
defined, 400
start-up firms and, 400
Net worth, 352
New Economy, 398–403
defined, 398
global competition and, 401
more rapid growth and, 401
permanence of, 402
productivity acceleration and, 398–403
start-up firms and, 400–401
technology and, 399
New York Stock Exchange, 48
New Zealand
Index of Economic Freedom and, 29
inflation targeting in, 384
interest rates in, 368
standardized budget surplus in, 319
Nicaragua, inflation in, 286
Nigeria, average income and, 9
Nokia, 184, 210
Nominal GDP, 269–272
defined, 270
real GDP versus, 269–271
transactions demand for money and, 367–368, 370
Nominal income, defined, 283
Nominal interest rate, 285
Noncash transfers
defined, 249
impact on income inequality, 246
Noninvestment transactions, 267
Nonprice competition, product differentiation and, 193
Nontariff barriers (NTBs), 422
Nordstrom, 87

Normal goods
defined, 52
income elasticity of demand and, 86
Normal profit
as cost, 118–119
defined, 118
North American Free Trade Agreement (NAFTA), 401, 431
North Korea
command system in, 27
Index of Economic Freedom and, 29
Norway, growth competitiveness index and, 403
Number of sellers, change in supply and, 57

Occupational licensing, 231
Office of Thrift Supervision, 348, 349n
Offshoring, 428
Oligopoly, 197–212
advertising and, 208–210
in beer industry, 211–212
characteristics of, 198–199
collusion in, 201, 205–208
defined, 141, 197
efficiency and, 210–212
game theory of, 200–201, 207
kinked-demand model of, 201–204
prices in, 198–199, 203–204, 211, 306
price wars and, 204, 306
Open economy, 412–413
Open-market operations, 348, 366, 371–372
Operational lag, 323
Opportunity cost
applications of, 4, 18, 98–99
Coase theorem and, 98–99
constant, 12
defined, 4
law of increasing, 16–17
in macroeconomics, 16–18, 21–22
in microeconomics, 12
in production possibilities model, 16–17, 18, 21–22
Organization for Economic Cooperation and Development (OECD), 319, 327, 368
Organization of Petroleum Exporting Countries (OPEC), 206, 301, 411
Other-things-equal assumption (*ceteris paribus*), 7
Output. *See also* Supply
distribution of, 35–36
inflation and, 285–286
in monopolistic competition, 193–195
in pure monopoly, 172–174
Output effect, 221

Pabst, 211–212
Packaging, in product differentiation, 192
Pakistan, average income and, 9
Patents, as barriers to entry, 168–169
Payoff matrix, oligopoly and, 200–201
Payroll taxes
  aggregate supply and, 302
  as regressive, 109
  Social Security trust fund and, 333
Pentagon attack (2001). *See* September 11, 2001 terrorist attacks
Pepsi, 7
Perfectly elastic demand, 72–73, 74, 143–144
Perfectly inelastic demand, 72–73, 74
Per se violations, 202
Personal consumption expenditures
  aggregate demand and, 291–293
  in GDP, 267
  trade deficit and, 433
Personal income tax, U.S., as regressive, 108
Personal Responsibility Act (1996), 260
Pet, 206
Pfizer, 115, 208
Philip Morris, 212
Picasso, Pablo, 89, 236
Plant, defined, 115
Poland, interest rates in, 368
Polaroid, 168
Politics
  government trade protections and, 424–425
  political business cycles and, 323
Pollution
  economic growth and, 404–405
  World Trade Organization (WTO) and, 430
Portugal, underground economy in, 271
Positive externalities, 97–98
  correcting for, 101
  government intervention and, 101–103
Post, 204
Potential output, 278
Poverty, 254–261
  defined, 255
  extent of, 242
  growth in low-income nations, 405–407
  incidence of, 255–256
  measuring, 257
  minimum wage and, 237
  trends concerning, 256
  U.S. income-maintenance system and, 257–261
  welfare reform and, 260–261
Poverty rate, 255
Preferences
  income inequality and, 248
  in market system, 35
Price. *See also* Inflation; Price ceilings; Price discrimination; Price elasticity of demand; Price elasticity of supply; Price floors; Price leadership
  aggregate supply and, 300–301
  as barriers to entry, 169
  change in demand and, 52–53, 61
  change in supply and, 56, 57, 61
  changes in labor, 219–221
  changes in other resource, 221
  of complementary goods, 221–222
  in determining exchange rates, 421
  domestic resource, 300–301
  equilibrium, 59, 152–154, 302–309
  expected, 53, 57
  government-set, 63–67
  imported resource, 301
  marginal revenue product of labor and, 218
  market power and, 301
  in market system, 30–31
  money and, 345–346
  in monopolistic competition, 193–195
  oligopoly and, 198–199, 203–204, 211, 306
  price makers and, 167, 172
  price takers and, 142, 156
  in product differentiation, 193
  in pure monopoly, 170–176
  rationing function of, 59–60
Price ceilings
  defined, 63
  on gasoline, 63–64
  rent controls and, 64–65
Price discrimination
  application of, 182–183
  conditions for, 180
  defined, 180
  dumping and, 427
  examples of, 181
  graphical analysis of, 181–182
  pure monopoly and, 180–183
Price elasticity of demand, 71–82
  along linear demand curve, 76–77
  applications of, 79–82
  defined, 71
  determinants of, 77–82
  examples of, 78
  formula for, 71–73
  price-elasticity coefficient and, 71–73
  total-revenue test for, 73–76
Price elasticity of supply, 82–86
  applications of, 85–86
  defined, 82–83
  formula for, 82–83
  long run, 85
  market period and, 83–84
  short run, 84–85
Price floors
  defined, 65
  on wheat, 65–66
Price leadership
  challenges to, 204
  defined, 203
  kinked demand and, 203–204
  tactics in, 203–204
Price makers
  defined, 167
  in pure monopoly, 167, 172
Price takers
  defined, 142
  pure competition and, 142, 167
Price wars, 204, 306
Prime interest rate, 380–381
Principal-agent problem, 116–117
Principles, defined, 7
Private goods, 91–92
  characteristics of, 91
  defined, 91
  efficient allocation of, 91–92
  profitable provision of, 91
Private property
  defined, 28
  liability rules and lawsuits concerning, 99–100
  in market system, 28
Private sector. *See also* Businesses; Corporations
  facts about U.S. businesses, 40–41
  facts about U.S. households, 42–43
Procter & Gamble, 208
Product attributes, in product differentiation, 192
Product demand
  changes in, 220
  elasticity of, 225
Product differentiation
  aspects of, 192–193
  defined, 192
  in monopolistic competition, 192–193
Product improvement, monopolistic competition and, 197
Production costs
  in long run, 130–136
  in short run, 125–130
Production possibilities model, 14–18
  aggregate supply and, 391
  applications of, 18, 21
  assumptions of, 14
  economic growth and, 19–21, 390–393
  law of increasing opportunity cost in, 16–17

Production possibilities model (*continued*)
- opportunity costs and, 16–17, 18, 21–22
- optimal allocation in, 17–18
- production possibilities curve and, 15–16
- production possibilities table in, 14–15
- unemployment and, 19

Productive efficiency
- defined, 91–92
- monopolistic competition and, 196–197
- in pure competition, 161–162
- pure monopoly and, 175–176

Productivity
- acceleration of, 398–403
- aggregate supply and, 301–302
- changes in, 220–221
- defined, 301
- downward price-level inflexibility and, 307
- economic growth and, 273, 392–393, 394, 398–403
- marginal revenue product of labor and, 217

Product markets, 39–40
- business population and, 115–117
- economic costs in, 117–121
- income inequality and, 248
- long-run production costs in, 130–136
- market models in, 141–142. *See also* Monopolistic competition; Oligopoly; Pure competition; Pure monopoly
- short-run production costs in, 125–130
- short-run production relationships in, 121–125

Product variety, monopolistic competition and, 197

Professional sports teams
- monopsony and, 230
- price discrimination and, 182–183
- as pure monopolies, 167, 182–183

Profit
- continuing economic, 34
- economic (pure), 119
- normal, 118–119
- private goods and, 91

Profit maximization
- applications of, 150
- in collusion, 205–207
- factors in, 145–147
- long-run, 150, 154–160
- in monopolistic competition, 195
- with pure competition, 145–160
- with pure monopoly, 172–174
- short-run, 145–154

Progressive taxes
- defined, 107–108
- in the United States, 108–109

Property taxes, U.S., as regressive, 109

Proportional taxes, 107–110
- defined, 107–108
- in the United States, 108–109

Protectionism, 422–427
- arguments for, 425–427
- economic impact of tariffs, 423–424
- methods of, 422–423
- net costs of tariffs, 424
- reasons for, 424–425

Public assistance programs, 258, 259–261

Public debt, 325–333
- defined, 325
- false concerns for, 327–328
- future generations and, 328
- GDP and, 325–326
- interest charges on, 327
- international comparisons of, 326–327
- ownership of, 325, 326
- Social Security and, 331–333
- substantive issues for, 328–333
- trade deficits and, 433

Public goods, 92–96
- characteristics of, 92
- cost-benefit analysis for, 95–96
- defined, 92
- examples of, 92–93
- free-rider problem and, 92–93
- measuring demand for, 94–95
- optimal quantity of, 94
- pure competition and, 161

Public investments, 330–331

Public sector. *See* Government

Purchasing power, 345

Pure capitalism, 28

Pure competition, 142–164
- characteristics of, 142
- defined, 141, 142
- demand as seen by seller in, 143–144
- efficiency and, 160–163
- in labor market, 217–218
- occurrence of, 142
- profit maximization in the long run, 154–160
- profit maximization in the short run, 145–154
- pure monopoly versus, 170
- supply in, 151–160

Purely competitive labor market, 217–218

Pure monopoly, 166–186
- antitrust policy and, 183–186, 199, 201–202
- barriers to entry and, 168–169
- characteristics of, 167
- defined, 142, 167
- demand in, 170–172
- economic effects of, 175–180
- efficiency and, 175–176
- examples of, 167, 179–180
- price and output in, 172–174
- price discrimination and, 180–183
- profit maximization in, 172–174
- supply in, 172–176

Purposeful behavior, 5. *See also* Utility

Quasi-public banks, Federal Reserve Banks as, 347

Quasi-public goods
- defined, 102
- positive externalities and, 102

Quotas, import, 422, 431

Ratchet effect, 307

Rationing function of prices, 59–60

Real GDP, 269–274
- changes in, 303–305
- defined, 270
- equilibrium price level and, 302–309
- growth of, 393, 394
- growth rates of, 272
- nominal GDP versus, 269–271

Real GDP per capita, 272–274, 393, 405–407

Real income, defined, 283

Real interest rate, 285, 294, 377

Recession
- collusion and, 208
- cyclical unemployment and, 277–278, 308
- defined, 275
- downward price level inflexibility and, 308–309
- easy money policy for, 374, 376, 378, 379
- in the United States, 275
- welfare reform and, 261

Recognition lag, 322

Refinancing, of public debt, 328

Regressive taxes, 107–110
- defined, 107–108
- in the United States, 108–109

Regulation. *See* Government regulation

Relative income, in determining exchange rates, 421

Rent controls, 64–65

Rent-seeking behavior, 178

Reproductions, price elasticity of supply and, 85

Required reserves, 348, 353–354, 372–373

Resale, price discrimination and, 180

Research and development (R&D)
as barrier to entry, 169, 211
start-up firms and, 400
Reserve ratio, 353–354, 372–373, 375
Reserves
actual, 354–355, 372–373
excess, 354–355, 372–373
fractional, 350–358
required, 348, 353–354, 372–373
Resource markets, 39. *See also* Economic resources; Income inequality; Poverty; Wage determination
income inequality and, 248
Ricardo, David, 413
Rivlin, Alice M., 404n
Rodriguez, Alex, 4
Roosevelt, Franklin, 362
Ross, David, 178n
Royal Dutch/Shell, 184
Royal Philips, 184
Rule of 70, 272
Rule of reason, 184, 199
Russia
exports of, 411
GDP in, 269
Index of Economic Freedom and, 29
Rwanda, average income and, 9

SABMiller, 211–212
Saffer, Henry, 81
Sales taxes
aggregate supply and, 302
as regressive, 108
Savers, inflation and, 283
Savings accounts, 342
Savings and loan associations, defined, 341
SBC Communications, 208
Scale
constant returns to, 135
diseconomies of, 135
economies of. *See* Economies of scale
minimum efficient (MES), 135–136, 177
Scalping, 60
Scarcity. *See also* Opportunity cost
in economic perspective, 4
of money, 345
Scherer, F. M., 178n
Schneider, Friedrich, 271n
Scientific method
defined, 6
elements of, 6–7
Secondhand sales, excluding, in GDP, 266
Self-interest
defined, 29
in market system, 29–30
September 11, 2001 terrorist attacks
administrative lag and, 322–323
insurance costs and, 130
monetary policy and, 382
production possibilities analysis and, 18
Serbia, inflation in, 287
Services
nature of, 43
in product differentiation, 192
Shell, 41, 115
Shepherd, William G., 178n
Sherman Act (1890), 183–185, 201–202
Shortage, defined, 59
Short run, 121–130
aggregate supply in, 298–299
defined, 84, 120
economic costs in, 120, 121–130
equilibrium prices in, 152–154
fixed plant and, 120
law of diminishing returns and, 121–125
in monopolistic competition, 194, 195
price elasticity of supply and, 84–85
production costs in, 125–130
production relationships in, 121–125
profit maximization under pure competition, 145–154
supply in, 151–154
Short-run aggregate supply curve, 298–299
Short-run supply curve, 151–154
defined, 152
equilibrium price and, 152–154
Shutdown. *See* Exit
Simultaneous consumption, 177
Singapore, growth competitiveness index and, 403
Single seller, in pure monopoly, 167
Smith, Adam, 36–37, 412–413
Smoot-Hawley Tariff Act (1930), 426
Social insurance programs, 258–259
Social Security
described, 257–258
fiscal imbalance due to, 331–333
inflation and, 284
policy options concerning, 332–333
Social Security trust fund, 331–333
Sole proprietorships, defined, 40
Sony, 184
Sotheby's, 207
South Africa, income inequality and, 249
South African Breweries (SAB), 212
South Korea
average income and, 9
exports of, 411–412
GDP in, 269
gross investment expenditures in, 295
interest rates in, 368
union membership in, 230
Soviet Union, former, command system in, 27, 37–38
Spain
exports of, 411–412
GDP in, 269
gross investment expenditures in, 295
Index of Economic Freedom and, 29
public debt of, 327
underground economy in, 271
Specialization, 31–32
defined, 31
gains from, 416
geographic, 32
international trade and, 412–413
of labor, 31, 132–133
managerial, 133–134
in market system, 31–32
start-up firms and, 400
Speculation, in determining exchange rates, 422
Spillover costs. *See* Negative externalities
Sports teams. *See* Professional sports teams
Standardized budget, 317–322
Standardized product, pure competition and, 142
Standard Oil, 184
Start-up firms, 400–401
State banks, 348
Stock options, 117
Stocks
defined, 115
wealth effect and, 293
Store of value
defined, 339
money as, 339, 345–346
Strategic behavior
defined, 198
example of, 198–199
oligopoly and, 198–199
Structural unemployment, 277
Subsidies
change in supply and, 57
export, 423
positive externalities and, 101–102
Substitute goods, 52–53
defined, 52
ease of resource substitutability, 225
price changes in, 221
price elasticity of demand and, 77–78, 79–80
in pure monopoly, 167
Substitution effect, 221
Sunk costs, 127
Sun Microsystems, 169
Supplemental Security Income (SSI), 258, 259

Supply, 54–58. *See also* Aggregate supply; Price elasticity of supply
- change in, 56–57, 61, 62–63
- change in quantity supplied, 57–58
- defined, 54
- determinants of, 55–56
- economic growth and, 389
- of labor, 225–227, 228
- law of supply, 55
- long-run, 158–160
- market, 55–56, 225–228
- market equilibrium and, 58–60
- market supply, 55–56, 225–227, 228
- in pure competition, 151–160
- in pure monopoly, 172–176
- short-run, 151–154

Supply curve, 56–57
Surplus, defined, 59
Sweden
- gross investment expenditures in, 295
- growth competitiveness index and, 403
- income inequality and, 249
- inflation targeting in, 384
- underground economy in, 271
- union membership in, 230

Switzerland
- average income and, 9
- growth competitiveness index and, 403
- underground economy in, 271

Taiwan
- exports of, 411–412
- growth competitiveness index and, 403

Tariffs
- defined, 422
- economic impact of, 423–424
- EU abolition of, 431
- net costs of, 424

Tastes
- change in demand and, 52
- in determining exchange rates, 421

Taxes, 106–109
- ability-to-pay principle and, 107
- aggregate supply and, 302
- apportioning tax burden, 106
- average, 107–108
- benefits-received principle and, 106–107
- business, 108, 109, 295, 302, 333
- change in supply and, 57
- consumer spending and, 293
- earned-income tax credit (EITC), 258, 259–260
- excise, 80, 302
- expected returns and, 295
- under feudalism, 282
- fiscal policy and increases in, 315
- fiscal policy and reductions in, 314, 321
- impact on income inequality, 246
- marginal, 107–108
- negative externalities and, 101
- net tax revenues, 316
- progressive, 107–110
- proportional, 107–110
- public debt and, 328
- regressive, 107–110

Technology
- advances in, 20–21, 36, 157, 178–179, 211, 221, 394–395, 399
- change in supply and, 57
- economic growth and, 20–21, 394–395, 399
- examples of, 21, 399
- expected returns and, 294
- marginal revenue product (MRP) and, 221
- in market system, 31, 36
- oligopoly and, 211
- in production of goods and services, 35
- productivity acceleration and, 399

Temporary Assistance for Needy Families (TANF), 258, 259, 260
Terms of trade, 415–416
Terrorism. *See* September 11, 2001 terrorist attacks
Thrift institutions
- defined, 341
- Federal Reserve lending to, 349
- types of, 341, 348

Ticket scalping, 60
Tight money policy
- defined, 374
- effects of, 378–379
- illustrated, 376

Till money, 352
Time and timing
- fiscal policy and, 322–323
- income inequality and, 249–251
- income mobility and, 245
- monetary policy lags and, 382
- price elasticity of demand and, 79
- time value of money, 370

Time deposits, 342, 343
Time Warner, 208
Token money, 340
Total cost (TC), 34, 126
- average total cost (ATC), 128–132, 181–182
- defined, 127
- ratio of labor cost to, 225

Total demand for money, 369–370
Total product (TP)
- defined, 121
- law of diminishing returns and, 123–125

Total revenue (TR), 34
- business population and, 41
- defined, 74, 143
- in pure competition, 143–144

Total-revenue test, 73–76
- defined, 74
- elastic demand and, 75–76
- inelastic demand and, 76
- unit elasticity and, 76

Toyota, 41, 184, 209, 210
Trade. *See* International trade
Trade Adjustment Assistance Act (2002), 427–428
Trade blocs, 431
Trade deficit
- causes of, 432–433
- defined, 411
- implications of, 433–434
- of the United States, 432–434

Trade surplus, defined, 411
Training. *See* Education and training
Transactions demand for money, 367–368, 370
Treble damages, 185

UBS, 349
UCAR International, 207
Unanticipated inflation, 283–284
Underground economy, 270–271
Unemployment, 276–279
- definition of full, 278
- downward price level inflexibility and, 308–309
- easy money policy for, 374, 376, 378, 379
- economic cost of, 278–279
- Great Depression and, 19, 278
- international comparisons of, 279
- measuring, 276–277
- in production possibilities analysis, 19
- types of, 277–278, 308
- wage increases and, 233

Unemployment compensation, 258, 259
Unemployment rate, 276–277
Unilever, 184
Union models, 230–233
- downward price-level inflexibility and, 307, 308–309
- exclusive unionism and, 231, 232–233
- income inequality and, 251
- inflation and, 284
- union membership and, 230
- wage advantage of, 233

United Kingdom
- central bank of, 347
- economic growth in, 274
- exports of, 411–412
- GDP in, 269
- gross investment expenditures in, 295

inflation in, 281
inflation targeting in, 384
interest rates in, 368
net exports and, 296
public debt of, 327
standardized budget deficit in, 319
underground economy in, 271
union membership in, 230
United States. *See also* Fiscal policy; Monetary policy
aggregate supply in, 297–302
agriculture in, 65–66, 79–80, 122, 157
antitrust policy in, 183–186
average income and, 9
backing for money supply in, 343–346
bank panics in, 362–363
budget deficit and surplus in, 319, 320–322
capitalism in, 28. *See also* Market system
downward price level inflexibility and, 308–309
economic growth in, 273–274, 393
educational attainment in, 395–397
exports of, 411–412
facts about businesses in, 40–41
facts about households in, 42
GDP in, 269
gross investment expenditures in, 295
growth competitiveness index and, 403
income elasticity of demand in, 87
income inequality in, 242, 243, 245–249
income-maintenance system and, 257–261
Index of Economic Freedom and, 29
inflation in, 280–281, 384
interest rates in, 368
international trade and, 411–412, 432–434
largest advertisers, 208
net exports and, 296
North American Free Trade Agreement (NAFTA) and, 401, 431
occupational employment trends in, 222–224
poverty in, 254–261
price discrimination in, 181
public debt of, 327
recessions in, 275
securities of. *See* U.S. securities
tax progressivity in, 108–109
trade deficits of, 432–434
underground economy in, 271
unemployment in, 276, 278
union membership in, 230
U.S. Bureau of Economic Analysis (BEA), 42, 265
U.S. Bureau of Labor Statistics, 223, 233, 276, 280, 281
U.S. Bureau of the Census, 243, 245
U.S. Department of Commerce, 265
U.S. Department of Defense, 18
U.S. Department of Justice, 169, 185, 207
U.S. Department of the Treasury, 348
U.S. Environmental Protection Agency (EPA), 105
U.S. Federal Communications Commission (FCC), 169
U.S. Federal Trade Commission (FTC), 185
U.S. Postal Service, 183, 209
U.S. securities
defined, 325
Federal Reserve as largest single holder of, 371
foreign ownership of, 329
future generations and, 328
open-market operations and, 348, 366, 371–372
public debt and, 325
U.S. Steel, 184
United States v. Microsoft, 185–186
Unit elasticity, 76
Unit elasticity of demand, defined, 72
Unit of account
defined, 339
money as, 339
UPS, 209
Uruguay Round, 429
Utility
defined, 5
in economic perspective, 5, 21–22
law of diminishing marginal, 252–253
maximizing total, 252–253

Variable costs
average variable cost (AVC), 128
defined, 127
Variable plant, 120–121
Variety, monopolistic competition and, 197
Vault money, 352
Verizon, 208
Verson, 134
Vertical integration, 115
Vietnam war, 304
Visa, 344
Voluntary export restriction (VER), 422–423

Wage contracts. *See also* Union models
downward price-level inflexibility and, 307
Wage determination, 216–239. *See also* Minimum wage
changes in labor demand and, 220–224
elasticity of labor demand and, 224–225
employment determination and, 226–227
labor demand and, 217–220, 224–225
market demand for labor and, 220–225
market supply of labor and, 225–227
monopsony and, 227–230
purely competitive labor market and, 217
union models and, 230–233
wage differentials and, 233–238
Wage differentials, 233–238. *See also* Income inequality
compensating differences and, 237
defined, 233
marginal revenue productivity and, 235
minimum wage and, 237–238
noncompeting groups and, 235–236
union membership and, 233
Wal-Mart, 41, 115, 116
Walt Disney, 208, 210
Wealth
consumer, 292, 293
unequal distribution of, 248
Wealth effect, 292, 293
Wealth of Nations, The (Smith), 36–37, 412–413
Welfare reform, 260–261
Wells Fargo Bank, 24
Wendy's, 138
Western Union, 167
Wham-O, 167
Wheat, price floors on, 65–66
Whites, poverty of, 255
Williams, Raburn M., 287n
Winfrey, Oprah, 4, 242
Woods, Tiger, 242
World Bank, 9, 269, 295
WorldCom, 117
World Economic Forum, 403
World Trade Center attacks (2001). *See* September 11, 2001 terrorist attacks
World Trade Organization (WTO), 296, 401, 411, 429–430, 431
establishment of, 429
protests and, 429–430

Xerox, 168
X-inefficiency, 178

Yahoo, 45

RELEVANT ECONOMIC STATISTICS, UNITED STATES, 1984–2004

	1984	1985	1986	1987	1988	1989	1990
1 Gross domestic product (billions of dollars)	3,933.2	4,220.3	4,462.8	4,739.5	5,103.8	5,484.4	5,803.1
2 Real gross domestic product (billions of 2000 dollars)	5,813.6	6,053.7	6,263.6	6,475.1	6,742.7	6,981.4	7,112.5
3 Economic growth rate (percent change in real GDP)	7.2	4.1	3.5	3.4	4.1	3.5	1.9
4 Consumption expenditures (billions of dollars)	2,503.3	2,720.3	2,899.7	3,100.2	3,353.6	3,598.5	3,839.9
5 Gross private domestic investment (billions of dollars)	735.6	736.2	746.5	785	821.6	874.9	861
6 Government purchases (billions of dollars)	797	879	949.3	999.5	1,039	1,099.1	1,180.2
7 Rate of inflation (percent change in CPI)	4.3	3.6	1.9	3.6	4.1	4.8	5.4
8 Money supply, M1	551.6	619.8	724.6	750.2	786.6	792.8	824.8
9 Federal funds interest rate (%)	10.23	8.1	6.8	6.66	7.57	9.21	8.1
10 Prime interest rate (%)	12.04	9.93	8.33	8.21	9.32	10.87	10.01
11 Population (millions)	236.3	238.5	240.7	242.8	245	247.3	250.1
12 Immigration (thousands)	543.9	570	601.7	601.5	643	1,091	1,536.5
13 Labor Force (millions)	113.5	115.5	117.8	119.9	121.7	123.9	125.8
14 Employment (millions)	105	107.2	109.6	112.4	115	117.3	118.8
15 Unemployment rate (%)	7.5	7.2	7	6.2	5.5	5.3	5.6
16 Federal budget surplus (+) or deficit (−)	−185.4	−212.3	−221.2	−149.7	−155.2	−152.6	−221.1
17 Public debt (billions of dollars)	1,564.6	1,817.4	2,120.5	2,346	2,601.1	2,867.8	3,206.3
18 Price of crude oil (dollars per barrel)	28.2	27.01	13.53	17.73	14.24	17.31	22.26
19 Average hourly earnings, private nonagricultiral industries (dollars)	8.48	8.73	8.92	9.13	9.43	9.8	10.19
20 Average weekly hours, private nonagriculatural industries	35.1	34.9	34.7	34.7	34.6	34.5	34.3
21 After-tax manufacturing profits per dollar of sales (cents)*	4.6	3.8	3.7	4.9	5.9	4.9	3.9
22 Industry research and development expenditures (billions of dollars)	73.1	82.4	85.9	90.2	94.9	99.9	107.4
23 Net farm income (billions of dollars)	26	28.5	31.1	38	39.6	46.5	46.3
24 Federal minimum wage (dollars per hour)	3.35	3.35	3.35	3.35	3.35	3.35	3.8
25 Poverty rate (% of population)	14.4	14	13.6	13.4	13	12.8	13.5
26 Gini ratio for household income distribution**	0.415	0.419	0.425	0.426	0.427	0.431	0.428
27 Productivity growth, business sector (%)	2.7	2.3	3	0.6	1.5	1	2
28 Trade surplus (+) or deficit (−) (billions)	−109.1	−121.9	−138.5	−151.7	−114.6	−93.1	−80.9

*Revised definition of this series beginning in 1973.
**Revised definitions have occurred within this series.

Sources: Bureau of Economic Analysis; Bureau of Labor Statistics; *Economic Report of the President, 2005;* U.S. Bureau of the Census; Federal Reserve System; National Science Foundation; U.S. Citizenship and Immigration Services; Organization of Petroleum Exporting Countries (OPEC).